*The Editor*

MARIA TATAR is the author of *The Hard Facts of the Grimms' Fairy Tales, Off with Their Heads! Fairy Tales and the Culture of Childhood,* and *Lustmord: Sexual Violence in Weimar Germany.* She holds the John L. Loeb chair for Germanic Languages and Literatures at Harvard University, where she teaches courses on German cultural studies, folklore, and children's literature.

P. 138 - 211

A NORTON CRITICAL EDITION

# THE
# CLASSIC FAIRY TALES

TEXTS

CRITICISM

*Edited by*

## MARIA TATAR

HARVARD UNIVERSITY

W • W • NORTON & COMPANY • *New York* • *London*

For Lauren and Daniel

The text of this book is composed in Electra with the display set in Bernhard Modern. Composition by PennSet, Inc. Book design by Antonina Krass.

Cover illustration: *The Enchanted Prince*, reproduced by permission of © Maxfield Parrish Family Trust/Licensed by ASAP and VAGA, NYC/Courtesy American Illustrated Gallery, NYC.

Library of Congress Cataloging-in-Publication Data

The classic fairy tales : texts, criticism / edited by Maria Tatar.
    p.    cm. — (Norton critical edition)
    Includes bibliographical references.

    ISBN 0-393-97277-1 (pbk.)

    1. Fairy tales — History and criticism.  I. Tatar, Maria M., 1945–
GR550.C57    1998
385.2 — dc21                                                        98-13552

W. W. Norton & Company, Inc., 500 Fifth Avenue, New York, N.Y. 10110
www.wwnorton.com
W. W. Norton & Company Ltd., Castle House, 75/76 Wells Street,
London W1T 3QT

9 0

# Contents

# Criticism                                            267

# Introduction

Fairy tales, Angela Carter tells us, are not "unique one-offs," and their narrators are neither "original" nor "godlike" nor "inspired." To the contrary, these stories circulate in multiple versions, reconfigured by each telling to form kaleidoscopic variations with distinctly different effects. When we say the word "Cinderella," we are referring not to a single text but to an entire array of stories with a persecuted heroine who may respond to her situation with defiance, cunning, ingenuity, self-pity, anguish, or grief. She will be called Yeh-hsien in China, Cendrillon in Italy, Aschenputtel in Germany, and Catskin in England. Her sisters may be named One-Eye and Three-Eyes, Anastasia and Drizella, or she may have just one sister named Haloek. Her tasks range from tending cows to sorting peas to fetching embers for a fire.

Although many variant forms of a tale can now be found between the covers of books and are attributed to individual authors, editors, or compilers, they derive largely from collective efforts. In reflecting on the origins of fairy tales, Carter asks us to consider: "Who first invented meatballs? In what country? Is there a definitive recipe for potato soup? Think in terms of the domestic arts. 'This is how *I* make potato soup.' "[1] The story of Little Red Riding Hood, for example, can be discovered the world over, yet it varies radically in texture and flavor from one culture to the next. Even in a single culture, that texture or flavor may be different enough that a listener will impatiently interrupt the telling of a tale to insist "That's not the way I heard it." In France, Little Red Riding Hood and her grandmother are devoured by the wolf. The Grimms' version, by contrast, stages a rescue scene in which a hunter intervenes to liberate Red Riding Hood and her grandmother from the belly of the wolf. Caterinella, an Italian Red Riding Hood, is invited to dine on the teeth and ears of her grandmother by a masquerading wolf. A Chinese "Goldflower" manages to slay the beast who wants to devour her by throwing a spear into his mouth. Local color often affects the premises of a tale. In Italy, the challenge facing one heroine is not spinning straw into gold but downing seven plates of lasagna.

Virtually every element of a tale, from the name of the hero or heroine through the nature of the beloved to the depiction of the villain, seems subject to change. In the British Isles, Cinderella goes by the name of Catskin, Mossycoat, or Rashin-Coatie. The mother of one Italian "Beauty" pleads with her daughter to marry a pig, while another mother runs interference for a snake. In Russia, the cannibalistic witch in the forest has a hut set on chicken legs surrounded by a fence with posts made of stacked

1. Angela Carter, ed., *The Virago Book of Fairy Tales* (London: Virago Press, 1990) x.

ix

human skulls. Rumpelstiltskin is also known as Titeliture, Ricdin-Ricdon, Tom Tit Tot, Batzibitzili, Panzimanzi, and Whuppity Stoorie.

While there is no "original" version of "Cinderella" or "Sleeping Beauty," there is a basic plot structure (what folklorists refer to as a "tale type") that appears despite rich cultural variation. "Beauty and the Beast," for example, according to the tale-type index compiled by the Finnish folklorist Antti Aarne and refined by the American folklorist Stith Thompson, has the following episodic structure:

    I. The monster as husband
    II. Disenchantment of the monster
    III. Loss of the husband
    IV. Search for the husband
    V. Recovery of the husband

While the monster as husband is a structural constant, the monster itself may (and does) take the form of virtually any beast—a goat, a mouse, a hedgehog, a crocodile, or a lion. The search for the husband may require the heroine to cover vast tracts of land in iron shoes, to sort out peas from lentils in an impossibly short time, or simply to wish herself back to the monster's castle. Despite certain limitations, the tale-type index is a convenient tool for defining the stable core of a story and for identifying those features subject to local variation.

Telling fairy tales has been considered a "domestic art" at least since Plato in the *Gorgias* referred to the "old wives' tales" told by nurses to amuse and to frighten children. Although virtually all of the national collections of fairy tales compiled in the nineteenth century were the work of men, the tales themselves were ascribed to women narrators. As early as the second century A.D., Apuleius, the North African author of *The Golden Ass*, had designated his story of "Cupid and Psyche" (told by a drunken and half-demented old woman) as belonging to the genre of "old wives' tales." The Venetian Giovanni Francesco Straparola claimed to have heard the stories that constituted his *Facetious Nights* of 1550 "from the lips of . . . lady storytellers" and he embedded those stories in a narrative frame featuring a circle of garrulous female narrators.[2] Giambattista Basile's seventeenth-century collection of Neapolitan tales, *The Pentamerone*, also has women storytellers—quick-witted, gossipy old crones who recount "those tales that old women tell to amuse children."[3] The renowned *Tales of Mother Goose* by Charles Perrault were designated by their author as old wives' tales, "told by governesses and grandmothers to little children."[4] And many of the most expansive storytellers consulted by the Grimms were women—family friends or servants who had at their disposal a rich repertoire of folklore.

The association of fairy tales with the domestic arts and with old wives' tales has not done much to enhance the status of these cultural stories.

---

2. Marina Warner, *From the Beast to the Blonde: On Fairy Tales and Their Tellers* (New York: Farrar, Straus and Giroux, 1994) 36.
3. *The Pentamerone*, trans. Benedetto Croce, ed. N. M. Penzer (John Lane: The Bodley Head, 1932) 9.
4. Charles Perrault, "Préface," *Contes en vers* (1694; reprint, Paris: Gallimard, 1981) 50.

"On a par with trifles," Marina Warner stresses, " 'mere old wives' tales' carry connotations of error, of false counsel, ignorance, prejudice and fallacious nostrums—against heartbreak as well as headache; similarly 'fairy tale,' as a derogatory term, implies fantasy, escapism, invention, the unreliable consolations of romance."[5]

Although fairy tales are still arguably the most powerfully formative tales of childhood and permeate mass media for children and adults, it is not unusual to find them deemed of marginal cultural importance and dismissed as unworthy of critical attention. Yet the staying power of these stories, their widespread and enduring popularity, suggests that they must be addressing issues that have a significant social function—whether critical, conservative, compensatory, or therapeutic. In a study of mass-produced fantasies for women, Tania Modleski points out that genres such as the soap opera, the Gothic novel, and the Harlequin romance "speak to very real problems and tensions in women's lives. The narrative strategies which have evolved for smoothing over these tensions can tell us much about how women have managed not only to live in oppressive circumstances but to invest their situations with some degree of dignity."[6] Fairy tales register an effort on the part of both women and men to develop maps for coping with personal anxieties, family conflicts, social frictions, and the myriad frustrations of everyday life.

Trivializing fairy tales leads to the mistaken conclusion that we should suspend our critical faculties while reading these "harmless" narratives. While it may be disturbing to hear voices disavowing the transformative influence of fairy tales and proclaiming them to be culturally insignificant, it is just as troubling to find fairy tales turned into inviolable cultural icons. The Grimms steadfastly insisted on the sacred quality of the fairy tales they collected. Their *Nursery and Household Tales*, they asserted, made an effort to capture the pure, artless simplicity of a people not yet tainted by the corrupting influences of civilization. "These stories are suffused with the same purity that makes children appear so marvelous and blessed," Wilhelm Grimm declared in his preface to the collection. Yet both brothers must also have recognized that fairy tales were far from culturally innocent, for they extolled the "civilizing" power of the tales and conceived of their collection as a "manual of manners" for children.[7]

The myth of fairy tales as a kind of holy scripture was energetically propagated by Charles Dickens, who brought to the literature of childhood the same devout reverence he accorded children. Like the Grimms, Dickens hailed the "simplicity," "purity," and "innocent extravagance" of fairy tales, yet also praised the tales as powerful instruments of constructive socialization: "It would be hard to estimate the amount of gentleness and mercy that has made its way among us through these slight channels. Forebearance, courtesy, consideration for the poor and aged, kind treatment of

5. Warner, *Beast* 19. (Excerpted below, p. 309.)
6. Tania Modleski, *Loving with a Vengeance: Mass-Produced Fantasies for Women* (Hamden, Conn.: Archon Books, 1982) 15.
7. From Jacob and Wilhelm Grimms' "Preface," *Nursery and Household Tales*, 1st ed., 2d ed., trans. Maria Tatar, in Maria Tatar, *The Hard Facts of the Grimms' Fairy Tales* (Princeton: Princeton UP, 1978) 206, 207.

animals, the love of nature, abhorrence of tyranny and brute force—many such good things have been first nourished in the child's heart by this powerful aid."[8]

Even in 1944, when Allied troops were locked in combat with German soldiers, W. H. Auden decreed the Grimms' fairy tales to be "among the few indispensable, common-property books upon which Western culture can be founded." "It is hardly too much to say," he added, "that these tales rank next to the Bible in importance."[9] Like the devaluation of fairy tales, the overvaluation of fairy tales promotes a suspension of critical faculties and prevents us from taking a good, hard look at stories that are so obviously instrumental in shaping our values, moral codes, and aspirations. The reverence brought by some readers to fairy tales mystifies these stories, making them appear to be a source of transcendent spiritual truth and authority. Such a mystification promotes a hands-off attitude and conceals the fact that fairy tales, like "high art," are squarely implicated in the complex, yet not impenetrable, symbolic codes that permeate our cultural stories.

Despite efforts to deflect critical attention from fairy tales, the stories themselves have attracted the attention of scholars in disciplinary corners ranging from psychology and anthropology through religion and history to cultural studies and literary theory. Every culture has its myths, fairy tales, and fables, but few cultures have mobilized as much critical energy as has ours of late to debate the merits of these stories. Margaret Atwood, whose personal and literary engagement with fairy tales is no secret, has written vividly about her childhood encounter with an unexpurgated version of *Grimms' Fairy Tales*: "Where else could I have gotten the idea," she asserts, "so early in life, that words can change you?"[1] Atwood's phrasing is magnificently ambiguous, referring on one level to the transformative spells cast on fairy-tale characters, but also implying that fairy tales can both shape our way of experiencing the world and endow us with the power to restructure our lives. As Stephen Greenblatt has observed, "the work of art is not the passive surface on which . . . historical experience leaves its stamp but one of the creative agents in the fashioning and refashioning of this experience."[2] As we read fairy tales, we simultaneously evoke the cultural experience of the past and allow it to work on our consciousness even as we reinterpret and reshape that experience.

Carolyn Heilbrun has also addressed the question of how the stories circulating in our culture regulate our lives and fashion our identities:

> Let us agree on this: that we live our lives through texts. These may
> be read, or chanted, or experienced electronically, or come to us, like
> the murmurings of our mothers, telling us of what conventions de-

8. Charles Dickens, "Frauds on the Fairies," in *Household Words: A Weekly Journal* (New York: McElrath and Barker, 1854) 97.
9. W. H. Auden, "In Praise of the Brothers Grimm," *New York Times Book Review*, 12 November 1944, 1.
1. Margaret Atwood, "Grimms' Remembered," in Donald Haase, ed., *The Reception of Grimms' Fairy Tales: Responses, Reactions, Revisions* (Detroit: Wayne State UP, 1993) 292.
2. Stephen Greenblatt, "Introduction," *Representing the English Renaissance*, ed. Stephen Greenblatt (Berkeley: U of California P, 1988) viii.

mand. Whatever their form or medium, these stories are what have formed us all, they are what we must use to make our new fictions. . . . Out of old tales, we must make new lives.[3]

Heilbrun endorses the notion of appropriating, revising, and revitalizing "old tales" in order to produce new social discourses that can, in turn, refashion our lives.

How we go about mobilizing fairy tales to help us form new social roles and identities is a hotly contested question. Some advocate the recuperation and critique of the classic canon; others have called for the revival of "heretical" texts (stories repressed and suppressed from cultural memory) and the formation of a new canon; still others champion rewriting the old tales or inventing new ones. This volume furnishes examples of each of these strategies, providing "classic" versions of specific tale types side by side with less well known versions from other cultures and inspired literary efforts to recast the tales. These projects for reclaiming folkloric legacies are not unproblematic, and they have each come under fire for failing to provide the answer to that perennial question of what makes an ideal cultural story.

For some observers, the classic canon of fairy tales is so hopelessly retrograde that it is futile to try to rehabilitate it. Andrea Dworkin refuses to countenance the possibility of preserving tales that were more or less forced upon us and that have been so effective in promoting stereotypical gender roles:

> We have not formed that ancient world [of fairy tales]—it has formed us. We ingested it as children whole, had its values and consciousness imprinted on our minds as cultural absolutes long before we were in fact men and women. We have taken the fairy tales of childhood with us into maturity, chewed but still lying in the stomach, as real identity. Between Snow-white and her heroic prince, our two great fictions, we never did have much of a chance. At some point the Great Divide took place: they (the boys) dreamed of mounting the Great Steed and buying Snow-white from the dwarfs; we (the girls) aspired to become that object of every necrophiliac's lust—the innocent, *victimized* Sleeping Beauty, beauteous lump of ultimate, sleeping good.[4]

Yet for every critic who is convinced that we need to sound the tocsin and make fairy tales off-limits to children, there is one who celebrates the liberating energy and revolutionary edge of fairy tales. Alison Lurie, for example, sees the tales as reflecting a commendable level of gender equality, along with a power asymmetry tilted in favor of older women:

> These stories suggest a society in which women are as competent and active as men, at every age and in every class. Gretel, not Hansel, defeats the Witch; and for every clever youngest son there is a youngest daughter equally resourceful. The contrast is greatest in maturity,

3. Carolyn Heilbrun, "What Was Penelope Unweaving?" in *Hamlet's Mother and Other Women* (New York: Columbia UP, 1990) 109.
4. Andrea Dworkin, *Woman-Hating* (New York: Dutton, 1974) 32–33.

where women are often more powerful than men. Real help for the
hero or heroine comes most frequently from a fairy godmother or wise
woman, and real trouble from a witch or wicked stepmother. . . . To
prepare children for women's liberation, therefore, and to protect
them against Future Shock, you had better buy at least one collection
of fairy tales.[5]

Whom are we to believe? Andrea Dworkin, who contends that fairy tales
perpetuate gender stereotypes, or Alison Lurie, who asserts that they unsettle gender roles? Do we side with those who denounce fairy tales for
their melodrama and violence or with the psychologist Bruno Bettelheim,
who finds them crucial to a child's healthy mental development? Margaret
Atwood would answer by saying "It depends." Astonished by reports that
*Grimms' Fairy Tales* was being denounced as sexist, she observed that one
finds in the volume "wicked wizards as well as wicked witches, stupid
women as well as stupid men." "When people say 'sexist fairy tales,' " she
added, "they probably mean the anthologies that concentrate on 'The
Sleeping Beauty,' 'Cinderella,' and 'Little Red Riding Hood' and leave out
everything else. But in 'my' version, there are a good many forgetful or
imprisoned princes who have to be rescued by the clever, brave, and resourceful princess, who is just as willing to undergo hardship and risk her
neck as are the princes engaged in dragon slaying and tower climbing."[6]
Few fairy tales dictate a single, univocal, uncontested meaning; most are
so elastic as to accommodate a wide variety of interpretations, and they
derive their meaning through a process of engaged negotiation on the part
of the reader. Just as there is no definitive version of "Little Red Riding
Hood," there is also no definitive interpretation of her story.

Some versions of Little Red Riding Hood's story or Snow White's story
may appear to reenforce stereotypes; others may have an emancipatory potential; still others may seem radically feminist. All are of historical interest,
revealing the ways in which a story has adapted to a culture and been
shaped by its social practices. The new story may be ideologically correct
or ideologically suspect, but it can always serve as the point of departure
for debate, critique, and dialogue. In this volume, I have tried to convey a
sense of the rich cultural archive behind stories that we tend to flatten out
with the monolithic labels "Little Red Riding Hood," "Snow White," or
"Cinderella."

Recovering fairy tales that have undergone a process of cultural suppression or that have succumbed to cultural amnesia has been the mission
of a number of folklorists in the past decades. Instead of reshaping canonical fairy tales or trying to reinvent them, these collectors seek to fill in the
many empty spaces on the shelves of our collective folkloric archive. Rosemary Minard's *Womenfolk and Fairy Tales* explicitly seeks to identify tales
in which women are "active, intelligent, capable, and courageous human
beings."[7] While Minard succeeds in reviving some resourceful folklore heroines, many of the faces in her anthology are familiar ones. A Chinese Red
Riding Hood, a Scandinavian Beauty, and a British wife of Bluebeard

5. Alison Lurie, "Fairy Tale Liberation," *New York Review of Books*, 17 December 1970, 42.
6. Atwood, "Grimms' Remembered," 291–92.
7. Rosemary Minard, ed., *Womenfolk and Fairy Tales* (Boston: Houghton Mifflin, 1975) viii.

mingle in her anthology with the more obscure Unanana, Kate Cracker-nuts, and Clever Manka.

Like Minard, Ethel Johnston Phelps aims to collect tales that feature "active and courageous girls and women in the leading roles" for her volume *Tatterhood and Other Tales*.[8] By contrast, Angela Carter's *Virago Book of Fairy Tales* chooses texts for their historical interest, for the way in which they provide models of how women struggled, succeeded, and also sometimes failed in the challenges of everyday life. "I wanted to demonstrate the extraordinary richness and diversity of responses to the same common predicament—being alive—and the richness and diversity with which femininity, in practice, is represented in 'unofficial' culture: its strategies, its plots, its hard work."[9]

Our own fairy-tale repertoire can now be said to consist of two competing traditions. On the one hand, we have the classical canon of tales collected by, among others, Joseph Jacobs in England, Charles Perrault in France, the Grimm brothers in Germany, and Alexander Afanasev in Russia. On the other hand, we have a rival tradition of heretical stories established by folklorists who have sought to unearth buried cultural treasures and to conduct archaeological exercises designed to connect us with a subversive dimension of our collective past. In addition to this twin folkloric legacy, we have the reinventions of such authors as Hans Christian Andersen and Oscar Wilde, who, in competing with the raconteurs of old, attempted to supplant their narratives and to provide new cultural texts on which to model our lives.

Hans Christian Andersen and Oscar Wilde can be seen as moving in an imitative mode, attempting to capture the style and spirit of folk raconteurs in their literary efforts. Yet their fairy tales, with their self-consciously artless expressions and calculated didactic effects, diverge dramatically from the traditional tales of folk cultures. What both Andersen and Wilde seem to have forgotten is that the folktale thrives on conflict and contrast, not on sentiment and pathos. P. L. Travers tellingly registers her response as a child to reading Andersen's fairy tales: "Ah, how pleasant to be manipulated, to feel one's heartstrings pulled this way and that—twang, twang, again and again, longing, self-pity, nostalgia, remorse—and to let fall the fullsome tear that would never be shed for Grimm."[1] Andersen wants to erase "the pagan world with its fortitude and strong contrasts." Still, Andersen's "Little Mermaid" reveals just how easily literary fairy tales can mutate into folklore, lending themselves to adaptation, transformation, and critique in a variety of media and becoming part of our collective cultural awareness.

Feminist writers have resisted the temptation to move in the imitative mode, choosing instead the route of critique and parody in their recastings of tales. For Anne Sexton, for example, the history and wisdom of the past embedded in fairy tales is less important than the construction of new cultural signposts for coping with "being alive." Anne Sexton's *Transfor-*

---

8. Ethel Johnston Phelps, ed., *Tatterhood and Other Tales* (Old Westbury, New York: Feminist Press, 1978) xv.
9. Carter, *Virago*, xiv.
1. P. L. Travers, *What the Bee Knows: Reflections on Myth, Symbol and Story* (Wellingborough, Northamptonshire: Aquarian Press, 1989) 232.

*mations* begins by staking a claim to producing fairy tales, by declaring herself to be the new source of folk wisdom and of oracular authority. She positions herself as speaker, "my face in a book" (presumably the Grimms' *Nursery and Household Tales*), with "mouth wide, ready to tell you a story or two." In a self-described appropriation of the Grimms' legacy ("I take the fairy tale and transform it into a poem of my own"), Sexton creates new stories that stage her own "very wry and cruel and sadistic and funny" psychic melodramas.[2] As "middle-aged witch," Sexton presents herself as master of the black arts, of an opaque art of illusion, and also as a disruptive force, a figure of anarchic energy who subverts conventional cultural wisdom. Nowhere is her critique of romantic love, of the "happily ever after" of fairy tales, more searingly expressed than in the final strophe of "Cinderella":

> Cinderella and the prince
> lived, they say, happily ever after,
> like two dolls in a museum case
> never bothered by diapers and dust,
> never arguing over the timing of an egg,
> never telling the same story twice,
> never getting a middle-aged spread,
> their darling smiles pasted on for eternity.
> Regular Bobbsey Twins.
> That story.

Sexton's transformations reveal the gap between "that story" and reality, yet at the same time expose the specious terms of "that story," showing how intolerable it would be, even if true.

Sexton enters into an impassioned dialogue with the Grimm brothers, contesting their premises, interrogating their plots, and reinventing their conclusions. Other writers, recognizing the social energy of these tales, have followed her lead, rewriting and recasting stories told by Perrault, the Grimms, Madame de Beaumont, and Hans Christian Andersen. The dialogue may not always be as emotionally charged as it is in Sexton's poetry. In some cases it will be so muted that many readers will be unaware of the intertextual connection with fairy tales. Few film reviewers, for example, recognized the allusive richness of Jane Campion's *The Piano*,[3] which opens with a bow to Andersen's "Little Mermaid," then nods repeatedly in the direction of the Grimms' "Robber Bridegroom" and Perrault's "Bluebeard."

With her collection of stories *The Bloody Chamber*, Angela Carter joined Anne Sexton in reworking the familiar script of fairy tales, in her case to mount "a critique of current relations between the sexes." Carter positions herself as a "moral pornographer," a writer seeking to "penetrate to the heart of the contempt for women that distorts our culture." "Beauty and the Beast," "Little Red Riding Hood," "Puss in Boots," and "Bluebeard":

2. Diane Wood Middlebrook, *Anne Sexton* (Boston: Houghton Mifflin, 1991) 336–37.
3. *The Piano*, dir. Jane Campion, Miramax, 1994.

all these stories have, according to Carter, a "violently sexual" side to them, a "latent content" that becomes manifest in her rescriptings of fairy tales for an adult audience.[4] Carter aims above all to demystify these sacred cultural texts, to show that we can break their magical spells and that social change is possible once we become aware of the stories that have guided our social, moral, and personal development. Margaret Atwood's novels and short stories also enact and critique the plots of fairy tales, showing the degree to which these stories inform our affective life, programming our responses to romance, defining our desires, and constructing our anxieties. Like Sally, the fictional heroine of Atwood's "Bluebeard's Egg," Atwood questions the seemingly timeless and universal truths of our cultural stories by reflecting on their assumptions and exploring the ways in which they can be subverted through rewritings.

It was Charlotte Brontë who inaugurated with full force the critique of fairy-tale romance in fiction by women for women. The life story of the heroine of *Jane Eyre* (1847) can be read as a one-woman crusade and act of resistance to the roles modeled for girls and women in fairy tales.[5] At Gateshead, Jane Eyre finds herself positioned as domestic slave, as a Cinderella figure in the Reed household. Employed as an "under-nurserymaid, to tidy the rooms, dust the chairs" (25), she is subjected on a daily basis to reproaches, persecuted by two unpleasant "stepsisters" and by a "stepmother" who has an "insuperable and rooted aversion" (23) to her, and excluded from the "usual festive cheer" (23) of holiday parties. Jane, although initially self-pitying and complicit, takes a defiant stance, refusing to be contained and framed by the cultural story that has inscribed itself on her life. Rather than passively enduring her storybook fate (which will keep her—as a "plain Jane"—forever locked in the first phase of "Cinderella"), she rebels against the social reflexes of her world and writes herself out of the script.

Just as Jane refuses to model her behavior on Cinderella, despite the seductive, though false, hopes of that story, so too she refrains from accepting the role of beloved in Rochester's fairy-tale fantasies. No beauty, Jane is nonetheless at first enchanted by the prospect of domesticating a man who is described as "metamorphosed into a lion" and who inhabits a house with "a corridor from some Bluebeard's castle," a house that contains the dreaded forbidden chamber familiar to readers of "Bluebeard." Jane recognizes what is at stake for her in succumbing to a fairy-tale concept of romance: "For a moment I am beyond my own mastery. What does it mean? I did not think I should tremble in this way when I saw him—or lose my voice or the power of motion in his presence" (214). Jane Eyre rejects the cult of suffering and self-effacement endorsed in fairy tales like "Cinderella" and "Beauty and the Beast" to construct her own story, renouncing prefabricated roles and creating her own identity. She reinvents herself and produces a radically new cultural script, the one embodied in

4. Robin Ann Sheets, "Pornography, Fairy Tales, and Feminism: Angela Carter's 'The Bloody Chamber,'" *Journal of the History of Sexuality* 1 (1991): 635, 642.
5. All parenthetical citations to *Jane Eyre* refer to Charlotte Brontë, *Jane Eyre*, ed. Richard J. Dunn (New York: Norton, 1987).

the written record that constitutes her own autobiography. Making productive use of fairy tales by reacting to them, resisting them, and rewriting them rather than passively consuming them until they are "lying in the stomach, as real identity," Jane Eyre offers us a splendidly legible and luminous map of reading for our cultural stories.

The Texts of
# THE CLASSIC FAIRY TALES

# INTRODUCTION: Little Red Riding Hood

Late in life, Charles Dickens confessed that Little Red Riding Hood was his "first love": "I felt that if I could have married Little Red Riding Hood, I should have known perfect bliss."[1] Dickens's sentimental attachment to a fairy-tale character brought to literary life by Charles Perrault and reincarnated by the Brothers Grimm as Little Red Cap is hardly remarkable. But had Dickens been aware of Red Riding Hood's folkloric origins, he might have been more guarded in his enthusiasm for Perrault's "pretty village girl" or the Grimms' "dear little girl." Fairy tales, as folklorists and historians never tire of reminding us, have their roots in a peasant culture relatively uninhibited in its expressive energy. For centuries, farm laborers and household workers relied on the telling of tales to shorten the hours devoted to repetitive harvesting tasks and domestic chores. Is it surprising that, in an age without radios, televisions, and other electronic wonders, they favored fast-paced narratives with heavy doses of burlesque comedy, melodramatic action, scatalogical humor, and free-wheeling violence?

The distinguished French folklorist Paul Delarue claims to have found an authentic peasant folk narrative in "The Story of Grandmother" [10–11], a version of Little Red Riding Hood recorded in Brittany in 1885 but presumably told by the fireside at least a century earlier. While the tale recounts a girl's trip to grandmother's house and her encounter with a wolf, the resemblance to Perrault's "Little Red Riding Hood" and the Grimms' "Little Red Cap" ends there. This Gallic heroine escapes falling victim to the wolf and instead joins the ranks of trickster figures. After arriving at grandmother's house and unwittingly eating "meat" and drinking "wine" that turns out to be the flesh and blood of her grandmother, she performs a striptease for the wolf, gets into bed with him, and escapes by pleading with the wolf for a chance to go outdoors and relieve herself.

Although Delarue's "Story of Grandmother" was not recorded until 1885 (almost two centuries after Perrault wrote down the story of "Little

---

Bracketed page numbers refer to this Norton Critical Edition.
1. Charles Dickens, "A Christmas Tree," *Christmas Stories* (London: Chaptman and Hall, 1898) 8.

Red Riding Hood" [11–13]), it is presumably more faithful to an oral tradition predating Perrault, in part because the folklorist recording it was not invested in producing a highly literary book of manners for aristocratic children and worked hard to capture the exact wording of the peasant raconteur, and in part because oral traditions are notoriously conservative and often preserve the flavor of narratives as they circulated centuries ago. The "peasant girl" of the oral tradition is, as Jack Zipes points out, "forthright, brave, and shrewd."[2] She is an expert at using her wits to escape danger. Perrault changed all that when he put her story between the covers of a book and eliminated vulgarities, coarse turns of phrase, and unmotivated plot elements. Gone are the references to bodily functions, the racy double entendres, and the gaps in narrative logic. As Delarue points out, Perrault removed those elements that would have shocked the society of his epoch with their cruelty (the girl's devouring of the grandmother's flesh and blood), their inanity (the choice between the path of needles and the path of pins), or their "impropriety" (the girl's question about her grandmother's hairy body).[3]

Perrault worked hard to craft a tale that excised the ribald grotesqueries from the original peasant tale and rescripted the events in such a way as to accommodate a rational discursive mode and moral economy. That he intended to send a message about vanity, idleness, and ignorance becomes clear from the "moralité" appended to the tale:

> From this story one learns that children,
> Especially young girls,
> Pretty, well-bred, and genteel,
> Are wrong to listen to just anyone,
> And it's not at all strange,
> If a wolf ends up eating them. [13]

Perrault's Little Red Riding Hood has no idea that it is "dangerous to stop and listen to wolves" [12]. She also makes the fatal error of having a "good time" gathering nuts, chasing butterflies, and picking flowers [12]. And, of course, she is not as savvy as Thurber's "little girl" who knows that "a wolf does not look any more like your grandmother than the Metro-Goldwyn lion looks like Calvin Coolidge" [17].

Little Red Riding Hood's failure to fight back or to resist in any way led the psychoanalytically oriented Bruno Bettelheim to declare that the girl must be "stupid or she wants to be seduced." Perrault, in his view, transformed a "naive, attractive young girl, who is induced to neglect Mother's warnings and enjoy herself in what she consciously

---

2. Jack Zipes, ed. *The Trials and Tribulations of Little Red Riding Hood*, 2d ed. (New York: Routledge, 1993) 26.
3. Paul Delarue, "Les Contes merveilleux de Perrault et la tradition populaire," *Bulletin folklorique de l'Ile-de-France* (1951): 26.

believes to be innocent ways, into nothing but a fallen woman."[4] No longer a trickster who survives through her powers of improvisation, she has become either a dimwit or a complicit victim. Bettelheim was also sensitive to the transformations endured by the wolf. Once a rapacious beast, he was turned by Perrault into a metaphor, a stand-in for male seducers who lure young women into their beds. While it may be true that peasant cultures figured the wolf as a savage predator, folk raconteurs had probably already gleefully taken advantage of the metaphorical possibilities of Little Red Riding Hood's encounter with the wolf and also exploited the full range and play of the tale's potential for sexual innuendo.

The Grimms' "Little Red Cap" [13–16] erased all traces of the erotic playfulness found in "The Story of Grandmother" and placed the action in the service of teaching lessons to the child inside and outside the story. Like many fairy tales, the Grimms' narrative begins by framing a prohibition, but it has difficulty moving out of that mode. Little Red Cap's mother hands her daughter cakes and wine for grandmother and proceeds to instruct her in the art of good behavior: "When you're out in the woods, walk properly and don't stray from the path. Otherwise you'll fall and break the glass, and then there'll be nothing for Grandmother. And when you enter her room, don't forget to say good morning, and don't go peeping in all the corners of the room" [14]. The Grimms' effort to encode lessons in "Little Red Cap" could hardly be called successful. The lecture on manners embedded in the narrative is not only alien to the spirit of fairy tales—which are so plot driven that they rarely traffic in the kind of pedagogical precision on display here—but also misfires in its lack of logic. The bottle never breaks even though Red Cap strays from the path, and the straying takes place only after the wolf has already spotted his prey.

The folly of trying to derive a clear moral message from "Little Red Riding Hood" in any of its versions becomes evident from Eric Berne's rendition of a Martian's reaction to the tale:

> What kind of a mother sends a little girl into a forest where there are wolves? Why didn't her mother do it herself, or go along with LRRH? If grandmother was so helpless, why did mother leave her all by herself in a hut far away? But if LRRH had to go, how come her mother had never warned her not to stop and talk to wolves? The story makes it clear that LRRH had never been told that this was dangerous. No mother could really be that stupid, so it sounds as if her mother didn't care much what happened to LRRH, or maybe even wanted to get rid of her. No little girl is that stupid either. How could LRRH look at the wolf's eyes, ears, hands, and

4. Bruno Bettelheim, *The Uses of Enchantment: The Meaning and Importance of Fairy Tales* (New York: Knopf, 1976).

teeth, and still think it was her grandmother? Why didn't she get
out of there as fast as she could?[5]

In analyzing the rhetoric of the text and showing how it subverts the
very terms it establishes, Berne performs a kind of protodeconstructive
analysis that challenges the notion of an unambiguous moral message
in "Little Red Riding Hood." Still, both Perrault and the Brothers
Grimm remained intent on sending a moral message, and they did so
by making the heroine responsible for the violence to which she is
subjected. By speaking to strangers (as Perrault has it) or by disobeying
her mother and straying from the path (as the Grimms have it), Red
Riding Hood courts her own downfall.

For every act of violence that befalls heroes and heroines of fairy
tales, it is easy enough to establish a cause by pointing to behavioral
flaws. The aggression of the witch in "Hansel and Gretel," for example,
is often traced to the gluttony of the children. A chain of events that
might once have been arbitrarily linked to create burlesque effects can
easily be restructured to produce a morally edifying tale. The shift from
violence in the service of slapstick to violence in the service of a disciplinary regime may have added a moral backbone to fairy tales, but
it rarely curbed their uninhibited display of violence. Nineteenth-
century rescriptings of "Little Red Riding Hood" are, in fact, among
the most frightening, in large part because they tap into discursive practices that rely on a pedagogy of fear to regulate behavior. A verse melodrama that appeared in 1862 made Little Red Riding Hood responsible
for her own death and for her grandmother's demise:

> If Little Red Riding Hood only had thought
> Of these little matters as much as she ought,
> In the trap of the Wolf she would ne'er have been caught,
> Nor her Grandmother killed in so cruel a sort. [6]

Or, as Red Riding Hood's father put it in a version of the tale by Sabine
Baring-Gould:

> A little maid,
> Must be afraid
> To do other than her mother told her.[7]

The story of Little Red Riding Hood seems to have lost more than
it gained in making the transition from adult oral entertainment to
literary fare for children. Once a folktale full of earthy humor and high
melodrama, it was transformed into a heavy-handed narrative with a
pedagogical agenda designed by adults. In the process, the surreal vi-

5. Eric Berne, *What Do You Say After You Say Hello? The Psychology of Human Destiny* (New
   York: Grove, 1972) 43.
6. Zipes, *Trials*, 158.
7. Ibid., 200.

olence of the original was converted into a frightening punishment for a relatively minor infraction. It is only in the past few decades that the tale has been reinvigorated through the efforts of writers who have contested the disciplinary edge to the story and challenged its basic assumptions. Although the strategies for reframing the story vary from one author to the next, they generally aim to turn Little Red Riding Hood into a clever, resourceful heroine ("It is not so easy to fool little girls nowadays as it used to be" [17], as Thurber notes) or to rehabilitate the wolf ("Sweet and sound she sleeps in granny's bed, between the paws of the tender wolf," is the final sentence of Angela Carter's story "The Company of Wolves").[8]

Just as writers have felt free to tamper and tinker with "Little Red Riding Hood" (often radically revising its terms, as does Roald Dahl [21–23]), critics have played fast and loose with the tale, displaying boundless confidence in their interpretive pronouncements. To be sure, the tale itself, by depicting a conflict between a weak, vulnerable protagonist and a large, powerful antagonist, lends itself to a certain interpretive elasticity. Allegorical readings invest the story with a kind of interpretive plenitude, giving it a meaning, relevance, and sense that claims to transcend historical variation. Yet these readings, whether they take the form of political or social allegories can turn out to be remarkably unstable.

Both Erich Fromm and Susan Brownmiller have trained their interpretive skills on "Little Red Riding Hood." Each has read the story in allegorical terms as depicting an eternal battle of the sexes, but those readings reach very different conclusions about what is at stake in that battle. Fromm, whose psychoanalytic account of "Little Red Riding Hood" came under heavy fire from the historian Robert Darnton, finds in the tale the "expression of a deep antagonism against men and sex."[9] This story, presumably passed on from one generation of women to the next, portrays men as ruthless and cunning animals, who turn the sexual act into a cannibalistic ritual.

> The hate and prejudice against men are even more clearly exhibited at the end of the story. . . . We must remember that the woman's superiority consists in her ability to bear children. How, then, is the wolf made ridiculous? By showing that he attempted to play the role of a pregnant woman, having living things in his belly. Little Red-Cap puts stones, a symbol of sterility, into his belly, and the wolf collapses and dies. His deed . . . is punished according to his crime: he is killed by the stones, the symbol of sterility, which mock his usurpation of the pregnant woman's role.[1]

8. In *The Bloody Chamber and Other Stories* (New York: Penguin, 1979) 118.
9. Erich Fromm, *The Forgotten Language: An Introduction to the Understanding of Dreams, Fairy Tales and Myths* (New York: Rinehart, 1951) 241.
1. Fromm, *Forgotten*, 241.

The notion of a wolf suffering from womb envy may seem preposterous, but Fromm is not the only interpreter of the tale to read the
wolf's act of devouring as a cover for the desire to conceive. Anne
Sexton's wolf appears to be "in his ninth month" after gobbling down
Red Riding Hood and her grandmother, and the two are liberated when
a hunter performs "a kind of caesarian section."[2] A recent children's
version of the tale shows the wolf peacefully sleeping with a glowing
belly, swollen to accommodate the body of a serene Little Red Riding
Hood.[3]

For Susan Brownmiller, "Little Red Riding Hood" recounts a cultural story that holds the gender bottom line by perpetuating the notion
that women are at once victims of male violence even as they must
position themselves as beneficiaries of male protection:

> Sweet, feminine Little Red Riding Hood is off to visit her dear old
> grandmother in the woods. The wolf lurks in the shadows, con-
> templating a tender morsel. Little Red Riding Hood and her grand-
> mother, we learn, are equally defenseless before the male wolf's
> strength and cunning. . . . The wolf swallows both females with
> no sign of a struggle. . . . *Red Riding Hood* is a parable of rape.
> There are frightening male figures abroad in the woods—we call
> them wolves, among other names—and females are helpless before
> them. Better stick close to the path, better not be adventurous. If
> you are lucky, a *good friendly* male may be able to save you from
> certain disaster.[4]

Both Fromm and Brownmiller's efforts to view "Little Red Riding
Hood" as a repository for certain timeless and universal truths founder
precisely because every critic seems to find a different timeless and
universal truth in the tale. Allegorical readings tend to undermine and
discredit each other by their very multiplicity. Their sheer number begins to suggest that the story targeted for interpretation is nothing but
nonsense, that it veers off in the direction of the absurd, signifying
nothing.

"The Story of Grandmother" seems to support the notion that fairy
tales function as little more than a diversion and that efforts to invest
them with meaning inevitably misfire. But the excessive number of
references to nourishment, starvation, cannibalism, and devouring in
"The Story of Grandmother" also suggests that the interpretive stakes
are high and challenges us to understand the story's engagement with
the basic conditions of our existence. Psychoanalytic criticism has
worked hard to understand what Alan Dundes refers to as the strong

2. Anne Sexton, "Red Riding Hood," *Transformations* (Boston: Houghton Mifflin, 1971) 72–
79.
3. Beni Montresor, *Little Red Riding Hood* (New York: Doubleday, 1991).
4. Susan Brownmiller, *Against Our Will: Men, Women, and Rape* (New York: Bantam, 1976)
343–44.

component of "infantile fantasy" at work in the tale.[5] Dundes points
out that "Little Red Riding Hood," identified in the Aarne-Thompson
tale-type index[6] as AT 333 and known by the title, "The Glutton," is
probably a cognate form of AT 123, "The Wolf and the Seven Kids."
The only real difference, Dundes insists, is that the ogre goes to the
house of the child in AT 123, while the child goes to the house of the
ogre in AT 333. Dundes further argues that "Little Red Riding Hood,"
at least in its early forms, had more to do with children's anxieties about
being devoured than with the adult sexual anxieties that came to be
foregrounded as the story evolved. Chiang Mi's "Goldflower and the
Bear" (19–21) gives us an Asian version of "The Wolf and the Seven
Kids" that reveals a clear kinship with early European versions of "Little
Red Riding Hood" and suggests just how child-centered the tale was
in its early forms.

Angela Carter recalls her first encounter with Perrault's Little Red
Riding Hood: "My maternal grandmother used to say, 'Lift up the latch
and walk in,' when she told it [to] me when I was a child; and at the
conclusion, when the wolf jumps on Little Red Riding Hood and gob-
bles her up, my grandmother used to pretend to eat me, which made
me squeak and gibber with excited pleasure."[7] Carter's grandmother,
by impersonating the grandmother-devouring wolf who also imperson-
ates grandmothers, turns the tables by turning on her granddaughter,
the girl who feasts on grandmother's flesh and blood in folk versions of
the tale. Carter's account of her experience with "Little Red Riding
Hood" shows the tale to be one of intergenerational rivalry, yet it also
reveals the degree to which the meaning of a tale is generated in its
performance. The scene of reading or acting out a text can affect its
reception far more powerfully than the morals and timeless truths in-
serted into the text by Perrault, the Grimms, and others.

Consider Luciano Pavarotti's childhood experience with "Little Red
Riding Hood" and how markedly it differs from Carter's:

> In my house, when I was a little boy, it was my grandfather who
> told the stories. He was wonderful. He told violent, mysterious tales
> that enchanted me. . . . My favorite one was *Little Red Riding
> Hood*. I identified with Little Red Riding Hood. I had the same
> fears as she. I didn't want her to die. I dreaded her death—or what
> we think death is. I waited anxiously for the hunter to come.[8]

Little Red Riding Hood's brush with death is no longer burlesque,
playful, or erotically charged. Instead, it has become the site of violence,

5. Alan Dundes, "Interpreting 'Little Red Riding Hood' Psychoanalytically," in *Little Red Riding
Hood: A Casebook*, ed. Alan Dundes (Madison: U of Wisconsin P, 1989) 225.
6. Antti Aarne and Stith Thompson, *The Types of the Folktales: A Classification and Bibliography*
(Helsinki: Academia Scientiarum Fennica, 1961).
7. Angela Carter, ed., *The Virago Book of Fairy Tales* (London: Virago, 1990) 240.
8. Luciano Pavarotti, "Introduction," in Montresor, *Little Red Riding Hood*.

melodrama, and mystery. The feeling of dread, coupled with a sense of enchantment, captures the fascination with matters from which children are usually shielded. Pavarotti, like Dickens, is enamored of Little Red Riding Hood, but his infatuation is driven by her ability to survive death, to emerge whole from the belly of the wolf even in the face of death's finality.

- wolf eats granny   skin+blood in pantry
- girl to strip   girl escapes attaches rope to plumb tree.

## The Story of Grandmother†

There was once a woman who had made some bread. She said to her daughter: "Take this loaf of hot bread and this bottle of milk over to granny's."

The little girl left. At the crossroads she met a wolf, who asked: "Where are you going?"

"I'm taking a loaf of hot bread and a bottle of milk to granny's."

"Which path are you going to take," asked the wolf, "the path of needles or the path of pins?"[1]

"The path of needles," said the little girl.

"Well, then, I'll take the path of pins."

The little girl had fun picking up needles. Meanwhile, the wolf arrived at granny's, killed her, put some of her flesh in the pantry and a bottle of her blood on the shelf. The little girl got there and knocked at the door.

"Push the door," said the wolf, "it's latched with a wet straw."

"Hello, granny. I'm bringing you a loaf of hot bread and a bottle of milk."

"Put it in the pantry, my child. Take some of the meat in there along with the bottle of wine on the shelf."[2]

There was a little cat in the room who watched her eat and said: "Phooey! You're a slut if you eat the flesh and drink the blood of granny."

"Take your clothes off, my child," said the wolf, "and come into bed with me."

"Where should I put my apron?"

"Throw it into the fire, my child. You won't be needing it any longer."

† Told by Louis and François Briffault in Nièvre, 1885. Originally published by Paul Delarue, in "Les Contes merveilleux de Perrault et la tradition populaire," *Bulletin folklorique de l'Ile-de-France* (1951): 221–22. Translated for this Norton Critical Edition by Maria Tatar. Copyright © 1999 by Maria Tatar.

1. Yvonne Verdier ("Grand-mères, si vous saviez . . . le Petit Chaperon Rouge dans la tradition orale," *Cahiers de Littérature Orale* 4 [1978]: 17–55) reads the path of pins and the path of needles as part of a social discourse pertaining to apprenticeships for girls in sewing. In another region of France, the paths are described as the path of little stones and the path of little thorns. An Italian version refers to a path of stones and a path of roots.

2. Local variations turn the flesh into tortellini in Italy and into sausage in France, while the blood is often said to be wine.

When she asked the wolf where to put all her other things, her bodice, her dress, her skirt, and her stockings, each time he said: "Throw them into the fire, my child. You won't be needing them any longer."[3]

"Oh, granny, how hairy you are!"

"The better to keep me warm, my child!"

"Oh, granny, what long nails you have!"

"The better to scratch myself with, my child!"

"Oh, granny, what big shoulders you have!"

"The better to carry firewood with, my child!"

"Oh, granny, what big ears you have!"

"The better to hear you with, my child!"

"Oh, granny, what big nostrils you have!"

"The better to sniff my tobacco with, my child!"

"Oh, granny, what a big mouth you have!"

"The better to eat you with, my child!"

"Oh, granny, I need to go badly. Let me go outside!"

"Do it in the bed, my child."

"No, granny, I want to go outside."

"All right, but don't stay out long."

The wolf tied a rope made of wool to her leg and let her go outside.

When the little girl got outside, she attached the end of the rope to a plum tree in the yard. The wolf became impatient and said: "Are you making cables out there? Are you making cables?"

When he realized that there was no answer, he jumped out of bed and discovered that the little girl had escaped. He followed her, but he reached her house only after she had gotten inside.

# CHARLES PERRAULT

## Little Red Riding Hood†

Once upon a time there was a village girl, the prettiest you can imagine. Her mother adored her. Her grandmother adored her even more and made a little red hood for her. The hood suited the child so much that everywhere she went she was known by the name Little Red Riding Hood.

One day, her mother baked some cakes and said to her: "I want you

---

3. Many oral renditions of the tale presumably drew out the story by dwelling at length on what happens to each article of clothing.

† Charles Perrault, "Le Petit Chaperon Rouge," in *Histoires ou Contes du temps passé. Avec des Moralités* (Paris: Barbin, 1697). Translated for this Norton Critical Edition by Maria Tatar. Copyright © 1999 by Maria Tatar.

to go and see how your grandmother is faring, for I've heard that she's ill. Take her some cakes and this little pot of butter."

Little Red Riding Hood left right away for her grandmother's house, which was in another village. As she was walking through the woods she met old Neighbor Wolf, who wanted to eat her right there on the spot. But he didn't dare because some woodcutters were in the forest. He asked where she was going. The poor child, who did not know that it was dangerous to stop and listen to wolves, said: "I'm going to see my grandmother and am taking her some cakes and a little pot of butter sent by my mother."

"Does she live very far away?" asked the wolf.

"Oh, yes," said Little Red Riding Hood. "She lives beyond the mill that you can see over there. Hers is the first house you come to in the village."

"Well, well," said the wolf. "I think I shall go and see her too. I'll take the path over here, and you take the path over there, and we'll see who gets there first."

The wolf ran as fast as he could on the shorter path, and the little girl continued on her way along the longer path. She had a good time gathering nuts, chasing butterflies, and picking bunches of flowers that she found.

The wolf did not take long to get to Grandmother's house. He knocked: Rat-a-tat-tat.

"Who's there?"

"It's your granddaughter, Little Red Riding Hood," said the wolf, disguising his voice. "And I'm bringing you some cake and a little pot of butter sent by my mother."

The dear grandmother, who was in bed because she was not feeling well, called out: "Pull the bolt and the latch will open."

The wolf pulled the bolt, and the door opened wide. He threw himself on the good woman and devoured her in no time, for he had eaten nothing in the last three days. Then he closed the door and lay down on Grandmother's bed, waiting for Little Red Riding Hood, who, before long, came knocking at the door: Rat-a-tat-tat.

"Who's there?"

Little Red Riding Hood was afraid at first when she heard the gruff voice of the wolf, but thinking that her grandmother must have caught cold, she said: "It's your granddaughter, Little Red Riding Hood, and I'm bringing you some cake and a little pot of butter sent by my mother."

The wolf tried to soften his voice as he called out to her: "Pull the bolt and the latch will open."

Little Red Riding Hood pulled the bolt, and the door opened wide. When the wolf saw her come in, he hid under the covers of the bed and said: "Put the cakes and the little pot of butter on the bin and climb into bed with me."

Little Red Riding Hood took off her clothes and climbed into the bed. She was astonished to see what her grandmother looked like in her nightgown.

"Grandmother," she said, "What big arms you have!"

"The better to hug you with, my child."

"Grandmother, what big legs you have!"

"The better to run with, my child."

"Grandmother, what big ears you have!"

"The better to hear with, my child."

"Grandmother, what big eyes you have!"

"The better to see with, my child."

"Grandmother, what big teeth you have!"

"The better to eat you with!"

Upon saying these words, the wicked wolf threw himself on Little Red Riding Hood and gobbled her up.

*Moral*

From this story one learns that children,
Especially young girls,
Pretty, well-bred, and genteel,
Are wrong to listen to just anyone,
And it's not at all strange,
If a wolf ends up eating them.
I say a wolf, but not all wolves
Are exactly the same.
Some are perfectly charming,
Not loud, brutal, or angry,
But tame, pleasant, and gentle,
Following young ladies
Right into their homes, into their chambers,
But watch out if you haven't learned that tame wolves
Are the most dangerous of all.

# BROTHERS GRIMM

## Little Red Cap†

Once upon a time there was a dear little girl. If you set eyes on her you could not but love her. The person who loved her most of all was her grandmother, and she could never give the child enough. Once she made her a little cap of red velvet. Since it was so becoming and

† Jacob and Wilhelm Grimm, "Rotkäppchen," in *Kinder- und Hausmärchen*, 7th ed. (Berlin: Dieterich, 1857; first published: Berlin: Realschulbuchhandlung, 1812). Translated for this Norton Critical Edition by Maria Tatar. Copyright © 1999 by Maria Tatar.

since she wanted to wear it all the time, everyone called her Little Red Cap.

One day her mother said to her: "Look, Little Red Cap. Here's a piece of cake and a bottle of wine. Take them to your grandmother. She is ill and feels weak, and they will give her strength. You'd better start now before it gets too hot, and when you're out in the woods, walk properly and don't stray from the path. Otherwise you'll fall and break the glass, and then there'll be nothing for Grandmother. And when you enter her room, don't forget to say good morning, and don't go peeping in all the corners of the room."

"I'll do just as you say," Little Red Cap promised her mother.

Grandmother lived deep in the woods, half an hour's walk from the village. No sooner had Little Red Cap set foot in the forest than she met the wolf. Little Red Cap had no idea what a wicked beast he was, and so she wasn't in the least afraid of him.

"Good morning, Little Red Cap," he said.

"Thank you kindly, wolf."

"Where are you headed so early in the morning, Little Red Cap?"

"To my grandmother's."

"What's that you've got under your apron?"

"Cake and wine. Yesterday we baked and Grandmother, who is sick and feels weak, needs something to make her feel better."

"Where does your grandmother live, Little Red Cap?"

"It's another quarter of an hour's walk into the woods. Her house is right under three large oaks. You must know the place from the hazel hedges near it," said Little Red Cap.

The wolf thought to himself: "That tender young thing will make a dainty morsel. She'll be even tastier than the old woman. If you're really crafty, you'll get them both."

He walked for a while beside Little Red Cap. Then he said: "Little Red Cap, have you seen the beautiful flowers all about? Why don't you look around for a while? I don't think you've even noticed how sweetly the birds are singing. You are walking along as if you were on the way to school, and yet it's so heavenly out here in the woods."

Little Red Cap opened her eyes wide and saw how the sunbeams were dancing this way and that through the trees and how there were beautiful flowers all about. She thought to herself: "If you bring a fresh bouquet to Grandmother, she will be overjoyed. It's still so early in the morning that I'm sure to get there in plenty of time."

She left the path and ran off into the woods looking for flowers. As soon as she picked one she saw an even more beautiful one somewhere else and went after it, and so she went deeper and deeper into the woods.

The wolf went straight to Grandmother's house and knocked at the door. "Who's there?"

"Little Red Cap, I've brought some cake and wine. Open the door."

"Just raise the latch," Grandmother called out. "I'm too weak to get out of bed."

The wolf raised the latch, and the door swung wide open. Without saying a word, he went straight to Grandmother's bed and gobbled her up. Then he put on her clothes and her nightcap, lay down in her bed, and drew the curtains.

Meanwhile, Little Red Cap had been running around looking for flowers. When she finally had so many that she couldn't carry them all, she suddenly remembered Grandmother and set off again on the path to her house. She was surprised to find the door open, and when she stepped into the house, she had such a strange feeling that she thought to herself: "Oh, my goodness, I'm usually so glad to be at Grandmother's, but today I feel so nervous."

She called out a greeting but there was no answer. Then she went to the bed and drew back the curtains. Grandmother was lying there with her nightcap pulled down over her face. She looked very strange.

"Oh, Grandmother, what big ears you have!"

"The better to hear you with."

"Oh, Grandmother, what big eyes you have!"

"The better to see you with."

"Oh, Grandmother, what big hands you have!"

"The better to grab you with!"

"Oh, Grandmother, what a big, scary mouth you have!"

"The better to eat you with!"

No sooner had the wolf spoken those words than he leaped out of bed and gobbled up poor Little Red Cap.

Once the wolf had satisfied his desires, he lay down again in bed, fell asleep, and began to snore very loudly. A huntsman happened to be passing by the house just then and thought to himself: "How the old woman is snoring! You'd better check to see what's wrong." He walked into the house and when he got to the bed he saw that the wolf was lying in it.

"I've found you at last, you old sinner," he said. "I've been after you for a while now."

He pulled out his musket and was about to take aim when he realized that the wolf might have eaten Grandmother and that she could still be saved. Instead of firing, he took out a pair of scissors and began cutting open the belly of the sleeping wolf. After making a few snips, he could see a red cap faintly. After making a few more cuts, the girl jumped out, crying: "Oh, how terrified I was! It was so dark in the wolf's belly!" And then the old grandmother found her way out alive, though she could hardly breathe. Little Red Cap quickly fetched some large stones and filled the wolf's belly with them. When he awoke, he was about to bound off, but the stones were so heavy that his legs collapsed and he fell down dead.

All three were overjoyed. The huntsman skinned the wolf and went home with the pelt. Grandmother ate the cake and drank the wine Little Red Cap had brought her and recovered her health. Little Red Cap thought to herself: "Never again will you stray from the path and go into the woods, when your mother has forbidden it."

There is also a story about another wolf who met Little Red Cap on the way to Grandmother's, as she was taking her some cakes. The wolf tried to divert her from the path, but Little Red Cap was on her guard and kept right on going. She told her grandmother that she had met the wolf and that he had greeted her. But he had looked at her in such an evil way that "If we hadn't been out in the open, he would have gobbled me right up."

"Well then," said Grandmother. "We'll just lock that door so he can't get in."

Not much later the wolf knocked at the door and called out: "Open the door, Grandmother, it's Little Red Cap. I'm bringing you some cakes."

The two kept quiet and didn't open the door. Then old Grayhead circled the house a few times and finally jumped up on the roof. He was planning on waiting until Little Red Cap went home. Then he was going to creep up after her and gobble her up in the dark. But Grandmother guessed what he had on his mind. There was a big stone trough in front of the house. She said to the child: "Here's a bucket, Little Red Cap. Yesterday I cooked some sausages. Take the water in which they were boiled and pour it into the trough."

Little Red Cap kept carrying water until that big, big trough was completely full. The smell of those sausages reached the wolf's nostrils. His neck was stretched out so long from sniffing and looking around that he lost his balance and began to slide down. He went right down the roof into the trough and was drowned. Little Red Cap walked home cheerfully, and no one did her any harm.

# JAMES THURBER

## The Little Girl and the Wolf†

One afternoon a big wolf waited in a dark forest for a little girl to come along carrying a basket of food to her grandmother. Finally a little girl did come along and she was carrying a basket of food. "Are you carrying that basket to your grandmother?" asked the wolf. The little girl said

† James Thurber, "The Little Girl and the Wolf," from *Fables for Our Time and Famous Poems Illustrated by James Thurber* (New York: Harpers, 1940). Copyright © 1940 by James Thurber, renewed 1968 by Helen Thurber and Rosemary A. Thurber. Reprinted by arrangement with Rosemary A. Thurber and the Barbara Hogenson Agency.

yes, she was. So the wolf asked her where her grandmother lived and the little girl told him and he disappeared into the wood.

When the little girl opened the door of her grandmother's house she saw that there was somebody in bed with a nightcap and nightgown on. She had approached no nearer than twenty-five feet from the bed when she saw that it was not her grandmother but the wolf, for even in a nightcap a wolf does not look any more like your grandmother than the Metro-Goldwyn lion looks like Calvin Coolidge. So the little girl took an automatic out of her basket and shot the wolf dead.

*Moral: It is not so easy to fool little girls nowadays as it used to be.*

*[handwritten: — pulls out automatic and shoots wolf — girls are prepared, aware of such dangers nowadays. her past safety you doesn't allow passes days.]*

# ITALO CALVINO

## The False Grandmother†

*[handwritten: — ogress eater granny — Jordan riverlets]*

A mother had to sift flour, and told her little girl to go to her grandmother's and borrow the sifter. The child packed a snack—ring-shaped cakes and bread with oil—and set out.

She came to the Jordan River.

"Jordan River, will you let me pass?"

"Yes, if you give me your ring-shaped cakes."

The Jordan River had a weakness for ring-shaped cakes, which he enjoyed twirling in his whirlpools.

The child tossed the ring-shaped cakes into the river, and the river lowered its waters and let her through.

The little girl came to the Rake Gate.

"Rake Gate, will you let me pass?"

"Yes, if you give me your bread with oil."

The Rake Gate had a weakness for bread with oil, since her hinges were rusty, and bread with oil oiled them for her.

The little girl gave the gate her bread with oil, and the gate opened and let her through.

She reached her grandmother's house, but the door was shut tight.

"Grandmother, Grandmother, come let me in."

"I'm in bed sick. Come through the window."

"I can't make it."

"Come through the cat door."

"I can't squeeze through."

"Well, wait a minute," she said, and lowered a rope, by which she pulled the little girl up through the window. The room was dark. In

† "The False Grandmother," recorded by Antonio de Nino, 1883, in *Italian Folktales*, selected and retold by Italo Calvino, trans. George Martin (New York: Pantheon Books, 1980). Copyright © 1980 by Harcourt Brace & Company, reprinted by permission of Harcourt Brace & Company.

bed was the ogress, not the grandmother, for the ogress had gobbled up Grandmother all in one piece from head to toe, all except her teeth, which she had put on to stew in a small stew pan, and her ears, which she had put on to fry in a frying pan.

"Grandmother, Mamma wants the sifter."

"It's late now. I'll give it to you tomorrow. Come to bed."

"Grandmother, I'm hungry, I want my supper first."

"Eat the beans boiling in the boiler."

In the pot were the teeth. The child stirred them around and said, "Grandmother, they're too hard."

"Well, eat the fritters in the frying pan."

In the frying pan were the ears. The child felt them with the fork and said, "Grandmother, they're not crisp."

"Well, come to bed. You can eat tomorrow."

The little girl got into bed beside Grandmother. She felt one of her hands and said, "Why are your hands so hairy, Grandmother?"

"From wearing too many rings on my fingers."

She felt her chest. "Why is your chest so hairy, Grandmother?"

"From wearing too many necklaces around my neck."

She felt her hips. "Why are your hips so hairy, Grandmother?"

"Because I wore my corset too tight."

She felt her tail and reasoned that, hairy or not, Grandmother had never had a tail. That had to be the ogress and nobody else. So she said, "Grandmother, I can't go to sleep unless I first go and take care of a little business."

Grandmother replied, "Go do it in the barn below. I'll let you down through the trapdoor and then draw you back up."

She tied a rope around her and lowered her into the barn. The minute the little girl was down she untied the rope and in her place attached a nanny goat. "Are you through?" asked Grandmother.

"Just a minute." She finished tying the rope around the nanny goat. "There, I've finished. Pull me back up."

The ogress pulled and pulled, and the little girl began yelling, "Hairy ogress! Hairy ogress!" She threw open the barn and fled. The ogress kept pulling, and up came the nanny goat. She jumped out of bed and ran after the little girl.

When the child reached the Rake Gate, the ogress yelled from a distance, "Rake Gate, don't let her pass!"

But the Rake Gate replied, "Of course I'll let her pass; she gave me her bread with oil."

When the child reached the Jordan River, the ogress shouted, "Jordan River, don't you let her pass!"

But the Jordan River answered, "Of course I'll let her pass; she gave me her ring-shaped cakes."

When the ogress tried to get through, the Jordan River did not lower his waters, and the ogress was swept away in the current. From the bank the little girl made faces at her.

# CHIANG MI

## Goldflower and the Bear[†]

*Goldflower decides to stay home alone with brother 3*

Long, long ago, there was a clever and brave girl called Goldflower who lived with her mother and brother. They were very happy.

One day, her mother said: "Your Aunty is ill. I'm going to see her and won't be back tonight. Look after your brother and ask your Granny to stay with you tonight!" Then she left with a basket of eggs and a hen.

At sunset, Goldflower herded the sheep home. After penning up the sheep, she shooed all the chickens into the coop. Then, she and her brother climbed a small hill to call Granny. Usually, after one shout, there would be an answer, but today there was no reply after several shouts. Goldflower thought: "It doesn't matter. I'm not afraid." They went home and she bolted the door.

Lighting a wick, they sat by the fire-pan and she began to tell her brother a story. Suddenly they heard a knock at the door. Brother hugged her and cried: "I'm afraid!"

They heard a strange but kindly voice saying: "I'm Granny." Brother was very happy and shouted: "Sister, open the door! Granny has come!"

Goldflower leaned against the door and asked: "Is that you, Granny? What's wrong with your voice?"

"I've a cold." Came the reply followed by coughs.

The boy urged his sister to open the door. Meanwhile, the voice continued: "My dear, there is something wrong with my eyes and I'm afraid of light. Please blow out the wick before letting me in."

It was so dark in the room that they couldn't see who was coming in. Goldflower invited "Granny" to a stool, but it cried out when sitting down. The children jumped in fright. The "Granny" said: "Dear, I've a boil so I can't sit on hard wood. Please give me a wicker basket."

The swishing of the Bear's tail in the dark caused Goldflower to ask: "What's making that noise?"

"Oh! It's the fly-swatter your grandpa bought for me," replied "Granny."

The clever girl stoked the fire brighter and, wow, there was a pair of hairy feet! Now she realized this isn't Granny. It's the Bear which likes to eat children. Goldflower calmed and pretended to have seen noth-

---

† "Goldflower and the Bear," in Jack Zipes, *The Trials and Tribulations of Little Red Riding Hood* (New York: Routledge, 1993). Recorded by Chiang Mi, 1979. Copyright © 1993. Reprinted by permission of Routledge, Inc.

ing. But how to deal with this wicked Bear? Her mother had told her that bears were afraid of lice. She grabbed a handful of seeds and took off her brother's hat, pretending to be catching lice in his hair. She threw the seeds into the fire. They crackled. The Bear growled: "Don't let him sleep with me with his lice. Let him sleep outside!"

Brother was so afraid that he began to sob. Goldflower coaxed him to go to the other room to sleep. She locked the door on her way back. When she got back, the Bear asked her to go to bed. The Bear was very happy because it could have a hearty meal at midnight. But the clever Goldflower was also thinking of a way out. After sleeping for a while, she cried: "My tummy hurts! I want to go on the pot."

The Bear thought: She would not be good to eat like this. So, it tied one end of a belt to Goldflower's hand and let her go outside. After a while, the Bear pulled and then pulled again. It seemed that the girl was still on the other end. A long time passed. The Bear called several times but there was no answer. It got worried and pulled hard. Clunk. Something tumbled. The Bear was puzzled and felt its way along the belt. There was nothing at the end but a pot. The Bear was very angry. It was already midnight and the Bear started bellowing for food like any beast. Failing to find Goldflower, it stopped to drink some water from a pond before continuing the search. It saw Goldflower in the water and was overjoyed. When the Bear reached into the water to grasp Goldflower, she disappeared. The Bear angrily watched. When the water became still, Goldflower reappeared. The Bear reached out but Goldflower again vanished. The Bear did not know what to do. A laugh came from above. The Bear quickly looked up and saw Goldflower in a tree. The image in the water was her reflection. The Bear wanted to climb the tree, but Goldflower had covered it with grease. The Bear slipped again and again. The Bear could only wait under the tree hapless while Goldflower laughed up on the tree. "Granny, do you want to eat some pears? Please get me the spear in the house."

The Bear was really happy to hear this and went to fetch the spear. The Bear handed her the spear and, pointing to a few big pears, it said: "Give me those."

"Granny, open your mouth. Here comes the pear!" Goldflower threw one at the Bear's mouth.

The Bear ate it in two bites and asked her to spear some more. "Granny, this time open your mouth wide. It is a real big one."

The Bear opened its mouth as wide as it could. And with all her might, Goldflower threw the spear into its mouth. With a groan, the Bear fell flat. Goldflower slid down the tree and kicked the dead Bear. "Do you still want to eat children?"

Roosters crowed. Goldflower opened the door to her brother's room. He was sleeping soundly. She woke him and took him to the dead body. Now he knew that it was the wicked old Bear. The sun was rising

red in the east. Mother came back. She was very pleased to hear what
had happened and praised the brave little girl. The story of Goldflower
and the Bear spread far and wide. *—bear pretends to be grandma.*
*—asks girl to come to bed.*
*— peartree, throws spear*
*down bear's throat*
*to kill it.*

# ROALD DAHL

## Little Red Riding Hood and the Wolf†

As soon as Wolf began to feel
That he would like a decent meal,
He went and knocked on Grandma's door.
When Grandma opened it, she saw
The sharp white teeth, the horrid grin,
And Wolfie said, 'May I come in?'
Poor Grandmamma was terrified,
'He's going to eat me up!' she cried.
And she was absolutely right.
He ate her up in one big bite.
But Grandmamma was small and tough,
And Wolfie wailed, 'That's not enough!
'I haven't yet begun to feel
'That I have had a decent meal!'
He ran around the kitchen yelping,
'I've *got* to have another helping!'
Then added with a frightful leer,
'I'm therefore going to wait right here
'Till Little Miss Red Riding Hood
'Comes home from walking in the wood.'
He quickly put on Grandma's clothes,
(Of course he hadn't eaten those.)
He dressed himself in coat and hat.
He put on shoes and after that
He even brushed and curled his hair,
Then sat himself in Grandma's chair.
In came the little girl in red.
She stopped. She stared. And then she said,

'*What great big ears you have, Grandma.*'
'*All the better to hear you with,*' the Wolf replied.
'*What great big eyes you have, Grandma,*'

---

† Roald Dahl, "Little Red Riding Hood and the Wolf," in *Roald Dahl's Revolting Rhymes* (New York: Penguin, Puffin Books, 1995). Copyright © 1982 by Roald Dahl. Reprinted by permission of Random House, Inc.

said Little Red Riding Hood.
'*All the better to see you with,*' the Wolf replied.

He sat there watching her and smiled.
He thought, I'm going to eat this child.
Compared with her old Grandmamma
She's going to taste like caviare.

Then Little Red Riding Hood said, '*But Grandma,*
*what a lovely great big furry coat you have on.*'
'That's wrong!' cried Wolf. 'Have you forgot
'To tell me what BIG TEETH I've got?
'Ah well, no matter what you say,
'I'm going to eat you anyway.'
The small girl smiles. One eyelid flickers.
She whips a pistol from her knickers.
She aims it at the creature's head
And *bang bang bang*, she shoots him dead.
A few weeks later, in the wood,
I came across Miss Riding Hood.
But what a change! No cloak of red,
No silly hood upon her head.
She said, 'Hello, and do please note
'My lovely furry WOLFSKIN COAT.'

## ROALD DAHL

## The Three Little Pigs†

The animal I really dig
Above all others is the pig.
Pigs are noble. Pigs are clever,
Pigs are courteous. However,
Now and then, to break this rule,
One meets a pig who is a fool.
What, for example, would you say
If strolling through the woods one day,
Right there in front of you you saw
A pig who'd built his house of STRAW?
The Wolf who saw it licked his lips,
And said, 'That pig has had his chips.'

---

† Roald Dahl, "The Three Little Pigs," in *Roald Dahl's Revolting Rhymes* (New York: Penguin, Puffin Books, 1995). Copyright © 1982 by Roald Dahl. Reprinted by permission of Random House, Inc.

*'Little pig, little pig, let me come in!'*
*'No, no, by the hairs on my chinny-chin-chin!'*
*'Then I'll huff and I'll puff and I'll blow your*
    *house in!'*

The little pig began to pray,
But Wolfie blew his house away.
He shouted, 'Bacon, pork and ham!
'Oh, what a lucky Wolf I am!'
And though he ate the pig quite fast,
He carefully kept the tail till last.
Wolf wandered on, a trifle bloated.
Surprise, surprise, for soon he noted
Another little house for pigs,
And this one had been built of TWIGS!

*'Little pig, little pig, let me come in!'*
*'No, no, by the hairs of my chinny-chin-chin!'*
*'Then I'll huff and I'll puff and I'll blow your*
    *house in!'*

The Wolf said, 'Okay, here we go!'
He then began to blow and blow.
The little pig began to squeal.
He cried, 'Oh Wolf, you've had *one* meal!
'Why can't we talk and make a deal?'
The Wolf replied, 'Not on your nelly!'
And soon the pig was in his belly.
'Two juicy little pigs!' Wolf cried,
'But still I am not satisfied!
'I know full well my Tummy's bulging,
'But oh, how I adore indulging.'
So creeping quietly as a mouse,
The Wolf approached another house,
A house which also had inside
A little piggy trying to hide.
But this one, Piggy Number Three,
Was bright and brainy as could be.
No straw for him, no twigs or sticks.
This pig had built his house of BRICKS.
'You'll not get *me*!' the Piggy cried.
'I'll blow you down!' the Wolf replied.
'You'll need,' Pig said, 'a lot of puff,
'And I don't think you've got enough.'
Wolf huffed and puffed and blew and blew.

The house stayed up as good as new.
'If I can't blow it *down*,' Wolf said,
'I'll have to blow it *up* instead.
'I'll come back in the dead of night
'And blow it up with dynamite!'
Pig cried, 'You brute! I might have known!'
Then, picking up the telephone,
He dialled as quickly as he could
The number of Red Riding Hood.
'Hello,' she said. 'Who's speaking? *Who?*
'Oh, hello Piggy, how d'you do?'
Pig cried, 'I need your help, Miss Hood!
'Oh help me, please! D'you think you could?'
'I'll try, of course,' Miss Hood replied.
'What's on your mind?' . . . 'A *Wolf!*' Pig cried.
'I know you've dealt with wolves before,
'And now I've got one at my door!'
'My darling Pig,' she said, 'my sweet,
'That's something *really* up my street.
'I've just begun to wash my hair.
'But when it's dry, I'll be right there.'
A short while later, through the wood,
Came striding brave Miss Riding Hood.
The Wolf stood there, his eyes ablaze
And yellowish, like mayonnaise.
His teeth were sharp, his gums were raw,
And spit was dripping from his jaw.
Once more the maiden's eyelid flickers.
She draws the pistol from her knickers.
Once more, she hits the vital spot,
And kills him with a single shot.
Pig, peeping through the window, stood
And yelled, 'Well done, Miss Riding Hood!'

Ah, Piglet, you must never trust
Young ladies from the upper crust.
For now, Miss Riding Hood, one notes,
Not only has *two* wolfskin coats,
But when she goes from place to place,
She has a PIGSKIN TRAVELLING CASE.

# INTRODUCTION:
# Beauty and the Beast

"Beauty and the Beast," unlike most fairy tales, accommodates two developmental trajectories. It not only charts the challenges facing Beauty but also registers the transformation sustained by Beast, showing how these two antithetical allegorical figures resolve their differences to be joined in wedlock. What makes this story especially attractive is the way in which it is deeply entrenched in the myth of romantic love even as its representational energy is channeled into the tense moral, economic, and emotional negotiations that complicate courtship rituals. Virtually every culture knows this story in at least one of the variant forms of the tale type designated by folklorists as "The Search for the Lost Husband" or "The Man on a Quest for His Lost Wife."[1] While we may be burdened with a version of "Beauty and the Beast" that reflects the social mores of centuries ago, we also have an array of adept rescriptings that address the rich complexities and troubling anxieties of contemporary romantic entanglements.

"Cupid and Psyche," the earliest known version of "Beauty and the Beast," appeared in the second century A.D. in Apuleius's *Transformations of Lucian, Otherwise Known as the Golden Ass.* Told by a "drunken and half-demented" woman to a young bride abducted by bandits on her wedding day, it is described as a fairy tale meant to console the distraught captive. While "Cupid and Psyche" shares many features with "Beauty and the Beast" as we know it today, it deviates from what has become our canonical version of the tale in a number of key ways. Eros, the first "Beast," is only rumored to be a monster, and it is he who abandons Psyche, after her sisters urge her to take a look at the "enormous snake" that is her husband. More importantly, Psyche's story is what one critic has declared a "paradigm of female heroism."[2] The intrepid heroine, jilted by Cupid, never indulges in self-pity but sets off on an epic quest fraught with risks and requiring her to accomplish one impossible task after another. Unlike her elo-

---

Bracketed page numbers refer to this Norton Critical Edition.
1. Antti Aarne and Stith Thompson, *The Types of the Folktale: A Classification and Bibliography* (Helsinki: Academia Scientiarum Fennica, 1961).
2. Lee Edwards, "The Labors of Psyche: Toward a Theory of Female Heroism," *Critical Inquiry* 6 (1979): 37.

quent avatars in European versions of "Beauty and the Beast," Psyche is all action and no words. She undertakes a mission that not only requires the performance of feats (sorting grains, fetching a hank of golden wool, bringing Venus a jar of ice-cold water from the river Styx), but also demands that she renounce that quintessential feminine virtue known as compassion—the very trait that comes to the fore in European variants of "Beauty and the Beast."

The version of "Beauty and the Beast" best known to Anglo-American audiences was penned in 1757 by Madame de Beaumont (Jeanne-Marie Leprince de Beaumont) for her *Magasin des Enfants*. Based on a baroque literary version of more than one hundred pages written in 1740 by Mademoiselle Gabrielle-Suzanne de Villeneuve, Madame de Beaumont's courtly "Beauty and the Beast" reflects a desire to transform fairy tales into what Angela Carter has called "parables of instruction," vehicles for indoctrinating and enlightening children about the virtues of good manners, good breeding, and good behavior. But the lessons and moral imperatives inscribed in Beaumont's "Beauty and the Beast" pertain almost unilaterally to the tale's young women, who, in a coda, are showered with either praise or blame. As Carter points out, the moral of Madame de Beaumont's tale has more to do with "being good" than with "doing well": "Beauty's happiness is founded on her abstract quality of virtue."[3] With nervous pedagogical zeal, Madame de Beaumont concludes her tale with a flurry of plaudits and aspersions. Beauty has "preferred virtue to looks" and has "many virtues" along with a marriage "founded on virtue" [42]. Her two sisters, by contrast, have hearts "filled with envy and malice" [42].

Beauty's virtues, as her story makes clear, stem from a willingness to sacrifice herself. After discovering that Beast is prepared to accept one of the daughters in place of the father, she declares: "I feel fortunate to be able to sacrifice myself for him, since I will have the pleasure of saving my father and proving my feelings of tenderness for him" [36]. To be sure, not all Beauties are such willing victims. In the Norwegian "East o' the Sun and West o' the Moon," the heroine has to be talked into marrying the beast (a white bear) by her father: "[He] kept on telling her of all the riches they would get, and how well off she would be herself; and so at last she thought better of it".[4] Marrying her daughter off to a swine does not appear to be a terrible prospect to a woman in Straparola's "Pig King," especially after she learns that the daughter stands to inherit a kingdom. And in words that read to us like a parody of paternal expectations, the king of Basile's "Serpent" pleads with his

3. Angela Carter, "About the Stories," in *Sleeping Beauty and Other Favourite Fairy Tales*, ed. Angela Carter (Boston: Otter Books, 1991) 128.
4. "East o' the Sun and West o' the Moon," in *The Blue Fairy Tale Book*, ed. Andrew Lang (Harmondsworth: Penguin, Puffin Books, 1987) 2.

daughter to take a snake as her husband: "Finding myself, I know not how, bound by my promise, I beg you, if you are a dutiful daughter, to enable me to keep my word and to content yourself with the husband Heaven sends and I am forced to give you."[5]

That the desire for wealth motivates parents to turn their daughters over to a beast points to the possibility that these tales mirror social practices of an earlier age. Many an arranged marriage must have seemed like marriage to a beast, and the telling of stories like "Beauty and the Beast" may have furnished women with a socially acceptable channel for providing therapeutic advice, comfort, and consolation. Yet what many of these tales seem to endorse in one cultural inflection after another is a reinscription of patriarchal norms, the subordination of female desire to male desire, and a glorification of filial duty and self-sacrifice. Angela Carter's "Courtship of Mr. Lyon" is unique in its effort to demystify these "natural" virtues by subjecting them to grotesque exaggeration. Her heroine, who is "possessed by a sense of obligation to an unusual degree," perceives herself to be "Miss Lamb, spotless, sacrificial."[6]

Madame de Beaumont's version of "Beauty and the Beast" not only endorses the importance of obedience and self-denial, but also uses the tale to preach the transformative power of love, more specifically the importance of valuing essences over appearances. That the latter lesson should be inscribed in a tale with a heroine who embodies physical perfection and a seamless fit between external appearances and inner essences is an irony that seems to have escaped the French governess. In men, by contrast, external appearances, and even charm, count for nothing. As Beauty puts it, in Madame de Beaumont's tale: "It is neither good looks nor great wit that makes a woman happy with her husband, but character, virtue, and kindness, and Beast has all those good qualities. I may not be in love with him, but I feel respect, friendship, and gratitude toward him" [40]. In an anonymous version of 1818, Beauty delivers a similar speech attesting to the way in which Beast's kindness makes his "deformity" virtually disappear.[7]

Just as "Beauty and the Beast" was entering print, it took various didactic turns that had been absent from many of the folk versions. Madame de Beaumont's tale, which has become the canonical text in Anglo-American and European cultures, erases the burlesque humor and bizarre twists and turns found in many folk versions of the tale. Written at the dawn of the Enlightenment, it attempted to steady the

---

5. Giambattista Basile, "Serpent," in *The Pentamerone*, trans. Benedetto Croce, ed. N. M. Penzer (New York: John Lane the Bodley Head, 1932) 1:163.

6. Angela Carter, "The Courtship of Mr. Lyon," in *The Bloody Chamber and Other Stories* (Harmondsworth: Penguin, 1993) 45.

7 Marina Warner, "Reluctant Brides: Beauty and the Beast I," in *From the Beast to the Blonde: On Fairy Tales and Their Tellers* (New York: Farrar, Straus and Giroux, 1994) 295.

fears of young women, to reconcile them to the custom of arranged marriages, and to brace them for an alliance that required them to efface their own desires and to submit to the will of a "monster."

That there are multiple alternatives to the social norms presented in Madame de Beaumont's story becomes evident not only in recent re-castings of "Beauty and the Beast" by Angela Carter and others, but also in earlier versions that found their way into print. Consider the comic possibilities inherent in tales about girls who marry pigs, hedge-hogs, snakes, frogs, or donkeys and the ways in which folk raconteurs no doubt elaborated on courtship rituals and grew expansive about the wedding night. When the transformation from beast to man does not take place until the morning after—or many mornings after, as in Stra-parola's "Pig King" in the Neapolitan *Pleasant Nights*—it is not difficult to extract humor from bedroom scenes:

> As soon as the time for retiring for the night had come, the bride went to bed and awaited her unseemly spouse, and, as soon as he came, she raised the coverlet and bade him lie near to her and put his head upon the pillow. . . . When morning had come the pig got up and ranged abroad to pasture. . . . The queen went to the bride's chamber, expecting to find that she had met with the same fate as her sisters; but when she saw [Meldina] lying in the bed, all defiled with mud as it was, and looking pleased and con-tented, she thanked God for this favor, that her son had at last found a spouse according to his liking.

Or imagine how the grotesqueries of the Russian "Snotty Goat" ("snot ran down his nose, slobber ran from his mouth")[8] and the Italian "Mouse with the Long Tail" ("a tail a mile long that smelled to high heaven")[9] might have enlivened long winter evenings devoted to house-hold chores.

These variants of "Beauty and the Beast" offered more than just the opportunity for pointed wisecracks, spirited banter, and bawdy humor. The heroine of "The Snotty Goat," for example, is no self-effacing Beauty. She is described as "not a bit squeamish," willing to tolerate the vulgar habits of her betrothed yet also defiantly slapping the cheeks of anyone who tries to belittle her. Defiance is, in fact, a characteristic trait of many of the folkloric heroines who find themselves pestered by beasts. In the Grimms' "Three Little Birds," the heroine and her two brothers encounter a large black dog who turns into "a handsome prince" after being struck on the face. The fairy-tale heroine who reacts with aversion, loathing, or anger to the beastly exterior of her prospec-

8. Alexander Afanasev, "The Snotty Goat," in *Russian Fairy Tales*, trans. Norbert Guterman (New York: Pantheon, 1945) 201.
9. "The Mouse with the Long Tale," in *Italian Folktales*, comp. Italo Calvino, trans. George Martin (New York: Pantheon, 1980) 653.

tive spouse seems no less likely to effect a magical transformation than her tenderly affectionate or compassionate counterpart.

The Grimms' "Frog King, or Iron Heinrich," although classified by folklorists as a tale type separate from "Beauty and the Beast," bears a distinct family resemblance to it. Like Beauty, the princess in the Grimms' tale must accept an animal suitor, but, despite her father's admonition ("You shouldn't scorn someone who helped you when you were in trouble!" [40]), she balks at the idea of letting the frog into her bed. Flying into a rage, she hurls the erotically ambitious frog against the wall: "Now you'll get your rest, you disgusting frog!" [50].

Some variant forms of the Grimms' tale feature a princess who admits the frog to her chamber despite his revolting appearance, but most give us a princess who is perfectly capable of committing acts rivaling the coldblooded violence of dashing a creature against a wall. Scottish and Gaelic versions of "The Frog King" show the princess beheading her suitor. A Polish variant replaces the frog with a snake and recounts in lavish detail the princess's act of tearing the creature in two. A more tame Lithuanian text requires the burning of the snake's skin before the prince is freed from his reptilian state. Acts of passion as much as acts of compassion have the power to disenchant. Although the princess of "The Frog King, or Iron Heinrich" is self-absorbed, ungrateful, and cruel, in the end she does as well for herself as all of the modest, obedient, and charitable Beauties of "Search for the Lost Husband" tales.

"Beauty and the Beast" stands as a model for a plot rich in opportunities for expressing a woman's anxieties about marriage, but, in recent years, it has turned into a story focused on Beast rather than on Beauty. As Marina Warner points out, "the attraction of the wild, and of the wild brother in twentieth-century culture, cannot be overestimated; as the century advanced, in the cascade of deliberate revisions of the tale, Beauty stands in need of the Beast, rather than vice versa, and the Beast's beastliness is good, even adorable."[1] While eighteenth- and nineteenth-century versions of the tale celebrated the civilizing power of feminine virtue and its triumph over crude animal desire, our own culture hails Beast's heroic defiance of civilization, with all its discontents.

The happy ending to Angela Carter's "Tiger's Bride" reverses the traditional terms of "Beauty and the Beast." Fulfilling a contract requiring her to strip before the beast, the heroine approaches her oppressor as if offering "the key to a peaceable kingdom in which his appetite need not be my extinction" [65]. Haunted by "the fear of devourment" [65], she nonetheless courageously approaches Beast, prepared to hold up her father's end of the bargain:

1. Warner, "Go Be a Beast: Beauty and the Beast II," in *Beast*, 307.

He dragged himself closer and closer to me, until I felt the harsh velvet of his head against my hand, then a tongue, abrasive as sandpaper. "He will lick the skin off me!" And each stroke of his tongue ripped off skin after successive skin, all the skins of a life in the world, and left behind a nascent patina of shining hairs. My earrings turned back to water and trickled down my shoulders; I shrugged the drops off my beautiful fur.

Jon Scieszka plays fast and loose with the ground rules of folk narratives in his recasting of "The Frog King" for children, *The Frog Prince Continued*. His story, which begins *after* the transformation into a prince, reveals "the shocking truth about life 'happily ever after.'" The princess and the prince live in such marital discord that the prince flees, searching for a witch who can effect his transformation back into a frog. Yet in the end, as in the conclusion to "The Tiger's Bride," an authentic happy ending is found in a return to nature for both partners: "The Prince kissed the Princess. They both turned into frogs. And they hopped off happily ever after."[2] Scieszka has done more than give a clever new twist to an old tale. He has effected a profound ideological shift, transforming the tale from one that celebrates the superiority of culture over nature to one that concedes nature's triumph over culture. Human beings, as it turns out, are the real beasts.

The profound shift in cultural values registered in Carter's "Tiger's Bride" and Scieszka's *Frog Prince Continued* also finds expression in the Disney Studio version of "Beauty and the Beast." The true villain in this cinematic tale is Gaston (Beast's rival for Belle), a man who endorses the rigid, self-destructive logic of Western civilization and sanctions ecological devastation. Disney's Beast, virile yet sensitive, remains attuned to nature and open to the notion of regeneration by cultivating his feminine side. The Disney version in this particular case gives us a Beast-centered narrative devoted almost exclusively to the development of the male figure in the story. Marina Warner finds in Belle nothing but a cover for telling the story of Beast: "While the Disney version ostensibly tells the story of the feisty, strong-willed heroine, and carries the audience along on the wave of her dash, her impatient ambitions, her bravery, her self-awareness, and her integrity, the principal burden of the film's message concerns maleness, its various faces and masks, and, in the spirit of romance, it offers hope of regeneration from within the unregenerate male."[3]

With such a profusion of tales about animal grooms, it is easy to forget that women also often fall victim to enchantments and suffer in silence as snakes, frogs, and ravens, waiting for the right man to come along. While these tales may have fallen into cultural disfavor, with few

2. Jon Scieszka, *The Frog Prince Continued* (New York: Viking, 1991).
3. Warner, "Go," *Beast,* 314.

incorporated into the current canon of children's literature, they are worth looking at to see the extent to which gender becomes destiny in folklore. Comparisons of the two tale types can reveal the degree to which the folkloric imagination constructs subjectivity and desire differently for men and for women.

To begin with, it is important to bear in mind that the titles "The Search for the Lost Husband" (AT 425) and "The Man on a Quest for His Lost Wife" (AT 420) already reflect a certain degree of critical distortion. The two different lexical registers ("search" versus "quest") speak for themselves (a quest is more noble than a search), as does the absence of the female subject in the title "The Search for the Lost Husband." That the term *quest* is not always appropriate for describing a husband's action becomes evident from a reading of "The Frog Princess," a Russian tale about an enchanted bride. So resourceful, enterprising, and accomplished is this amphibious wife that she succeeds in earning the devotion of a human husband who does little more than burn her animal skin (and too soon at that). Yet the early burning of the skin leads to a second phase of action that demonstrates the husband's willingness to go to the ends of the earth for his wife's sake and culminates in a joyous reunion of the pair.

One cultural variant of "The Man on a Quest for His Lost Wife" is particularly prescient in its representation of nostalgia for a return to an original, primordial state of being. "The Swan Maiden," a tale widespread in Scandinavian regions, discloses the secretly oppressive nature of marriage with its attendant housekeeping and childrearing responsibilities. Swan maidens, domesticated by an act of violence, eventually seize the opportunity to return to an unsullied natural condition. The tormented Nora of Ibsen's *Doll's House*, a figure identified again and again as a bird or creature of nature, was clearly inspired to some extent by the swan maiden and her domestic tribulations. Instead of donning feathers (as swan maidens do), Nora rediscovers a diaphanous dancing dress and, after executing the tarantella, takes leave of Torvald. The symbolic nexus connecting animal skins, costumes, and dancing is so prominent in this tale type that it points to a possible underlying link with the Cinderella, Donkeyskin, and Catskin stories.

Barbara Fass Leavy has argued that tales of swan maidens must once have been far more widespread than they are today. She theorizes that the tales could be found "in virtually every corner of the world," because in most cultures "woman *was* a symbolic outsider, was the *other*, and marriage demanded an intimate involvement in a world never quite her own."[4] Yet Leavy is also well aware that some female animal brides lure their mortal husbands into a hermetic world of timeless beauty, a world in which the husbands revel in pleasure yet never feel

---

4. Barbara Fass Leavy, *In Search of the Swan Maiden: A Narrative on Folklore and Gender* (New York: New York UP, 1994) 2.

completely at home. Like Tannhäuser, who becomes Venus's captive, Urashima, a Japanese fisherman, and his many folkloric brothers dwell in a realm where they are the outsiders. Their stories reveal that the gender roles in "Beauty and the Beast" and other tale types are not as fixed as we are accustomed to believe. A look at the many extant variants of "The Search for the Lost Husband" can unsettle our expectations and show the extent to which fairy tales take us into regions that require constant reorientation.

# JEANNE-MARIE LEPRINCE DE BEAUMONT

## Beauty and the Beast†

Once upon a time there was a very wealthy merchant who lived with his six children, three boys and three girls. Since he was a man of intelligence and good sense, he spared no expense in educating his children and hiring all kinds of tutors for them. His daughters were all very beautiful, but the youngest was admired by everyone. When she was little, people used to refer to her as "the beautiful child." The name "Beauty" stuck, and, as a result, her two sisters were always very jealous. The youngest daughter was not only more beautiful than her sisters, she was also better behaved. The two older sisters were vain and proud because the family had money. They tried to act like ladies of the court and paid no attention at all to girls from merchant families. They chose to spend time only with people of rank. Every day they went to balls, to the theater, to the park, and they made fun of their younger sister, who spent most of her time reading good books.

Since the girls were known to be very wealthy, many prominent merchants were interested in marrying them. But the two older sisters always insisted that they would never marry unless they found a duke or, at the very least, a count. Beauty (as I noted, this was the name of the youngest daughter) very politely thanked all those who proposed to her, but she told them that she was still too young for marriage and that she planned to keep her father company for some years to come.

Out of the blue, the merchant lost his fortune, and he had nothing left but a small country house quite far from town. With tears in his eyes, he told his children that they would have to live in that house from now on and that, by working there like peasants, they could manage to make ends meet. The two elder daughters said that they did not want to leave town and that they had many admirers who would be more than happy to marry them, even though they were no longer

† Jeanne-Marie Leprince de Beaumont, "La Belle et la Bête," in *Le Magasin des Enfants* (London: Haberkorn, 1756). Translated for this Norton Critical Edition by Maria Tatar. Copyright © 1999 by Maria Tatar.

wealthy. But the fine young ladies were wrong. Their admirers had lost all interest in them now that they were poor. And since they were disliked because of their pride, people said: "Those two girls don't deserve our sympathy. It's quite satisfying to see pride take a fall. Let them play the ladies while tending their sheep."

At the same time, people were saying: "As for Beauty, we are very upset by her misfortune. She's such a good girl! She speaks so kindly to the poor. She is so sweet and sincere."

There were a number of gentlemen who would have been happy to marry Beauty, even though she didn't have a penny. She told them that she could not bring herself to abandon her poor father in his distress and that she would go with him to the country in order to comfort him and help him with his work. Poor Beauty had been upset at first by the loss of the family fortune, but she said to herself: "No matter how much I cry, my tears won't bring our fortune back. I must try to be happy without it."

When they arrived at the country house, the merchant and his three sons began working the land. Beauty got up every day at four in the morning and started cleaning the house and preparing breakfast for the family. It was hard for her at first, because she was not used to working like a servant. At the end of two months, however, she became stronger, and the hard work made her very healthy. After finishing her housework, she read or sang while spinning. Her two sisters, by contrast, were bored to death. They got up at ten in the morning, took walks all day long, and talked endlessly about the beautiful clothes they used to wear.

"Look at our sister," they said to each other. "She is so stupid and such a simpleton that she is perfectly satisfied with her miserable lot."

The good merchant did not agree with his daughters. He knew that Beauty could stand out in company in a way that her sisters could not. He admired the virtue of his daughter, above all her patience. The sisters not only made her do all the housework, they also insulted her whenever they could.

The family had lived an entire year in seclusion when the merchant received a letter informing him that a ship containing his merchandise had just arrived safely in its home port. The news made the two elder sisters giddy with excitement, for they thought they would finally be able to leave the countryside where they were so bored. When they saw that their father was ready to leave, they begged him to bring them dresses, furs, laces, and all kinds of baubles. Beauty did not ask for anything, because she thought that all the money from the merchandise would not be enough to buy everything her sisters wanted.

"Don't you want me to buy anything for you?" asked her father.

"You are so kind to think of me," Beauty answered. "Can you bring me a rose, for there are none here?"

It was not that Beauty was anxious to have a rose, but she did not want to set an example that would make her sisters look bad. Her sisters would have said that she was asking for nothing in order to make herself look good.

The good man left home, but when he arrived at the port he found that there was a lawsuit over his merchandise. After much trouble, he set off for home as impoverished as he had been on his departure. He had only thirty miles left to go and was already overjoyed at the prospect of seeing his children again when he had to cross a dense forest and got lost. There was a fierce snowstorm, and the wind was so strong that it knocked him off his horse twice. When night fell, he was sure that he was going to die of hunger or of the cold or that he would be eaten by the wolves that he could hear howling all around. All of a sudden he saw a bright light at the end of a long avenue of trees. The bright light seemed very far away. He walked in its direction and realized that it was coming from an immense castle that was completely lit up. The merchant thanked God for sending help, and he hurried toward the castle. He was surprised that no one was in the courtyard. His horse went inside a large, open stable, where he found some hay and oats. The poor animal, near death from hunger, began eating voraciously. The merchant tied the horse up in the stable and walked toward the house, where not a soul was in sight. Once he entered the great hall, however, he found a warm fire and a table laden with food, with just a single place setting. Since the rain and snow had soaked him to the bone, he went over to the fire to get dry. He thought to himself: "The master of the house, or his servants, will not be offended by the liberties I am taking. No doubt someone will be back soon."

He waited a long time. Once the clock struck eleven and there was still no one in sight, he could not resist the pangs of hunger and, trembling with fear, he took a chicken and ate it all up in two big bites. He also drank several glasses of wine and, feeling more daring, he left the great hall and crossed many large, magnificently furnished apartments. Finally he found a room with a good bed. Since it was past midnight and he was exhausted, he took it upon himself to close the door and go to bed.

When he got up the next day, it was already ten in the morning. He was greatly surprised to find clean clothes in the place of the ones that had been completely ruined by the rain. "Surely," he thought to himself, "this palace belongs to some good fairy who has taken pity on me."

He looked out the window and saw that it was no longer snowing. Before his eyes a magnificent vista of gardens and flowers unfolded. He returned to the great hall where he had dined the night before and found a small table with a cup of hot chocolate on it. "Thank you, Madame Fairy," he said out loud, "for being so kind as to remember my breakfast."

After finishing his hot chocolate, the good man left to go find his horse. Passing beneath a magnificent arbor of roses, he remembered that Beauty had asked him for a rose, and he plucked one from a branch with many flowers on it. At that very moment, he heard a loud noise and saw a beast coming toward him. It looked so dreadful that he almost fainted.

"You are very ungrateful," said the beast in a terrible voice. "I have saved your life by sheltering you in my castle, and you repay me by stealing my roses, which I love more than anything in the world. You will have to pay for your offense. I'm going to give you exactly a quarter of an hour to beg God's forgiveness."

The merchant fell to his knees and, hands clasped, pleaded with the beast: "My Liege, pardon me. I did not think I would be offending you by plucking a rose for my daughter, who asked me to bring her one or two."

"I am not called 'My Liege,'" said the monster. "My name is Beast. I don't like flattery, and I prefer that people say what they think. So don't try to move me with your compliments. But you said that you have some daughters. I am prepared to forgive you if one of your daughters consents to die in your place. Don't argue with me. Just go. If your daughters refuse to die for you, swear that you will return in three days."

The good man was not about to sacrifice one of his daughters to this hideous monster, but he thought: "At least I will have the pleasure of embracing them one last time."

He swore that he would return, and Beast told him that he could leave whenever he wished. "But I don't want you to leave empty-handed," he added. "Return to the room in which you slept. There you will find a large empty chest. You can fill it up with whatever you like, and I will have it delivered to your door."

The beast withdrew, and the good man thought to himself: "If I must die, I will at least have the consolation of leaving something for my poor children to live on."

The merchant returned to the room where he had slept. He filled the great chest that Beast had described with the many gold pieces he found there. After he found his horse in the stable, he left the palace with a sadness equal to the joy he had felt on entering it. His horse instinctively took one of the forest paths, and in just a few hours, the good man arrived at his little house. His children gathered around him, but instead of responding to their caresses, the merchant burst into tears as he gazed on them. In his hand, he was holding the branch of roses he had brought for Beauty. He gave it to her and said: "Beauty, take these roses. They have cost your poor father dearly."

Then the merchant told his family about the woeful events that had befallen him. Upon hearing the tale, the two sisters uttered loud cries and said derogatory things to Beauty, who was not crying: "See what the pride of this little creature has brought down on us!" they said.

"Why didn't she ask for fine clothes the way we did. No, she wanted to get all the attention. She's responsible for Father's death, and she's not even shedding a tear!"

"That would be quite pointless," Beauty replied. "Why should I shed tears about Father when he is not going to die. Since the monster is willing to accept one of his daughters, I am prepared to risk all his fury. I feel fortunate to be able to sacrifice myself for him, since I will have the pleasure of saving my father and proving my feelings of tenderness for him."

"No, sister," said her three brothers. "You won't die. We will find this monster, and we are prepared to die under his blows if we are unable to slay him."

"Don't count on that, children," said the merchant. "The beast's power is so great that I don't have the least hope of killing him. I am moved by the goodness of Beauty's heart, but I refuse to risk her life. I'm old and don't have many years left. I will only lose a few years of my life, and I don't regret losing them for your sake, my dear children."

"Rest assured, Father," said Beauty, "that you will not go to that palace without me. You can't keep me from following you. I may be young, but I am not all that attached to life, and I would rather be devoured by that monster than die of the grief which your loss would cause me."

It was no use arguing with Beauty. She was determined to go to the palace. Her sisters were delighted, for the virtues of their younger sister had filled them with a good deal of envy. The merchant was so pre-occupied by the sad prospect of losing his daughter that he forgot about the chest he had filled with gold. But as soon as he repaired to his room to get some sleep, he was astonished to find it beside his bed. He decided not to tell his children that he had become rich, for his daughters would then want to return to town, and he was determined to die in the country. He did confide his secret to Beauty, who told him that several gentlemen had come during his absence and that two of them wanted to marry her sisters. Beauty begged her father to let them marry. She was so kind that she still loved her sisters with all her heart and forgave them the evil they had done her.

When Beauty left with her father, the two mean sisters rubbed their eyes with an onion in order to draw tears. But the brothers cried real tears, as did the merchant. Only Beauty did not cry at all, because she did not want to make everyone even more sad.

The horse took the road to the palace, and, when night fell, they could see that it was all lit up. The horse went by itself to the stable, and the good man went with his daughter into the hall, where there was a magnificently set table with two place settings. The merchant did not have the stomach to eat, but Beauty, forcing herself to appear calm, sat down and served her father. "You see, Father," she said while forc-

ing a laugh, "the beast wants to fatten me up before eating me, since
he paid so dearly for me."

After they had dined, they heard a loud noise, and the merchant
tearfully bid adieu to his poor daughter, for he knew it was the beast.
Beauty could not help but tremble at the sight of this horrible figure,
but she tried as hard as she could to stay calm. The monster asked her
if she had come of her own free will and, trembling, she replied that
she had.

"You are very kind," said Beast, "and I am very grateful to you. As
for you, my good man, get out of here by tomorrow morning and don't
think of coming back here ever again. Goodbye, Beauty."

"Goodbye, Beast," she replied. Suddenly the monster vanished.

"Oh my daughter!" cried the merchant, embracing Beauty. "I am
half dead with fear. Believe me, you have to let me stay," he said.

"No, Father," Beauty said firmly. "You must go tomorrow morning
and leave me to the mercy of heaven. Heaven may still take pity on
me."

They both went to bed thinking that they would not be able to sleep
all night long, but they had hardly gotten into their beds when their
eyes closed. While she was sleeping, Beauty saw a woman who said to
her: "I am pleased with your kind heart, Beauty. The good deed you
have done in saving your father's life will not go unrewarded."

Upon waking, Beauty recounted this dream to her father. While it
comforted him a little, it did not keep him from crying out loud when
he had to leave his dear daughter. After he had left, Beauty sat down
in the great hall and began to cry as well. But since she was courageous,
she put herself in God's hands and resolved not to bemoan her fate
during the short time she had left to live. Convinced that Beast planned
to eat her that very evening, she decided to walk around the grounds
and to explore the castle while awaiting her fate. She could not help
but admire the castle's beauty, and she was very surprised to find a door
upon which was written: "Beauty's Room." She opened the door hastily
and was dazzled by the radiant beauty of that room. She was especially
impressed by a huge bookcase, a harpsichord, and various music books.
"Someone does not want me to get bored!" she said softly. Then she
realized: "If I had only one hour to live here, no one would have made
such a fuss about the room." This thought lifted her spirits.

She opened the bookcase and saw a book, on the cover of which
was written in gold letters: "Your wish is our command. Here you are
queen and mistress."

"Alas," she sighed, "I only wish to see my poor father again and to
know what he's doing now."

She had said this to herself, so you can imagine how surprised she
was when she looked in a large mirror and saw her father arriving at
his house with a dejected expression. Her sisters went out to meet him,

and, despite the faces they made in order to look as if they were distressed, they were visibly happy to have lost their sister. A moment later, everything in the mirror vanished. Beauty could not help thinking that Beast was most obliging and that she had nothing to fear from him.

At noon, Beauty found the table set and, during her meal, she heard an excellent concert, even though she could not see a soul. That evening, as she was about to sit down at the table, she heard Beast making noises, and she could not help but tremble.

"Beauty," said the monster, "will you let me watch you dine?"

"You are my master," said Beauty, trembling.

"No, you are the only mistress here," replied Beast. "If I bother you, order me to go, and I will leave at once. Tell me, don't you find me very ugly?"

"Yes, I do," said Beauty. "I don't know how to lie. But I do think that you are very kind."

"You are right," said the monster. "But in addition to being ugly, I also lack intelligence. I know very well that I am nothing but a beast."

"You can't be a beast," replied Beauty, "if you know that you lack intelligence. A fool never knows that he is stupid."

"Go ahead and eat, Beauty," said the monster, "and try not to be bored in your house, for everything here is yours, and I would be upset if you were not happy."

"You are very kind," said Beauty. "I swear to you that I am completely pleased with your good heart. When I think of it, you no longer seem ugly to me."

"Oh, of course," Beast replied. "I have a kind heart, but I am still a monster."

"There are certainly men more monstrous than you," said Beauty. "I like you better, even with your looks, than men who hide false, corrupt, and ungrateful hearts behind charming manners."

"If I were intelligent," said Beast, "I would pay you a great compliment to thank you. But I am so stupid that all I can say is that I am very much obliged."

Beauty ate with a good appetite. She no longer dreaded the monster, but she thought that she would die of fright when he said: "Beauty, would you be my wife?"

It took her a moment to get to the point of answering. She was afraid to provoke the monster by refusing him. Trembling, she said to him: "No, Beast."

At that moment, the poor monster meant to sigh deeply, but he made such a frightful whistling sound that it echoed throughout the palace. Beauty felt better soon, however, because Beast, turning to look at her from time to time, left the room and said adieu in a sad voice. Finding herself alone, Beauty felt great compassion for poor Beast. "Alas," she said, "it is too bad he is so ugly, for he is so kind."

Beauty spent three peaceful months at the castle. Every evening, Beast paid her a visit and, while she was eating, entertained her with good plain talk, though not with what the world would call wit. Each day Beauty discovered new good qualities in the monster. Once she began seeing him every day, she became accustomed to his ugliness, and, far from fearing his arrival, she often looked at her watch to see if it was nine o'clock yet. Beast never failed to appear at that hour. There was only one thing that still bothered Beauty. The monster, before leaving, always asked her if she wanted to be his wife, and he seemed deeply wounded when she refused.

One day she said to him: "You are making me feel upset, Beast. I would like to be able to marry you, but I am far too candid to allow you to believe that that could ever happen. I will always be your friend. Try to be satisfied with that."

"I will have to," Beast replied. "I don't flatter myself, and I know that I'm horrible looking, but I love you very much. However, I am very happy that you want to stay here. Promise me that you will never leave."

Beauty blushed at these words. She had seen in her mirror that her father was sick at heart at having lost her. She had been hoping to see him again. "I can promise you that I will never leave you," she said to Beast. "But right now I am so longing to see my father again that I would die of grief if you were to deny me this wish."

"I would rather die myself than cause you pain," said Beast. "I will send you back to your father. Stay there, and your poor beast will die of grief."

"No," Beauty said, bursting into tears, "I love you too much to be the cause of your death. I promise to return in a week. You have let me see that my sisters are married and that my brothers have left to serve in the army. Father is living all alone. Let me stay with him for just a week."

"You will be there tomorrow morning," said Beast. "But don't forget your promise. All you have to do is put your ring on the table before going to sleep when you want to return. Goodbye, Beauty."

As was his habit, Beast sighed deeply after speaking, and Beauty went to bed feeling very sad to see him so dejected. The next morning, on waking up, she was in her father's house. She pulled a cord at the side of her bed and a bell summoned a servant, who uttered a loud cry upon seeing her. The good man of the house came running when he heard the cry, and he almost died of joy when he saw his beloved daughter. They held each other tight for over a quarter of an hour. After the first excitement subsided, Beauty realized that she didn't have any clothes to go out in. But the servant told her that she had just discovered in the room next door a huge trunk full of silk dresses embroidered with gold and encrusted with diamonds. Beauty thanked Beast for his thoughtfulness. She took the least ornate of the dresses and told the servant to lock up the others, for she wanted to make a present of them to her sisters. Hardly had she spoken these words when the chest disappeared. When her father told her that Beast wanted her to keep everything for herself, the dresses and the chest reappeared on the spot.

While Beauty was getting dressed, her two sisters learned about her arrival and rushed to the scene with their husbands. Both sisters were very unhappy. The older one had married a remarkably handsome gentleman, but he was so enamored of his own looks that he spent all day in front of the mirror. The other one had married a man of great wit, but he used it to infuriate everybody, first and foremost his wife. Beauty's sisters were so mortified that they felt ready to die when they saw her dressed like a princess and more beautiful than the bright day. Beauty tried in vain to shower them with attention, but nothing could restrain their jealousy, which only increased when Beauty told them how happy she was. These two envious women walked down to the garden so that they could weep freely. They both asked themselves: "Why should this little beast enjoy more happiness than we do? Aren't we more likable than she is?"

"Dearest sister," the older one said, "I have an idea. Let's try to keep Beauty here for more than a week. Her stupid beast will get angry when he sees that she has broken her promise, and maybe he'll eat her up."

"You're right," the other one replied. "To make that work, we will have to shower her with affection and act as if we are delighted to have her here."

Having made this decision, the two nasty creatures returned to Beauty's room and showed her so much affection that she nearly wept for joy. When the week had gone by, the two sisters started tearing out their hair and performed so well that Beauty promised to stay another four or five days. At the same time she felt guilty about the grief she was causing poor Beast, whom she loved with all her heart and missed seeing. On the tenth night she spent at her father's house, she dreamed that she was in a garden of the palace when she saw Beast lying in the grass, nearly dead and reproaching her for her ingratitude. Beauty woke up with a start and began crying. "Aren't I terrible," she said, "for causing grief to someone who has done so much to please me? Is it his fault that he's ugly and lacks intelligence? He is kind. That's worth more than anything else. Why haven't I wanted to marry him? I would be more happy with him than my sisters are with their husbands. It is neither good looks nor great wit that makes a woman happy with her husband, but character, virtue, and kindness, and Beast has all those good qualities. I may not be in love with him, but I feel respect, friendship, and gratitude toward him. If I made him unhappy, my lack of appreciation would make me feel guilty for the rest of my life." With these words, Beauty got up, wrote a few lines to her father to explain why she was leaving, put her ring on the table, and went back to bed. She had hardly gotten into bed when she fell sound asleep. And when she awoke in the morning, she was overjoyed to find herself in Beast's palace. She dressed up in magnificent clothes just to make him happy and spent the day feeling bored to death while waiting for the clock to strike nine. But the clock struck nine in vain. Beast was nowhere in sight.

Beauty feared that she might be responsible for his death. She ran into every room of the castle, crying out loud. She was in a state of despair. After having searched everywhere, she remembered her dream and ran into the garden, toward the canal where she had seen Beast in her sleep. She found poor Beast stretched out unconscious, and she was sure that he was dead. Feeling no revulsion at his looks, she threw herself on him and, realizing that his heart was still beating, she got some water from the canal and threw it on him. Beast opened his eyes and told Beauty: "You forgot your promise. The thought of having lost you made me decide to starve myself. But now I will die happy, for I have the pleasure of seeing you one more time."

"No, my dear Beast, you will not die," said Beauty. "You will live and become my husband. From this moment on, I give you my hand in marriage, and I swear that I belong only to you. Alas, I thought that I felt only friendship for you, but the grief I am feeling makes me realize that I can't live without you." — b/c of guilt? - seems implied on no.

Scarcely had Beauty uttered these words when the castle became radiant with light. Fireworks and music alike signaled a celebration. But these attractions did not engage her attention for long. She turned back to look at her dear beast, whose perilous condition made her tremble with fear. How great was her surprise when she discovered that Beast had disappeared and that a young prince more beautiful than the day was bright was lying at her feet, thanking her for having broken a magic spell. Even though she was worried about the prince, she could not keep herself from asking about Beast. "You see him at your feet," the prince said. "An evil fairy condemned me to remain in that form until a beautiful girl would consent to marry me. She barred me from revealing my intelligence. You were the only person in the world kind enough to be touched by the goodness of my character. Even by offering you a crown, I still can't fully discharge the obligation I feel to you." rewarded you preferred virtue to good looks.

Pleasantly surprised, Beauty offered her hand to the handsome prince to help him get up. Together, they went to the castle, and Beauty nearly swooned with joy when she found her father and the entire family in the large hall. The beautiful lady who had appeared to her in a dream had transported them to the castle.

"Beauty," said the lady, who was a grand fairy, "come and receive the reward for your wise choice. You preferred virtue to looks and intelligence, and so you deserve to see those qualities united in a single person. You will become a noble queen, and I hope that sitting on a throne will not destroy your many virtues. As for you, my dear ladies," the fairy continued, speaking to Beauty's two sisters, "I know your hearts and all the malice that is in them. You will be turned into two statues, but you will keep your senses beneath the stone that envelops you. You will be transported to the door of your sister's palace, and I can think of no better punishment than being a witness to her happiness. You will not return to your former state until you recognize your faults. I fear that you may remain statues forever. You can correct pride, anger, gluttony, and laziness. But a miracle is needed to convert a heart filled with malice and envy."

The fairy waved her wand, and everyone there was transported to the great hall of the prince's realm, where the subjects were overjoyed to see him. The prince married Beauty, who lived with him for a long time in perfect happiness, for their marriage was founded on virtue.

# GIOVANNI FRANCESCO STRAPAROLA

## The Pig King†

Fair ladies,[1] if man were to spend a thousand years in rendering thanks to his Creator for having made him in the form of a human and not of a brute beast, he could not speak gratitude enough. This reflection calls to mind the story of one who was born as a pig, but afterwards became a comely youth. Nevertheless, to his dying day he was known to the people over whom he ruled as King Pig.

You must know, dear ladies, that Galeotto, King of Anglia, was a man highly blessed in worldly riches, and in his wife Ersilia, the daughter of Matthias, King of Hungary, a princess who, in virtue and beauty, outshone all the other ladies of the time. And Galeotto was a wise king, ruling his land so that no man could hear complaint against him. Though they had been married several years they had no child, wherefore they both were much aggrieved. While Ersilia was walking one day in her garden she felt suddenly weary, and catching sight of a spot covered with fresh green turf, she went up to it and sat down, and, overcome with weariness and soothed by the sweet singing of the birds in the green foliage, she fell asleep.

And it chanced that while she slept there passed by three fairies who held mankind somewhat in scorn, and these, when they beheld the

---

† Giovanni Francesco Straparola, "The Pig King," in *The Facetious Nights of Straparola*, trans. W. G. Waters (London: Society of Bibliophiles, 1891).

1. The tales in Straparola's collection are told by a circle of ladies living in exile in Murano to pass the time during the nights of the Venetian carnival.

sleeping queen, halted, and gazing upon her beauty, took counsel together how they might protect her and throw a spell upon her. When they were agreed the first cried out, 'I will that no man shall be able to harm her, and that, the next time she lie with her husband, she may be with child and bear a son who shall not have his equal in all the world for beauty.' Then the second said, 'I will that no one shall ever have power to offend her, and that the prince who shall be born of her shall be gifted with every virtue under the sun.' And the third said, 'And I will that she shall be the wisest among women, but that the son whom she shall conceive shall be born in the skin of a pig, with a pig's ways and manners, and in this state he shall be constrained to abide till he shall have three times taken a woman to wife.'

As soon as the three fairies had flown away Ersilia awoke, and straightway arose and went back to the palace, taking with her the flowers she had plucked. Not many days had passed before she knew herself to be with child, and when the time of her delivery was come, she gave birth to a son with members like those of a pig and not of a human being. When tidings of this prodigy came to the ears of the king and queen they were greatly aggrieved, and the king, bearing in mind how good and wise his queen was, often felt moved to put this offspring of hers to death and cast it into the sea, in order that she might be spared the shame of having given birth to him. But when he debated in his mind and considered that this son, let him be what he might, was of his own begetting, he put aside the cruel purpose which he had been harbouring, and, seized with pity and grief, he made up his mind that the son should be brought up and nurtured like a rational being and not as a brute beast. The child, therefore, being nursed with the greatest care, would often be brought to the queen and put his little snout and his little paws in his mother's lap, and she, moved by natural affection, would caress him by stroking his bristly back with her hand, and embracing and kissing him as if he had been of human form. Then he would wag his tail and give other signs to show that he was conscious of his mother's affection.

The pigling, when he grew older, began to talk like a human being, and to wander abroad in the city, but whenever he came near to any mud or dirt he would always wallow therein, after the manner of pigs, and return all covered with filth. Then, when he approached the king and queen, he would rub his sides against their fair garments, defiling them with all manner of dirt, but because he was indeed their own son they bore it all.

One day he came home covered with mud and filth, as was his wont, and lay down on his mother's rich robe, and said in a grunting tone, 'Mother, I wish to get married.' When the queen heard this, she replied, 'Do not talk so foolishly. What maid would ever take you for a husband, and do you think that any noble or knight would give his daughter to one so dirty and ill-savoured as you?' But he kept on grunting that he must have a wife of one sort or another. The queen, not knowing how to manage him in this matter, asked the king what they should do in their trouble: 'Our son wishes to marry, but where shall we find anyone who will take him as a husband?' Every day the pig would come back to his mother with the same demand: 'I must have a wife, and I will never leave you in peace until you procure for me a certain maiden I have seen to-day, who pleases me greatly.'

It happened that this maiden was a daughter of a poor woman who had three daughters, each one of them being very lovely. When the queen heard this, she had brought before her the poor woman and her eldest daughter, and said, 'Good mother, you are poor and burdened with children. If you will agree to what I shall say to you, you will be rich. I have this son who is, as you see, in form a pig, and I would like to marry him to your eldest daughter. Do not consider him, but think of the king and of me, and remember that your daughter will inherit this whole kingdom when the king and I shall be dead.'

When the young girl listened to the words of the queen she was greatly disturbed in her mind and blushed red for shame, and then said that on no account would she listen to the queen's proposition; but the poor mother pleaded so urgently with her that at last she yielded. When the pig came home one day, all covered with dirt as usual, his mother said to him, 'My son, we have found for you the wife you desire.' And then she had the bride brought in, who by this time had been robed in sumptuous regal attire, and presented her to the pig prince. When he saw how lovely and desirable she was he was filled with joy, and, all foul and dirty as he was, jumped round about her, endeavouring by his pawing and nuzzling to show some sign of his affection. But she, when she found he was soiling her beautiful dress, thrust him aside; whereupon the pig said to her, 'Why do you push me thus? Have I not had these garments made for you myself?' Then she answered disdainfully, 'No, neither you nor any other of the whole kingdom of hogs has done this thing.' And when it was time to go to bed, the young girl said to herself, 'What am I to do with this foul beast? This very night, while he lies asleep, I will kill him.' The pig prince, who was not far off, heard these words, but said nothing, and when the two retired to their chamber he got into the bed, stinking and dirty as he was, and defiled the sumptuous bed with his filthy paws and snout. He lay down by his spouse, who was not long in falling asleep, and then he struck her with his sharp hoofs and drove them into her breast so that he killed her.

The next morning the queen went to visit her daughter-in-law, and to her great grief found that the pig had killed her; and when he came back from wandering about the city he said, in reply to the queen's bitter reproaches, that he had only dealt with his wife as she intended to deal with him, and then withdrew in an ill humour. Not many days

had passed before the pig prince again began to plead with the queen
to allow him to marry one of the other sisters, and when the queen at
first would not listen to his petition he persisted in his purpose, and
threatened to ruin everything in the place if he could not have her as
wife. The queen, when she heard this, went to the king and told him
everything, and he answered that perhaps it would be wiser to kill their
ill-fated offspring before he might work some fatal mischief in the city.
But the queen felt all the tenderness of a mother towards him, and
loved him very dearly in spite of his brutal person, and could not endure the thought of being parted from him; so she summoned once
more to the palace the poor woman, together with her second daughter,
and held a long discourse with her, begging her the while to give her
daughter in marriage. At last the girl assented to take the pig prince for
a husband; but her fate was no happier than her sister's, for the bridegroom killed her, as he had killed his other bride, and then fled headlong from the palace.

When he came back, dirty as usual and smelling so foully that no
one could approach him, the king and queen censured him gravely for
the outrage he had committed; but again he cried out boldly that if he
had not killed her she would have killed him. As it had happened
before, the pig in a very short time began to plead with his mother
again to let him marry the youngest sister, who was much more beautiful than either of the others; and when this request of his was refused,
he became more insistent than ever, and in the end began to threaten
the queen's life in violent and bloodthirsty words, unless he should have
given to him the young girl for his wife. The queen, when she heard
this shameful and unnatural speech, was well-nigh broken-hearted and
about to go out of her mind; but, putting all other considerations aside,
she called for the poor woman and her third daughter, who was named
Meldina, and thus addressed her: 'Meldina, my child, I should be
greatly pleased if you would take the pig prince for a husband; pay no
regard to him, but to his father and to me; then, if you will be prudent
and bear patiently with him, you may be the happiest woman in the
world.' To this speech Meldina answered, with a grateful smile upon
her face, that she was quite content to do as the queen asked her, and
thanked her humbly for deigning to choose her as a daughter-in-law;
for, seeing that she herself had nothing in the world, it was indeed great
good fortune that she, a poor girl, should become the daughter-in-law
of a potent sovereign. The queen, when she heard this modest and
amiable reply, could not keep back her tears for the happiness she felt;
but she feared all the time that the same fate might be in store for
Meldina as her sisters.

When the new bride had been clothed in rich attire and decked with
jewels, and was awaiting the bridegroom, the pig prince came in, filth-
ier and more muddy than ever; but she spread out her rich gown and

besought him to lie down by her side. Whereupon the queen told her to thrust him away, but to this she would not consent, and spoke thus to the queen: 'There are three wise sayings, gracious lady, which I remember having heard. The first is that it is folly to waste time in searching for that which cannot be found. The second is that we should believe nothing we may hear, except those things which bear the marks of sense and reason. The third is that, when once you have got possession of some rare and precious treasure, prize it well and keep a firm hold upon it.'

When the maiden had finished speaking, the pig prince, who had been wide awake and had heard all that she had said, got up, kissed her on the face and neck and bosom and shoulders with his tongue, and she was not backward in returning his caresses; so that he was fired with a warm love for her. As soon as the time for retiring for the night had come, the bride went to bed and awaited her unseemly spouse, and, as soon as he came, she raised the coverlet and bade him lie near to her and put his head upon the pillow, covering him carefully with the bed-clothes and drawing the curtains so that he might feel no cold. When morning came the pig got up and ranged abroad to pasture, as was his wont, and very soon after the queen went to the bride's chamber, expecting to find that she had met with the same fate as her sisters; but when she saw her lying in the bed, all defiled with mud as it was, and looking pleased and contented, she thanked God for this favour, that her son had at last found a spouse according to his liking.

One day, soon after this, when the pig prince was conversing pleasantly with his wife, he said to her: 'Meldina, my beloved wife, if I could be fully sure that you could keep a secret, I would now tell you one of mine; something I have kept hidden for many years. I know you to be very prudent and wise, and that you love me truly; so I wish to make you the sharer of my secret.' 'You may safely tell it to me, if you will,' said Meldina, 'for I promise never to reveal it to anyone without your consent.' Whereupon, being now sure of his wife's discretion and fidelity, he straightaway shook off from his body the foul and dirty skin of the pig, and stood revealed as a handsome and well-shaped young man, and all that night rested closely folded in the arms of his beloved wife. But he charged her solemnly to keep silence about this wonder she had seen, for the time had not yet come for his complete delivery from this misery. So when he left the bed he donned the dirty pig's hide once more. I leave you to imagine for yourselves how great was the joy of Meldina when she discovered that, instead of a pig, she had gained a handsome and gallant young prince for a husband. Not long after this she proved to be with child, and when the time of her delivery came she gave birth to a fair and shapely boy. The joy of the king and queen was unbounded, especially when they found that the newborn child had the form of a human being and not that of a beast.

But the burden of the strange and weighty secret which her husband had confided to her pressed heavily upon Meldina, and one day she went to her mother-in-law and said: 'Gracious queen, when first I married your son I believed I was married to a beast, but now I find that you have given me the comeliest, the worthiest, and the most gallant young man ever born into the world to be my husband. For know that when he comes into my chamber to lie by my side, he casts off his dirty hide and leaves it on the ground, and is changed into a graceful handsome youth. No one could believe this marvel unless they saw it with their own eyes.' When the queen heard these words she was sure that her daughter-in-law must be jesting with her, but Meldina insisted that what she said was true. And when the queen demanded to know how she might witness with her own eyes the truth of this thing, Meldina replied: 'Come to my chamber tonight, when we shall be in our first sleep; the door will be open, and you will find that what I tell you is the truth.'

That same night, when the time came, and all were gone to rest, the queen let some torches be kindled and went, accompanied by the king, to the chamber of her son, and when she had entered she saw the pig's skin lying on the floor in the corner of the room, and having gone to the bedside, found a handsome young man in whose arms Meldina was lying. And when they saw this, the delight of the king and queen was very great, and the king gave order that before anyone should leave the chamber the pig's hide should be torn to shreds. So great was their joy over the recovery of their son that they nearly died from it.

And King Galeotto, when he saw that he had so fine a son, and a grandchild as well, laid aside his diadem and his royal robes, and advanced to his place his son, whom he let be crowned with the greatest pomp, and who was ever afterwards known as King Pig. Thus, to the great contentment of all the people, the young king began his reign, and he lived long and happily with Meldina his beloved wife.

\* \* \*

# BROTHERS GRIMM

## The Frog King, or Iron Heinrich†

In the olden days, when wishing could help you, there lived a king whose daughters were all beautiful. But the youngest was so beautiful that even the sun, which had seen so much, was filled with wonder

---

† Jacob and Wilhelm Grimm, "Der Froschkönig oder der eiserne Heinrich," in *Kinder- und Hausmärchen*, 7th ed. (Berlin: Dieterich, 1857; first published: Berlin: Realschulbuchhandlung, 1812). Translated for this Norton Critical Edition by Maria Tatar. Copyright © 1999 by Maria Tatar.

when it shone upon her face. There was a dark, vast forest near the king's castle, and in that forest, beneath an old linden tree, was a well. When the weather was really hot, the king's daughter would go out into the woods and sit down at the edge of the cool fountain. And when she got bored, she would take out her golden ball, throw it up in the air, and catch it again. That was her favorite toy.

One day it happened that the golden ball didn't land in the princess's hands when she reached up to catch it, but fell down on the ground and rolled right into the water. The princess followed it with her eyes, but the ball had disappeared, and the fountain was so very deep that you couldn't see the bottom. She began to weep and wept louder and louder, unable to stop herself. While she was wailing, a voice called out to her: "What's going on, princess? Stones would be moved to pity if they could hear you."

She turned around to see where the voice was coming from and saw a frog, which had stuck its big ugly head out of the water.

"Oh, it's you, you old splasher," she said. "I'm crying because my golden ball has fallen into the well."

"Be quiet and stop crying," said the frog. "I can help you, but what will you give me if I fetch your toy?"

"Whatever you want, dear frog," she said. "My dresses, my pearls and jewels, even the golden crown I'm wearing."

The frog said: "I don't want your dresses, your pearls and jewels, or your golden crown. But if you promise to cherish me and let me be your companion and playmate, and let me sit beside you at the table and eat from your little golden plate, drink from your little cup, and sleep in your little bed, if you promise me that, I will crawl down into the well and bring back your golden ball."

"Oh, yes," she said. "I'll give you anything you want as long as you get my ball back." But to herself she thought: "What nonsense that stupid frog is talking! He's down there in the water croaking away with all the other frogs. How could anyone want him for a companion?"

Once the frog had her word, he dove down into the water head first. After a while he came paddling back up with the ball in his mouth and tossed it onto the grass. When the princess caught sight of her beautiful toy, she was overjoyed. She picked it up and ran off with it.

"Wait for me," the frog cried out. "Take me with you. I can't run the way you do."

He croaked as loudly as he could after her, but it was no use. She paid no attention, sped home, and quickly forgot about the poor frog, who crawled back down into the well.

The next day, after she had sat down for dinner with the king and all the other courtiers and was eating from her little golden plate, something came crawling up the marble staircase, splish, splash, splish, splash. When it reached the top of the stairs, it knocked at the door and called out: "Princess, youngest princess, let me in!"

She ran to the door to see who it was, and when she opened the door, the frog was waiting right there. Terrified, she slammed the door as fast as she could and went back to the table. The king could see that her heart was pounding and said: "My child, why are you afraid? Was there a giant at the door coming to get you?"

"Oh, no," she replied. "It wasn't a giant, but it was a disgusting frog."

"What does a frog want from you?"

"Oh, father dear, yesterday when I was playing at the well, my golden ball fell into the water. And because I was crying so hard, the frog fetched it for me, and because he insisted, I promised that he could be my companion. I never thought that he would be able to leave the water. Now he's outside and wants to come in to see me." Just then there was a second knock at the door, and a voice called out:

> Princess, youngest princess,
> Let me in.
> Did you forget
> Yesterday's promise
> Down by the chilly waters?
> Princess, youngest princess,
> Let me in.

Then the king said: "When you make a promise, you must keep it. Just go and let him in."

She went and opened the door. The frog hopped into the room and followed close on her heels until she reached her chair. Then he sat down and called out: "Lift me up beside you."

She hesitated, but the king ordered her to obey. Once the frog was up on the chair, he wanted to get on the table, and once he was there he said: "Push your little golden plate closer to me so that we can eat together."

She did as he said, but it was obvious that she was not happy about it. The frog enjoyed his meal, but for her almost every little morsel stuck in her throat. Finally he said: "I've had enough to eat and am tired. Carry me up to your little room and prepare your little bed with the silken covers."

The princess began to cry, and was afraid of the clammy frog. She didn't dare touch him, and now he was going to sleep in her beautiful, clean bed. The king grew angry and said: "You shouldn't scorn some-one who helped you when you were in trouble."

The princess picked up the frog with two fingers, carried him up to her room, and put him in a corner. While she was lying in bed, he came crawling over and said: "I'm tired and want to sleep as much as you do. Lift me up or I'll tell your father."

*[handwritten annotation: she's rewarded for throwing frog against wall.]*

Then she became really cross, picked him up, and threw him with all her might against the wall. "Now you'll get your rest, you disgusting frog!"

When he fell to the ground, he was no longer a frog but a prince with beautiful, beaming eyes. At her father's bidding, he became her dear companion and husband. He told her that a wicked witch had cast a spell on him and that she alone could release him from the well. The next day they would set out together for his kingdom. They fell asleep, and, in the morning, after the sun had woken them, a coach drove up drawn by eight white horses in golden harnesses, with white ostrich plumes on their heads. At the back of the coach stood Faithful Heinrich, the servant of the young king. Faithful Heinrich had been so saddened by the transformation of his master into a frog that he had to have three hoops placed around his heart to keep it from bursting with pain and sorrow. Now the coach was there to take the young king back to his kingdom, and Faithful Heinrich lifted the two of them in and took his place in the back again. He was overjoyed by the transformation. When they had covered some distance, the prince heard a cracking noise behind him, as if something had broken. He turned around and called out:

*[handwritten annotation: 3 times]*

> "Heinrich, the coach is falling apart!"
> "No, my lord, 'tis not the coach,
> But a hoop from round my heart,
> Which was in such pain,
> While you were down in the well,
> Living there as a frog."

Two more times the prince heard the cracking noise, and he was sure that the coach was falling apart. But it was only the sounds of the hoops breaking off from Faithful Heinrich's heart, for his master had been set free and was happy.

*[handwritten annotation: -handsome, rich, prince that's usually all we care about in fairy tales.]*

# ANGELA CARTER

## The Tiger's Bride†

My father lost me to The Beast at cards.

There's a special madness strikes travellers from the North when they reach the lovely land where the lemon trees grow.[1] We come from

---

† From Angela Carter, "The Tiger's Bride," in *The Bloody Chamber and Other Stories* (New York: Penguin, 1993). Copyright © the Estate of Angela Carter 1995. Reprinted by permission of the Estate of Angela Carter c/o Rogers, Coleridge & White Ltd., 20 Powis Mews, London W11 1JN.

1. A reference to Italy, which was described in a poem by Johann Wolfgang von Goethe (1749–1832) as the "land where the lemon trees blossom."

countries of cold weather; at home, we are at war with nature but here, ah! you think you've come to the blessed plot where the lion lies down with the lamb. Everything flowers; no harsh wind stirs the voluptuous air. The sun spills fruit for you. And the deathly, sensual lethargy of the sweet South infects the starved brain; it gasps: "Luxury! more luxury!" But then the snow comes, you cannot escape it, it followed us from Russia as if it ran behind our carriage, and in this dark, bitter city has caught up with us at last, flocking against the windowpanes to mock my father's expectations of perpetual pleasure as the veins in his forehead stand out and throb, his hands shake as he deals the Devil's picture books.

The candles dropped hot, acrid gouts of wax on my bare shoulders. I watched with the furious cynicism peculiar to women whom circumstances force mutely to witness folly, while my father, fired in his desperation by more and yet more draughts of the firewater they call "grappa," rids himself of the last scraps of my inheritance. When we left Russia, we owned black earth, blue forest with bear and wild boar, serfs, cornfields, farmyards, my beloved horses, white nights of cool summer, the fireworks of the northern lights. What a burden all those possessions must have been to him, because he laughs as if with glee as he beggars himself; he is in such a passion to donate all to The Beast.

Everyone who comes to this city must play a hand with the *grand seigneur*;[2] few come. They did not warn us at Milan, or, if they did, we did not understand them—my limping Italian, the bewildering dialect of the region. Indeed, I myself spoke up in favour of this remote, provincial place, out of fashion two hundred years, because, oh irony, it boasted no casino. I did not know that the price of a stay in its Decembral solitude was a game with Milord.

The hour was late. The chill damp of this place creeps into the stones, into your bones, into the spongy pith of the lungs; it insinuated itself with a shiver into our parlour, where Milord came to play in the privacy essential to him. Who could refuse the invitation his valet brought to our lodging? Not my profligate father, certainly; the mirror above the table gave me back his frenzy, my impassivity, the withering candles, the emptying bottles, the coloured tide of the cards as they rose and fell, the still mask that concealed all the features of The Beast but for the yellow eyes that strayed, now and then, from his unfurled hand towards myself.

"La Bestia!" said our landlady, gingerly fingering an envelope with his huge crest of a tiger rampant on it, something of fear, something of wonder in her face. And I could not ask her why they called the master of the place, "La Bestia"—was it to do with that heraldic

2. French term for the lord of the manor or, in this case, the most powerful figure in the city.

signature?—because her tongue was so thickened by the phlegmy, bron-
chitic speech of the region I scarcely managed to make out a thing she
said except, when she saw me: "Che bella!"[3]

Since I could toddle, always the pretty one, with my glossy, nut-
brown curls, my rosy cheeks. And born on Christmas Day—her "Christmas rose," my English nurse called me. The peasants said: "The living
image of her mother," crossing themselves out of respect for the dead.
My mother did not blossom long; bartered for her dowry to such a
feckless sprig of the Russian nobility that she soon died of his gaming,
his whoring, his agonizing repentances. And The Beast gave me the
rose from his own impeccable if outmoded buttonhole when he arrived,
the valet brushing the snow off his black cloak. This white rose, unnatural, out of season, that now my nervous fingers ripped, petal by
petal, apart as my father magnificently concluded the career he had
made of catastrophe.

This is a melancholy, introspective region; a sunless, featureless landscape, the sullen river sweating fog, the shorn, hunkering willows. And
a cruel city; the sombre piazza, a place uniquely suited to public executions, under the beetling shadow of that malign barn of a church.
They used to hang condemned men in cages from the city walls; un-
kindness comes naturally to them, their eyes are set too close together,
they have thin lips. Poor food, pasta soaked in oil, boiled beef with
sauce of bitter herbs. A funereal hush about the place, the inhabitants
huddled up against the cold so you can hardly see their faces. And they
lie to you and cheat you, innkeepers, coachmen, everybody. God, how
they fleeced us!

The treacherous South, where you think there is no winter but forget
you take it with you.

My senses were increasingly troubled by the fuddling perfume of
Milord, far too potent a reek of purplish civet at such close quarters in
so small a room. He must bathe himself in scent, soak his shirts and
underlinen in it; what can he smell of, that needs so much camouflage?

I never saw a man so big look so two-dimensional, in spite of the
quaint elegance of The Beast, in the old-fashioned tailcoat that might,
from its looks, have been bought in those distant years before he imposed seclusion on himself; he does not feel he need keep up with the
times. There is a crude clumsiness about his outlines, that are on the
ungainly, giant side; and he has an odd air of self-imposed restraint, as
if fighting a battle with himself to remain upright when he would far
rather drop down on all fours. He throws our human aspirations to the
godlike sadly awry, poor fellow; only from a distance would you think
The Beast not much different from any other man, although he wears
a mask with a man's face painted most beautifully on it. Oh, yes, a

3. "What a beauty she is!" (Italian).

beautiful face; but one with too much formal symmetry of feature to be entirely human: one profile of his mask is the mirror image of the other, too perfect, uncanny. He wears a wig, too, false hair tied at the nape with a bow, a wig of the kind you see in old-fashioned portraits. A chaste silk stock stuck with a pearl hides his throat. And gloves of blond kid that are yet so huge and clumsy they do not seem to cover hands.

He is a carnival figure made of papier mâché and crêpe hair; and yet he has the Devil's knack at cards.

His masked voice echoes as from a great distance as he stoops over his hand and he has such a growling impediment in his speech that only his valet, who understands him, can interpret for him, as if his master were the clumsy doll and he the ventriloquist.

The wick slumped in the eroded wax, the candles guttered. By the time my rose had lost all its petals, my father, too, was left with nothing.

"Except the girl."

Gambling is a sickness. My father said he loved me yet he staked his daughter on a hand of cards. He fanned them out; in the mirror, I saw wild hope light up his eyes. His collar was unfastened, his rumpled hair stood up on end, he had the anguish of a man in the last stages of debauchery. The draughts came out of the old walls and bit me, I was colder than I'd ever been in Russia, when nights are coldest there.

A queen, a king, an ace. I saw them in the mirror. Oh, I know he thought he could not lose me; besides, back with me would come all he had lost, the unravelled fortunes of our family at one blow restored. And would he not win, as well, The Beast's hereditary palazzo outside the city; his immense revenues; his lands around the river; his rents, his treasure chest, his Mantegnas, his Giulio Romanos, his Cellini salt-cellars, his titles . . . the very city itself.[4]

You must not think my father valued me at less than a king's ransom; but, at *no more* than a king's ransom.

It was cold as hell in the parlour. And it seemed to me, child of the severe North, that it was not my flesh but, truly, my father's soul that was in peril.

My father, of course, believed in miracles; what gambler does not? In pursuit of just such a miracle as this, had we not travelled from the land of bears and shooting stars?

So we teetered on the brink.

The Beast bayed; laid down all three remaining aces.

The indifferent servants now glided smoothly forward as on wheels to douse the candles one by one. To look at them you would think that nothing of any moment had occurred. They yawned a little re-sentfully; it was almost morning, we had kept them out of bed. The

*[margin, handwritten: daughter staked on a hand of cards]*

4. Andrea Mantegna (1431–1506): Italian painter and engraver; Giulio Romano (1499–1546): Italian architect and painter; Benvenuto Cellini (1500–71): Italian sculptor and metalsmith.

Beast's man brought his cloak. My father sat amongst these preparations for departure, staring on at the betrayal of his cards upon the table.

The Beast's man informed me crisply that he, the valet, would call for me and my bags tomorrow, at ten, and conduct me forthwith to The Beast's palazzo. Capisco?[5] So shocked was I that I scarcely did "capisco"; he repeated my orders patiently, he was a strange, thin, quick little man who walked with an irregular, jolting rhythm upon splayed feet in curious, wedge-shaped shoes.

Where my father had been red as fire, now he was white as the snow that caked the window-pane. His eyes swam; soon he would cry.

" 'Like the base Indian,' " he said; he loved rhetoric. " 'One whose hand, / Like the base Indian, threw a pearl away / Richer than all his tribe . . .' I have lost my pearl, my pearl beyond price."[6]

At that, The Beast made a sudden, dreadful noise, halfway between a growl and a roar; the candles flared. The quick valet, the prim hypocrite, interpreted unblinking: "My master says: If you are so careless of your treasures, you should expect them to be taken from you."

He gave us the bow and smile his master could not offer us and they departed.

I watched the snow until, just before dawn, it stopped falling; a hard frost settled, next morning there was a light like iron.

The Beast's carriage, of an elegant if antique design, was black as a hearse and it was drawn by a dashing black gelding who blew smoke from his nostrils and stamped upon the packed snow with enough sprightly appearance of life to give me some hope that not all the world was locked in ice, as I was. I had always held a little towards Gulliver's opinion, that horses are better than we are,[7] and, that day, I would have been glad to depart with him to the kingdom of horses, if I'd been given the chance.

The valet sat up on the box in a natty black and gold livery, clasping, of all things, a bunch of his master's damned white roses as if a gift of flowers would reconcile a woman to any humiliation. He sprang down with preternatural agility to place them ceremoniously in my reluctant hand. My tear-beslobbered father wants a rose to show that I forgive him. When I break off a stem, I prick my finger and so he gets his rose all smeared with blood.

The valet crouched at my feet to tuck the rugs about me with a

---

5. Understand? (Italian).
6. "Like the base Indian . . .": from Shakespeare's *Othello*, V.ii.346–48; ". . . pearl beyond price": see Matthew 13.44–46, "Again, the kingdom of heaven is like a merchant in search of fine pearls who, on finding one pearl of great value, went and sold all that he had and bought it."
7. In part IV of Jonathan Swift's *Gulliver's Travels*, a visit to the Houyhnhnms leads Gulliver to compare horses favorably with human beings.

strange kind of unflattering obsequiousness yet he forgot his station sufficiently to scratch busily beneath his white periwig with an over-supple index finger as he offered me what my old nurse would have called an "old-fashioned look," ironic, sly, a smidgen of disdain in it. And pity? No pity. His eyes were moist and brown, his face seamed with the innocent cunning of an ancient baby. He had an irritating habit of chattering to himself under his breath all the time as he packed up his master's winnings. I drew the curtains to conceal the sight of my father's farewell; my spite was sharp as broken glass.

Lost to The Beast! And what, I wondered, might be the exact nature of his "beastliness"? My English nurse once told me about a tiger-man she saw in London, when she was a little girl, to scare me into good behaviour, for I was a wild wee thing and she could not tame me into submission with a frown or the bribe of a spoonful of jam. If you don't stop plaguing the nursemaids, my beauty, the tiger-man will come and take you away. They'd brought him from Sumatra, in the Indies, she said; his hinder parts were all hairy and only from the head downwards did he resemble a man.

And yet The Beast goes always masked; it cannot be his face that looks like mine.

But the tiger-man, in spite of his hairiness, could take a glass of ale in his hand like a good Christian and drink it down. Had she not seen him do so, at the sign of The George, by the steps of Upper Moor Fields when she was just as high as me and lisped and toddled, too. Then she would sigh for London, across the North Sea of the lapse of years. But, if this young lady was not a good little girl and did not eat her boiled beetroot, then the tiger-man would put on his big black travelling cloak lined with fur, just like your daddy's, and hire the Erl-King's galloper[8] of wind and ride through the night straight to the nursery and—

Yes, my beauty! GOBBLE YOU UP!

How I'd squeal in delighted terror, half believing her, half knowing that she teased me. And there were things I knew that I must not tell her. In our lost farmyard, where the giggling nursemaids initiated me into the mysteries of what the bull did to the cows, I heard about the waggoner's daughter. Hush, hush, don't let on to your nursie we said so; the waggoner's lass, hare-lipped, squint-eyed, ugly as sin, who would have taken her? Yet, to her shame, her belly swelled amid the cruel mockery of the ostlers[9] and her son was born of a bear, they whispered. Born with a full pelt and teeth; that proved it. But, when he grew up, he was a good shepherd, although he never married, lived in a hut

8. An allusion to another poem by Goethe, "The Erl-King," in which a father tries in vain to rescue his child from the enchantments of the title figure.
9. People who care for horses, especially at inns.

outside the village and could make the wind blow any way he wanted
to besides being able to tell which eggs would become cocks, which
hens.

The wondering peasants once brought my father a skull with horns
four inches long on either side of it and would not go back to the field
where their poor plough disturbed it until the priest went with them;
for this skull had the jaw-bone of a *man*, had it not?

Old wives' tales, nursery fears! I knew well enough the reason for the
trepidation I cosily titillated with superstitious marvels of my childhood
on the day my childhood ended. For now my own skin was my sole
capital in the world and today I'd make my first investment.

We had left the city far behind us and were now traversing a wide,
flat dish of snow where the mutilated stumps of the willows flourished
their ciliate heads athwart frozen ditches; mist diminished the horizon,
brought down the sky until it seemed no more than a few inches above
us. As far as eye could see, not one thing living. How starveling, how
bereft the dead season of this spurious Eden in which all the fruit was
blighted by cold! And my frail roses, already faded. I opened the carriage door and tossed the defunct bouquet into the rucked, frost-stiff
mud of the road. Suddenly a sharp, freezing wind arose and pelted my
face with a dry rice of powdered snow. The mist lifted sufficiently to
reveal before me an acreage of half-derelict façades of sheer red brick,
the vast man-trap, the megalomaniac citadel of his palazzo.

It was a world in itself but a dead one, a burned-out planet. I saw
The Beast bought solitude, not luxury, with his money.

The little black horse trotted smartly through the figured bronze
doors that stood open to the weather like those of a barn and the valet
handed me out of the carriage on to the scarred tiles of the great hall
itself, into the odorous warmth of a stable, sweet with hay, acrid with
horse dung. An equine chorus of neighings and soft drummings of
hooves broke out beneath the tall roof, where the beams were scabbed
with last summer's swallows' nests; a dozen gracile muzzles lifted from
their mangers and turned towards us, ears erect. The Beast had given
his horses the use of the dining room. The walls were painted, aptly
enough, with a fresco of horses, dogs and men in a wood where fruit
and blossom grew on the bough together.

The valet tweaked politely at my sleeve. Milord is waiting.

Gaping doors and broken windows let the wind in everywhere. We
mounted one staircase after another, our feet clopping on the marble.
Through archways and open doors, I glimpsed suites of vaulted chambers opening one out of another like systems of Chinese boxes into the
infinite complexity of the innards of the place. He and I and the wind
were the only things stirring; and all the furniture was under dust sheets,
the chandeliers bundled up in cloth, pictures taken from their hooks
and propped with their faces to the walls as if their master could not

bear to look at them. The palace was dismantled, as if its owner were about to move house or had never properly moved in; The Beast had chosen to live in an uninhabited place.

The valet darted me a reassuring glance from his brown, eloquent eyes, yet a glance with so much queer superciliousness in it that it did not comfort me, and went bounding ahead of me on his bandy legs, softly chattering to himself. I held my head high and followed him; but, for all my pride, my heart was heavy.

Milord has his eyrie high above the house, a small, stifling, darkened room; he keeps his shutters locked at noon. I was out of breath by the time we reached it and returned to him the silence with which he greeted me. I will not smile. He cannot smile.

In his rarely disturbed privacy, The Beast wears a garment of Ottoman design, a loose, dull purple gown with gold embroidery round the neck that falls from his shoulders to conceal his feet. The feet of the chair he sits in are handsomely clawed. He hides his hands in his ample sleeves. The artificial masterpiece of his face appals me. A small fire in a small grate. A rushing wind rattles the shutters.

The valet coughed. To him fell the delicate task of transmitting to me his master's wishes.

"My master—"

A stick fell in the grate. It made a mighty clatter in that dreadful silence; the valet started; lost his place in his speech, began again.

"My master has but one desire."

The thick, rich, wild scent with which Milord had soaked himself the previous evening hangs all about us, ascends in cursive blue from the smoke of a precious Chinese pot.

"He wishes only—"

Now, in the face of my impassivity, the valet twittered, his ironic composure gone, for the desire of a master, however trivial, may yet sound unbearably insolent in the mouth of a servant and his role of go-between clearly caused him a good deal of embarrassment. He gulped; he swallowed, at last contrived to unleash an unpunctuated flood.

"My master's sole desire is to see the pretty young lady unclothed nude without her dress and that only for the one time after which she will be returned to her father undamaged with bankers' orders for the sum which he lost to my master at cards and also a number of fine presents such as furs, jewels and horses—"

I remained standing. During this interview, my eyes were level with those inside the mask that now evaded mine as if, to his credit, he was ashamed of his own request even as his mouthpiece made it for him. Agitato, molto agitato,[1] the valet wrung his white-gloved hands.

_beast wants to see her nude_

---

1. Agitated, very agitated (Italian).

"Desnuda—"[2]

I could scarcely believe my ears. I let out a raucous guffaw; no young lady laughs like that! my old nurse used to remonstrate. But I did. And do. At the clamour of my heartless mirth, the valet danced backwards with perturbation, palpitating his fingers as if attempting to wrench them off, expostulating, wordlessly pleading. I felt that I owed it to him to make my reply in as exquisite a Tuscan as I could master.

"You may put me in a windowless room, sir, and I promise you I will pull my skirt up to my waist, ready for you. But there must be a sheet over my face, to hide it; though the sheet must be laid over me so lightly that it will not choke me. So I shall be covered completely from the waist upwards, and no lights. There you can visit me once, sir, and only the once. After that I must be driven directly to the city and deposited in the public square, in front of the church. If you wish to give me money, then I should be pleased to receive it. But I must stress that you should give me only the same amount of money that you would give to any other woman in such circumstances. However, if you choose not to give me a present, then that is your right."

How pleased I was to see I struck The Beast to the heart! For, after a baker's dozen heartbeats, one single tear swelled, glittering, at the corner of the masked eye. A tear! A tear, I hoped, of shame. The tear trembled for a moment on an edge of painted bone, then tumbled down the painted cheek to fall, with an abrupt tinkle, on the tiled floor.

The valet, ticking and clucking to himself, hastily ushered me out of the room. A mauve cloud of his master's perfume billowed out into the chill corridor with us and dissipated itself on the spinning winds.

A cell had been prepared for me, a veritable cell, windowless, airless, lightless, in the viscera of the palace. The valet lit a lamp for me; a narrow bed, a dark cupboard with fruit and flowers carved on it bulked out of the gloom.

"I shall twist a noose out of my bed linen and hang myself with it," I said.

"Oh, no," said the valet, fixing upon me wide and suddenly melancholy eyes. "Oh, no, you will not. You are a woman of honour."

And what was *he* doing in my bedroom, this jigging caricature of a man? Was he to be my warder until I submitted to The Beast's whim or he to mine? Am I in such reduced circumstances that I may not have a lady's maid? As if in reply to my unspoken demand, the valet clapped his hands.

"To assuage your loneliness, madame . . ."

A knocking and clattering behind the door of the cupboard; the door swings open and out glides a soubrette from an operetta, with glossy, nut-brown curls, rosy cheeks, blue, rolling eyes; it takes me a moment

2. "Undressed" (Italian).

to recognize her, in her little cap, her white stockings, her frilled petticoats. She carries a looking glass in one hand and a powder puff in the other and there is a musical box where her heart should be; she tinkles as she rolls towards me on her tiny wheels.

"Nothing human lives here," said the valet.

My maid halted, bowed; from a split seam at the side of her bodice protrudes the handle of a key. She is a marvellous machine, the most delicately balanced system of cords and pulleys in the world.

"We have dispensed with servants," the valet said. "We surround ourselves, instead, for utility and pleasure, with simulacra and find it no less convenient than do most gentlemen."

This clockwork twin of mine halted before me, her bowels churning out a settecento[3] minuet, and offered me the bold carnation of her smile. Click, click—she raises her arm and busily dusts my cheeks with pink, powdered chalk that makes me cough; then thrusts towards me her little mirror.

I saw within it not my own face but that of my father, as if I had put on his face when I arrived at The Beast's palace as the discharge of his debt. What, you self-deluding fool, are you crying still? And drunk, too. He tossed back his grappa and hurled the tumbler away.

Seeing my astonished fright, the valet took the mirror away from me, breathed on it, polished it with the ham of his gloved fist, handed it back to me. Now all I saw was myself, haggard from a sleepless night, pale enough to need my maid's supply of rouge.

I heard the key turn in the heavy door and the valet's footsteps patter down the stone passage. Meanwhile, my double continued to powder the air, emitting her jangling tune but, as it turned out, she was not inexhaustible; soon she was powdering more and yet more languorously, her metal heart slowed in imitation of fatigue, her musical box ran down until the notes separated themselves out of the tune and plopped like single raindrops and, as if sleep had overtaken her, at last she moved no longer. As she succumbed to sleep, I had no option but to do so, too. I dropped on that narrow bed as if felled.

Time passed but I do not know how much; then the valet woke me with rolls and honey. I gestured the tray away but he set it down firmly beside the lamp and took from it a little shagreen box, which he offered to me.

I turned away my head.

"Oh, my lady!" Such hurt cracked his high-pitched voice! He dextrously unfastened the gold clasp; on a bed of crimson velvet lay a single diamond earring, perfect as a tear.

I snapped the box shut and tossed it into a corner. This sudden, sharp movement must have disturbed the mechanism of the doll; she

3. Seventeenth-century (Italian).

jerked her arm almost as if to reprimand me, letting out a rippling fart of gavotte.[4] Then was still again.

"Very well," said the valet, put out. And indicated it was time for me to visit my host again. He did not let me wash or comb my hair. There was so little natural light in the interior of the palace that I could not tell whether it was day or night.

You would not think The Beast had budged an inch since I last saw him; he sat in his huge chair, with his hands in his sleeves, and the heavy air never moved. I might have slept an hour, a night, or a month, but his sculptured calm, the stifling air remained just as it had been. The incense rose from the pot, still traced the same signature on the air. The same fire burned.

Take off my clothes for you, like a ballet girl? Is that all you want of me?

"The sight of a young lady's skin that no man has seen before—" stammered the valet.

I wished I'd rolled in the hay with every lad on my father's farm, to disqualify myself from this humiliating bargain. That he should want so little was the reason why I could not give it; I did not need to speak for The Beast to understand me.

A tear came from his other eye. And then he moved; he buried his cardboard carnival head with its ribboned weight of false hair in, I would say, his arms; he withdrew his, I might say, hands from his sleeves and I saw his furred pads, his excoriating claws.

The dropped tear caught upon his fur and shone. And in my room for hours I hear those paws pad back and forth outside my door.

When the valet arrived again with his silver salver, I had a pair of diamond earrings of the finest water in the world; I threw the other into the corner where the first one lay. The valet twittered with aggrieved regret but did not offer to lead me to The Beast again. Instead, he smiled ingratiatingly and confided: "My master, he say: invite the young lady to go riding."

"What's this?"

He briskly mimicked the action of a gallop and, to my amazement, tunelessly croaked: "Tantivy! tantivy![5] a-hunting we will go!"

"I'll run away, I'll ride to the city."

"Oh, no," he said. "Are you not a woman of honour?"

He clapped his hands and my maidservant clicked and jangled into the imitation of life. She rolled towards the cupboard where she had come from and reached inside it to fetch out over her synthetic arm my riding habit. Of all things. My very own riding habit, that I'd left

4. A French dance.
5. A hunting cry used when the chase is at full speed.

behind me in a trunk in a loft in that country house outside Petersburg that we'd lost long ago, before, even, we set out on this wild pilgrimage to the cruel South. Either the very riding habit my old nurse had sewn for me or else a copy of it perfect to the lost button on the right sleeve, the ripped hem held up with a pin. I turned the worn cloth about in my hands, looking for a clue. The wind that sprinted through the palace made the door tremble in its frame; had the north wind blown my garments across Europe to me? At home, the bear's son directed the winds at his pleasure; what democracy of magic held this palace and the fir forest in common? Or, should I be prepared to accept it as proof of the axiom my father had drummed into me: that, if you have enough money, anything is possible?

"Tantivy," suggested the now twinkling valet, evidently charmed at the pleasure mixed with my bewilderment. The clockwork maid held my jacket out to me and I allowed myself to shrug into it as if reluctantly, although I was half mad to get out into the open air, away from this deathly palace, even in such company.

The doors of the hall let the bright day in; I saw that it was morning. Our horses, saddled and bridled, beasts in bondage, were waiting for us, striking sparks from the tiles with their impatient hooves while their stablemates lolled at ease among the straw, conversing with one another in the mute speech of horses. A pigeon or two, feathers puffed to keep out the cold, strutted about, pecking at ears of corn. The little black gelding who had brought me here greeted me with a ringing neigh that resonated inside the misty roof as in a sounding box and I knew he was meant for me to ride.

I always adored horses, noblest of creatures, such wounded sensitivity in their wise eyes, such rational restraint of energy at their high-strung hindquarters. I lirruped and hurrumphed to my shining black companion and he acknowledged my greeting with a kiss on the forehead from his soft lips. There was a little shaggy pony nuzzling away at the *trompe l'œil*[6] foliage beneath the hooves of the painted horses on the wall, into whose saddle the valet sprang with a flourish as of the circus. Then The Beast, wrapped in a black fur-lined cloak, came to heave himself aloft a grave grey mare. No natural horseman he; he clung to her mane like a shipwrecked sailor to a spar.

Cold, that morning, yet dazzling with the sharp winter sunlight that wounds the retina. There was a scurrying wind about that seemed to go with us, as if the masked, immense one who did not speak carried it inside his cloak and let it out at his pleasure, for it stirred the horses' manes but did not lift the lowland mists.

A bereft landscape in the sad browns and sepias of winter lay all

6. A visual deception or a painting that gives the illusion of being real (French).

about us, the marshland drearily protracting itself towards the wide river. Those decapitated willows. Now and then, the swoop of a bird, its irreconcilable cry.

A profound sense of strangeness slowly began to possess me. I knew my two companions were not, in any way, as other men, the simian retainer and the master for whom he spoke, the one with clawed fore-paws who was in a plot with the witches who let the winds out of their knotted handkerchiefs up towards the Finnish border. I knew they lived according to a different logic than I had done until my father abandoned me to the wild beasts by his human carelessness. This knowledge gave me a certain fearfulness still; but, I would say, not much . . . I was a young girl, a virgin, and therefore men denied me rationality just as they denied it to all those who were not exactly like themselves, in all their unreason. If I could see not one single soul in that wilderness of desolation all around me, then the six of us—mounts and riders, both—could boast amongst us not one soul, either, since all the best religions in the world state categorically that not beasts nor women were equipped with the flimsy, insubstantial things when the good Lord opened the gates of Eden and let Eve and her familiars tumble out. Understand, then, that though I would not say I privately engaged in metaphysical speculation as we rode through the reedy approaches to the river, I certainly meditated on the nature of my own state, how I had been bought and sold, passed from hand to hand. That clockwork girl who powdered my cheeks for me; had I not been allotted only the same kind of imitative life amongst men that the doll-maker had given her?

Yet, as to the true nature of the being of this clawed magus[7] who rode his pale horse in a style that made me recall how Kublai Khan's leopards went out hunting on horseback, of that I had no notion.

We came to the bank of the river that was so wide we could not see across it, so still with winter that it scarcely seemed to flow. The horses lowered their heads to drink. The valet cleared his throat, about to speak; we were in a place of perfect privacy, beyond a brake of winter-bare rushes, a hedge of reeds.

"If you will not let him see you without your clothes—"

I involuntarily shook my head—

"—you must, then, prepare yourself for the sight of my master, naked."

The river broke on the pebbles with a diminishing sigh. My composure deserted me; all at once I was on the brink of panic. I did not think that I could bear the sight of him, whatever he was. The mare raised her dripping muzzle and looked at me keenly, as if urging me. This river broke again at my feet. I was far from home.

---

7. Magician, sorcerer.

"You," said the valet, "must."

When I saw how scared he was I might refuse, I nodded.

The reed bowed down in a sudden snarl of wind that brought with it a gust of the heavy odour of his disguise. The valet held out his master's cloak to screen him from me as he removed the mask. The horses stirred.

The tiger will never lie down with the lamb; he acknowledges no pact that is not reciprocal. The lamb must learn to run with the tigers.

A great, feline, tawny shape whose pelt was barred with a savage geometry of bars the colour of burned wood. His domed, heavy head, so terrible he must hide it. How subtle the muscles, how profound the tread. The annihilating vehemence of his eyes, like twin suns.

I felt my breast ripped apart as if I suffered a marvellous wound.

The valet moved forward as if to cover up his master now the girl had acknowledged him, but I said: "No." The tiger sat still as a heraldic beast, in the pact he had made with his own ferocity to do me no harm. He was far larger than I could have imagined, from the poor, shabby things I'd seen once, in the Czar's menagerie at Petersburg, the golden fruit of their eyes dimming, withering in the far North of captivity. Nothing about him reminded me of humanity.

I therefore, shivering, now unfastened my jacket, to show him I would do him no harm. Yet I was clumsy and blushed a little, for no man had seen me naked and I was a proud girl. Pride it was, not shame, that thwarted my fingers so; and a certain trepidation lest this frail little article of human upholstery before him might not be, in itself, grand enough to satisfy his expectations of us, since those, for all I knew, might have grown infinite during the endless time he had been waiting. The wind clattered in the rushes, purled and eddied in the river.

I showed his grave silence my white skin, my red nipples, and the horses turned their heads to watch me, also, as if they, too, were courteously curious as to the fleshly nature of women. Then The Beast lowered his massive head; Enough! said the valet with a gesture. The wind died down, all was still again.

Then they went off together, the valet on his pony, the tiger running before him like a hound, and I walked along the river bank for a while. I felt I was at liberty for the first time in my life. Then the winter sun began to tarnish, a few flakes of snow drifted from the darkening sky and, when I returned to the horses, I found The Beast mounted again on his grey mare, cloaked and masked and once more, to all appearances, a man, while the valet had a fine catch of waterfowl dangling from his hand and the corpse of a young roebuck slung behind his saddle. I climbed up on the black gelding in silence and so we returned to the palace as the snow fell more and more heavily, obscuring the tracks that we had left behind us.

The valet did not return me to my cell but, instead, to an elegant, if old-fashioned boudoir with sofas of faded pink brocade, a jinn's treasury of Oriental carpets, tintinnabulation of cut-glass chandeliers. Candles in antlered holders struck rainbows from the prismatic hearts of my diamond earrings, that lay on my new dressing table at which my attentive maid stood ready with her powder puff and mirror. Intending to fix the ornaments in my ears, I took the looking glass from her hand, but it was in the midst of one of its magic fits again and I did not see my own face in it but that of my father; at first I thought he smiled at me. Then I saw he was smiling with pure gratification.

He sat, I saw, in the parlour of our lodgings, at the very table where he had lost me, but now he was busily engaged in counting out a tremendous pile of banknotes. My father's circumstances had changed already; well-shaven, neatly barbered, smart new clothes. A frosted glass of sparkling wine sat convenient to his hand beside an ice bucket. The Beast had clearly paid cash on the nail for his glimpse of my bosom, and paid up promptly, as if it had not been a sight I might have died of showing. Then I saw my father's trunks were packed, ready for departure. Could he so easily leave me here?

There was a note on the table with the money, in a fine hand. I could read it quite clearly. "The young lady will arrive immediately." Some harlot with whom he'd briskly negotiated a liaison on the strength of his spoils? Not at all. For, at that moment, the valet knocked at my door to announce that I might leave the palace at any time hereafter, and he bore over his arm a handsome sable cloak, my very own little gratuity, The Beast's morning gift, in which he proposed to pack me up and send me off.

When I looked at the mirror again, my father had disappeared and all I saw was a pale, hollow-eyed girl whom I scarcely recognized. The valet asked politely when he should prepare the carriage, as if he did not doubt that I would leave with my booty at the first opportunity while my maid, whose face was no longer the spit of my own, continued bonnily to beam. I will dress her in my own clothes, wind her up, send her back to perform the part of my father's daughter.

"Leave me alone," I said to the valet.

He did not need to lock the door, now. I fixed the earrings in my ears. They were very heavy. Then I took off my riding habit, left it where it lay on the floor. But, when I got down to my shift, my arms dropped to my sides. I was unaccustomed to nakedness. I was so unused to my own skin that to take off all my clothes involved a kind of flaying. I thought The Beast had wanted a little thing compared with what I was prepared to give him; but it is not natural for humankind to go naked, not since first we hid our loins with fig leaves. He had demanded the abominable. I felt as much atrocious pain as if I was stripping off my own underpelt and the smiling girl stood poised in the oblivion of her balked simulation of life, watching me peel down to the cold, white meat of contract and, if she did not see me, then so much more like the market place, where the eyes that watch you take no account of your existence.

And it seemed my entire life, since I had left the North, had passed under the indifferent gaze of eyes like hers.

Then I was flinching stark, except for his irreproachable tears.

I huddled in the furs I must return to him, to keep me from the lacerating winds that raced along the corridors. I knew the way to his den without the valet to guide me.

No response to my tentative rap on his door.

Then the wind blew the valet whirling along the passage. He must have decided that, if one should go naked, then all should go naked; without his livery, he revealed himself, as I had suspected, a delicate creature, covered with silken moth-grey fur, brown fingers supple as leather, chocolate muzzle, the gentlest creature in the world. He gibbered a little to see my fine furs and jewels as if I were dressed up for the opera and, with a great deal of tender ceremony, removed the sables from my shoulders. The sables thereupon resolved themselves into a pack of black, squeaking rats that rattled immediately down the stairs on their hard little feet and were lost to sight.

The valet bowed me inside The Beast's room.

The purple dressing gown, the mask, the wig, were laid out on his chair; a glove was planted on each arm. The empty house of his appearance was ready for him but he had abandoned it. There was a reek of fur and piss; the incense pot lay broken in pieces on the floor. Half-burned sticks were scattered from the extinguished fire. A candle stuck by its own grease to the mantelpiece lit two narrow flames in the pupils of the tiger's eyes.

He was pacing backwards and forwards, backwards and forwards, the tip of his heavy tail twitching as he paced out the length and breadth of his imprisonment between the gnawed and bloody bones.

He will gobble you up.

Nursery fears made flesh and sinew; earliest and most archaic of fears, fear of devourment. The beast and his carnivorous bed of bone and I, white, shaking, raw, approaching him as if offering, in myself, the key to a peaceable kingdom in which his appetite need not be my extinction.

He went still as stone. He was far more frightened of me than I was of him.

I squatted on the wet straw and stretched out my hand. I was now within the field of force of his golden eyes. He growled at the back of his throat, lowered his head, sank on to his forepaws, snarled, showed me his red gullet, his yellow teeth. I never moved. He snuffed the air, as if to smell my fear; he could not.

Slowly, slowly he began to drag his heavy, gleaming weight across the floor towards me.

A tremendous throbbing, as of the engine that makes the earth turn, filled the little room; he had begun to purr.

The sweet thunder of this purr shook the old walls, made the shutters batter the windows until they burst apart and let in the white light of the snowy moon. Tiles came crashing down from the roof; I heard them fall into the courtyard far below. The reverberations of his purring rocked the foundations of the house, the walls began to dance. I thought: "It will all fall, everything will disintegrate."

He dragged himself closer and closer to me, until I felt the harsh velvet of his head against my hand, then a tongue, abrasive as sandpaper. "He will lick the skin off me!"

And each stroke of his tongue ripped off skin after successive skin, all the skins of a life in the world, and left behind a nascent patina of shining hairs. My earrings turned back to water and trickled down my shoulders; I shrugged the drops off my beautiful fur.

# Urashima the Fisherman†

Young Urashima lived in Tango province, in the village of Tsutsu-gawa. One day in the fall of 477 (it was Emperor Yūryaku's reign), he rowed out alone on the sea to fish. After catching nothing for three days and nights, he was surprised to find that he had taken a five-colored turtle. He got the turtle into the boat and lay down to sleep.

When the turtle changed into a dazzlingly lovely girl, the mystified Urashima asked her who she was.

"I saw you here, alone at sea," she answered with a smile, "and I wanted so much to talk to you! I came on the clouds and the wind."

"But where did you come from, then, on the clouds and wind?"

"I'm an Immortal and I live in the sky. Don't doubt me! Oh, be kind and speak to me tenderly!"

Urashima understood she was divine, and all his fear of her melted away.

"I'll love you as long as the sky and earth last," she promised him, "as long as there's a sun and a moon! But tell me, will you have me?"

"Your wish is mine," he answered. "How could I not love you?"

"Then lean on your oars, my darling, and take us to my Eternal Mountain!"

She told him to close his eyes. In no time they reached a large island

† From *Tango fudoki* (Account of the Province of Tango), 713 A.D., in *Japanese Tales*, comp. and trans. Royall Tyler (New York: Pantheon, 1987). Copyright © 1987 by Royall Tyler. Reprinted by permission of Pantheon Books, a division of Random House.

with earth like jade. Watchtowers on it shone darkly, and palaces gleamed like gems. It was a wonder no eye had seen and no ear had ever heard tell of before.

They landed and strolled on hand in hand to a splendid mansion, where she asked him to wait; then she opened the gate and went in. Seven young girls soon came out of the gate, telling each other as they passed him that he was Turtle's husband; and eight girls who came after them told each other the same. That was how he learned her name.

He mentioned the girls when she came back out. She said the seven were the seven stars of the Pleiades, and the eight the cluster of Aldebaran. Then she led him inside.

Her father and mother greeted him warmly and invited him to sit down. They explained the difference between the human and the divine worlds, and they let him know how glad this rare meeting between the gods and a man had made them. He tasted a hundred fragrant delicacies and exchanged cups of wine with the girl's brothers and sisters. Young girls with glowing faces flocked to the happy gathering, while the gods sang their songs sweetly and clearly and danced with fluid grace. The feast was a thousand times more beautiful than any ever enjoyed by mortals in their far-off land.

Urashima never noticed the sun going down, but as twilight came on the Immortals all slipped away. He and the maiden, now alone, lay down in each other's arms and made love. They were man and wife at last.

For three years he forgot his old life and lived in paradise with the Immortals. Then one day he felt a pang of longing for the village where he had been born and the parents he had left behind. After that, he missed them more each day.

"Darling," said his wife, "you haven't looked yourself lately. Won't you tell me what's wrong?"

"They say the dying fox turns toward his lair and the lesser man longs to go home. I'd never believed it, but now I know it's true."

"Do you want to go back?"

"Here I am in the land of the gods, far from all my family and friends. I shouldn't feel this way, I know, but I can't help being homesick for them. I want so much to go back and see my mother and father!"

His wife brushed away her tears. "We gave ourselves to each other forever!" she lamented. "We promised we'd be as true as gold or the rocks of the mountains! How could a little homesickness make you want to leave me?"

They went for a walk hand in hand, sadly talking it all over. Finally they embraced, and when they separated their parting was sealed.

Urashima's parents-in-law were sad to see him go. His wife gave him a jeweled box. "Dearest," she said, "if you don't forget me and find you want to come back, then grip this box hard. But you mustn't open it, ever."

He got into his boat and they told him to close his eyes. In no time he was at Tsutsugawa, his home. The place looked entirely different. He recognized nothing there at all.

"Where's Urashima's family—Urashima the fisherman?" he asked a villager.

"Who are you?" the villager answered. "Where are you from? Why are you looking for a man who lived long ago? Yes, I've heard old people mention someone named Urashima. He went out alone on the sea and never came back. That was three hundred years ago. What do you want with him now?"

Bewildered, Urashima roamed the village for ten days without finding any sign of family or old friends. At last he stroked the box his divine lady had given him and thought of her; then, forgetting his recent promise, he opened it. Before his eyes her fragrant form, borne by the clouds and the wind, floated up and vanished into the blue sky. He understood he had disobeyed her and would never see her again. All he could do was gaze after her, then pace weeping along the shore.

When he dried his tears, he sang about her far, cloud-girdled realm. The clouds, he sang, would bring her the message of his love. Her sweet voice answered him, across the vastness of the sky, entreating him never to forget her. Then a last song burst from him as he struggled with his loss: "My love, when after a night of longing, day dawns and I stand at my open door, I hear far-off waves breaking on the shores of your paradise!"

If only he hadn't opened that jeweled box, people have said since, he could have been with her again. But the clouds hid her paradise from him and left him nothing but his grief.

*(margin handwriting: broke promise (opened box) never return)*

# ALEXANDER AFANASEV

## The Frog Princess†

Long ago, in ancient times, there was a king who had three sons, all of them grown. The king said: "My children, let each of you make a bow for himself and shoot an arrow. She who brings back your arrow will be your bride; he whose arrow is not brought back will not marry." The eldest son shot his arrow, and a prince's daughter brought it back to him. The middle son shot his arrow, and a general's daughter

---

† From *Russian Fairy Tales* by Norbert Guterman, ed. and trans.; coll. by Alexander Afanasev. Copyright © 1945 by Pantheon Books, Inc. and renewed 1973 by Random House, Inc. Reprinted by permission of Pantheon Books, a division of Random House, Inc. Afanasev's collection was originally published over a period of several years, 1855–64.

brought it back to him. But little Prince Ivan's arrow was brought back from the marsh by a frog who held it between her teeth. His brothers were joyous and happy, but Prince Ivan became thoughtful and wept: "How will I live with a frog? After all, this is a life task, not like wading across a river or walking across a field!" He wept and wept, but there was no way out of it, so he took the frog to wife. All three sons and their brides were wed in accordance with the customs of their country; the frog was held on a dish.

They began living together. One day the king asked that all three brides make him gifts, so that he could see which of them was the most skillful. Prince Ivan again became thoughtful and wept: "What can my frog make? Everyone will laugh at me!" The frog only hopped about on the floor and croaked. When Prince Ivan fell asleep, she went out into the street, cast off her skin, turned into a lovely maiden, and cried: "Nurses, nurses! Make something!" The nurses at once brought a finely woven shirt. She took it, folded it, placed it beside Prince Ivan, and again turned herself into a frog, as though she had never been anything else! Prince Ivan awoke, was overjoyed with the shirt, and brought it to the king. The king received it, examined it, and said: "Well, this is indeed a shirt to wear on holidays!" Then the second brother brought a shirt. The king said: "This one is good only to wear to the bath!" And of the shirt the eldest brother brought he said: "This one is fit to be worn only in a lowly peasant hut!" The king's sons left, and the two elder ones decided between themselves: "We were wrong to make fun of Prince Ivan's wife; she is not a frog, but a cunning witch!"

The king again issued a command to his daughters-in-law—this time that they should bake bread, and show it to him, so that he might see which of them baked best. Before the first contest, the brides of the two elder sons had made fun of the frog; but now they sent a chambermaid to spy on her and see how she would go about baking her loaf. The frog was aware of this, so she mixed her dough, rolled it, hollowed out the oven from above, and poured her dough right there. The chambermaid saw this and ran to tell her mistresses, who forthwith did the same. But the cunning frog had deceived them; the moment the chambermaid left, she dug the dough out of the oven, cleaned and plastered up everything as though nothing had happened, then went on the porch, got out of her frog's skin, and cried: "Nurses, nurses! Bake me such a loaf of bread as my dear father ate only on Sundays and holidays!" The nurses brought the bread at once. She took it, placed it beside the sleeping Prince Ivan, and turned into a frog again. Prince Ivan awoke, took the bread, and went with it to his father. Just then the king was examining the loaves of bread brought by his elder sons. Their wives had dropped the dough into the oven just as the frog had, and all they had pulled out was formless lumps. First the king took the eldest son's loaf, looked at it, and sent it back to the kitchen;

then he took the second son's loaf and sent it back too. Then came Prince Ivan's turn: he presented his loaf. The father received it, examined it, and said: "Now this bread is good enough for a holiday! It is not slack-baked, like that of my elder daughters-in-law!"

After that the king decided to hold a ball in order to see which of his daughters-in-law danced best. All the guests and the daughters-in-law assembled, and also the sons, except Prince Ivan, who became thoughtful: how could he go to a ball with a frog? And our Prince Ivan began to sob. The frog said to him: "Weep not, Prince Ivan! Go to the ball. I will join you in an hour." Prince Ivan was somewhat heartened when he heard the frog's words; he left for the ball, and the frog cast off her skin, and dressed herself in marvelous raiment. She came to the ball; Prince Ivan was overjoyed, and all the guests clapped their hands when they beheld her: what a beauty! The guests began to eat and drink; the princess would pick a bone and put it in her sleeve; she would drink of a cup and pour the last drops into her other sleeve. The wives of the elder brothers saw what she did, and they too put the bones in their sleeves, and whenever they drank of a cup, poured the last drops into their other sleeves. The time came for dancing; the tsar called upon his elder daughters-in-law, but they deferred to the frog. She straightway took Prince Ivan's arm and came forward to dance. She danced and danced, and whirled and whirled, a marvel to behold! She waved her right hand, and lakes and woods appeared; she waved her left hand, and various birds began to fly about. Everyone was amazed. She finished dancing, and all that she had created vanished. Then the other daughters-in-law came forward to dance. They wanted to do as the frog had done: they waved their right hands, and the bones flew straight at the guests; and from their left sleeves water spattered, that too on the guests. The king was displeased by this and cried: "Enough, enough!" The daughters-in-law stopped dancing.

The ball was over. Prince Ivan went home first, found his wife's skin somewhere, took it and burned it. She arrived, looked for the skin, but it was gone, burned. She lay down to sleep with Prince Ivan, but before daybreak she said to him: "If you had waited a little, I would have been yours; now only God knows when we will be together again. Farewell! Seek me beyond the thrice ninth land, in the thrice tenth kingdom!" And the princess vanished.

A year went by, and Prince Ivan longed for his wife. In the second year, he made ready for his journey, obtained his father's and mother's blessing, and left. He walked a long time and suddenly he saw a little hut standing with its front to the woods and its back to him. He said: "Little hut, little hut, stand the old way, as thy mother stood thee, with thy back to the woods and thy front to me!" The hut turned around. He entered. An old woman was sitting there, who said: "Fie, fie! Of a

Russian bone not a sound was heard, not a glimpse was seen, and now a Russian bone has come to my house of its own free will. Whither goest thou, Prince Ivan?" "First of all, old woman, give me to eat and to drink, then ask me questions." The old woman gave him to eat and to drink and put him to bed. Prince Ivan said to her: "Little grandmother, I have set out to find Elena the Fair." "Oh, my child, how long you have been away! At the beginning she often remembered thee, but now she no longer remembers thee, and has not come to see me for a long time. Go now to my middle sister, she knows more than I do."

In the morning Prince Ivan set out, came to a hut, and said: "Little hut, little hut, stand the old way, as thy mother stood thee, with thy back to the woods and thy front to me." The hut turned around. He entered, and saw an old woman sitting there, who said: "Fie, fie! Of a Russian bone not a sound was heard, not a glimpse was seen, and now a Russian bone has come to my house of its own free will. Whither goest thou, Prince Ivan?" "To get Elena the Fair, little grandmother." "Oh, Prince Ivan," said the old woman, "thou hast been long a-coming! She has begun to forget thee, she is marrying someone else; the wedding will take place soon! She is now living with my eldest sister. Go there, but be careful. When thou approachest their house, they will sense it; Elena will turn into a spindle, and her dress will turn into gold thread. My sister will wind the gold thread; when she has wound it around the spindle, and put it into a box and locked the box, thou must find the key, open the box, break the spindle, throw the top of it in back of thee, and the bottom of it in front of thee. Then she will appear before thee."

Prince Ivan went, came to the third old woman's house, and entered. The old woman was winding gold thread; she wound it around the spindle and put it in a box, locked the box, and put the key somewhere. He took the key, opened the box, took out the spindle, broke it just as he had been told, cast the top in back of him and the bottom in front of him. Suddenly Elena the Fair stood before him and greeted him: "Oh, you have been a long time coming, Prince Ivan! I almost married someone else." And she told him that the other bridegroom was expected soon. Elena the Fair took a magic carpet from the old woman, sat on it with Prince Ivan, and they took off and flew like birds. The other bridegroom suddenly arrived and learned that they had left. He too was cunning! He began to pursue them, and chased and chased them, and came within ten yards of overtaking them: but on their carpet they flew into Russia, and for some reason he could not get into Russia, so he turned back. The happy bride and groom came home; everyone rejoiced, and soon Ivan and Elena began to live and prosper, for the glory of all the people.

## The Swan Maiden†

A young peasant, in the parish of Mellby, who often amused himself with hunting, saw one day three swans flying toward him, which settled down upon the strand of a sound near by.

Approaching the place, he was astonished at seeing the three swans divest themselves of their feathery attire, which they threw into the grass, and three maidens of dazzling beauty step forth and spring into the water.

After sporting in the waves awhile they returned to the land, where they resumed their former garb and shape and flew away in the same direction from which they came.

One of them, the youngest and fairest, had, in the meantime, so smitten the young hunter that neither night nor day could he tear his thoughts from the bright image.

His mother, noticing that something was wrong with her son, and that the chase, which had formerly been his favorite pleasure, had lost its attractions, asked him finally the cause of his melancholy, where-upon he related to her what he had seen, and declared that there was no longer any happiness in this life for him if he would not possess the fair swan maiden.

"Nothing is easier," said the mother. "Go at sunset next Thursday evening to the place where you last saw her. When the three swans come, give attention to where your chosen one lays her feathery garb, take it and hasten away."

The young man listened to his mother's instructions, and, betaking himself, the following Thursday evening, to a convenient hiding place near the sound, he waited, with impatience, the coming of the swans. The sun was just sinking behind the trees when the young man's ears were greeted by a whizzing in the air, and the three swans settled down upon the beach, as on their former visit.

As soon as they had laid off their swan attire they were again trans-formed into the most beautiful maidens, and, springing out upon the white sand, they were soon enjoying themselves in the water.

From his hiding place the young hunter had taken careful note of where his enchantress had laid her swan feathers. Stealing softly forth, he took them and returned to his place of concealment in the sur-rounding foliage.

Soon thereafter two of the swans were heard to fly away, but the third, in search of her clothes, discovered the young man, before whom, believing him responsible for their disappearance, she fell upon her knees and prayed that her swan attire might be returned to her. The

† "The Swan Maiden," in *Scandinavian Folk and Fairy Tales*, comp. Claire Booss (New York: Avenel Books, 1984). Reprinted from Herman Hofberg, *Swedish Fairy Tales*, 1895.

hunter was, however, unwilling to yield the beautiful prize, and, casting a cloak around her shoulders, carried her home.

Preparations were soon made for a magnificent wedding, which took place in due form, and the young couple dwelt lovingly and contentedly together.

One Thursday evening, seven years later, the hunter related to her how he had sought and won his wife. He brought forth and showed her, also, the white swan feathers of her former days. No sooner were they placed in her hands than she was transformed once more into a swan, and instantly took flight through the open window. In breathless astonishment, the man stared wildly after his rapidly vanishing wife, and before a year and a day had passed, he was laid, with his longings and sorrows, in his allotted place in the village church-yard.

# INTRODUCTION: Snow White

Walt Disney's *Snow White and the Seven Dwarfs* has so eclipsed other versions of the story that it is easy to forget that hundreds of variants have been collected over the past century in Europe, Asia, Africa, and the Americas. The heroine may ingest a poisoned apple in her cinematic incarnation, but in Italy she is just as likely to fall victim to a toxic comb, a contaminated cake, or a suffocating braid. Disney's queen, who demands Snow White's heart from the huntsman who takes her into the woods, seems restrained by comparison with the Grimms' evil queen, who orders the huntsman to return with the girl's lungs and liver (she plans to eat both after boiling them in salt water). In Spain, the queen is even more bloodthirsty, asking for a bottle of blood stoppered with the girl's toe. In Italy, she instructs the huntsman to return with the girl's intestines and her blood-soaked shirt. Disney's film has made much of Snow White's coffin being made of glass, but in other versions that coffin is made of gold, silver, or lead or is jewel-encrusted. While it is often displayed on a mountaintop, it can also be set adrift on a river, placed under a tree, hung from the rafters of a room, or locked in a room and surrounded with candles.

"Snow White" may vary tremendously from culture to culture in its details, but it has an easily identifiable, stable core. Steven Swann Jones, modifying and refining the structure outline in the Aarne-Thompson index, emphasizes nine episodes: origin (birth of the heroine), jealousy, expulsion, adoption, renewed jealousy, death, exhibition, resuscitation, and resolution. But while Swann captures the defining features of the tale and reveals how the story's narrative structure is sustained by the tension of binary oppositions (birth/death, expulsion/adoption, jealousy/affection, etc.), he is at a loss when it comes to accounting for the staying power of this cultural story. Rather than drawing definite conclusions about what is at stake in a plot driven by competitive energy, he cautiously formulates what he perceives to be the tale's shaping force: "The most plausible explanation for the form that the overall plot structure of 'Snow White' assumes," he declares, "is that it is a reflection of a young woman's development."[1]

Page numbers in brackets refer to this Norton Critical Edition.
1. Steven Swann Jones, *The Comparative Method: Structural and Symbolic Analysis of the Allomotifs of "Snow White"* (Helsinki: Academia Scientiarum Fennica, 1990) 32.

To account for the remarkable narrative stability and cultural dura-
bility of "Snow White," most critics point to the tale's powerful staging
of mother/daughter conflicts. Bruno Bettelheim defines those conflicts
as oedipal and asserts that they are "left to our imagination" because
"the person for whose love the two are in competition is never mentioned."[2] Basing his interpretation of the story on the Grimms' "Snow
White," which features a "good" biological mother who dies in childbirth and an "evil" queen who persecutes her seven-year-old stepdaughter, he advances the thesis that this splitting of the maternal function
has a strong emotional resonance for fairy-tale audiences. The oedipal
child, he argues, has a deep need to preserve a positive image of
mother, one uncontaminated by the natural feelings of anger and hostility that arise as differences develop between mother and child. The
wicked stepmother of fairy tales "permits anger at this bad 'stepmother'
without endangering the goodwill of the true mother, who is viewed as
a different person."[3]

For Bettelheim, the malice of the stepmother is, in the end, nothing
more than a projection of the heroine's imagination. Fairy tales, he
argues, do not stage scenarios that correspond to psychological realities
of family life; rather, they dramatize *projections* of trouble brewing in
the young child's mind. Thus the jealousy of the evil queen has nothing
whatsoever to do with a mother's possible competition with her daughter and reflects only the daughter's envy of the mother: "If a child
cannot permit himself to feel his jealousy of a parent . . . he projects
his feelings onto the parent. Then 'I am jealous of all the advantages
and prerogatives of Mother' turns into the wishful thought 'Mother is
jealous of me.' "[4]

The struggle between Snow White and the wicked queen so dominates the psychological landscape of this fairy tale that Sandra Gilbert
and Susan Gubar have proposed renaming it "Snow White and Her
Wicked Stepmother." These two feminist critics, for whom the
Grimms' tale enacts "the essential but equivocal relationship between
the angel-woman and the monster-woman" of Western patriarchy, emphasize the contrast between protagonist and antagonist:

> The central action of the tale—indeed its only real action—arises
> from the relationship between these two women: the one fair,
> young, pale, the other just as fair, but older, fiercer; the one a
> daughter, the other a mother; the one sweet, ignorant, passive, the
> other both artful and active; the one a sort of angel, the other an
> undeniable witch.[5]

2. Bruno Bettelheim, *The Uses of Enchantment: The Meaning and Importance of Fairy Tales*
   (New York: Knopf, 1976) 201.
3. Bettelheim, *Uses*, 690.
4. Bettelheim, *Uses*, 204.
5. Sandra M. Gilbert and Susan Gubar, *The Madwoman in the Attic: The Woman Writer and
   the Nineteenth-Century Literary Imagination* (New Haven: Yale UP, 1979) 36.

*(handwritten marginal notes, rotated along left edge: "at stake approval of father for both", "—long affection" / "of father approval")*

For both Bettelheim and for Gilbert and Gubar, the absent father occupies a central, if invisible, position in this domestic drama. Although we know nothing about Snow White's relationship to her father, Bettelheim insists that "it is reasonable to assume that it is competition for him which sets (step)mother against daughter."[6] Gilbert and Gubar find the father acoustically present if physically absent: "His, surely, is the voice of the looking glass, the patriarchal voice of judgment that rules the Queen's—and every woman's—self-evaluation."[7] The absence of the father is framed as an emphatic narrative denial that only reveals the extent to which he occupies center stage. What is at stake for the two female characters is, in sum, the love, affection, or approval of the father, a father whom we see only briefly as the huntsman and hear as the voice in the mirror. Although the centrality of the father does not become explicit in many versions of "Snow White," one Scottish folktale, "Lasair Gheug, the King of Ireland's Daughter," puts the father in the foreground of this family melodrama, but suggests that what is really at issue has more to do with inheritance customs than with sexual jealousy.

In "The Young Slave" of Giambattista Basile's 1634 collection of tales published under the title *The Pentamerone*, the persecution of the heroine is explicitly motivated by her aunt's (unwarranted) sexual jealousy. Lisa, a Neapolitan Snow White, falls into a coma and is preserved for many years in a casket of crystal. When she awakens, she finds herself the target of sexual rage and jealousy, for her aunt believes that she has been the clandestine mistress of her husband. In the end, Lisa's uncle, who has been a model of marital fidelity, reveals a distinct preference for his niece when he drives his cruel wife out of the house. Basile's tale, one of the earliest recorded versions of "Snow White," suggests that the complex psychosexual motivations shaping the plots of fairy tales underwent a process of repression once the social venue for the stories shifted from the household to the nursery.

Where Bettelheim sees a generational conflict between mother and daughter, Gilbert and Gubar see an intrapsychic drama played out between two possible developmental trajectories, one passive, docile, and compliant with patriarchal norms, the other nomadic, creative, and socially subversive. Gilbert and Gubar invest the figure of the wicked queen with narrative energy so powerful that she becomes the story's most admirable character. For them, she is a "plotter, a plot-maker, a schemer, a witch, an artist, and impersonator, a woman of almost infinite creative energy, witty, wily, and self-absorbed as all artists traditionally are."[8] And it is the queen who foreshadows the destiny of Snow White; once Snow White gains the throne, she will exchange her glass

6. Bettelheim, *Uses*, 203.
7. Gilbert and Gubar, *Madwoman*, 38.
8. Gilbert and Gubar, *Madwoman*, 38–39.

coffin for the imprisonment of the looking-glass: "Renouncing 'contemplative purity,' she must now embark on that life of 'significant action' which, for a woman, is defined as a witch's life because it is so monstrous, so unnatural."[9]

Gilbert and Gubar surely took an interpretive cue from Anne Sexton's poetic transformation of the Grimms' "Snow White," in which an aging Queen ("brown spots on her hand / and four whiskers over her lips") is pitted against a thirteen-year-old "lovely virgin." "Beauty is a simple passion," Sexton declares, "but, oh my friends, in the end / you will dance the fire dance in iron shoes" [96–97]. The scene that stages the Queen's death juxtaposes a mobile Queen, dancing herself to death with "her tongue flicking in and out / like a gas jet," with a frozen Snow White, "rolling her china-blue doll eyes open and shut / and sometimes referring to her mirror / as women do" [100]. Sexton's inert Snow White is destined one day to become her mother, galvanized into action and turned into an agent of persecution by the divisive gaze into the mirror.

The mirror image and the glass coffin, not surprisingly, have become the privileged sites for feminist interpretive projects. For Gilbert and Gubar, the magic looking glass and the enchanted glass coffin are "the tools patriarchy suggests that women use to kill themselves into art, the two women literally try to kill each other with art."[1] "In the mirrored reduplication of the self," Elisabeth Bronfen finds both the "ego's narcissistic desire for integrity and immortality" and its "division and mortality."[2] Beauty may mask death but its image (both in the magic mirror and on the face of Snow White in her coffin) reveals its connection with death. "For the queen to eliminate Snow White," Bronfen adds, "means reassuring herself that she as a unity exists independent of difference, Otherness and temporality."[3] For these critics, the story of "Snow White" reproduces a cultural script in which women are enmeshed in a discourse connecting beauty, death, and femininity. Beauty, as reflected in the glass and seen through the coffin, may be attractive, but its seductions have a sinister, lethal side.

The version of "Snow White" that has had the most significant impact on children today is Disney's "Snow White and the Seven Dwarfs." Disney Studios bears the responsibility for turning Snow White into a cultural icon, making her the best known fairy-tale character in this country. The Grimms' "Snow White" may never have fared particularly well in the United States, but its cinematic reincarnation continues to fill the coffers of its corporate producer fifty years after its release. If Gilbert and Gubar believe that "Snow White" should be renamed to

9. Gilbert and Gubar, *Madwoman*, 42.
1. Gilbert and Gubar, *Madwoman*, 36.
2. Elisabeth Bronfen, *Over Her Dead Body: Death, Femininity, and the Aesthetic* (New York: Routledge, 1992) 104.
3. Bronfen, *Over*, 105.

include the wicked stepmother in that tale's title, it is largely because they use the Disney version as their interpretive point of departure. Covers for the video version of "Snow White" may foreground the heroine, the prince, and the seven dwarfs, but it is the wicked queen who dominates the action of the film and virtually monopolizes the film's visual and narrative energy. Interestingly, Disney Studios erased the Grimms' prefatory episode describing the death of Snow White's biological mother in childbirth—the only maternal figure is the step-mother in her double incarnation as beautiful, proud, and evil queen and as ugly, sinister, and wicked witch. Notes taken at story conferences reveal that the queen was planned as "a mixture of Lady Macbeth and the Big Bad Wolf," fiercely treacherous and mercilessly cruel.[4] Disney himself, who referred to the transformation of the queen into an old hag as a "Jekyll and Hyde thing,"[5] seemed unaware that there is no Jekyll component to this figure's personality, only two Hydes. Instead of the splitting of the mother image into a good mother who dies in childbirth and an evil queen who persecutes her stepchild, the maternal figure appears only in the realm of evil.

The Disney version of "Snow White" relentlessly polarizes the notion of the feminine to produce a murderously jealous and forbiddingly cold woman on the one hand and an innocently sweet girl accomplished in the art of good housekeeping on the other. Beginning with the Grimms, it is through a combination of labor and good looks that Snow White earns a prince for herself. Here is how the Grimms describe the house-keeping contract extended to Snow White by the dwarfs: "If you will keep house for us, cook, make the beds, wash, sew, knit, and keep everything neat and clean, then you can stay with us, and we'll give you everything you need" [85]. But the dwarfs in the Grimms' tale are hardly in need of a housekeeper, for they appear to be models of tidi-ness. Everything in their cottage is "indescribably dainty and spotless" [84]; the table has a white cloth with tiny plates, cups, knives, forks, and spoons, and the beds are covered with sheets "as white as snow" [84]. Compare this description of the dwarfs' cottage with the following one taken from a book based on Disney's version of "Snow White":

> Skipping across a little bridge to the house, Snow White peeked in through one window pane. There seemed to be no one at home, but the sink was piled high with cups and saucers and plates which looked as though they had never been washed. Dirty little shirts and wrinkled little trousers hung over chairs, and everything was blanketed with dust.
>
> "Maybe the children who live here have no mother," said Snow

4. Richard Holliss and Brian Sibley, *Walt Disney's "Snow White and the Seven Dwarfs" and the Making of the Classic Film* (New York: Simon and Schuster, 1987) 14.
5. Holliss and Sibley, *Disney*, 14.

White, "and need someone to take care of them. Let's clean their house and surprise them."

So in she went, followed by her forest friends. Snow White found an old broom in the corner and swept the floor, while the little animals all did their best to help.

Then Snow White washed all the crumpled little clothes, and set a kettle of delicious soup to bubbling on the hearth.[6]

In one post-Disney American variant of the story after another, Snow White makes it her mission to clean up after the the dwarfs ("seven dirty little boys") and is represented as serving an apprenticeship in home economics ("Snow White, for her part, was becoming an excellent housekeeper and cook.").[7] The Disney version itself transforms household drudgery into frolicking good fun, less work than play, since it requires no real effort, is carried out with the help of wonderfully dextrous woodland creatures, and achieves such a dazzling result. Disney made a point of placing the housekeeping sequence before the encounter with the dwarfs and of presenting the dwarfs as "naturally messy," just as Snow White is "by nature" tidy. When she comes upon the dwarfs' cottage, her first instinct is "to clean it up and surprise them when they come home and maybe they'll let me stay and keep house for them."[8]

"We just try to make a good picture," Walt Disney once observed in connection with *Snow White and the Seven Dwarfs*. "And then the professors come along and tell us what we do."[9] In a sense, Gilbert and Gubar have become the professors who tell us what Disney did, for their critical intervention is above all a response to Disney's film, to a motion picture that positions the evil queen as the figure of cinematic fascination and that makes Snow White so dull that she requires a supporting cast of seven to enliven her scenes (Disney's is the only version of "Snow White" that presents the dwarfs as individualized figures). With a voice in which "the accents of Betty Boop are far too prominent" and with a figure that has been described as a "pasty, sepulchral, sewing-pattern design scissored out of context," the Snow White character lacks the narrative charge and élan so potently present in the representation of her stepmother.[1] Ultimately it is the stepmother's disruptive, disturbing, and divisive presence that invests the story

---

6. *55 Favorite Stories Adapted from Disney Films*, A Golden Book (n.p.: Western Publishing, 1960).
7. The phrase about the dwarfs is from *Snow White*, illus. Rex Irvine and Judie Clarke (n.p.: Superscope, 1973). The description of Snow White comes from *Storytime Treasury* (New York: McCall, 1969).
8. These are the thoughts that Walt Disney put into Snow White's mind in transcripts of a story conference in preparation for *Snow White*. See Rudy Behlmer, "They Called It 'Disney's Folly': Snow White and the Seven Dwarfs (1937)," *America's Favorite Movies: Behind the Scenes* (New York: Ungar, 1982) 53.
9. "Mouse & Man," *Time* (27 December 1937): 21.
1. "The accents of Betty Boop . . .": Holliss and Sibley, *Disney*, 65; "pasty, sepulchral . . .": "The Snow White Fiasco," *Current History* (June 1938): 46.

with a degree of fascination that has facilitated its widespread circulation and that has allowed it to take hold in our culture.

# GIAMBATTISTA BASILE

## The Young Slave†

\*   \*   \*

There was once a Baron of Selvascura who had an unmarried sister. This sister used to go and play in a garden with other girls her own age. One day they found a lovely rose in full bloom, so they made a compact that whoever jumped clean over it without touching a single leaf, should win something. But although many of the girls jumped leapfrog over it, they all hit it, and not one of them jumped clean over. But when the turn came to Lilla, the Baron's sister, she stood back a little and took such a run at it that she jumped right over to the other side of the rose. Nevertheless, one leaf fell, but she was so quick and ready that she picked it up from the ground without anyone noticing and swallowed it, thereby winning the prize.

Not less than three days later, Lilla felt herself to be pregnant, and nearly died of grief, for she knew that she had done nothing compromising or dishonest, and could not understand how it was possible for her belly to have swollen. She ran at once to some fairies who were her friends, and when they heard her story, they told her not to worry, for the cause of it all was the rose-leaf she had swallowed.

When Lilla understood this, she took precautions to conceal her condition as much as possible, and when the hour of her deliverance came, she gave birth in hiding to a lovely little girl whom she named Lisa. She sent her to the fairies and they each gave her some charm, but the last one slipped and twisted her foot so badly as she was running to see the child, that in her acute pain she hurled a curse at her, to the effect that when she was seven years old, her mother, whilst combing out her hair, would leave the comb in her tresses, stuck into the head, and from this the child would perish.

At the end of seven years the disaster occurred, and the despairing mother, lamenting bitterly, encased the body in seven caskets of crystal, one within the other, and placed her in a distant room of the palace, keeping the key in her pocket. However, after some time her grief brought her to her grave. When she felt the end to be near, she called her brother and said to him, "My brother, I feel death's hook dragging me away inch by inch. I leave you all my belongings for you to have

† Giambattista Basile, "The Young Slave," in *The Pentamerone*, trans. Benedetto Croce (London: John Lane the Bodley Head, 1932). Reprinted by permission.

and dispose of as you like; but you must promise me never to open the last room in this house, and always keep the key safely in the casket." The brother, who loved her above all things, gave her his word; at the same moment she breathed, "Adieu, for the beans are ripe."

At the end of some years, this lord (who had in the meantime taken a wife) was invited to a hunting-party. He recommended the care of the house to his wife, and begged her above all not to open the room, the key of which he kept in the casket. However, as soon as he had turned his back, she began to feel suspicious, and impelled by jealousy and consumed by curiosity, which is woman's first attribute, took the key and went to open the room. There she saw the young girl, clearly visible through the crystal caskets, so she opened them one by one and found that she seemed to be asleep. Lisa had grown like any other woman, and the caskets had lengthened with her, keeping pace as she grew.

When she beheld this lovely creature, the jealous woman at once thought, "By my life, this is a fine thing! Keys at one's girdle, yet nature makes horns![1] No wonder he never let anyone open the door and see the Mahomet[2] that he worshipped inside the caskets!" Saying this, she seized the girl by the hair, dragged her out, and in so doing caused the comb to drop out, so that the sleeping Lisa awoke, calling out, "Mother, mother!"

"I'll give you mother, and father too!" cried the Baroness, who was as bitter as a slave, as angry as a bitch with a litter of pups, and as venomous as a snake. She straightaway cut off the girl's hair and thrashed her with the tresses, dressed her in rags, and every day heaped blows on her head and bruises on her face, blackening her eyes and making her mouth look as if she had eaten raw pigeons.[3]

When her husband came back from his hunting-party and saw this girl being so hardly used, he asked who she was. His wife answered that she was a slave sent her by her aunt, only fit for the rope's end, and that one had to be forever beating her.

Now it happened one day, when the Baron had occasion to go to a fair, that he asked everyone in the house, including even the cats, what they would like him to buy for them, and when they had all chosen, one one thing and one another, he turned at last to the slave. But his wife flew into a rage and acted unbecomingly to a Christian, saying, "That's right, class her with all the others, this thick-lipped slave, let everyone be brought down to the same level and all use the urinal.[4] Don't pay so much attention to a worthless bitch, let her go to the devil." But the Baron who was kind and courteous insisted that the

1. The husband or wife is cuckolded.
2. The body of Mahomet was rumored to have been preserved in a coffin suspended between heaven and earth. The Baron, it is implied, has been worshipping a false god.
3. Dripping with blood.
4. All have the same privileges (reflects a time in which using the urinal was considered a luxury).

slave should also ask for something. And she said to him, "I want nothing but a doll, a knife and a pumice-stone; and if you forget them, may
you never be able to cross the first river that you come to on your
journey!"

The Baron bought all the other things, but forgot just those for which
his niece had asked him; so when he came to a river that carried down
stones and trees to the shore to lay foundations of fears and raise walls
of wonder, he found it impossible to ford it. Then he remembered the
spell put on him by the slave, and turned back and bought the three
articles in question. When he arrived home he gave out to each one
the thing for which they had asked.

When Lisa had what she wanted, she went into the kitchen, and,
putting the doll in front of her, began to weep and lament and recount
all the story of her troubles to that bundle of cloth just as if it had been
a real person. When it did not reply, she took the knife and sharpened
it on the pumice-stone and said, "Mind, if you don't answer me, I will
dig this into you, and that will put an end to the game!" And the doll,
swelling up like a reed when it has been blown into, answered at last,
"All right, I have understood you! I'm not deaf!"

This music had already gone on for a couple of days, when the
Baron, who had a little room on the other side of the kitchen, chanced
to hear this, and putting his eye to the keyhole, saw Lisa telling
the doll all about her mother's jump over the rose-leaf, how she swallowed it, her own birth, the spell, the curse of the last fairy, the comb
left in her hair, her death, how she was shut into the seven caskets and
placed in that room, her mother's death, the key entrusted to the
brother, his departure for the hunt, the jealousy of his wife, how she
opened the room against her husband's commands, how she cut off
her hair and treated her like a slave, and the many, many torments she
had inflicted on her. And all the while she wept and said, "Answer me,
dolly, or I will kill myself with this knife." And sharpening it on the
pumice-stone, she would have plunged it into herself had not the Baron
kicked down the door and snatched the knife out of her hand.

He made her tell him the story again at greater length, and then he
embraced his niece and took her away from that house, and left her in
charge of one of his relations in order that she should get better, for
the hard usage inflicted on her by that heart of a Medea[5] had made
her quite thin and pale. After several months, when she had become
as beautiful as a goddess, the Baron brought her home and told everyone that she was his niece. He ordered a great banquet, and when the
viands had been cleared away, he asked Lisa to tell the story of the
hardships she had undergone and of the cruelty of his wife—a tale
which made all the guests weep. Then he drove his wife away, sending

5. Princess and sorceress of Colchis who helped Jason obtain the Golden Fleece and murdered
her two sons when she was betrayed.

her back to her parents, and gave his niece a handsome husband of her own choice. Thus Lisa testified that

*Heaven rains favors on us when we least expect it.*

# BROTHERS GRIMM

## Snow White†

Once upon a time in the middle of winter, when snow flakes were falling from the sky like feathers, a queen was sitting and sewing by a window with a black ebony frame. While she was sewing and looking out at the snow, she pricked her finger with a needle, and three drops of blood fell onto the snow. The red looked so beautiful against the white snow that she thought to herself: "If only I had a child as white as snow, as red as blood, and as black as the wood of the window frame." Soon thereafter she gave birth to a little girl, who was as white as snow, as red as blood, and as black as ebony, and she was called Snow White. The queen died after the child was born.

A year later the king married another woman. She was a beautiful lady, but proud and arrogant and could not bear being second to anyone in beauty. She had a magic mirror, and when she stood in front of it and looked at herself, she would say:

> "Mirror, mirror, on the wall,
> Who's the fairest one of all?"

The mirror would reply:

> "You, oh queen, are the fairest of all."

Then she was satisfied, for she knew that the mirror always spoke the truth.

Snow White was growing up and becoming more and more beautiful. When she was seven years old, she was as beautiful as the bright day and more beautiful than the queen herself. One day the queen asked the mirror:

> "Mirror, mirror, on the wall,
> Who's the fairest one of all?"

The mirror replied:

> "My queen, you are the fairest one here,
> But Snow White is a thousand times more fair than you!"

† Jacob and Wilhelm Grimm, "Schneewittchen," in *Kinder- und Hausmärchen*, 7th ed. (Berlin: Dieterich, 1857; first published: Berlin: Realschulbuchhandlung, 1812). Translated for this Norton Critical Edition by Maria Tatar. Copyright © 1999 by Maria Tatar.

When the Queen heard these words, she trembled and turned green with envy. From that moment on, she hated Snow White, and whenever she set eyes on her, her heart turned as cold as a stone. Envy and pride grew like weeds in her heart. Day and night, she never had a moment's peace. One day, she summoned a huntsman and said: "Take the child out into the forest. I don't want to have to lay eyes on her ever again. You must kill her and bring me her lungs and liver as proof of your deed." The huntsman obeyed and took her out into the woods, but just as he was pulling out his hunting knife and about to take aim at her innocent heart, she began weeping and pleading with him. "Alas, dear huntsman, spare my life. I promise to run into the woods and never return."

Snow White was so beautiful that the huntsman took pity on her and said: "Just run away, you poor child."

"The wild animals will devour you before long," he thought to himself. He felt as if a great weight had been lifted from his heart, for at least he did not have to kill her. Just then a young boar ran past him, and the huntsman stabbed it to death. He took out the lungs and liver and brought them to the queen as proof that he had murdered the child. The cook was told to boil them in brine, and the wicked woman ate them up, thinking that she had eaten Snow White's lungs and liver.

The poor child was left all alone in the vast forest. She was so frightened that she just stared at all the leaves on the trees and had no idea what to do next. She started running and raced over sharp stones and through thornbushes. Wild beasts darted near her at times, but they did her no harm. She ran as far as her legs could carry her. When night fell, she saw a little cottage and went inside to rest. Everything in the house was tiny, and indescribably dainty and spotless. There was a little table, with seven little plates on a white cloth. Each little plate had a little spoon, seven little knives and forks, and seven little cups. Against the wall were seven little beds in a row, each made up with sheets as white as snow. Snow White was so hungry and thirsty that she ate a few vegetables and some bread from each little plate and drank a drop of wine out of each little cup. She didn't want to take everything away from one place. Later, she was so tired that she tried out the beds, but they did not seem to be the right size. The first was too long, the second too short, but the seventh one was just right, and she stayed in it. Then she said her prayers and fell fast asleep.

After it was completely dark outside, the owners of the cottage returned. They were seven dwarfs who spent their days in the mountains mining ore and digging for minerals. They lighted their seven little lanterns, and when the cottage brightened up, they saw that someone had been there, for some things were not the way they had left them.

The first one asked: "Who's been sitting on my little chair?"

The second asked: "Who's been eating from my little plate?"

The third asked: "Who's been eating my little loaf of bread?"

The fourth asked: "Who's been eating from my little plate of vegetables?"

The fifth asked: "Who's been using my little fork?"

The sixth asked: "Who's been cutting with my little knife?"

The seventh asked: "Who's been drinking from my little cup?"

The first one turned around and saw some wrinkles on his sheets and said: "Who climbed into my little bed?"

The others came running and each shouted: "Someone's been sleeping in my bed too."

When the seventh dwarf looked in his little bed, he saw Snow White lying there, fast asleep. He shouted to the others who came running and who were so astonished that they raised their seven little lanterns to let the light shine on Snow White.

"My goodness, oh my goodness!" they exclaimed. "What a beautiful child!"

They were so delighted to see her that they decided not to wake her up and let her continue sleeping in her little bed. The seventh dwarf slept for one hour with each of his companions until the night was over.

In the morning, Snow White woke up. When she saw the dwarfs, she was frightened, but they were friendly and asked "What's your name?"

"My name is Snow White," she replied.

"How did you get to our house?" asked the dwarfs.

Then she told them how her stepmother had tried to kill her and that the huntsman had spared her life. She had run all day long until she had arrived at their cottage.

The dwarfs told her: "If you will keep house for us, cook, make the beds, wash, sew, knit, and keep everything neat and tidy, then you can stay with us, and we'll give you everything you need."

"Yes, with pleasure," Snow White replied, and she stayed with them.

She kept house for them. In the morning, they went up to the mountains in search of minerals and gold. In the evening, they returned, and dinner had to be ready for them. Since the girl was by herself during the day, the good dwarfs gave her a strong warning:

"Beware of your stepmother. She'll know soon enough that you're here. Don't let anyone in the house."

After the queen had finished eating what she thought were Snow White's lungs and liver, she was sure that she was once again the fairest of all in the land. She went to the mirror and said:

> "Mirror, mirror, on the wall,
> Who's the fairest of them all?"

The mirror replied:

*[handwritten marginal note: dwarfs offer snow white housekeeper job]*

"Here you're the fairest, dearest queen,
But little Snow White, who plans to stay
With the seven dwarfs far far away,
Is now the fairest ever seen."

When the queen heard this she was horrified, for she knew that the mirror could not tell a lie. She realized that the huntsman had deceived her and that Snow White must still be alive. She thought long and hard about how she could kill Snow White. Unless she herself was the fairest in the land, she would never be able to feel anything but envy. Finally, she came up with a plan. After staining her face and dressing up as an old peddler woman, she was completely unrecognizable. She traveled beyond the seven hills to the seven dwarfs in that disguise. Then she knocked on the door and called out: "Pretty wares for a good price."

Snow White peeked out of the window and said: "Good day, old woman, what do you have for sale?"

"Nice things, pretty things," she replied. "Staylaces[1] in all kinds of colors," and she took out a silk lace woven of many colors.

"I can let this good woman in," Snow White thought to herself, and she unbolted the door and bought the pretty lace.

"Oh my child, what a sight you are. Come, let me lace you up properly."

Snow White wasn't the least bit suspicious. She stood in front of the old woman and let her put on the new lace. The old woman laced her up so quickly and so tightly that Snow White's breath was cut off, and she fell down as if dead.

"So much for being the fairest of them all," she said and hurried away.

Not much later, in the evening, the seven dwarfs came home. When they saw their beloved Snow White lying on the ground, they were horrified. She didn't move in the slightest, and they were sure she was dead. They lifted her up, and when they saw that she had been laced too tightly, they cut the staylace in two. Snow White began to breathe, and little by little she came back to life. When the dwarfs heard what had happened, they said: "The old peddler woman was none other than the wicked queen. Beware, and don't let anyone in unless we're at home."

When the wicked woman returned home, she went to the mirror and asked:

"Mirror, mirror, on the wall,
Who's the fairest of them all?"

The mirror replied as usual:

1. Laces used to tighten the band of strips in a corset.

> "Here you're the fairest, dearest queen,
> But little Snow White, who plans to stay
> With the seven dwarfs far far away,
> Is now the fairest ever seen."

The blood froze in her veins when she heard those words. She was horrified, for she knew that Snow White was still alive. "But this time," she said, "I will dream up something that will destroy you."

Using all the witchcraft in her power, she made a poisoned comb. She then changed her clothes and disguised herself as another old woman. Once again she traveled beyond the seven hills to the seven dwarfs, knocked on the door, and called out: "Pretty wares at a good price."

Snow White peeked out of the window and said: "Go away, I can't let anyone in."

"But you can at least take a look," said the old woman, and she took out the poisoned comb and held it up in the air. The child liked it so much that she was completely fooled and opened the door. When they had agreed on a price, the old woman said: "Now I'll give your hair a good combing."

Poor Snow White suspected nothing and let the woman go ahead, but no sooner had the comb touched her hair when the poison took effect, and the girl fell senseless to the ground.

"There, my beauty," said the wicked woman, "now you're finished," and she rushed away.

Fortunately, it was almost evening, and the seven dwarfs were on their way home. When they saw Snow White lying on the ground as though dead, they suspected the stepmother right away. They examined Snow White and found the poisoned comb. As soon as they pulled it out, Snow White came back to life and told them what had happened. Again they warned her to be on her guard and not to open the door to anyone.

At home, the queen stood before the mirror and said:

> "Mirror, mirror, on the wall,
> Who's the fairest of them all?"

The mirror answered as before:

> "Here you're the fairest, dearest queen,
> But little Snow White, who plans to stay
> With the seven dwarfs far far away,
> Is now the fairest ever seen."

When the queen heard the words of the mirror, she began trembling with rage. "Snow White must die!" she cried out. "Even if it costs me my life."

Then she went into a remote, hidden chamber where no one ever set foot and made an apple full of poison. On the outside it looked beautiful—white with red cheeks—so that if you saw it you longed for it. But anyone who took the tiniest bite would die. When the apple was finished, she stained her face, dressed up as a peasant woman, and traveled beyond the seven hills to the seven dwarfs.

She knocked at the door, and Snow White put her head out the window to say: "I can't let anyone in. The seven dwarfs won't allow it."

"That's all right," replied the peasant woman. "I'll get rid of my apples soon enough. Here, I'll give you one."

"No," said Snow White, "I'm not supposed to take anything."

"Are you afraid that it's poisoned?" asked the old woman. "Here, I'll cut the apple in two. You eat the red part, I'll eat the white."

The apple had been made so artfully that only the red part of it was poison. Snow White felt a craving for the beautiful apple, and when she saw that the peasant woman was eating it, she could no longer resist. She put her hand out the window and took the poisoned half. But no sooner had she taken a bite when she fell down on the ground dead. The queen stared at her with savage eyes and burst out laughing: "White as snow, red as blood, black as ebony! This time the dwarfs won't be able to bring you back to life!"

At home, she asked the mirror:

> "Mirror, mirror, on the wall,
> Who's the fairest of them all?"

And finally it replied:

> "Oh queen, you are the fairest in the land."

Her envious heart was finally at peace, as much as an envious heart can be.

When the little dwarfs returned home in the evening, they found Snow White lying on the ground. Not a breath of air was coming from her lips. She was dead. They lifted her up and looked around for something that might be poisonous. They unlaced her, combed her hair, washed her with water and wine, but it was all in vain. The dear child was dead and nothing could bring her back. They placed her on a bier, and all seven of them sat down on it and mourned her. They wept for three days. They were about to bury her, but she still looked just like a living person with beautiful red cheeks.

They said: "We can't possibly lower her into the dark ground." And so they had a transparent glass coffin made that allowed Snow White to be seen from all sides. They put her in it, wrote her name on it in golden letters, and added that she was the daughter of a king. They brought the coffin up to the top of a mountain, and one of them was always there to keep vigil. Animals also came to mourn Snow White, first an owl, then a raven, and finally a dove.

Snow White lay in the coffin for a long, long time. But she did not decay and looked as if she were sleeping, for she was still white as snow, red as blood, and with hair as black as ebony.

One day the son of a king was traveling through the woods and arrived at the dwarfs' cottage. He wanted to spend the night there. On top of the mountain, he saw the coffin with beautiful Snow White lying in it, and he read what had been written in golden letters. Then he said to the dwarfs: "Let me have the coffin. I will give you whatever you want for it."

The dwarfs answered: "We wouldn't sell it for all the gold in the world."

Then he said: "Make me a present of it, for I can't live without seeing Snow White. I will honor and cherish her as if she were my beloved."

The good dwarfs took pity on him when they heard these words, and they gave him the coffin. The prince ordered his servants to carry the coffin away on their shoulders. It happened that they stumbled over a shrub, and the jolt freed the poisonous piece of apple lodged in Snow White's throat. She came to life. "Good heavens, where am I?" she cried out.

The prince was overjoyed and said: "You are with me," and he described what had happened and said: "I love you more than anything else on earth. Come with me to my father's castle. You shall be my bride." Snow White had tender feelings for him, and she departed with him. Their marriage was celebrated with great splendor.

Snow White's wicked stepmother was also invited to the wedding feast. She put on beautiful clothes, stepped up to the mirror, and said:

> "Mirror, mirror on the wall:
> Who's the fairest of them all?"

The mirror replied:

> "My queen, you may be the fairest here,
> But the young queen is a thousand times more fair."

The wicked women let loose a curse, and she became so petrified with fear that she didn't know what to do. At first she didn't want to go to the wedding feast. But she never had a moment's peace after that and had to go see the young queen. When she entered, Snow White recognized her right away. The queen was so terrified that she just stood there and couldn't budge an inch. Iron slippers had already been heated up over a fire of coals. They were brought in with tongs and set right in front of her. She had to put on the red hot iron shoes and dance in them until she dropped to the ground dead.

## Lasair Gheug, the King of Ireland's Daughter†

There was a king once, and he married a queen, and she had a daughter. The mother died then, and he married another queen. The queen was good to her stepdaughter. But one day the *eachrais ùrlair*[1] came in, and she said to the queen that she was a fool to be so good to her stepdaughter "when you know that the day the king dies, your share of the inheritance will be a small one to your stepdaughter's share."

"What can be done about it?" said the queen. "If my stepdaughter does well, I will get a share."

"If you give me what I ask," said the *eachrais ùrlair*, "I will do something about it."

"What would you want, old woman?" said the queen.

"I have a little saucepan, I only put it on occasionally. I want meal enough to thicken it, and butter enough to thin it, and the full of my ear of wool."

"How much meal will thicken it?"

"The increase of seven granaries of oats in seven years."

"How much butter will thin it?" said the queen.

"The increase of seven byres[2] of cattle in seven years."

"And how much wool will your ear hold?"

"The increase of seven folds of sheep in seven years."

"You have asked much, old woman," said the queen, "but though it is much, you shall have it."

"We will kill the king's greyhound bitch and leave it on the landing of the stairs, so that the king thinks that it is Lasair Gheug[3] who has done it. We will make Lasair Gheug swear three baptismal oaths, that she will not be on foot, she will not be on horseback, and she will not be on the green earth the day she tells of it."

The king came home, and saw the greyhound bitch on the landing. Roared, roared, roared the king: "Who did the deed?"

"Who do you think, but your own eldest daughter?" said the queen.

"That cannot be," said the king, and he went to bed, and he ate not a bite, and he drank not a drop: and if day came early, the king rose earlier than that, and went to the hill to hunt.

In came the *eachrais ùrlair*. "What did the king do to his daughter last night?" she asked.

---

† "A Scottish Gaelic Version of 'Snow White,'  " in *Scottish Studies* 9 (1969): 162–70. Narrated by Mrs. Macmillan and recorded by Lady Evelyn Stewart-Murray (1891); translated by Alan Bruford.

1. Malicious old woman (a stock villain of the Gaelic folktale, the figure sometimes called the henwife).
2. Cowbarns or sheds.
3. Flame of Branches, the King's daughter.

"He did nothing at all, old woman," said the queen. "Go home, and never let us see you again after the rage you put the king in last night."

"I will be bound that he will kill his daughter tonight," said the *eachrais ùrlair*. "We will kill the king's graceful black palfrey, and leave it on the landing. We will make Lasair Gheug swear three baptismal oaths, that she will not be on foot, she will not be on horseback, and she will not be on the green earth the day she tells of it."

The king came home, and saw the graceful black palfrey on the landing. Roared, roared, roared the king: "Who did the deed?"

"Who do you think, but your own eldest daughter?" said the queen.

"That cannot be," said the king. He went to bed, and he ate not a bite, and he drank not a drop: and if day came early, the king rose earlier than that, and went to the hill to hunt.

In came the *eachrais ùrlair*. "What did the king do to his daughter last night?" she asked.

"He did nothing at all, old woman," said the queen. "Go home, and don't come here again, after the rage you put the king in last night."

"I will be bound," said the *eachrais ùrlair*, "that he will kill his daughter tonight. We will kill your own eldest son," said she, "and leave him on the landing. We will make Lasair Gheug swear three baptismal oaths, that she will not be on foot, she will not be on horseback, and she will not be on the green earth the day she tells of it."

The king came home, then, and saw his eldest son on the landing. Roared, roared, roared the king: "Who did the deed?"

"Who do you think, but your own eldest daughter?" said the queen.

"That cannot be," said the king. He went to bed, and he ate not a bite, and he drank not a drop: and if day came early, the king rose earlier than that, and went to the hill to hunt.

In came the *eachrais ùrlair*. "What did the king do to his daughter last night?" she asked.

"He did nothing at all, old woman," said the queen. "Go home, and don't come here again, after the rage you put the king in last night."

"I will be bound," said the *eachrais ùrlair*, "that he will kill his daughter tonight. You must pretend that you are sick, sore and sorry."

Men leapt on horses and horses on men to look for the king. The king came. He asked the queen what in the seven continents of the world he could get to help her, that he would not get.

"There is something to help me," said she, "but what will help me you will not give me."

"If there is something to help you," said he, "you shall have it."

"Give me the heart and liver of Lasair Gheug, the King of Ireland's daughter," said the queen.

"Well," said the king, "it hurts me to give you that, but you shall have that," said the king. He went to the squinting sandy cook and asked him if he would hide his child for one night.

"I will," said the cook. They killed a sucking pig, and they took out the heart and liver. They put its blood on Lasair Gheug's clothes. The king went home with the heart and the liver, and gave it to the queen. Then the queen was as well as she had ever been.

The king went again to the squinting sandy cook, and he asked him if he would hide his child for one night again. The cook said he would. Next day the king took with him the best horse in the stable, a peck of gold, a peck of silver, and Lasair Gheug. He came to a great forest, with no edge and no end, and he was going to leave Lasair Gheug there. He cut off the end of one of her fingers.

"Does that hurt you, daughter?" he said.

"It doesn't hurt me, father," she said, "because it is you who did it."

"It hurts me more," said the king, "to have lost the greyhound bitch." With that he cut off another of her fingers.

"Does that hurt you, daughter?"

"It doesn't hurt me, father, because it is you who did it."

"It hurts me more than that to have lost the graceful black palfrey." With that he cut off another of her fingers.

"Does that hurt you, daughter?" said the king.

"It doesn't hurt me, father," said she, "because it is you who did it."

"It hurts me more," said he, "to have lost my eldest son." He gave her the peck of gold and the peck of silver, and he left her there. He went home, and he lay down on his bed, blind and deaf to the world.

Lasair Gheug was frightened in the forest that wild beasts would come and eat her. The highest tree she could see in the forest, she climbed that tree. She was not there long when she saw twelve cats coming, and a one-eyed grey cat along with them. They had a cow and a cauldron, and they lit a fire at the foot of the tree she was in. They killed the cow and put it in the cauldron to cook. The steam was rising, and her fingers were getting warm. She began to bleed, and drop after drop fell into the cauldron. The one-eyed grey cat told one of the other cats to go up the tree and see what was there: for king's blood or knight's blood was falling into the cauldron. The cat went up. She gave it a handful of gold and a handful of silver not to tell that she was there. But the blood would not stop. The one-eyed grey cat sent every one of them up, one after another, until all twelve had been up, and they all got a handful of gold and a handful of silver. The one-eyed grey cat climbed up himself, and he found Lasair Gheug and brought her down.

When the supper was ready, the one-eyed grey cat asked her whether she would rather have her supper with him, or with the others. She said she would rather have her supper with him, he was the one she liked the look of best. They had their supper, and then they were going to bed. The one-eyed grey cat asked her which she would rather, to go to bed with him, or to sleep with the others. She said she would rather go with him, he was the one she liked the look of best. They went to bed, and when they got up in the morning, they were in Lochlann. The one-eyed grey cat was really the King of Lochlann's son, and his twelve squires along with him. They had been bewitched by his step-mother, and now the spell was loosed.

They were married then, and Lasair Gheug had three sons. She asked the king as a favor not to have them christened.

There was a well in the King of Ireland's garden, and there was a trout in the well, and the queen used to go every year to wash in the well. She went there this time, and when she had washed, she said to the trout, "Little trout, little trout," said she, "am not I," said she, "the most beautiful woman that ever was in Ireland?"

"Indeed and indeed then, you are not," said the trout, "while Lasair Gheug, the King of Ireland's daughter, is alive."

"Is she alive still?" said the queen.

"She is, and will be in spite of you," said the trout. "She is in Lochlann, and has three unchristened children."

"I will set a snare to catch her," said the queen, "and a net to destroy you."

"You have tried to do that once or twice before," said the trout, "but you haven't managed it yet," said he, "and though I am here now, many is the mighty water I can be on before night comes."

The queen went home, and she gave the king a piece of her mind for making her believe that he had given her Lasair Gheug's heart and liver, when she was alive and well in Lochlann still. She wanted the king to go with her to see Lasair Gheug, but the king would not budge, and he would not believe that she was there. She sent her twelve maids-in-waiting to Lochlann, and she gave a box to her own maid to give Lasair Gheug, and she asked her to tell her not to open it until she was with her three unchristened children.

Lasair Gheug was sitting at the window, sewing. She saw her father's banner coming. In her delight she did not know whether to run out of the door or fly out of the window. They gave her the box, and she was so delighted with it that she did not wait to be with her three unchristened children. She opened the box when the others had gone home. When she opened the box, there were three grains in it . . . one grain of ice stuck in her forehead and another in each of her palms, and she fell dead and cold.

The king came home and found her dead. That would have beaten a wiser man than he. He was so fond of her, he would not let her be buried. He put her in a leaden coffin and kept it locked up in a room. He used to visit her early and late. He used to look twice as well when he went in as when he came out. This had been going on for a while when his companions persuaded him to marry again. He gave every key in the house to the queen, except the key of that room. She wondered what was in the room, when he looked so poorly coming out,

compared with the way he was when he went in. She told one of the
boys one day, if he was playing near the king, to see if he could manage
to steal that key out of his pocket. The lad stole the key and gave it to
his stepmother. She went in, and what was there but the king's first
wife. She looked her over; she saw the grain of ice in her forehead and
she took a pin and picked it out. The woman in the coffin gave a sigh.
She saw another one in one of her palms, and took it out. The woman
sat up. She found another one in the other palm, and took it out. Then
she was as well as she had ever been. She brought her out with her
and put her in another room. She sent the boy with the key to meet
his father coming home and put it back in his pocket without his
knowledge.

The king came home. The first thing he did was to go into that room
as usual. There was nothing there. He came out then to ask what had
happened to the thing that had been in the room. The queen said she
had never had the key of that room. She asked what had been in the
room. He said it was his first wife, and with the love he had for her he
would not bury her: he liked to see her, dead though she was.

"What will you give me," said the queen, "if I bring you her alive?"

"I don't expect to see her alive," said he, "but I would be glad to see
her even though she were dead."

The queen went then and brought her in on her arm, alive and well.
He did not know whether to laugh or cry with his delight. The other
queen said then that she might as well go home, there was no more
need for her there. Lasair Gheug said that she was not to go home: she
should stay along with her, and should have food and drink as good as
herself, every day as long as she lived.

At the end of this another year had gone by. The Queen of Ireland
went to the well to wash there again.

"Little trout, little trout," said she, "am not I the most beautiful
woman that ever was in Ireland?"

"Indeed and indeed you are not," said the trout, "while Lasair
Gheug, the king of Ireland's daughter, is alive."

"Is she alive still?" said she.

"Oh yes, and she will be in spite of you," said the trout.

"I will set a snare to catch her," said the queen, "and a net to destroy
you."

"You have tried to do that once or twice before," said the trout, "but
you haven't managed it yet," said he. "Though I am here now, many
is the mighty water I can be on before night comes."

The queen went home then, and she got the king moving, and they
went to visit Lasair Gheug. Lasair Gheug was sitting at the window this
time, but she showed no pleasure at all at the sight of her father's
banner.

When Sunday came, they went to church. She had sent people to
catch a wild boar that was in the wood, and others to get faggots and
sticks and stuff to make a big fire. She got the wild boar; she got on to
the boar's back, went in at one door of the church and out at the other
door. She called her three unchristened children to her side.

"I am not going to tell my story to anyone at all," said she, "but to
you three unchristened children.

"When I was in my own father's kingdom in Ireland, my stepmother
and the *eachrais ùrlair* killed my father's greyhound bitch and left it on
the landing. They made me swear three baptismal oaths, that I would
not be on foot, I would not be on horseback, and I would not be on
the green earth the day I told of it. But I am on the wild boar's back.
They expected that my father would kill me, but my father has not
killed me yet."

She went in at one door, and she went out at the other door, and
she called her three unchristened children along with her.

"I am not going to tell my story to anyone at all," said she, "but to
you unchristened children.

"When I was in my own father's kingdom in Ireland, my stepmother
and the *eachrais ùrlair* killed my father's graceful black palfrey and left
it on the landing. They made me swear three baptismal oaths, that I
would not be on foot, I would not be on horseback, and I would not
be on the green earth the day I told of it. But I am on the wild boar's
back. They expected that my father would kill me, but my father has
not killed me yet."

She went in at one door, and she went out at the other door, and
she called her three unchristened children along with her.

"I am not going to tell my story to anyone at all," said she, "but to
you three unchristened children.

"When I was in my own father's kingdom in Ireland, my stepmother
and the *eachrais ùrlair* killed my eldest brother and left him on the
landing. They made me swear three baptismal oaths, that I would not
be on foot, I would not be on horseback, and I would not be on the
green earth the day I told of it. But I am on the wild boar's back. They
expected that my father would kill me, but my father has not killed me
yet. Now," said she, "I have nothing more to tell you."

The wild boar was set free. When they came out of the church, the
Queen of Ireland was caught and burnt in the fire.

When the king was going home, he said to his daughter, Lasair
Gheug, that she had done ill by him: he had come from home with a
wife, and he was going home now without one. And Lasair Gheug said:
"It wasn't that way: you came here with a monster, but I have a woman
friend, and you shall have her, and you will go home with a wife." And
they made a great, merry, mirthful, happy, hospitable, wonderful wed-

ding; it was kept up for a year and a day. I[4] got shoes of paper there on a glass pavement, a bit of butter on an ember, porridge in a creel,[5] a greatcoat of chaff[6] and a short coat of buttermilk. I hadn't gone far when I fell, and the glass pavement broke, the short coat of buttermilk spilt, the butter melted on the ember, a gust of wind came and blew away the greatcoat of chaff. All I had had was gone, and I was as poor as I was to start with. And I left them there.

# ANNE SEXTON

## Snow White and the Seven Dwarfs†

No matter what life you lead
the virgin is a lovely number:
cheeks as fragile as cigarette paper,
arms and legs made of Limoges,
lips like Vin Du Rhône,[1]
rolling her china-blue doll eyes
open and shut.
Open to say,
Good Day Mama,
and shut for the thrust
of the unicorn.
She is unsoiled.
She is as white as a bonefish.

Once there was a lovely virgin
called Snow White.
Say she was thirteen.
Her stepmother,
a beauty in her own right,
though eaten, of course, by age,
would hear of no beauty surpassing her own.
Beauty is a simple passion,
but, oh my friends, in the end

4. Folk raconteurs frequently concluded their tales with the kind of comic twist introduced at the end of this story. The tellers often used the conclusion as an opportunity to insist that the events told are true (they were, after all, witnesses) and to underscore the contrast between the protagonists' good fortune and their own hard luck (perhaps an appeal for generosity in rewarding the teller for spinning a good yarn).
5. *creel*: a wicker basket, usually used for carrying fish.
6. A heavy overcoat unlikely to last long, since it is made of husks of grain.
† Anne Sexton, "Snow White and the Seven Dwarfs," in *Transformations* (Boston: Houghton Mifflin, 1971). Copyright © 1971 by Anne Sexton. Reprinted by permission of Houghton Mifflin Company and Sterling Lord Literistic, Inc. All rights reserved.
1. Limoges: a type of fine porcelain; Vin Du Rhône: wine from the Rhône valley.

you will dance the fire dance in iron shoes.
The stepmother had a mirror to which she referred—

something like the weather forecast—
a mirror that proclaimed
the one beauty of the land.
She would ask,
Looking glass upon the wall,
who is fairest of us all?
And the mirror would reply,
You are fairest of us all.
Pride pumped in her like poison.

Suddenly one day the mirror replied,
Queen, you are full fair, 'tis true,
but Snow White is fairer than you.
Until that moment Snow White
had been no more important
than a dust mouse under the bed.
But now the queen saw brown spots on her hand
and four whiskers over her lip
so she condemned Snow White
to be hacked to death.
Bring me her heart, she said to the hunter,
and I will salt it and eat it.
The hunter, however, let his prisoner go
and brought a boar's heart back to the castle.
The queen chewed it up like a cube steak.
Now I am fairest, she said,
lapping her slim white fingers.

Snow White walked in the wildwood
for weeks and weeks.
At each turn there were twenty doorways
and at each stood a hungry wolf,
his tongue lolling out like a worm.
The birds called out lewdly,
talking like pink parrots,
and the snakes hung down in loops,
each a noose for her sweet white neck.
On the seventh week
she came to the seventh mountain
and there she found the dwarf house.
It was as droll as a honeymoon cottage
and completely equipped with

seven beds, seven chairs, seven forks
and seven chamber pots.
Snow White ate seven chicken livers
and lay down, at last, to sleep.

*[handwritten: hot dogs]* The dwarfs, those little hot dogs,
walked three times around Snow White,
the sleeping virgin. They were wise
and wattled like small czars.
Yes. It's a good omen,
they said, and will bring us luck.
They stood on tiptoes to watch
Snow White wake up. She told them
about the mirror and the killer-queen
and they asked her to stay and keep house.
Beware of your stepmother,
they said.
Soon she will know you are here.
While we are away in the mines
during the day, you must not
open the door.

Looking glass upon the wall . . .
The mirror told
and so the queen dressed herself in rags
and went out like a peddler to trap Snow White.
She went across seven mountains.
She came to the dwarf house
and Snow White opened the door
and bought a bit of lacing.
The queen fastened it tightly
*[handwritten: Ace bandage]* around her bodice,
as tight as an Ace bandage,
so tight that Snow White swooned.
She lay on the floor, a plucked daisy.
When the dwarfs came home they undid the lace
and she revived miraculously.
She was as full of life as soda pop.
*[handwritten: soda pop]* Beware of your stepmother,
they said.
She will try once more.

Looking glass upon the wall . . .
Once more the mirror told
and once more the queen dressed in rags

and once more Snow White opened the door.
This time she bought a poison comb,
a curved eight-inch scorpion,
and put it in her hair and swooned again.
The dwarfs returned and took out the comb
and she revived miraculously.
She opened her eyes as wide as Orphan Annie.
Beware, beware, they said,
but the mirror told,
the queen came,
Snow White, the dumb bunny,
opened the door
and she bit into a poison apple
and fell down for the final time.
When the dwarfs returned
they undid her bodice,
they looked for a comb,
but it did no good.
Though they washed her with wine
and rubbed her with butter
it was to no avail.
She lay as still as a gold piece.

The seven dwarfs could not bring themselves
to bury her in the black ground
so they made a glass coffin
and set it upon the seventh mountain
so that all who passed by
could peek in upon her beauty.
A prince came one June day
and would not budge.
He stayed so long his hair turned green
and still he would not leave.
The dwarfs took pity upon him
and gave him the glass Snow White—
its doll's eyes shut forever—
to keep in his far-off castle.
As the prince's men carried the coffin
they stumbled and dropped it
and the chunk of apple flew out
of her throat and she woke up miraculously.

And thus Snow White became the prince's bride.
The wicked queen was invited to the wedding feast
and when she arrived there were

*roller skates*

red-hot iron shoes,
in the manner of red-hot roller skates,
clamped upon her feet.
First your toes will smoke
and then your heels will turn black
and you will fry upward like a frog,
she was told.
And so she danced until she was dead,
a subterranean figure,
her tongue flicking in and out
like a gas jet.
Meanwhile Snow White held court,
rolling her china-blue doll eyes open and shut
and sometimes referring to her mirror
as women do.

*– humility*
*└ sometimes*
*looking*
*in mirror*

# INTRODUCTION:
## Cinderella

Cinderella may live happily ever after in virtually every version of her story, but her stepsisters rarely fare very well. Who can forget the final scene of the Grimms' "Cinderella," which graphically describes the fate of those ill-tempered, disagreeable pretenders to the throne?

> When the couple went to church, the elder sister was on the right, the younger on the left side: the doves pecked one eye from each one. Later, when they left the church, the elder sister was on the left, and the younger on the right. The doves pecked out the other eye from each one. [122]

For their "wickedness and malice" [122] the sisters are punished with blindness for the rest of their lives. This ending, along with the details of the mutilation of their feet, is often cited as evidence of the brutal, violent turn taken by German fairy tales. Yet the Grimms' punishment for the stepsisters is relatively mild when compared to what befalls their counterparts in other cultures. An Indonesian Cinderella forces her stepsister into a cauldron of boiling water, then has the body cut up, pickled, and sent to the girl's mother as "salt meat" for her next meal. A Filipino variant shows the stepmother and her daughters "pulled to pieces by wild horses." And a Japanese stepsister is dragged around in a basket, tumbles over the edge of a deep ditch, and falls to her death.[1]

Many versions of "Cinderella," however, end on a conciliatory note. Charles Perrault offers what is perhaps the fullest elaboration of a reconciliation between the heroine and her stepsisters, who throw themselves at Cinderella's feet and beg her forgiveness. This Cinderella, who is as good as she is beautiful, not only pardons the sisters, but also invites them to join her in the palace and loses no time in marrying them to two high-ranking court officials. An Armenian Cinderella falls at the feet of her wicked sisters as they are leaving church, weeps copious tears with them, and bears them no grudge.[2] And finally, a recent American version marketed through elementary schools stages a crudely

---

Page numbers in brackets refer to this Norton Critical Edition.
1. Neil Philip, *The Cinderella Story: The Origins and Variations of the Story Known as 'Cinderella'* (London: Penguin, 1989) 21–31, 113–21, 32–35.
2. Philip, *The Cinderella Story*, 46–51.

sentimental reconciliation scene, presumably designed to appeal to the
educators and parents buying the book:

> [The sisters] begged Cinderella to forgive them for being so
> mean to her.
> Cinderella told them they were forgiven.
> "I am sure you will never be mean to me again," she said.
> "Oh, never," said the older sister.
> "Never, ever," said the younger sister.[3]

Cinderella has been reinvented by so many different cultures that it
is hardly surprising to find that she is sometimes cruel and vindictive,
at other times compassionate and kind. Even within a single culture,
she can appear genteel and self-effacing in one story, clever and enterprising in another, coy and manipulative in a third.[4] Despite the elasticity of Cinderella's character within any given culture, Jane Yolen
may have a point when she asserts that the shrewd, resourceful heroine
of folktales from earlier centuries has been supplanted by a "passive
princess" waiting for Prince Charming to rescue her. Disney's Cinderella, as we shall see, is no match for some of her folkloric ancestors,
who refuse to stay at home suffering in silence and who become adept
at engineering their own rescues.

Just how spirited and resourceful was Cinderella in her earliest incarnations? Answering that question requires surveying a vast array of
tales featuring heroines known not only as Cinderella, Cendrillon, Ash
Girl, and Cennerentola, but also as Rashin Coatie, Mossy Coat, Catskin, Katie Woodencloak, and Donkeyskin. The Aarne-Thompson index of tale types[5] identifies two distinct Cinderella tales: AT 510A
("Cinderella") and AT 510B ("The Dress of Gold, of Silver, and of
Stars," also known as "Catskin"). The two narratives encoded in the
tale-type index seem virtually unrelated at first glance. The plots of
"Cinderella" stories are driven by the anxious jealousy of biological
mothers and stepmothers who subject the heroine to one ordeal of
domestic drudgery after another; the plots of "Catskin" tales are fueled
by the sexual desire of fathers, whose unseemly behavior drives their
daughters from home.

In tales depicting the social persecution of a girl by her stepmother,
the central focus comes to rest on the unbearable family situation produced by a father's remarriage. But while the father's responsibility for
creating turmoil by choosing a monstrous marriage partner recedes into
the background or is suppressed (even as the father himself is virtually

3. Jane Yolen, "America's Cinderella," *Children's Literature in Education* 8 (1977): 21–29.
4. Ruth B. Bottigheimer, "Fairy Tales and Children's Literature: A Feminist Perspective," in
   *Teaching Children's Literature: Issues, Pedagogy, Resources*, ed. Glen Edward Sadler (New
   York: Modern Language Association of America, 1992), 101–8.
5. Antti Aarne and Stith Thompson, *The Types of the Folktale: A Classification and Bibliography*
   (Helsinki: Academia Scientiarum Fennica, 1961).

eliminated as a character), the foul deeds of his wife come to occupy center stage. We see her throwing her stepdaughter into a river, instructing a hunter to kill her and recover her lungs and liver for dinner, sending her into a snowstorm wearing nothing but a shift, depriving her of food, and making her life wretched in every way.

In tales depicting erotic persecution of a daughter by her father, stepmothers and their daughters tend to vanish from the central arena of action. Yet the father's desire for his daughter in the second tale type furnishes a powerful motive for a stepmother's jealous rages and unnatural deeds in the first tale type. The two plots can be seen as conveniently dovetailing to produce an intrigue that corresponds to the oedipal fantasies of girls. Psychoanalytic criticism has indeed seen "Cinderella" and "Catskin" as enactments of oedipal desires, with each tale suppressing one component (love for the father or hatred of the mother) of the oedipal plot. Many "Catskin" narratives, among them Perrault's "Donkeyskin" and the Grimms' "Thousandfurs," mount two phases of action: in the first the heroine is persecuted by her father, in the second she turns into a Cinderella figure, obliged to spend her days in domestic servitude under the supervision of a despotic cook or a queen.

While wicked stepmothers figure prominently in fairy tales disseminated in our culture, fathers who persecute their daughters by showing them too much affection are virtually unknown. "Cinderella," "Snow White," and "Hansel and Gretel" are the tales from Perrault and from the Grimms that continue to thrive even on foreign soil, while stories such as "Donkeyskin" and "Thousandfurs" have either failed to take root or have been modified beyond recognition, with the result that fathers have a surprisingly limited role in fairy tales transmitted today.

It is important to bear in mind that the passive or absent father was, even a century ago, not the rule in fairy tales. As Marian Cox's nineteenth-century study of 345 variants of "Cinderella" makes clear, at least two widespread and pervasive versions of the tale attributed the heroine's social degradation either to what Cox describes in characteristic Victorian language as an "unnatural father" or to a father who attempts to extract from his daughter a statement about her filial devotion.[6] Of the 226 tales belonging unambiguously to one of the three categories labeled by Cox as (1) ill-treated heroine (with mothers, stepmothers, and their progeny as victimizers), (2) unnatural father, and (3) King Lear judgment, 130 belong to the first class, 77 to the second, and 19 to the third. Thus in the tales examined by Cox, the versions that cast (step)mothers in the role of villain only slightly outnumber those that ascribe Cinderella's misfortune to an importunate father. Cinderella and her cousins were, therefore, once almost as likely to flee the household because of their father's perverse erotic attachment to them or

6. Marian Roalfe Cox, *Cinderella: Three Hundred and Forty-five Variants of Cinderella, Catskin, and Cap o' Rushes,* ed. Andrew Lang (London: David Nutt, 1893).

because of his insistence on a verbal declaration of love, as they were to be banished to the hearth and degraded to domestic servitude by an ill-tempered stepmother.

That our own culture would suppress the theme of paternal erotic pursuit and indulge freely in elaborate variations on the theme of maternal tyranny is perhaps not surprising on a number of counts. Since tales such as Perrault's "Donkeyskin" and the Grimms' "Thousandfurs" make for troubling reading matter for adults, it hardly seems advisable to put them between the covers of books for children. But Marina Warner has argued that there is something more at stake in this evolutionary turn in the Cinderella story:

> When interest in psychological realism is at work in the mind of the receiver of traditional folklore, the proposed marriage of a father to his daughter becomes too hard to accept. But it is only too hard to accept precisely because it belongs to a different order of reality/fantasy from the donkeyskin disguise or the gold excrement or the other magical motifs: because it is not impossible, because it could actually happen, and is know to have done so. It is when fairy tales coincide with experience that they begin to suffer from censoring, rather than the other way around.[7]

The censorship to which Warner refers seems to have led to dramatic editorial interventions very early on, perhaps as the tale made its way from an oral culture to a literary tradition. In Straparola's seventeenth-century "Catskin" tale, the king is described as a "wicked father" with "evil designs," "execrable lust," and a "wicked and treacherous passion." Yet it is his wife who decrees that the object of his lust and passion be their daughter Doralice. On her deathbed, the queen beseeches her husband Tebaldo never to take anyone as wife whose finger does not perfectly fit her own wedding ring. Faithful husband that he is, Tebaldo makes it a condition "that any damsel who might be offered to him in marriage should first try on her finger his wife's ring, to see whether it fitted." When the king fails to find a woman whose finger fits the ring, he turns to his daughter and discovers that the fit is perfect. As Tebaldo tells his daughter, he is obliged to marry her for it is the only way "I shall satisfy my own desire without violating the promise I made to your mother."[8]

While some readers will not be persuaded by Tebaldo's logic and by the narrator's efforts to exonerate the king, many others have clearly bought right into the rhetoric of self-justification set forth in other Catskin tales. Consider one critic's gloss on the family dynamics in Perrault's "Donkeyskin": "The dying queen had a vengeful streak: she

7. Marina Warner, "The Silence of the Fathers: Donkeyskin II," in *From the Beast to the Blonde: On Fairy Tales and Their Tellers* (New York: Farrar, Straus and Giroux, 1994) 349.
8. Giovanni Francesco Straparola, *The Facetious Nights of Straparola*, trans. W. G. Waters (London: Society of Bibliophiles, 1901) 82.

made her husband . . . swear not to remarry unless he found a woman superior to her in beauty and goodness. Entrapped, the king eventually discovers that only his lovely daughter can fill the bill."[9] Another critic finds that "Rashie-Coat's degradation is consequent upon her dying mother's unfortunate imprudence."[1] Again and again, mothers are the real villains, extracting promises that end by victimizing both father and daughter. Everywhere we look, the tendency to defame women and to magnify maternal evil emerges. Even when a tale turns on a father's incestuous desires, the mother becomes more than complicit: she has stirred up the trouble in the first place by setting the conditions for her husband's remarriage.

The ring episode in Straparola's "Catskin" does suggest one hitherto neglected point of contact between "Cinderella" tales and "Catskin" tales. Finding the perfect fit between fingers and rings and between feet and shoes becomes a task set both fathers and princes, who now and then collaborate with each other (as in the Grimms' "Cinderella"), who sometimes work in succession (as in Perrault's "Donkeyskin"), and who are occasionally concurrent rivals, as in an Indian tale entitled "The Father Who Wanted to Marry His Daughter."[2] What these stories demonstrate, perhaps more forcefully than anything else, is the way in which the path to happy heterosexual unions depends on a successful transfer of filial love and devotion from a father to a "prince," on a move from a false "perfect fit" to a true "perfect fit."

While Catskin tales raise the charged issue of incestuous desire and place the heroine in jeopardy, they also furnish a rare stage for creative action. Unlike Cinderella, who endures humiliation at home and becomes the beneficiary of lavish gifts, the heroine of Catskin tales is mobile, active, and resourceful. She begins with a strong assertion of will, resistant to the paternal desires that would claim her. Fleeing the household, she moves out into an alien world that requires her to be inventive, energetic, and enterprising if she is to reestablish herself, to reclaim her royal rank, and to marry the prince. To be sure, her resourcefulness is confined largely to sartorial and culinary arts, but these were, after all, the two areas in which women traditionally could distinguish themselves. The Grimms' Thousandfurs dazzles with her dress, and she successfully uses her cuisine to lure the prince. Donkeyskin's powers of attraction are also explicitly linked to her wardrobe and her baking skills.

That these stories are disappearing from the folkloric arena is perhaps not surprising. The theme of incest alone would account for the steady erosion of interest in anthologizing the tale. But in addition, the story's

9. Philip Lewis, *Seeing through the Mother Goose Tales; Visual Turns in the Writings of Charles Perrault* (Stanford: Stanford UP, 1996) 155.
1. W. R. S. Ralston, "Cinderella," in *Cinderella: A Casebook*, ed. Alan Dundes (Madison: U of Wisconsin P, 1981) 41.
2. A. K. Ramanujan, ed., *Folktales from India* (New York: Pantheon, 1991) 186–89.

critique of paternal authority and its endorsement of filial disobedience turn it into an unlikely candidate for bedtime reading. What are we to make of a story that positions a father as the agent of transgressive sexuality and the daughter as the enforcer of cultural law and order? Charles Perrault, who felt that fairy tales ought to transmit lessons to children about virtue and vice, was so mystified by "Donkeyskin" that he appended a moral that is absurdly irrelevant to the premises of the text: "The story of Donkeyskin may be hard to believe, but as long as there are children, mothers, and grandmothers in this world, it will be fondly remembered by all" [116]. What is far harder to believe than the story itself is the idea that this particular tale could generate "fond" memories.

In staging the attempted violation of our most sacred taboo, Catskin stories celebrate daughters as agents of resistance, yet also enshrine them as maintaining the sanctity of cultural codes. Giambattista Basile captured exactly what made this story unacceptable to later generations when he spelled out its moral:

> The wise man spoke well when he said that one cannot obey commands of gall with obedience sweet as sugar. Man must give only well-measured commands if he expects well-weighed obedience, and resistance springs from wrongful orders, as happened in the case of the King of Roccaspra, who, by asking for what was unseemly from his daughter, caused her to run away at the peril of her life and honor.[3]

While there are virtually no male counterparts to Catskin (mother/son incest seems to resist representation in folktales), male Cinderellas abound in the folklore of many cultures. Antti Aarne and Stith Thompson felt obliged to accommodate these male Cinderellas in their index of tale types by setting up a separate category of Cinderella tales identified by the rubric AT 511 ("One-Eye, Two-Eyes, and Three-Eyes" for female Cinderellas) and AT 511A ("The Little Red Ox" for male Cinderellas). The distinction is little more than theoretical, for in practice, tales such as "The Little Red Ox" (a story in which the protagonist's mother returns in the form of a donor-ox) seem to feature girls almost as often as boys. These tales neutralize the persecutions of a wicked stepmother with the sustenance, nurturing, and rescue provided by an animal that is clearly identified with the dead mother. The Indian "Story of the Black Cow" belongs to a tale type that has virtually disappeared from our folkloristic repertoire but once enjoyed the kind of popularity that "Cinderella" has attained today. That male Cinderellas have disappeared from our own cultural horizon challenges us to un-

3. Giambattista Basile, "The She-Bear," in *The Pentamerone of Giambattista Basile*, trans. Benedetto Croce, ed. N. M. Penzer (London: John Lane the Bodley Head, 1932) 170.

derstand exactly what it was that once allowed both girls and boys to participate in the developmental trajectory outlined in the tale.

## Yeh-hsien†

Among the people of the south there is a tradition that before the Ch'in and Han dynasties there was a cave-master called Wu. The aborigines called the place the Wu cave. He married two wives. One wife died. She had a daughter called Yeh-hsien, who from childhood was intelligent and good at making pottery on the wheel. Her father loved her. After some years the father died, and she was ill-treated by her step-mother, who always made her collect firewood in dangerous places and draw water from deep pools. She once got a fish about two inches long, with red fins and golden eyes. She put it into a bowl of water. It grew bigger every day, and after she had changed the bowl several times she could find no bowl big enough for it, so she threw it into the back pond. Whatever food was left over from meals she put into the water to feed it. When she came to the pond, the fish always exposed its head and pillowed it on the bank; but when anyone else came, it did not come out. The step-mother knew about this, but when she watched for it, it did not once appear. So she tricked the girl, saying, "Haven't you worked hard! I am going to give you a new dress." She then made the girl change out of her tattered clothing. Afterwards she sent her to get water from another spring and reckoning that it was several hundred leagues, the step-mother at her leisure put on her daughter's clothes, hid a sharp blade up her sleeve, and went to the pond. She called to the fish. The fish at once put its head out, and she chopped it off and killed it. The fish was now more than ten feet long. She served it up and it tasted twice as good as an ordinary fish. She hid the bones under the dung-hill. Next day, when the girl came to the pond, no fish appeared. She howled with grief in the open countryside, and suddenly there appeared a man with his hair loose over his shoulders and coarse clothes. He came down from the sky. He consoled her saying, "Don't howl! Your step-mother has killed the fish and its bones are under the dung. You go back, take the fish's bones and hide them in your room. Whatever you want, you have only to pray to them for it. It is bound to be granted." The girl followed his advice, and was able to provide herself with gold, pearls, dresses and food whenever she wanted them.

When the time came for the cave-festival, the step-mother went, leaving the girl to keep watch over the fruit-trees in the garden. She waited till the step-mother was some way off, and then went herself, wearing

---

† "The Chinese Cinderella Story," *Folk-Lore*, vol. 58 (London: The Folklore Society, 1947), 18–20. Narrated by Li Shih-yüan and recorded by Tuan Ch'eng-shih (c. 850 A.D.); translated by Arthur Waley (1947). Reprinted by permission.

a cloak of stuff spun from kingfisher feathers and shoes of gold. Her step-sister recognized her and said to the step-mother, "That's very like my sister." The step-mother suspected the same thing. The girl was aware of this and went away in such a hurry that she lost one shoe. It was picked up by one of the people of the cave. When the step-mother got home, she found the girl asleep, with her arms round one of the trees in the garden, and thought no more about it.

This cave was near to an island in the sea. On this island was a kingdom called T'o-han. Its soldiers had subdued twenty or thirty other islands and it had a coast-line of several thousand leagues. The cave-man sold the shoe in T'o-han, and the ruler of T'o-han got it. He told those about him to put it on; but it was an inch too small even for the one among them that had the smallest foot. He ordered all the women in his kingdom to try it on; but there was not one that it fitted. It was light as down and made no noise even when treading on stone. The king of T'o-han thought the cave-man had got it unlawfully. He put him in prison and tortured him, but did not end by finding out where it had come from. So he threw it down at the wayside. Then they went everywhere through all the people's houses and arrested them. If there was a woman's shoe, they arrested them and told the king of T'o-han. He thought it strange, searched the inner-rooms and found Yeh-hsien. He made her put on the shoe, and it was true.

Yeh-hsien then came forward, wearing her cloak spun from halcyon feathers and her shoes. She was as beautiful as a heavenly being. She now began to render service to the king, and he took the fish-bones and Yeh-hsien, and brought them back to his country.

The step-mother and step-sister were shortly afterwards struck by flying stones, and died. The cave people were sorry for them and buried them in a stone-pit, which was called the Tomb of the Distressed Women. The men of the cave made mating-offerings there; any girl they prayed for there, they got. The king of T'o-han, when he got back to his kingdom made Yeh-hsien his chief wife. The first year the king was very greedy and by his prayers to the fish-bones got treasures and jade without limit. Next year, there was no response, so the king buried the fish-bones on the sea-shore. He covered them with a hundred bushels of pearls and bordered them with gold. Later there was a mutiny of some soldiers who had been conscripted and their general opened (the hiding-place) in order to make better provision for his army. One night they (the bones) were washed away by the tide.

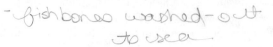

# CHARLES PERRAULT

## Donkeyskin†

Once upon a time there lived a king who was the most powerful ruler on earth. Gentle in peace and terrifying in war, he had no rivals. While his neighbors feared him, his subjects were perfectly content. Under his protection, civic virtues and the fine arts flourished everywhere. His better half, his faithful companion, was so charming and so beautiful, with a disposition so sweet and generous, that he was prouder about being her husband than about being king. From their pure, tender marriage, which was full of affection and pleasure, was born a girl with so many virtues that they easily compensated for the lack of additional progeny.

Everything in the king's palatial, luxurious castle was magnificent. It was teeming with vast numbers of courtiers and servants. In the stables were steeds large and small, of every description, covered with handsome trappings, embroidery, and braids of gold. But what surprised everyone on entering was that the most visible place in the castle was occupied by Master Donkey, who displayed his two immense ears for everyone to see. This incongruity may surprise you, but once you become aware of the superlative virtues of this creature, you too will agree that he was well worth his keep. Nature had formed him in such a way that instead of dropping dung he excreted all kinds of beautiful gold coins that were gathered from his golden litter every morning when he awoke.

Heaven sometimes tires of letting people enjoy happiness and always mingles the good with the bad just like rain with good weather. Out of the blue, a nasty illness attacked the queen and ended her days of joy. Help was summoned from all quarters, but neither erudite physicians nor the charlatans who appeared were able to arrest the fire started by the fever and fueled by it.

In her dying hour, the queen said to her husband the king: "Before I die I want to make one request of you. If you desire to remarry when I am no more. . . ."

"Oh," said the king," your fears are unnecessary. I'd never in my life think of it. Rest assured of that."

"I believe you," answered the queen. "Your ardent love proves it to me. But just to be absolutely certain, I want you to swear that you will pledge your love and marry only if you meet a woman more beautiful, more accomplished, and more wise than I am. Confidence in her own

† From Charles Perrault, *Griselidis, Nouvelle, avec le conte de Peau d'Ane et celui des Souhaits ridicules* (Paris: Coignard, 1694). Translated for this Norton Critical Edition by Maria Tatar. Copyright © 1999 Maria Tatar.

qualities convinced the queen that the promise, cunningly extracted, was as good as an oath never to marry. His eyes bathed in tears, the king swore to do everything the queen desired. And the queen died in his arms. Never did a king make such a display of his emotions. To hear him sobbing both day and night one would have thought that his grief could not endure and that he was mourning his deceased wife like a man eager to put an end to the affair quickly.

And indeed, that was the case. After a few months, he wanted to go ahead and choose a new wife. But this was not an easy matter. He had to keep the promise that the new wife would be more charming and attractive than the one who had just been buried. Neither the court with its many beauties, nor the country, nor the city, nor the neighboring kingdoms where they were making the rounds could provide such a woman. Only his own daughter was more beautiful, and she even possessed certain charms that his dead wife never had. The king noticed it himself and, burning with a desire that drove him mad, he took it into his head that she ought to marry him. He even found a sophist who agreed that a case could be made for the marriage. But the young princess, saddened by this kind of love, grieved and wept night and day.

With a heart grieving with a thousand sorrows, the princess went to find her godmother, who lived some distance in a remote grotto made of pearls and lavishly adorned with coral. She was an extraordinary fairy, unrivaled in her art. There is no need to tell you what a fairy was in those radiant days, for I am sure that your loved ones told you about them when you were very young.

"I know what has brought you here," the fairy godmother said, looking at the princess. "I understand the deep sadness in your heart. But with me by your side, there is no need to worry. Nothing can harm you so long as you follow my advice. It is true that your father wants to marry you, and it would be a fatal mistake to pay attention to his mad demand. But there is a way of refusing him without defying him. Tell him that before you are willing to give your heart to him, he must satisfy your desires and give you a dress the color of the seasons. No matter how rich and powerful he is and no matter how much he is favored by the heavens, he will never be able to fulfill your request."

Trembling with fear, the young princess went right away to her amorous father, who instantly ordered the most renowned tailors in the land to make a dress the color of the sky without delay. If not, they could rest assured that he would have them all hanged.

It was not yet dawn the next day when the desired dress was brought in. The most beautiful blue of the firmament, even when it is encircled with large clouds of gold, is not a deeper azure. Transfixed with joy and with sorrow, the child did not know what to say or how to get around the agreement. The godmother said to her in a low voice: "Ask for a dress more brilliant and less commonplace, one the color of the moon. He will never be able to give it to you."

No sooner had the princess placed the request when the king said to his embroiderer: "I want a dress more splendid than the star of the night, and I want it ready without fail in four days."

The elegant dress was ready on the designated day, just as the king had decreed. When the night unfurls its veils in the skies, the moon, whose brilliant voyage makes the stars turn pale, was no more majestic than this dress. The princess admired the wonderful dress and was about to give her consent when, inspired by her godmother, she said to the amorous king: "I can't be satisfied until I have a dress the color of the sun, but even more radiant."

The king, who loved the princess with a passion beyond compare, summoned a wealthy jeweler and ordered him to make a superb garment of gold and diamonds. He told him that if he failed to carry out the work in satisfactory fashion, he would have him tortured to death.

The king did not have to go to that trouble, for the industrious worker brought him the precious work before the week was over. It was so beautiful, vibrant, and radiant that the blonde lover of Clymene,[1] who drives his chariot of gold along the arch of the heavens, was not dazzled by a more brilliant light.

These gifts so confused the child that she did not know what to say to her father, the king. Her godmother took her by the hand and whispered in her ear: "You don't have to stay on this lovely path. Are these gifts that you have received really so marvelous when he has a donkey that, as you know, continually fills his coffers with gold coins? Ask him for the skin of that extraordinary animal. Unless I'm badly mistaken, you won't get it from him, since it is the sole source of his wealth."

This fairy was very learned, and yet she was unaware that passionate love, provided that it has a chance, takes no notice of money or gold. The skin was gallantly bestowed on the child as soon as she asked for it. When the skin was brought to her, she was filled with horror and complained bitterly about her fate. Her godmother arrived and explained that as long as she did the right thing, she would not have to be afraid. She should let the king believe that she was completely prepared to take her wedding vows with him, but at the same time she must disguise herself and flee all alone to a distant country to avoid an evil destiny so certain and so near.

"Here's a large trunk," she added. "We'll put all your clothes, your mirror, your toilet articles, your diamonds and your rubies into it. I will also give you my wand. If you hold it in your hand, the trunk will remain hidden beneath the ground and follow wherever you go. And if you ever want to open it, as soon as my wand touches the ground, it

1. Reference to Apollo, the Greek god of light and of the sun.

will appear right before your eyes. The hide of the donkey will be the perfect disguise to make you unrecognizable. Conceal yourself carefully under that skin. It is so hideous that no one will ever believe it covers anything beautiful."

The princess put on her disguise and left the wise fairy while the dew was still in the air. The king, who was just then preparing for his joyous wedding feast, learned with horror of the dark turn of events. Every house, road, and avenue was searched forthwith, but it was all in vain. No one could imagine what had become of her. A deep and dark sadness spread throughout the land. No more weddings, no more feasts, no more tarts, no more sugared almonds. Most of the ladies of the court were completely disappointed that they were unable to dine, but the priest felt the greatest sorrow, for he not only missed a meal but, what's worse, nothing was put on the offering plate.

In the meantime, the child continued her journey, her face dirtied with mud. She put out a hand to everyone who passed by her, trying to find a place to work. But these vulgar and unfortunate people saw someone so disagreeable and unkempt that they were not inclined to pay attention to her, let alone to take in a creature so dirty.

And so she journeyed farther and farther, and farther still, until she arrived at a farm where the farmer's wife needed a scullery maid who would be energetic enough to wash the dish rags and to clean the trough for the pigs. She was put into a back corner of the kitchen, where the valets, those insolent scoundrels, ridiculed, attacked, and mocked her all the time. They played tricks on her whenever they could, tormenting her at every turn. She became the butt of all their jokes, and they jeered at her day and night.

On Sundays she was able to get a little more rest than usual. Having done her chores early in the morning, she went to her room and closed the door. She cleaned herself, then opened her chest, carefully set up a dressing table for herself, with her little jars on top. Cheerful and pleased with herself, she stood before a large mirror and first put on the dress of the moon, then the one from which the fire of the sun burst forth, and finally the beautiful blue dress, which all the blue of the heavens could not match. Her only regret was that there was not enough room on the floor to spread out their long trains. She loved to see herself looking youthful, in ruby and white, a hundred times more elegant than anyone else. This sweet pleasure kept her going from one Sunday to the next.

I forgot to mention in passing that on that large farm owned by a powerful and regal king there was an aviary. There, chickens from Barbary, rails, guinea fowls, cormorants, goslings raised on musk, ducks, and thousands of other types of exotic birds, each different from the other, could fill with envy the hearts of ten whole courts.

After hunting, the king's son frequently went over to that charming place to rest for a while and to raise a glass with the nobles of the court. Even the handsome Cephalus[2] could not compete with him, with his regal air, his martial bearing, which could fill the most proud battalions with fear. Donkeyskin watched him with tenderness from a distance. She had the confidence to know that, beneath the dirt and rags covering her, she preserved the heart of a princess.

"What a grand manner he has, even though he is dressed casually. How agreeable he is," she said to herself. "And how happy must be the beauty who has won his heart! If he honored me with the most modest dress, I would feel myself graced far more than by all the dresses I have here."

One day the young prince was wandering aimlessly from one court-yard to another and came upon an obscure path where Donkeyskin had her humble abode. By chance, he put an eye to the keyhole. Since it was a holiday that day, she had dressed up in elegant clothes, and her magnificent dress, which was made of fine gold and of large diamonds, rivaled the sun in its pure brightness. The prince looked at her and was at the mercy of his desires. He almost lost his breath while he was gazing at her, so taken was he with her. No matter what her dress was like, the beauty of her face, her lovely profile, her warm, ivory skin, her fine features, and her fresh youthfulness moved him a hundred times more. But most of all, his heart was captured by a wise and modest reserve that bore witness to the beauty of her soul.

Three times he was about to push her door open; but each time his arm was arrested by the admiration he felt for this seemingly divine creature. He returned to the palace, where, day and night, he sighed pensively. He didn't want to attend the balls, even though it was the season of Carnival. He hated the idea of hunting or of going to the theater. His appetite was gone, and everything seemed to pain him. A deep, lethal melancholy was at the root of his ailment.

He made inquiries about the remarkable nymph who was living in one of the lower courtyards at the end of a squalid alley where you couldn't see a thing, even in broad daylight.

"It's Donkeyskin," he was told. "There's nothing beautiful about her, and she is not at all a nymph." She is called Donkeyskin because of the skin that she wears on her back. She's the ideal remedy for someone in love. Simply put, only wolves are uglier than she is." They spoke in vain, for he never believed them. The traces left by love were so powerfully inscribed in his memory that they could never be erased.

Meanwhile, his mother the queen, whose only child he was, wept in her anguish. She urged him to tell her what was wrong, but it was

2. A hunter of Greek mythology who was carried away for his beauty by the goddess of the dawn.

no use. He moaned, he wept, he sighed, but he didn't say a thing except that he wanted Donkeyskin to make him a cake with her own hands. The mother had no idea what her son meant.

"Good heavens, madam," everyone said. "Donkeyskin is nothing but a black drab, uglier and dirtier than the most filthy scullion."

"It doesn't matter," the queen said. "We must satisfy his wish, and that's all that counts." His mother loved him so much that she would have given him gold, if he wanted to eat that.

Donkeyskin took some flour that she had ground to make her dough as fine as possible and mixed it with salt, butter, and fresh eggs. Then she locked herself up in her room to make the cake as carefully as she could. First she washed her hands, her arms and her face. Then she put on a silver smock in honor of the work she was about to undertake and laced it up.

It is said that she worked a little too hastily and that one of her precious rings accidentally fell from her finger into the dough. But those thought to be knowledgeable about the outcome to this story claim that she put it in there with a purpose. As for me, quite frankly, I believe it, for I am sure that when the prince stopped at her door and saw her through the keyhole, she knew exactly what was happening. In these matters, women are so discerning and their eyes are so sharp that you can't look at them for a moment without their knowing it. I have no doubts, and I give you my word that she was confident that her young admirer would accept the ring with gratitude.

No one had ever kneaded a morsel so dainty, and the prince thought that the cake tasted so good that if he had been just a little more famished, he would have swallowed the ring along with the cake. When he saw the wonderful emerald and the narrow band of gold which revealed the shape of a finger, he was so moved that he felt incredible joy in his heart. He put it by his bedside right away. But his ailment became more serious, and the doctors observed how he was wasting away from day to day. Wise with experience, they used their great scientific erudition to conclude that he was lovesick.

People may say bad things about marriage, but it is an excellent remedy for lovesickness. The prince, it was decided, was to marry. He took some time to think about it, then said: "I'll be happy to get married provided that it is to the person whose finger fits this ring."

The queen and the king were greatly surprised by this strange demand, but their son was ailing so badly that they did not dare say no. And so a search was undertaken to find the woman who would be elevated to a high rank by the ring, no matter what her background. There was not a woman around who was not prepared to present her finger, and not a one around who was willing to give up the right to try the ring.

Since a rumor had been spreading that you had to have a very slender finger to aspire to marry the prince, every charlatan around, in order to make his reputation, claimed to possess the secret of making fingers small. One woman, following a strange whim, scraped her finger as if it were a radish. Another cut off a small piece of it. A third squeezed it so that it would become smaller. A fourth used a certain kind of liquid to make the skin fall off so that her finger would be smaller. There was not a single trick left unused by women trying to make their fingers fit the ring.

The selection began with young princesses, marquesses, and duchesses, but no matter how delicate their fingers were, they were always too large to get into the ring. Countesses, baronesses, and all manner of nobility presented their hands one at a time, but they presented them in vain. Next came the working girls, whose fingers, pretty and slender (for there are many who are well-proportioned), seemed almost to fit the ring. But each time the ring, which rejected everyone with equal disdain, was either too small or too large.

Finally they had to summon servants, scullery maids, chambermaids, and peasant girls, in short, all the riffraff whose reddened and blackened hands aspired, no less than the delicate hands, to a happy fate. Many girls arrived with big, thick fingers which fit the ring of the prince about as well as a rope trying to get through the eye of a needle.

They all believed that it was over, for there was really no one left but poor Donkeyskin in the corner of the kitchen. But who could believe that the heavens had destined her to rule!

The prince said: "Why not? Let her come here."

Everyone began laughing and shouted out loud: "You mean to say that you are going to let that dirty little fright come in here?"

But when she drew a little hand as white as ivory and colored by a touch of crimson from under the black skin and when the destined ring fit her little finger with unmatched precision, the court was in a state of astonishment and shock.

Everyone wanted to take her to the king right away, but she insisted that she wanted some time to change her clothes before appearing before her lord and master. If truth be told, everyone was about to burst out laughing because of those clothes. She arrived at the king's chambers and crossed the rooms in her ceremonial clothes whose radiant beauty had never before been seen. Her lovely blond hair glittered with diamonds that emitted a bright light with their many rays. Her blue eyes, large and soft, were filled with a proud majesty, but never inflicted pain and gave only pleasure when they looked at you. Her waist was so small and fine that you could encircle it with two hands. Even showing their charms and their divine grace, the women of the court and all their ornaments lost any kind of appeal by comparison.

With all the rejoicing and commotion of those assembled, the good king was beside himself when he saw the charms of his daughter-in-law. The queen was taken with her as well. And the prince, her ardent lover, found his heart filled with a hundred pleasures and succumbed to the sway of his passion.

Preparations were made right away for the wedding. The monarch invited all the kings from the surrounding countries, who, radiant in their diverse finery, left their lands to attend the great event. You could see those from the East mounted on huge elephants; and from distant shores came the Moors, who were so black and ugly that they frightened little children. Guests arrived from every corner of the world and descended on the court in great numbers.

No prince or potentate arrived there with as much splendor as the father of the bride, who, though he had once been in love with her, had since purified the fires that had inflamed his heart. He had purged himself of all lawless desires and all that was left in his heart of that wicked flame had been transformed into paternal devotion. When he saw her, he said: "May the heavens be blessed for allowing me to see you again, dearest child." With tears of joy in his eyes, he rushed over to embrace her tenderly. Everyone was deeply moved by his happiness, and the future husband of the bride was delighted to learn that he was going to be the son-in-law of such a powerful king. Just then the godmother arrived to tell the whole story, and through her narrative she succeeded in covering Donkeyskin with glory.

It is not difficult to see that the moral to this story teaches children that it is better to expose yourself to harsh adversity than to neglect your duty. Virtue may sometimes seem ill-fated, but it is always crowned with success. Even the most powerful logic is no defense against frenzied love and ardent ecstasy, especially when a lover is prepared to squander his rich treasures. Finally this story shows that pure water and brown bread are enough nourishment for young women, so long as they have beautiful clothes, and that there is no woman on earth who does not believe that she is beautiful and who does not see herself as getting the golden apple if she were to be mixed in with the three beauties of that famous contest.[3]

The story of Donkeyskin may be hard to believe, but as long as there are children, mothers, and grandmothers in this world, it will be fondly remembered by all.

---

3. Reference to the golden apple thrown by Eris down among the assembled gods. Inscribed "For the fairest," it became the prize of beauty in a contest including Hera, Athena, and Aphrodite.

# BROTHERS GRIMM

## Cinderella†

The wife of a rich man fell ill. When she realized that the end was near, she called her only daughter to her bedside and said: "Dear child, if you are good and say your prayers, our dear Lord will always be with you, and I shall look down on you from heaven and always be with you." Then she shut her eyes and passed away.

Every day the girl went to the grave of her mother and wept. She was always good and said her prayers. When winter came, the snow covered the grave with a white blanket, and when the sun had taken it off again in the spring, the rich man remarried.

His new wife brought with her two daughters, whose features were beautiful and white, but whose hearts were foul and black. This meant the beginning of a hard time for the poor stepchild. "Why should this silly goose be allowed to sit in the parlor with us?" the girls said. "If you want to eat bread, you'll have to earn it. Out with the kitchen maid!"

They took away her beautiful clothes, dressed her in an old grey smock, and gave her some wooden shoes. "Just look at the proud princess in her finery!" they shouted and laughed, taking her out to the kitchen. From morning until night she had to work hard. Every day, she got up before daybreak to carry water, start the fire, cook, and wash. On top of that the two sisters did everything imaginable to make her miserable. They ridiculed her and threw peas and lentils into the ashes so that she would have to sit down in the ashes and pick them out. In the evening, when she was completely exhausted from work, she didn't have a bed but had to lie down next to the hearth in ashes. She always looked so dusty and dirty that people started to call her Cinderella.

One day, the father was going to the fair and he asked his two step-daughters what he could bring back for them. "Beautiful dresses," said one.

"Pearls and jewels," said the other.

"But you, Cinderella," he asked, "What do you want?"

"Father," she said, "break off the first branch that brushes against your hat on the way home and bring it to me."

And so he bought beautiful dresses, pearls, and jewels for the two stepsisters. On the way home, when he was riding through a thicket of green bushes, a hazel branch brushed against him and knocked his hat off. When he arrived home, he gave his stepdaughters what they had

---

† Jacob and Wilhelm Grimm, "Aschenputtel," in *Kinder- und Hausmärchen*, 7th ed. (Berlin: Dieterich, 1857; first published: Berlin: Realschulbuchhandlung, 1812). Translated for this Norton Critical Edition by Maria Tatar. Copyright © 1999 by Maria Tatar.

asked for, and to Cinderella he gave the branch from the hazel bush. Cinderella thanked him, went to her mother's grave, and planted a hazel sprig on it. She wept so hard that her tears fell to the ground and watered it. It grew and became a beautiful tree. Three times a day Cinderella went and sat under it, and wept and prayed. Each time a little white bird would also fly to the tree, and if she made a wish, the little bird would toss down what she had wished for.

It happened that one day the king announced a festival that was to last for three days and to which all the beautiful young ladies of the land were invited from whom his son might choose a bride. When the two stepsisters heard that they too had been asked to attend, they were in fine spirits. They called Cinderella and said: "Comb our hair, brush our shoes, and fasten our buckles. We're going to the wedding at the king's palace."

Cinderella did as she was told, but she wept, for she too would have liked to go to the ball, and she begged her stepmother to let her go.

"Cinderella," she said, "How can you go to a wedding when you're covered with dust and dirt? How can you want to go to a ball when you have neither a dress nor shoes?"

Cinderella kept pleading with her, and so she finally said: "Here, I've dumped a bowlful of lentils into the ashes. If you can pick out the lentils in the next two hours, then you may go."

The girl went out the back door into the garden and called out: "O tame little doves, little turtledoves, and all you little birds in the sky, come and help me put

> the good ones into the little pot,
> the bad ones into your little crop."

Two little white doves came flying in through the kitchen window, followed by little turtle doves. And finally all the birds in the sky came swooping and fluttering and settled down in the ashes. The little doves nodded their heads and began to peck, peck, peck, peck, and then the others began to peck, peck, peck, peck and put all the good lentils into the bowl. Barely an hour had passed when they were finished and flew back out the window.

The girl brought the bowl to her stepmother and was overjoyed because she was sure that she would now be able to go to the wedding. But the stepmother said: "No, Cinderella, you have nothing to wear, and you don't know how to dance. Everybody would just laugh at you."

When Cinderella began to cry, the stepmother said: "If you can pick out two bowlfuls of lentils from the ashes in the next hour, then you can go."

But she thought to herself: "She'll never be able to do it."

After she had dumped the two bowlfuls of lentils into the ashes, the girl went out the back door into the garden and called out: "O tame little doves, little turtledoves, and all you little birds in the sky, come and help me put

the good ones into the little pot,
the bad ones into your little crop."

Two little white doves came flying in through the kitchen window, followed by little turtle doves. And finally all the birds in the sky came swooping and fluttering and settled down in the ashes. The little doves nodded their heads and began to peck, peck, peck, peck, and then the others began to peck, peck, peck, peck and put all the good lentils into the bowl. Barely a half hour had passed when they were finished and flew back out the window.

The girl brought the bowls back to her stepmother and was overjoyed because she was sure that she would now be able to go to the wedding. But her stepmother said: "It's no use. You can't come along since you have nothing to wear and don't know how to dance. We would be so embarrassed." Turning her back on Cinderella, she hurried off with her two proud daughters.

Now that no one was at home any longer, Cinderella went to her mother's grave under the hazel tree and called:

"Shake your branches, little tree,
Toss gold and silver down on me."

The bird tossed down a dress of gold and silver, with slippers embroidered with silk and silver. She slipped the dress on hastily and left for the wedding. Her sister and her stepmother had no idea who she was. She looked so beautiful in the dress of gold that they thought she must be the daughter of a foreign king. They never imagined it could be Cinderella for they were sure that she was at home, sitting in the dirt and picking lentils out of the ashes.

The prince approached Cinderella, took her by the hand, and danced with her. He didn't intend to dance with anyone else and never let go of her hand. Whenever anyone else asked her to dance, he would say: "She is my partner."

Cinderella danced until it was night, then she wanted to go home. The prince said: "I will go with you and be your escort," for he wanted to find out about the beautiful girl's family. But she managed to slip away from him and bounded into a dovecote. The prince waited until Cinderella's father arrived and told him that the strange girl had bounded into the dovecote. The old man thought: "Could it be Cinderella?" He sent for an ax and pick and broke into the dovecote, but no one was inside it. And when they went back to the house, there was Cinderella, lying in the ashes in her filthy clothes with a dim little oil lamp burning on the mantel. Cinderella had jumped down from the back of the dovecote and had run over to the little hazel tree, where she slipped out of her beautiful dress and put it on the grave. The bird took the dress back, and Cinderella had slipped into her grey smock and settled back into the ashes in the kitchen.

The next day, when the festivities started up again and the parents had left with the stepsisters, Cinderella went to the hazel tree and said:

> "Shake your branches, little tree,
> Toss gold and silver down on me."

The bird tossed down a dress that was even more splendid than the previous one. And when she appeared at the wedding in this dress, everyone was dazzled by her beauty. The Prince, who had been waiting for her to arrive, took her by the hand and danced with her alone. Whenever anyone came and asked her to dance, he would say: "She is my partner."

At night she wanted to leave, and the prince followed her, hoping to see which house she would enter. But she bounded away and disappeared into the garden behind the house, where there was a beautiful, tall tree from whose branches hung magnificent pears. She climbed up through the branches as nimbly as a squirrel, and the prince had no idea where she was. He waited until her father got there and said to him: "The strange girl has escaped, but I believe that she climbed up into the pear tree."

The father thought: "Could it be Cinderella?" and he sent for an ax and chopped down the tree. But no one was in it. When they went into the kitchen, Cinderella was, as usual, lying in the ashes, for she had jumped down on the other side of the tree, taken the beautiful dress to the bird on the hazel tree, and slipped on her little grey smock again.

On the third day, when the parents and sisters had left, Cinderella went to her mother's grave and said to the little tree:

> "Shake your branches, little tree,
> Toss gold and silver down on me."

The bird tossed down a dress which was more splendid and radiant than anything she had ever had, and the slippers were covered in gold. When she got to the wedding in that dress, everyone was speechless with amazement. The prince danced with her alone, and if someone asked her to dance, he would say: "She is my partner."

At night, Cinderella wanted to leave, and the prince wanted to escort her, but she slipped away so quickly that he was unable to follow her. The prince had planned a trick. The entire staircase had been coated with pitch, and as the girl went running down the stairs, her left slipper got stuck. The prince lifted it up: it was a dainty little shoe covered with gold.

The next morning he went with it to the father and said to him: "No one else will be my bride but the women whose foot fits this golden shoe." The two sisters were overjoyed, for they both had beautiful feet. The elder went with her mother into a room to try it on. But the shoe was too small for her, for she couldn't get her big toe into it. Her mother handed her a knife and said: "Cut the toe off. Once you're queen, you won't need to go on foot any more."

The girl sliced off her toe, forced her foot into the shoe, gritted her teeth, and went out to meet the prince. He lifted her up on his horse as his bride, and rode away with her. But they had to pass by the grave, where two little doves were perched in the little hazel tree, calling out:

> "Roo coo coo, roo coo coo,
> blood's in the shoe:
> the shoe's too tight,
> the real bride's waiting another night."

When he looked down at her foot, he saw blood spurting from it and turned his horse around. He brought the false bride back home, and said that since she was not the true bride, her sister should try the shoe on. The sister went into her room and succeeded in getting her toes into the shoe, but her heel was too big. Her mother handed her a knife and said: "Cut off part of your heel. Once you're queen, you won't need to go on foot any more."

The girl sliced off a piece of her heel, forced her foot into the shoe, gritted her teeth, and went out to meet the prince. He lifted her up on his horse as his bride, and rode away with her. When they passed by the little hazel tree, two little doves were perched there, calling out:

> "Roo coo coo, roo coo coo,
> blood's in the shoe:
> the shoe's too tight,
> the real bride's waiting another night."

When he looked down at her foot, he saw blood spurting from it and staining her white stockings completely red. Then he turned his horse around and brought the false bride back home. "She's not the true bride either," he said. "Don't you have another daughter?"

"No," said the man, "there's only puny little Cinderella, my dead wife's daughter, but she can't possibly be the bride."

The prince asked that she be sent for, but the mother said: "Oh no, she's much too dirty to be seen."

The prince insisted, and Cinderella was summoned. First she washed her hands and face completely clean, then she went and curtsied before the prince, who handed her the golden shoe. She sat down on a stool, took her foot out of the heavy wooden shoe, and put it into the slipper. It fit perfectly. And when she stood up and the prince looked her straight in the face, he recognized the beautiful girl with whom he had danced and exclaimed: "She is the true bride." The stepmother and the two sisters were horrified and turned pale with rage. But the prince lifted Cinderella up on his horse and rode away with her. When they passed by the little hazel tree, the two little white doves called out:

> "Roo coo coo, roo coo coo,
> no blood in the shoe:
> the shoe's not tight,
> the real bride's here tonight."

After they had called out these words, the doves both came flying down and perched on Cinderella's shoulders, one on the right, the other on the left, and there they stayed.

On the day of the wedding to the prince, the two false sisters came and tried to ingratiate themselves and share in Cinderella's good fortune. When the couple went to church, the elder sister was on the right, the younger on the left side: the doves pecked one eye from each one. Later, when they left the church, the elder sister was on the left, the younger on the right. The doves pecked the other eye from each one. And so they were punished for their wickedness and malice with blindness for the rest of their lives.

# JOSEPH JACOBS

## Catskin†

Well, there was once a gentleman who had fine lands and houses, and he very much wanted to have a son to be heir to them. So when his wife brought him a daughter, bonny as bonny could be, he cared nought for her, and said, "Let me never see her face." So she grew up a bonny girl, though her father never set eyes on her till she was fifteen years old and was ready to be married. But her father said, "Let her marry the first that comes for her." And when this was known, who should be first but a nasty rough old man. So she didn't know what to do, and went to the hen-wife and asked her advice. The hen-wife said, "Say you will not take him unless they give you a coat of silver cloth." Well, they gave her a coat of silver cloth, but she wouldn't take him for all that, but went again to the hen-wife, who said, "Say you will not take him unless they give you a coat of beaten gold." Well, they gave her a coat of beaten gold, but still she would not take him, but went to the hen-wife, who said, "Say you will not take him unless they give you a coat made of the feathers of all the birds of the air." So they sent a man with a great heap of peas; and the

---

† Joseph Jacobs, "Catskin," in *English Fairy Tales* (London: David Nutt, 1890).

man cried to all the birds of the air, "Each bird take a pea, and put down a feather." So each bird took a pea and put down one of its feathers: and they took all the feathers and made a coat of them and gave it to her; but still she would not, but asked the hen-wife once again, who said, "Say they must first make you a coat of catskin." So they made her a coat of catskin; and she put it on, and tied up her other coats, and ran away into the woods.

So she went along and went along and went along, till she came to the end of the wood, and saw a fine castle. So there she hid her fine dresses, and went up to the castle gates, and asked for work. The lady of the castle saw her, and told her, "I'm sorry I have no better place, but if you like you may be our scullion." So down she went into the kitchen, and they called her Catskin, because of her dress. But the cook was very cruel to her and led her a sad life.

Well, it happened soon after that the young lord of the castle was coming home, and there was to be a grand ball in honour of the occasion. And when they were speaking about it among the servants, "Dear me, Mrs Cook," said Catskin, "how much I should like to go."

"What! you dirty impudent slut," said the cook, "you go among all the fine lords and ladies with your filthy catskin? A fine figure you'd cut!" and with that she took a basin of water and dashed it into Catskin's face. But she only briskly shook her ears, and said nothing.

When the day of the ball arrived Catskin slipped out of the house and went to the edge of the forest, where she had hidden her dresses. So she bathed herself in a crystal waterfall, and then put on her coat of silver cloth, and hastened away to the ball. As soon as she entered all were overcome by her beauty and grace, while the young lord at once lost his heart to her. He asked her to be his partner for the first dance, and he would dance with none other the livelong night.

When it came to parting-time, the young lord said, "Pray tell me, fair maid, where you live." But Catskin curtsied and said:

> "Kind sir, if the truth I must tell,
> At the sign of the 'Basin of Water' I dwell."

Then she flew from the castle and donned her catskin robe again, and slipped into the scullery again, unbeknown to the cook.

The young lord went the very next day to his mother, the lady of the castle, and declared he would wed none other but the lady of the silver dress, and would never rest till he had found her. So another ball was soon arranged for, in hope that the beautiful maid would appear again. So Catskin said to the cook, "Oh, how I should like to go!" Whereupon the cook screamed out in a rage, "What, you, you dirty impudent slut! You would cut a fine figure among all the fine lords and ladies." And with that she up with a ladle and broke it across Catskin's back. But she only shook her ears, and ran off to the forest, where she first of all bathed, and then put on her coat of beaten gold, and off she went to the ballroom.

As soon as she entered all eyes were upon her; and the young lord soon recognized her as the lady of the "Basin of Water," and claimed her hand for the first dance, and did not leave her till the last. When that came, he again asked her where she lived. But all that she would say was:

> "Kind sir, if the truth I must tell,
> At the sign of the 'Broken Ladle' I dwell."

and with that she curtsied, and flew from the ball, off with her golden robe, on with her catskin, and into the scullery without the cook's knowing.

Next day when the young lord could not find where was the sign of the "Basin of Water," or of the "Broken Ladle," he begged his mother to have another grand ball, so that he might meet the beautiful maid once more.

All happened as before. Catskin told the cook how much she would like to go to the ball, the cook called her "a dirty slut," and broke the skimmer across her head. But she only shook her ears, and went off to the forest, where she first bathed in the crystal spring, and then donned her coat of feathers, and so off to the ballroom.

When she entered everyone was surprised at so beautiful a face and form dressed in so rich and rare a dress; but the young lord soon recognized his beautiful sweetheart, and would dance with none but her the whole evening. When the ball came to an end, he pressed her to tell him where she lived, but all she would answer was:

> "Kind sir, if the truth I must tell,
> At the sign of the 'Broken Skimmer' I dwell;"

and with that she curtsied, and was off to the forest. But this time the young lord followed her, and watched her change her fine dress of feathers for her catskin dress, and then he knew her for his own scullery-maid.

Next day he went to his mother, the lady of the castle, and told her that he wished to marry the scullery-maid, Catskin. "Never," said the lady, and rushed from the room. Well, the young lord was so grieved at that, that he took to his bed and was very ill. The doctor tried to cure him, but he would not take any medicine unless from the hands of Catskin. So the doctor went to the lady of the castle, and told her her son would die if she did not consent to his marriage with Catskin. So she had to give way, and summoned Catskin to her. But she put on her coat of beaten gold, and went to the lady, who soon was glad to wed her son to so beautiful a maid.

Well, so they were married, and after a time a dear little son came to them, and grew up a bonny lad; and one day, when he was four years old, a beggar woman came to the door, so Lady Catskin gave some money to the little lord and told him to go and give it to the beggar woman. So he went and gave it, but put it into the hand of the woman's child, who leant forward and kissed the little lord. Now the wicked old cook—why hadn't she been sent away?—was looking on, so she said, "Only see how beggars' brats take to one another." This insult went to Catskin's heart, so she went to her husband, the young lord, and told him all about her father, and begged he would go and find out what had become of her parents. So they set out in the lord's grand coach, and travelled through the forest till they came to Catskin's father's house, and put up at an inn near, where Catskin stopped, while her husband went to see if her father would own her.

Now her father had never had any other child, and his wife had died; he was all alone in the world and sat moping and miserable. When the young lord came in he hardly looked up, till he saw a chair close up to him, and asked him: "Pray, sir, had you not once a young daughter whom you would never see or own?"

The old gentleman said: "It is true; I am a hardened sinner. But I would give all my worldly goods if I could but see her once before I die." Then the young lord told him what had happened to Catskin, and took him to the inn, and brought his father-in-law to his own castle, where they lived happy ever afterwards.

## The Story of the Black Cow†

There was a certain Brahmin whose wife died leaving him one little son. For some time the two lived happily together, but at last the Brahmin married for a second time, and the woman, who had a daughter of her own, was very unkind to her little stepson.

Each day the two children went out together to attend to the cattle, and at night they returned home to eat their food. But the cakes made by the Brahmin's wife for her stepson were of ashes, with just a little flour mixed in to give them the appearance of food, that the Brahmin might not notice; and the child ate in silence, for he was afraid to complain, yet, when he was alone in the forest he wept from hunger, and a black cow, one of the herd, saw this, and asked him what was the matter.

The boy told her everything, and presently she beat her hoofs upon the ground. As she did so, sweets of all kinds appeared, which the child ate greedily, and shared with his little sister, warning her the while not

† Alice Elizabeth Dracott, "The Story of the Black Cow," in *Simla Village Tales, or Folk Tales from the Himalayas* (London: John Murray, 1906).

to mention at home what the black cow had done, lest the stepmother should be angry.

The stepmother meanwhile wondered to see how well the boy looked, and she resolved to keep watch, for she suspected that he drank the milk while tending her cows; so she told her little daughter to keep a good look-out on all his doings, and to let her know. At last the girl confessed that they ate sweets every day, and the black cow provided the feast.

That day when the Brahmin came home his wife begged him to sell the black cow, and said she would neither sleep nor eat until this was done.

The poor boy was sad indeed when he heard this, and went at once to his favourite, where, throwing himself on the black cow's neck, he wept bitterly.

"Do not weep, my child, but get up on my back, and I will carry you to a place of safety where we can still be together."

So they escaped to a forest, and there lived in peace and security for many days.

Now, in the forest was a hole, which led to the home of the Great Snake, which, together with a bull, holds up the universe. Into this hole the black cow poured five seers of milk daily to feed the snake. This pleased the snake so much that he said one day: "I must go up into the world and see for myself the creature who is so good to me and who sends me such good milk to drink."

When he came he saw the black cow grazing with the boy beside her.

The cow asked no favours for herself, but when the snake asked what she would like, she said she would like her son, as she called the Brahmin's son, to be clothed in gold from head to foot, and that all his body might shine as gold.

This wish the snake readily granted, but both cow and boy afterwards regretted their request, for they feared robbers.

One day as the boy had his bath by the river, and combed his long locks of pure gold, some of his golden hair fell into the water, and was swallowed by a fish. This fish was caught by a fisherman, and taken for sale to the King's Palace. When they cut it open all present admired the lovely golden hair, and when the Princess saw it, she said she would never be happy again until she met the owner. The fisherman was asked where he caught the fish, and people were dispatched in all directions in boats to search both far and wide.

At last a man in one of the boats espied in the distance a beautiful shining object taking a bath by the river-side. Little by little the boat came closer and closer, until it was alongside; then the man called out and asked the bather to come a little nearer. At first the Brahmin's son would not listen, but after a time he came up to the boat, when, to his surprise, he was at once seized, tied up, and carried away.

Arrived at the King's Palace he met the Princess, who was very beautiful; and when he saw her he forgot everything else, and thought only of her.

After a short time they were married, and spent many happy days together; but some one chanced to offer them a sweetmeat made of curds, such as the black cow often gave her boy, and in a frenzy of remorse, the Brahmin's son remembered his faithful friend and hastened to the place in the distant forest where he had last seen her. Arrived there he found only a few bones of dead cattle strewn about.

He was heart-broken at the sight, and gathered all the bones together into a funeral pyre, upon which he declared he would lay down his own life; but just as he was about to do this who should appear but his old friend, the black cow.

They were overjoyed to see each other, and she told him she had only kept the bones there to test his affection; but now that she was satisfied that he had not forgotten her, the meeting was full of happiness and joy, so they held a great feast for many days and then went their separate ways as before.

# LIN LAN

## Cinderella†

There were once two sisters. The elder was very beautiful, and everyone called her Beauty. But the younger had a face covered with pock marks, so that everyone called her Pock Face. She was the daughter of the second wife, and was so spoiled that she was a very unpleasant girl. Beauty's real mother had died when Beauty was very young. After her death she turned into a yellow cow and lived in the garden. Beauty adored the yellow cow, but it had a miserable existence because the stepmother treated it so badly.

One day the stepmother took the ugly daughter to the theater and left Beauty at home. Beauty wanted to accompany them, but the stepmother said, "I will take you tomorrow if you straighten the hemp in my room."

Beauty went off and sat down in front of the stack of hemp, but after a long time she had only divided half of it. Bursting into tears, she took it off to the yellow cow, who swallowed the whole mass and then spat

† Lin Lan, "San-ko yüan-wang (Three Wishes)" (Shanghai, 1933), in *Folktales of China*, trans. Wolfram Eberhard and Desmond Parsons (Chicago: U of Chicago P, 1965). Copyright © 1965. Reprinted by permission of the University of Chicago Press.

it out again all neatly arranged piece by piece. Beauty dried her tears, and gave the hemp to her mother on her return home. "Mother, here is the hemp. I can go to the theater tomorrow, can't I?"

When the next day came, her stepmother again refused to take her saying, "You can go when you have separated the sesame seeds from the beans."

The poor girl had to divide them seed by seed, until the exhausting task made her eyes ache. Again she went to the yellow cow, who said to her, "You stupid girl! You must separate them with a fan." Now she understood, and the sesame and beans were soon divided. When she brought the seeds all nicely separated, her stepmother knew that she could no longer prevent her going to the theater. However, she asked her, "How can a servant girl be so clever? Who helped you?"

Beauty had to admit that the yellow cow had advised her, which made the stepmother very angry. Therefore, without saying a word, she killed and ate the cow. Beauty had loved the cow so dearly that she could not eat its flesh. Instead, she put the bones in an earthenware pot and hid them in her bedroom.

Day after day, the stepmother would still not take Beauty to the theater. One evening, when the stepmother had gone to the theater with Pock Face, Beauty was so cross that she smashed everything in the house, including the earthenware pot containing the cow's bones. Whereupon there was a loud crackling sound, and a white horse, a new dress, and a pair of embroidered shoes came out. The sudden appearance of these things gave Beauty a terrible start, but she soon saw that they were real objects. Quickly pulling on the new dress and the shoes, she jumped on the horse and rode out of the gate.

While she was riding along, one of her shoes slipped off and fell into the ditch. She wanted to dismount and pick it up, but could not do so; at the same time she did not want to leave it lying there.

She was in a real quandary, when a fishmonger appeared. "Brother fishmonger, please pick up my shoe," she said to him. He answered with a grin, "With great pleasure, if you will marry me." "Who could marry you?" she said crossly. "Fishmongers always stink." Seeing that he had no chance, the fishmonger went on his way.

Next, a clerk from a rice shop went by, and she said to him, "Brother rice broker, please give me my shoe." "Certainly, if you will marry me," said the young man. "Marry a rice broker! Their bodies are all covered with dust."

The rice broker departed, and soon an oil merchant came by, whom she also asked to pick up her shoe. "I will pick it up if you consent to marry me," he replied. "Who could want to marry you?" Beauty said with a sigh. "Oil merchants are always so greasy."

Shortly a scholar came by, whom she also asked to pick up her shoe. The scholar turned to look at her, and then said, "I will do so at once if you promise to marry me." The scholar was very handsome, and so she nodded her head in agreement. He picked up the shoe and put it on her foot. Then he took her back to his house and made her his wife.

Three days later, Beauty went with her husband to pay the necessary respects to her parents. Her stepmother and sister had quite changed their manner, and treated them both in the most friendly and attentive fashion. In the evening they wanted to keep Beauty at home, and she, thinking they meant it kindly, agreed to stay and to follow her husband in a few days.

The next morning her sister took her by the hand and said to her with a laugh, "Sister, come and look into the well. We will see which of us is the more beautiful." Suspecting nothing, Beauty went to the well and leaned over to look down. At this moment her sister gave her a shove and pushed her into the well; then she quickly covered the well with a basket. Poor Beauty lost consciousness and was drowned.

*[handwritten margin note: Beauty pushed into a well and drowned]*

After ten days the scholar began to wonder why his wife had still not returned. He sent a messenger to inquire, and the stepmother sent back a message that his wife was suffering from a bad attack of smallpox and would not be well enough to return for some time. The scholar believed this, and every day he sent salted eggs and other sickbed delicacies, all of which found their way into the stomach of the ugly sister.

After two months the stepmother was irritated by the continual messages from the scholar, and decided to deceive him by sending back her own daughter as his wife. The scholar was horrified when he saw Pock Face, and said, "Goodness! How changed you are! Surely you are not Beauty. My wife was never such a monster. Good Heavens!" Pock Face replied seriously, "If I am not Beauty, who do you think I am then? You know perfectly well I was very ill with smallpox, and now you want to disown me. I shall die! I shall die!" She began to howl. The tender-hearted scholar could not bear to see her weeping, and although he still had some doubts he begged her forgiveness and tried to console her. Gradually she stopped weeping.

Beauty, however, had been transformed into a sparrow, and she used to come and call out when Pock Face was combing her hair, "Comb once, peep; comb twice, peep; comb thrice, up to the spine of Pock Face." The wicked wife answered, "Comb once, comb twice, comb thrice, to the spine of Beauty." The scholar was very mystified by this conversation, and he said to the sparrow, "Why do you sing like that? Are you by any chance my wife? If you are, call three times, and I will put you in a golden cage and keep you as a pet." The sparrow called out three times, and the scholar brought a golden cage to keep it in.

The ugly sister was very angry when she saw that her husband was keeping the sparrow, and so she secretly killed it and threw it into the garden. It was at once transformed into a bamboo with many shoots.

When Pock Face ate the bamboo shoots, an ulcer formed on her tongue, but the scholar found them excellent. The wicked woman became suspicious again, and had the bamboo cut down and made into a bed. When she lay on it, innumerable needles pricked her, but the scholar found it extremely comfortable. Again she became very cross and threw the bed away.

Next door to the scholar lived an old woman who sold money bags. One day on her way home she saw the bed and thought to herself, "No one has died here; why have they thrown the bed away? I shall take it." She took the bed into her house and had a very comfortable night.

The next day she saw that the food in the kitchen was already cooked. She ate it up, but naturally she felt a little nervous, not having any idea who could have prepared it. For several days she found she could have dinner the moment she came home. Finally, being no longer able to contain her anxiety, she came back early one afternoon and went into the kitchen, where she saw a dark shadow washing rice. She ran up quickly and clasped the shadow round the waist. "Who are you?" she asked, "and why do you cook food for me?" The shadow replied, "I will tell you everything. I am the wife of your neighbor the scholar and am called Beauty. My sister threw me into the well; I was drowned, but my soul was not destroyed. Please give me a rice pot as head, a stick as hand, a dish cloth as entrails, and firehooks as feet, and then I can assume my former shape again."

The old woman gave her what she asked for, and in a moment a beautiful girl appeared. The old woman was delighted at seeing such a charming girl, and she questioned her very closely about who she was and what had happened to her. She told the old woman everything, and then said, "Old woman, I have a bag which you must offer for sale outside the scholar's house. If he comes out, you must sell it to him." And she gave her an embroidered bag.

The next day the old woman stood outside the scholar's house and shouted that she had a bag for sale. Maddened by the noise, he came out to ask what kind of bags she sold, and she showed him Beauty's embroidered bag. "Where did you get this bag?" he asked, "I once gave it to my wife." The old woman then told the whole story to the scholar, who was overjoyed to hear that his wife was still alive. He arranged everything with the old woman, put a red cloth on the ground, and brought Beauty back to his house.

When Pock Face saw her sister return, she gave her no peace. She began to grumble and say that the woman was only pretending to be Beauty, and that actually she was a spirit. She wanted to have a trial to see which was the genuine wife. Beauty, of course, knew that she herself was the real bride. She said, "Good. We will have a test." Pock Face suggested that they should walk on eggs, and whoever broke the shells would be the loser. Although Pock Face broke all the eggs, and Beauty none, Pock Face refused to admit her loss and insisted on another trial.

This time they were to walk up a ladder made of knives. Beauty went up and down first without receiving the tiniest scratch, but before Pock Face had gone two steps her feet were cut to the bone. Although she had lost again, she insisted on another test—that of jumping into a caldron of hot oil. She hoped that Beauty, who would have to jump first, would be burned. Beauty, however, was quite unharmed by the boiling oil, but the wicked sister jumped into it and did not come up again.

Beauty put the roasted bones of the wicked sister into a box and sent them over to her stepmother by a stuttering old servant woman, who was told to say, "Your daughter's flesh." But the stepmother loved carp and understood "carp flesh" instead of "your daughter's flesh." She thought her daughter had sent her over some carp, and opened the box in a state of great excitement; but when she saw the charred bones of her daughter lying inside, she let out a piercing scream and fell down dead.

# The Princess in the Suit of Leather[†]

Neither here nor elsewhere lived a king who had a wife whom he loved with all his heart and a daughter who was the light of his eyes. The princess had hardly reached womanhood when the queen fell ill and died. For one whole year the king kept vigil, sitting with bowed head beside her tomb. Then he summoned the matchmakers, elderly women wise in the ways of living, and said, "I wish to marry again. Here is my poor queen's anklet. Find me the girl, rich or poor, humble or well-born, whose foot this anklet will fit. For I promised the queen as she lay dying that I would marry that girl and no other."

The matchmakers traveled up and down the kingdom looking for the king's new bride. But search and search as they would, they could not find a single girl around whose ankle the jewel would close. The queen had been such that there was no woman like her. Then one old woman said, "We have entered the house of every maiden in the land except the house of the king's own daughter. Let us go to the palace."

When they slipped the anklet onto the princess's foot, it suited as if it had been made to her measure. Out of the seraglio went the women at a run, straight into the king's presence, and said, "We have visited every maiden in your kingdom, but none was able to squeeze her foot into the late queen's anklet. None, that is, except the princess your daughter. She wears it as easily as if it were her own." A wrinkled

† "The Princess in the Suit of Leather" (Egyptian folktale), *Arab Folktales*, trans. and ed. Inea Bushnaq (New York: Pantheon, 1986). Copyright © 1986 by Inea Bushnaq Books, a division of Random House, Inc.

matron spoke up. "Why not marry the princess? Why give her to a stranger and deprive yourself?" The words were hardly spoken when the king summoned the *qadi*[1] to pen the papers for the marriage. To the princess he made no mention of his plan.

Now there was a bustle in the palace as the jewelers, the clothiers, and the furnishers came to outfit the bride. The princess was pleased to know that she was to be wed. But who her husband was she had no inkling. As late as the "night of the entering," when the groom first sees the bride, she remained in ignorance even though the servants with their whispers were busy around her, combing and pinning and making her beautiful. At last the minister's daughter, who had come to admire her in her finery, said, "Why are you frowning? Were not women created for marriage with men? And is there any man whose standing is higher than the king's?"

"What is the meaning of such talk?" cried the princess. "I won't tell you," said the girl, "unless you give me your golden bangle to keep." The princess pulled off the bracelet, and the girl explained how everything had come about so that the bridegroom was no other than the princess's own father.

The princess turned whiter than the cloth on her head and trembled like one who is sick with the forty-day fever. She rose to her feet and sent away all who were with her. Then, knowing only that she must escape, she ran onto the terrace and leaped over the palace wall, landing in a tanner's yard which lay below. She pressed a handful of gold into the tanner's palm and said, "Can you make me a suit of leather to hide me from head to heels, showing nothing but my eyes? I want it by tomorrow's dawn."

The poor man was overjoyed to earn the coins. He set to work with his wife and children. Cutting and stitching through the night they had the suit ready, before it was light enough to know a white thread from a dark. Wait a little! and here comes our lady, the princess. She put on the suit—such a strange spectacle that anyone looking at her would think he was seeing nothing but a pile of hides. In this disguise she left the tanner and lay down beside the city gate, waiting for the day.

Now to return to my lord the king. When he entered the bridal chamber and found the princess gone, he sent his army into the city to search for her. Time and again a soldier would stumble upon the princess lying at the gate and ask, "Have you seen the king's daughter?" And she would reply,

> My name is Juleidah for my coat of skins,
> My eyes are weak, my sight is dim,
> My ears are deaf, I cannot hear.
> I care for no one far or near.

1. Judge of an Islamic court of justice.

When it was day and the city gate was unbarred, she shuffled out until she was beyond the walls. Then she turned her face away from her father's city and fled.

Walking and running, one foot lifting her and one foot setting her down, there was a day when, with the setting of the sun, the princess came to another city. Too weary to travel a step farther, she fell to the ground. Now her resting place was in the shadow of the wall of the women's quarters, the harem of the sultan's palace. A slave girl, leaning from the window to toss out the crumbs from the royal table, noticed the heap of skins on the ground and thought nothing of it. But when she saw two bright eyes staring out at her from the middle of the hides, she sprang back in terror and said to the queen, "My lady, there is something monstrous crouching under our window. I have seen it, and it looks like nothing less than an Afreet!"[2] "Bring it up for me to see and judge," said the queen.

The slave girl went down shivering with fear, not knowing which was the easier thing to face, the monster outside or her mistress's rage should she fail to do her bidding. But the princess in her suit made no sound when the slave girl tugged at a corner of the leather. The girl took courage and dragged her all the way into the presence of the sultan's wife.

Never had such an astonishing creature been seen in that country. Lifting both palms in amazement, the queen asked her servant, "What is it?" and then turned to the monster and asked, "Who are you?" When the heap of skins answered—

> My name is Juleidah for my coat of skins,
> My eyes are weak, my sight is dim,
> My ears are deaf, I cannot hear.
> I care for no one far or near.

—how the queen laughed at the quaint reply! "Go bring food and drink for our guest," she said, holding her side. "We shall keep her to amuse us." When Juleidah had eaten, the queen said, "Tell us what you can do, so that we may put you to work about the palace." "Anything you ask me to do, I am ready to try," said Juleidah. Then the queen called, "Mistress cook! Take this broken-winged soul into your kitchen. Maybe for her sake God will reward us with His blessings."

So now our fine princess was a kitchen skivvy, feeding the fires and raking out the ashes. And whenever the queen lacked company and felt bored, she called Juleidah and laughed at her prattle.

One day the *wazir*[3] sent word that all the sultan's harem was invited to a night's entertainment in his house. All day long there was a stir of excitement in the women's quarters. As the queen prepared to set out

2. A cunning demon or spirit from the Djinn world.
3. Minister or chief courtier.

in the evening, she stopped by Juleidah and said, "Won't you come with us tonight? All the servants and slaves are invited. Aren't you afraid to stay alone?" But Juleidah only repeated her refrain,

> My ears are deaf, I cannot hear.
> I care for no one far or near.

One of the serving girls sniffed and said, "What is there to make her afraid? She is blind and deaf and wouldn't notice an Afreet even if he were to jump on top of her in the dark!" So they left.

In the women's reception hall of the *wazir*'s house there was dining and feasting and music and much merriment. Suddenly at the height of the talk and enjoyment, such a one entered that they all stopped in the middle of the word they were speaking. Tall as a cypress, with a face like a rose and the silks and jewels of a king's bride, she seemed to fill the room with light. Who was it? Juleidah, who had shaken off her coat of leather as soon as the sultan's harem had gone. She had followed them to the *wazir*'s, and now the ladies who had been so merry began to quarrel, each wanting to sit beside the newcomer.

When dawn was near, Juleidah took a handful of gold sequins from the fold of her sash and scattered them on the floor. The ladies scrambled to pick up the bright treasure. And while they were occupied, Juleidah left the hall. Quickly, quickly she raced back to the palace kitchen and put on the coat of leather. Soon the others returned. Seeing the heap of hides on the kitchen floor, the queen poked it with the toe of her red slipper and said, "Truly, I wish you had been with us to admire the lady who was at the entertainment." But Juleidah only mumbled, "My eyes are weak, I cannot see . . ." and they all went to their own beds to sleep.

When the queen woke up next day, the sun was high in the sky. As was his habit, the sultan's son came in to kiss his mother's hands and bid her good morning. But she could talk only of the visitor at the *wazir*'s feast. "O my son," she sighed, "it was a woman with such a face and such a neck and such a form that all who saw her said, 'She is the daughter of neither a king nor a sultan, but of someone greater yet!' " On and on the queen poured out her praises of the woman, until the prince's heart was on fire. Finally his mother concluded, "I wish I had asked her father's name so that I could engage her to be your bride." And the sultan's son replied, "When you return tonight to continue your entertainment, I shall stand outside the *wazir*'s door and wait until she leaves. I'll ask her then about her father and her station."

At sunset the women dressed themselves once more. With the folds of their robes smelling of orange blossom and incense and their bracelets chinking on their arms, they passed by Juleidah lying on the kitchen floor and said, "Will you come with us tonight?" But Juleidah only turned her back on them. Then as soon as they were safely gone, she threw off her suit of leather and hurried after them.

In the *wazir*'s hall the guests pressed close around Juleidah, wanting to see her and ask where she came from. But to all their questions she gave no answer, whether yes or no, although she sat with them until the dawning of the day. Then she threw a fistful of pearls on the marble tiles, and while the women pushed one another to catch them, she slipped away as easily as a hair is pulled out of the dough.

Now who was standing at the door? The prince, of course. He had been waiting for this moment. Blocking her path, he grasped her arm and asked who her father was and from what land she came. But the princess had to be back in her kitchen or her secret would be known. So she fought to get away, and in the scuffle, she pulled the prince's ring clean off his hand. "At least tell me where you come from!" he shouted after her as she ran. "By Allah, tell me where!" And she replied, "I live in a land of paddles and ladles." Then she fled into the palace and hid in her coat of hides.

In came the others, talking and laughing. The prince told his mother what had taken place and announced that he intended to make a journey. "I must go to the land of the paddles and ladles," he said. "Be patient, my son," said the queen. "Give me time to prepare your provisions." Eager as he was, the prince agreed to delay his departure for two days—"But not one hour more!"

Now the kitchen became the busiest corner of the palace. The grinding and the sieving, the kneading and the baking began and Juleidah stood watching. "Away with you," cried the cook, "this is no work for you!" "I want to serve the prince our master like the rest!" said Juleidah. Willing and not willing to let her help, the cook gave her a piece of dough to shape. Juleidah began to make a cake, and when no one was watching, she pushed the prince's ring inside it. And when the food was packed Juleidah placed her own little cake on top of the rest.

Early on the third morning the rations were strapped into the saddlebags, and the prince set off with his servants and his men. He rode without slackening until the sun grew hot. Then he said, "Let us rest the horses while we ourselves eat a mouthful." A servant, seeing Juleidah's tiny loaf lying on top of all the rest, flung it to one side. "Why did you throw that one away?" asked the prince. "It was the work of the creature Juleidah; I saw her make it," said the servant. "It is as misshapen as she is." The prince felt pity for the strange half-wit and asked the servant to bring back her cake. When he tore open the loaf, look, his own ring was inside! The ring he lost the night of the *wazir*'s entertainment. Understanding now where lay the land of ladles and paddles, the prince gave orders to turn back.

When the king and queen had greeted him, the prince said,

"Mother, send me my supper with Juleidah." "She can barely see or even hear," said the queen. "How can she bring your supper to you?" "I shall not eat unless Juleidah brings the food," said the prince. So when the time came, the cooks arranged the dishes on a tray and helped Juleidah lift it onto her head. Up the stairs she went, but before she reached the prince's room she tipped the dishes and sent them crashing to the floor. "I told you she cannot see," the queen said to her son. "And I will only eat what Juleidah brings," said the prince.

The cooks prepared a second meal, and when they had balanced the loaded tray upon Juleidah's head, they sent two slave girls to hold her by either hand and guide her to the prince's door. "Go," said the prince to the two slaves, "and you, Juleidah, come." Juleidah began to say,

> My eyes are weak, my sight is dim,
> I'm called Juleidah for my coat of skins,
> My ears are deaf, I cannot hear.
> I care for no one far or near.

But the prince told her, "Come and fill my cup." As she approached, he drew the dagger that hung at his side and slashed her leather coat from collar to hem. It fell into a heap upon the floor—and there stood the maiden his mother had described, one who could say to the moon, "Set that I may shine in your stead."

Hiding Juleidah in a corner of the room, the prince sent for the queen. Our mistress cried out when she saw the pile of skins upon the floor. "Why, my son, did you bring her death upon your neck? The poor thing deserved your pity more than your punishment!" "Come in, Mother," said the prince, "Come and look at our Juleidah before you mourn her." And he led his mother to where our fine princess sat revealed, her fairness filling the room like a ray of light. The queen threw herself upon the girl and kissed her on this side and on that, and bade her sit with the prince and eat. Then she summoned the *qadi* to write the paper that would bind our lord the prince to the fair princess, after which they lived together in the sweetest bliss.

Now we make our way back to the king, Juleidah's father. When he entered the bridal chamber to unveil his own daughter's face and found her gone, and when he had searched the city in vain for her, he called his minister and his servants and dressed himself for travel. From country to country he journeyed, entering one city and leaving the next, taking with him in chains the old woman who had first suggested to him that he marry his own daughter. At last he reached the city where Juleidah was living with her husband the prince.

Now, the princess was sitting in her window when they entered the gate, and she knew them as soon as she saw them. Straightway she sent to her husband urging him to invite the strangers. Our lord went to meet them and succeeded in detaining them only after much pressing, for they were impatient to continue their quest. They dined in the prince's guest hall, then thanked their host and took leave with the words, "The proverb says: 'Have your fill to eat, but then up, onto your feet!' "—while he delayed them further with the proverb, "Where you break your bread, there spread out your bed!"

In the end the prince's kindness forced the tired strangers to lie in his house as guests for the night. "But why did you single out these strangers?" the prince asked Juleidah. "Lend me your robes and head-cloth and let me go to them," she said. "Soon you will know my reasons."

Thus disguised, Juleidah sat with her guests. When the coffee cups had been filled and emptied, she said, "Let us tell stories to pass the time. Will you speak first, or shall I?" "Leave us to our sorrows, my son," said the king her father. "We have not the spirit to tell tales." "I'll entertain you, then, and distract your mind," said Juleidah. "There once was a king," she began, and went on to tell the history of her own adventures from the beginning to the end. Every now and then the old woman would interrupt and say, "Can you find no better story than this, my son?" But Juleidah kept right on, and when she had finished she said, "I am your daughter the princess, upon whom all these troubles fell through the words of this old sinner and daughter of shame!"

In the morning they flung the old woman over a tall cliff into the *wadi*.[4] Then the king gave half his kingdom to his daughter and the prince, and they lived in happiness and contentment until death, the parter of the truest lovers, divided them.

4. Riverbed or ravine.

# INTRODUCTION: Bluebeard

"Bluebeard" is the stuff of nightmares: raised scimitars, forbidden chambers, corpses hanging from hooks, bloody basins, and dismembered bodies. The tale made its literary debut in Charles Perrault's seventeenth-century *Tales of Mother Goose*, a collection that took the lead in transforming the oral narratives of a peasant culture into bedtime reading for children. Like many of the fairy tales in Perrault's collection, "Bluebeard" has a happy ending: the heroine marries "a very worthy man who banished the memory of the miserable days she had spent with Bluebeard" [148]. Yet most readers—even those willing to suspend disbelief about the pleasures of the next marriage—will find themselves unable to erase the graphic impressions left by the "miserable time" of the first marriage. In the narrative economy of Perrault's text, the verbal energy is invested almost exclusively in exposing Bluebeard's wife to horrors of extraordinary vividness and power.

Just who was Bluebeard and how did he come by his bad name? As Anatole France reminds us in his story "The Seven Wives of Bluebeard," Charles Perrault composed "the first biography of this *seigneur*" and established his reputation as "an accomplished villain" and "the most perfect model of cruelty that ever trod the earth."[1] Cultural historians have been quick to claim that Perrault's "Bluebeard" is based on fact, that it broadcasts the misdeeds of various noblemen, among them Cunmar of Brittany and Gilles de Rais. But neither Cunmar the Accursed, who decapitated his pregnant wife Triphine, nor Gilles de Rais, the Marshal of France who was hanged in 1440 for murdering hundreds of children, present themselves as compelling models for Bluebeard. This French aristocrat remains a construction of collective fantasy, a figure firmly anchored in the realm of folklore.

Perrault's "Bluebeard" recounts the story of an aristocratic gentleman (known in Italy as "Silver Nose," in England as "Mr Fox") and his marriage to a young woman whose desire for opulence conquers her feelings of revulsion for blue beards. The French tale contains what folklorists have identified as the three distinctive features of Bluebeard narratives: a forbidden chamber, an agent of prohibition who also metes

Page numbers in brackets refer to this Norton Critical Edition.
1. Anatole France, "The Seven Wives of Bluebeard," in *Spells of Enchantment: The Wondrous Fairy Tales of Western Culture*, ed. Jack Zipes (New York: Viking, 1991) 567.

out punishments, and a figure who violates the prohibition. From Perrault's time onward, the tale has been framed as a story about transgressive desire, as a text that enunciates the dire consequences of curiosity and disobedience.

Perrault presents Bluebeard's wife as a figure who suffers from an excess of desire for knowledge of what lies beyond the door. Bluebeard's wife enters the forbidden chamber and sees a pool of clotted blood in which are reflected the bodies of her husband's wives, hanging from the wall. Horrified, she drops the key (in some versions it is an egg, a straw, or a rose) into the pool of blood and is unable to remove the tell-tale stain from the key. But Bluebeard's wife, both in Perrault's rendition and in its many cultural inflections, is a canny survivor. Her husband may try to behead her for her act of disobedience, but she succeeds in delaying the execution long enough that her brothers, summoned by Sister Anne, arrive in time to rescue her and to cut Bluebeard down with their swords.

"Bluebeard" stands virtually alone among fairy tales in its depiction of marriage as an institution haunted by the threat of murder. While canonical fairy tales like "Cinderella," "Snow White," and "Beauty and the Beast" begin with unhappy situations at home, center on a romantic quest, and end in visions of marital bliss, "Bluebeard" stories show us women leaving the safety of home and entering the risky domains of their husband's castles. In these tales, mothers, sisters, and brothers mobilize to rescue the heroine rather than to do her in. "Bluebeard," as Bruno Bettelheim argues, represents a troubling flip side to "Beauty and the Beast." According to Bettelheim, "Beauty and the Beast" is a wonderfully reassuring story that relieves the "anxious sexual fantasies" to which children are prey: "While sex may at first seem beastlike, in reality love between woman and man is the most satisfying of all emotions, and the only one which makes for permanent happiness."[2] Perrault's "Bluebeard," by contrast, confirms a child's "worst fears about sex," for it reveals marriage as charged with life-threatening perils.

Bettelheim clearly prefers the "permanent happiness" promised by the myth of perfect romantic love in "Beauty and the Beast" to the disturbing anxieties about love and marriage aroused by "Bluebeard." To be sure, "Beauty and the Beast," with its messages about the transformative power of love, makes for better bedtime reading, and that fact alone may explain the apparent erosion of cultural interest in "Bluebeard" in the United States. But while "Bluebeard" may not necessarily be an appropriate story for children, it remains a powerful text challenging the myth of romantic love encapsulated in the "happily ever after" of fairy tales and presenting a message with a social logic compelling for Perrault's day and age. Anxious fantasies about sex and mar-

2. Bruno Bettelheim, *The Uses of Enchantment* (New York: Knopf, 1977) 306.

*women conditions
of the time*

riage would hardly be surprising in seventeenth- and eighteenth-century
Europe, where women married at a relatively young age, where the
mortality rate for women in childbirth was high, and where a move
away from home might rightly be charged with fears about isolation,
violence, abuse, and marital estrangement. While it is tempting to promote stories that stage the joys of heterosexual romantic unions and to
banish grisly stories about murderous husbands (especially once the
venue for the tales shifted to the nursery), it is important to preserve
our cultural memory of this particular story and to understand exactly
what is at stake in it. "Bluebeard" may not appear with great frequency
between the covers of twentieth-century anthologies of fairy tales, but
it is a story whose cultural resilience becomes quickly evident when we
enter the arena of contemporary literary and cinematic production for
adults.

Folklore often trades in the sensational—breaking taboos, enacting
the forbidden, staging transgressive desires, and exploring pathologies
with uninhibited investigative energy. The story of Bluebeard is without
doubt the most stunning piece of evidence that folktales can be seen
as the legitimate precursors of cinematic horror, another genre notorious for trading on collective fears and fantasies. Stories like "Bluebeard"
prefigure the gothic plots of modern horror and construct desires and
fears that remain remarkably intact (despite cultural variations) as we
move from one century to the next and as we cross from one popular
form of entertainment to another. In "Bluebeard," as in cinematic horror, we have not only a killer who is propelled by psychotic rage, but
also the abject victims of his serial murders, along with a "final girl"
(Bluebeard's wife), who either saves herself or arranges her own rescue.
The "terrible place" of horror, a dark, tomblike site that harbors grisly
evidence of the killer's derangement, manifests itself as Bluebeard's forbidden chamber.[3]

It is not only in cinematic horror from the 1970s onward that the
Bluebeard story manifests its cultural staying power. In what one critic
has tellingly called "paranoid woman's films," we also find the Bluebeard syndrome at work.[4] These films, which were made in the wake
of Hitchcock's *Rebecca* (1940) and include such classic thrillers as Robert Stevenson's *Jane Eyre* (1944), George Cukor's *Gaslight* (1944), and
Fritz Lang's *Secret beyond the Door* (1948), all feature a heroine who
is beset by fears that her husband is planning to murder her. Driven
by hermeneutic desire, these women investigators search for the key to
understanding the sinisterly cryptic behavior of their husbands, always
by penetrating the mysteries of a chamber in the house where they

3. Carol J. Clover draws up an inventory of generic properties of the horror film in *Men, Women,
and Chainsaws: Gender in the Modern Horror Film* (Princeton: Princeton UP, 1992)
26–44.
4. Mary Ann Doane, "Paranoia and the Specular," in *The Desire to Desire: The Woman's Film
of the 1940s* (Bloomington: Indiana UP, 1987) 123–54.

have taken up residence. In Hitchcock's *Rebecca*, the boathouse and Rebecca's bedroom are forbidden or uncanny spaces for the character played by Joan Fontaine; in *Jane Eyre* the title character must unlock the secret of the tower room in which Bertha Mason is housed; in *Gaslight* it is the attic, along with the husband's locked desk, that are taboo; and in *Secret beyond the Door*, the heroine is barred from entering room 7, a replica of her own bedroom built to provide her husband with the scene of his next crime.

In much the same way that cinema criticism has been obsessed with the "paranoia" of a wife rather than by the very real threat posed by a husband who seems to be rescripting the Bluebeard story, folklorists have shown surprising interpretive confidence in reading Perrault's "Bluebeard" as a story about a woman's marital disobedience or sexual infidelity rather than about her husband's murderous violence. "Bloody key as sign of disobedience"—this is the motif that folklorists consistently read as the defining moment in the tale. The blood-stained key points to a double transgression, one that is at once moral and sexual. For one critic, it becomes a sign of "marital infidelity";[5] for another it marks the heroine's "irreversible loss of her virginity";[6] for a third, it stands as a sign of "defloration."[7] If we recall that the bloody chamber in Bluebeard's castle is strewn with the corpses of previous wives, this reading of the blood-stained key as a marker of sexual infidelity becomes willfully wrongheaded in its effort to vilify Bluebeard's wife.

Illustrators, commentators, and retellers alike seem to have fallen in line with Perrault's stated view in his moral to the story that "Bluebeard" is about the evils of female curiosity. Walter Crane's illustration of Bluebeard's wife on her way to the forbidden chamber shows her descending the stairs, framed by a tapestry of Eve giving in to temptation in the Garden of Eden. "Succumbing to temptation" is the "sin of the fall, the sin of Eve," one representative critical voice asserts. A nineteenth-century Scottish version of the tale summarizes in its title what appears to be the collective critical wisdom on this tale: "The Story of Bluebeard, or, the effects of female curiosity."[8]

Bluebeard's wife may suffer from an excess of transgressive curiosity, but that curiosity is clearly intellectual rather than sexual. Her curiosity turns her into an energetic investigator, determined to acquire knowledge of the secrets hidden behind the door of the castle's forbidden chamber. Perrault's story, by underscoring the heroine's kinship with certain literary, biblical, and mythical figures (most notably Psyche, Eve, and Pandora), gives us a tale that willfully undermines a robust

5. Bruno Bettelheim, *Uses*, 302.
6. Carl-Heinz Mallett, *Kopf ab! Gewalt im Märchen* (Hamburg: Rasch und Röhring, 1985), 201.
7. Alan Dundes, "Projection in Folklore: A Plea for Psychoanalytic Semiotics," in *Interpreting Folklore* (Bloomington: Indiana UP, 1980) 46.
8. These critical voices are cited in Maria Tatar, *The Hard Facts of the Grimms' Fairy Tales* (Princeton: Princeton UP, 1987) 157–64.

folkloric tradition in which the heroine is a resourceful agent of her own salvation. Rather than celebrating the courage and wisdom of Bluebeard's wife in discovering the dreadful truth about her husband's murderous deeds, Perrault and other tellers of the tale often cast aspersions on her for engaging in an unruly act of insubordination.

The French folklorist Paul Delarue has mapped out the evolution of "Bluebeard," documenting the liberties taken by Perrault in transforming an oral folktale into a literary text.[9] The folk heroines of "Bluebeard" delay their executions by insisting on donning bridal clothes for the event (thus buttressing the folkloric connection between marriage and death) and prolong the possibility of rescue by recounting each and every item of clothing. Perrault's heroine, by contrast, who asks her husband for "a little time to say my prayers" [146], becomes a model of repentent piety. Unlike many folk heroines, who become agents of their own rescue by dispatching fleet-footed pet dogs or talking birds to their families with urgent calls for help, Perrault's heroine sends her sister up to the castle tower to watch for the brothers who were to visit her that very day. Most importantly, folk versions of the tale do not fault the heroine for her curiosity. To the contrary, when the young women stand before the forbidden chamber, they feel duty-bound to open its door. "I have to know what is in there," one young woman reflects just before turning the key. The pangs of conscience that beset Perrault's heroine are absent. These folkloric figures are often described as courageous: curiosity and valor enable them to come to the rescue of their sisters by reconstituting them physically (putting their dismembered parts back together again) and by providing them with safe passage home.

While the story of Bluebeard has been read by countless contemporary commentators as turning on the issue of sexual fidelity, what really seems to be at issue, if one considers the folkloric evidence, is the heroine's discovery of her husband's misdeeds, her craft in delaying the execution of his murderous plans, and her ability to engineer her own rescue. In its bold proclamation of the perils of some marriages, "Bluebeard" endorses, above all, allegiance to family and celebrates a return to the safety and security of home, a regressive move back to the household of the heroine's childhood. Bluebeard's wife becomes a double of the British Jack, liquidating the ogre and climbing back down the beanstalk to live happily ever after with his mother.

When we consider the form in which "Bluebeard" circulated in an oral culture, it quickly becomes evident that the story must be closely related to two tales recorded by the brothers Grimm. The first of these, "Fitcher's Bird," shows us the youngest of three sisters using her "cunning" to escape the snares set by a clever sorcerer and to rescue her

9. Paul Delarue, "Barbe-Bleue," in *Le Conte populaire français* (Paris: Editions Erasme, 1976) I: 182–99.

two sisters. The heroine of "The Robber Bridegroom" also engineers a rescue, mobilizing her wits and her narrative skills to escape from the thieves with whom her betrothed consorts. Oddly enough, however, these two variants of the "Bluebeard" story seem to have fallen into a cultural black hole, while tales like Perrault's "Bluebeard" have been preserved and rewritten as cautionary tales warning women about the hazards of disobedience and curiosity. It is telling that an author like Margaret Atwood has turned to "Fitcher's Bird" and "The Robber Bridegroom" for narrative inspiration and that a visual artist like Cindy Sherman has created a picture book of the Grimms' "Fitcher's Bird." This new cultural investment in old tales about bad marriages clearly has something to do with the discovery that older versions of "Bluebeard" stressed the resourcefulness of the heroine and with the revelation that Perrault's "Bluebeard" was not the sole source of narrative authority for this particular marriage tale.

Margaret Atwood, who grew up reading the Grimms, recognized that fairy tales were not at all as culturally repressive as some feminist critics had made them out to be.

> The unexpurgated *Grimm's Fairy Tales* contain a number of fairy tales in which women are not only the central characters but win by using their own intelligence. Some people feel fairy tales are bad for women. This is true if the only ones they're referring to are those tarted-up French versions of "Cinderella" and "Bluebeard," in which the female protagonist gets rescued by her brothers. But in many of them, women rather than men have the magic powers.[1]

Atwood, who weaves fairy-tale motifs throughout her narratives with almost unprecedented insistence, also produced a new version of "Bluebeard," one that has embedded in it the Grimms' story "Fitcher's Bird." "Bluebeard's Egg," unlike any fairy tale, is told from the protagonist's point of view: it charts Sally's drive to solve "the puzzle . . . Ed" [169] and reveals that Ed Bear (who may not sport a beard on his face but surely has one encrypted in his nickname) is not as transparent as Sally once assumed. His inner life becomes a kind of secret chamber, a space that Sally is unable to penetrate. But Atwood challenges our interpretive faculties by refusing to write a text that offers unproblematic parallels with "Bluebeard." In the profusion of references to other fairy tales (Ed is a "third son" [157], a "brainless beast" [157], and a "Sleeping Beauty" [158] waiting to be wakened by Sally, who is both a princess and a false bride), Atwood makes it clear that she taps multiple cultural stories for this work. And by transforming the forbidden chamber of Bluebeard's castle into everything from Ed's enigmatic mind and his

1. Sharon R. Wilson, *Margaret Atwood's Fairy-Tale Sexual Politics* (Jackson: UP of Mississippi, 1993) 11–12.

"new facility" [164] to the anatomical cavities of the human heart and the keyhole desk before which Ed betrays his sexual infidelity, Atwood unsettles the traditional story of "Bluebeard" and challenges us to understand the complexities of what she calls "power politics." Ed cannot be reduced to Bluebeard, and Sally is more than his investigative wife. In focalizing the story through Sally and showing how her effort to come to terms with the Grimms' "Fitcher's Bird" leads her to powerful revelations about her own life, Atwood suggests that engagement with our cultural stories can open our eyes to realities that—however disruptive, painful, and disturbing—are not without a liberating potential. Hence the story ends on an ambiguous note, with a sense of anxiety but also with the possibility of hope about what will hatch from the "almost pulsing" [178] egg of Sally's dream vision.

# CHARLES PERRAULT

## Bluebeard†

There once lived a man who had fine houses, both in the city and in the country, dinner services of gold and silver, chairs covered with tapestries, and coaches covered with gold. But this man had the misfortune of having a blue beard, which made him look so ugly and frightful that women and girls alike fled at the sight of him.

One of his neighbors, a respectable lady, had two daughters who were perfect beauties. He asked for the hand of one, but left it up to the mother to choose which one. Neither of the two girls wanted to marry him, and the offer went back and forth between them, since they could not bring themselves to marry a man with a blue beard. What added even more to their sense of disgust was that he had already married several women, and no one knew what had become of them.

In order to cultivate their acquaintance, Bluebeard threw a party for the two girls with their mother, three or four of their closest friends, and a few young men from the neighborhood in one of his country houses. It lasted an entire week. Everyday there were parties of pleasure, hunting, fishing, dancing, and dining. The guests never even slept, but cavorted and caroused all night long. Everything went so well that the younger of the two sisters began to think that the beard of the master of the house was not so blue after all and that he was in fact a fine fellow. As soon as they returned to town, the marriage was celebrated.

After a month had passed, Bluebeard told his wife that he had to travel to take care of some urgent business in the provinces and that

† Charles Perrault, "Le Barbe bleue," in *Histoires ou Contes du temps passé. Avec des Moralités* (Paris: Barbin, 1697). Translated for this Norton Critical Edition by Maria Tatar. Copyright © 1999 Maria Tatar.

he would be away for at least six weeks. He urged her to enjoy herself while he was away, to invite her close friends and to take them out to the country if she wished. Above all, she was to stay in good spirits.

"Here," he said, "are the keys to my two large store rooms. Here are the ones for the gold and silver china that is too good for everyday use. Here are the ones for my strongboxes, where my gold and silver are kept. Here are the ones for the caskets where my jewels are stored. And finally, this is the passkey to all the rooms in my mansion. As for this particular key, it is the key to the small room at the end of the long passage on the lower floor. Open anything you want. Go anywhere you wish. But I absolutely forbid you to enter that little room, and if you so much as open it a crack, there will be no limit to my anger."

She promised to follow the orders he had just given exactly. After kissing his wife, Bluebeard got into the carriage and embarked on his journey.

Friends and neighbors of the young bride did not wait for an invitation before coming to call, so great was their impatience to see the splendors of the house. They had not dared to call while the husband was there, because of his blue beard, which frightened them. In no time they were darting through the rooms, the closets, and the wardrobes, each of which was more splendid and sumptuous than the next. Then they went upstairs to the storerooms, where they could not find words to describe the number and beauty of the tapestries, beds, sofas, cabinets, stands, and tables. There were looking glasses, in which you could see yourself from head to toe, some of which had frames of glass, others of silver or gilded lacquer, but all of which were more splendid and magnificent than anyone there had ever seen. They kept on expressing praise even as they felt envy for the good fortune of their friend who, however, was unable to take any pleasure at all from the sight of these riches because she was so anxious to get into that room on the lower floor. So tormented was she by her curiosity that, without stopping to think about how rude it was to leave her friends, she raced down a little staircase so fast that more than once she thought she was going to break her neck. When she reached the door to the room, she stopped to think for a moment about how her husband had forbidden her to enter, and she reflected on the harm that might come her way for being disobedient. But the temptation was so great that she was unable to resist it. She took the little key and, trembling, opened the door.

At first she saw nothing, for the windows were closed. After a few moments, she began to realize that the floor was covered with clotted blood and that the blood reflected the bodies of several dead women hung up on the walls (these were all the women Bluebeard had married and then murdered one after another).

She thought she would die of fright, and the key to the room, which she was about to pull out of the lock, dropped from her hand. When she regained her senses, she picked up the key, closed the door, and went back to her room to compose herself. But she didn't succeed, for her nerves were too frayed. Having noticed that the key to the room was stained with blood, she wiped it two or three times, but the blood would not come off at all. She tried to wash it off and even to scrub it with sand and grit. The blood stain would not come off because the key was enchanted and nothing could clean it completely. When you cleaned the stain from one side, it just returned on the other.

That very night, Bluebeard returned unexpectedly from his journey and reported that, on the road, he had received letters informing him that the business upon which he had set forth had just been settled to his satisfaction. His wife did everything that she could to make it appear that she was thrilled with his speedy return. The next day, he asked to have the keys back, and she returned them, but with a hand trembling so much that he knew at once what had happened.

"How is it," he asked, "that the key to the little room isn't with the others?"

"I must have left it upstairs on my dressing table," she replied.

"Don't forget to bring it to me soon," Bluebeard told her.

After making one excuse after another, she had to bring him the key. Bluebeard examined it and said to his wife: "Why is there blood on this key?"

"I have no idea," answered the poor woman, paler than death.

"You have no idea," Bluebeard replied. "But I have an idea. You tried to enter that little room. Well, madam, now that you have opened it, you can go right in and take your place beside the ladies whom you saw there."

She threw herself at her husband's feet, weeping and begging his pardon, with all the signs of genuine regret for disobeying him. She looked so beautiful and was so distressed that she would have melted a heart of stone, but Bluebeard had a heart harder than any rock.

"You must die, madam," he declared, "and it will be right away."

"Since I must die," she replied, gazing at him with eyes full of tears, "give me a little time to say my prayers."

"I will give you a quarter of an hour," Bluebeard said, "but not a moment more."

When she was alone, she called her sister and said to her: "Sister Anne"—for that was her name—"I implore you to go up to the top of the tower to see if my brothers are on the way here. They told me that they were coming to visit today. If you catch sight of them, signal them to hurry."

Sister Anne went up to the top of the tower, and the poor distressed girl cried out to her from time to time: "Anne, Sister Anne, do you see anyone coming?"

Sister Anne replied: "I see nothing but the sun shining and the green grass growing."

In the meantime, Bluebeard took an enormous cutlass in hand and cried out at the top of his voice to his wife: "Come down at once or I'll go up there!"

"Just a moment more, I beg you," his wife replied and at the same time she called out softly: "Anne, Sister Anne, do you see anyone coming?"

And Sister Anne replied: "I see nothing but the sun shining and the green grass growing."

"Come down at once," Bluebeard called, "or I'll go up there!"

"I'm coming," his wife replied, and then she called: "Anne, Sister Anne, do you see anyone coming?"

"I can see a great cloud of dust coming this way," replied Sister Anne.

"Is it my brothers?"

"No, oh no, sister, it's just a flock of sheep."

"Are you coming down?" Bluebeard roared.

"Just one moment more," his wife replied, and then she called: "Anne, Sister Anne, do you see anyone coming?"

"I see two horsemen coming this way, but they're still far away," she replied. "Thank God," she shouted a moment later, "it must be our brothers. I'll signal to them to hurry up."

Bluebeard began shouting so loudly that the entire house shook. His poor wife came downstairs, in tears and with disheveled hair. She threw herself at his feet.

"That won't do you any good," said Bluebeard. "Prepare to die." Then, taking her by the hair with one hand and raising his cutlass with the other, he was about to chop off her head. The poor woman turned to him and implored him with a gaze that had death written on it. She begged for one last moment to prepare herself for death. "No, no," he said, "prepare to meet your maker." And lifting his arm . . .

Just at that moment there was such a loud pounding at the gate that Bluebeard stopped short. The gate was opened, and two horsemen, swords in hand, dashed in and made straight for Bluebeard. He realized that they were the brothers of his wife: the one a dragoon and the other a musketeer. He fled instantly in an effort to escape. But the two brothers were so hot in pursuit that they trapped him before he could get to the stairs. They plunged their swords through his body and left him for dead. Bluebeard's wife was as close to death as her husband and barely had the strength to rise and embrace her brothers.

It turned out that Bluebeard had left no heirs, and so his wife took possession of the entire estate. She devoted a portion of it to arranging a marriage between her sister Anne and a young gentleman with whom she had been in love for a long time. Another portion of it was used to buy commissions for her two brothers. She used the rest to marry herself to a very worthy man, who banished the memory of the miserable days she had spent with Bluebeard.

## Moral

Curiosity, in spite of its many charms,
Can bring with it serious regrets;
You can see a thousand examples of it every day.
Women succumb, but it's a fleeting pleasure;
As soon as you satisfy it, it ceases to be.
And it always proves very, very costly.

## Another Moral

If you just take a sensible point of view,
And study this grim little story,
You will understand that this tale
Is one that took place many years ago.
No longer are husbands so terrible,
Demanding the impossible,
Acting unhappy and jealous.
With their wives they toe the line;
And whatever color their beards might be,
It's not hard to tell which of the pair is master.

# BROTHERS GRIMM

## Fitcher's Bird†

There was once a sorcerer who would disguise himself as a poor man, then go begging from door to door in order to capture pretty girls. No one knew what he did with them, for they were never seen again.

One day he appeared at the door of a man who had three beautiful daughters. He looked like a poor, weak beggar and had a basket on his back, as if to collect alms. He asked for something to eat, and when the eldest girl went to the door and was about to hand him a piece of bread, he just touched her and she jumped into his basket. Then he made long legs and rushed off to get her to his house, which was in the middle of a dark forest.

Everything in the house was splendid. He gave the girl everything she wanted, and said: "My darling, I'm sure you'll be happy here with me, for you'll have everything your heart desires." After a few days went

† Jacob and Wilhelm Grimm, "Fitchers Vogel," in *Kinder- und Hausmärchen*, 7th ed. (Berlin: Dieterich, 1857; first published: Berlin: Realschulbuchhandlung, 1812). Translated for this Norton Critical Edition by Maria Tatar. Copyright © 1999 by Maria Tatar.

by, he said: "I have to take a journey and must leave you alone for a short while. Here are the keys for the house. You can go anywhere you want and look around at everything, but don't go into the room that this little key opens. I forbid it under penalty of death."

He also gave her an egg and said: "Carry it with you wherever you go, because if it gets lost, something terrible will happen." She took the keys and the egg and promised to do exactly what he had said. After he left, she went over the house from top to bottom, taking a good look at everything. The rooms glittered with silver and gold, and it seemed to her that she had never before seen such magnificence. Finally she came to the forbidden door and planned to walk right by it, but curiosity got the better of her. She examined the key, and it was just like the others. When she put it in the lock and just turned it a little bit, the door sprang open.

But what did she see when she entered! In the middle of the room was a large, bloody basin filled with dead people who had been chopped to pieces. Next to the basin was a block of wood with a gleaming ax on it. She was so horrified that she dropped the egg she was holding into the basin. She took it right out and wiped off the blood, but to no avail, for the stain immediately returned. She wiped it and scraped at it, but it just wouldn't come off.

Not much later the man returned from his journey, and the first things he demanded were the keys and the egg. She gave them to him, but she was trembling, and when he saw the red stains, he knew she had been in the bloody chamber. "You entered the chamber against my wishes," he said. "Now you will go back in against yours. Your life is over."

He threw her down, dragged her in by the hair, chopped her head off on the block, and hacked her into pieces so that her blood flowed all over the floor. Then he tossed her into the basin with the others.

"Now I'll go and get the second one," said the sorcerer, and he went back to the house dressed as a poor man begging for alms. When the second daughter brought him a piece of bread, he caught her as he had the first just by touching her. He carried her off, and she fared no better than her sister. Her curiosity got the better of her: she opened the door to the bloody chamber, looked inside it, and when he returned she had to pay with her life.

The man went to fetch the third daughter, but she was clever and cunning. After handing over the keys and egg, he went away, and she put the egg in a safe place. She explored the house and entered the forbidden chamber. And what did she see! There in the basin were her two sisters, cruelly murdered and chopped to pieces. But she set to work gathering all their body parts and put them in their proper places: heads, torsos, arms, legs. When everything was in place, the pieces began to move and joined themselves together. The two girls opened their eyes and came back to life. Overjoyed, they kissed and hugged each other.

On his return, the man asked at once for the keys and egg. When he could not find a trace of blood on the egg, he declared: "You have passed the test, and you shall be my bride." He no longer had any power over her and had to do her bidding. "Very well," she replied. "But first you must take a basketful of gold to my father and mother, and you must carry it on your own back. In the meantime, I'll make the wedding arrangements."

She ran to her sisters, whom she had hidden in a little room and said: "Now is the time when I can save you. That brute will be the one who carries you home. But as soon as you get home, send help for me."

She put both girls into a basket and covered them with gold until they could not be seen. Then she summoned the sorcerer and said: "Pick up the basket and go. But don't you dare stop to rest along the way. I'll be looking out of my little window, keeping an eye on you."

The sorcerer lifted the basket onto his shoulders and set off with it. But it weighed so much that sweat began to pour down his face. He sat down to rest for a moment, but right away one of the girls cried out from the basket: "I'm looking out my little window, and I see that you're resting. Get a move on." He thought his bride was calling to him, and he went on his way. A second time he wanted to sit down, but again the voice called out: "I'm looking out my little window and I see that you're resting. Get a move on." Whenever he stopped, the voice called out and he had to move along until finally, gasping for breath and groaning, he carried the basket with the gold and the two girls in it into their parent's house.

Back at home the bride was preparing the wedding celebration to which she had invited all the sorcerer's friends. She took a skull with grinning teeth, crowned it with jewels and a garland of flowers, carried it upstairs and set it down at an attic window, facing out. When everything was ready, she crawled into a barrel of honey, cut open a featherbed and rolled in the feathers until she looked like a strange bird that not a soul would recognize. She left the house and on her way met some wedding guests, who asked:

> "Oh, Fitcher's feathered bird, where are you from?"
> "From feathered Fitze Fitcher's house I've come."
> "And the young bride there, what has she done?"
> "She's swept the house all the way through,
> And from the attic window, she's looking right at you."

She met the bridegroom, who was walking back home very slowly. He too asked:

"Oh, Fitcher's feathered bird, where are you from?"
"From feathered Fitze Fitcher's house I've come."
"And my young bride there, what has she done?"
"She's swept the house all the way through,
And from the attic window, she's looking right at you."

The bridegroom looked up and saw the decorated skull. He thought it was his bride, nodded, and waved to her. But when he got to the house with his guests, the brothers and relatives who had been sent to rescue the bride were already there. They locked the doors to the house so that no one could escape. Then they set fire to it so that the sorcerer and his crew burned to death.

# BROTHERS GRIMM

## The Robber Bridegroom†

There was once a miller who had a beautiful daughter, and when she was grown, he wanted to make sure that she was provided for and well married. He thought: "If the right kind of suitor comes along and asks for her hand, I shall give her to him."

Not much later a suitor turned up who seemed to be rich, and since the miller could find nothing wrong with him, he promised him his daughter. But the girl didn't care for him as a girl should care for her betrothed, and she didn't trust him. Whenever she looked at him or thought of him, her heart filled with dread.

One day he said to her: "You're engaged to me, and yet you've never once visited me."

The girl replied: "I don't know where you live."

The bridegroom answered: "My house is out in the dark forest."

The girl made excuses and claimed that she couldn't find the way there. But the bridegroom said: "Next Sunday you have to come to my place. I've already invited the guests, and I'll put ashes on the path so that you can find your way through the woods."

When Sunday came and the girl was supposed to leave, she became dreadfully frightened without knowing why, and she filled both her pockets with peas and lentils to mark the way. At the entrance to the woods she found the trail of ashes and followed it, but at every step she threw some peas on the ground, first to the right and then to the left. She walked almost the entire day until she got to the middle of the

† Jacob and Wilhelm Grimm, "Der Räuberbräutigam," In *Kinder- und Hausmärchen*, 7th ed. (Berlin: Dieterich, 1857; first published: Berlin: Realschulbuchhandlung, 1812). Translated for this Norton Critical Edition by Maria Tatar. Copyright © 1999 by Maria Tatar.

forest, where it was the gloomiest. There she saw a house standing by itself, but she didn't like the look of it because it seemed dark and spooky. She walked in. It was deadly silent, and no one was around. Suddenly a voice cried out:

> "Turn back, turn back, my pretty young bride,
> In a house of murderers you've arrived."

The girl looked up and saw that the voice was coming from a bird in a cage hanging on the wall. Once again it cried out:

> "Turn back, turn back, my pretty young bride,
> In a house of murderers you've arrived."

The beautiful bride went all over the house from one room to the next, but it was completely empty and not a soul could be found in it. Finally she went down to the cellar, where she found a woman as old as the hills, her head bobbing up and down.

"Can you tell me if my betrothed lives here?" asked the girl.

"Oh, you poor child!" said the old woman. "How did you get here? This is a den of murderers. You think you're a bride about to be married, but the only wedding you'll celebrate is one with death. Look over here! I had to heat up this big pot of water for them. When you get into their hands, they'll show no mercy and chop you into pieces, cook you, and eat you, for they are cannibals. You're lost unless I take pity on you and try to save you."

The old woman hid her behind a big barrel, where no one could see her. "Be still as a mouse," she said. "Don't stir and don't move or it'll be the end of you. At night, when the robbers are sleeping, we'll escape. I've been waiting for this moment for a long time."

No sooner had she spoken when the ungodly crew returned home, dragging another maiden in with them. They were drunk and paid no attention to her screams and sobs. They gave her wine to drink, three glasses full, one white, one red, one yellow, and soon her heart burst in two. They tore off her fine clothes, put her on a table, chopped her beautiful body into pieces, and sprinkled them with salt.

The poor girl was trembling and shaking from her hiding place behind the barrel, for she now understood what the robbers had in store for her. One of them caught sight of a gold ring on the little finger of the murdered girl, and when he couldn't pull it off right away, he took an ax and chopped the finger off. The finger went flying through the air up over the barrel and landed right in the girl's lap. The robber took a candle and wanted to go looking for it but couldn't find it. Another of the robbers asked: "Have you looked over there behind that big barrel?" Just then the old woman called out: "Come and eat! You can look again tomorrow. The finger isn't going to go running off."

"The old woman's right," the robbers said, and they put an end to their search and sat down to eat. The old woman put a few drops of a sleeping potion into their wine, and soon they retired to the cellar where they were snoring away in their sleep.

When the bride heard them snoring, she came out from behind the barrel and made her way over the sleeping bodies arranged in rows on the ground. She was terrified that she might wake one of them up, but God guided her footsteps. The old woman went up the stairs with her, opened the door, and they ran as fast as they could from the den of murderers. The wind had scattered the ashes, but the peas and lentils had sprouted and showed the way in the moonlight. The two walked all night long. In the morning they reached the mill, and the girl told her father about everything that had happened.

When the day of the wedding celebration arrived, the groom appeared, as did all the friends and relatives invited by the miller. When they sat down for dinner, each person was asked to tell a story. The bride sat quietly and didn't utter a word. Finally the bridegroom said to his bride: "Don't you have anything to say, my love? You have to tell us something."

"Very well," she replied, "I will tell you about a dream I had. I was walking alone through the woods and came across a house. Not a soul was living in it, but on the wall there was a cage, and in it was a bird that cried out:

'Turn back, turn back, my pretty young bride,
In a house of murderers you've arrived.'

"Then it repeated those words. My dear, I must have been dreaming all this. Then I walked from room to room and each was completely empty. Everything was so spooky. Finally I went down to the cellar, and there I saw a woman as old as the hills, her head bobbing up and down. I asked her: 'Does my betrothed live here?' She replied: 'Oh, you poor child, you have stumbled into a den of murderers. Your betrothed lives here, but he is planning to chop you up and kill you, and then he'll cook you and eat you up.' My dear, I must have been dreaming all this. The old woman hid me behind a big barrel, and no sooner was I hidden when the robbers returned home, dragging a maiden with them. They gave her three kinds of wine to drink, white, red, yellow, and her heart burst in two. My dear, I must have been dreaming all this. Then they tore off her fine clothes, chopped her beautiful body into pieces, and sprinkled it with salt. My dear, I must have been dreaming all this. One of the robbers caught sight of a gold ring on her finger and since it was hard to pull off, he took an ax and chopped it off. The finger flew through the air up behind the big barrel and landed in my lap. And here is the finger with the ring."

With these words, she pulled it out and showed it to everyone there.

The robber, who had turned white as a ghost while she was telling the story, jumped up and tried to escape, but the guests seized him and turned him over to the authorities. He and his band were executed for their dreadful deeds.

# JOSEPH JACOBS

## Mr. Fox†

*—Woman engaged to see him*
*sneaks over to see*
*his house*
*—gets finger*
*kill women*
*shows to*
*family*
*kill him*

Lady Mary was young, and Lady Mary was fair. She had two brothers, and more lovers than she could count. But of them all, the bravest and most gallant was a Mr. Fox, whom she met when she was down at her father's country house. No one knew who Mr. Fox was; but he was certainly brave, and surely rich, and of all her lovers Lady Mary cared for him alone. At last it was agreed upon between them that they should be married. Lady Mary asked Mr. Fox where they should live, and he described to her his castle, and where it was; but, strange to say, did not ask her or her brothers to come and see it.

So one day, near the wedding day, when her brothers were out, and Mr. Fox was away for a day or two on business, as he said, Lady Mary set out for Mr. Fox's castle. And after many searchings, she came at last to it, and a fine strong house it was, with high walls and a deep moat. And when she came up to the gateway she saw written on it:

Be bold, be bold.[1]

But as the gate was open, she went through it, and found no one there. So she went up to the doorway, and over it she found written:

Be bold, be bold, but not too bold.

Still she went on, till she came into the hall, and went up the broad stairs till she came to a door in the gallery, over which was written:

Be bold, be bold, but not too bold,
Lest that your heart's blood should run cold.

But Lady Mary was a brave one, she was, and she opened the door, and what do you think she saw? Why, bodies and skeletons of beautiful young ladies all stained with blood. So Lady Mary thought it was high time to get out of that horrid place, and she closed the door, went through the gallery, and was just going down the stairs, and out of the hall, when who should she see through the window but Mr. Fox dragging a beautiful young lady along from the gateway to the door. Lady

---

† Joseph Jacobs, "Mr. Fox," in *English Fairy Tales* (London: David Nutt, 1890).

1. The admonition "Be bold" appears also in Edmund Spenser's *Faerie Queen* (1590): "How over that same door was likewise writ, / *Be bold, be bold*, and everywhere *Be bold*" (11, st. 54).

Mary rushed downstairs, and hid herself behind a cask, just in time, as Mr. Fox came in with the poor young lady, who seemed to have fainted. Just as he got near Lady Mary, Mr. Fox saw a diamond ring glittering on the finger of the young lady he was dragging, and he tried to pull it off. But it was tightly fixed, and would not come off, so Mr. Fox cursed and swore, and drew his sword, raised it, and brought it down upon the hand of the poor lady. The sword cut off the hand, which jumped up into the air, and fell of all places in the world into Lady Mary's lap. Mr. Fox looked about a bit, but did not think of looking behind the cask, so at last he went on dragging the young lady up the stairs into the Bloody Chamber.

As soon as she heard him pass through the gallery, Lady Mary crept out of the door, down through the gateway, and ran home as fast as she could.

Now it happened that the very next day the marriage contract of Lady Mary and Mr. Fox was to be signed, and there was a splendid breakfast before that. And when Mr. Fox was seated at table opposite Lady Mary, he looked at her. "How pale you are this morning, my dear." "Yes," said she, "I had a bad night's rest last night. I had horrible dreams." "Dreams go by contraries," said Mr. Fox; "but tell us your dream, and your sweet voice will make the time pass till the happy hour comes."

"I dreamed," said Lady Mary, "that I went yestermorn to your castle, and I found it in the woods, with high walls, and a deep moat, and over the gateway was written:

> Be bold, be bold."

"But it is not so, nor it was not so,"[2] said Mr. Fox.

"And when I came to the doorway, over it was written:

> Be bold, be bold, but not too bold."

"It is not so, nor it was not so," said Mr. Fox.

"And then I went upstairs, and came to a gallery, at the end of which was a door, on which was written:

> Be bold, be bold, but not too bold,
> Lest that your heart's blood should run cold."

"It is not so, nor it was not so," said Mr. Fox.

"And then—and then I opened the door, and the room was filled with bodies and skeletons of poor dead women, all stained with their blood."

"It is not so, nor it was not so. And God forbid it should be so," said Mr. Fox.

2. Cf. Shakespeare, *Much Ado about Nothing* (I.i.146): "Like the old tale, my Lord, 'It is not so, nor t'was not so, but, indeed, God forbid it should be so!'"

"I then dreamed that I rushed down the gallery, and just as I was going down the stairs I saw you, Mr. Fox, coming up to the hall door, dragging after you a poor young lady, rich and beautiful."

"It is not so, nor it was not so. And God forbid it should be so," said Mr. Fox.

"I rushed downstairs, just in time to hide myself behind a cask, when you, Mr. Fox, came in dragging the young lady by the arm. And, as you passed me, Mr. Fox, I thought I saw you try and get off her diamond ring, and when you could not, Mr. Fox, it seemed to me in my dream, that you out with your sword and hacked off the poor lady's hand to get the ring."

"It is not so, nor it was not so. And God forbid it should be so," said Mr. Fox, and was going to say something else as he rose from his seat, when Lady Mary cried out:

"But it is so, and it was so. Here's hand and ring I have to show," and pulled out the lady's hand from her dress, and pointed it straight at Mr. Fox.

At once her brothers and her friends drew their swords and cut Mr. Fox into a thousand pieces.

# MARGARET ATWOOD

## Bluebeard's Egg†

Sally stands at the kitchen window, waiting for the sauce she's reducing to come to a simmer, looking out. Past the garage the lot sweeps downwards, into the ravine; it's a wilderness there, of bushes and branches and what Sally thinks of as vines. It was her idea to have a kind of terrace, built of old railroad ties, with wild flowers growing between them, but Edward says he likes it the way it is. There's a playhouse down at the bottom, near the fence; from here she can just see the roof. It has nothing to do with Edward's kids, in their earlier incarnations, before Sally's time; it's more ancient than that, and falling apart. Sally would like it cleared away. She thinks drunks sleep in it, the men who live under the bridges down there, who occasionally wander over the fence (which is broken down, from where they step on it) and up the hill, to emerge squinting like moles into the light of Sally's well-kept back lawn.

Off to the left is Ed, in his windbreaker; it's officially spring, Sally's blue scylla is in flower, but it's chilly for this time of year. Ed's windbreaker is an old one he won't throw out; it still says WILDCATS, relic

† From *Bluebeard's Egg and Other Stories* by Margaret Atwood. Copyright © 1983, 1986 by O. W. Toad Ltd. Reprinted by permission of Houghton Mifflin Company, McClelland & Stewart, Inc. *The Canadian Publishers*, and Jonathan Cape Ltd.

of some team he was on in high school, an era so prehistoric Sally can barely imagine it; though picturing Ed at high school is not all that difficult. Girls would have had crushes on him, he would have been unconscious of it; things like that don't change. He's puttering around the rock garden now; some of the rocks stick out too far and are in danger of grazing the side of Sally's Peugeot, on its way to the garage, and he's moving them around. He likes doing things like that, puttering, humming to himself. He won't wear work gloves, though she keeps telling him he could squash his fingers.

Watching his bent back with its frayed, poignant lettering, Sally dissolves; which is not infrequent with her. *My darling Edward*, she thinks. *Edward Bear,*[1] *of little brain. How I love you.* At times like this she feels very protective of him.

Sally knows for a fact that dumb blondes were loved, not because they were blondes, but because they were dumb. It was their helplessness and confusion that were so sexually attractive, once; not their hair. It wasn't false, the rush of tenderness men must have felt for such women. Sally understands it.

For it must be admitted: Sally is in love with Ed because of his stupidity, his monumental and almost energetic stupidity: energetic, because Ed's stupidity is not passive. He's no mere blockhead;[2] you'd have to be working at it to be that stupid. Does it make Sally feel smug, or smarter than he is, or even smarter than she really is herself? No; on the contrary, it makes her humble. It fills her with wonder that the world can contain such marvels as Ed's colossal and endearing thickness. He is just so *stupid*. Every time he gives her another piece of evidence, another tile that she can glue into place in the vast mosaic of his stupidity she's continually piecing together, she wants to hug him, and often does; and he is so stupid he can never figure out what for.

Because Ed is so stupid he doesn't even know he's stupid. He's a child of luck, a third son who, armed with nothing but a certain feeble-minded amiability, manages to make it through the forest with all its witches and traps and pitfalls and end up with the princess, who is Sally, of course. It helps that he's handsome.

On good days she sees his stupidity as innocence, lamblike, shining with the light of (for instance) green daisied meadows in the sun. (When Sally starts thinking this way about Ed, in terms of the calendar art from the service-station washrooms of her childhood, dredging up images of a boy with curly golden hair, his arm thrown around the neck of an Irish setter—a notorious brainless beast, she reminds herself—she knows she is sliding over the edge, into a ghastly kind of sentimentality, and that she must stop at once, or Ed will vanish, to be replaced by a stuffed facsimile, useful for little else but an umbrella

1. Christopher Robin's formal name for Winnie-the-Pooh.
2. Reference to blockheads and numbskulls in folklore.

stand. Ed is a real person, with a lot more to him than these simplistic renditions allow for; which sometimes worries her.) On bad days though, she sees his stupidity as wilfullness, a stubborn determination to shut things out. His obtuseness is a wall, within which he can go about his business, humming to himself, while Sally, locked outside, must hack her way through the brambles[3] with hardly so much as a transparent raincoat between them and her skin.

Why did she choose him (or, to be precise, as she tries to be with herself and sometimes is even out loud, *hunt him down*), when it's clear to everyone she had other options? To Marylynn, who is her best though most recent friend, she's explained it by saying she was spoiled when young by reading too many Agatha Christie murder mysteries, of the kind in which the clever and witty heroine passes over the equally clever and witty first-lead male, who's helped solve the crime, in order to marry the second-lead male, the stupid one, the one who would have been arrested and condemned and executed if it hadn't been for her cleverness. Maybe this is how she sees Ed: if it weren't for her, his blundering too-many-thumbs kindness would get him into all sorts of quagmires, all sorts of sink-holes he'd never be able to get himself out of, and then he'd be done for.

"Sink-hole" and "quagmire" are not flattering ways of speaking about other women, but this is what is at the back of Sally's mind; specifically, Ed's two previous wives. Sally didn't exactly extricate him from their clutches. She's never even met the first one, who moved to the west coast fourteen years ago and sends Christmas cards, and the second one was middle-aged and already in the act of severing herself from Ed before Sally came along. (For Sally, "middle-aged" means anyone five years older than she is. It has always meant this. She applies it only to women, however. She doesn't think of Ed as middle-aged, although the gap between them is considerably more than five years.)

Ed doesn't know what happened with these marriages, what went wrong. His protestations of ignorance, his refusal to discuss the finer points, is frustrating to Sally, because she would like to hear the whole story. But it's also cause for anxiety: if he doesn't know what happened with the other two, maybe the same thing could be happening with her and he doesn't know about that, either. Stupidity like Ed's can be a health hazard, for other people. What if he wakes up one day and decides that she isn't the true bride[4] after all, but the false one? Then she will be put into a barrel stuck full of nails[5] and rolled downhill, endlessly, while he is sitting in yet another bridal bed, drinking champagne. She remembers the brand name, because she bought it herself.

3. An allusion to "Briar Rose" or "Sleeping Beauty."
4. A reference to fairy tales that pit a false bride against the heroine, or true bride.
5. A punishment frequently meted out to fairy-tale villains.

Champagne isn't the sort of finishing touch that would occur to Ed, though he enjoyed it enough at the time.

But outwardly Sally makes a joke of all this. "He doesn't know," she says to Marylynn, laughing a little, and they shake their heads. If it were them, they'd know, all right. Marylynn is in fact divorced, and she can list every single thing that went wrong, item by item. After doing this, she adds that her divorce was one of the best things that ever happened to her. "I was just a nothing before," she says. "It made me pull myself together."

Sally, looking across the kitchen table at Marylynn, has to agree that she is far from being a nothing now. She started out re-doing people's closets, and has worked that up into her own interior-design firm. She does the houses of the newly rich, those who lack ancestral furniture and the confidence to be shabby, and who wish their interiors to reflect a personal taste they do not in reality possess.

"What they want are mausoleums," Marylynn says, "or hotels," and she cheerfully supplies them. "Right down to the ash-trays. Imagine having someone else pick out your ash-trays for you."

By saying this, Marylynn lets Sally know that she's not including her in that category, though Sally did in fact hire her, at the very first, to help with a few details around the house. It was Marylynn who redesigned the wall of closets in the master bedroom and who found Sally's massive Chinese mahogany table, which cost her another seven hundred dollars to have stripped. But it turned out to be perfect, as Marylynn said it would. Now she's dug up a nineteenth-century keyhole desk, which both she and Sally know will be exactly right for the bay-windowed alcove off the living room. "Why do you need it?" Ed said in his puzzled way. "I thought you worked in your study." Sally admitted this, but said they could keep the telephone bills in it, which appeared to satisfy him. She knows exactly what she needs it for: she needs it to sit at, in something flowing, backlit by the morning sunlight, gracefully dashing off notes. She saw a 1940's advertisement for coffee like this once; and the husband was standing behind the chair, leaning over, with a worshipful expression on his face.

Marylynn is the kind of friend Sally does not have to explain any of this to, because it's assumed between them. Her intelligence is the kind Sally respects.

Marylynn is tall and elegant, and makes anything she is wearing seem fashionable. Her hair is prematurely grey and she leaves it that way. She goes in for loose blouses in cream-coloured silk, and eccentric scarves gathered from interesting shops and odd corners of the world, thrown carelessly around her neck and over one shoulder. (Sally has tried this toss in the mirror, but it doesn't work.) Marylynn has a large collection of unusual shoes; she says they're unusual because her feet are so big, but Sally knows better. Sally, who used to think of herself as pretty enough and now thinks of herself as doing quite well for her age, envies Marylynn her bone structure, which will serve her well when the inevitable happens.

Whenever Marylynn is coming to dinner, as she is today—she's bringing the desk, too—Sally takes especial care with her clothes and make-up. Marylynn, she knows, is her real audience for such things, since no changes she effects in herself seem to affect Ed one way or the other, or even to register with him. "You look fine to me" is all he says, no matter how she really looks. (But does she want him to see her more clearly, or not? Most likely not. If he did he would notice the incipient wrinkles, the small pouches of flesh that are not quite there yet, the network forming beneath her eyes. It's better as it is.)

Sally has repeated this remark of Ed's to Marylynn, adding that he said it the day the Jacuzzi overflowed because the smoke alarm went off, because an English muffin she was heating to eat in the bathtub got stuck in the toaster, and she had to spend an hour putting down newspaper and mopping up, and only had half an hour to dress for a dinner they were going to. "Really I looked like the wrath of God," said Sally. These days she finds herself repeating to Marylynn many of the things Ed says: the stupid things. Marylynn is the only one of Sally's friends she has confided in to this extent.

"Ed is cute as a button," Marylynn said. "In fact, he's just like a button: he's so bright and shiny. If he were mine, I'd get him bronzed and keep him on the mantelpiece."

Marylynn is even better than Sally at concocting formulations for Ed's particular brand of stupidity, which can irritate Sally: coming from herself, this sort of comment appears to her indulgent and loving, but from Marylynn it borders on the patronizing. So then she sticks up for Ed, who is by no means stupid about everything. When you narrow it down, there's only one area of life he's hopeless about. The rest of the time he's intelligent enough, some even say brilliant: otherwise, how could he be so successful?

Ed is a heart man, one of the best, and the irony of this is not lost on Sally: who could possibly know less about the workings of hearts, real hearts, the kind symbolized by red satin surrounded by lace and topped by pink bows, than Ed? Hearts with arrows in them. At the same time, the fact that he's a heart man is a large part of his allure. Women corner him on sofas, trap him in bay-windows at cocktail parties, mutter to him in confidential voices at dinner parties. They behave this way right in front of Sally, under her very nose, as if she's invisible, and Ed lets them do it. This would never happen if he were in banking or construction.

As it is, everywhere he goes he is beset by sirens. They want him to fix their hearts. Each of them seems to have a little something wrong

—a murmur, a whisper. Or they faint a lot and want him to tell them why. This is always what the conversations are about, according to Ed, and Sally believes it. Once she'd wanted it herself, that mirage. What had she invented for him, in the beginning? A heavy heart, that beat too hard after meals. And he'd been so sweet, looking at her with those stunned brown eyes of his, as if her heart were the genuine topic, listening to her gravely as if he'd never heard any of this twaddle before, advising her to drink less coffee. And she'd felt such triumph, to have carried off her imposture, pried out of him that miniscule token of concern.

Thinking back on this incident makes her uneasy, now that she's seen her own performance repeated so many times, including the hand placed lightly on the heart, to call attention of course to the breasts. Some of these women have been within inches of getting Ed to put his head down on their chests, right there in Sally's living room. Watching all this out of the corners of her eyes while serving the liqueurs, Sally feels the Aztec rise within her. *Trouble with your heart? Get it removed*, she thinks. *Then you'll have no more problems.*

Sometimes Sally worries that she's a nothing, the way Marylynn was before she got a divorce and a job. But Sally isn't a nothing; therefore, she doesn't need a divorce to stop being one. And she's always had a job of some sort; in fact she has one now. Luckily Ed has no objection; he doesn't have much of an objection to anything she does.

Her job is supposed to be full-time, but in effect it's part-time, because Sally can take a lot of the work away and do it at home, and, as she says, with one arm tied behind her back. When Sally is being ornery, when she's playing the dull wife of a fascinating heart man— she does this with people she can't be bothered with—she says she works in a bank, nothing important. Then she watches their eyes dismiss her. When, on the other hand, she's trying to impress, she says she's in P.R. In reality she runs the in-house organ for a trust company, a medium-sized one. This is a thin magazine, nicely printed, which is supposed to make the employees feel that some of the boys are doing worthwhile things out there and are human beings as well. It's still the boys, though the few women in anything resembling key positions are wheeled out regularly, bloused and suited and smiling brightly, with what they hope will come across as confidence rather than aggression.

This is the latest in a string of such jobs Sally has held over the years: comfortable enough jobs that engage only half of her cogs and wheels, and that end up leading nowhere. Technically she's second-in-command: over her is a man who wasn't working out in management, but who couldn't be fired because his wife was related to the chairman of the board. He goes out for long alcoholic lunches and plays a lot of golf, and Sally runs the show. This man gets the official credit for everything Sally does right, but the senior executives in the company take Sally aside when no one is looking and tell her what a great gal she is and what a whiz she is at holding up her end.

The real pay-off for Sally, though, is that her boss provides her with an endless supply of anecdotes. She dines out on stories about his dim-wittedness and pomposity, his lobotomized suggestions about what the two of them should cook up for the magazine; *the organ*, as she says he always calls it. "He says we need some fresh blood to perk up the organ," Sally says, and the heart men grin at her. "He actually said that?" Talking like this about her boss would be reckless—you never know what might get back to him, with the world as small as it is—if Sally were afraid of losing her job, but she isn't. There's an unspoken agreement between her and this man: they both know that if she goes, he goes, because who else would put up with him? Sally might angle for his job, if she were stupid enough to disregard his family connections, if she coveted the trappings of power. But she's just fine where she is. Jokingly, she says she's reached her level of incompetence. She says she suffers from fear of success.

Her boss is white-haired, slender, and tanned, and looks like an English gin ad. Despite his vapidity he's outwardly distinguished, she allows him that. In truth she pampers him outrageously, indulges him, covers up for him at every turn, though she stops short of behaving like a secretary: she doesn't bring him coffee. They both have a secretary who does that anyway. The one time he made a pass at her, when he came in from lunch visibly reeling, Sally was kind about it.

Occasionally, though not often, Sally has to travel in connection with her job. She's sent off to places like Edmonton, where they have a branch. She interviews the boys at the middle and senior levels; they have lunch, and the boys talk about ups and downs in oil or the slump in the real-estate market. Then she gets taken on tours of shopping plazas under construction. It's always windy, and grit blows into her face. She comes back to home base and writes a piece on the youthfulness and vitality of the West.

She teases Ed, while she packs, saying she's going off for a rendezvous with a dashing financier or two. Ed isn't threatened; he tells her to enjoy herself, and she hugs him and tells him how much she will miss him. He's so dumb it doesn't occur to him she might not be joking. In point of fact, it would have been quite possible for Sally to have had an affair, or at least a one- or two-night stand, on several of these occasions: she knows when those chalk lines are being drawn, when she's being dared to step over them. But she isn't interested in having an affair with anyone but Ed.

She doesn't eat much on the planes; she doesn't like the food. But on the return trip, she invariably saves the pre-packaged parts of the meal, the cheese in its plastic wrap, the miniature chocolate bar, the bag of pretzels. She ferrets them away in her purse. She thinks of them as supplies, that she may need if she gets stuck in a strange airport, if they have to change course because of snow or fog, for instance. All kinds of things could happen, although they never have. When she gets home she takes the things from her purse and throws them out.

Outside the window Ed straightens up and wipes his earth-smeared hands down the sides of his pants. He begins to turn, and Sally moves back from the window so he won't see that she's watching. She doesn't like it to be too obvious. She shifts her attention to the sauce: it's in the second stage of a *sauce suprême*, which will make all the difference to the chicken. When Sally was learning this sauce, her cooking instructor quoted one of the great chefs, to the effect that the chicken was merely a canvas. He meant as in painting, but Sally, in an undertone to the woman next to her, turned it around. "Mine's canvas anyway, sauce or no sauce," or words to that effect.

Gourmet cooking was the third night course Sally has taken. At the moment she's on her fifth, which is called *Forms of Narrative Fiction*. It's half reading and half writing assignments—the instructor doesn't believe you can understand an art form without at least trying it yourself—and Sally purports to be enjoying it. She tells her friends she takes night courses to keep her brain from atrophying, and her friends find this amusing: whatever else may become of Sally's brain, they say, they don't see atrophying as an option. Sally knows better, but in any case there's always room for improvement. She may have begun taking the courses in the belief that this would make her more interesting to Ed, but she soon gave up on that idea: she appears to be neither more nor less interesting to Ed now than she was before.

Most of the food for tonight is already made. Sally tries to be well organized: the overflowing Jacuzzi was an aberration. The cold watercress soup with walnuts is chilling in the refrigerator, the chocolate mousse ditto. Ed, being Ed, prefers meatloaf to sweetbreads with pine nuts, butterscotch pudding made from a package to chestnut purée topped with whipped cream. (Sally burnt her fingers peeling the chestnuts. She couldn't do it the easy way and buy it tinned.) Sally says Ed's preference for this type of food comes from being pre-programmed by hospital cafeterias when he was younger: show him a burned sausage and a scoop of instant mashed potatoes and he salivates. So it's only for company that she can unfurl her *boeuf en daube* and her salmon *en papillote*, spread them forth to be savoured and praised.[6]

What she likes best about these dinners though is setting the table,

6. *boeuf en daube*: braised beef, *en papillote*: baked in paper.

deciding who will sit where and, when she's feeling mischievous, even what they are likely to say. Then she can sit and listen to them say it. Occasionally she prompts a little.

Tonight will not be very challenging, since it's only the heart men and their wives, and Marylynn, whom Sally hopes will dilute them. The heart men are forbidden to talk shop at Sally's dinner table, but they do it anyway. "Not what you really want to listen to while you're eating," says Sally. "All those tubes and valves." Privately she thinks they're a conceited lot, all except Ed. She can't resist needling them from time to time.

"I mean," she said to one of the leading surgeons, "basically it's just an exalted form of dress-making, don't you think?"

"Come again?" said the surgeon, smiling. The heart men think Sally is one hell of a tease.

"It's really just cutting and sewing, isn't it?" Sally murmured. The surgeon laughed.

"There's more to it than that," Ed said, unexpectedly, solemnly.

"What more, Ed?" said the surgeon. "You could say there's a lot of embroidery, but that's in the billing." He chuckled at himself.

Sally held her breath. She could hear Ed's verbal thought processes lurching into gear. He was delectable.

"Good judgement," Ed said. His earnestness hit the table like a wet fish. The surgeon hastily downed his wine.

Sally smiled. This was supposed to be a reprimand to her, she knew, for not taking things seriously enough. *Oh, come on, Ed,* she could say. But she knows also, most of the time, when to keep her trap shut. She should have a light-up JOKE sign on her forehead, so Ed would be able to tell the difference.

The heart men do well. Most of them appear to be doing better than Ed, but that's only because they have, on the whole, more expensive tastes and fewer wives. Sally can calculate these things and she figures Ed is about par.

These days there's much talk about advanced technologies, which Sally tries to keep up on, since they interest Ed. A few years ago the heart men got themselves a new facility. Ed was so revved up that he told Sally about it, which was unusual for him. A week later Sally said she would drop by the hospital at the end of the day and pick Ed up and take him out for dinner; she didn't feel like cooking, she said. Really she wanted to check out the facility; she likes to check out anything that causes the line on Ed's excitement chart to move above level.

At first Ed said he was tired, that when the day came to an end he didn't want to prolong it. But Sally wheedled and was respectful, and finally Ed took her to see his new gizmo. It was in a cramped, darkened room with an examining table in it. The thing itself looked like a television screen hooked up to some complicated hardware. Ed said that they could wire a patient up and bounce sound waves off the heart and pick up the echoes, and they would get a picture on the screen, an actual picture, of the heart in motion. It was a thousand times better than an electrocardiogram, he said: they could see the faults, the thickenings and cloggings, much more clearly.

"Colour?" said Sally.

"Black and white," said Ed.

Then Sally was possessed by a desire to see her own heart, in motion, in black and white, on the screen. At the dentist's she always wants to see the X-rays of her teeth, too, solid and glittering in her cloudy head. "Do it," she said, "I want to see how it works," and though this was the kind of thing Ed would ordinarily evade or tell her she was being silly about, he didn't need much persuading. He was fascinated by the thing himself, and he wanted to show it off.

He checked to make sure there was nobody real booked for the room. Then he told Sally to slip out of her clothes, the top half, brassière and all. He gave her a paper gown and turned his back modestly while she slipped it on, as if he didn't see her body every night of the week. He attached electrodes to her, the ankles and one wrist, and turned a switch and fiddled with the dials. Really a technician was supposed to do this, he told her, but he knew how to run the machine himself. He was good with small appliances.

Sally lay prone on the table, feeling strangely naked. "What do I do?" she said.

"Just lie there," said Ed. He came over to her and tore a hole in the paper gown, above her left breast. Then he started running a probe over her skin. It was wet and slippery and cold, and felt like the roller on a roll-on deodorant.

"There," he said, and Sally turned her head. On the screen was a large grey object, like a giant fig, paler in the middle, a dark line running down the centre. The sides moved in and out; two wings fluttered in it, like an uncertain moth's.

"That's it?" said Sally dubiously. Her heart looked so insubstantial, like a bag of gelatin, something that would melt, fade, disintegrate, if you squeezed it even a little.

Ed moved the probe, and they looked at the heart from the bottom, then the top. Then he stopped the frame, then changed it from a positive to a negative image. Sally began to shiver.

"That's wonderful," she said. He seemed so distant, absorbed in his machine, taking the measure of her heart, which was beating over there all by itself, detached from her, exposed and under his control.

Ed unwired her and she put on her clothes again, neutrally, as if he were actually a doctor. Nevertheless this transaction, this whole room, was sexual in a way she didn't quite understand; it was clearly a dangerous place. It was like a massage parlour, only for women. Put a batch of women in there with Ed and they would never want to come out. They'd want to stay in there while he ran his probe over their wet skins and pointed out to them the defects of their beating hearts.

"Thank you," said Sally.

Sally hears the back door open and close. She feels Ed approaching, coming through the passages of the house towards her, like a small wind or a ball of static electricity. The hair stands up on her arms. Sometimes he makes her so happy she thinks she's about to burst; other times she thinks she's about to burst anyway.

He comes into the kitchen, and she pretends not to notice. He puts his arms around her from behind, kisses her on the neck. She leans back, pressing herself into him. What they should do now is go into the bedroom (or even the living room, even the den) and make love, but it wouldn't occur to Ed to make love in the middle of the day. Sally often comes across articles in magazines about how to improve your sex life, which leave her feeling disappointed, or reminiscent: Ed is not Sally's first and only man. But she knows she shouldn't expect too much of Ed. If Ed were more experimental, more interested in variety, he would be a different kind of man altogether: slyer, more devious, more observant, harder to deal with.

As it is, Ed makes love in the same way, time after time, each movement following the others in an exact order. But it seems to satisfy him. Of course it satisfies him: you can always tell when men are satisfied. It's Sally who lies awake, afterwards, watching the pictures unroll across her closed eyes.

Sally steps away from Ed, smiles at him. "How did you make out with the women today?" she says.

"What women?" says Ed absently, going towards the sink. He knows what women.

"The ones out there, hiding in the forsythia," says Sally. "I counted at least ten. They were just waiting for a chance."

She teases him frequently about these troops of women, which follow him around everywhere, which are invisible to Ed but which she can see as plain as day.

"I bet they hang around outside the front door of the hospital," she will say, "just waiting till you come out. I bet they hide in the linen closets and jump out at you from behind, and then pretend to be lost so you'll take them by the short cut. It's the white coat that does it.

None of those women can resist the white coats. They've been conditioned by Young Doctor Kildare."[7]

"Don't be silly," says Ed today, with equanimity. Is he blushing, is he embarrassed? Sally examines his face closely, like a geologist with an aerial photograph, looking for telltale signs of mineral treasure: markings, bumps, hollows. Everything about Ed means something, though it's difficult at times to say what.

Now he's washing his hands at the sink, to get the earth off. In a minute he'll wipe them on the dish towel instead of using the hand towel the way he's supposed to. Is that complacency, in the back turned to her? Maybe there really are these hordes of women, even though she's made them up. Maybe they really do behave that way. His shoulders are slightly drawn up: is he shutting her out?

"I know what they want," she goes on. "They want to get into that little dark room of yours and climb up onto your table. They think you're delicious. They'll gobble you up. They'll chew you into tiny pieces. There won't be anything left of you at all, only a stethoscope and a couple of shoelaces."

Once Ed would have laughed at this, but today he doesn't. Maybe she's said it, or something like it, a few times too often. He smiles though, wipes his hands on the dish towel, peers into the fridge. He likes to snack.

"There's some cold roast beef," Sally says, baffled.

Sally takes the sauce off the stove and sets it aside for later: she'll do the last steps just before serving. It's only two-thirty. Ed has disappeared into the cellar, where Sally knows he will be safe for a while. She goes into her study, which used to be one of the kids' bedrooms, and sits down at her desk. The room has never been completely redecorated: there's still a bed in it, and a dressing table with a blue flowered flounce Sally helped pick out, long before the kids went off to university: "flew the coop," as Ed puts it.

Sally doesn't comment on the expression, though she would like to say that it wasn't the first coop they flew. Her house isn't even the real coop, since neither of the kids is hers. She'd hoped for a baby of her own when she married Ed, but she didn't want to force the issue. Ed didn't object to the idea, exactly, but he was neutral about it, and Sally got the feeling he'd had enough babies already. Anyway, the other two wives had babies, and look what happened to them. Since their actual fates have always been vague to Sally, she's free to imagine all kinds of things, from drug addiction to madness. Whatever it was resulted in Sally having to bring up their kids, at least from puberty onwards. The

7. A physician in a television series of the 1960s.

way it was presented by the first wife was that it was Ed's turn now. The second wife was more oblique: she said that the child wanted to spend some time with her father. Sally was left out of both these equations, as if the house wasn't a place she lived in, not really, so she couldn't be expected to have any opinion.

Considering everything, she hasn't done badly. She likes the kids and tries to be a friend to them, since she can hardly pretend to be a mother. She describes the three of them as having an easy relationship. Ed wasn't around much for the kids, but it's him they want approval from, not Sally; it's him they respect. Sally is more like a confederate, helping them get what they want from Ed.

When the kids were younger, Sally used to play Monopoly with them, up at the summer place in Muskoka Ed owned then but has since sold. Ed would play too, on his vacations and on the weekends when he could make it up. These games would all proceed along the same lines. Sally would have an initial run of luck and would buy up everything she had a chance at. She didn't care whether it was classy real estate, like Boardwalk or Park Place, or those dingy little houses on the other side of the tracks; she would even buy train stations, which the kids would pass over, preferring to save their cash reserves for better investments. Ed, on the other hand, would plod along, getting a little here, a little there. Then, when Sally was feeling flush, she would blow her money on next-to-useless luxuries such as the electric light company; and when the kids started to lose, as they invariably did, Sally would lend them money at cheap rates or trade them things of her own, at a loss. Why not? She could afford it.

Ed meanwhile would be hedging his bets, building up blocks of property, sticking houses and hotels on them. He preferred the middle range, respectable streets but not flashy. Sally would land on his spaces and have to shell out hard cash. Ed never offered deals, and never accepted them. He played a lone game, and won more often than not. Then Sally would feel thwarted. She would say she guessed she lacked the killer instinct; or she would say that for herself she didn't care, because after all it was only a game, but he ought to allow the kids to win, once in a while. Ed couldn't grasp the concept of allowing other people to win. He said it would be condescending towards the children, and anyway you couldn't arrange to have a dice game turn out the way you wanted it to, since it was partly a matter of chance. If it was chance, Sally would think, why were the games so similar to one another? At the end, there would be Ed, counting up his paper cash, sorting it out into piles of bills of varying denominations, and Sally, her vast holdings dwindled to a few shoddy blocks on Baltic Avenue, doomed to foreclosure: extravagant, generous, bankrupt.

On these nights, after the kids were asleep, Sally would have two or three more rye-and-gingers than were good for her. Ed would go to bed early—winning made him satisfied and drowsy—and Sally would ramble about the house or read the endings of murder mysteries she had already read once before, and finally she would slip into bed and wake Ed up and stroke him into arousal, seeking comfort.

Sally has almost forgotten these games. Right now the kids are receding, fading like old ink; Ed on the contrary looms larger and larger, the outlines around him darkening. He's constantly developing, like a Polaroid print, new colours emerging, but the result remains the same: Ed is a surface, one she has trouble getting beneath.

"Explore your inner world," said Sally's instructor in *Forms of Narrative Fiction*, a middle-aged woman of scant fame who goes in for astrology and the Tarot pack and writes short stories, which are not published in any of the magazines Sally reads. "Then there's your outer one," Sally said afterwards, to her friends. "For instance, she should really get something done about her hair." She made this trivial and mean remark because she's fed up with her inner world; she doesn't need to explore it. In her inner world is Ed, like a doll within a Russian wooden doll, and in Ed is Ed's inner world, which she can't get at.

She takes a crack at it anyway: Ed's inner world is a forest, which looks something like the bottom part of their ravine lot, but without the fence. He wanders around in there, among the trees, not heading in any special direction. Every once in a while he comes upon a strange-looking plant, a sickly plant choked with weeds and briars. Ed kneels, clears a space around it, does some pruning, a little skillful snipping and cutting, props it up. The plant revives, flushes with health, sends out a grateful red blossom. Ed continues on his way. Or it may be a conked-out squirrel, which he restores with a drop from his flask of magic elixir. At set intervals an angel appears, bringing him food. It's always meatloaf. That's fine with Ed, who hardly notices what he eats, but the angel is getting tired of being an angel. Now Sally begins thinking about the angel: why are its wings frayed and dingy grey around the edges, why is it looking so withered and frantic? This is where all Sally's attempts to explore Ed's inner world end up.

She knows she thinks about Ed too much. She knows she should stop. She knows she shouldn't ask, "Do you still love me?" in the plaintive tone that sets even her own teeth on edge. All it achieves is that Ed shakes his head, as if not understanding why she would ask this, and pats her hand. "Sally, Sally," he says, and everything proceeds as usual; except for the dread that seeps into things, the most ordinary things, such as rearranging the chairs and changing the burntout lightbulbs. But what is it she's afraid of? She has what they call everything: Ed, their wonderful house on a ravine lot, something she's always wanted. (But the hill is jungly, and the house is made of ice. It's held together only by Sally, who sits in the middle of it, working on a puzzle.

The puzzle is Ed. If she should ever solve it, if she should ever fit the
last cold splinter into place, the house will melt and flow away down
the hill, and then . . .) It's a bad habit, fooling around with her head
this way. It does no good. She knows that if she could quit she'd be
happier. She ought to be able to: she's given up smoking.

She needs to concentrate her attention on other things. This is the
real reason for the night courses, which she picks almost at random, to
coincide with the evenings Ed isn't in. He has meetings, he's on the
boards of charities, he has trouble saying no. She runs the courses past
herself, mediaeval history, cooking, anthropology, hoping her mind will
snag on something; she's even taken a course in geology, which was
fascinating, she told her friends, all that magma. That's just it: everything is fascinating, but nothing enters her. She's always a star pupil,
she does well on the exams and impresses the teachers, for which she
despises them. She is familiar with her brightness, her techniques; she's
surprised other people are still taken in by them.

*Forms of Narrative Fiction* started out the same way. Sally was full
of good ideas, brimming with helpful suggestions. The workshop part
of it was anyway just like a committee meeting, and Sally knew how
to run those, from behind, without seeming to run them: she'd done
it lots of times at work. Bertha, the instructor, told Sally she had a vivid
imagination and a lot of untapped creative energy. "No wonder she
never gets anywhere, with a name like Bertha," Sally said, while having
coffee afterwards with two of the other night-coursers. "It goes with her
outfits, though." (Bertha sports the macramé look, with health-food san-
dals and bulky-knit sweaters and hand-weave skirts that don't do a thing
for her square figure, and too many Mexican rings on her hands, which
she doesn't wash often enough.) Bertha goes in for assignments, which
she calls learning by doing. Sally likes assignments: she likes things that
can be completed and then discarded, and for which she gets marks.

The first thing Bertha assigned was The Epic. They read *The Odyssey*
(selected passages, in translation, with a plot summary of the rest); then
they poked around in James Joyce's *Ulysses*, to see how Joyce had
adapted the epic form to the modern-day novel. Bertha had them keep
a Toronto notebook, in which they had to pick out various spots around
town as the ports of call in *The Odyssey*, and say why they had chosen
them. The notebooks were read out loud in class, and it was a scream
to see who had chosen what for Hades. (The Mount Pleasant Cemetery,
McDonald's, where, if you eat the forbidden food, you never get back
to the land of the living, the University Club with its dead ancestral
souls, and so forth.) Sally's was the hospital, of course; she had no
difficulty with the trench filled with blood, and she put the ghosts in
wheelchairs.

After that they did The Ballad, and read gruesome accounts of murders and betrayed love. Bertha played them tapes of wheezy old men

singing traditionally, in the Doric mode, and assigned a newspaper scrapbook, in which you had to clip and paste up-to-the-minute equivalents. The *Sun* was the best newspaper for these. The fiction that turned out to go with this kind of plot was the kind Sally liked anyway, and she had no difficulty concocting a five-page murder mystery, complete with revenge.

But now they are on Folk Tales and the Oral Tradition, and Sally is having trouble. This time, Bertha wouldn't let them read anything. Instead she read to them, in a voice, Sally said, that was like a gravel truck and was not conducive to reverie. Since it was the Oral Tradition, they weren't even allowed to take notes; Bertha said the original hearers of these stories couldn't read, so the stories were memorized. "To re-create the atmosphere," said Bertha, "I should turn out the lights. These stories were always told at night." "To make them creepier?" someone offered. "No," said Bertha. "In the days, they worked." She didn't do that, though she did make them sit in a circle.

"You should have seen us," Sally said afterwards to Ed, "sitting in a circle, listening to fairy stories. It was just like kindergarten. Some of them even had their mouths open. I kept expecting her to say, 'If you need to go, put up your hand.'" She was meaning to be funny, to amuse Ed with this account of Bertha's eccentricity and the foolish appearance of the students, most of them middle-aged, sitting in a circle as if they had never grown up at all. She was also intending to belittle the course, just slightly. She always did this with her night courses, so Ed wouldn't get the idea there was anything in her life that was even remotely as important as he was. But Ed didn't seem to need this amusement or this belittlement. He took her information earnestly, gravely, as if Bertha's behaviour was, after all, only the procedure of a specialist. No one knew better than he did that the procedures of specialists often looked bizarre or incomprehensible to onlookers. "She probably has her reasons," was all he would say.

The first stories Bertha read them, for warm-ups ("No memorizing for *her*," said Sally), were about princes who got amnesia and forgot about their true loves and married girls their mothers had picked out for them. Then they had to be rescued, with the aid of magic. The stories didn't say what happened to the women the princes had already married, though Sally wondered about it. Then Bertha read them another story, and this time they were supposed to remember the features that stood out for them and write a five-page transposition, set in the present and cast in the realistic mode. ("In other words," said Bertha, "no real magic.") They couldn't use the Universal Narrator, however: they had done that in their Ballad assignment. This time they had to choose a point of view. It could be the point of view of anyone or anything in the story, but they were limited to one only. The story she was about to read, she said, was a variant of the Bluebeard motif, much earlier than Perrault's sentimental rewriting of it. In Perrault, said Bertha, the girl has to be rescued by her brothers; but in the earlier version things were quite otherwise.[8]

This is what Bertha read, as far as Sally can remember:

There were once three young sisters. One day a beggar with a large basket on his back came to the door and asked for some bread. The eldest sister brought him some, but no sooner had she touched him than she was compelled to jump into his basket, for the beggar was really a wizard in disguise. ("So much for United Appeal," Sally murmured. "She should have said, 'I gave at the office.'") The wizard carried her away to his house in the forest, which was large and richly furnished. "Here you will be happy with me, my darling," said the wizard, "for you will have everything your heart could desire."

This lasted for a few days. Then the wizard gave the girl an egg and a bunch of keys. "I must go away on a journey," he said, "and I am leaving the house in your charge. Preserve this egg for me, and carry it about with you everywhere; for a great misfortune will follow from its loss. The keys open every room in the house. You may go into each of them and enjoy what you find there, but do not go into the small room at the top of the house, on pain of death." The girl promised, and the wizard disappeared.

At first the girl contented herself with exploring the rooms, which contained many treasures. But finally her curiosity would not let her alone. She sought out the smallest key, and, with beating heart, opened the little door at the top of the house. Inside it was a large basin full of blood, within which were the bodies of many women, which had been cut to pieces; nearby were a chopping block and an axe. In her horror, she let go of the egg which fell into the basin of blood. In vain did she try to wipe away the stain: every time she succeeded in removing it, back it would come.

The wizard returned, and in a stern voice asked for the egg and the keys. When he saw the egg, he knew at once she had disobeyed him and gone into the forbidden room. "Since you have gone into the room against my will," he said, "you shall go back into it against your own." Despite her pleas he threw her down, dragged her by the hair into the little room, hacked her into pieces and threw her body into the basin with the others.

Then he went for the second girl, who fared no better than her sister. But the third was clever and wily. As soon as the wizard had gone, she set the egg on a shelf, out of harm's way, and then went immediately and opened the forbidden door. Imagine her distress when she saw the cut-up bodies of her two beloved sisters; but she set the parts in order,

---

8. What follows is an abbreviated version of the Grimms' "Fitcher's Bird" (pp. 148–51, above).

and they joined together and her sisters stood up and moved, and were living and well. They embraced each other, and the third sister hid the other two in a cupboard.

When the wizard returned he at once asked for the egg. This time it was spotless. "You have passed the test," he said to the third sister. "You shall be my bride." ("And second prize," said Sally, to herself this time, "is *two* weeks in Niagara Falls.") The wizard no longer had any power over her, and had to do whatever she asked. There was more, about how the wizard met his come-uppance and was burned to death, but Sally already knew which features stood out for her.

At first she thought the most important thing in the story was the forbidden room. What would she put in the forbidden room, in her present-day realistic version? Certainly not chopped-up women. It wasn't that they were too unrealistic, but they were certainly too sick, as well as being too obvious. She wanted to do something more clever. She thought it might be a good idea to have the curious woman open the door and find nothing there at all, but after mulling it over she set this notion aside. It would leave her with the problem of why the wizard would have a forbidden room in which he kept nothing.

That was the way she was thinking right after she got the assignment, which was a full two weeks ago. So far she's written nothing. The great temptation is to cast herself in the role of the cunning heroine, but again it's too predictable. And Ed certainly isn't the wizard; he's no-where near sinister enough. If Ed were the wizard, the room would contain a forest, some ailing plants and feeble squirrels, and Ed himself, fixing them up; but then, if it were Ed the room wouldn't even be locked, and there would be no story.

Now, as she sits at her desk, fiddling with her felt-tip pen, it comes to Sally that the intriguing thing about the story, the thing she should fasten on, is the egg. Why an egg? From the night course in Comparative Folklore she took four years ago, she remembers that the egg can be a fertility symbol, or a necessary object in African spells, or something the world hatched out of. Maybe in this story it's a symbol of virginity, and that is why the wizard requires it unbloodied. Women with dirty eggs get murdered, those with clean ones get married.

But this isn't useful either. The concept is so outmoded. Sally doesn't see how she can transpose it into real life without making it ridiculous, unless she sets the story in, for instance, an immigrant Portuguese family, and what would she know about that?

Sally opens the drawer of her desk and hunts around in it for her nail file. As she's doing this, she gets the brilliant idea of writing the story from the point of view of the egg. Other people will do the other things: the clever girl, the wizard, the two blundering sisters, who weren't smart enough to lie, and who will have problems afterwards, because of the thin red lines running all over their bodies, from where their parts joined together. But no one will think of the egg. How does it feel, to be the innocent and passive cause of so much misfortune?

(Ed isn't the Bluebeard: Ed is the egg. Ed Egg, blank and pristine and lovely. Stupid, too. Boiled, probably. Sally smiles fondly.)

But how can there be a story from the egg's point of view, if the egg is so closed and unaware? Sally ponders this, doodling on her pad of lined paper. Then she resumes the search for her nail file. Already it's time to begin getting ready for her dinner party. She can sleep on the problem of the egg and finish the assignment tomorrow, which is Sunday. It's due on Monday, but Sally's mother used to say she was a whiz at getting things done at the last minute.

After painting her nails with *Nuit Magique*,[9] Sally takes a bath, eating her habitual toasted English muffin while she lies in the tub. She begins to dress, dawdling; she has plenty of time. She hears Ed coming up out of the cellar; then she hears him in the bathroom, which he has entered from the hall door. Sally goes in through the other door, still in her slip. Ed is standing at the sink with his shirt off, shaving. On the weekends he leaves it until necessary, or until Sally tells him he's too scratchy.

Sally slides her hands around his waist, nuzzling against his naked back. He has very smooth skin, for a man. Sally smiles to herself: she can't stop thinking of him as an egg.

"Mmm," says Ed. It could be appreciation, or the answer to a question Sally hasn't asked and he hasn't heard, or just an acknowledgement that she's there.

"Don't you ever wonder what I think about?" Sally says. She's said this more than once, in bed or at the dinner table, after dessert. She stands behind him, watching the swaths the razor cuts in the white of his face, looking at her own face reflected in the mirror, just the eyes visible above his naked shoulder. Ed, lathered, is Assyrian, sterner than usual; or a frost-covered Arctic explorer; or demi-human, a white-bearded forest mutant. He scrapes away at himself, methodically destroying the illusion.

"But I already know what you think about," says Ed.

"How?" Sally says, taken aback.

"You're always telling me," Ed says, with what might be resignation or sadness; or maybe this is only a simple statement of fact.

Sally is relieved. If that's all he's going on, she's safe.

Marylynn arrives half an hour early, her pearl-coloured Porsche leading two men in a delivery truck up the driveway. The men install the keyhole desk, while Marylynn supervises: it looks, in the alcove, exactly

9. Magic Night (French).

as Marylynn has said it would, and Sally is delighted. She sits at it to write the cheque. Then she and Marylynn go into the kitchen, where Sally is finishing up her sauce, and Sally pours them each a Kir. She's glad Marylynn is here: it will keep her from dithering, as she tends to do just before people arrive. Though it's only the heart men, she's still a bit nervous. Ed is more likely to notice when things are wrong than when they're exactly right.

Marylynn sits at the kitchen table, one arm draped over the chair-back, her chin on the other hand; she's in soft grey which makes her hair look silver, and Sally feels once again how banal it is to have ordinary dark hair like her own, however well-cut, however shiny. It's the confidence she envies, the negligence. Marylynn doesn't seem to be trying at all, ever.

"Guess what Ed said today?" Sally says.

Marylynn leans further forward. "What?" she says, with the eagerness of one joining in a familiar game.

"He said, 'Some of these femininists go too far,' " Sally reports. " 'Femininists.' Isn't that sweet?"

Marylynn holds the pause too long, and Sally has a sudden awful thought: maybe Marylynn thinks she's showing off, about Ed. Marylynn has always said she's not ready for another marriage yet; still, Sally should watch herself, not rub her nose in it. But then Marylynn laughs indulgently, and Sally, relieved, joins in.

"Ed is unbelievable," says Marylynn. "You should pin his mittens to his sleeves when he goes out in the morning."

"He shouldn't be let out alone," says Sally.

"You should get him a seeing-eye dog," says Marylynn, "to bark at women."

"Why?" says Sally, still laughing but alert now, the cold beginning at the ends of her fingers. Maybe Marylynn knows something she doesn't; maybe the house is beginning to crumble, after all.

"Because he can't see them coming," says Marylynn. "That's what you're always telling me."

She sips her Kir; Sally stirs the sauce. "I bet he thinks I'm a feminist," says Marylynn.

"You?" says Sally. "Never." She would like to add that Ed has given no indication of thinking anything at all about Marylynn, but she doesn't. She doesn't want to take the risk of hurting her feelings.

The wives of the heart men admire Sally's sauce; the heart men talk shop, all except Walter Morly, who is good at by-passes. He's sitting beside Marylynn, and paying far too much attention to her for Sally's comfort. Mrs. Morly is at the other end of the table, not saying much of anything, which Marylynn appears not to notice. She keeps on talking to Walter about St. Lucia, where they've both been.

So after dinner, when Sally has herded them all into the living room for coffee and liqueurs, she takes Marylynn by the elbow. "Ed hasn't seen our desk yet," she says, "not up close. Take him away and give him your lecture on nineteenth-century antiques. Show him all the pigeon-holes. Ed loves pigeon-holes." Ed appears not to get this.

Marylynn knows exactly what Sally is up to. "Don't worry," she says, "I won't rape Dr. Morly; the poor creature would never survive the shock," but she allows herself to be shunted off to the side with Ed.

Sally moves from guest to guest, smiling, making sure everything is in order. Although she never looks directly, she's always conscious of Ed's presence in the room, any room; she perceives him as a shadow, a shape seen dimly at the edge of her field of vision, recognizable by the outline. She likes to know where he is, that's all. Some people are on their second cup of coffee. She walks towards the alcove: they must have finished with the desk by now.

But they haven't, they're still in there. Marylynn is bending forward, one hand on the veneer. Ed is standing too close to her, and as Sally comes up behind them she sees his left arm, held close to his side, the back of it pressed against Marylynn, her shimmering upper thigh, her ass to be exact. Marylynn does not move away.

It's a split second, and then Ed sees Sally and the hand is gone; there it is, on top of the desk, reaching for a liqueur glass.

"Marylynn needs more Tia Maria," he says. "I just told her that people who drink a little now and again live longer." His voice is even, his face is as level as ever, a flat plain with no signposts.

Marylynn laughs. "I once had a dentist who I swear drilled tiny holes in my teeth, so he could fix them later," she says.

Sally sees Ed's hand outstretched towards her, holding the empty glass. She takes it, smiling, and turns away. There's a roaring sound at the back of her head; blackness appears around the edges of the picture she is seeing, like a television screen going dead. She walks into the kitchen and puts her cheek against the refrigerator and her arms around it, as far as they will go. She remains that way, hugging it; it hums steadily, with a sound like comfort. After a while she lets go of it and touches her hair, and walks back into the living room with the filled glass.

Marylynn is over by the french doors, talking with Walter Morly. Ed is standing by himself, in front of the fireplace, one arm on the mantelpiece, his left hand out of sight in his pocket.

Sally goes to Marylynn, hands her the glass. "Is that enough?" she says.

Marylynn is unchanged. "Thanks, Sally," she says, and goes on listening to Walter, who has dragged out his usual piece of mischief: some day, when they've perfected it, he says, all hearts will be plastic, and this will be a vast improvement on the current model. It's an obscure form of flirtation. Marylynn winks at Sally, to show that she knows he's tedious. Sally, after a pause, winks back.

She looks over at Ed, who is staring off into space, like a robot which has been parked and switched off. Now she isn't sure whether she really saw what she thought she saw. Even if she did, what does it mean? Maybe it's just that Ed, in a wayward intoxicated moment, put his hand on the nearest buttock, and Marylynn refrained from a shriek or a flinch out of good breeding or the desire not to offend him. Things like this have happened to Sally.

Or it could mean something more sinister: a familiarity between them, an understanding. If this is it, Sally has been wrong about Ed, for years, forever. Her version of Ed is not something she's perceived but something that's been perpetrated on her, by Ed himself, for reasons of his own. Possibly Ed is not stupid. Possibly he's enormously clever. She thinks of moment after moment when this cleverness, this cunning, would have shown itself if it were there, but didn't. She has watched him so carefully. She remembers playing Pick Up Sticks, with the kids, Ed's kids, years ago: how if you moved one stick in the tangle, even slightly, everything else moved also.

She won't say anything to him. She can't say anything: she can't afford to be wrong, or to be right either. She goes back into the kitchen and begins to scrape the plates. This is unlike her—usually she sticks right with the party until it's over—and after a while Ed wanders out. He stands silently, watching her. Sally concentrates on the scraping: dollops of *sauce suprême* slide into the plastic bag, shreds of lettuce, rice, congealed and lumpy. What is left of her afternoon.

"What are you doing out here?" Ed asks at last.

"Scraping the plates," Sally says, cheerful, neutral. "I just thought I'd get a head start on tidying up."

"Leave it," says Ed. "The woman can do that in the morning." That's how he refers to Mrs. Rudge, although she's been with them for three years now: *the woman*. And Mrs. Bird before her, as though they are interchangeable. This has never bothered Sally before. "Go on out there and have a good time."

Sally puts down the spatula, wipes her hands on the hand towel, puts her arms around him, holds on tighter than she should. Ed pats her shoulder. "What's up?" he says; then, "Sally, Sally." If she looks up, she will see him shaking his head a little, as if he doesn't know what to do about her. She doesn't look up.

Ed has gone to bed. Sally roams the house, fidgeting with the debris left by the party. She collects empty glasses, picks up peanuts from the rug. After a while she realizes that she's down on her knees, looking under a chair, and she's forgotten what for. She goes upstairs, creams off her make-up, does her teeth, undresses in the darkened bedroom and slides into bed beside Ed, who is breathing deeply as if asleep. *As if.*

   Sally lies in bed with her eyes closed. What she sees is her own heart, in black and white, beating with that insubstantial moth-like flutter, a ghostly heart, torn out of her and floating in space, an animated valentine with no colour. It will go on and on forever; she has no control over it. But now she's seeing the egg, which is not small and cold and white and inert but larger than a real egg and golden pink, resting in a nest of brambles, glowing softly as though there's something red and hot inside it. It's almost pulsing; Sally is afraid of it. As she looks it darkens: rose-red, crimson. This is something the story left out, Sally thinks: the egg is alive, and one day it will hatch. But what will come out of it?

Secret room - Ed's secret life
           ↳ Women?
Egg - Sally? - naïve (innocent)
         - being carried along
            for ride unknowingly.

# INTRODUCTION:
# Hansel and Gretel

Food—its presence and its absence—shapes the social world of fairy tales in profound ways. It is not at all uncommon for a peasant hero, faced with three wishes, to ask first for a plate of meat and potatoes, or to be so distracted by hunger that he yearns out loud for a sausage while contemplating the limitless possibilities before him. "What shall I command?" asks the hero of a Greek tale when told he can have anything he wants. Without a moment's hesitation, he responds by asking for "Food to eat!"[1] Wish-fulfillment in fairy tales often has more to do with the stomach than with the heart. As Robert Darnton has pointed out in his discussion of the origins of fairy tales in an adult peasant culture, "To eat one's fill, eat until the exhaustion of the appetite (*manger à sa faim*), was the principal pleasure that the peasants dangled before their imaginations, and one that they rarely realized in their lives."[2] The same could be said about small children. While many folktales take us into the rugged and often brutal world of peasant life, where survival depends on getting your next meal, fairy tales often take us squarely into the household, where everyone seems to be anxious both about what's for dinner and about who's for dinner. The peasants of folktales may have to worry about famines, but children in fairy tales live perpetually under the double threat of starvation and cannibalism.

"I've got to kill you so that I can have something to eat!" a woman cries out in desperation to her two daughters in the Grimms' story "The Children of Famine." Happily, this tale cannot be found between the covers of most standard editions of the Grimms' *Nursery and Household Tales*, but that it was ever included at all is telling, for it makes clear that the threat of being devoured was not seen as arising from supernatural monsters alone. The sheer number of cannibalistic fiends in fairy tales is impressive. Giants, ogres, stepmothers, cooks, witches, and mothers-in-law all seem driven by a voracious appetite for human fare,

Bracketed page numbers refer to this Norton Critical Edition.
1. "The Grateful Animals and the Talisman," in *Modern Greek Folktales*, comp. and trans. R. M. Dawkins (Oxford: Clarendon Press, 1953) 42.
2. Robert Darnton, "Peasants Tell Tales: The Meaning of Mother Goose," in *The Great Cat Massacre and Other Episodes in French Cultural History* (New York: Random House, Vintage Books, 1985) 34.

for the flesh and blood (in some cases the liver and lungs will do) of the weak and vulnerable. The victims, both potential and real, are often children: a boy is chopped up and cooked into a stew eagerly devoured by his father ("The Juniper Tree"); siblings are served up to their grandmother in a sauce Robert (Perrault's "Sleeping Beauty in the Wood"); and a child is fattened up for a feast of human flesh ("Hansel and Gretel").

Like many fairy tales, the Grimms' "Hansel and Gretel" is set in a time of famine. While the parents of Perrault's Tom Thumb take their children into the woods because they cannot bear to see them starve to death, the stepmother of Hansel and Gretel is driven to abandon the children by brutish self-interest. She urges her husband to lead the children deep into the forest and is glad to be "rid of them," for their needs jeopardize her own survival. Some critics have explained the grotesque cruelty of the children's stepmother by pointing to the harsh social realities of an earlier age, in which "wicked stepmothers were not a subject of fantasy any more than castout children."[3] In their view, "Hansel and Gretel" does not so much stage a child's fears about starvation, exposure, and abandonment as mirror the hard facts of the premodern era.

A look at the version of "Hansel and Gretel" first recorded by the Grimms reveals that the children's cruel stepmother was in fact a creation of Wilhelm Grimm's fantasy. The tale, as the brothers first heard it, featured a biological mother who conspires with her husband to abandon the children. To be sure, Wilhelm Grimm may have made the change in order to align the tale with the realities of nineteenth-century family life, but, more likely, he transformed the mother into a stepmother simply because he could not bear to pass on stories about mothers so intent on surviving a famine that they are willing to sacrifice their own children.

The villainous stepmother in "Hansel and Gretel" reemerges in the woods as a monster equipped with powers far more formidable than those she exercised at home. In the woods, the children are no longer pitted against a hostile, human adversary, but locked in combat with a superhuman opponent armed with daunting powers. Just what is at stake in the conflict between children and witch? The Grimms strained their verbal resources in representing the cannibalistic fiend in the forest. Originally described simply as "a witch," she grew, by the final edition of the tales, into a creature with an elaborate history:

> The old woman had only pretended to be so friendly. She was
> really a wicked witch, who lay in wait for children. She had built
> the little house of bread just to lure them inside. As soon as a child

3. Eugen Weber, "Fairies and Hard Facts: The Reality of Folktales," *Journal of the History of Ideas* 42 (1981): 94.

was in her power, she killed it, cooked it, and ate it. That was a real feast day for her. Witches have red eyes and can't see very far, but they have a keen sense of smell, like animals, and they can always tell when a human being is around. When Hansel and Gretel got near her, she laughed fiendishly and sneered: "They're mine! This time they won't get away from me!" [188]

While the stepmother at home was intent on starving the children, providing neither food nor nurturing care, the witch in the forest initially appears to be a splendidly bountiful figure, offering the children a supper of pancakes with sugar, apples, and nuts and putting them in beds so comfortable that they feel as if they are "in heaven." But it quickly becomes clear that the witch is an even more exaggerated form of maternal malice than the stepmother, for she feeds the children only in order to fatten them up for her next meal.

How do we explain the profusion of references to food in this tale of parental abandonment that ends by reuniting the children with their father? Does "Hansel and Gretel" perhaps address a child's real anxieties about starvation, abandonment, and being devoured by enacting a drama in which children are perpetually at risk but eventually delivered from want and deprivation? Or is the tale really about the oral greed, denial, and regression of the children, as Bruno Bettelheim insists? Disavowing the manifest content of the tale, Bettelheim suggests that the real problem turns on the children's "unrestrained giving in to gluttony," their "cannibalistic inclinations," and their "oral greediness."[4] For Bettelheim, the mother, who nourishes the child but who also imposes restrictions on it in the course of its development, becomes the target of the child's hostility and of a projected form of oral aggression. "Hansel and Gretel" enacts these childhood feelings of hostility to the omnipotent mother and takes revenge by showing the triumph of the powerless children over the figure who, in her role as supreme provider, is always also a withholder of nourishment.

Bettelheim cheerfully outlines the triumph of "the child" in "Hansel and Gretel": "Having overcome his oedipal difficulties, mastered his oral anxieties, and sublimated those of his cravings which cannot be satisfied realistically, and learned that wishful thinking has to be replaced by intelligent action, the child is ready to live happily again with his parents."[5] This optimistic analysis willfully ignores the fact that the children do not live happily ever after with their parents, but with their father alone. Both stepmother and witch have been eradicated in this tale that celebrates a reunion with the father who collaborated in the plot to abandon them. The tale's triumphant ending—the three do not just live happily ever after, "Their worries were over, and they lived

4. Bruno Bettelheim, *The Uses of Enchantment: The Meaning and Importance of Fairy Tales* (New York: Vintage Books, 1976) 163–64.
5. Bettelheim, *Uses*, 165.

together in perfect happiness" [190]—underscores the notion that the death of the mother eliminates the twin dreads of starvation and the fear of being devoured.

In the vast majority of variants of the tale type known as "The Children and the Ogre" (AT 327),[6] fathers are rehabilitated and reunited with their children, while mothers and stepmothers alike epitomize menacing cruelty to the bitter end. Nancy Chodorow has observed that, in psychoanalytic terms, "representations of the father relationship do not become so internalized and subject to ambivalence, repression, and splitting of good and bad aspects" as representations of the mother.[7] In fact, the father often becomes, because of the "separate" and "special" status assigned him by virtue of his traditional absence from early child-rearing, the representative of autonomy and of the public, social world. Development is thus conventionally defined in terms of growing away from the mother, who represents dependence and domesticity, and turning toward the father. "Hansel and Gretel" enacts this very process in its exclusion of the maternal component from the domestic tableau that closes the tale. The children have successfully negotiated the path from dependence to autonomy by eradicating the mother and joining forces with the father.

That ill will and evil are so often personified as adult female figures in fairy tales raises some weighty questions that challenge the notion of fairy tales as therapeutic reading for children. However satisfying the tales may seem from a child's point of view, however much they may map developmental paths endorsed by orthodox Freudians, they still perpetuate strangely inappropriate notions about what it means to live happily ever after. Jack Zipes objects to "Hansel and Gretel" on the grounds that it is a story that "rationalizes child abuse in the name of the symbolic order of the father."[8] For him, "Hansel and Gretel" should be taken at face value: it is an account of fathers who engage in abusive behavior to secure the submission of their children to a patriarchal order.

In "The Juniper Tree," a tale that can be seen as presenting the male counterpart to the female developmental trajectory mapped out in "Snow White," the stepmother is also a troublemaker *par excellence*, stirring things up and unsettling the family in an unspeakably radical fashion. At the end of the Grimms' version of the tale, she gets into real trouble for her wicked ways: "Bam! the bird dropped a millstone on her head and crushed her to death!"

6. In Antti Aarne and Stith Thompson, *The Types of the Folktale: A Classification and Bibliography* (Helsinki: Academia Scientiarum Fennica, 1961).
7. Nancy Chodorow, *The Reproduction of Mothering: Psychoanalysis and the Sociology of Gender* (Berkeley: U of California P, 1978) 97.
8. Jack Zipes, "The Rationalization of Abandonment and Abuse in Fairy Tales: The Case of Hansel and Gretel," in *Happily Ever After: Fairy Tales, Children and the Culture Industry* (New York: Routledge, 1997) 41.

With its lurid descriptions of decapitation and cannibalism, "The Juniper Tree" (also known as "My Mother Slew Me; My Father Ate Me" [AT 706]) is probably the most shocking of all fairy tales. In most versions, the central character is a boy, yet occasionally, as in the British story "The Rose-Tree" (collected by Joseph Jacobs), a girl undergoes the transformation into a bird. The scenes of the boy's beheading by the mother and consumption by the father have not prevented P. L. Travers from referring to the tale as "beautiful," nor have they deterred Tolkien from describing it as a story of "beauty and horror" with an "exquisite and tragic beginning."[9] The "beauty" of the story probably turns less on its aesthetic appeal than on its engagement with cultural anxieties that fascinate us in their evocation of sheer dread. In the stepmother, we have a figure who represents maternal power run mad, an incarnation of a natural force so cruel and inexorable that it heightens our own sense of weakness and helplessness. In the Grimms' version, the boy is transformed back to human form and reunited with his father and sister to live in a motherless household. But in some versions, as in the Scottish "Pippety Pew" included here, the boy remains a bird while "the goodman and his daughter lived happy and died happy" [209].

Fathers and father figures do not always fare as well as they do in "Hansel and Gretel," "The Juniper Tree," and "Pippety Pew." Who can forget the downfall of the Goliath-like ogres in British folklore who "eat little children" and the defeat of the giants who hunt down diminutive boys in French folklore? Molly Whuppie, in the tale of that title, is one of three girls abandoned in a shockingly matter-of-fact fashion by parents who have "too many children" [209]. The youngest and cleverest of the three, Molly is a trickster figure who lies, cheats, and steals her way to happiness. It is she who succeeds in engineering her own marriage and the marriages of her sisters. One of the few popular folkloric heroines to outwit an ogre and earn her own fortune, Molly never even considers returning home to the parents who left her and her siblings in the woods. Tom Thumb may go back home to endow his family with material comforts, but he too is very much on his own by the end of the tale.

While "Hansel and Gretel" and "The Juniper Tree" give us high melodrama—abandonment, treachery, betrayal, and joyous reunions— "Molly Whuppie" and "Tom Thumb" offer comic relief in the form of spunky adventurers who use their wits to turn the tables on adversaries with daunting powers. Interestingly, stories about spirited adventurers who conquer ogres and giants seem to be no match for the seductive sentimentality of "Hansel and Gretel" or the tragic power of

9. P. L. Travers, "The Black Sheep," in *What the Bee Knows: Reflections on Myth, Symbol, and Story* (Wellingborough, Northamptonshire: Aquarian, 1989) 232; J. R. R. Tolkien, "On Fairy-Stories," in *The Tolkien Reader* (New York: Balantine, 1966) 31.

"The Juniper Tree." What George Cruikshank had to say about "Puss in Boots" goes far in explaining why child tricksters have not enjoyed the success of other fairy tale characters: "As it stood, the tale was a succession of successful falsehoods—a clever lesson in lying!—a system of imposture rewarded by the greatest worldly advantage!—a useful lesson, truly, to be impressed upon the minds of children!"[1] It is not surprising that adults are more likely to prefer the sufferings of the "God-fearing" siblings in "Hansel and Gretel" to the irreverent antics of Molly Whuppie or Tom Thumb.

# BROTHERS GRIMM

## Hansel and Gretel†

At the edge of a great forest, there once lived a poor woodcutter with his wife and two children. The little boy was called Hansel, and the girl's name was Gretel. There was never much to eat in the house, and once, during a famine, the woodcutter could no longer put bread on the table. At night, he lay in bed worrying, tossing and turning in his distress. He sighed and said to his wife: "What will become of us? How can we provide for our poor children when we don't even have enough for ourselves?"

"Listen to me," answered the wife. "Tomorrow at the break of day we'll take the children out into the darkest part of the woods. We'll make a fire for them and give them each a piece of bread. Then we'll go about our work and leave them alone. They'll never find their way home, and then we'll be rid of them."

"No," her husband replied. "I won't do it. How could I have the heart to leave the children all alone in the woods when wild beasts would surely come and tear them to pieces?"

"You fool," she said. "Then all four of us will starve to death. You might as well start planing the boards for our coffins."

She didn't give him a moment's peace until he consented. "But still, I feel sorry for the poor children," he said.

The two children hadn't been able to sleep either, because they were so hungry, and they heard everything that their stepmother had said to their father. Gretel wept bitter tears and said to Hansel: "Well, now we're lost."

"Be quiet, Gretel," said Hansel, "and stop worrying. I'll figure out something."

---

1. George Cruikshank, *Puss in Boots* (London: Arnold, 1864) 1.
† Jacob and Wilhelm Grimm, "Hänsel und Gretel," in *Kinder- und Hausmärchen*, 7th ed. (Berlin: Dieterich, 1857; first published: Berlin: Realschulbuchhandlung, 1812). Translated for this Norton Critical Edition by Maria Tatar. Copyright © 1999 by Maria Tatar.

As soon as the old folks had fallen asleep, he got up, put on his little
jacket, opened the lower half of the door, and slipped out. The moon
was shining brightly, and the white pebbles in front of the house were
glittering like silver coins. Hansel stooped down and put as many as
would fit into his jacket pocket. Then he went back and said to Gretel:
"Don't worry, dear little sister. Sleep peacefully. God will not forsake
us." And he went back to bed.

At daybreak, just before the sun had risen, the wife came and woke
the two children. "Get up, you lazybones, we're going to go into the
forest to get some wood."

The wife gave each child a little piece of bread and said: "Here's
something for lunch. But don't eat it before then, because you're not
getting anything else."

Gretel put the bread under her apron because Hansel had the pebbles in his pocket. Then they all set out together on the path into the
forest. After a little while, Hansel stopped to look back at the house.
He did that again and again. His father said: "Hansel, why are you
always stopping and staring? Watch out, and don't forget what your legs
are for."

"Oh, Father," said Hansel. "I'm looking at my white kitten, which
is sitting up on the roof trying to bid me farewell."

The woman said: "You fool, that's not your kitten. Those are the rays
of the sun, shining on the chimney."

But Hansel had not been looking at the kitten. He had been taking
the shiny pebbles from his pocket and dropping them on the ground.

When they arrived in the middle of the forest, the father said: "Go
gather some wood, children. I'll build a fire so that you won't get cold."

Hansel and Gretel gathered brushwood until they had a little pile of
it. The brushwood was lit, and when the flames were high enough, the
woman said: "Now lie down by the fire, children, and get some rest.
We're going into the forest to chop some wood. When we're done,
we'll come back to get you."

Hansel and Gretel sat by the fire. At noon they ate their little pieces
of bread. Since they could hear the sounds of an ax, they were sure
that their father was close by. But it wasn't an ax that they heard, it was
a branch that their father had fastened to a dead tree, and the wind
was banging it back and forth. They were sitting there for such a long
time that finally their eyes closed from fatigue, and they fell fast asleep.
When they awoke, it was pitch dark. Gretel began to cry and said: "How
will we ever get out of the woods!"

Hansel comforted her: "Just wait until the moon has risen. Then we
will find the way back."

And when the full moon had risen, Hansel took his sister by the
hand and followed the pebbles, which were shimmering like newly
minted coins and pointed the way for them. They walked all night long

and arrived at their father's house just as day was breaking. They knocked at the door, and when the woman opened the door and saw that it was Hansel and Gretel, she said: "You wicked children! Why did you sleep so long in the woods? We thought you weren't ever going to come back."

But the father was overjoyed, because he had been upset at how he had abandoned them in the forest.

Not long after that, every square inch of the country was stricken by famine, and one night the children could hear what the mother was saying to their father when they were in bed: "We've eaten everything up again. All that's left is half a loaf of bread, then the jig's up. The children have to go. This time we'll take them deeper into the forest so that they won't find the way out. Otherwise there's no hope for us."

Her husband's heart was heavy, and he thought: "It would be better if you shared the last crumb of bread with your children." But the woman would not listen to anything that he said. She fussed and berated him. In for a penny, in for a pound, and since he had given in the first time, he had to give in a second time.

The children were still awake and had heard the conversation. When their parents had fallen asleep, Hansel got up and wanted to go out to pick up some pebbles as he had the last time, but the woman had locked the door, and Hansel couldn't get out. But he comforted his sister and said: "Don't cry, Gretel. Just sleep peacefully. The Lord will protect us."

Early the next morning the woman came and woke the children up. They each got a little piece of bread, this time even smaller than last time. On the way into the woods, Hansel crushed the bread in his pocket and would often stop to scatter crumbs on the ground.

"Hansel, why are you stopping and staring?" asked the father. "Keep going!"

"I'm looking at my little dove, the one sitting on the roof and trying to bid me farewell," Hansel replied.

"Fool," said the woman. "That isn't your little dove. Those are the rays of the morning sun shining up on the chimney."

After a while, Hansel had scattered all the crumbs on the path.

The woman took the children even deeper into the woods, where they had never been before in their lives. Once again a large fire was built, and the mother said: "Don't move from there, children. If you get tired, you can sleep for a while. We're going to go into the forest to chop wood. In the evening, when we're done, we'll come to get you."

At noon Gretel shared her bread with Hansel, who had scattered bits of his piece on the path. Then they fell asleep. The evening went by, but no one came to get the poor children. They awoke when it was pitch dark, and Hansel comforted his sister by saying: "Just wait, Gretel, until the moon rises. Than we will be able to see the crumbs of bread I scattered. They will point the way home for us."

When the moon rose, they set off, but they couldn't find the crumbs because the many thousands of birds flying about in the forest and over the fields had eaten them. Hansel said to Gretel: "We'll find the way back," but they didn't find it. They walked all night long and then another day from early in the morning until late at night. But they couldn't find their way out of the woods, and they got more and more hungry, for they had nothing to eat but a few berries they found on the ground. When they became so tired that their legs would no longer carry them, they lay down under a tree and fell asleep.

It was now the third morning after they had left their father's house. They started walking again, but they just got deeper and deeper into the woods. If they didn't get help soon, they were sure to perish. At noon they saw a beautiful bird, white as snow, perched on a branch. It was singing so beautifully that they stopped to listen. When it had finished its song, it flapped its wings and flew on ahead of them. They followed it until they came to a little house, and the bird perched on its roof. As they approached the house, they realized that it was built of bread and had a roof made of cake and transparent windows of sugar.

"Let's see what it tastes like," said Hansel. "May the Lord bless our meal. I'll try a piece of the roof, Gretel, and you can try the window. That's sure to taste sweet." Hansel reached up and broke off a small piece of the roof to see what it tasted like. Gretel went over to the windowpane and nibbled on it. Suddenly a gentle voice called from inside:

> "Nibble, nibble, is it a mouse?
> Who's that nibbling at my house?"

The children replied:

> "The wind so mild,
> The heavenly child."

and they continued eating, without getting distracted. Hansel, who liked the taste of the roof, tore off a big piece of it, and Gretel knocked out an entire windowpane and sat down on the ground to savor it. Suddenly the door opened, and a woman as old as the hills, leaning on a crutch, hobbled out. Hansel and Gretel were so terrified that they dropped everything in their hands. The old woman said, with her head shaking: "Well, dear children, how in the world did you get here? Come right inside and stay with me. You will not meet with any harm here."

She took them by the hand and led them into her little house. They were served a wonderful meal of milk and pancakes with sugar, apples, and nuts. Later, two beautiful little beds were made up with white sheets. Hansel and Gretel lay down in them and felt as if they were in heaven.

The old woman had only pretended to be so friendly. She was really a wicked witch, who lay in wait for children. She had built the little house of bread just to lure them inside. As soon as a child was in her power, she killed it, cooked it, and ate it. That was a real feast day for her. Witches have red eyes and can't see very far, but they have a keen sense of smell, like animals, and they can always tell when a human being is around. When Hansel and Gretel got near her, she laughed fiendishly and sneered: "They're mine! This time they won't get away from me!" Early in the morning, before the children were awake, she got out of bed and looked at the two of them resting so sweetly, with their full red cheeks. She muttered to herself: "They will make a tasty morsel."

Then she grabbed Hansel with her scrawny hand, took him to a small shed, and closed the barred door on him. He could cry as loud as he wanted, it did him no good. Then she went over to Gretel, shook her until she woke up, and cried out: "Get up, lazy bones, fetch some water and cook your brother something good. He's staying outside in a shed, waiting to be fattened up. When he's put on enough weight, I'll eat him."

Gretel began to cry bitter tears, but it did no good. She had to do what the wicked witch demanded. The finest food was cooked for poor Hansel, and Gretel got nothing but crab shells. Every morning the old woman would slink over to the little shed and cry out: "Hansel, hold out your finger so that I can tell if you're plump enough."

Hansel would stick a little bone out, and the old woman, who had poor eyesight, thought that it was Hansel's finger and wondered why he wasn't putting on weight. When four weeks had passed and Hansel was still as scrawny as ever, she lost her patience and decided not to wait any longer. "Hey there, Gretel," she called out to the girl, "go get some water and be quick about it. I don't care whether Hansel's plump or scrawny. He's going to be slaughtered tomorrow, and then I'll cook him."

"Oh," the poor little sister wailed, and how the tears flowed down her cheeks! "Dear God, help us," she cried out. "If only the wild animals in the forest had eaten us, at least then we would have died together."

"Spare me your blubbering!" the old woman said. "Nothing can help you now."

Early in the morning Gretel had to go fill the kettle with water and light the fire. "First we'll do some baking," the old woman said. "I've already heated up the oven and kneaded the dough."

She pushed poor Gretel over to the oven, from which flames were lcaping. "Crawl in," said the witch, "and see if it's hot enough to slide the bread in."

The witch was planning to shut the door as soon as Gretel got into the oven. Then she was going to bake her and eat her up too. But Gretel saw what was on her mind and said: "I don't know how to get in there. How can I manage it?"

"Silly goose," said the old woman. "The opening is big enough. Just look. Even I can get in," and she scrambled over to it and stuck her head in the oven. Gretel gave her a big push that sent her sprawling. Then she shut the iron door and bolted it. Phew! the witch began screeching dreadfully. But Gretel ran away and the godless witch burned miserably to death.

Gretel ran straight to Hansel, opened the little shed and cried out: "Hansel, we're saved! The old witch is dead."

Hansel hopped out as soon as the door opened, like a bird leaving its cage. How thrilled they were: they hugged and kissed, and jumped up and down for joy! Since there was nothing more to fear, they went right into the witch's house. In every corner there were chests filled with pearls and jewels. "These are even better than pebbles," said Hansel and put what he could into his pockets.

Gretel said, "I'll take something home too," and she filled up her little apron.

"Let's get going now," said Hansel. "We need to get out of this witch's forest."

When they had walked for a few hours, they reached a large body of water. "We can't get across," said Hansel. "There's not a bridge in sight."

"There aren't any ships around," Gretel said, "but here comes a white duck. It will help us cross, if I ask it." She called out:

> "Help us, help us, little duck
> Hansel and Gretel are out of luck.
> There's no bridge, not far or wide,
> Help us, give us both a ride."

The duck came paddling over. Hansel got on it and told his sister to sit down next to him. "No," said Gretel, "that would be too heavy a load for the little duck. It can take us over one at a time."

That's just what the good little creature did. When they were safely on the other side and had walked for some time, the woods became more and more familiar. Finally they could see their father's house from afar. They began running, and then they raced into their father's house, throwing their arms around him. The man had not had a happy hour since the day that he had abandoned the children in the forest. His wife had died. Gretel emptied her apron and the pearls and jewels rolled all over the floor. Hansel reached into his pockets and pulled out one handful of jewels after another. Their worries were over, and they lived together in perfect happiness.

My fairy tale is done. See the mouse run. Whoever catches it can make a great big fur hat out of it.

# BROTHERS GRIMM

## The Juniper Tree†

A long time ago, as many as two thousand years ago, there was a rich man who had a beautiful and pious wife. They loved each other dearly, but they had no children, even though they longed for them. Day and night the wife prayed for a child, but still they had no children.

Now in front of the house there was a garden, and in the garden there grew a juniper tree. Once in the wintertime, the wife was peeling an apple under the tree, and while she was peeling it, she cut her finger. Blood dripped on the snow. "Ah," said the woman, and she sighed deeply. "If only I had a child as red as blood and as white as snow!" Having said that, she began to feel better, for she had a feeling that something would come of it. Then she went back in the house.

A month went by, and the snow was gone. Two months passed, and everything was green. Three months went by, and the flowers sprouted from the ground. Four months passed, and all the trees in the woods grew tall, with their green branches intertwining. The woods resounded with the singing of birds, and the blossoms were falling from the trees. And so the fifth month went by. And when the woman was under the juniper tree, her heart leaped for joy because it smelled so sweet. She fell to her knees and was beside herself with joy. When the sixth month had passed, the fruit grew large and firm, and she became quite still. In the seventh month she picked the juniper berries and so gorged herself that she became sad and ill. After the eighth month went by, she called her husband and, weeping, said to him: "If I die, bury me under the juniper tree." After that she felt better and was happy until the ninth month had passed. Then she bore a child as white as snow and as red as blood. When she saw the child she was so happy that she died.

Her husband buried her under the juniper tree, and he wept day after day. After a while he felt better, but he still wept from time to time. Eventually he stopped and then he took a second wife.

The man had a daughter with his second wife. The child from the

† Jacob and Wilhelm Grimm, "Von dem Machandelboom," in *Kinder- und Hausmärchen*, 7th ed. (Berlin: Dieterich, 1857; first published: Berlin: Realschulbuchhandlung, 1812). Translated for this Norton Critical Edition by Maria Tatar. Copyright © 1999 by Maria Tatar.

first marriage was a little boy, as red as blood and as white as snow. Whenever the woman looked at her daughter, she felt love for her, but whenever she looked at the little boy, she was sick at heart. It seemed that wherever he went, he was always in the way, and she kept wondering how she could get the entire family fortune for her daughter. The devil got hold of her so that she began to hate the little boy, and she slapped him around and pinched him here and cuffed him there. The poor child lived in terror, and when he came home from school, he had no peace at all.

One day the woman went to the pantry. Her little daughter followed her and said: "Mother, give me an apple."

"All right, my child," said the woman, and she give her a beautiful apple from a chest that had a big heavy lid with a sharp iron lock on it.

"Mother," said the little girl, "Can't brother have one too?"

This irritated the woman, but she said: "Yes, he can have one when he gets back from school."

When she looked out the window and saw the boy coming home, it was as if the devil had taken hold of her, and she snatched the apple out of her daughter's hand and said: "You can't have one before your brother." Then she tossed the apple into the chest and shut it.

The little boy walked in the door, and the devil got her to speak sweetly to him and say: "My son, would you like an apple?" But she gave him a look full of hate.

"Mother," said the little boy, "How dreadful you look! Yes, give me an apple."

Then she felt as if she had to keep leading him on. "Come over here," she said, and she lifted the lid. "Now pick out an apple."

And when the little boy bent down, the devil prompted her, and *bam!* She slammed the lid down so hard that the boy's head flew off and fell into the chest with the apples. Then she was overcome with fear and thought: "How am I going to get out of this?" She went to her room and took a white kerchief from her dresser drawer. She put the boy's head back on his neck and tied the scarf around it so that you couldn't see anything was wrong. Then she sat him down on a chair in front of the door and put an apple in his hand.

Later on Little Marlene came into the kitchen to see her mother, who was standing by the fire, stirring a pot of hot water round and round. "Mother," said Little Marlene, "brother is sitting by the door and looks pale. He has an apple in his hand, and when I asked him to give me the apple, he didn't answer. It was very scary."

"Go back to him," the mother said, "and if he doesn't answer, slap his face."

And so Little Marlene went back to him and said: "Brother, give me the apple."

But he wouldn't answer. So she gave him a slap, and his head went flying off. She was so terrified that she began to howl and weep. Then she ran to her mother and said: "Mother, I've knocked my brother's head off!" And she cried so hard that she couldn't stop.

"Little Marlene," said her mother, "what a dreadful thing you've done! But don't breathe a word to anyone, for there's nothing we can do. We'll cook him up in a stew."

And so the mother took the little boy and chopped him up. Then she put the pieces into a pot and cooked him up into a stew. Little Marlene stood nearby and wept so hard that the stew didn't need salt because of all her tears.

When the father came home, he sat down at the table and said: "Where's my son?"

The mother brought in a huge dish of stew, and Little Marlene wept so hard that she couldn't stop.

"Where's my son?" the father asked again.

"Oh," said the mother, "he went off to the country to visit his mother's great uncle. He plans to stay there a while."

"What's he going to do there? He didn't even say good-bye to me."

"Well, he really wanted to go and he asked if he could stay for six weeks. They'll take good care of him."

"Oh, that makes me so sad," said the husband. "It's not right. He should have said good-bye."

Then he began eating and said: "Little Marlene, why are you crying? Your brother will be back soon." Then he said: "Oh, wife, this stew tastes so good! Give me some more."

The more he ate the more he wanted. "Give me some more," he said. "No one else will get any. Somehow I feel as if it's all mine."

And he kept eating and threw the bones under the table until he had eaten everything. Meanwhile, Little Marlene went to her dresser and got her best silk kerchief. She picked up all the bones from beneath the table, tied them up in her silk kerchief, and carried them outside. Then she wept bitter tears. She put the bones down in the green grass under the juniper tree. When she had put them down, she suddenly felt much better and stopped crying. The juniper tree began stirring. Its branches parted and came back together again as though it were clapping its hands for joy. A mist arose from the tree, and in the middle of the mist burned a flame, and from the flame a beautiful bird emerged and began singing gloriously. It soared up in the air, then vanished. The tree was as it had been before, but the kerchief with the bones was gone. Little Marlene was as happy and relieved as if her brother were still alive. She returned home feeling happy and sat down at the table to eat.

Meanwhile the bird flew away, perched on a goldsmith's house, and began singing:

> "My mother, she slew me,
> My father, he ate me,
> My sister, Little Marlene,
> Gathered up my bones,
> Tied them up in silk,
> And put them under the juniper tree.
> Tweet, tweet, what a fine bird I am!"

The goldsmith was sitting in his shop, making a gold chain. He heard the bird singing on his roof and found its song very beautiful. He got up and, when he walked across the threshold, he lost a slipper. Still, he kept right on going out into the middle of the street with only one sock and one slipper on. He was also wearing his apron, and in one hand he had the gold chain, in the other his tongs. The sun was shining brightly on the street. He stopped to look at the bird and said: "Bird, you sing so beautifully. Sing me that song again."

"No," said the bird. "I never sing the second time for nothing. Give me that golden chain, and I'll sing it for you again."

"Here," said the goldsmith. "Here's the golden chain. Now sing the song again."

The bird came flying down. Taking the golden chain in its right claw, it perched in front of the goldsmith and began singing:

> "My mother, she slew me,
> My father, he ate me,
> My sister, Little Marlene,
> Gathered up my bones,
> Tied them up in silk,
> And put them under the juniper tree.
> Tweet, tweet, what a fine bird I am!"

Then the bird flew off to a shoemaker's house, perched on the roof, and sang:

> "My mother, she slew me,
> My father, he ate me,
> My sister, Little Marlene,
> Gathered up my bones,
> Tied them up in silk,
> And put them under the juniper tree.
> Tweet, tweet, what a fine bird I am!"

When the shoemaker heard the song, he ran out the door in his shirtsleeves and looked up at the roof. He had to put his hand over his eyes to keep the sun from blinding him. "Bird," he said, "You sing so beautifully." Then he called into the house: "Wife, come out here for a moment. There's a bird up there. See it? How beautifully it sings!"

He called his daughter and her children, apprentices, hired hand

and maid. They all came running out into the street to look at the bird
and see how beautiful it was. It had red and green feathers, and around
its neck was pure gold, and the eyes in its head sparkled like stars.

"Bird," said the shoemaker, "sing that song again."

"No," said the bird, "I never sing the second time for nothing. You
have to give me something."

"Wife," said the man, "go up to the attic. On the top shelf you'll
find a pair of red shoes. Get them for me."

His wife went and got the shoes.

"Here," said the man. "Now sing that song again."

The bird came flying down. Taking the shoes in its left claw, it flew
back up on the roof and sang:

> "My mother, she slew me,
> My father, he ate me,
> My sister, Little Marlene,
> Gathered up my bones,
> Tied them up in silk,
> And put them under the juniper tree.
> Tweet, tweet, what a fine bird I am!"

When the bird had finished the song, it flew away. It had the chain
in its right claw and the shoes in its left, and it flew far away to a mill.
The mill went "clickety-clack, clickety-clack, clickety-clack." Inside the
mill sat twenty of the miller's men, hewing a stone, "hick hack hick
hack hick hack." And the mill kept going "clickety-clack, clickety-clack,
clickety-clack." And so the bird went and perched on a linden tree
outside the mill and sang:

> "My mother, she slew me,"

and one of the men stopped working,

> "My father, he ate me,"

and two more stopped working and listened,

> "My sister, Little Marlene,"

then four men stopped working,

> "Gathered up my bones,
> Tied them up in silk,"

now only eight kept hewing,

> "And put them under . . ."

now only five,

> ". . . the juniper tree."

now only one.

"Tweet, tweet, what a fine bird I am!"

The last one stopped to listen to the final words. "Bird," he said, "you sing so beautifully! Let me hear the whole thing too. Sing that song again."

"I never sing the second time for nothing. If you give me the mill-stone, I'll sing the song again."

"If it belonged to me alone," he said. "I would give it to you."

"If the bird sings again," the others said, "it can have the millstone."

Then the bird swooped down, and the miller's men, all twenty of them, set the beam to and raised up the stone. "Heave-ho-hup, heave-ho-hup, heave-ho-hup." And the bird stuck its neck through the hole, put the stone on as if it were a collar, flew back to the tree, and sang:

> "My mother, she slew me,
> My father, he ate me,
> My sister, Little Marlene,
> Gathered up my bones,
> Tied them up in silk,
> And put them under the juniper tree.
> Tweet, tweet, what a fine bird I am!"

When the bird had finished its song, it spread its wings. In its right claw was the chain, in its left claw the shoes, and round its neck was the millstone. Then it flew away, far away to the house of its father.

The father, mother, and Little Marlene were sitting at the table in the parlor, and the father said: "How happy I feel! My heart feels so easy."

"Not me," said the mother. "I feel frightened, as if a big storm were on its way."

Meanwhile, Little Marlene just sat there weeping. The bird flew up and, when it landed on the roof, the father said: "How happy I'm feeling. And outside the sun is shining so brightly! I feel as if I'm about to see an old friend again."

"I don't," said the woman. "I'm so scared that my teeth are chatter-ing, and I feel as if there's fire running through my veins."

She tore at her bodice to loosen it, while little Marlene sat there weeping. She held her apron up to her eyes and wept so hard that it was completely soaked with tears. The bird swooped down to the ju-niper tree, perched on a branch, and sang:

> "My mother, she slew me . . ."

The mother stopped up her ears and closed her eyes, for she didn't want to see or hear anything, but the roaring in her ears was like the wildest of storms, and her eyes burned and flashed like lightning.

"My father, he ate me . . ."

"Oh, Mother," said the man, "there's a beautiful bird out there, and it's singing so gloriously. The sun is shining so warmly, and the air smells like cinnamon."

"My sister, Little Marlene . . ."

Little Marlene put her head in her lap and just kept crying and crying. But the husband said: "I'm going outside. I've got to see this bird close up."

"Oh, don't go," said the wife. "It feels as if the whole house is shaking and about to go up in flames!"

But the husband went out and looked at the bird.

> "Gathered up my bones,
> Tied them up in silk,
> And put them under the juniper tree.
> Tweet, tweet, what a fine bird I am!"

After finishing its song, the bird dropped the golden chain, and it fell right around the man's neck, fitting him perfectly. He went inside and said: "Just see what a fine bird is out there! It gave me this beautiful golden chain, as beautiful as it is."

But the woman was so terrified that she fell full length on the floor, and the cap she was wearing came off her head. And the bird sang once again:

"My mother, she slew me . . ."

"Oh, if only I were a thousand feet under the ground so that I wouldn't have to hear this!"

"My father, he ate me . . ."

Then the woman fell down again as if dead.

"My sister, Little Marlene . . ."

"Oh," said Little Marlene, "I want to go outside and see if the bird will give me something too." And she went out.

> "Gathered up my bones,
> Tied them up in silk,"

And the bird tossed her the shoes.

> "And put them under the juniper tree.
> Tweet, tweet, what a fine bird I am!"

Little Marlene felt lighthearted and happy. She put on the new red shoes and came dancing and skipping into the house.

"Oh," she said, "I was so sad when I went out, and now I feel so cheerful. What a fine bird is out there. It gave me a pair of red shoes."

The woman jumped to her feet and her hair stood straight on end like tongues of flame. "I have a feeling that the world is coming to an end. Maybe I'd feel better if I went outside."

As she went out the door, *bam!* the bird dropped the millstone on her head and crushed her to death. The father and Little Marlene heard the crash and went outside. Smoke, flames, and fire were rising up from the spot, and when they vanished, little brother was standing there. He took his father and Little Marlene by the hand, and the three of them were overjoyed. Then they went into the house, sat down at the table, and ate.

# JOSEPH JACOBS

## The Rose-Tree†

There was once upon a time a good man who had two children: a girl by a first wife, and a boy by the second. The girl was as white as milk, and her lips were like cherries. Her hair was like golden silk, and it hung to the ground. Her brother loved her dearly, but her wicked stepmother hated her. "Child," said the stepmother one day, "go to the grocer's shop and buy me a pound of candles." She gave her the money; and the little girl went, bought the candles, and started on her return. There was a stile to cross. She put down the candles whilst she got over the stile. Up came a dog and ran off with the candles.

She went back to the grocer's, and she got a second bunch. She came to the stile, set down the candles, and proceeded to climb over. Up came the dog and ran off with the candles.

She went again to the grocer's, and she got a third bunch; and just the same happened. Then she came to her stepmother crying, for she had spent all the money and had lost three bunches of candles.

The stepmother was angry, but she pretended not to mind the loss. She said to the child: "Come, lay your head on my lap that I may comb your hair." So the little one laid her head in the woman's lap, who proceeded to comb the yellow silken hair. And when she combed, the hair fell over her knees, and rolled right down to the ground.

Then the stepmother hated her more for the beauty of her hair; so she said to her, "I cannot part your hair on my knee, fetch a billet of wood." So she fetched it. Then said the stepmother, "I cannot part your hair with a comb, fetch me an axe." So she fetched it.

"Now," said the wicked woman, "lay your head down on the billet whilst I part your hair."

† Joseph Jacobs, "The Rose-Tree," in *English Fairy Tales* (London: David Nutt, 1890).

Well! she laid down her little golden head without fear; and whist! down came the axe, and it was off. So the mother wiped the axe and laughed.

Then she took the heart and liver of the little girl, and she stewed them and brought them into the house for supper. The husband tasted them and shook his head. He said they tasted very strangely. She gave some to the little boy, but he would not eat. She tried to force him, but he refused, and ran out into the garden, and took up his little sister, and put her in a box, and buried the box under a rose-tree; and every day he went to the tree and wept, till his tears ran down on the box.

One day the rose-tree flowered. It was spring, and there among the flowers was a white bird; and it sang, and sang, and sang like an angel out of heaven. Away it flew, and it went to a cobbler's shop, and perched itself on a tree hard by; and thus it sang:

> "My wicked mother slew me,
> My dear father ate me,
> My little brother whom I love
> Sits below, and I sing above
>    Stick, stock, stone dead."

"Sing again that beautiful song," said the shoemaker. "If you will first give me those little red shoes you are making." The cobbler gave the shoes, and the bird sang the song; then flew to a tree in front of the watchmaker's, and sang:

> "My wicked mother slew me
> My dear father ate me,
> My little brother whom I love
> Sits below, and I sing above
>    Stick, stock, stone dead."

"Oh, the beautiful song! sing it again, sweet bird," said the watch-maker. "If you will give me first that gold watch and chain in your hand." The jeweller gave the watch and chain. The bird took it in one foot, the shoes in the other, and, after having repeated the song, flew away to where three millers were picking a millstone. The bird perched on a tree and sang:

> "My wicked mother slew me,
> My dear father ate me,
> My little brother whom I love
> Sits below, and I sing above
>    Stick!"

Then one of the men put down his tool and looked up from his work,

> "Stock!"

Then the second miller's man laid aside his tool and looked up,

"Stone!"

Then the third miller's man laid down his tool and looked up,

"Dead!"

Then all three cried out with one voice: "Oh, what a beautiful song! Sing it, sweet bird, again." "If you will put the millstone round my neck," said the bird. The men did what the bird wanted and away to the tree it flew with the millstone round its neck, the red shoes in one foot, and the gold watch and chain in the other. It sang the song and then flew home. It rattled the millstone against the eaves of the house, and the stepmother said: "It thunders." Then the little boy ran out to see the thunder, and down dropped the red shoes at his feet. It rattled the millstone against the eaves of the house once more, and the stepmother said again: "It thunders." Then the father ran out and down fell the chain about his neck.

In ran father and son, laughing and saying, "See, what fine things the thunder has brought us!" Then the bird rattled the millstone against the eaves of the house a third time; and the stepmother said: "It thunders again; perhaps the thunder has brought something for me," and she ran out; but the moment she stepped outside the door, down fell the millstone on her head; and so she died.

# CHARLES PERRAULT

## Little Thumbling†

Once upon a time there lived a woodcutter and his wife who had seven children, all boys. The oldest was only ten years old, and the youngest was only seven. Everyone was astonished that the woodcutter had had so many children in so short a time, but his wife didn't waste any time, and she never had fewer than two at a time.

These people were very poor. Having seven children was a great burden, because not one of them was able to earn his own living. To their great distress, the youngest was very sickly and did not speak a word. They mistook for stupidity what was in reality the sign of a kind and generous nature.

This youngest boy was very small. At birth he was hardly larger than a thumb, and as a result he was called "Little Thumbling." The poor child was the underdog in the family, and he got the blame for ev-

---

† Charles Perrault, "Le Petit Poucet," in *Histoires ou Contes du temps passé. Avec des Moralités* (Paris: Barbin, 1697). Translated for this Norton Critical Edition by Maria Tatar. Copyright © 1999 by Maria Tatar.

erything. All the same, he was the wisest and shrewdest of the brothers, and though he may have spoken little, he listened carefully to
everything.

There came a year of misfortune, when famine was so widespread
that these poor people resolved to get rid of their children. One evening, after the children had gone to bed, the woodcutter was sitting
by the fire with his wife. His heart was heavy with sorrow when he said
to her: "It must be obvious to you that we can no longer feed our
children. I refuse to watch them die of hunger before my very eyes,
and I've made up my mind to take them out into the woods tomorrow
and to leave them there. It won't be difficult, for collecting firewood
will distract them, and we can disappear without their noticing it."
"Oh," cried the woodcutter's wife, "do you mean to say that you
have the heart to abandon your own children?" Her husband tried in
vain to remind her of their terrible poverty, but she would not give her
consent. She was poor, but she was still their mother. In the end, however, when she thought about how distressing it would be to watch
them die of hunger, she agreed to the plan and, weeping, went off to
bed.

Little Thumbling heard everything that was said. While lying in bed,
he realized that serious things were being discussed, and he got up
quietly and slipped under his father's stool in order to listen without
being seen. He went back to bed, but didn't sleep a wink for the rest
of the night, for he was thinking about what to do. In the morning, he
got up very early and went to the bank of the river. There he filled his
pockets with little white pebbles and returned home.

The family set out for the woods, and Little Thumbling did not say
a word to his brothers about what he knew. They entered a forest so
dense that at ten paces they could not see each other. The woodcutter
began his work, and the children started collecting twigs for firewood.
The father and mother, seeing them busy at their work, stole gradually
away, and then suddenly dashed off along a little sidepath.

When the children realized that they were all alone, they began to
weep and sob with all their might. Little Thumbling let them cry, since
he was confident that he would be able to get them back home. On
the way, he had dropped the little white pebbles which he had been
carrying in his pocket.

"Don't be afraid, brothers," he said to them. "Mother and Father
have left us here, but I will take you back home again. Just follow me."

They fell in behind him, and he took them straight home by the
same path they had taken into the forest. At first they were afraid to go
into the house. Instead, they leaned against the door to hear what their
father and mother were saying. Now the woodcutter and his wife had
no sooner reached home when the lord of the manor sent them a sum

of ten crowns that he had owed them for a long time and that they had despaired of ever getting. This gave them a new lease on life, for the poor creatures had been dying of hunger.

The woodcutter sent his wife off to the butcher at once, and since it had been such a long time since they had eaten anything, she bought three times more meat than was needed for two people to dine. When they sat down at the table, the woodcutter's wife said: "Alas! where are our poor children now! They could get a good meal from our leftovers. Mind you, William, it was you who wanted to abandon them. I said over and over again that we would regret it. What are they doing now in the forest? God in heaven, the wolves may already have eaten them! What a monster you are for having abandoned your children."

The woodcutter finally lost his patience, for she had repeated more than twenty times that he would regret it and that she had told him so. He threatened to beat her if she did not hold her tongue. It was not that the woodcutter was any less distressed than his wife, but she drove him crazy, and he was of the same opinion as many other people, who like women to say the right thing, but are troubled when they are always right. The woodcutter's wife burst into tears: "Alas, where are my children now, my poor children?"

She said it so loudly that the children, who were at the door, heard it and began to cry out at once: "Here we are! Here we are!"

She rushed to open the door for them, and, as she kissed them, she said: "How happy I am to see you again, dear children! You must be very tired and very hungry. And you, little Pierrot, how muddy you are! Come and let me wash you!"

Pierrot was the oldest son, whom she loved more than all the others because he was something of a redhead, and she herself had reddish hair.

They sat down at the table and ate with an appetite that gave pleasure to their father and mother. They all talked at once as they told of how afraid they had been in the forest.

The good people were overjoyed to have their children back with them again, but the pleasure lasted only as long as the ten crowns. When the money was spent, they lapsed back into their previous despair. Once again they decided to abandon the children, and to make sure they would not fail this time, they took them much farther away than the first time. But they were not able to talk about it quietly enough to escape being heard by Little Thumbling, who made up his mind to get out of this difficulty just as he had on the previous occasion. Although he was up early in the morning to go and collect his little stones, this time he could not carry out his plan because he found the door to the house had a double lock on it.

He could not think what to do until the woodcutter's wife gave them

-bread crumbs

each a piece of bread for breakfast. Then it occurred to him to use the bread instead of the stones, by scattering crumbs along the path they were taking. He tucked his piece tightly into his pocket.

The father and mother took them into the deepest and darkest part of the forest, and as soon as they got there, they slipped off on a sidepath and abandoned them. This did not cause Little Thumbling much distress, for he was sure that he would be able to find the way back by following the bread crumbs he had scattered on the path. But to his dismay he could not find a single crumb. Birds had come along and eaten them all up.

They were in real trouble now, for with every step they went further astray and plunged deeper and deeper into the forest. Night fell, and a strong wind arose, which made them feel anxious and scared. Everywhere they seemed to hear the howling of wolves who were coming toward them to eat them up. They hardly dared to talk with each other or even to turn their heads. Then it began raining so heavily that they were soaked to the bone. At every step they tripped and fell into the mud, getting up again all covered with mud and not knowing what to do with their hands.

– Candle

Little Thumbling climbed to the top of a tree to take a look around. Surveying the area, he could see a little light that looked like a candle far away on the other side of the forest. He climbed down the tree and was disappointed to find that, once back on the ground, he couldn't see the light any more. After walking some distance in the direction of the light, however, he caught a glimpse of it as they were about to leave the forest. At last they reached the house where the light was burning, not without a good deal of anxiety, for they lost sight of it every time they had to go down into a hollow. They knocked at the door, and a good woman opened the door. She asked them what they wanted.

Little Thumbling explained that they were poor children who had lost their way in the forest and who had come begging for a night's lodging. Noticing what lovely children they were, the woman began to weep: "Alas, my poor children! Don't you realize where you are? Haven't you ever heard that this house belongs to an ogre who eats little children?"

– ogre's house.

"Alas, Madam!" answered Little Thumbling, who was trembling as visibly as his brothers. "What shall we do? If you don't take us in, the wolves in the forest will surely devour us this very night. That being the case, we might as well be eaten by your husband. If you plead for us, maybe he will take pity on us."

The ogre's wife, who thought she might be able to hide them from her husband until the next morning, let them come in and warm themselves by a roaring fire, where a whole sheep was cooking on the spit for the ogre's supper. Just as the boys were beginning to get warm, they heard three or four loud bangs at the door. The ogre had returned. His wife hid the boys quickly under the bed and went to open the door.

The ogre asked right away whether supper was ready and whether the wine had been drawn. Then he sat down to eat dinner. Blood was still dripping from the sheep, but it seemed all the better for that. He sniffed to the right, then to the left, insisting that he could smell fresh meat. His wife said: "You must be smelling the calf that I just dressed."

"I'll tell you again that I smell fresh meat," the ogre responded, looking at his wife suspiciously, "and there's something going on here that I don't get."

At that he got up from the table and went straight to the bed. "Aha!" he said. "So that's how you deceive me, you cursed woman! I don't know what's stopping me from eating you too! It's lucky for you that you're an old beast! I'm expecting three ogre friends for a visit in the next few days, and this excellent game will come in handy to entertain them!"

He pulled the children out from under the bed, one after another. The poor things fell to their knees, begging for mercy, but they were dealing with the most cruel of all ogres. Far from feeling pity for them, he was already devouring them with his eyes. He told his wife that if she cooked them with a tasty sauce, they would make dainty morsels. He went to get a big knife, which he sharpened on a long stone in his left hand as he walked toward the poor children. He had already grabbed one of them when his wife said to him: "Why are you doing this now? Can't it wait until tomorrow?"

"Hold your tongue," replied the ogre. "They will be all the more tender."

"But you already have plenty of meat on your plate," his wife countered. "There's a calf, two sheep, and half a pig."

"You're right," said the ogre. "Give them a good supper to eat so they won't lose any weight and put them to bed."

The good woman was overjoyed and brought them a tasty supper, but the boys were so overcome with fear that they couldn't eat a thing. As for the ogre, he went back to his drinking, thrilled at the prospect of having such a treat to regale his friends. He drank a dozen glasses more than usual, and had to go to bed early, for the wine had gone to his head.

Now the ogre had seven daughters who were still just little children. These ogresses all had the most lovely complexions, because, like their father, they ate fresh meat. But they had little grey eyes which were completely round, crooked noses, and very large mouths, with long and dreadfully sharp teeth, set far apart. They were not yet terribly vicious, but they showed great promise, for already they were in the habit of killing little children to suck their blood.

They had gone to bed early, and all seven were in one large bed, each wearing a crown of gold upon her head. In that same room was another bed of the same size. The ogre's wife had put the seven boys into it. Then she lay down next to her husband and went to sleep.

Little Thumbling was afraid that the ogre might suddenly regret not having cut the throats of the boys that evening. Having noticed that the ogre's daughters all had golden crowns upon their heads, he got up in the middle of the night and gently put his own cap and those of his brothers on their heads, after having removed the crowns of gold and put them on his own and on his brothers' heads. In this way, the ogre would take them for his daughters and his daughters for the boys whom he wanted to eat.

Everything worked just as Little Thumbling had predicted. The ogre, waking up at midnight, regretted having postponed until tomorrow what he could have done that night. He leaped headlong out of bed and grabbed a knife, saying: "Now then, let's see how the little rascals are faring. I won't make the same mistake twice!"

He stole his way up to the room where his daughters were sleeping and walked over to the bed with the seven little boys, who were all asleep except for Little Thumbling. When the ogre's hand moved from the heads of each of his brothers to his own head, Thumbling was paralyzed with fear.

"Well, well," said the ogre, when he felt the golden crowns. "I almost made a mess of this job! It's obvious that I had a little too much to drink last night!"

He went straight to the bed where his daughters were sleeping, and after feeling the boys' little caps, he cried: "Aha, here are the little rascals. Now let's get down to work!"

At that, without a moment's hesitation, he cut the throats of his seven daughters. Completely satisfied with his work, he got back into bed and lay down next to his wife.

As soon as Little Thumbling heard the ogre snoring, he woke his brothers up and told them to get dressed fast and to follow him. They crawled quietly down to the garden and jumped over the walls. They ran almost all night, trembling with fear and having no idea where they were going.

When the ogre woke up, he said to his wife: "Go upstairs and dress those little rascals who were here last night."

The wife was surprised by her husband's good will, never once suspecting the manner in which he was ordering to have them dressed. She thought that he was telling her to go and put on their clothes. When she got upstairs, she was horrified to find her seven daughters with their throats cut, bathed in blood. She fainted instantly (the first resort of almost all women in similar circumstances). The ogre, fearing that his wife was taking too long to carry out his orders, went upstairs to help her. He was no less horrified than his wife at the terrible spectacle that met his eyes.

"What have I done?" he shouted. "I will make those wretches pay, and it will be now."

He threw a jugful of water in his wife's face, and after reviving her, said: "Fetch me my seven-league boots so that I can catch the children."

He got right down to it and, after having run far and wide in all directions, he came to the road the poor children were traveling. They were not more than a hundred steps from their father's house when they saw the ogre striding from one mountain to another, and stepping across rivers as though they were nothing but little brooks. Little Thumbling, who noticed a cave in some rocks close to where they were, hid his six brothers there and squeezed inside, always keeping an eye on the ogre's movements.

Now the ogre was feeling exhausted after having traveled so far in vain (for seven-league boots are very fatiguing to their owner), and he wanted to rest for a while. By chance, he happened to sit down on the very rock beneath which the boys were concealed. Since he could go no farther, he fell asleep after a while and began snoring so dreadfully that the poor children were no less frightened than when he had put his long knife to their throats. Little Thumbling was not as alarmed, and he told his brothers to race at once to the house while the ogre was still sleeping so soundly. They were not to worry about him. The brothers took his advice and got home fast.

Little Thumbling went over to the ogre and gently pulled off his boots and put them on his own feet. The boots were very roomy and very long, but since they were enchanted, they had the power to become larger or smaller according to the feet wearing them. As a result they fit his feet and his ankles as if they had been made expressly for him. He went straight to the ogre's house, where he found the ogre's wife weeping over her murdered daughters.

"Your husband," said Little Thumbling, "is in great danger, for he has been captured by a band of thieves who have sworn to kill him if he does not hand over all his gold and silver. Just as they were putting a dagger to his throat, he caught sight of me and begged me to come to you and to alert you to the plight he is in. He said that you should give me everything he has of value, without holding back anything, otherwise he'll be slain without mercy. Since time is of the essence, he wanted me to take his seven-league boots, to make haste, and also to show you that I am no impostor.

The ogre's wife was terribly frightened and immediately gave Thumbling everything she had, for the ogre had always been a very good husband, even though he ate little children. Loaded down with the ogre's entire wealth, Little Thumbling returned to his father's house, where he was welcomed with open arms.

———

Many people do not agree about this last adventure and claim that Little Thumbling never stole money from the ogre, just the seven-league boots about which he had no qualms, since they had been used to chase little children. These people insist that they are in a position to know, having been wined and dined at the woodcutter's cottage. They claim that when Little Thumbling put on the ogre's boots, he went to the court, where he knew there was great anxiety about the army and about the outcome of a battle being fought two hundred leagues away. They say that Little Thumbling went to look for the king and told him that if he was interested he could get news of the army before the day was out. The king promised him a large sum of money if he were to succeed.

Little Thumbling brought news that very night, and this first errand having made his reputation, he could then earn as much as he wanted. The king paid him handsomely to carry orders to the army, but countless ladies gave him any price he named to get news of their lovers, and this became his best source of income. Some wives entrusted him with letters to their husbands, but they paid him so badly, and this activity brought him in so little, that he didn't even bother to keep track of what he made from it.

After working as courier for some time and amassing a small fortune, Little Thumbling returned to his father's house, where everyone was overjoyed to see him again. He saw to it that the entire family lived comfortably, buying newly created positions for his father and brothers. In this way he got them all established at the same time that he managed to do perfectly well for himself at the court.

### Moral

You never worry about having too many children
When they are handsome, well bred, strong,
And when they shine.
But if one is sickly or mute,
He is despised, scorned, ridiculed.
But sometimes it is the little runt
Who makes the family's happiness.

# Pippety Pew†

There was once a man who worked in the fields, and he had a wife, a son and a daughter. One day he caught a hare, took it home to his wife and told her to make it ready for his dinner.

† Comp., Norah and William Montgomerie, "Pippety Pew," in *The Well at the World's End: Folk Tales of Scotland* (London: The Bodley Head, 1956). Copyright © 1956. Reprinted by permission of The Bodley Head.

While it was on the fire cooking, the goodwife kept on tasting it till she had tasted it all away, and she didn't know what to do for her husband's dinner. So she called Johnnie, her son, to come and have his hair combed. When she was combing his head, she slew him, and put him into the pot.

The goodman came home for his dinner, and his wife set down Johnnie to him well boiled. When he was eating, he took up a foot.

"Surely that's my Johnnie's foot," said he.

"Nonsense. It is one of the hare's," said she.

Then he took up a hand.

"That's surely my Johnnie's hand," said he.

"You're talking nonsense, goodman," said she. "That's another of the hare's feet."

When the goodman had eaten his dinner, his daughter Katy gathered all the bones and put them below a stone at the cheek of the door.

> Where they grew, and they grew,
> To a milk-white doo,
> That took to its wings,
> And away it flew.

The dove flew till it came to a burn where two women were washing clothes. It sat down on a stone, and cried:

> *"Pippety pew!*
> *My mammy me slew,*
> *My daddy me ate,*
> *My sister Kate*
> *Gathered all my banes,*
> *And laid them between*
> *Two milk-white stanes.*
> *So a bird I grew,*
> *And away I flew,*
> *Sing Pippety Pew!"*

"Say that again, my pretty bird, and we'll give you all these clothes," said one of the women.

> *"Pippety Pew!*
> *My mammy me slew,*
> *My daddy me ate,*
> *My sister Kate*
> *Gathered all my banes,*
> *And laid them between*
> *Two milk-white stanes.*
> *So a bird I grew,*
> *And away I flew,*
> *Sing Pippety Pew!"*

The bird took the clothes, and away it flew till it came to a man counting a great heap of silver. It sat down beside him and cried:

*— Silver*

> "*Pippety Pew!*
> *My mammy me slew,*
> *My daddy me ate,*
> *My sister Kate*
> *Gathered all my banes,*
> *And laid them between*
> *Two milk-white stanes.*
> *So a bird I grew,*
> *And away I flew,*
> *Sing Pippety Pew!*"

"Say that again, my bonny bird, and I'll give you all this silver," said the man.

> "*Pippety Pew!*
> *My mammy me slew,*
> *My daddy me ate,*
> *My sister Kate*
> *Gathered all my banes,*
> *And laid them between*
> *Two milk-white stanes.*
> *So a bird I grew,*
> *And away I flew,*
> *Sing Pippety Pew!*"

The man gave the bird all the silver. It flew till it came to a miller grinding corn, and cried:

*millsto*

> "*Pippety Pew!*
> *My mammy me slew,*
> *My daddy me ate,*
> *My sister Kate*
> *Gathered all my banes,*
> *And laid them between*
> *Two milk-white stanes.*
> *So a bird I grew,*
> *And away I flew,*
> *Sing Pippety Pew!*"

"Say that again, my bonny bird, and I'll give you this millstone," said the miller.

> "*Pippety Pew!*
> *My mammy me slew,*
> *My daddy me ate,*
> *My sister Kate*
> *Gathered all my banes,*

*And laid them between*
*Two milk-white stanes.*
*So a bird I grew,*
*And away I flew,*
*Sing Pippety Pew!"*

The miller gave the millstone to the bird, and away it flew till it lighted on its father's housetop. It threw small stones down the chimney, and Katy came out to see what was the matter. The dove threw all the clothes down to her. Then the father came out, and the dove threw all the silver down to him. Then the mother came out. The dove threw the millstone down on her and killed her.

Then the dove flew away, and after that the goodman and his daughter lived happy and died happy.

# JOSEPH JACOBS

## Molly Whuppie†

Once upon a time there was a man and a wife had too many children, and they could not get meat for them, so they took the three youngest and left them in a wood. They travelled and travelled and could never see a house. It began to be dark, and they were hungry. At last they saw a light and made for it; it turned out to be a house. They knocked at the door, and a woman came to it, who said: "What do you want?" They said: "Please let us in and give us something to eat." The woman said: "I can't do that, as my man is a giant, and he would kill you if he comes home." They begged hard. "Let us stop for a little while," said they, "and we will go away before he comes." So she took them in, and set them down before the fire, and gave them milk and bread; but just as they had begun to eat, a great knock came to the door, and a dreadful voice said:

"Fee, fie, fo, fum,
I smell the blood of some earthly one.

Who have you there, wife?" "Eh," said the wife, "it's three poor lassies cold and hungry, and they will go away. Ye won't touch 'em, man." He said nothing, but ate up a big supper, and ordered them to stay all night. Now he had three lassies of his own, and they were to sleep in the same bed with the three strangers. The youngest of the three strange lassies was called Molly Whuppie, and she was very clever. She noticed that before they went to bed the giant put straw ropes round her neck and her sisters', and round his own lassies' necks, he put gold chains.

† Joseph Jacobs, "Molly Whuppie," in *English Fairy Tales* (London: The Bodley Head, 1890).

So Molly took care and did not fall asleep, but waited till she was sure
everyone was sleeping sound. Then she slipped out of the bed, and
took the straw ropes off her own and her sisters' necks, and took the
gold chains off the giant's lassies. She then put the straw ropes on the
giant's lassies and the gold on herself and her sisters, and lay down.
And in the middle of the night up rose the giant, armed with a great
club, and felt for the necks with the straw. It was dark. He took his own
lassies out of the bed on to the floor, and battered them until they were
dead, and then lay down again, thinking he had managed finely. Molly
thought it time she and her sisters were off and away, so she wakened
them and told them to be quiet, and they slipped out of the house.
They all got out safe, and they ran and ran, and never stopped until
morning, when they saw a grand house before them. It turned out to
be a king's house: so Molly went in, and told her story to the king. He
said: "Well, Molly, you are a clever girl, and you have managed well;
but, if you would manage better, and go back, and steal the giant's
sword that hangs on the back of his bed, I would give your eldest sister
my eldest son to marry." Molly said she would try. So she went back,
and managed to slip into the giant's house, and crept in below the bed.
The giant came home, and ate up a great supper, and went to bed.
Molly waited until he was snoring, and she crept out, and reached over
the giant and got down the sword; but just as she got it out over the
bed it gave a rattle, and up jumped the giant, and Molly ran out at the
door and the sword with her; and she ran, and he ran, till they came
to the "Bridge of one hair"; and she got over, but he couldn't and he
says, "Woe worth ye, Molly Whuppie! never ye come again." And she
says: "Twice yet, carle," quoth she, "I'll come to Spain." So Molly took
the sword to the king, and her sister was married to his son.

Well, the king he says: "Ye've managed well, Molly; but if ye would
manage better, and steal the purse that lies below the giant's pillow, I
would marry your second sister to my second son." And Molly said she
would try. So she set out for the giant's house, and slipped in, and hid
again below the bed, and waited till the giant had eaten his supper,
and was snoring sound asleep. She slipped out and slipped her hand
below the pillow, and got out the purse; but just as she was going out
the giant wakened, and ran after her; and she ran, and he ran, till they
came to the "Bridge of one hair," and she got over, but he couldn't,
and he said, "Woe worth ye, Molly Whuppie! never you come again."
"Once yet, carle," quoth she, "I'll come to Spain." So Molly took the
purse to the king, and her second sister was married to the king's second
son.

After that the king says to Molly: "Molly, you are a clever girl, but
if you would do better yet, and steal the giant's ring that he wears on
his finger, I will give you my youngest son for yourself." Molly said she
would try. So back she goes to the giant's house, and hides herself below

the bed. The giant wasn't long ere he came home, and, after he had eaten a great big supper, he went to his bed, and shortly was snoring loud. Molly crept out and reached over the bed, and got hold of the giant's hand, and she pulled and she pulled until she got off the ring; but just as she got it off the giant got up, and gripped her by the hand and he says: "Now I have caught you, Molly Whuppie, and, if I had done as much ill to you as ye have done to me, what would ye do to me?"

Molly says: "I would put you into a sack, and I'd put the cat inside wi' you, and the dog aside you, and a needle and thread and a shears, and I'd hang you up upon the wall, and I'd go to the wood, and choose the thickest stick I could get, and I would come home, and take you down, and bang you till you were dead."

"Well, Molly," says the giant, "I'll just do that to you."

So he gets a sack, and puts Molly into it, and the cat and the dog beside her, and a needle and thread and shears, and hangs her up upon the wall, and goes to the wood to choose a stick.

Molly she sings out: "Oh, if ye saw what I see."

"Oh," says the giant's wife, "what do ye see, Molly?"

But Molly never said a word but, "Oh, if ye saw what I see!"

The giant's wife begged that Molly would take her up into the sack till she would see what Molly saw. So Molly took the shears and cut a hole in the sack, and took out the needle and thread with her, and jumped down and helped the giant's wife up into the sack, and sewed up the hole.

The giant's wife saw nothing, and began to ask to get down again; but Molly never minded, but hid herself at the back of the door. Home came the giant, and a great big tree in his hand, and he took down the sack, and began to batter it. His wife cried, "It's me, man"; but the dog barked and the cat mewed, and he did not know his wife's voice. But Molly came out from the back of the door, and the giant saw her and he after her; and he ran, and she ran, till they came to the "Bridge of one hair," and she got over but he couldn't; and he said, "Woe worth you, Mollie Whuppie! never you come again." "Never more, carle," quoth she, "will I come again to Spain."

So Molly took the ring to the king, and she was married to his youngest son, and she never saw the giant again.

# INTRODUCTION:
# Hans Christian Andersen

Cruelty and violence have often been seen as the signature of German fairy tales, but P. L. Travers, the British writer who created Mary Poppins, found the Grimms' tales downright tame by comparison to the stories composed by Hans Christian Andersen:

> How much rather would I see wicked stepmothers boiled in oil— all over in half a second—than bear the protracted agony of the Little Mermaid or the girl who wore the Red Shoes. There, if you like, is cruelty, sustained, deliberate, contrived. Hans Andersen lets no blood. But his tortures, disguised as piety, are subtle, often demoralizing.[1]

Travers's objection, framed as a protest against the duration and function of the punishment, fails to make a more important point about the target of torture. While the Grimms may boil stepmothers in oil or send them down hills in barrels studded with nails, they rarely allow children to endure torture. Andersen, by contrast, promotes what many readers might perceive as a cult of suffering, death, and transcendence for children rivaled only by what passed for the spiritual edification of children in Puritan cultures.

Nowhere is the effort to celebrate the virtues of physical distress and spiritual anguish more pronounced than in "The Little Match Girl," a story with remarkable staying power. Hardly a year goes by without a new American edition, in large format, with lavish illustrations, clearly intended to appeal to children and often issued in the holiday season. Yet this is a tale hardly designed to buoy spirits. To the contrary, Andersen strains his verbal resources to construct a scene of abject suffering. The "hungry and shivering" [233] heroine in the story's title is not only subjected to freezing temperatures, she must also witness the gay festivities around her (lights shine through the windows). Although she has a home (wind whistles through its cracks), she dares not return to it, for she has not earned a single penny and her father is sure to beat

---

Bracketed page numbers refer to this Norton Critical Edition.
1. P. L. Travers, "The Black Sheep," in *What the Bee Knows: Reflections on Myth, Symbol and Story* (Wellingborough, Northamptonshire: Aquarium, 1989) 229–34.

her. Punctuated with increasingly urgent reports of the dropping tem-
perature, Andersen's narrative builds to a climactic finale in which the
little match girl is embraced by her dead grandmother ("the only one
who had been kind to her" [234]).

Just what is it that compels us to read to children a story that culminates in a "little dead body" [234], a girl "frozen to death" [234]?
William Bennett gives us one answer in the caption that introduces the
story in his best-selling *Book of Virtues*: "To feel another's anguish—
this is the essence of compassion. Here is a Hans Christian Andersen
masterpiece, a simple, tragic story that stirs pity in every child's heart."[2]
What is odd about this gloss on the tale is the way in which it so
passionately endorses a story that "stirs pity" and defines identification
with the victim ("to feel another's anguish") as the source of compassion. To be sure, part of the appeal of the Little Match Girl is her
innocent fragility. John Griffith has pointed out that virtually all of
Andersen's central characters are "small, frail, more likely to be female
than male—above all, *delicate*, an embodiment of that innocence
which is harmlessness, that purity which is incapacity for lust."[3] Their
deaths become what the cultural historian Philippe Ariès has called
"beautiful deaths," sites of radiant spirituality and transcendent meaning.

On occasion the frailty of Andersen's protagonists takes a form so
extreme that it manifests itself in some form of immobility. Think of
Thumbelina, who has to be carried from place to place as if she were
lame, or of the little mermaid, for whom every step is like "treading on
sharp knives," or of the numerous statues and figurines endowed with
emotional lives of extraordinary range and play. The ugly duckling has
to endure glacial incarceration as a precondition for his metamorphosis:
every night the pond in which he swims grows smaller and smaller
until it freezes over completely, holding him fast as frozen ornament,
dead to the world. For Andersen, a turn away from carnality (sometimes
taking the extreme form of mortification of the flesh and physical pa-
ralysis) becomes the prerequisite for spiritual plenitude and salvation.

In "The Red Shoes," the moment of Karen's deepest personal degradation and social disgrace comes when she is in perpetual motion, a
socially disruptive nomadic figure unable to remove the shoes that signal her pride. The dancing Karen is subjected not only to agonizing
pain, but also to public humiliation, for she is held up as an example
of moral depravity:

> "Dance you shall," said the angel, "dance in your red shoes until
> you are cold and pale, until your skin shrivels up like a skeleton's.
> Dance you shall from door to door, and at all the houses where

2. William J. Bennett, "The Little Match Girl," in *The Book of Virtues: A Treasury of Great
Moral Stories* (New York: Simon and Schuster, 1993) 124.
3. John Griffith, "Personal Fantasy in Andersen's Fairy Tales," *Kansas Quarterly* 16 (1984): 82.

the children are vain and proud you shall knock till they hear you
and are frightened." [243]

Only once the offending limbs are cut off by an executioner, leaving
Karen virtually housebound, is there hope for salvation. In a reprise of
the final scene of "The Little Match Girl," the liberation of Karen's
soul offers a glorious vision of what awaits those who are sufficiently
humble, indigent, immobile, and contrite.

In "The Girl Who Trod on the Loaf," we have another example of
how the life of a "proud and vain" [234] child comes to form the basis
for a cautionary tale in public circulation. Ballads are sung "all over
the country" about "the proud young girl who trod on the loaf to save
her pretty shoes" [238], and stories about "Wicked Inger" [238] are
broadcast throughout the land. Inger's one false step figures as the most
vile of all possible sins. Sinking down into the mud, she disappears
from the face of the earth to materialize in the realm of the marsh-
woman. There she is turned into a hideous, living statue, destined to
serve as an ornament for the Devil's entrance hall.

The "protracted agony" to which P. L. Travers refers is on full display
in Inger's story:

> Her clothes seemed to be smeared over with one great blotch of
> slime; a snake had got caught in her hair and was dangling down
> her neck, and from each fold in her dress a toad peeped out with
> a croak like the bark of a wheezy pug-dog. . . . Her back had
> stiffened, her arms and hands had stiffened, her whole body was
> like a stone pillar; all she could turn were the eyes in her head,
> turn them right round, so that they could see backwards—and that
> was a ghastly sight, that was. Then the flies came and crawled over
> her eyes, to and fro. [237]

This image of Inger is permeated with narrative energy and becomes
the most compelling element in the story. The girl's beleaguered body
is described in such loving detail that it becomes a shockingly aesthet-
icized icon of a child suffering a deserved punishment. Andersen's protagonist is not just suffering; she is presented in her death throes, from
which she is released only after years of torment, when she is transformed into a bird by the prayers of a stranger.

Of all Andersen's characters, it is probably the little mermaid who is
the real virtuoso in the art of silent suffering. With her tongue cut out
by the sea witch, she drinks a potion designed to endow her with legs
and feels a "two-edged sword" piercing her "delicate body" [227]. After
suffering the pangs of unrequited love, she is sentenced to three hundred years of good deeds to earn an immortal soul. Here again, much
of the representational energy in the text is channeled in the direction
of portraying anguish and pain, transforming mortal agony into transcendent beauty.

To gain mobility in the human world, Andersen's mermaid must sacrifice her voice to the sea witch, a figure who, in her affiliation with biological corruption, grotesque sensuality, and ugly deaths, is diametrically opposed to the promise of eternal salvation. The "slimy open space" [225] where she resides, the fat water-snakes that feed on her "great spongy bosom" [225] and the bones of human folk that support her house all point to a regime that is emphatically anchored in nature rather than culture, pointing to the condition of human mortality and bodily decay. Initially attracted to what the sea witch can provide, the little mermaid ultimately renounces her black magic when she flings the knife meant to kill the prince into the sea and is rewarded with the possibility of earning immortality.

Our own culture's answer to Andersen's spiritually triumphant mermaid appears in the adventurous, rebellious, curious, and "upwardly mobile"[4] Ariel created by Disney Studio. As one shrewd critic of *The Little Mermaid* observes, the Disney film establishes a powerful hierarchical relationship dividing the blithe Caribbean-equivalent sea creatures from the humans above who engage in labor and transform nature into culture. Ariel's longing for this realm, which manifests itself in the commodity fetishism of her enthusiastic collecting of booty from shipwrecks, is fulfilled through Ursula, a grotesque Medusa-like octopus who, like Andersen's sea witch, represents the monstrosity of feminine power. Ariel may regain her voice when she is assimilated to the human world in the end, but Disney conveniently leaves us in the dark about the cost, allowing the couple's final embrace to erase Ariel's rebelliousness, her troubled relationship with the feminine, and the painful self-mutilation involved in her transformation. As Patrick D. Murphy points out, "the escapist character of the film" is especially evident in its avoidance of the problem that will inevitably arise when "Ariel's former friend Flounder shows up on the dinner table one evening."[5]

Maurice Sendak, renowned for creating vibrantly spirited and scrappy child characters, was disturbed by the "disquieting passivity" in Andersen's books for children. "At his worst," Sendak comments on Andersen, "he dreadfully sentimentalizes children; they rarely have the spunk, shrewdness, and character with which he endows inanimate objects."[6] The little mermaid, the little match girl, and Karen of "The Red Shoes" he found particularly "irritating," surely in part for the simple reason that the stories of all these creatures end with their deaths. "His heroines always wind up going to the bosom of God (if they're good), or else

---

4. Laura Sells, " 'Where Do the Mermaids Stand?' Voice and Body in *The Little Mermaid*," in *From Mouse to Mermaid: The Politics of Film, Gender and Culture*, ed. Elizabeth Bell, Lynda Haas, Laura Sells (Bloomington: Indiana UP, 1995) 179.
5. Patrick D. Murphy, " 'The Whole Wide World Was Scrubbed Clean': The Androcentric Animation of Denatured Disney," in *From Mouse to Mermaid*, 133.
6. Maurice Sendak, "Hans Christian Andersen," in *Caldecott & Co.: Notes on Books & Pictures* (New York: Farrar, Straus and Giroux, Michael di Capua Books, 1988) 33, 34.

they're praying or being saved from Hell by someone else's prayers," the illustrator Trina Schart Hyman observed in recollecting her childhood reading of Andersen.[7]

Cheerful self-effacement becomes the badge of Andersen's characters. Joyfully embracing death, they reproach themselves for their sins and endorse piety, humility, passivity, and a host of other "virtues" designed to promote subservient behavior. Jack Zipes succinctly captures the contradictory logic of Andersen's narratives: "true virtue and self-realization can be obtained through self-denial."[8] For Zipes, the message of Andersen's stories is based on "Andersen's astute perception and his own experience as a lower-class clumsy youth who sought to cultivate himself: by becoming voiceless, walking with legs like knives, and denying one's needs, one (as a non-entity) gains divine recognition."[9] While the stories may reflect Andersen's own troubled psyche and his personal experience as an upwardly mobile writer, they have also engaged generations of children and adults alike with their melodramatic depictions of desire, loss, and self-immolation.

## The Little Mermaid†

Far out at sea the water's as blue as the petals of the loveliest cornflower, and as clear as the purest glass; but it's very deep, deeper than any anchor can reach. Many church steeples would have to be piled up one above the other to reach from the bottom of the sea to the surface. Right down there live the sea people.

Now you mustn't for a moment suppose that it's a bare white sandy bottom. Oh, no. The most wonderful trees and plants are growing down there, with stalks and leaves that bend so easily that they stir at the very slightest movement of the water, just as though they were alive. All the fishes, big ones and little ones, slip in and out of the branches just like birds in the air up here. Down in the deepest part of all is the sea King's palace. Its walls are made of coral, and the long pointed windows of the clearest amber; but the roof is made of cockle-shells that open and shut with the current. It's a pretty sight, for in each shell is a dazzling pearl; any single one of them would be a splendid ornament in a Queen's crown.

The sea King down there had been a widower for some years, but

7. Trina Schart Hyman, " 'Cut It Down, and You Will Find Something at the Roots,' " in *The Reception of Grimms' Fairy Tales: Responses, Reactions, Revisions*, ed. Donald Haase (Detroit: Wayne State UP, 1993) 294.
8. Jack Zipes, "Hans Christian Andersen," in *Fairy Tales and the Art of Subversion: The Classical Genre for Children and the Process of Civilization* (New York: Wildman Press, 1983) 85.
9. Zipes, "Andersen," 85.
† From *Eighty Fairy Tales* by Hans Christian Andersen, trans. R. P. Keigwin. Translation copyright © 1976 by Skandinavisk Bogforlag, Flensteds Forlag. Reprinted by permission of Pantheon Books, a division of Random House, Inc.

his old mother kept house for him. She was a clever woman, but proud of her noble birth; that's why she went about with twelve oysters on her tail, while the rest of the nobility had to put up with only six. But apart from that, she was deserving of special praise, because she was so fond of the little sea Princesses, her grandchildren. They were six pretty children, but the youngest was the loveliest of them all. Her skin was as clear and delicate as a rose-leaf, her eyes were as blue as the deepest lake, but like the others she had no feet; her body ended in a fish's tail.

All the long day they could play down there in the palace, in the great halls where living flowers grew out of the walls. The fishes would swim in to them, just as with us the swallows fly in when we open the windows; but the fishes swam right up to the little Princesses, fed out of their hands, and let themselves be patted.

Outside the palace was a large garden with trees of deep blue and fiery red; the fruit all shone like gold, and the flowers like a blazing fire with stalks and leaves that were never still. The soil itself was the finest sand, but blue like a sulphur flame. Over everything down there lay a strange blue gleam; you really might have thought you were standing high up in the air with nothing to see but sky above and below you, rather than that you were at the bottom of the sea. When there was a dead calm you caught a glimpse of the sun, which looked like a purple flower pouring out all light from its cup.

Each of the small Princesses had her own little plot in the garden, where she could dig and plant at will. One of them gave her flower-bed the shape of a whale, another thought it nicer for hers to look like a little mermaid; but the youngest made hers quite round like the sun, and would only have flowers that shone red like it. She was a curious child, silent and thoughtful; and when the other sisters decorated their gardens with the most wonderful things they had got from sunken ships, she would have nothing but the rose-red flowers that were like the sun high above, and a beautiful marble statue. It was the statue of a handsome boy, hewn from the clear white stone and come down to the bottom of the sea from a wreck. Beside the statue she planted a rose-red weeping willow, which grew splendidly and let its fresh foliage droop over the statue right down to the blue sandy bottom. Here the shadow took on a violet tinge and, like the branches, was never still; roots and treetop looked as though they were playing at kissing each other.

Nothing pleased her more than to hear about the world of humans up above the sea. The old grandmother had to tell her all she knew about ships and towns, people and animals. One thing especially surprised her with its beauty, and this was that the flowers had a smell—at the bottom of the sea they hadn't any—and also that the woods were green and the fishes you saw in among the branches could sing as clearly and prettily as possible. It was the little birds that the grandmother called fishes; otherwise, never having seen a bird, the small sea Princesses would never have understood her.

"As soon as you are fifteen," the grandmother told them, "you shall be allowed to rise to the surface, and to sit in the moonlight on the rocks and watch the great ships sailing past; you shall see woods and towns." That coming year one of the sisters was to have her fifteenth birthday, but the rest of them—well, they were each one year younger than the other; so the youngest of them had a whole five years to wait before she could rise up from the bottom and see how things are with us. But each promised to tell the others what she had seen and found most interesting on the first day; for their grandmother didn't really tell them enough—there were so many things they were longing to hear about.

None of them was so full of longing as the youngest: the very one who had most time to wait and was so silent and thoughtful. Many a night she stood at the open window and gazed up through the dark-blue water, where the fishes frisked their tails and fins. She could see the moon and the stars, though it's true their light was rather pale; and yet through the water they looked much larger than they do to us, and if ever a kind of black cloud went gliding along below them, she knew it was either a whale swimming above her or else a vessel with many passengers; these certainly never imagined that a lovely little mermaid was standing beneath and stretching up her white hands towards the keel of their ship.

By now the eldest Princess was fifteen and allowed to go up to the surface.

When she came back, she had a hundred things to tell; but the loveliest, she said, was to lie in the moonlight on a sandbank in a calm sea and there, close in to the shore, to look at the big town where the lights were twinkling like a hundred stars; to listen to the sound of music and the noise and clatter of carts and people; to see all the towers and spires on the churches and hear the bells ringing. And just because she couldn't get there, it was this above everything that she longed for.

Oh, how the youngest sister drank it all in! And, when later in the evening she stood at the open window and gazed up through the dark-blue water, she thought of the big town with all its noise and clatter, and then she seemed to catch the sound of the churchbells ringing down to her.

The following year, the second sister was allowed to go up through the water and swim wherever she liked. She came to the surface just as the sun was setting, and that was the sight she found most beautiful. The whole sky had looked like gold, she said, and the clouds—well, she just couldn't describe how beautiful they were as they sailed, all crimson and violet, over her head. And yet, much faster than they, a flock of wild swans flew like a long white veil across the water where the sun was setting. She swam off in that direction, but the sun sank, and its rosy light was swallowed up by sea and cloud.

The year after that, the third sister went up. She was the boldest of them all, and she swam up a wide river that flowed into the sea. She saw delightful green slopes with grape-vines; manors and farms peeped out among magnificent woods; she heard all the birds singing; and the sun was so hot that she often had to dive under the water to cool her burning face. In a small cove she came upon a swarm of little human children splashing about quite naked in the water. She wanted to play with them, but they ran away terrified, and a little black animal came up; it was a dog. She had never seen a dog before. It barked at her so dreadfully that she got frightened and made for the open sea. But never could she forget the magnificent woods, the green slopes and the darling children, who could swim on the water although they had no fishes' tails.

The fourth sister was not so bold. She kept far out in the wild waste of ocean, and told them that was just what was so wonderful: you could see for miles and miles around you, and the sky hung above like a big glass bell. She had seen ships, but a long way off, looking like sea-gulls. The jolly dolphins had been turning somersaults, and enormous whales had spurted up water from their nostrils, so that they seemed to be surrounded by a hundred fountains.

And now it was the turn of the fifth sister. Her birthday happened to come in winter, and so she saw things that the others hadn't seen the first time. The sea appeared quite green, and great icebergs were floating about; they looked like pearls, she said, and yet were much larger than the church-towers put up by human beings. They were to be seen in the most fantastic shapes, and they glittered like diamonds. She had sat down on one of the biggest, and all the ships gave it a wide berth as they sailed in terror past where she sat with her long hair streaming in the wind. But late in the evening the sky became overcast with clouds; it lightened and thundered, as the dark waves lifted the great blocks of ice right up, so that they flashed in the fierce red lightning. All the ships took in sail, and amidst the general horror and alarm, she sat calmly on her floating iceberg and watched the blue lightning zigzag into the glittering sea.

The first time one of the sisters went up to the surface, she would always be delighted to see so much that was new and beautiful; but afterwards, when they were older and could go up as often as they liked, it no longer interested them; they longed to be back again, and when a month had passed they said that, after all, it was nicest down below —it was such a comfort to be home.

Often of an evening the five sisters used to link arms and float up together out of the water. They had lovely voices, more beautiful than any human voice; and when a gale sprang up threatening shipwreck, they would swim in front of the ships and sing tempting songs of how delightful it was at the bottom of the sea. And they told the sailors not to be afraid of coming down there, but the sailors couldn't make out the words of their song; they thought it was the noise of the gale, nor did they ever see any of the delights the mermaids promised, because when the ship sank the crew were drowned, and only as dead men did they come to the palace of the sea King.

When of an evening the sisters floated up through the sea like this, arm in arm, their little sister stayed back all alone gazing after them. She would have cried, only a mermaid hasn't any tears, and so she suffers all the more.

"Oh, if only I were fifteen!" she said. "I'm sure I shall love that world up there and the people who live in it."

And then at last she was fifteen.

"There, now you'll soon be off our hands," said her grandmother, the old Dowager Queen. "Come now, let me dress you up like your sisters;" and she put a wreath of white lilies on her hair, but every petal of the flowers was half a pearl. And the old lady made eight big oysters nip tight on to the Princess's tail to show her high rank.

"Oo! that hurts," said the little mermaid.

"Yes," said the grandmother, "one can't have beauty for nothing."

How she would have liked to shake off all this finery and put away the heavy wreath! The red flowers in her garden suited her much better, but she didn't dare make any change. "Goodbye," she said, and went up through the water as light and clear as a bubble.

The sun had just set, as she put her head up out of the sea, but the clouds had still a gleam of rose and gold; and up in the pale pink sky the evening star shone clear and beautiful. The air was soft and fresh, and the sea dead calm. A large three-masted ship was lying there, with only one sail hoisted because not a breath of wind was stirring, and sailors were lolling about in the rigging and on the yards. There was music and singing, and as it grew dark hundreds of lanterns were lit that, with their many different colours, looked as if the flags of all nations were flying in the breeze.

The little mermaid swam right up to the porthole of the cabin and, every time she rose with the swell of the wave, she could see through the clear glass a crowd of splendidly dressed people; but the handsomest of them all was a young Prince with large dark eyes. He couldn't have been much more than sixteen; it was his birthday, and that's why there was all this set-out. As the young Prince came out on to the deck where sailors were dancing, over a hundred rockets swished up into the sky— and broke into a glitter like broad daylight. That frightened the little mermaid, and she dived down under the water; but she quickly popped up her head again, and look! it was just as if all the stars in heaven were falling down on her. Never had she seen such fireworks. Great suns went spinning around, gorgeous firefishes swerving into the blue air, and all this glitter was mirrored in the clear still water. On board the ship herself it was so light that you could make out every little rope, let alone the passengers. Oh, how handsome the young Prince was; he shook hands with the sailors, he laughed and smiled, while the music went floating out into the loveliness of the night.

It grew late, but the little mermaid couldn't take her eyes off the ship and the beautiful Prince. The coloured lanterns were put out, the rockets no longer climbed into the sky, and the cannon were heard no more; but deep down in the sea there was a mumbling and a rumbling. Meanwhile the mermaid stayed on the water, rocking up and down so that she could look into the cabin. But the ship now gathered speed; one after another her sails were spread. The waves increased, heavy clouds blew up, and lightning flashed in the distance. Yes, they were in for a terrible storm; so the sailors took in their sails, as the great ship rocked and scudded through the raging sea. The waves rose higher and higher like huge black mountains, threatening to bring down the mast, but the ship dived like a swan into the trough of the waves and then rode up again on their towering crests. The little mermaid thought, why, it must be fun for a ship to sail like that—but the crew didn't. The vessel creaked and cracked, the stout planks crumpled up under the heavy pounding of the sea against the ship, the mast snapped in the middle like a stick, and then the ship gave a lurch to one side as the water came rushing into the hold. At last the little mermaid realized that they were in danger; she herself had to look out for the beams and bits of wreckage that were drifting on the water. One moment it was so pitch dark that she couldn't see a thing, but then when the lightning came it was so bright that she could make out everyone on board. It was now a case of each man for himself. The young Prince was the one she was looking for and, as the ship broke up, she saw him disappear into the depths of the sea. Just for one moment she felt quite pleased, for now he would come down to her; but then she remembered that humans can't live under the water and that only as a dead man could he come down to her father's palace. No, no, he mustn't die. So she swam in among the drifting beams and planks, with no thought for the danger of being crushed by them; she dived deep down and came right up again among the waves, and at last she found the young Prince. He could hardly swim any longer in the heavy sea; his arms and legs were beginning to tire, the fine eyes were closed, he would certainly have drowned if the little mermaid had not come. She held his head above water and then let the waves carry her along with him.

By morning the gale had quite gone; not the smallest trace of the ship was to be seen. The sun rose red and glowing out of the water and seemed to bring life to the Prince's cheeks, but his eyes were still shut. The mermaid kissed his fine high forehead and smoothed back his dripping hair. He was like the marble statue down in her little garden; she kissed him again and wished that he might live.

Presently she saw the mainland in front of her, high blue mountains with the white snow glittering on their peaks like nestling swans. Down by the shore were lovely green woods and, in front of them, a church or a convent—she wasn't sure which, but anyhow a building. Lemon and orange trees were growing in the garden, and tall palm trees in front of the gate. At this point the sea formed a little inlet, where the water was quite smooth but very deep close in to the rock where the fine white sand had silted up. She swam here with the handsome Prince and laid him on the sand with his head carefully pillowed in the warm sunshine.

Now there was a sound of bells from the large white building, and a number of young girls came through the garden. So the little mermaid swam farther out behind some large boulders that were sticking out of the water and covered her hair and breast with seafoam, so that her face wouldn't show; and then she watched to see who would come to the help of the unfortunate Prince.

It wasn't long before a young girl came along. She seemed quite frightened, but only for a moment; then she fetched several others, and the mermaid saw the Prince come round and smile at those about him; but no smile came out to her, for of course he didn't know she had rescued him. She felt so sad that, when he was taken away into the large building, she dived down sorrowfully into the sea and went back to her father's palace.

Silent and thoughtful as she had always been, she now became much more so. Her sisters asked her what she had seen on her first visit to the surface, but she wouldn't say.

Many a morning and many an evening she rose up to where she had left the Prince. She saw the fruit in the garden ripen and be gathered, she saw the snow melt on the peaks, but she never saw the Prince, and so she always turned back more despondent than ever. Her one comfort was to sit in the little garden with her arms round the beautiful marble statue which was so like the Prince. She never looked after her flowers, and they grew into a sort of wilderness, out over the paths, and braided their long stalks and leaves on to the branches of the trees, until the light was quite shut out.

At last she could keep it to herself no longer, but told one of her sisters; and immediately all the rest got to know, but nobody else—except a few other mermaids who didn't breathe a word to any but their nearest friends. One of these was able to say who the Prince was; she, too, had seen the party that was held on board the ship, and knew where he came from and whereabouts his kingdom was.

"Come on, little sister!" said the other Princesses. And with arms round each other's shoulders they rose in one line out of the sea, just in front of where the Prince's castle stood. It was built in a glistening stone of pale yellow with great flights of marble steps; one of these led straight into the sea. Splendid gilt domes curved above the roof, and between the pillars that went right round the building were lifelike sculptures in marble. Through the clear glass in the tall windows you could see into the most magnificent rooms; these were hung with sumptuous silk curtains and tapestries and their walls were covered with large paintings that were a delight to the eye. In the middle of the biggest room was a huge splashing fountain; its spray was flung high up to the glass dome in the ceiling, through which the sun shone down on to the water and the beautiful plants growing in the great pool.

Now she knew where he lived, and many an evening and many a night she would come to the surface at that spot. She swam much closer to the shore than any of the others had ever dared. She even went up the narrow creek under the fine marble balcony that threw its long shadow across the water. Here she would sit and gaze at the young Prince, who imagined he was quite alone in the clear moonlight.

Often in the evening she saw him go out to the strains of music in his splendid vessel that was dressed with flags. She peeped out from among the green rushes and, when the wind caught her long silvery veil and someone saw it, they fancied it was a swan spreading its wings.

On many nights, when the fishermen were at sea with their torches, she heard them speaking so well of the young Prince, and that made her glad she had saved his life when he drifted about half-dead on the waves; and she thought of how closely his head had rested on her bosom and how lovingly she had kissed him. But he knew nothing whatsoever about that, never even dreamed she existed.

Fonder and fonder she became of human beings, more and more she longed for their company. Their world seemed to her to be so much larger than her own. You see, they could fly across the ocean in ships, climb the tall mountains high above the clouds; and the lands they owned stretched with woods and meadows further than her eyes could see. There was so much she would have liked to know, but her sisters couldn't answer all her questions, and so she asked the old grandmother, for she knew all about the upper world—as she so aptly called the countries above the sea.

"If people don't drown," asked the little mermaid, "can they go on living for ever? Don't they die, as we do down here in the sea?"

"Yes, yes," said the old lady, "They, too, have to die; their lifetime is even shorter than ours. We can live for three hundred years, but when our life here comes to an end we merely turn into foam on the water; we haven't even a grave down here among those we love. We've no immortal soul; we shall never have another life. We're like the green rush—once it's been cut it can't grow green again. But human beings

have a soul which lives for ever; still lives after the body is turned to
dust. The soul goes climbing up through the clear air, up till it reaches
the shining stars. Just as we rise up out of the sea and look at the
countries of human beings, so they rise up to beautiful unknown
regions—ones we shall never see."

"Why haven't we got an immortal soul?" the little mermaid asked
sadly. "I would give the whole three hundred years I have to live, to
become for one day a human being and then share in that heavenly
world."

"You mustn't go worrying about that," said the grandmother. "We're
much happier and better off here than the people who live up there."

"So then I'm doomed to die and float like foam on the sea, never
to hear the music of the waves or see the lovely flowers and the red
sun. Isn't there anything at all I can do to win an immortal soul?"

"No," said the old lady. "Only if a human being loved you so much
that you were more to him than father and mother—if he clung to you
with all his heart and soul, and let the priest put his right hand in yours
as a promise to be faithful and true here and in all eternity—then his
soul would flow over into your body and you, too, would get a share
in human happiness. He would give you a soul and yet keep his own.
But that can never happen. The very thing that's so beautiful here in
the sea, your fish's tail, seems ugly to people on the earth; they know
so little about it that they have to have two clumsy supports called legs,
in order to look nice."

That made the little mermaid sigh and look sadly at her fish's tail.

"We must be content," said the old lady. "Let's dance and be gay
for the three hundred years we have to live—that's a good time, isn't
it?—then one can have one's fill of sleep in the grave all the more
pleasantly afterwards. To-night we're having a Court ball."

That was something more magnificent than we ever see on the earth.
In the great ballroom, walls and ceiling were made of thick but quite
clear glass. Several hundred enormous shells, rose-red and grass-green,
were ranged on either side, each with a blue-burning flame which lit
up the whole room and, shining out through the walls, lit up the sea
outside as well. Countless fishes, big and small, could be seen swimming towards the glass walls; the scales on some of them shone purple-
red, and on others like silver and gold . . . Through the middle of the
ballroom flowed a wide running stream, on which mermen and mermaids danced to their own beautiful singing. No human beings have
voices so lovely. The little mermaid sang the most sweetly of them all,
and they clapped their hands for her, and for a moment there was joy
in her heart, for she knew that she had the most beautiful voice on
earth or sea. But then her thoughts soon returned to the world above
her; she couldn't forget the handsome Prince and her sorrow at not
possessing, like him, an immortal soul. So she crept out of her father's

palace and, while all in there was song and merriment, she sat grieving in her little garden. Suddenly she caught the sound of a horn echoing down through the water, and she thought, "Ah, there he is, sailing up above—he whom I love more than father or mother, he who is always in my thoughts and in whose hands I would gladly place the happiness of my life. I will dare anything to win him and an immortal soul. While my sisters are dancing there in my father's palace, I will go to the sea witch; I've always been dreadfully afraid of her, but perhaps she can help me and tell me what to do."

So the little mermaid left her garden and set off for the place where the witch lived, on the far side of the roaring whirlpools. She had never been that way before. There were no flowers growing, no sea grass, nothing but the bare grey sandy bottom stretching right up to the whirlpools, where the water went swirling round like roaring mill-wheels and pulled everything it could clutch down with it to the depths. She had to pass through the middle of these battering eddies in order to get to the sea witch's domain; and here for a long stretch there was no other way than over hot bubbling mud—the witch called it her swamp. Her house lay behind it in the middle of an extraordinary wood. All the trees and bushes were polyps, half animals and half plants. They looked like hundred-headed snakes growing out of the earth; all the branches were long slimy arms with supple worm-like fingers, and joint by joint from the root up to the very tip they were continuously on the move. They wound themselves tight round everything they could clutch hold of in the sea, and they never let go. The little mermaid was terribly scared as she paused at the edge of the wood. Her heart was throbbing with fear; she nearly turned back. But then she remembered the Prince and the human soul, and that gave her courage. She wound her long flowing hair tightly round her head, so that the polyps shouldn't have that to clutch her by, she folded both her hands across her breast and darted off just as a fish darts through the water, in among the hideous polyps which reached out for her with their supple arms and fingers. She noticed how each of them had something they had caught, held fast by a hundred little arms like hoops of iron. White skeletons of folk who had been lost at sea and had sunk to the bottom looked out from the arms of the polyps. Ship's rudders and chests were gripped tight, skeletons of land animals, and—most horrible of all—a small mermaid whom they had caught and throttled.

Now she came to a large slimy open space in the wood where big fat water-snakes were frisking about and showing their hideous whitish-yellow bellies. In the middle was a house built of the bones of human folk who had been wrecked. There sat the sea witch letting a toad feed out of her mouth, just as we might let a little canary come and peck sugar. She called the horrible fat water-snakes her little chicks and allowed them to sprawl about her great spongy bosom.

"I know well enough what you're after," said the sea witch. "How stupid of you! Still, you shall have your way, and it'll bring you into misfortune, my lovely Princess. You want to get rid of your fish's tail and in its place have a couple of stumps to walk on like a human being, so that the young Prince can fall in love with you and you can win him and an immortal soul"—and with that the witch gave such a loud repulsive laugh that the toad and the snakes fell to the ground and remained sprawling there. "You've just come at the right time," said the witch. "Tomorrow, once the sun's up, I couldn't help you for another year. I shall make you a drink, and before sunrise you must swim to land, sit down on the shore and drink it up. Then your tail will divide in two and shrink into what humans call 'pretty legs'. But it'll hurt; it'll be like a sharp sword going through you. Everyone who sees you will say you are the loveliest human child they have ever seen. You will keep your graceful movements—no dancer can glide so lightly—but every step you take will feel as if you were treading on a sharp knife, enough to make your feet bleed. Are you ready to bear all that? If you are, I'll help you."

"Yes," said the little mermaid, and her voice trembled; but she thought of her Prince and the prize of an immortal soul.

"Still, don't forget this," said the witch: "once you've got human shape, you can never become a mermaid again. You can never go down through the water to your sisters and to your father's palace; and if you don't win the Prince's love, so that he forgets father and mother for you and always has you in his thoughts and lets the priest join your hands together to be man and wife, then you won't get an immortal soul. The first morning after the Prince marries someone else, your heart must break and you become foam on the water."

"I'm ready," said the little mermaid, pale as death.

"Then there's me to be paid," said the witch, "and you're not getting my help for nothing. You have the loveliest voice of all down here at the bottom of the sea. With that voice, no doubt, you think to enchant him; but that voice you shall hand over to me. I demand the best that you have for me to make a rich drink. You see, I have to give you my own blood, in order that the drink may be as sharp as a two-edged sword."

"But if you take my voice," said the little mermaid, "what shall I have left?"

"Your lovely form," said the witch, "your graceful movements, and your speaking eyes. With those you can so easily enchant a human heart . . . Well, where's your spunk? Put out your little tongue and let me cut it off in payment; then you shall be given the potent mixture."

"Go on, then," said the little mermaid, and the witch put the kettle on for brewing the magic drink. "Cleanliness before everything," she said, as she scoured out the kettle with a bundle of snakes she had knotted together. Next, she scratched her breast and let her black blood drip down into the kettle; the steam took on the weirdest shapes, terrifying to look at. The witch kept popping fresh things into the kettle, and when it boiled up properly it sounded like a crocodile in tears. At last the brew was ready; it looked like the clearest water.

"There you are!" said the witch and cut off the little mermaid's tongue; she was now dumb and could neither sing nor speak.

"If the polyps should catch hold of you, as you go back through the wood," said the witch, "throw but a single drop of this drink on them, and their arms and fingers will burst into a thousand pieces." But the little mermaid had no need to do that. The polyps shrank from her in terror when they saw the dazzling drink that shone in her hand like a glittering star. So she quickly came through the wood, the swamp and the roaring whirlpools.

She could see her father's palace; the lights were out in the great ballroom. They were all certain to be asleep in there by this time; but she didn't anyhow dare to look for them, now that she was dumb and was going to leave them for ever. She felt as if her heart must break for grief. She stole into the garden, picked one flower from each of her sisters' flower-beds, blew a thousand finger kisses towards the palace, and rose then through the dark-blue sea.

The sun was not yet up, as she sighted the Prince's castle and climbed the magnificent marble steps. The moon was shining wonderfully clear. The little mermaid drank the sharp burning potion, and it was as if a two-edged sword pierced through her delicate body—she fainted and lay as though dead. Then the sun, streaming over the sea, woke her up, and she felt a sharp pain. But there in front of her stood the handsome young Prince. He stared at her with his coal-black eyes, so that she cast down her own—and saw that her fish's tail had gone and she had the sweetest little white legs that any young girl could wish for; but she was quite naked and so she wrapped herself in her long flowing hair. The Prince asked who she was and how she had come there, and she could only look back at him so gently and yet so sadly out of her deep-blue eyes; for of course she couldn't speak. Then he took her by the hand and led her into the castle. Every step she took, as the witch had foretold, was as though she were treading on sharp knives and pricking gimlets; but she gladly put up with that. By the side of the Prince she went along as lightly as a bubble; and he and all of them marvelled at the charm of her graceful movements.

Costly dresses were given her of silk and muslin; she was the most beautiful in all the castle. But she was dumb; she could neither sing nor speak. Lovely slave-girls in gold and silk came out and danced before the Prince and his royal parents; one of them sang more beautifully than all the rest, and the Prince clapped his hands and smiled at her. This saddened the little mermaid, for she knew that she herself had sung far more beautifully. And she thought, "Oh, if only he knew that I gave my voice away for ever, in order to be with him!"

Next, the slave-girls danced a graceful gliding dance to the most delightful music; and then the little mermaid raised her pretty white arms, lingered on the tips of her toes and then glided across the floor, dancing as no one had danced before. She looked more and more lovely with every movement, and her eyes spoke more deeply to the heart than the slave-girls' singing.

Everyone was enchanted, and especially the Prince, who called her his little foundling. Still she went on dancing, although every time her foot touched the ground it felt as though she was treading on sharp knives. The Prince said that she must never leave him, and she was allowed to sleep on a velvet cushion outside his door.

He had boys' clothes made for her, so that she could go riding with him on horseback. They rode through the sweet-smelling woods, where the green boughs grazed her shoulders and the little birds sang among the cool foliage. She went climbing with the Prince up high mountains and, although her delicate feet bled so that others could see it, she only laughed and went on and on with him, until they could see the clouds sailing below them like a flock of birds migrating to other lands.

Back at the Prince's castle, when at night the others were asleep, she would go out on to the broad marble steps and cool her tingling feet in the cold sea-water; and then she would think of those down there in the depths of the sea.

One night her sisters rose up arm in arm singing so mournfully as they swam on the water. She made signs to them, and they recognized her and told her how unhappy she had made them all. After that, they used to visit her every night; and once, in the far distance, she saw her old grandmother who hadn't been above the water for many years, and also the sea King wearing his crown. They both stretched out their hands towards her, but they didn't venture in so near to the shore as the five sisters.

Day by day she became dearer to the Prince. He loved her as one loves a dear good child, but he didn't dream of making her his Queen; and yet she had to become his wife, or else she would never win an immortal soul, but on his wedding morning would be turned to foam on the sea.

"Do you like me best of all?" the little mermaid's eyes seemed to say, when he took her in his arms and kissed her lovely brow.

"Yes," said the prince, "You're the dearest of all, because you have the kindest heart. You are the most devoted to me, and you remind me of a young girl I once saw but shall probably never see again. I was sailing in a ship that was wrecked; the waves drove me ashore near a sacred temple where a number of young girls were serving. The youngest, who found me on the beach and saved my life—I only saw her twice. She was the only one I could ever love in this world, but you are so like her that you almost take the place of her image in my heart. She belongs to the holy temple, so that fortune has been kind in sending you to me. We will never part."

"Ah, little does he know that it was I who saved his life," thought the mermaid; "that I carried him across the sea to the temple in the wood; that I waited in the foam and watched if anyone would come. I saw the pretty girl he loves better than me"—and the mermaid sighed deeply, for she didn't know how to cry. "The girl belongs to the sacred temple, he says; she'll never come out into the world, and they'll never meet again. I am with him. I see him every day. I will take care of him, love him, give up my life to him."

But now the Prince was getting married they said—married to the pretty daughter of the neighbouring King, and that was why he was fitting out such a splendid ship. The Prince was going off to take a look at his neighbour's kingdom—that was how they put it, meaning that it was really to take a look at his neighbour's daughter. A large suite was to go with him, but the little mermaid shook her head and laughed. She knew the Prince's thoughts far better than all the others. "I shall have to go," he said to her. "I shall have to visit the pretty Princess, as my parents are so insistent. But force me to bring her back here as my wife, that they will never do. I can't love her. She's not like the beautiful girl in the temple, as you are. If I ever had to find a bride, I would rather have you, my dear mute foundling with the speaking eyes," and he kissed her red mouth, played with her long hair and laid his head against her heart, so that it dreamed of human happiness and an immortal soul.

"You've no fear of the sea, have you, my dumb child?" he asked, as they stood on board the splendid ship that was to take him to the neighbouring kingdom. And he told her of stormy gales and dead calms, of strange fishes at the bottom of the ocean, and all that the diver had seen there; and she smiled at his tales, for she knew better than anyone else about the bottom of the sea.

At night, when there was an unclouded moon and all were asleep but the helmsman at his wheel, she sat by the ship's rail and stared down through the clear water; and she seemed to see her father's palace, with her old grandmother standing on the top of it in her silver crown and gazing up through the swift current at the keel of the vessel. Then her sisters came up on to the water and looked at her with eyes full of sorrow, wringing their white hands. She beckoned to them and smiled and would have liked to tell them that all was going well and happily with her; but the cabin-boy came up at that moment, and the sisters dived down, so that the boy felt satisfied that the white something he had seen was foam on the water.

Next morning the ship sailed into the harbour of the neighbouring King's magnificent capital. The church-bells all rang out; and trumpets were blown from the tall battlements, while the soldiers saluted with gleaming bayonets and flying colours. Every day there was a fête. Balls and parties were given one after another, but nothing had yet been seen of the Princess; it was said that she was being educated abroad in a sacred temple, where she had lessons in all the royal virtues. At last she arrived.

The little mermaid was eager for a glimpse of her beauty, and she had to admit that she had never seen anyone more charming to look at. Her complexion was so clear and delicate, and behind the long dark lashes smiled a pair of trusting deep-blue eyes.

"It's you!" cried the Prince. "You who rescued me, when I was lying half-dead on the shore." And he clasped his blushing bride in his arms. "Oh, I'm too, too happy," he said to the little mermaid. "My dearest wish—more than I ever dared to hope for—has been granted me. My happiness will give you pleasure, because you're fonder of me than any of the others." Then the little mermaid kissed his hand, and already she felt as if her heart was breaking. The morrow of his wedding would mean death to her and change her to foam on the sea.

All the church-bells were ringing, as the heralds rode round the streets to proclaim the betrothal. On every altar sweet oil was burning in rich lamps of silver. The priests swung their censers, and bride and bridegroom joined hands and received the blessing of the bishop. Dressed in silk and gold, the little mermaid stood holding the bride's train; but her ears never heard the festive music, her eyes never saw the holy rites; she was thinking of her last night on earth, of all she had lost in this world.

That same evening, bride and bridegroom went on board the ship; the cannon thundered, the flags were all flying, and amidships they had put up a royal tent of gold and purple, strewn with luxurious cushions; here the wedded couple were to sleep that calm cool night.

The sails filled with the breeze and the ship glided lightly and smoothly over the clear water.

As darkness fell, coloured lanterns were lit, and the crew danced merrily on the deck. The little mermaid could not help thinking of the first time she came up out of the sea and gazed on just such a scene of joy and splendour. And now she joined in the dance, swerving and swooping as lightly as a swallow that avoids pursuit; and shouts of admiration greeted her on every side. Never had she danced so brilliantly. It was as if sharp knives were wounding her delicate feet, but she never felt it; more painful was the wound in her heart. She knew that this was the last evening she would see the Prince for whom she had turned her back on kindred and home, given up her beautiful voice, and every day suffered hours of agony without his suspecting a thing. This was the last night she would breathe the same air as he, gaze on the deep sea and the star-blue sky. An endless night, without thoughts, without dreams, awaited her who had no soul and could never win one . . . All was joy and merriment on board until long past midnight. She laughed and danced with the thought of death in her heart. The Prince kissed his lovely bride, and she toyed with his dark hair, and arm in arm they went to rest in the magnificent tent.

The ship was now hushed and still; only the helmsman was there at his wheel. And the little mermaid leaned with her white arms on the rail and looked eastward for a sign of the pink dawn. The first ray of sun, she knew, would kill her. Suddenly she saw her sisters rising out of the sea. They were pale, like her; no more was their beautiful long hair fluttering in the wind—it had been cut off.

"We have given it to the witch, so that she might help us to save you from dying when to-night is over. She has given us a knife—look, here it is—do you see how sharp it is? Before sunrise you must stab it into the Prince's heart. Then, when his warm blood splashes over your feet, they will grow together into a fish's tail, and you will become a mermaid once more; you will be able to come down to us in the water and live out your three hundred years before being changed into the dead salt foam of the sea. Make haste! Either he or you must die before the sun rises. Our old grandmother has been sorrowing till her white hair has fallen away, as ours fell before the witch's scissors. Kill the Prince and come back to us! But make haste—look at that red gleam in the sky. In a few minutes the sun will rise, and then you must die." And with a strange deep sigh they sank beneath the waves.

The little mermaid drew aside the purple curtain of the tent, and she saw the lovely bride sleeping with her head on the Prince's breast. She stopped and kissed his handsome brow, looked at the sky where the pink dawn glowed brighter and brighter, looked at the sharp knife in her hand, and again fixed her eyes on the Prince, who murmured in his dreams the name of his bride—she alone was in his thoughts. The knife quivered in the mermaid's hand—but then she flung it far out into the waves; they glimmered red where it fell, and what looked like drops of blood came oozing out of the water. With a last glance at the Prince from eyes half-dimmed in death she hurled herself from the ship into the sea and felt her body dissolving into foam.

And now the sun came rising from the sea. Its rays fell gentle and warm on the death chilled foam, and the little mermaid had no feeling of death. She saw the bright sun and, hovering above her, hundreds of lovely creatures—she could see right through them, see the white sails of the ship and the pink clouds in the sky. And their voice was the voice of melody, yet so spiritual that no human ear could hear it, just as no earthly eye could see them. They had no wings, but their own lightness bore them up as they floated through the air. The little mermaid saw that she had a body like theirs, raising itself freer and freer from the foam.

"To whom am I coming?" she asked, and her voice sounded like that of the other beings, more spiritual than any earthly music can record.

"To the daughters of the air," answered the others. "A mermaid has no immortal soul and can never have one unless she wins the love of a mortal. Eternity, for her, depends on a power outside her. Neither have the daughters of the air an everlasting soul, but by good deeds they can shape one for themselves. We shall fly to the hot countries, where the stifling air of pestilence means death to mankind; we shall bring them cool breezes. We shall scatter the fragrance of flowers through the air and send them comfort and healing. When for three hundred years we have striven to do the good we can, then we shall win an immortal soul and have a share in mankind's eternal happiness. You, poor little mermaid, have striven for that with all your heart; you have suffered and endured, and have raised yourself into the world of the spirits of the air. Now, by three hundred years of good deeds, you too can shape for yourself an immortal soul."

And the little mermaid raised her crystal arms toward God's sun, and for the first time she knew the feeling of tears.

On board the ship there was bustle and life once more. She saw the Prince with his pretty bride looking about for her; sorrowfully they stared at the heaving foam, as if they knew she had thrown herself into the waves. Unseen, she kissed the forehead of the bride, gave a smile to the Prince, and then with the other children of the air she climbed to a rose-red cloud that was sailing to the sky.

"So we shall float for three hundred years, till at last we come into the heavenly kingdom."

"And we may reach it even sooner," whispered one. "Unseen we float into human homes where there are children and, for every day we find a good child who makes father and mother happy and earns their love, God shortens our time of trial. The child never knows when we fly through the room and, if that makes us smile with joy, then a year is taken away from the three hundred. But if we see a child who is naughty or spiteful, then we have to weep tears of sorrow, and every tear adds one more day to our time of trial."

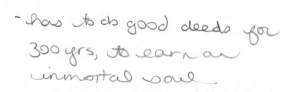
- has to do good deeds for
300 yrs, to earn an
immortal soul

# The Little Match Girl†

It was terribly cold. Snow was falling and soon it would be quite dark; for it was the last day in the year—New Year's Eve. Along the street, in that same cold and dark, went a poor little girl in bare feet—well, yes, it's true, she had slippers on when she left home; but what was the good of that? They were great big slippers which her mother used to wear, so you can imagine the size of them; and they both came off when the little girl scurried across the road just as two carts went whizzing by at a fearful rate. One slipper was not to be found, and a boy ran off with the other, saying it would do for a cradle one day when he had children of his own.

So there was the little girl walking along in her bare feet that were simply blue with cold. In an old apron she was carrying a whole lot of matches, and she had one bunch of them in her hand. She hadn't sold anything all day, and no one had given her a single penny. Poor mite, she looked so downcast as she trudged along hungry and shivering. The snowflakes settled on her long flaxen hair, which hung in pretty curls over her shoulder; but you may be sure she wasn't thinking about her looks. Lights were shining in every window, and out into the street came the lovely smell of roast goose. You see, it was New Year's Eve; that's what she was thinking about.

Over in a little corner between two houses—one of them jutted out rather more into the street than the other—there she crouched and huddled with her legs tucked under her; but she only got colder and colder. She didn't dare to go home, for she hadn't sold a match nor earned a single penny. Her father would beat her, and besides it was so cold at home. They had only the bare roof over their heads and the wind whistled through that although the worst cracks had been stopped up with rags and straw. Her hands were really quite numb with cold. Ah, but a little match—that would be a comfort. If only she dared pull one out of the bunch, just one, strike it on the wall and warm her fingers! She pulled one out . . . ritch! . . . how it spirted and blazed! Such a clear warm flame, like a little candle, as she put her hand round it—yes, and what a curious light it was! The little girl fancied she was sitting in front of a big iron stove with shiny brass knobs and brass facings, with such a warm friendly fire burning . . . why, whatever was that? She was just stretching out her toes, so as to warm them too, when—out went the flame, and the stove vanished. There she sat with a little stub of burnt-out match in her hand.

She struck another one. It burned up so brightly, and where the

† From *Eighty Fairy Tales* by Hans Christian Andersen, trans. R. P. Keigwin. Translation copyright © 1976 by Skandinavisk Bogforlag, Flensteds Forlag. Reprinted by permission of Pantheon Books, a division of Random House, Inc.

gleam fell on the wall this became transparent like gauze. She could see right into the room, where the table was laid with a glittering white cloth and with delicate china; and there, steaming deliciously, was the roast goose stuffed with prunes and apples. Then, what was even finer, the goose jumped off the dish and waddled along the floor with the carving knife and fork in its back. Right up to the poor little girl it came . . . but then the match went out, and nothing could be seen but the massive cold wall.

She lighted another match. Now she was sitting under the loveliest Christmas tree; it was even bigger and prettier than the one she had seen through the glass-door at the rich merchant's at Christmas. Hundreds of candles were burning on the green branches, and gay-coloured prints, like the ones they hang in the shop-windows, looked down at her. The little girl reached up both her hands . . . then the match went out; all the Christmas candles rose higher and higher, until now she could see they were the shining stars. One of them rushed down the sky with a long fiery streak.

"That's somebody dying," said the little girl, for her dead Grannie, who was the only one who had been kind to her, had told her that a falling star shows that a soul is going up to God.

She struck yet another match on the wall. It gave a glow all around, and there in the midst of it stood her old grandmother, looking so very bright and gentle and loving. "Oh, Grannie", cried the little girl, "do take me with you! I know you'll disappear as soon as the match goes out—just as the warm stove did, and the lovely roast goose, and the wonderful great Christmas-tree." And she quickly struck the rest of the matches in the bunch, for she did so want to keep her Grannie there. And the matches flared up so gloriously that it became brighter than broad daylight. Never had Grannie looked so tall and beautiful. She took the little girl into her arms, and together they flew in joy and splendour, up, up, to where there was no cold, no hunger, no fear. They were with God.

But in the cold early morning huddled between the two houses, sat the little girl with rosy cheeks and a smile on her lips, frozen to death on the last night of the old year. The New Year dawned on the little dead body leaning there with the matches, one lot of them nearly all used up. "She was trying to get warm," people said. Nobody knew what lovely things she had seen and in what glory she had gone with her old Grannie to the happiness of the New Year.

## The Girl Who Trod on the Loaf†

I expect you've heard of the girl who trod on the loaf so as not to dirty her shoes, and of how she came to a bad end. The story's been written, and printed too.

She was a poor child, proud and vain; there was a bad streak in her, as the saying is. When quite a little child she enjoyed catching flies and pulling off their wings, so making creeping things of them. She would take a cockchafer and a beetle, stick each of them on a pin, and then place a green leaf or a little bit of paper up against their feet. The poor creature would hold on tight to it, turning and twisting it to try and get off the pin.

"Now the cockchafer's reading," said little Inger. "Look how it's turning over the page."

As she grew older, she got worse rather than better; but she was very pretty, and that was her misfortune, for otherwise she'd have been slapped a good deal oftener than she was.

"It'll need a desperate remedy to cure *your* disease," said her own mother. "Often, when you were little, you trod on my apron; now you're older, I'm afraid you'll end by treading on my heart."

And, sure enough, she did.

She now went out to service with a good family who lived in the country. They treated her as if she was their own child and dressed her in the same way; she was very goodlooking, and she grew vainer than ever.

After she had been with them for a year, her mistress said to her. "Don't you think you ought to go some time and see your parents, Inger dear?"

So she went, though it was only to show herself off and let them see how fine she had become. But when she got to the outskirts of the town and saw some girls and young fellows gossiping together by the pond and her mother, too, resting on a stone with a bundle of faggots she had gathered in the wood, she felt ashamed that she who was so finely dressed should have a mother who went about in rags collecting sticks. She wasn't in the least sorry at having to turn back; she was only annoyed.

And now another six months went by.

"You really ought to go home one day and see your old father and mother, Inger dear," said her mistress. "Look—here's a big white loaf; you can take that with you. They'll be so glad to see you."

† From *Eighty Fairy Tales* by Hans Christian Andersen, trans. R. P. Keigwin. Translation copyright © 1976 by Skandinavisk Bogforlag, Flensteds Forlag. Reprinted by permission of Pantheon Books, a division of Random House, Inc.

So Inger put on her best things and her new shoes, and she caught up her skirt and looked well where she was going, so as to keep her shoes nice and clean; and of course she couldn't be blamed for that. But when she came to where the path led across marshy ground and there was a long strip of puddles and slush, she flung the loaf down into the mud, so as to tread on this and get across without wetting her shoes. But as she stood with one foot on the loaf and lifted the other, the loaf sank down with her deeper and deeper, and she disappeared altogether, till there was nothing to be seen but a black bubbling swamp.

That's the story.

What became of her? She came down to the marsh-woman, who goes in for brewing. The marsh-woman is aunt to the elf-maids; they are well enough known—they've had ballads written about them and pictures drawn of them. But all that people know about the marsh-woman is that, when the meadows are steaming in summer, that's the marsh-woman brewing. It was down into her brewery that Inger sank, and that's not a place you can stand for long. A cesspit is a gay palatial apartment compared with the marsh-woman's brewery. Every vat stinks enough to make a man faint and, besides, the vats are all pressed up against each other; and if there is somewhere a little gap between them through which you might squeeze yourself out, you can't do it because of all the slimy toads and fat snakes that get entangled here together. This was where Inger sank down. All that nasty living mess was so icy cold that she shuddered in every limb, and it made her more and more stiff and numb. The loaf still clung to her feet and dragged her on, just as an amber button may drag a bit of straw.

The marsh-woman was at home; the brewery that day was being inspected by the Devil and his great-grandmother, an extremely venomous old female who is never idle. She never goes out without her needlework, and she had it with her now. She had her pin-cushion with her, so as to give people pins and needles in their legs. She embroidered lies and did crochet from rash remarks that had fallen to the ground—anything, in fact, that could lead to injury and corruption. Oh yes, she knew all about sewing, embroidery and crochet work did old great-granny.

She caught sight of Inger, put on her spectacles and then had another look at her. "That's a girl with talent," she said. "I'd like her as a memento of my visit here. She will do very well as a statue for my great-grandson's entrance-hall."

And she got her. In this way Inger came to hell. People can't always go straight down, but they can get there by a roundabout way if they have talent.

It was an entrance-hall that never seemed to end. It made you giddy to look ahead and giddy to look back. And then there was a forlorn crowd waiting for the door of mercy to be opened; they might have to wait a long time. Great fat waddling spiders spun a thousand-year web over their feet, and these toils cut into the feet like screws and clamped them like copper chains; and, added to this, there was a never-ending disquiet in every soul, a disquiet that was itself a torment. Among them was the miser who had lost the key of his safe and now remembered he had left it in the lock. But there—it would take too long to go through all the different pains and torments that were felt there. Inger felt that it was ghastly to be standing as a statue; she was just as though riveted from below to the loaf.

"This comes of taking care to keep your shoes clean," she said to herself. "Look how they're staring at me"—and, it's true, they were all looking at her. Their evil passions gleamed from their eyes and spoke silently from the corners of their mouths; they were a horrible sight.

"I must be delightful to look at," thought Inger. "I have a pretty face and nice clothes," and then she turned her eyes—her neck was too stiff for that to be turned. Goodness, how dirty she had got in the marsh-woman's brewhouse! She hadn't thought of that. Her clothes seemed to be smeared over with one great blotch of slime; a snake had got caught in her hair and was dangling down her neck, and from each fold in her dress a toad peeped out with a croak like the bark of a wheezy pug-dog. It was most unpleasant. "Still," she consoled herself, "the others down here really look just as dreadful."

Worst of all was the terrible hunger she felt. Couldn't she at least stoop down and break off a bit of the loaf she was standing on? No, for her back had stiffened, her arms and hands had stiffened, her whole body was like a stone pillar; all she could turn were the eyes in her head, turn them right round, so that they could see backwards—and that was a ghastly sight, that was. Then the flies came and crawled over her eyes, to and fro. She blinked her eyes, but the flies didn't fly away; they couldn't, because their wings had been pulled off and they had become creeping things. That was torment for her, and as for her hunger—well, at last she felt that her innards were eating themselves up, and she became quite empty inside, so appallingly empty.

"If it goes on much longer, I shan't be able to bear it," she said; but she had to bear it, and it still went on.

Then a burning tear fell on her head. It trickled down her face and breast right down to the loaf. Another tear fell—and many more beside. Who was it crying over Inger? Well, hadn't she up on earth a mother? Sorrowing tears that a mother sheds for her child will always reach it, but they don't set it free; they burn, they only make the torment greater. And now this unbearable hunger—and not to be able to get at the loaf she was treading with her foot! At last she got a feeling that everything inside her must have eaten itself up. She was like a thin hollow reed that drew every sound inside it. She could hear distinctly everything up on earth that concerned her, and what she heard was harsh and spiteful. Her mother, to be sure, wept in deep sorrow, but she added, "Pride goes before a fall—that was your misfortune, Inger. How you have grieved your mother!"

Her mother and all the others up there knew about her sin, how she had trodden on the loaf and had sunk down and disappeared. The cowherd had told them, for he had seen it all himself from the slope.

"How you have grieved your mother, Inger!" said the mother. "Yes, and I always felt you would."

"I wish I had never been born," thought Inger. "It would have been far better. What's the good now of my mother snivelling like that?"

Inger heard how her master and mistress were speaking, those two good-natured people who had been like father and mother to her: "She was a wicked child," they said. "She had no respect for God's gifts, but trod them underfoot; the door of mercy will be hard for her to open."

"They should have corrected me more often," thought Inger, "cured me of my bad ways if I had any."

She heard that a whole ballad about her had been brought out—*The proud young girl who trod on the loaf to save her pretty shoes*—and it was sung all over the country.

"To think of being blamed so much for it and suffering so much for it," thought Inger. "Why aren't the others punished for what they've done? Yes, and what a lot there would be to punish! Ooh, how I'm tormented!"

And her heart grew even harder than her shell.

"I shall never get any better while I'm down here in this company, and I don't want to get any better. Look how they're glaring."

And she felt angry and vicious towards all mankind.

"Now I dare say they'll have something to talk about up there—ooh, how I'm tormented!"

And she heard them telling her story to the children, and the little ones called her Wicked Inger. "She was so horrid," they said, "so nasty, she deserves to be well punished."

There were nothing but hard words against her in children's mouths.

And yet one day, as hunger and resentment were gnawing deep in her hollow shell and she heard her name mentioned and her story told to an innocent child, a small girl, she noticed that the little one burst into tears at the story of the proud Inger and her love of finery.

"But won't she ever come up again?" asked the small girl. And she was told, "No, she'll never come up again."

"Yes, but if she will ask to be forgiven and promise never to do it again?"

"But she won't ask to be forgiven," they told the child.

"Oh, I do wish she would," said the little girl, and refused to be comforted. "I'll give up my doll's house, if they let her come up. It's so horrible for poor Inger."

These words went right down into Inger's heart; they seemed to do her good. It was the first time anyone had said "poor Inger" without adding the least thing about her faults. An innocent little child cried and pleaded for her; it gave her such a queer feeling that she would like to have cried herself, but she couldn't cry, and that too was a torment.

As the years passed by up there—there were no changes below—she heard sounds from above less often and there was less talk about her. Then one day she heard a sigh, "Inger, Inger, what sorrow you have brought me! I always said you would." It was her mother dying.

Sometimes she heard her name mentioned by her old master and mistress, and the mildest remark was when the housewife said, "I wonder if I shall ever see you again, Inger. There's no knowing what may become of one."

But Inger knew well enough that her honest mistress never could come where she was.

In that way another long and bitter time went by. Then Inger again heard her name spoken and saw above what seemed to be two bright stars shining. They were two gentle eyes that were closing on earth. So many years had passed since the time when the small girl cried inconsolably for "poor Inger" that the child had now become an old woman, whom God would soon be calling to himself; and at that very moment, when the thoughts of her whole life were rising before her, she also remembered how as a little child she couldn't help crying bitterly when she heard the story about Inger. That time and the impression it made on her stood so vividly before the old woman in her hour of death that she burst out aloud, "Lord, my God, haven't I too, like Inger, sometimes trodden thoughtlessly on the blessings you gave? Haven't I, too, gone with pride in my heart? And yet you, in your mercy, did not let me sink, held me up. Do not abandon me in my last hour."

And her old eyes closed, and the soul's eyes opened to what lies hidden; and as Inger was there so vividly in her last thoughts, she saw Inger—saw to what depths she had been dragged down—and at the sight of her the saintly soul burst into tears. She stood like a child in the kingdom of heaven and wept for poor Inger; her tears and prayers rang like an echo down into the hollow empty shell that hemmed in the imprisoned tormented soul, and it was overcome by all this undreamed affection from above. To think that an angel of God should be weeping for her! Why was she granted this favour? The tortured soul seemed to gather up into its thoughts every deed it had ever done in its life on earth, and it shook with weeping; Inger could never have wept like that. She was filled with sorrow for herself, and she felt that never could the gate of mercy be opened for her. As in her contrite heart she realized this, at that moment a beam of light flashed down into the bottomless pit—a beam stronger even than the sunbeam that thaws the snowman made by the boys in the yard. Then, far quicker than the snowflake falling on a child's warm lips melts away to a drop, Inger's stiffened stony figure evaporated; a little bird soared like forked lightning up towards the world of men. But it was timid and shy of everything near; it felt ashamed of itself in the sight of all living creatures and hurriedly looked for shelter in a dark hole, and found it in a crumbling wall. Here it perched cowering and trembling all over without uttering a sound, for it had no voice. It stayed there a long while before it felt calm enough to see and appreciate all the beauty that lay before it. Yes, indeed, beauty there was. The air was so fresh and genial, the moon shone so bright, trees and shrubs smelt sweet; and then the spot where it perched was so cosy, its feather coat so clean and delicate. What a revelation of love and splendour in all created things! All the thoughts stirring in the heart of the bird strove to find utterance in song, but the bird didn't know how. It would have liked to sing as the cuckoo and nightingale do in spring. God, who also hears the worm's silent song of praise, hearkened now to the song of praise that rose in harmonies of thought, just as a psalm used to ring in David's heart before it found words and music.

For days and weeks these noiseless songs grew and grew; surely they must break out at the first beat of wings in a good deed; such a deed must now be done.

The holy festival of Christmas was here. The farmer put up a pole close against the wall and tied on it an unthreshed bundle of oats, so that the birds of the air might also have a merry Christmas and a cheerful dinner at this season of the Saviour's.

And the sun rose up on Christmas morning and shone on to the sheaf of oats, and all the twittering birds flew round the dinnerpole. Then, too, a "tweet, tweet!" sounded from the wall. The swelling thought turned into sound; the feeble chirp became a whole paean of joy. The idea of a good deed had awakened, and the bird flew out from its hiding-place. In heaven they knew well enough the kind of bird it was.

Winter began in earnest, the waters were frozen deep, and birds and forest animals were often pinched for food. The little bird flew along the high road and there in the tracks of the sledges it managed to find, in places, a grain of corn. At coaching inns it might come across a few breadcrumbs, but would only eat one of these and then let all the other famishing sparrows know that here they could find food. It also flew to the towns, scouted around, and wherever a kind hand had scattered crumbs from the window for the birds, it ate only a single crumb itself and gave the rest to the others.

In the course of the winter the bird had collected and given away so many crumbs that the weight of them all would have equalled that of the whole loaf that Inger had trodden on so as not to dirty her shoes; and when the last crumb had been found and given away, the bird's grey wings turned white and spread themselves out.

"Look! There's a tern flying off across the lake," cried the children who saw the white bird. First, it dipped down on to the lake, then it rose into the bright sunshine; the bird was so dazzling white that there was no chance of seeing what became of it. They said that it flew straight into the sun. — heaven?

*[handwritten annotation:]* — Sounds very spiritual Christian yet Han.C.A. so graphic + dark in detail.

## The Red Shoes†

There was once a little girl, very delicate and pretty, and yet so poor that in summer she always had to go barefooted and in winter she had to wear big wooden clogs which chafed her insteps most horribly, until they were quite red.

In the middle of the village lived a shoemaker's widow, who had some strips of old red cloth, and out of these she did her best to sew a little pair of shoes. They were rather clumsy-looking shoes, but the old widow meant well; they were for the little girl, whose name was Karen. As it happened, she got the red shoes and put them on for the first time on the very day that her mother was buried. Of course they weren't exactly the right shoes for a funeral, but they were the only ones she had; and so she wore them on her bare feet, as she followed the humble straw coffin.

Just then a large old-looking carriage drove up with a large old-looking lady inside it. She caught sight of the little girl and felt sorry for her. So she said to the parson: "Look here, if you let me have the little girl, I'll take care of her."

Karen thought this was all because of the red shoes, but the old lady said they were hideous and had them burnt; Karen herself was given nice new clothes and was taught to read and sew. People said how pretty she was, but the looking-glass said to her: "You are more than pretty, you are lovely."

On one occasion the Queen was passing through the country with her little daughter, who was a Princess. People flocked around the castle, and Karen was there too; and the little Princess showed herself at one of the windows. She was wearing a beautiful white dress; no train nor golden crown, but lovely red morocco shoes—far, far prettier than

† From *Eighty Fairy Tales* by Hans Christian Andersen, trans. R. P. Keigwin. Translation copyright © 1976 by Skandinavisk Bogforlag, Flensteds Forlag. Reprinted by permission of Pantheon Books, a division of Random House, Inc.

the ones the shoemaker's widow had made for little Karen. No, there was really nothing in the world like red shoes.

But now Karen was old enough to be confirmed. She was given new clothes, and she was also to have new shoes. The best shoemaker in town took the measurement of her feet in his own private room, where there were big glass cabinets with elegant shoes and shiny boots. They made a brave shoe, but the old lady's sight was far from good, and so it gave her no pleasure. Among the shoes was a red pair just like the ones the Princess had been wearing—oh, they were pretty! The shoemaker explained that they had been made for an earl's daughter but didn't quite fit. "That must be patent leather from the way they shine," said the old lady.

"Yes, don't they shine!" said Karen; and as they were a good fit, the shoes were bought. But the old lady didn't realize that they were red, for she would never have allowed Karen to go to Confirmation in red shoes. And yet that's just what happened.

Everybody stared at her feet and, as she walked up the aisle to the chancel, she felt that even the old pictures over the tombs, those portraits of the clergy and their wives in stiff ruffs and long black garments, were fastening their eyes on the red shoes. It was these that filled her thoughts, when the priest laid his hand on her head and spoke of holy baptism, of the covenant with God, and of her duty now to become a fully-fledged Christian. And the organ played so solemnly, and the children sang so beautifully, and the old choirmaster sang, too; but Karen thought of nothing but her red shoes.

By the afternoon, sure enough, the old lady had heard from everybody about the shoes being red, and she said how shocking it was; they were quite out of place and in future, when Karen went to church, she must always wear black shoes, however old they were.

Next Sunday there was Communion, and Karen looked at the black shoes, and she looked at the red ones . . . And then she looked at the red ones again—and put the red ones on.

It was a beautiful sunny day. Karen and the old lady took the path through the cornfield, where it was a bit dusty. At the churchdoor stood an old soldier with a crutch and a funny long beard which was more red than white—in fact, it really was red. He made a deep bow to the old lady and asked if he might dust her shoes. And when Karen also put out her foot, "My! what lovely dancingshoes!" said the soldier. "Stay on tight when you dance!" and he gave the soles a tap with his hand.

The old lady gave the soldier something for himself and went with Karen into the church. The whole congregation stared at Karen's red shoes, and so did all the portraits; and when Karen knelt before the altar and put the gold chalice to her lips, she thought of nothing but the red shoes—it seemed as if they were floating in front of her. She forgot to sing the hymns, and she forgot to say the prayers.

Presently everyone came out of church, and the old lady stepped into her carriage. As Karen raised her foot to get in after her, the old soldier, who was standing close by, said: "My! what lovely dancing-shoes!" Karen couldn't resist—she had to dance a few steps and, once she had started, her feet went on dancing just as though the shoes had some power over them. She danced round the corner of the church—she couldn't stop; the coachman had to run after her and pick her up and carry her back into the carriage. But still her feet went on dancing and gave the kind old lady some dreadful kicks. At last they got the shoes off, and her legs kept still.

When they came home, the shoes were put away in a cupboard, but Karen still kept taking a peep at them. By and by the old lady fell ill; it was said she would never get better. She had to be nursed and cared for, and nobody was more suited for this than Karen. But a big ball was being given in the town, and Karen was invited. She looked at the old lady, who after all couldn't live long, and she looked at the red shoes. She couldn't see there would be any harm. She put on the red shoes, she had a perfect right to do that . . . But then she went to the ball and began to dance.

But when she wanted to go to the right, the shoes went dancing off to the left; and when she wanted to go up the room, the shoes went dancing down the room—down the stairs through the street and out by the town-gate. Dance she did and dance she must, away into the dark forest.

Up among the trees she saw something shining. It looked like a face, and so she thought it was the moon; but it was the old soldier with the red beard, sitting and nodding and saying: "My! what lovely dancing-shoes!"

This made her frightened, and she tried to kick off the red shoes, but they still stuck on tight. She tore off her stockings, but the shoes had grown fast to her feet, and so dance she did and dance she must, over field and furrow, in rain and sun, by night and day; but the night-time was the worst.

She danced into the open churchyard, but the dead there didn't dance; they had something better to do. She wanted to sit down by the poor man's grave, where the bitter tansy grew; but peace and quiet were not for her and, when she danced towards the open church-door, she found an angel there in long white robes and with wings reaching from his shoulders to the ground. His face was stern and solemn, and in his hand he held a sword with broad shining blade.

"Dance you shall," said the angel, "dance in your red shoes until you are cold and pale, until your skin shrivels up like a skeleton's! Dance you shall from door to door, and at all the houses where the children are vain and proud you shall knock till they hear you and are frightened. You shall dance, you shall dance . . . !"

"Mercy! Mercy!" cried Karen. But she never heard the angel's answer, for the shoes whirled her away through the gate and the field, along highway and byway, dancing, dancing, all the time.

One morning she danced past a door she knew well. From inside came the sound of a hymn; then out came a coffin all covered with flowers. She realized then that the old lady was dead, and she felt that now she was deserted by everyone, as well as cursed by the angel of God.

Dance she did and dance she must, dance on in the dark night . . . The shoes whirled her away over thorns and stubble, until she was scratched and bleeding. She danced across the heath up to a lonely little house. She knew that the executioner lived here, and she rapped the window-pane with her knuckles and said: "Please come out! I can't come in, because I'm dancing."

"Do you mean to say you don't know who I am? I cut off wicked people's heads—my goodness, how my axe is quivering!"

"Please don't cut off my head!" said Karen, "for then I can't show that I'm sorry for my sins. Cut off my feet with the red shoes."

Then she confessed all her sins, and the executioner cut off her feet with the red shoes. But the shoes went dancing with the little feet across the fields into the depths of the forest. And he made her wooden feet and crutches; he taught her a hymn—the Psalm for Sinners—and she kissed the hand that had wielded the axe and went her way across the heath.

"Surely by now I must have done penance for the red shoes," she said. "I'll go to church and let everyone see me." And she did; she went quickly towards the church-door but, when she reached it, there were the red shoes dancing in front of her, and she grew frightened and turned back.

All the next week she was miserable and did nothing but cry, but when Sunday came round she said to herself: "Dear me, I really feel I've been through enough. Surely I'm just as good as many of those that sit so perkily there in church." And she plucked up her courage and started off, but she got no further than the gate, when she saw the red shoes dancing in front of her, and she grew frightened and turned back and repented deeply of her sins.

Next she made her way to the parsonage and asked to be taken in there as a servant; she would work so hard and do her very best. She never gave a thought to the wages, only that she might have a roof over her head and be with kind people.

The parson's wife felt sorry for her and took her into her service and found her hard-working and sensible. In the evenings Karen sat and listened in silence, while the parson read aloud from the Bible. All the little ones were very fond of her but, when there was talk of dress and finery and of being as pretty as a picture, she would shake her head.

The following Sunday they all went to church, and they asked her to go with them; but with tears in her eyes she looked sadly at her crutches and, when the others went off to hear the word of God, she went alone to her tiny room, where there was just enough space for a bed and a chair, and here she sat devoutly reading her prayerbook. As she did so, the wind brought the sound of the organ to her from the church, and her eyes filled with tears as she lifted up her face, exclaiming: "Help me, O God"!

Then the sun came out so brightly, and straight in front of her stood the same angel in white robes that she had seen that night at the church-door. But instead of the sharp sword he was holding a beautiful green bough that was covered with roses; and he touched the ceiling with it so that it arched itself higher, and where he touched it there shone a golden star. And he touched the walls so that they grew wider; and she saw the organ which was still playing, she saw the old pictures of the clergy and their wives, and the congregation sitting in the carved pews and singing from their hymn-books . . . You see, the church itself had come to the poor girl in her narrow little room—or was it she who had come to the church? She was sitting in the pew with all the others from the parsonage and, when they had finished the hymn and looked up from their books, they nodded to her and said: "It was right you should come, Karen." "It was God's mercy!" she answered.

And the organ pealed forth and the young voices of the choir sounded so soft and pure. The bright warm sunshine streamed in through the church-window to the place where Karen was sitting. Her heart was so full of sunshine and peace and joy that at last it broke, and her soul flew on the sunbeams to heaven, where there was no one to ask about the red shoes.

# INTRODUCTION: Oscar Wilde

It is hard to imagine that a writer who believed that his "first duty in life" was to be "as artificial as possible" would have turned to the genre of the fairy tale.[1] But Oscar Wilde has never been known for his consistency, and this teller of tales found in fairy tales a congenial vehicle for displaying the flip slide to his natural talent for inventive satire and coruscating wit. Admirers of Wilde's urbane and sophisticated prose have anxiously tried to explain the interest in writing fairy tales as the symptom of a developmental defect, of a perverse sexuality, or of an identity confusion. One critic claims that Wilde was drawn to fairy tales because he was "emotionally undeveloped"; a second attributes his decision to embrace the genre to "homosexual tendencies"; and a third traces the engagement with fairy tales to "sexual ambivalence."[2] The literary "degeneration" seen to manifest itself in Wilde's fairy tales has even been explicitly and directly linked to homosexual practices: "Something had happened to Wilde. He met Mr. Robert Baldwin Ross. The effect of this unfortunate encounter is to be seen in Wilde's work. . . . *The Happy Prince* appeared in 1888; and was followed up in the year 1891, when Wilde made his second unfortunate friendship, with Lord Alfred Douglas, by *The House of Pomegranates*. . . . There is nothing here for exultation."[3]

That Wilde's fairy tales are considered aesthetically and ethically suspect (one critic finds their style "fleshy" and unsuitable for children) seems peculiar in light of their emphatic articulation of moral truths.[4] The same author who recited with glee such dandyish maxims as "To love oneself is the beginning of a life-long romance" embedded in his fairy tales stinging critiques of boorish self-absorption, willful selfishness, and brazen greed. Wilde clearly modeled his stories more on Andersen's literary tales, with their ostentatious moral pronouncements and

Bracketed page numbers refer to this Norton Critical Edition.
1. Alvin Redman, ed., *The Epigrams of Oscar Wilde* (London: Alvin Redman, 1952) 116.
2. "Emotionally undeveloped": Hesketh Pearson, *The Life of Oscar Wilde* (London: Methuen, 1946) 141; "homosexual tendencies": Leon Lémonnier, *Oscar Wilde* (Paris: Didier, 1938) 122; "sexual ambivalence": Robert Merle, *Oscar Wilde* (Paris: Editions, 1948) 261.
3. St. John Ervine, *Oscar Wilde: A Present Time Appraisal* (New York: William Morrow, 1952) p. 167.
4. Review of *A House of Pomegranates*, by Oscar Wilde, *Pall Mall Gazette*, as quoted in Maria Edelson, "The Language of Allegory in Oscar Wilde's Tales," in *Anglo-Irish and Irish Literature*, ed. Birgit Bramsbäck and Martin Croghan (Stockholm: Almqvist and Wiksell and Bromsbäck, 1985) 167.

their displays of pious self-denial, than on the Irish folklore that his mother collected. The kinship between Wilde's tales and Andersen's stories did not escape contemporary reviewers, who found Wilde to be writing "somewhat after the manner of Hans Andersen," whose works had been available in English translation since 1846.[5] That Wilde deeply respected the Danish writer becomes evident from "The Fisherman and His Soul" (clearly inspired by "The Little Mermaid") and by the unmistakable tribute to "The Little Match Girl" in one of the many visions of human misery in "The Happy Prince."

In a note to his friend G. H. Kersely, Wilde commented on the implied audience for his collection. The tales, he insisted, were "an attempt to mirror modern life in a form remote from reality." Conceding that the stories were meant "partly for children," Wilde in the same breath declared the tales to be "slight and fanciful, and written, not for children, but for childlike people from eighteen to eighty!"[6]

Why would Wilde exclude children from his implied audience, as he ultimately does in setting a lower limit of eighteen years for the stories? Wilde, like Andersen, may have begun some of his fairy tales with the phrase "Once upon a time," but he never ended them with "They lived happily ever after." In fact, almost every story culminates in death. The statue of the "Happy Prince" is razed. After his conversion, the "Selfish Giant" is found "lying dead . . . all covered with white blossoms" [253]. The self-sacrificing little Hans in "The Devoted Friend" is found drowned, floating in a ditch. "The Fisherman and his Soul" ends with the death of both mermaid and fisherman. The dwarf enamored of a princess in "The Birthday of the Infanta" dies of a broken heart. Even the eponymous hero of the "Remarkable Rocket" expires, without a trace of the glory to which he aspires.

No fairy tale by Wilde is more expansive in its description of the mortal agony of death throes than "The Nightingale and the Rose." Hoping to produce a red rose of unsurpassed beauty for a lovelorn student, a nightingale sings all night, with its breast pressed against the thorn of a rosebush:

> The nightingale pressed closer against the thorn, and the thorn touched her heart, and a fierce pang of pain shot through her. Bitter, bitter was the pain, and wilder and wilder grew her song, for she sang of the Love that is perfected by Death, of the Love that dies not in the tomb. [264]

The songbird's bid for a love of transcendent beauty becomes a form of sacrificial suffering, missing its mark (for the student and his beloved have no emotional depth whatsoever) but leading to the expression of

5. Norbert Kohl, *Oscar Wilde: The Works of a Conformist Rebel*, trans. David Henry Wilson (Cambridge: Cambridge UP, 1989) 58.
6. *The Letters of Oscar Wilde*, ed. Rupert Hart-Davis (London: Rupert Hart-Davis, 1962) 219.

her own peerless longing for spiritual release. Beauty, if not salvation, emerges from passionate self-sacrifice, which often takes the form of mortification of the flesh.

"There is no Mystery as great as Misery," the Happy Prince confides to a swallow. "You tell me of marvelous things," he avows, "but more marvelous than anything is the suffering of men and of women" [259]. That there is something sacred about anguish, grief, and distress is not an argument one expects to hear in a fairy tale. Even more surprising, especially from the hand of an artist who has been seen as an apostle of art and artifice, is the celebration of the unsightly, bizarre, and grotesque in a genre traditionally directed at children. In "The Birthday of the Infanta," what is conventionally beautiful becomes rank and fetid: "The pomegranates split and cracked with the heat, and showed their bleeding hearts." The grotesque has the power to vanquish beauty, as becomes evident when the dwarf in that story discovers his mirror image:

> Of all the rooms this was the brightest and the most beautiful. The walls were covered with a pink-flowered Lucca damask, patterned with birds and dotted with dainty blossoms of silver; the furniture was of massive silver, festooned with florid wreaths, and swinging Cupids; in front of the two large fire-places stood great screens broidered with parrots and peacocks, and the floor, which was of sea-green onyx, seemed to stretch far away into the distance. Nor was he alone. Standing under the shadow of the doorway, at the extreme end of the room, he saw a little figure watching him. . . .
>
> It was a monster, the most grotesque monster he had ever beheld. Not properly shaped as all other people were, but hunchbacked, and crooked-limbed, with a huge lolling head and mane of black hair.[7]

The elaborate spatial description is not merely a foil to the dwarf's hideous appearance, it also frames him, turning him into an icon of abject despair, foregrounded by his startling ugliness. The monster in the mirror is as riveting to the reader as it is to the dwarf, and the enthralling spectacle of the misshapen body becomes a powerful magnet of narrative interest.

Hans Christian Andersen might have seen in the dwarf's afflictions a moment of pure transcendent suffering, but Wilde deflates such expectations in the coda to his stories. When the Spanish infanta learns that the dwarf's heart has broken in two, she curls her lip "in pretty disdain" and declares: "For the future let those who come to play with me have no hearts."[8] Just as the dwarf's deformed body becomes the

7. Oscar Wilde, "The Birthday of the Infanta," in *Complete Short Fiction*, ed. Ian Small (New York: Penguin, 1994) 97, 112.
8. Wilde, "Birthday," 114.

dominant figure in the decorative background of the palace's "brightest and most beautiful" room,[9] so too the infanta's sneering remark takes center stage, effacing the tragic pathos of the truth that dawns on the dwarf as he looks in the mirror. Wilde may find suffering marvelous and charged with mystery, but he also is not always willing to endow it with transcendent meaning.

The promise of redemption typically rings hollow in Wilde's tales. The nightingale may be Christlike in its martyrdom, but it suffers in vain, unable to transform the cynical selfishness of the student and his beloved. In "The Happy Prince," both the statue and the swallow annihilate themselves in their effort to do good works, but end by demonstrating how charity consumes itself. In a sense, they could be seen as staging Wilde's maxim that "No good deed goes unpunished."

Wilde, unlike Andersen, does not seem to find salvation, Christian or otherwise, in suffering. In "The Soul of Man under Socialism," Wilde made it clear that pain was not for him "the ultimate mode of perfection," as it appears to be for Andersen's little match girl or the girl who trod on the loaf. Pain, he asserted in that essay, is "provisional and a protest":

> It has reference to wrong, unhealthy, unjust surroundings. When the wrong, and the disease, and the injustice are removed, it will have no further place. It will have done its work. . . .
>
> Nor will man miss it. *For what man has sought for is, indeed, neither pain nor pleasure, but simply Life.* Man has sought to live intensely, fully, perfectly. When he can do so without exercising restraint on others, or suffering it ever, and his activities are all pleasurable to him, he will be saner, healthier, more civilized, more himself. Pleasure is Nature's test, her sign of approval.[1]

Despite the superficial resemblance to Andersen's tales, Wilde's stories sound very different ideological chords. Jack Zipes points out that Wilde was not only a more sophisticated writer, but also a shrewder social critic, one who wanted to "subvert the messages conveyed by Andersen's tales."[2] "The Happy Prince," for example, reveals that "the individual actions of a Christlike person are not enough to put an end to poverty, injustice, and exploitation."[3] The mayor and the town councilors, as Zipes emphasizes, control the city, and they work hard to ensure that Christian charity ends when the statue of the prince is melted down.

9. Wilde, "Birthday," 112.
1. Oscar Wilde, "The Soul of Man Under Socialism," in *The Artist as Critic: Critical Writings of Oscar Wilde*, ed. Richard Ellmann (New York: Random House, Vintage Books, 1968) 288–89.
2. Jack Zipes, "Inverting and Subverting the World with Hope: The Fairy Tales of George McDonald, Oscar Wilde and L. Frank Baum," in *Fairy Tales and the Art of Subversion: The Classical Genre for Children and the Process of Civilization* (New York: Wildman, 1983) 114.
3. Zipes, "Inverting," 117.

"Charity creates a multitude of sins," Wilde declared in "The Soul of Man under Socialism."[4] "The Star-Child," which ends with the death of the title figure, reveals the ephemeral nature of deeds motivated by compassion and suggests that it takes more than a single savior to redeem mankind. The Star-Child may usher in an era of "peace and plenty in the land," but he does not rule for long: "After the space of three years he died. And he who came after him ruled evilly."[5] If Wilde himself really believed that "the people who do most harm are the people who try to do the most good,"[6] then the efforts of the Happy Prince, the Selfish Giant, and the prodigal nightingale to alleviate misery and heartache are in vain. That the world is more likely to be improved by resisting the impulse to demonstrate charity and compassion may have been a lesson preached in "The Soul of Man under Socialism," but it did not carry over perfectly into Wilde's literary practice, where altruistic impulses remain stubbornly admirable even if they do not improve matters in the grand scheme of things.

# The Selfish Giant†

Every afternoon, as they were coming from school, the children used to go and play in the Giant's garden.

It was a large lovely garden, with soft green grass. Here and there over the grass stood beautiful flowers like stars, and there were twelve peach-trees that in the spring-time broke out into delicate blossoms of pink and pearl, and in the autumn bore rich fruit. The birds sat on the trees and sang so sweetly that the children used to stop their games in order to listen to them. "How happy we are here!" they cried to each other.

One day the Giant came back. He had been to visit his friend the Cornish ogre, and had stayed with him for seven years. After the seven years were over he had said all that he had to say, for his conversation was limited, and he determined to return to his own castle. When he arrived he saw the children playing in the garden.

"What are you doing here?" he cried in a very gruff voice, and the children ran away.

"My own garden is my own garden," said the Giant; "any one can understand that, and I will allow nobody to play in it but myself." So he built a high wall all round it, and put up a notice-board.

---

4. Wilde, "Soul," 256.
5. Oscar Wilde, "The Star-Child," in *Complete*, 164.
6. Wilde, "Soul," 256.
† From *Oscar Wilde: Complete Short Fiction*, ed. Ian Small (London: Penguin Books, 1994).

```
TRESPASSERS
  WILL BE
PROSECUTED
```

He was a very selfish Giant.

The poor children had now nowhere to play. They tried to play on the road, but the road was very dusty and full of hard stones, and they did not like it. They used to wander round the high wall when their lessons were over, and talk about the beautiful garden inside.

"How happy we were there," they said to each other.

Then the Spring came, and all over the country there were little blossoms and little birds. Only in the garden of the Selfish Giant it was still Winter. The birds did not care to sing in it as there were no children, and the trees forgot to blossom. Once a beautiful flower put its head out from the grass, but when it saw the notice-board it was so sorry for the children that it slipped back into the ground again, and went off to sleep. The only people who were pleased were the Snow and the Frost. "Spring has forgotten this garden," they cried, "so we will live here all the year round." The Snow covered up the grass with her great white cloak, and the Frost painted all the trees silver. Then they invited the North Wind to stay with them, and he came. He was wrapped in furs, and he roared all day about the garden, and blew the chimney-pots down. "This is a delightful spot," he said, "we must ask the Hail on a visit." So the Hail came. Every day for three hours he rattled on the roof of the castle till he broke most of the slates, and then he ran round and round the garden as fast as he could go. He was dressed in grey, and his breath was like ice.

"I cannot understand why the Spring is so late in coming," said the Selfish Giant, as he sat at the window and looked out at his cold white garden; "I hope there will be a change in the weather."

But the Spring never came, nor the Summer. The Autumn gave golden fruit to every garden, but to the Giant's garden she gave none. "He is too selfish," she said. So it was always Winter there, and the North Wind, and the Hail, and the Frost, and the Snow danced about through the trees.

One morning the Giant was lying awake in bed when he heard some lovely music. It sounded so sweet to his ears that he thought it must be the King's musicians passing by. It was really only a little linnet singing outside his window, but it was so long since he had heard a bird sing in his garden that it seemed to him to be the most beautiful music in the world. Then the Hail stopped dancing over his head, and the North Wind ceased roaring, and a delicious perfume came to him through the open casement. "I believe the Spring has come at last," said the Giant; and he jumped out of bed and looked out.

What did he see?

He saw a most wonderful sight. Through a little hole in the wall the children had crept in, and they were sitting in the branches of the trees. In every tree that he could see there was a little child. And the trees were so glad to have the children back again that they had covered themselves with blossoms, and were waving their arms gently above the children's heads. The birds were flying about and twittering with delight, and the flowers were looking up through the green grass and laughing. It was a lovely scene, only in one corner it was still Winter. It was the farthest corner of the garden, and in it was standing a little boy. He was so small that he could not reach up to the branches of the tree, and he was wandering all round it, crying bitterly. The poor tree was still quite covered with frost and snow, and the North Wind was blowing and roaring above it. "Climb up! little boy," said the Tree, and it bent its branches down as low as it could; but the boy was too tiny.

And the Giant's heart melted as he looked out. "How selfish I have been!" he said; "now I know why the Spring would not come here. I will put that poor little boy on the top of the tree, and then I will knock down the wall, and my garden shall be the children's playground for ever and ever." He was really very sorry for what he had done.

So he crept downstairs and opened the front door quite softly, and went out into the garden. But when the children saw him they were so frightened that they all ran away, and the garden became Winter again. Only the little boy did not run, for his eyes were so full of tears that he did not see the Giant coming. And the Giant stole up behind him and took him gently in his hand, and put him up into the tree. And the tree broke at once into blossom, and the birds came and sang on it, and the little boy stretched out his two arms and flung them round the Giant's neck, and kissed him. And the other children, when they saw that the Giant was not wicked any longer, came running back, and with them came the Spring. "It is your garden now, little children," said the Giant, and he took a great axe and knocked down the wall. And when the people were going to market at twelve o'clock they found the Giant playing with the children in the most beautiful garden they had ever seen.

All day long they played, and in the evening they came to the Giant to bid him good-bye.

"But where is your little companion?" he said: "the boy I put into the tree." The Giant loved him the best because he had kissed him.

"We don't know," answered the children; "he has gone away."

"You must tell him to be sure and come here to-morrow," said the

Giant. But the children said that they did not know where he lived, and had never seen him before; and the Giant felt very sad.

Every afternoon, when school was over, the children came and played with the Giant. But the little boy whom the Giant loved was never seen again. The Giant was very kind to all the children, yet he longed for his first little friend, and often spoke of him. "How I would like to see him!" he used to say.

Years went over, and the Giant grew very old and feeble. He could not play about any more, so he sat in a huge armchair, and watched the children at their games, and admired his garden. "I have many beautiful flowers," he said; "but the children are the most beautiful flowers of all."

One winter morning he looked out of his window as he was dressing. He did not hate the Winter now, for he knew that it was merely the Spring asleep, and that the flowers were resting.

Suddenly he rubbed his eyes in wonder, and looked and looked. It certainly was a marvellous sight. In the farthest corner of the garden was a tree quite covered with lovely white blossoms. Its branches were all golden, and silver fruit hung down from them, and underneath it stood the little boy he had loved.

Downstairs ran the Giant in great joy, and out into the garden. He hastened across the grass, and came near to the child. And when he came quite close his face grew red with anger, and he said, "Who hath dared to wound thee?" For on the palms of the child's hands were the prints of two nails, and the prints of two nails were on the little feet.

"Who hath dared to wound thee?" cried the Giant; "tell me, that I may take my big sword and slay him."

"Nay!" answered the child; "but these are the wounds of Love."

"Who art thou?" said the Giant, and a strange awe fell on him, and he knelt before the little child.

And the child smiled on the Giant, and said to him, "You let me play once in your garden, to-day you shall come with me to my garden, which is Paradise."

And when the children ran in that afternoon, they found the Giant lying dead under the tree, all covered with white blossoms.

# The Happy Prince†

High above the city, on a tall column, stood the statue of the Happy Prince. He was gilded all over with thin leaves of fine gold, for eyes he had two bright sapphires, and a large red ruby glowed on his sword-hilt.

† From *Oscar Wilde: Complete Short Fiction*, ed. Ian Small (London: Penguin Books, 1994).

He was very much admired indeed. "He is as beautiful as a weathercock," remarked one of the Town Councillors who wished to gain a reputation for having artistic tastes; "only not quite so useful," he added, fearing lest people should think him unpractical, which he really was not.

"Why can't you be like the Happy Prince?" asked a sensible mother of her little boy who was crying for the moon. "The Happy Prince never dreams of crying for anything."

"I am glad there is some one in the world who is quite happy," muttered a disappointed man as he gazed at the wonderful statue.

"He looks just like an angel," said the Charity Children[1] as they came out of the cathedral in their bright scarlet cloaks, and their clean white pinafores.

"How do you know?" said the Mathematical Master, "you have never seen one."

"Ah! but we have, in our dreams," answered the children; and the Mathematical Master frowned and looked very severe, for he did not approve of children dreaming.

One night there flew over the city a little Swallow. His friends had gone away to Egypt six weeks before, but he had stayed behind, for he was in love with the most beautiful Reed. He had met her early in the spring as he was flying down the river after a big yellow moth, and had been so attracted by her slender waist that he had stopped to talk to her.

"Shall I love you?" said the Swallow, who liked to come to the point at once, and the Reed made him a low bow. So he flew round and round her, touching the water with his wings, and making silver ripples. This was his courtship, and it lasted all through the summer.

"It is a ridiculous attachment," twittered the other Swallows, "she has no money, and far too many relations"; and indeed the river was quite full of Reeds. Then, when the autumn came, they all flew away.

After they had gone he felt lonely, and began to tire of his lady-love. "She has no conversation," he said, "and I am afraid that she is a coquette, for she is always flirting with the wind." And certainly, whenever the wind blew, the Reed made the most graceful curtsies. "I admit that she is domestic," he continued, "but I love travelling, and my wife, consequently, should love travelling also."

"Will you come away with me?" he said finally to her; but the Reed shook her head, she was so attached to her home.

"You have been trifling with me," he cried, "I am off to the Pyramids. Good-bye!" and he flew away.

All day long he flew, and at night-time he arrived at the city. "Where shall I put up?" he said; "I hope the town has made preparations."

---

1. Pupils in institutions known as Charity Schools, which are funded by public endowments.

Then he saw the statue on the tall column. "I will put up there," he cried; "it is a fine position with plenty of fresh air." So he alighted just between the feet of the Happy Prince.

"I have a golden bedroom," he said softly to himself as he looked round, and he prepared to go to sleep; but just as he was putting his head under his wing a large drop of water fell on him. "What a curious thing!" he cried, "there is not a single cloud in the sky, the stars are quite clear and bright, and yet it is raining. The climate in the north of Europe is really dreadful. The Reed used to like the rain, but that was merely her selfishness."

Then another drop fell.

"What is the use of a statue if it cannot keep the rain off?" he said; "I must look for a good chimney-pot," and he determined to fly away.

But before he had opened his wings, a third drop fell, and he looked up, and saw—Ah! what did he see?

The eyes of the Happy Prince were filled with tears, and tears were running down his golden cheeks. His face was so beautiful in the moonlight that the little Swallow was filled with pity.

"Who are you?" he said.

"I am the Happy Prince."

"Why are you weeping then?" asked the Swallow; "you have quite drenched me."

"When I was alive and had a human heart," answered the statue, "I did not know what tears were, for I lived in the Palace of Sans-Souci[2] where sorrow is not allowed to enter. In the daytime I played with my companions in the garden, and in the evening I led the dance in the Great Hall. Round the garden ran a very lofty wall, but I never cared to ask what lay beyond it, everything about me was so beautiful. My courtiers called me the Happy Prince, and happy indeed I was, if pleasure be happiness. So I lived, and so I died. And now that I am dead they have set me up here so high that I can see all the ugliness and all the misery of my city, and though my heart is made of lead yet I cannot choose but weep."

"What, is he not solid gold?" said the Swallow to himself. He was too polite to make any personal remarks out loud.

"Far away," continued the statue in a low musical voice, "far away in a little street there is a poor house. One of the windows is open, and through it I can see a woman seated at a table. Her face is thin and worn, and she has coarse, red hands, all pricked by the needle, for she is a seamstress. She is embroidering passion-flowers on a satin gown for the loveliest of the Queen's maids-of-honour to wear at the next Court-ball. In a bed in the corner of the room her little boy is lying ill. He has a fever, and is asking for oranges. His mother has nothing to give

2. Without Care (French). Sans-Souci was the name of Frederick the Great's palace in Potsdam.

him but river water, so he is crying. Swallow, Swallow, little Swallow, will you not bring her the ruby out of my sword-hilt? My feet arc fastened to this pedestal and I cannot move."

"I am waited for in Egypt," said the Swallow. "My friends are flying up and down the Nile, and talking to the large lotus-flowers. Soon they will go to sleep in the tomb of the great King. The King is there himself in his painted coffin. He is wrapped in yellow linen, and embalmed with spices. Round his neck is a chain of pale green jade, and his hands are like withered leaves."

"Swallow, Swallow, little Swallow," said the Prince, "will you not stay with me for one night, and be my messenger? The boy is so thirsty, and the mother so sad."

"I don't think I like boys," answered the Swallow. "Last summer, when I was staying on the river, there were two rude boys, the miller's sons, who were always throwing stones at me. They never hit me, of course; we swallows fly far too well for that, and besides, I come of a family famous for its agility; but still, it was a mark of disrespect."

But the Happy Prince looked so sad that the little Swallow was sorry. "It is very cold here," he said; "but I will stay with you for one night, and be your messenger."

"Thank you, little Swallow," said the Prince.

So the Swallow picked out the great ruby from the Prince's sword, and flew away with it in his beak over the roofs of the town.

He passed by the cathedral tower, where the white marble angels were sculptured. He passed by the palace and heard the sound of dancing. A beautiful girl came out on the balcony with her lover. "How wonderful the stars are," he said to her, "and how wonderful is the power of love!" "I hope my dress will be ready in time for the State-ball," she answered; "I have ordered passion-flowers to be embroidered on it; but the seamstresses are so lazy."

He passed over the river, and saw the lanterns hanging to the masts of the ships. He passed over the Ghetto, and saw the old Jews bargaining with each other, and weighing out money in copper scales. At last he came to the poor house and looked in. The boy was tossing feverishly on his bed, and the mother had fallen asleep, she was so tired. In he hopped, and laid the great ruby on the table beside the woman's thimble. Then he flew gently round the bed, fanning the boy's forehead with his wings. "How cool I feel," said the boy, "I must be getting better"; and he sank into a delicious slumber.

Then the Swallow flew back to the Happy Prince, and told him what he had done. "It is curious," he remarked, "but I feel quite warm now, although it is so cold."

"That is because you have done a good action," said the Prince. And the little Swallow began to think, and then he fell asleep. Thinking always made him sleepy.

When day broke he flew down to the river and had a bath.

"What a remarkable phenomenon," said the Professor of Ornithology as he was passing over the bridge. "A swallow in winter!" And he wrote a long letter about it to the local newspaper. Every one quoted it, it was full of so many words that they could not understand.

"To-night I go to Egypt," said the Swallow, and he was in high spirits at the prospect. He visited all the public monuments, and sat a long time on top of the church steeple. Wherever he went the Sparrows chirruped, and said to each other, "What a distinguished stranger!" so he enjoyed himself very much.

When the moon rose he flew back to the Happy Prince. "Have you any commissions for Egypt?" he cried; "I am just starting."

"Swallow, Swallow, little Swallow," said the Prince, "will you not stay with me one night longer?"

"I am waited for in Egypt," answered the Swallow. "To-morrow my friends will fly up to the Second Cataract.[3] The river-horse couches there among the bulrushes, and on a great granite throne sits the God Memnon.[4] All night long he watches the stars, and when the morning star shines he utters one cry of joy, and then he is silent. At noon the yellow lions come down to the water's edge to drink. They have eyes like green beryls,[5] and their roar is louder than the roar of the cataract."

"Swallow, Swallow, little Swallow," said the Prince, "far away across the city I see a young man in a garret. He is leaning over a desk covered with papers, and in a tumbler by his side there is a bunch of withered violets. His hair is brown and crisp, and his lips are red as a pomegranate, and he has large and dreamy eyes. He is trying to finish a play for the Director of the Theatre, but he is too cold to write any more. There is no fire in the grate, and hunger has made him faint."

"I will wait with you one night longer," said the Swallow, who really had a good heart. "Shall I take him another ruby?"

"Alas! I have no ruby now," said the Prince; "my eyes are all that I have left. They are made of rare sapphires, which were brought out of India a thousand years ago. Pluck out one of them and take it to him. He will sell it to the jeweller, and buy food and firewood, and finish his play."

"Dear Prince," said the Swallow, "I cannot do that;" and he began to weep.

"Swallow, Swallow, little Swallow," said the Prince, "do as I command you."

So the Swallow plucked out the Prince's eye, and flew away to the

3. This reference and other details of the journey (including the stay at the Temple of Baalbec) are taken from a poem by Emile Gautier, "Ce que disent les hirondelles" ("What the swallows say").
4. Reference to the statue of Memnon at Thebes, which is said to emit music when struck by the sun's rays.
5. Transparent pale green stones.

student's garret. It was easy enough to get in, as there was a hole in the roof. Through this he darted, and came into the room. The young man had his head buried in his hands, so he did not hear the flutter of the bird's wings, and when he looked up he found the beautiful sapphire lying on the withered violets.

"I am beginning to be appreciated," he cried; "this is from some great admirer. Now I can finish my play," and he looked quite happy.

The next day the Swallow flew down to the harbour. He sat on the mast of a large vessel and watched the sailors hauling big chests out of the hold with ropes. "Heave a-hoy!" they shouted as each chest came up. "I am going to Egypt!" cried the Swallow, but nobody minded, and when the moon rose he flew back to the Happy Prince.

"I am come to bid you good-bye," he cried.

"Swallow, Swallow, little Swallow," said the Prince, "will you not stay with me one night longer?"

"It is winter," answered the Swallow, "and the chill snow will soon be here. In Egypt the sun is warm on the green palm-trees, and the crocodiles lie in the mud and look lazily about them. My companions are building a nest in the Temple of Baalbec, and the pink and white doves are watching them, and cooing to each other. Dear Prince, I must leave you, but I will never forget you, and next spring I will bring you back two beautiful jewels in place of those you have given away. The ruby shall be redder than a red rose, and the sapphire shall be as blue as the great sea."

"In the square below," said the Happy Prince, "there stands a little match-girl. She has let her matches fall in the gutter, and they are all spoiled. Her father will beat her if she does not bring home some money, and she is crying. She has no shoes or stockings, and her little head is bare. Pluck out my other eye, and give it to her, and her father will not beat her."

"I will stay with you one night longer," said the Swallow, "but I cannot pluck out your eye. You would be quite blind then."

"Swallow, Swallow, little Swallow," said the Prince, "do as I command you."

So he plucked out the Prince's other eye, and darted down with it. He swooped past the match-girl, and slipped the jewel into the palm of her hand. "What a lovely bit of glass," cried the little girl; and she ran home, laughing.

Then the Swallow came back to the Prince. "You are blind now," he said, "so I will stay with you always."

"No, little Swallow," said the poor Prince, "you must go away to Egypt."

"I will stay with you always," said the Swallow, and he slept at the Prince's feet.

All the next day he sat on the Prince's shoulder, and told him stories of what he had seen in strange lands. He told him of the red ibises, who stand in long rows on the banks of the Nile, and catch gold fish in their beaks; of the Sphinx, who is as old as the world itself, and lives in the desert, and knows everything; of the merchants, who walk slowly by the side of their camels, and carry amber beads in their hands; of the King of the Mountains of the Moon,[6] who is as black as ebony, and worships a large crystal; of the great green snake that sleeps in a palm-tree, and has twenty priests to feed it with honey-cakes; and of the pygmies who sail over a big lake on large flat leaves, and are always at war with the butterflies.

"Dear little Swallow," said the Prince, "you tell me of marvellous things, but more marvellous than anything is the suffering of men and of women. There is no Mystery so great as Misery. Fly over my city, little Swallow, and tell me what you see there."

So the Swallow flew over the great city, and saw the rich making merry in their beautiful houses, while the beggars were sitting at the gates. He flew into dark lanes, and saw the white faces of starving children looking out listlessly at the black streets. Under the archway of a bridge two little boys were lying in one another's arms to try and keep themselves warm. "How hungry we are!" they said. "You must not lie here," shouted the Watchman, and they wandered out into the rain.

Then he flew back and told the Prince what he had seen.

"I am covered with fine gold," said the Prince, "you must take it off, leaf by leaf, and give it to my poor; the living always think that gold can make them happy."

Leaf after leaf of the fine gold the Swallow picked off, till the Happy Prince looked quite dull and grey. Leaf after leaf of the fine gold he brought to the poor, and the children's faces grew rosier, and they laughed and played games in the street. "We have bread now!" they cried.

Then the snow came, and after the snow came the frost. The streets looked as if they were made of silver, they were so bright and glistening; long icicles like crystal daggers hung down from the eaves of the houses, everybody went about in furs, and the little boys wore scarlet caps and skated on the ice.

The poor little Swallow grew colder and colder, but he would not leave the Prince, he loved him too well. He picked up crumbs outside the baker's door when the baker was not looking, and tried to keep himself warm by flapping his wings.

But at last he knew that he was going to die. He had just strength to fly up to the Prince's shoulder once more. "Good-bye, dear Prince!" he murmured, "will you let me kiss your hand?"

"I am glad that you are going to Egypt at last, little Swallow," said

6. The Mountains of the Moon are a range in Uganda.

the Prince, "you have stayed too long here; but you must kiss me on the lips, for I love you."

"It is not to Egypt that I am going," said the Swallow. "I am going to the House of Death. Death is the brother of Sleep, is he not?"

And he kissed the Happy Prince on the lips, and fell down dead at his feet.

At that moment a curious crack sounded inside the statue, as if something had broken. The fact is that the leaden heart had snapped right in two. It certainly was a dreadfully hard frost.

Early the next morning the Mayor was walking in the square below in company with the Town Councillors. As they passed the column he looked up at the statue: "Dear me! how shabby the Happy Prince looks!" he said.

"How shabby indeed!" cried the Town Councillors, who always agreed with the Mayor, and they went up to look at it.

"The ruby has fallen out of his sword, his eyes are gone, and he is golden no longer," said the Mayor; "in fact, he is little better than a beggar!"

"Little better than a beggar," said the Town Councillors.

"And here is actually a dead bird at his feet!" continued the Mayor. "We must really issue a proclamation that birds are not to be allowed to die here." And the Town Clerk made a note of the suggestion.

So they pulled down the statue of the Happy Prince. "As he is no longer beautiful he is no longer useful,"[7] said the Art Professor at the University.

Then they melted the statue in a furnace, and the Mayor held a meeting of the Corporation to decide what was to be done with the metal. "We must have another statue, of course," he said, "and it shall be a statue of myself."

"Of myself," said each of the Town Councillors, and they quarrelled. When I last heard of them they were quarrelling still.

"What a strange thing!" said the overseer of the workmen at the foundry. "This broken lead heart will not melt in the furnace. We must throw it away." So they threw it on a dust-heap where the dead Swallow was also lying.

"Bring me the two most precious things in the city," said God to one of His Angels; and the Angel brought Him the leaden heart and the dead bird.

"You have rightly chosen," said God, "for in my garden of Paradise this little bird shall sing for evermore, and in my city of gold the Happy Prince shall praise me."

*— sparrow dies & goes to heaven w̅ the Happy prince.*

7. Note Wilde's aphorism "All art is quite useless."

# The Nightingale and the Rose†

"She said that she would dance with me if I brought her red roses," cried the young Student; "but in all my garden there is no red rose."

From her nest in the holm-oak tree the Nightingale heard him, and she looked out through the leaves, and wondered.

"No red rose in all my garden!" he cried, and his beautiful eyes filled with tears. "Ah, on what little things does happiness depend! I have read all that the wise men have written, and all the secrets of philosophy are mine, yet for want of a red rose is my life made wretched."

"Here at last is a true lover," said the Nightingale. "Night after night have I sung of him, though I knew him not: night after night have I told his story to the stars, and now I see him. His hair is dark as the hyacinth-blossom, and his lips are red as the rose of his desire; but passion has made his face like pale ivory, and sorrow has set her seal upon his brow."

"The Prince gives a ball to-morrow night," murmured the young Student, "and my love will be of the company. If I bring her a red rose she will dance with me till dawn. If I bring her a red rose, I shall hold her in my arms, and she will lean her head upon my shoulder, and her hand will be clasped in mine. But there is no red rose in my garden, so I shall sit lonely, and she will pass me by. She will have no heed of me, and my heart will break."

"Here indeed is the true lover," said the Nightingale. "What I sing of, he suffers: what is joy to me, to him is pain. Surely Love is a wonderful thing. It is more precious than emeralds, and dearer than fine opals. Pearls and pomegranates cannot buy it, nor is it set forth in the market-place. It may not be purchased of the merchants, nor can it be weighed out in the balance for gold."

"The musicians will sit in their gallery," said the young Student, "and play upon their stringed instruments, and my love will dance to the sound of the harp and the violin. She will dance so lightly that her feet will not touch the floor, and the courtiers in their gay dresses will throng round her. But with me she will not dance, for I have no red rose to give her"; and he flung himself down on the grass, and buried his face in his hands, and wept.

"Why is he weeping?" asked a little Green Lizard, as he ran past him with his tail in the air.

"Why, indeed?" said a Butterfly, who was fluttering about after a sunbeam.

"Why, indeed?" whispered a Daisy to his neighbour, in a soft, low voice.

† From *Oscar Wilde: Complete Short Fiction*, ed. Ian Small (London: Penguin Books, 1994).

"He is weeping for a red rose," said the Nightingale.

"For a red rose!" they cried; "how very ridiculous!" and the little Lizard, who was something of a cynic, laughed outright.

But the Nightingale understood the secret of the Student's sorrow, and she sat silent in the oak-tree, and thought about the mystery of Love.

Suddenly she spread her brown wings for flight, and soared into the air. She passed through the grove like a shadow, and like a shadow she sailed across the garden.

In the centre of the grass-plot was standing a beautiful Rose-tree, and when she saw it, she flew over to it, and lit upon a spray.

"Give me a red rose," she cried, "and I will sing you my sweetest song."

But the Tree shook its head.

"My roses are white," it answered; "as white as the foam of the sea, and whiter than the snow upon the mountain. But go to my brother who grows round the old sun-dial, and perhaps he will give you what you want."

So the Nightingale flew over to the Rose-tree that was growing round the old sun-dial.

"Give me a red rose," she cried, "and I will sing you my sweetest song."

But the Tree shook its head.

"My roses are yellow," it answered; "as yellow as the hair of the mermaiden who sits upon an amber throne, and yellower than the daffodil that blooms in the meadow before the mower comes with his scythe. But go to my brother who grows beneath the Student's window, and perhaps he will give you what you want."

So the Nightingale flew over to the Rose-tree that was growing beneath the Student's window.

"Give me a red rose," she cried, "and I will sing you my sweetest song."

But the Tree shook its head.

"My roses are red," it answered, "as red as the feet of the dove, and redder than the great fans of coral that wave and wave in the ocean-cavern. But the winter has chilled my veins, and the frost has nipped my buds, and the storm has broken my branches, and I shall have no roses at all this year."

"One red rose is all I want," cried the Nightingale, "only one red rose! Is there no way by which I can get it?"

"There is a way," answered the Tree; "but it is so terrible that I dare not tell it to you."

"Tell it to me," said the Nightingale, "I am not afraid."

"If you want a red rose," said the Tree, "you must build it out of music by moonlight, and stain it with your own heart's-blood. You must sing to me with your breast against a thorn. All night long you must sing to me, and the thorn must pierce your heart, and your life-blood must flow into my veins, and become mine."

"Death is a great price to pay for a red rose," cried the Nightingale, "and Life is very dear to all. It is pleasant to sit in the green wood, and to watch the Sun in his chariot of gold, and the Moon in her chariot of pearl. Sweet is the scent of the hawthorn, and sweet are the bluebells that hide in the valley, and the heather that blows on the hill. Yet Love is better than Life, and what is the heart of a bird compared to the heart of a man?"

So she spread her brown wings for flight, and soared into the air. She swept over the garden like a shadow, and like a shadow she sailed through the grove.

The young Student was still lying on the grass, where she had left him, and the tears were not yet dry in his beautiful eyes.

"Be happy," cried the Nightingale, "be happy; you shall have your red rose. I will build it out of music by moonlight, and stain it with my own heart's-blood. All that I ask of you in return is that you will be a true lover, for Love is wiser than Philosophy, though she is wise, and mightier than Power, though he is mighty. Flame-coloured are his wings, and coloured like flame is his body. His lips are sweet as honey, and his breath is like frankincense."

The Student looked up from the grass, and listened, but he could not understand what the Nightingale was saying to him, for he only knew the things that are written down in books.

But the Oak-tree understood, and felt sad, for he was very fond of the little Nightingale who had built her nest in his branches.

"Sing me one last song," he whispered; "I shall feel very lonely when you are gone."

So the Nightingale sang to the Oak-tree, and her voice was like water bubbling from a silver jar.

When she had finished her song the Student got up, and pulled a note-book and a lead-pencil out of his pocket.

"She has form," he said to himself, as he walked away through the grove—"that cannot be denied to her; but has she got feeling? I am afraid not. In fact, she is like most artists; she is all style, without any sincerity. She would not sacrifice herself for others. She thinks merely of music, and everybody knows that the arts are selfish. Still, it must be admitted that she has some beautiful notes in her voice. What a pity it is that they do not mean anything, or do any practical good." And he went into his room, and lay down on his little pallet-bed, and began to think of his love; and, after a time, he fell asleep.

And when the Moon shone in the heavens the Nightingale flew to the Rose-tree, and set her breast against the thorn. All night long she sang with her breast against the thorn, and the cold crystal Moon leaned down and listened. All night long she sang, and the thorn went deeper and deeper into her breast, and her life-blood ebbed away from her.

She sang first of the birth of love in the heart of a boy and a girl. And on the topmost spray of the Rose-tree there blossomed a marvellous rose, petal following petal, as song followed song. Pale was it, at first, as the mist that hangs over the river—pale as the feet of the morning, and silver as the wings of the dawn. As the shadow of a rose in a mirror of silver, as the shadow of a rose in a water-pool, so was the rose that blossomed on the topmost spray of the Tree.

But the Tree cried to the Nightingale to press closer against the thorn. "Press closer, little Nightingale," cried the Tree, "or the Day will come before the rose is finished."

So the Nightingale pressed closer against the thorn, and louder and louder grew her song, for she sang of the birth of passion in the soul of a man and a maid.

And a delicate flush of pink came into the leaves of the rose, like the flush in the face of the bridegroom when he kisses the lips of the bride. But the thorn had not yet reached her heart, so the rose's heart remained white, for only a Nightingale's heart's-blood can crimson the heart of a rose.

And the Tree cried to the Nightingale to press closer against the thorn. "Press closer, little Nightingale," cried the Tree, "or the Day will come before the rose is finished."

So the Nightingale pressed closer against the thorn, and the thorn touched her heart, and a fierce pang of pain shot through her. Bitter, bitter was the pain, and wilder and wilder grew her song, for she sang of the Love that is perfected by Death, of the Love that dies not in the tomb.

And the marvellous rose became crimson, like the rose of the eastern sky. Crimson was the girdle of petals, and crimson as a ruby was the heart.

But the Nightingale's voice grew fainter, and her little wings began to beat, and a film came over her eyes. Fainter and fainter grew her song, and she felt something choking her in her throat.

Then she gave one last burst of music. The white Moon heard it, and she forgot the dawn, and lingered on in the sky. The red rose heard it, and it trembled all over with ecstasy, and opened its petals to the cold morning air. Echo[1] bore it to her purple cavern in the hills, and woke the sleeping shepherds from their dreams. It floated through the reeds of the river, and they carried its message to the sea.

"Look, look!" cried the Tree, "the rose is finished now"; but the Nightingale made no answer, for she was lying dead in the long grass, with the thorn in her heart.

---

1. In classical mythology, a mountain nymph who repeats the last words uttered by others.

And at noon the Student opened his window and looked out.

"Why, what a wonderful piece of luck!" he cried; "here is a red rose! I have never seen any rose like it in all my life. It is so beautiful that I am sure it has a long Latin name"; and he leaned down and plucked it.

Then he put on his hat, and ran up to the Professor's house with the rose in his hand.

The daughter of the Professor was sitting in the doorway winding blue silk on a reel, and her little dog was lying at her feet.

"You said that you would dance with me if I brought you a red rose," cried the Student. "Here is the reddest rose in all the world. You will wear it to-night next your heart, and as we dance together it will tell you how I love you."

But the girl frowned.

"I am afraid it will not go with my dress," she answered; "and, besides, the Chamberlain's nephew has sent me some real jewels, and everybody knows that jewels cost far more than flowers."

"Well, upon my word, you are very ungrateful," said the Student angrily; and he threw the rose into the street, where it fell into the gutter, and a cart-wheel went over it.

"Ungrateful!" said the girl. "I tell you what, you are very rude; and, after all, who are you? Only a Student. Why, I don't believe you have even got silver buckles to your shoes as the Chamberlain's nephew has"; and she got up from her chair and went into the house.

"What a silly thing Love is," said the Student as he walked away. "It is not half as useful as Logic, for it does not prove anything, and it is always telling one of things that are not going to happen, and making one believe things that are not true. In fact, it is quite unpractical, and, as in this age to be practical is everything, I shall go back to Philosophy and study Metaphysics."

So he returned to his room and pulled out a great dusty book, and began to read.

# CRITICISM

# BRUNO BETTELHEIM

# [The Struggle for Meaning]†

\* \* \*

Today, as in times past, the most important and also the most difficult task in raising a child is helping him to find meaning in life. Many growth experiences are needed to achieve this. The child, as he develops, must learn step by step to understand himself better; with this he becomes more able to understand others, and eventually can relate to them in ways which are mutually satisfying and meaningful.

To find deeper meaning, one must become able to transcend the narrow confines of a self-centered existence and believe that one will make a significant contribution to life—if not right now, then at some future time. This feeling is necessary if a person is to be satisfied with himself and with what he is doing. In order not to be at the mercy of the vagaries of life, one must develop one's inner resources, so that one's emotions, imagination, and intellect mutually support and enrich one another. Our positive feelings give us the strength to develop our rationality; only hope for the future can sustain us in the adversities we unavoidably encounter.

As an educator and therapist of severely disturbed children, my main task was to restore meaning to their lives. This work made it obvious to me that if children were reared so that life was meaningful to them, they would not need special help. I was confronted with the problem of deducing what experiences in a child's life are most suited to promote his ability to find meaning in his life; to endow life in general with more meaning. Regarding this task, nothing is more important than the impact of parents and others who take care of the child; second in importance is our cultural heritage, when transmitted to the child in the right manner. When children are young, it is literature that carries such information best.

Given this fact, I became deeply dissatisfied with much of the literature intended to develop the child's mind and personality, because it fails to stimulate and nurture those resources he needs most in order to cope with his difficult inner problems. The preprimers and primers from which he is taught to read in school are designed to teach the necessary skills, irrespective of meaning. The overwhelming bulk of the rest of so-called "children's literature" attempts to entertain or to inform, or both. But most of these books are so shallow in substance that little of significance can be gained from them. The acquisition of skills,

† From Bruno Bettelheim, *The Uses of Enchantment: The Meaning and Importance of Fairy Tales* (New York: Knopf, 1976) 3–8. Copyright © 1976. Reprinted by permission of Alfred A. Knopf, Inc.

including the ability to read, becomes devalued when what one has learned to read adds nothing of importance to one's life.

We all tend to assess the future merits of an activity on the basis of what it offers now. But this is especially true for the child, who, much more than the adult, lives in the present and, although he has anxieties about his future, has only the vaguest notions of what it may require or be like. The idea that learning to read may enable one later to enrich one's life is experienced as an empty promise when the stories the child listens to, or is reading at the moment, are vacuous. The worst feature of these children's books is that they cheat the child of what he ought to gain from the experience of literature: access to deeper meaning, and that which is meaningful to him at his stage of development.

For a story truly to hold the child's attention, it must entertain him and arouse his curiosity. But to enrich his life, it must stimulate his imagination; help him to develop his intellect and to clarify his emotions; be attuned to his anxieties and aspirations; give full recognition to his difficulties, while at the same time suggesting solutions to the problems which perturb him. In short, it must at one and the same time relate to all aspects of his personality—and this without ever belittling but, on the contrary, giving full credence to the seriousness of the child's predicaments, while simultaneously promoting confidence in himself and in his future.

In all these and many other respects, of the entire "children's literature"—with rare exceptions—nothing can be as enriching and satisfying to child and adult alike as the folk fairy tale. True, on an overt level fairy tales teach little about the specific conditions of life in modern mass society; these tales were created long before it came into being. But more can be learned from them about the inner problems of human beings, and of the right solutions to their predicaments in any society, than from any other type of story within a child's comprehension. Since the child at every moment of his life is exposed to the society in which he lives, he will certainly learn to cope with its conditions, provided his inner resources permit him to do so.

Just because his life is often bewildering to him, the child needs even more to be given the chance to understand himself in this complex world with which he must learn to cope. To be able to do so, the child must be helped to make some coherent sense out of the turmoil of his feelings. He needs ideas on how to bring his inner house into order, and on that basis be able to create order in his life. He needs—and this hardly requires emphasis at this moment in our history—a moral education which subtly, and by implication only, conveys to him the advantages of moral behavior, not through abstract ethical concepts but through that which seems tangibly right and therefore meaningful to him.

The child finds this kind of meaning through fairy tales. Like many other modern psychological insights, this was anticipated long ago by poets. The German poet Schiller wrote: "Deeper meaning resides in the fairy tales told to me in my childhood than in the truth that is taught by life." (*The Piccolomini*, III, 4.)

Through the centuries (if not millennia) during which, in their re-telling, fairy tales became ever more refined, they came to convey at the same time overt and covert meanings—came to speak simultane-ously to all levels of the human personality, communicating in a man-ner which reaches the uneducated mind of the child as well as that of the sophisticated adult. Applying the psychoanalytic model of the hu-man personality, fairy tales carry important messages to the conscious, the preconscious, and the unconscious mind, on whatever level each is functioning at the time. By dealing with universal human problems, particularly those which preoccupy the child's mind, these stories speak to his budding ego and encourage its development, while at the same time relieving preconscious and unconscious pressures. As the stories unfold, they give conscious credence and body to id pressures and show ways to satisfy these that are in line with ego and superego require-ments.

But my interest in fairy tales is not the result of such a technical analysis of their merits. It is, on the contrary, the consequence of asking myself why, in my experience, children—normal and abnormal alike, and at all levels of intelligence—find folk fairy tales more satisfying than all other children's stories.

The more I tried to understand why these stories are so successful at enriching the inner life of the child, the more I realized that these tales, in a much deeper sense than any other reading material, start where the child really is in his psychological and emotional being. They speak about his severe inner pressures in a way that the child uncon-sciously understands, and—without belittling the most serious inner struggles which growing up entails—offer examples of both temporary and permanent solutions to pressing difficulties.

*     *     *

## Fairy Tales and the Existential Predicament

In order to master the psychological problems of growing up—over-coming narcissistic disappointments, oedipal dilemmas, sibling rivalries; becoming able to relinquish childhood dependencies; gaining a feeling of selfhood and of self-worth, and a sense of moral obligation—a child needs to understand what is going on within his conscious self so that he can also cope with that which goes on in his unconscious. He can achieve this understanding, and with it the ability to cope, not through rational comprehension of the nature and content of his unconscious, but by becoming familiar with it through spinning out daydreams—

ruminating, rearranging, and fantasizing about suitable story elements in response to unconscious pressures. By doing this, the child fits unconscious content into conscious fantasies, which then enable him to deal with that content. It is here that fairy tales have unequaled value, because they offer new dimensions to the child's imagination which would be impossible for him to discover as truly on his own. Even more important, the form and structure of fairy tales suggest images to the child by which he can structure his daydreams and with them give better direction to his life.

In child or adult, the unconscious is a powerful determinant of behavior. When the unconscious is repressed and its content denied entrance into awareness, then eventually the person's conscious mind will be partially overwhelmed by derivatives of these unconscious elements, or else he is forced to keep such rigid, compulsive control over them that his personality may become severely crippled. But when unconscious material *is* to some degree permitted to come to awareness and worked through in imagination, its potential for causing harm—to ourselves or others—is much reduced; some of its forces can then be made to serve positive purposes. However, the prevalent parental belief is that a child must be diverted from what troubles him most: his formless, nameless anxieties, and his chaotic, angry, and even violent fantasies. Many parents believe that only conscious reality or pleasant and wishfulfilling images should be presented to the child—that he should be exposed only to the sunny side of things. But such one-sided fare nourishes the mind only in a one-sided way, and real life is not all sunny.

There is a widespread refusal to let children know that the source of much that goes wrong in life is due to our very own natures—the propensity of all men for acting aggressively, asocially, selfishly, out of anger and anxiety. Instead, we want our children to believe that, inherently, all men are good. But children know that *they* are not always good; and often, even when they are, they would prefer not to be. This contradicts what they are told by their parents, and therefore makes the child a monster in his own eyes.

The dominant culture wishes to pretend, particularly where children are concerned, that the dark side of man does not exist, and professes a belief in an optimistic meliorism. Psychoanalysis itself is viewed as having the purpose of making life easy—but this is not what its founder intended. Psychoanalysis was created to enable man to accept the problematic nature of life without being defeated by it, or giving in to escapism. Freud's prescription is that only by struggling courageously against what seem like overwhelming odds can man succeed in wringing meaning out of his existence.

This is exactly the message that fairy tales get across to the child in manifold form: that a struggle against severe difficulties in life is unavoidable, is an intrinsic part of human existence—but that if one does not shy away, but steadfastly meets unexpected and often unjust hardships, one masters all obstacles and at the end emerges victorious.

Modern stories written for young children mainly avoid these existential problems, although they are crucial issues for all of us. The child needs most particularly to be given suggestions in symbolic form about how he may deal with these issues and grow safely into maturity. "Safe" stories mention neither death nor aging, the limits to our existence, nor the wish for eternal life. The fairy tale, by contrast, confronts the child squarely with the basic human predicaments.

\* \* \*

# BRUNO BETTELHEIM

## "Hansel and Gretel"†

"Hansel and Gretel" begins realistically. The parents are poor, and they worry about how they will be able to take care of their children. Together at night they discuss their predicament, and how they can deal with it. Even taken on this surface level, the folk fairy tale conveys an important, although unpleasant, truth: poverty and deprivation do not improve man's character, but rather make him more selfish, less sensitive to the sufferings of others, and thus prone to embark on evil deeds.

The fairy tale expresses in words and actions the things which go on in children's minds. In terms of the child's dominant anxiety, Hansel and Gretel believe that their parents are talking about a plot to desert them. A small child, awakening hungry in the darkness of the night, feels threatened by complete rejection and desertion, which he experiences in the form of fear of starvation. By projecting their inner anxiety onto those they fear might cut them off, Hansel and Gretel are convinced that their parents plan to starve them to death! In line with the child's anxious fantasies, the story tells that until then the parents had been able to feed their children, but had now fallen upon lean times.

The mother represents the source of all food to the children, so it is she who now is experienced as abandoning them, as if in a wilderness. It is the child's anxiety and deep disappointment when Mother is no longer willing to meet all his oral demands which leads him to believe that suddenly Mother has become unloving, selfish, rejecting. Since the children know they need their parents desperately, they attempt to

† From Bruno Bettelheim, *The Uses of Enchantment: The Meaning and Importance of Fairy Tales* (New York: Knopf, 1976) 159–66. Copyright © 1975, 1976 by Bruno Bettelheim. Reprinted by permission of Alfred A. Knopf, Inc.

return home after being deserted. In fact, Hansel succeeds in finding their way back from the forest the first time they are abandoned. Before a child has the courage to embark on the voyage of finding himself, of becoming an independent person through meeting the world, he can develop initiative only in trying to return to passivity, to secure for himself eternally dependent gratification. "Hansel and Gretel" tells that this will not work in the long run.

The children's successful return home does not solve anything. Their effort to continue life as before, as if nothing had happened, is to no avail. The frustrations continue, and the mother becomes more shrewd in her plans for getting rid of the children.

By implication, the story tells about the debilitating consequences of trying to deal with life's problems by means of regression and denial, which reduce one's ability to solve problems. The first time in the forest Hansel used his intelligence appropriately by putting down white pebbles to mark the path home. The second time he did not use his intelligence as well—he, who lived close to a big forest, should have known that birds would eat the bread crumbs. Hansel might instead have studied landmarks on the way in, to find his way back out. But having engaged in denial and regression—the return home—Hansel has lost much of his initiative and ability to think clearly. Starvation anxiety has driven him back, so now he can think only of food as offering a solution to the problem of finding his way out of a serious predicament. Bread stands here for food in general, man's "life line"—an image which Hansel takes literally, out of his anxiety. This shows the limiting effects of fixations to primitive levels of development, engaged in out of fear.

The story of "Hansel and Gretel" gives body to the anxieties and learning tasks of the young child who must overcome and sublimate his primitive incorporative and hence destructive desires.[1] The child must learn that if he does not free himself of these, his parents or society will force him to do so against his will, as earlier his mother had stopped nursing the child when she felt the time had come to do so. This tale gives symbolic expression to these inner experiences directly linked to the mother. Therefore, the father remains a shadowy and ineffectual figure throughout the story, as he appears to the child during his early life when Mother is all-important, in both her benign and her threatening aspects.

Frustrated in their ability to find a solution to their problem in reality because reliance on food for safety (bread crumbs to mark the path) fails them, Hansel and Gretel now give full rein to their oral regression. The gingerbread house represents an existence based on the most primitive satisfactions. Carried away by their uncontrolled craving, the chil-

---

1. The wish to devour, or incorporate, whatever appears threatening [*Editor*].

dren think nothing of destroying what should give shelter and safety, even though the birds' having eaten the crumbs should have warned them about eating up things.

By devouring the gingerbread house's roof and window, the children show how ready they are to eat somebody out of house and home, a fear which they had projected onto their parents as the reason for their desertion. Despite the warning voice which asks, "Who is nibbling at my little house?" the children lie to themselves and blame it on the wind and "[go] on eating without disturbing themselves."

The gingerbread house is an image nobody forgets: how incredibly appealing and tempting a picture this is, and how terrible the risk one runs if one gives in to the temptation. The child recognizes that, like Hansel and Gretel, he would wish to eat up the gingerbread house, no matter what the dangers. The house stands for oral greediness and how attractive it is to give in to it. The fairy tale is the primer from which the child learns to read his mind in the language of images, the only language which permits understanding before intellectual maturity has been achieved. The child needs to be exposed to this language, and must learn to be responsive to it, if he is to become master of his soul.

The preconscious content of fairy-tale images is much richer than even the following simple illustrations convey. For example, in dreams as well as in fantasies and the child's imagination, a house, as the place in which we dwell, can symbolize the body, usually the mother's. A gingerbread house, which one can "eat up," is a symbol of the mother, who in fact nurses the infant from her body. Thus, the house at which Hansel and Gretel are eating away blissfully and without a care stands in the unconscious for the good mother, who offers her body as a source of nourishment. It is the original all-giving mother, whom every child hopes to find again later somewhere out in the world, when his own mother begins to make demands and to impose restrictions. This is why, carried away by their hopes, Hansel and Gretel do not heed the soft voice that calls out to them, asking what they are up to—a voice that is their externalized conscience. Carried away by their greediness, and fooled by the pleasures of oral satisfaction which seem to deny all previous oral anxiety, the children "thought they were in heaven."

But, as the story tells, such unrestrained giving in to gluttony threatens destruction. Regression to the earliest "heavenly" state of being—when on the mother's breast one lived symbiotically off her—does away with all individuation and independence. It even endangers one's very existence, as cannibalistic inclinations are given body in the figure of the witch.

The witch, who is a personification of the destructive aspects of orality, is as bent on eating up the children as they are on demolishing her gingerbread house. When the children give in to untamed id impulses, as symbolized by their uncontrolled voraciousness, they risk being destroyed. The children eat only the symbolic representation of the mother, the gingerbread house; the witch wants to eat the children themselves. This teaches the hearer a valuable lesson: dealing in symbols is safe when compared with acting on the real thing. Turning the tables on the witch is justified also on another level: children who have little experience and are still learning self-control are not to be measured by the same yardstick as older people, who are supposed to be able to restrain their instinctual desires better. Thus, the punishment of the witch is as justified as the children's rescue.

The witch's evil designs finally force the children to recognize the dangers of unrestrained oral greed and dependence. To survive, they must develop initiative and realize that their only recourse lies in intelligent planning and acting. They must exchange subservience to the pressures of the id for acting in accordance with the ego. Goal-directed behavior based on intelligent assessment of the situation in which they find themselves must take the place of wish-fulfilling fantasies: the substitution of the bone for the finger, tricking the witch to climb into the oven.

Only when the dangers inherent in remaining fixed to primitive orality with its destructive propensities are recognized does the way to a higher stage of development open up. Then it turns out that the good, giving mother was hidden deep down in the bad, destructive one, because there are treasures to be gained: the children inherit the witch's jewels, which become valuable to them after their return home—that is, after they can again find the good parent. This suggests that as the children transcend their oral anxiety, and free themselves of relying on oral satisfaction for security, they can also free themselves of the image of the threatening mother—the witch—and rediscover the good parents, whose greater wisdom—the shared jewels—then benefit all.

On repeated hearing of "Hansel and Gretel," no child remains unaware of the fact that birds eat the bread crumbs and thus prevent the children from returning home without first meeting their great adventure. It is also a bird which guides Hansel and Gretel to the gingerbread house, and thanks only to another bird do they manage to get back home. This gives the child—who thinks differently about animals than older persons do—pause to think: these birds must have a purpose, otherwise they would not first prevent Hansel and Gretel from finding their way back, then take them to the witch, and finally provide passage home.

Obviously, since all turns out for the best, the birds must have known that it is preferable for Hansel and Gretel not to find their way directly back home out of the forest, but rather to risk facing the dangers of the world. In consequence of their threatening encounter with the witch, not only the children but also their parents live much more happily ever afterward. The different birds offer a clue to the path the children must follow to gain their reward.

After they have become familiar with "Hansel and Gretel," most children comprehend, at least unconsciously, that what happens in the parental home and at the witch's house are but separate aspects of what in reality is one total experience. Initially, the witch is a perfectly gratifying mother figure, as we are told how "she took them both by the hand, and led them into her little house. Then good food was set before them, milk and pancakes with sugar, apples, and nuts. Afterwards two pretty little beds were covered with clean white linen, and Hansel and Gretel lay down in them, and thought they were in heaven." Only on the following morning comes a rude awakening from such dreams of infantile bliss. "The old woman had only pretended to be so kind; she was in reality a wicked witch. . . ."

This is how the child feels when devastated by the ambivalent feelings, frustrations, and anxieties of the oedipal stage of development, as well as his previous disappointment and rage at failures on his mother's part to gratify his needs and desires as fully as he expected. Severely upset that Mother no longer serves him unquestioningly but makes demands on him and devotes herself ever more to her own interests—something which the child had not permitted to come to his awareness before—he imagines that Mother, as she nursed him and created a world of oral bliss, did so only to fool him—like the witch of the story.

Thus, the parental home "hard by a great forest" and the fateful house in the depths of the same woods are on an unconscious level but the two aspects of the parental home: the gratifying one and the frustrating one.

The child who ponders on his own the details of "Hansel and Gretel" finds meaning in how it begins. That the parental home is located at the very edge of the forest where everything happens suggests that what is to follow was imminent from the start. This is again the fairy tale's way to express thoughts through impressive images which lead the child to use his own imagination to derive deeper understanding.

Mentioned before was how the behavior of the birds symbolizes that the entire adventure was arranged for the children's benefit. Since early Christian times the white dove has symbolized superior benevolent powers. Hansel claims to be looking back at a white dove that is sitting on the roof of the parental home, wanting to say goodbye to him. It is a snow-white bird, singing delightfully, which leads the children to the gingerbread house and then settles on its roof, suggesting that this is the right place for them to arrive at. Another white bird is needed to guide the children back to safety: their way home is blocked by a "big water" which they can cross only with the help of a white duck.

The children do not encounter any expanse of water on their way in. Having to cross one on their return symbolizes a transition, and a new beginning on a higher level of existence (as in baptism). Up to the time they have to cross this water, the children have never separated. The school-age child should develop consciousness of his personal uniqueness, of his individuality, which means that he can no longer share everything with others, has to live to some degree by himself and stride out on his own. This is symbolically expressed by the children not being able to remain together in crossing the water. As they arrive there, Hansel sees no way to get across, but Gretel spies a white duck and asks it to help them cross the water. Hansel seats himself on its back and asks his sister to join him. But she knows better: this will not do. They have to cross over separately, and they do.

The children's experience at the witch's house has purged them of their oral fixations; after having crossed the water, they arrive at the other shore as more mature children, ready to rely on their own intelligence and initiative to solve life's problems. As dependent children they had been a burden to their parents; on their return they have become the family's support, as they bring home the treasures they have gained. These treasures are the children's new-won independence in thought and action, a new self-reliance which is the opposite of the passive dependence which characterized them when they were deserted in the woods.

It is females—the stepmother and the witch—who are the inimical forces in this story. Gretel's importance in the children's deliverance reassures the child that a female can be a rescuer as well as a destroyer. Probably even more important is the fact that Hansel saves them once and then later Gretel saves them again, which suggests to children that as they grow up they must come to rely more and more on their age mates for mutual help and understanding. This idea reinforces the story's main thrust, which is a warning against regression, and an encouragement of growth toward a higher plane of psychological and intellectual existence.

"Hansel and Gretel" ends with the heroes returning to the home from which they started, and now finding happiness there. This is psychologically correct, because a young child, driven into his adventures by oral or oedipal problems, cannot hope to find happiness outside the home. If all is to go well in his development, he must work these problems out while still dependent on his parents. Only through good relations with his parents can a child successfully mature into adolescence.

Having overcome his oedipal difficulties, mastered his oral anxieties, sublimated those of his cravings which cannot be satisfied realistically, and learned that wishful thinking has to be replaced by intelligent action, the child is ready to live happily again with his parents. This is symbolized by the treasures Hansel and Gretel bring home to share with their father. Rather than expecting everything good to come from the parents, the older child needs to be able to make some contribution to the emotional well-being of himself and his family.

As "Hansel and Gretel" begins matter-of-factly with the worries of a poor woodcutter's family unable to make ends meet, it ends on an equally down-to-earth level. Although the story tells that the children brought home a pile of pearls and precious stones, nothing further suggests that their economic way of life was changed. This emphasizes the symbolic nature of these jewels. The tale concludes: "Then all worries ended, and they lived together in perfect joy. My tale is ended; there runs a mouse, who catches it may make himself a big fur cap out of it." Nothing has changed by the end of "Hansel and Gretel" but inner attitudes; or, more correctly, all has changed because inner attitudes have changed. No more will the children feel pushed out, deserted, and lost in the darkness of the forest; nor will they seek for the miraculous gingerbread house. But neither will they encounter or fear the witch, since they have proved to themselves that through their combined efforts they can outsmart her and be victorious. Industry, making something good even out of unpromising material (such as by using the fur of a mouse intelligently for making a cap), is the virtue and real achievement of the school-age child who has fought through and mastered the oedipal difficulties.

"Hansel and Gretel" is one of many fairy tales where two siblings cooperate in rescuing each other and succeed because of their combined efforts. These stories direct the child toward transcending his immature dependence on his parents and reaching the next higher stage of development: cherishing also the support of age mates. Cooperating with them in meeting life's tasks will eventually have to replace the child's single-minded reliance on his parents only. The child of school age often cannot yet believe that he ever will be able to meet the world without his parents; that is why he wishes to hold on to them beyond the necessary point. He needs to learn to trust that someday he will master the dangers of the world, even in the exaggerated form in which his fears depict them, and be enriched by it.

The child views existential dangers not objectively, but fantastically exaggerated in line with his immature dread—for example, personified as a child-devouring witch. "Hansel and Gretel" encourages the child to explore on his own even the figments of his anxious imagination, because such fairy tales give him confidence that he can master not only the real dangers which his parents told him about, but even those vastly exaggerated ones which he fears exist.

A witch as created by the child's anxious fantasies will haunt him; but a witch he can push into her own oven and burn to death is a witch the child can believe himself rid of. As long as children continue to believe in witches—they always have and always will, up to the age when they no longer are compelled to give their formless apprehensions humanlike appearance—they need to be told stories in which children, by being ingenious, rid themselves of these persecuting figures of their imagination. By succeeding in doing so, they gain immensely from the experience, as did Hansel and Gretel.

# ROBERT DARNTON

## Peasants Tell Tales: The Meaning of Mother Goose†

The mental world of the unenlightened during the Enlightenment seems to be irretrievably lost. It is so difficult, if not impossible, to locate the common man in the eighteenth century that it seems foolish to search for his cosmology. But before abandoning the attempt, it might be useful to suspend one's disbelief and to consider a story—a story everyone knows, though not in the following version, which is the tale more or less as it was told around firesides in peasant cottages during long winter evenings in eighteenth-century France.[1]

> Once a little girl was told by her mother to bring some bread and milk to her grandmother. As the girl was walking through the forest, a wolf came up to her and asked where she was going.
> "To grandmother's house," she replied.
> "Which path are you taking, the path of the pins or the path of the needles?"
> "The path of the needles."
> So the wolf took the path of the pins and arrived first at the house. He killed grandmother, poured her blood into a bottle, and sliced her flesh onto a platter. Then he got into her nightclothes and waited in bed.

> "Knock, knock."
> "Come in, my dear."
> "Hello, grandmother. I've brought you some bread and milk."
> "Have something yourself, my dear. There is meat and wine in the pantry."
> So the little girl ate what was offered; and as she did, a little cat

---

† From Robert Darnton, "Peasants Tell Tales: The Meaning of Mother Goose," in *The Great Cat Massacre and Other Episodes in French Cultural History* (New York: Basic Books, 1984) 9–22. Copyright © 1984 by Basic Books, Inc. Reprinted by permission of Basic Books, a division of HarperCollins Publishers, Inc. The author's footnotes have been edited for this Norton Critical Edition.

1. This text and those of the other French folktales discussed in this essay come from Paul Delarue and Marie-Louise Tenèze, *Le Conte populaire français* (Paris, 1976), 3 vols., which is the best of the French folktale collections because it provides all the recorded versions of each tale along with background information about how they were gathered from oral sources.

said, "Slut! To eat the flesh and drink the blood of your grandmother!"

Then the wolf said, "Undress and get into bed with me."

"Where shall I put my apron?"

"Throw it on the fire; you won't need it any more."

For each garment—bodice, skirt, petticoat, and stockings—the girl asked the same question; and each time the wolf answered, "Throw it on the fire; you won't need it any more."

When the girl got in bed, she said, "Oh, grandmother! How hairy you are!"

"It's to keep me warmer, my dear."

"Oh, grandmother! What big shoulders you have!"

"It's for better carrying firewood, my dear."

"Oh, grandmother! What long nails you have!"

"It's for scratching myself better, my dear."

"Oh, grandmother! What big teeth you have!"

"It's for eating you better, my dear."

And he ate her.

What is the moral of this story? For little girls, clearly: stay away from wolves. For historians, it seems to be saying something about the mental world of the early modern peasantry. But what? How can one begin to interpret such a text? One way leads through psychoanalysis. The analysts have given folktales a thorough going-over, picking out hidden symbols, unconscious motifs, and psychic mechanisms. Consider, for example, the exegesis of "Little Red Riding Hood" by two of the best known psychoanalysts, Erich Fromm and Bruno Bettelheim.

Fromm interpreted the tale as a riddle about the collective unconscious in primitive society, and he solved it "without difficulty" by decoding its "symbolic language." The story concerns an adolescent's confrontation with adult sexuality, he explained. Its hidden meaning shows through its symbolism—but the symbols he saw in his version of the text were based on details that did not exist in the versions known to peasants in the seventeenth and eighteenth centuries. Thus he makes a great deal of the (nonexistent) red riding hood as a symbol of menstruation and of the (nonexistent) bottle carried by the girl as a symbol of virginity: hence the mother's (nonexistent) admonition not to stray from the path into wild terrain where she might break it. The wolf is the ravishing male. And the two (nonexistent) stones that are placed in the wolf's belly after the (nonexistent) hunter extricates the girl and her grandmother, stand for sterility, the punishment for breaking a sexual taboo. So, with an uncanny sensitivity to detail that did not occur in the original folktale, the psychoanalyst takes us into a mental universe that never existed, at least not before the advent of psychoanalysis.[2]

2. Erich Fromm, The Forgotten Language: An Introduction to the Understanding of Dreams, Fairy Tales and Myths (New York, 1951), pp. 235–41, quotation from p. 240.

How could anyone get a text so wrong? The difficulty does not derive from professional dogmatism—for psychoanalysts need not be more rigid than poets in their manipulation of symbols—but rather from blindness to the historical dimension of folktales.

Fromm did not bother to mention his source, but apparently he took his text from the brothers Grimm. The Grimms got it, along with "Puss 'n Boots," "Bluebeard," and a few other stories, from Jeannette Hassenpflug, a neighbor and close friend of theirs in Cassel; and she learned it from her mother, who came from a French Huguenot family. The Huguenots brought their own repertory of tales into Germany when they fled from the persecution of Louis XIV. But they did not draw them directly from popular oral tradition. They read them in books written by Charles Perrault, Marie Cathérine d'Aulnoy, and others during the vogue for fairy tales in fashionable Parisian circles at the end of the seventeenth century. Perrault, the master of the genre, did indeed take his material from the oral tradition of the common people (his principal source probably was his son's nurse). But he touched it up so that it would suit the taste of the salon sophisticates, *précieuses*,[3] and courtiers to whom he directed the first printed version of Mother Goose, his *Contes de ma mère l'oye* of 1697. Thus the tales that reached the Grimms through the Hassenpflugs were neither very German nor very representative of folk tradition. Indeed, the Grimms recognized their literary and Frenchified character and therefore eliminated them from the second edition of the *Kinder- und Hausmärchen*—all but "Little Red Riding Hood." It remained in the collection, evidently, because Jeannette Hassenpflug had grafted on to it a happy ending derived from "The Wolf and the Kids" (tale type 123 according to the standard classification scheme developed by Antti Aarne and Stith Thompson), which was one of the most popular in Germany. So Little Red Riding Hood slipped into the German and later the English literary tradition with her French origins undetected. She changed character considerably as she passed from the French peasantry to Perrault's nursery, into print, across the Rhine, back into an oral tradition but this time as part of the Huguenot diaspora, and back into book form but now as a product of the Teutonic forest rather than the village hearths of the Old Regime in France.

Fromm and a host of other psychoanalytical exegetes did not worry about the transformations of the text—indeed, they did not know about them—because they got the tale they wanted. It begins with pubertal sex (the red hood, which does not exist in the French oral tradition) and ends with the triumph of the ego (the rescued girl, who is usually eaten in the French tales) over the id (the wolf, who is never killed in the traditional versions). All's well that ends well.

3. Literati [*Editor*].

The ending is particularly important for Bruno Bettelheim, the latest in the line of psychoanalysts who have had a go at "Little Red Riding Hood." For him, the key to the story, and to all such stories, is the affirmative message of its denouement. By ending happily, he maintains, folktales permit children to confront their unconscious desires and fears and to emerge unscathed, id subdued and ego triumphant. The id is the villain of "Little Red Riding Hood" in Bettelheim's version. It is the pleasure principle, which leads the girl astray when she is too old for oral fixation (the stage represented by "Hansel and Gretel") and too young for adult sex. The id is also the wolf, who is also the father, who is also the hunter, who is also the ego and, somehow, the superego as well. By directing the wolf to her grandmother, Little Red Riding Hood manages in oedipal fashion to do away with her mother, because mothers can also be grandmothers in the moral economy of the soul and the houses on either side of the woods are actually the same house, as in "Hansel and Gretel," where they are also the mother's body. This adroit mixing of symbols gives Little Red Riding Hood an opportunity to get into bed with her father, the wolf, thereby giving vent to her oedipal fantasies. She survives in the end because she is reborn on a higher level of existence when her father reappears as ego-superego-hunter and cuts her out of the belly of her father as wolf-id, so that everyone lives happily ever after.[4]

Bettelheim's generous view of symbolism makes for a less mechanistic interpretation of the tale than does Fromm's notion of a secret code, but it, too, proceeds from some unquestioned assumptions about the text. Although he cites enough commentators on Grimm and Perrault to indicate some awareness of folklore as an academic discipline, Bettelheim reads "Little Red Riding Hood" and the other tales as if they had no history. He treats them, so to speak, flattened out, like patients on a couch, in a timeless contemporaneity. He does not question their origins or worry over other meanings that they might have had in other contexts because he knows how the soul works and how it has always worked. In fact, however, folktales are historical documents. They have evolved over many centuries and have taken different turns in different cultural traditions. Far from expressing the unchanging operations of man's inner being, they suggest that *mentalités* themselves have changed. We can appreciate the distance between our mental world and that of our ancestors if we imagine lulling a child of our own to sleep with the primitive peasant version of "Little Red Riding Hood." Perhaps, then, the moral of the story should be: beware of psychoanalysts—and be careful in your use of sources. We seem to be back at historicism.

Not quite, however, for "Little Red Riding Hood" has a terrifying

4. Bruno Bettelheim, *The Uses of Enchantment: The Meaning and Importance of Fairy Tales* (New York, 1977), pp. 166–83.

irrationality that seems out of place in the Age of Reason. In fact, the peasants' version outdoes the psychoanalysts' in violence and sex. (Following the Grimms and Perrault, Fromm and Bettelheim do not mention the cannibalizing of grandmother and the strip-tease prelude to the devouring of the girl.) Evidently the peasants did not need a secret code to talk about taboos.

The other stories in the French peasant Mother Goose have the same nightmare quality. In one early version of "Sleeping Beauty" (tale type 410),[5] for example, Prince Charming, who is already married, ravishes the princess, and she bears him several children, without waking up. The infants finally break the spell by biting her while nursing, and the tale then takes up its second theme: the attempts of the prince's mother-in-law, an ogress, to eat his illicit offspring. The original "Bluebeard" (tale type 312) is the story of a bride who cannot resist the temptation to open a forbidden door in the house of her husband, a strange man who has already gone through six wives. She enters a dark room and discovers the corpses of the previous wives, hanging on the wall. Horrified, she lets the forbidden key drop from her hand into a pool of blood on the floor. She cannot wipe it clean; so Bluebeard discovers her disobedience, when he inspects the keys. As he sharpens his knife in preparation for making her his seventh victim, she withdraws to her bedroom and puts on her wedding costume. But she delays her toilette long enough to be saved by her brothers, who gallop to the rescue after receiving a warning from her pet dove. In one early tale from the Cinderella cycle (tale type 510B), the heroine becomes a domestic servant in order to prevent her father from forcing her to marry him. In another, the wicked stepmother tries to push her in an oven but incinerates one of the mean stepsisters by mistake. In the French peasant's "Hansel and Gretel" (tale type 327), the hero tricks an ogre into slitting the throats of his own children. A husband eats a succession of brides in the wedding bed in "La Belle et le monstre" (tale type 433), one of the hundreds of tales that never made it into the printed versions of Mother Goose. In a nastier tale, "Les Trois Chiens" (tale type 315), a sister kills her brother by hiding spikes in the mattress of his wedding bed. In the nastiest of all, "Ma mère m'a tué, mon père m'a mangé" (tale type 720), a mother chops her son up into a Lyonnais-style casserole, which her daughter serves to the father. And so it goes, from rape and sodomy to incest and cannibalism. Far from veiling their message with symbols, the storytellers of eighteenth-century France portrayed a world of raw and naked brutality.

How can the historian make sense of this world? One way for him to keep his footing in the psychic undertow of early Mother Goose is

5. See discussion below and note 6, p. 285 [Editor].

to hold fast to two disciplines: anthropology and folklore. When they discuss theory, anthropologists disagree about the fundamentals of their science. But when they go into the bush, they use techniques for understanding oral traditions that can, with discretion, be applied to Western folklore. Except for some structuralists, they relate tales to the art of tale telling and to the context in which it takes place. They look for the way a raconteur adapts an inherited theme to his audience so that the specificity of time and place shows through the universality of the topos. They do not expect to find direct social comment or metaphysical allegories so much as a tone of discourse or a cultural style, which communicates a particular ethos and world view. "Scientific" folklore, as the French call it (American specialists often distinguish between folklore and "fakelore"), involves the compilation and comparison of tales according to the standardized schemata of tale types developed by Antti Aarne and Stith Thompson. It does not necessarily exclude formalistic analysis such as that of Vladimir Propp, but it stresses rigorous documentation—the occasion of the telling, the background of the teller, and the degree of contamination from written sources.[6]

French folklorists have recorded about ten thousand tales, in many different dialects and in every corner of France and of French-speaking territories. For example, while on an expedition in Berry for the Musée des arts et traditions populaires in 1945, Ariane de Félice recorded a version of "Le Petit Poucet" ("Tom Thumb" or "Thumbling," tale type 327) by a peasant woman, Euphrasie Pichon, who had been born in 1862 in the village of Eguzon (Indre). In 1879 Jean Drouillet wrote down another version as he listened to his mother Eugénie, who had learned it from her mother, Octavie Riffet, in the village of Teillay (Cher). The two versions are nearly identical and owe nothing to the first printed account of the tale, which Charles Perrault published in 1697. They and eighty other "Petits Poucets," which folklorists have compiled and compared, motif by motif, belong to an oral tradition that survived with remarkably little contamination from print culture until late in the nineteenth century. Most of the tales in the French repertory were recorded between 1870 and 1914 during "the Golden Age of folktale research in France," and they were recounted by peasants who had learned them as children, long before literacy had spread throughout the countryside. Thus in 1874 Nannette Levesque, an illiterate peasant woman born in 1794, dictated a version of "Little Red Riding Hood" that went back to the eighteenth century; and in 1865 Louis Grolleau, a domestic servant born

6. See Aarne and Thompson, *The Types of the Folktale: A Classification and Bibliography* (2nd rev.; Helsinki, 1973); Thompson, *The Folktale* (Berkeley and Los Angeles, 1977; 1st ed. 1946); and Vladimir Propp, *Morphology of the Folktale*, trans. Laurence Scott (Austin, 1968). Aarne and Thompson used the "historical-geographical" or "Finnish" method, developed by Kaarle Krohn, to produce a world-wide survey and classification of folktales.

in 1803, dictated a rendition of "Le Pou" (tale type 621) that he had first heard under the Empire. Like all tellers of tales, the peasant raconteurs adjusted the setting of their stories to their own milieux; but they kept the main elements intact, using repetitions, rhymes, and other mnemonic devices. Although the "performance" element, which is central to the study of contemporary folklore, does not show through the old texts, folklorists argue that the recordings of the Third Republic provide enough evidence for them to reconstruct the rough outlines of an oral tradition that existed two centuries ago.[7]

That claim may seem extravagant, but comparative studies have revealed striking similarities in different recordings of the same tale, even though they were made in remote villages, far removed from one another and from the circulation of books. In a study of "Little Red Riding Hood," for example, Paul Delarue compared thirty-five versions recorded throughout a vast zone of the *langue d'oïl*. Twenty versions correspond exactly to the primitive "Conte de la mère grand" quoted above, except for a few details (sometimes the girl is eaten, sometimes she escapes by a ruse). Two versions follow Perrault's tale (the first to mention the red hood). And the rest contain a mixture of the oral and written accounts, whose elements stand out as distinctly as the garlic and mustard in a French salad dressing.[8]

Written evidence proves that the tales existed long before anyone conceived of "folklore," a nineteenth-century neologism.[9] Medieval preachers drew on the oral tradition in order to illustrate moral arguments. Their sermons, transcribed in collections of "Exempla" from the twelfth to the fifteenth century, refer to the same stories as those taken down in peasant cottages by folklorists in the nineteenth century. Despite the obscurity surrounding the origins of chivalric romances, *chansons de geste*, and *fabliaux*, it seems that a good deal of medieval literature drew on popular oral tradition, rather than vice versa. "Sleeping Beauty" appeared in an Arthurian romance of the fourteenth century, and "Cinderella" surfaced in Noël du Fail's *Propos rustiques* of 1547, a book that traced the tales to peasant lore and that showed how they were transmitted; for du Fail wrote the first account of an important French institution, the *veillée*, an evening fireside gathering, where men repaired tools and women sewed while listening to stories that would be recorded by folklorists three hundred years later and that were

---

7. This information comes from Paul Delarue's introduction to *Le Conte populaire français*, I, 7–99, which is the best general account of folklore research in France and which also contains a thorough bibliography.
8. Delarue, "Les contes merveilleux de Perrault et la tradition populaire," *Bulletin folklorique d'Ile-de-France*, n.s. (July–Oct., 1951).
9. William Thoms launched the term "folklore" in 1846, two decades before Edward Tylor introduced a similar term, "culture," among English-speaking anthropologists. See Thoms, "Folklore" and William R. Bascom, "Folklore and Anthropology" in Dundes, *Study of Folklore*, pp. 4–6 and 25–33.

already centuries old.[1] Whether they were meant to amuse adults or to frighten children, as in the case of cautionary tales like "Little Red Riding Hood," the stories belonged to a fund of popular culture, which peasants hoarded over the centuries with remarkably little loss.

The great collections of folktales made in the late nineteenth and early twentieth centuries therefore provide a rare opportunity to make contact with the illiterate masses who have disappeared into the past without leaving a trace. To reject folktales because they cannot be dated and situated with precision like other historical documents is to turn one's back on one of the few points of entry into the mental world of peasants under the Old Regime. But to attempt to penetrate that world is to face a set of obstacles as daunting as those confronted by Jean de l'Ours (tale type 301) when he tried to rescue the three Spanish princesses from the underworld or by little Parle (tale type 328) when he set out to capture the ogre's treasure.

The greatest obstacle is the impossibility of listening in on the story tellers. No matter how accurate they may be, the recorded versions of the tales cannot convey the effects that must have brought the stories to life in the eighteenth century: the dramatic pauses, the sly glances, the use of gestures to set scenes—a Snow White at a spinning wheel, a Cinderella delousing a stepsister—and the use of sounds to punctuate actions—a knock on the door (often done by rapping on a listener's forehead) or a cudgeling or a fart. All of those devices shaped the meaning of the tales, and all of them elude the historian. He cannot be sure that the limp and lifeless text that he holds between the covers of a book provides an accurate account of the performance that took place in the eighteenth century. He cannot even be certain that the text corresponds to the unrecorded versions that existed a century earlier. Although he may turn up plenty of evidence to prove that the tale itself existed, he cannot quiet his suspicions that it could have changed a great deal before it reached the folklorists of the Third Republic.

Given those uncertainties, it seems unwise to build an interpretation on a single version of a single tale, and more hazardous still to base symbolic analysis on details—riding hoods and hunters—that may not have occurred in the peasant versions. But there are enough recordings of those versions—35 "Little Red Riding Hoods," 90 "Tom Thumbs," 105 "Cinderellas"—for one to picture the general outline of a tale as it existed in the oral tradition. One can study it on the level of structure, noting the way the narrative is framed and the motifs are combined, instead of concentrating on fine points of detail. Then one can compare it with other stories. And finally, by working through the entire body of French folktales, one can distinguish general characteristics, over-arching themes, and pervasive elements of style and tone.

1. Noël du Fail, *Propos rustiques de Maistre Leon Ladulfi Champenois*, chap. 5, in *Conteurs français du XVIe siècle*, ed. Pierre Jourda (Paris, 1956), pp. 620–21.

ROBERT DARNTON

ян also seek aid and comfort from specialists in the study of
iture. Milman Parry and Albert Lord have shown how folk
epics as long as *The Iliad* are passed on faithfully from bard to bard
among the illiterate peasants of Yugoslavia. These "singers of tales" do
not possess the fabulous powers of memorization sometimes attributed
to "primitive" peoples. They do not memorize very much at all. Instead,
they combine stock phrases, formulas, and narrative segments in patterns improvised according to the response of their audience. Recordings of the same epic by the same singer demonstrate that each
performance is unique. Yet recordings made in 1950 do not differ in
essentials from those made in 1934. In each case, the singer proceeds
as if he were walking down a well-known path. He may branch off here
to take a shortcut or pause there to enjoy a panorama, but he always
remains on familiar ground—so familiar, in fact, that he will say that
he repeated every step exactly as he has done before. He does not
conceive of repetition in the same way as a literate person, for he has
no notion of words, lines, and verses. Texts are not rigidly fixed for him
as they are for readers of the printed page. He creates his text as he
goes, picking new routes through old themes. He can even work in
material derived from printed sources, for the epic as a whole is so
much greater than the sum of its parts that modifications of detail barely
disturb the general configuration.[2]

Lord's investigation confirms conclusions that Vladimir Propp
reached by a different mode of analysis, one that showed how variations
of detail remain subordinate to stable structures in Russian folktales.[3]
Field workers among illiterate peoples in Polynesia, Africa, and North
and South America have also found that oral traditions have enormous
staying power. Opinions divide on the separate question of whether or
not oral sources can provide a reliable account of past events. Robert
Lowie, who collected narratives from the Crow Indians in the early
twentieth century, took up a position of extreme skepticism: "I cannot
attach to oral traditions any historical value whatsoever under any conditions whatsoever."[4] By historical value, however, Lowie meant factual
accuracy. (In 1910 he recorded a Crow account of a battle against the
Dakota; in 1931 the same informant described the battle to him, but
claimed that it had taken place against the Cheyenne.) Lowie conceded
that the stories, taken as stories, remained quite consistent; they forked
and branched in the standard patterns of Crow narrative. So his findings
actually support the view that in traditional story telling continuities in
form and style outweigh variations in detail, among North American
Indians as well as Yugoslav peasants. Frank Hamilton Cushing noted a

2. Albert B. Lord, *The Singer of Tales* (Cambridge, Mass., 1960).
3. Propp, *Morphology of the Folktale*.
4. Lowie's remark is quoted in Richard Dorson, "The Debate over the Trustworthiness of Oral
Traditional History" in Dorson, *Folklore: Selected Essays* (Bloomington, Ind., 1972), p. 202.

spectacular example of this tendency among the Zuni almost a century ago. In 1886 he served as interpreter to a Zuni delegation in the eastern United States. During a round robin of story telling one evening, he recounted as his contribution the tale of "The Cock and the Mouse," which he had picked up from a book of Italian folktales. About a year later, he was astonished to hear the same tale from one of the Indians back at Zuni. The Italian motifs remained recognizable enough for one to be able to classify the tale in the Aarne-Thompson scheme (it is tale type 2032). But everything else about the story—its frame, figures of speech, allusions, style, and general feel—had become intensely Zuni. Instead of Italianizing the native lore, the story had been Zunified.[5]

No doubt the transmission process affects stories differently in different cultures. Some bodies of folklore can resist "contamination" while absorbing new material more effectively than can others. But oral traditions seem to be tenacious and long-lived nearly everywhere among illiterate peoples. Nor do they collapse at their first exposure to the printed word. Despite Jack Goody's contention that a literacy line cuts through all history, dividing oral from "written" or "print" cultures, it seems that traditional tale telling can flourish long after the onset of literacy. To anthropologists and folklorists who have tracked tales through the bush, there is nothing extravagant about the idea that peasant raconteurs in late nineteenth-century France told stories to one another pretty much as their ancestors had done a century or more earlier.[6]

Comforting as this expert testimony may be, it does not clear all the difficulties in the way of interpreting the French tales. The texts are accessible enough, for they lie unexploited in treasure houses like the Musée des arts et traditions populaires in Paris and in scholarly collections like Le Conte populaire français by Paul Delarue and Marie-Louise Tenèze. But one cannot lift them from such sources and hold them up to inspection as if they were so many photographs of the Old Regime, taken with the innocent eye of an extinct peasantry. They are stories.

As in most kinds of narration, they develop standardized plots from conventional motifs, picked up here, there, and everywhere. They have a distressing lack of specificity for anyone who wants to pin them down to precise points in time and place. Raymond Jameson has studied the case of a Chinese Cinderella from the ninth century. She gets her slippers from a magic fish instead of a fairy godmother and loses one of them at a village fête instead of a royal ball, but she bears an unmistakable resemblance to Perrault's heroine.[7] Folklorists have recog-

---

5. Frank Hamilton Cushing, Zuni Folk Tales (New York and London, 1901), pp. 411–22.
6. Jack Goody, The Domestication of the Savage Mind (Cambridge, 1977). See also the studies published by Goody as Literacy in Traditional Societies (Cambridge, 1968).
7. Raymond D. Jameson, Three Lectures on Chinese Folklore (Peking, 1932).

nized their tales in Herodotus and Homer, on ancient Egyptian papyruses and Chaldean stone tablets; and they have recorded them all over the world, in Scandinavia and Africa, among Indians on the banks of the Bengal and Indians along the Missouri. The dispersion is so striking that some have come to believe in Ur-stories and a basic Indo-European repertory of myths, legends, and tales. This tendency feeds into the cosmic theories of Frazer and Jung and Lévi-Strauss, but it does not help anyone attempting to penetrate the peasant mentalities of early modern France.

Fortunately, a more down-to-earth tendency in folklore makes it possible to isolate the peculiar characteristics of traditional French tales. *Le Conte populaire français* arranges them according to the Aarne-Thompson classification scheme, which covers all varieties of Indo-European folktales. It therefore provides the basis for comparative study, and the comparisons suggest the way general themes took root and grew in French soil. "Tom Thumb" ("Le Petit Poucet," tale type 327), for example, has a strong French flavor, in Perrault as well as the peasant versions, if one compares it with its German cousin, "Hansel and Gretel." The Grimms' tale emphasizes the mysterious forest and the naïveté of the children in the face of inscrutable evil, and it has more fanciful and poetic touches, as in the details about the bread-and-cake house and the magic birds. The French children confront an ogre, but in a very real house. Monsieur and Madame Ogre discuss their plans for a dinner party as if they were any married couple, and they carp at each other just as Tom Thumb's parents did. In fact, it is hard to tell the two couples apart. Both simple-minded wives throw away their family's fortunes; and their husbands berate them in the same manner, except that the ogre tells his wife that she deserves to be eaten and that he would do the job himself if she were not such an unappetizing *vieille bête* (old beast).[8] Unlike their German relatives, the French ogres appear in the role of *le bourgeois de la maison* (burgher head of household),[9] as if they were rich local landowners. They play fiddles, visit friends, snore contentedly in bed beside fat ogress wives;[1] and for all their boorishness, they never fail to be good family men and good providers. Hence the joy of the ogre in "Pitchin-Pitchot" as he bounds into the house, a sack on his back: "Catherine, put on the big kettle. I've caught Pitchin-Pitchot."[2]

Where the German tales maintain a tone of terror and fantasy, the French strike a note of humor and domesticity. Firebirds settle down into hen yards. Elves, genii, forest spirits, the whole Indo-European

---

8. This remark occurs in Perrault's version, which contains a sophisticated reworking of the dialogue in the peasant versions. See Delarue and Tenèze, *Le Conte populaire français*, I, 306–24.
9. "Jean de l'Ours," tale type 301B.
1. See "Le Conte de Parle," tale type 328 and "La Belle Eulalie," tale type 313.
2. "Pitchin-Pitchot," tale type 327C.

panoply of magical beings become reduced in France to two species, ogres and fairies. And those vestigial creatures acquire human foibles and generally let humans solve their problems by their own devices, that is, by cunning and "Cartesianism"—a term that the French apply vulgarly to their propensity for craftiness and intrigue. The Gallic touch is clear in many of the tales that Perrault did not rework for his own Gallicized Mother Goose of 1697: the *panache* of the young blacksmith in "Le Petit Forgeron" (tale type 317), for example, who kills giants on a classic *tour de France*; or the provincialism of the Breton peasant in "Jean Bête" (tale type 675), who is given anything he wishes and asks for *un bon péché de piquette et une écuelle de patates du lait* ("crude wine and a bowl of potatoes in milk"); or the professional jealousy of the master gardener, who fails to prune vines as well as his apprentice in "Jean le Teigneux" (tale type 314); or the cleverness of the devil's daughter in "La Belle Eulalie" (tale type 313), who escapes with her lover by leaving two talking pâtés in their beds. Just as one cannot attach the French tales to specific events, one should not dilute them in a timeless universal mythology. They really belong to a middle ground: *la France moderne* or the France that existed from the fifteenth through the eighteenth century.

\* \* \*

# SANDRA M. GILBERT AND SUSAN GUBAR

## [Snow White and Her Wicked Stepmother]†

\* \* \*

As the legend of Lilith[1] shows, and as psychoanalysts from Freud and Jung onward have observed, myths and fairy tales often both state and enforce culture's sentences with greater accuracy than more sophisticated literary texts. If Lilith's story summarizes the genesis of the female monster in a single useful parable, the Grimm tale of "Little Snow White" dramatizes the essential but equivocal relationship between the angel-woman and the monster-woman. \* \* \* "Little Snow White," which Walt Disney entitled "Snow White and the Seven Dwarves," should really be called Snow White and Her Wicked Stepmother, for the central action of the tale—indeed, its only real action—arises from the relationship between these two women: the one fair, young, pale, the other just as fair, but older, fiercer; the one a daughter, the

† From Sandra M. Gilbert and Susan Gubar, *The Madwoman in the Attic: The Woman Writer and the Nineteenth-Century Literary Imagination* (New Haven: Yale UP, 1979) 36–43. Copyright © 1979. Reprinted by permission of Yale University Press.
1. Adam's first wife, before Eve was created.

other a mother; the one sweet, ignorant, passive, the other both artful and active; the one a sort of angel, the other an undeniable witch.

Significantly, the conflict between these two women is fought out largely in the transparent enclosures into which * * * both have been locked: a magic looking glass, an enchanted and enchanting glass coffin. Here, wielding as weapons the tools patriarchy suggests that women use to kill themselves into art, the two women literally try to kill each other with art. Shadow fights shadow, image destroys image in the crystal prison. * * *

The story begins in midwinter, with a Queen sitting and sewing, framed by a window. As in so many fairy tales, she pricks her finger, bleeds, and is thereby assumed into the cycle of sexuality William Blake called the realm of "generation," giving birth "soon after" to a daughter "as white as snow, as red as blood, and as black as the wood of the window frame."[2] All the motifs introduced in this prefatory first paragraph—sewing, snow, blood, enclosure—are associated with key themes in female lives (hence in female writing), and they are thus themes we shall be studying throughout this book. But for our purposes here the tale's opening *is* merely prefatory. The real story begins when the Queen, having become a mother, metamorphoses also into a witch—that is, into a wicked "step" mother: ". . . when the child was born, the Queen died," and "After a year had passed the King took to himself another wife."

When we first encounter this "new" wife, she is framed in a magic looking glass, just as her predecessor—that is, her earlier self—had been framed in a window. To be caught and trapped in a mirror rather than a window, however, is to be driven inward, obsessively studying self-images as if seeking a viable self. The first Queen seems still to have had prospects; not yet fallen into sexuality, she looked outward, if only upon the snow. The second Queen is doomed to the inward search that psychoanalysts like Bruno Bettelheim censoriously define as "narcissism,"[3] but which * * * is necessitated by a state from which all outward prospects have been removed.

That outward prospects *have* been removed—or lost or dissolved away—is suggested not only by the Queen's mirror obsession but by the absence of the King from the story as it is related in the Grimm version. The Queen's husband and Snow White's father (for whose attentions, according to Bettelheim, the two women are battling in a feminized Oedipal struggle) never actually appears in this story at all, a fact that emphasizes the almost stifling intensity with which the tale concentrates on the conflict in the mirror between mother and daughter, woman

2. "Little Snow White." All references are to the text as given in *The Complete Grimm's Fairy Tales* (New York: Random House, 1972).
3. Bruno Bettelheim, *The Uses of Enchantment: The Meaning and Importance of Fairy Tales* (New York: Knopf, 1976), pp. 202–03.

and woman, self and self. At the same time, though, there is clearly at least one way in which the King *is* present. His, surely, is the voice of the looking glass, the patriarchal voice of judgment that rules the Queen's—and every woman's—self-evaluation. He it is who decides, first, that his consort is "the fairest of all," and then, as she becomes maddened, rebellious, witchlike, that she must be replaced by his angelically innocent and dutiful daughter, a girl who is therefore defined as "more beautiful still" than the Queen. To the extent, then, that the King, and only the King, constituted the first Queen's prospects, he need no longer appear in the story because, having assimilated the meaning of her own sexuality (and having, thus, become the second Queen) the woman has internalized the King's rules: his voice resides now in her own mirror, her own mind.

But if Snow White is "really" the daughter of the second as well as of the first Queen (i.e., if the two Queens are identical), why does the Queen hate her so much? The traditional explanation—that the mother is as threatened by her daughter's "budding sexuality" as the daughter is by the mother's "possession" of the father—is helpful but does not seem entirely adequate, considering the depth and ferocity of the Queen's rage. It is true, of course, that in the patriarchal Kingdom of the text these women inhabit the Queen's life can be literally imperiled by her daughter's beauty, and true (as we shall see throughout this study) that, given the female vulnerability such perils imply, female bonding is extraordinarily difficult in patriarchy: women almost inevitably turn against women because the voice of the looking glass sets them against each other. But, beyond all this, it seems as if there is a sense in which the intense desperation with which the Queen enacts her rituals of self-absorption causes (or is caused by) her hatred of Snow White. Innocent, passive, and self-lessly free of the mirror madness that consumes the Queen, Snow White represents the ideal of renunciation that the Queen has already renounced at the beginning of the story. Thus Snow White is destined to replace the Queen *because* the Queen hates her, rather than vice versa. The Queen's hatred of Snow White, in other words, exists before the looking glass has provided an obvious reason for hatred.

For the Queen, as we come to see more clearly in the course of the story, is a plotter, a plot-maker, a schemer, a witch, an artist, an impersonator, a woman of almost infinite creative energy, witty, wily, and self-absorbed as all artists traditionally are. On the other hand, in her absolute chastity, her frozen innocence, her sweet nullity, Snow White represents precisely the ideal of "contemplative purity" we have already discussed, an ideal that could quite literally kill the Queen. An angel in the house of myth, Snow White is not only a child but (as female angels always are) childlike, docile, submissive, the heroine of a life that *has no story*. But the Queen, adult and demonic, plainly wants a life of "significant action," by definition an "unfeminine" life of stories and story-telling. And therefore, to the extent that Snow White, as her daughter, is a part of herself, she wants to kill the Snow White *in herself,* the angel who would keep deeds and dramas out of her own house.

The first death plot the Queen invents is a naively straightforward murder story: she commands one of her huntsmen to kill Snow White. But, as Bruno Bettelheim has shown, the huntsman is really a surrogate for the King, a parental—or, more specifically, patriarchal—figure "who dominates, controls, and subdues wild ferocious beasts" and who thus "represents the subjugation of the animal, asocial, violent tendencies in man."[4] In a sense, then, the Queen has foolishly asked her patriarchal master to act for her in doing the subversive deed she wants to do in part to retain power over him and in part to steal his power from him. Obviously, he will not do this. As patriarchy's angelic daughter, Snow White is, after all, *his* child, and he must save her, not kill her. Hence he kills a wild boar in her stead, and brings its lung and liver to the Queen as proof that he has murdered the child. Thinking that she is devouring her ice-pure enemy, therefore, the Queen consumes, instead, the wild boar's organs; that is, symbolically speaking, she devours her own beastly rage, and becomes (of course) even more enraged.

When she learns that her first plot has failed, then, the Queen's story-telling becomes angrier as well as more inventive, more sophisticated, more subversive. Significantly, each of the three "tales" she tells—that is, each of the three plots she invents—depends on a poisonous or parodic use of a distinctively female device as a murder weapon, and in each case she reinforces the sardonic commentary on "femininity" that such weaponry makes by impersonating a "wise" woman, a "good" mother, or, as Ellen Moers would put it, an "educating heroine."[5] As a "kind" old pedlar woman, she offers to lace Snow White "properly" for once—then suffocates her with a very Victorian set of tight laces. As another wise old expert in female beauty, she promises to comb Snow White's hair "properly," then assaults her with a poisonous comb. Finally, as a wholesome farmer's wife, she gives Snow White a "very poisonous apple," which she has made in "a quite secret, lonely room, where no one ever came." The girl finally falls, killed, so it seems, by the female arts of cosmetology and cookery. Paradoxically, however, even though the Queen has been using such feminine wiles as the sirens' comb and Eve's apple subversively, to destroy angelic Snow White so that she (the Queen) can assert and aggrandize herself, these arts have had on her daughter an opposite effect from those she intended. Strengthening the chaste maiden in her passivity, they have made her into precisely the eternally beautiful, inanimate *objet d'art*

4. Bettelheim, p. 205.
5. See Ellen Moers, *Literary Women* (New York: Doubleday, 1976), pp. 211–42.

patriarchal aesthetics want a girl to be. From the point of view of the mad, self-assertive Queen, conventional female arts *kill*. But from the point of view of the docile and selfless princess, such arts, even while they kill, confer the only measure of power available to a woman in a patriarchal culture.

Certainly when the kindly huntsman-father saved her life by abandoning her in the forest at the edge of his kingdom, Snow White discovered her own powerlessness. Though she had been allowed to live because she was a "good" girl, she had to find her own devious way of resisting the onslaughts of the maddened Queen, both inside and outside her self. In this connection, the seven dwarves probably represent her own dwarfed powers, her stunted selfhood, for, as Bettelheim points out, they can do little to help save the girl from the Queen. At the same time, however, her life with them is an important part of her education in submissive femininity, for in serving them she learns essential lessons of service, of selflessness, of domesticity. Finally, that at this point Snow White is a housekeeping angel in a *tiny* house conveys the story's attitude toward "woman's world and woman's work": the realm of domesticity is a miniaturized kingdom in which the best of women is not only like a dwarf but like a dwarf's servant.

Does the irony and bitterness consequent upon such a perception lead to Snow White's few small acts of disobedience? Or would Snow White ultimately have rebelled anyway, precisely because she *is* the Queen's true daughter? The story does not, of course, answer such questions, but it does seem to imply them, since its turning point comes from Snow White's significant willingness to be tempted by the Queen's "gifts," despite the dwarves' admonitions. Indeed, the only hint of self-interest that Snow White displays throughout the whole story comes in her "narcissistic" desire for the stay-laces, the comb, and the apple that the disguised murderess offers. As Bettelheim remarks, this "suggests how close the stepmother's temptations are to Snow White's inner desires."[6] Indeed, it suggests that, as we have already noted, the Queen and Snow White are in some sense one: while the Queen struggles to free herself from the passive Snow White in herself, Snow White must struggle to repress the assertive Queen in herself. That both women eat from the same deadly apple in the third temptation episode merely clarifies and dramatizes this point. The Queen's lonely art has enabled her to contrive a two-faced fruit—one white and one red "cheek"—that represents her ambiguous relationship to this angelic girl who is both her daughter and her enemy, her self and her opposite. Her intention is that the girl will die of the apple's poisoned red half—red with her sexual energy, her assertive desire for deeds of blood and triumph— while she herself will be unharmed by the passivity of the white half.

6. Bettelheim, p. 211.

But though at first this seems to have happened, the apple's effect is, finally, of course, quite different. After the Queen's artfulness has killed Snow White into art, the girl becomes if anything even more dangerous to her "step" mother's autonomy than she was before, because even more opposed to it in both mind and body. For, dead and self-less in her glass coffin, she is an object, to be displayed and desired, patriarchy's marble "opus," the decorative and decorous Galatea[7] with whom every ruler would like to grace his parlor. Thus, when the Prince first sees Snow White in her coffin, he begs the dwarves to give "it" to him as a gift, "for I cannot live without seeing Snow White. I will honor and prize her as my dearest possession." An "it," a possession, Snow White has become an idealized image of herself, and as such she has definitively proven herself to be patriarchy's ideal woman, the perfect candidate for Queen. At this point, therefore, she regurgitates the poison apple (whose madness had stuck in her throat) and rises from her coffin. The fairest in the land, she will marry the most powerful in the land; bidden to their wedding, the egotistically assertive, plotting Queen will become a former Queen, dancing herself to death in red-hot iron shoes.

What does the future hold for Snow White, however? When her Prince becomes a King and she becomes a Queen, what will her life be like? Trained to domesticity by her dwarf instructors, will she sit in the window, gazing out on the wild forest of her past, and sigh, and sew, and prick her finger, and conceive a child white as snow, red as blood, black as ebony wood? Surely, fairest of them all, Snow White has exchanged one glass coffin for another, delivered from the prison where the Queen put her only to be imprisoned in the looking glass from which the King's voice speaks daily. There is, after all, no female model for her in this tale except the "good" (dead) mother and her living avatar the "bad" mother. And if Snow White escaped her first glass coffin by her goodness, her passivity and docility, her only escape from her second glass coffin, the imprisoning mirror, must evidently be through "badness," through plots and stories, duplicitous schemes, wild dreams, fierce fictions, mad impersonations. The cycle of her fate seems inexorable. Renouncing "contemplative purity," she must now embark on that life of "significant action" which, for a woman, is defined as a witch's life because it is so monstrous, so unnatural.* * * She will become a murderess bent on the self-slaughter implicit in her murderous attempts against the life of her own child. Finally, in fiery shoes that parody the costumes of femininity as surely as the comb and stays she herself contrived, she will do a silent terrible death-dance out of the story, the looking glass, the transparent coffin of her own image.

7. An ivory statue carved by Pygmalion and brought to life by Aphrodite in response to the sculptor's longing for his creation [*Editor*].

Her only deed, this death will imply, can be a deed of death, her only action the pernicious action of self-destruction.

In this connection, it seems especially significant that the Queen's dance of death is a silent one. In "The Juniper Tree" [190–97] a version of "Little Snow White" in which a *boy's* mother tries to kill him (for different reasons, of course) the dead boy is transformed not into a silent art object but into a furious golden bird who sings a song of vengeance against his murderess and finally crushes her to death with a millstone. The male child's progress toward adulthood is a growth toward both self-assertion and self-articulation, "The Juniper Tree" implies, a development of the *powers* of speech. But the girl child must learn the arts of silence either as herself a silent image invented and defined by the magic looking glass of the male-authored text, or as a silent dancer of her own woes, a dancer who enacts rather than articulates. \* \* \*

\* \* \*

# KAREN E. ROWE

## To Spin a Yarn: The Female Voice in Folklore and Fairy Tale†

I begin not, as one might expect, with a *conte de fées* or a *Märchen*[1] but instead with a story, which provides us with a more ancient paradigm for understanding the female voice in folklore and fairy tale. But to speak about voice in a tale so singularly about the voiceless is immediately to recognize that to tell a tale for women may be a way of breaking enforced silences. I refer to Ovid's account in the *Metamorphoses* of Philomela and Procne, which in Western tradition can serve as a type for the narrative power of the female, capable of weaving in tapestry the brutal story of rape that leads to the enactment of a terrible revenge.[2] Since the image of Philomela as weaver and nightingale becomes the quintessential type of the woman as tale-teller, it is best to review the story, noticing Ovid's preoccupation with the varieties of utterance and silence and the analogy that can be drawn between the story of Philomela and the art of creating a tale itself. Based upon this paradigm we can begin to explore the lineage of women as tale-tellers

---

† From Karen E. Rowe, "To Spin a Yarn: The Female Voice in Folklore and Fairy Tale," in *Fairy Tales and Society: Illusion, Allusion, and Paradigm*, ed. Ruth B. Bottigheimer (Philadelphia: U of Pennsylvania P, 1986) 53–73. Copyright © 1986. Reprinted by permission of the University of Pennsylvania Press.

1. French and German terms for "fairy tale" (respectively) [*Editor*].

2. Ovid, *Metamorphoses*, trans. Rolfe Humphries (Bloomington: Indiana University Press, 1963), bk. 6, pp. 143–51. All future references from book 6 will be cited parenthetically in the text by page.

in a history that stretches from Philomela and Scheherazade to the
raconteurs of French veillées[3] and salons, to English peasants, governesses, and novelists, and to the German Spinnerinnen[4] and the Brothers
Grimm. It is a complex history, which I can only highlight in this essay.

To return to Ovid. With "flame bursting out of his breast," Tereus,
as Ovid recounts, in his "unbridled passion" is granted a perverse elo-
quence (p. 144). Although he disguises them as the pleadings of a "most
devoted husband," the "crime-contriver" Tereus speaks only false re-
assurances of protection, honor, and kinship (p. 144). The voyage to
Thrace accomplished, Tereus violently seizes Philomela and

> told her then
> What he was going to do, and straightway did it,
> Raped her, a virgin, all alone, and calling
> For her father, for her sister, but most often
> For the great gods. In vain. (p. 146)

Trembling "as a frightened lamb which a gray wolf has mangled," she
vows to "proclaim" the vile ravishment, to "go where people are / Tell
everybody," and "if there is any god in Heaven, [He] will hear me"
(pp. 146, 147). Fearing already the potency of Philomela's voice, the
cruel king Tereus

> seized her tongue
> With pincers, though it cried against the outrage,
> Babbled and made a sound something like Father,
> Till the sword cut it off. The mangled root
> Quivered, the severed tongue along the ground
> Lay quivering, making a little murmur,
> Jerking and twitching . . .
> . . . [and] even then, Tereus
> Took her, and took her again, the injured body
> Still giving satisfaction to his lust. (p. 147)

What Tereus has injured, we might keep in mind, is not only the organ
of speech, but the orifice of sexuality itself—and when the ravaged
Philomela speaks later through another medium, it is on behalf of a
body and spirit doubly mutilated. Philomela, who supposedly lacks the
"power of speech / To help her tell her wrongs," discovers that

> grief has taught her
> Sharpness of wit, and cunning comes in trouble.
> She had a loom to work with, and with purple
> On a white background, wove her story in,
> Her story in and out, and when it was finished,
> Gave it to one old woman, with signs and gestures

3. Evening gatherings [Editor].
4. German for "female spinners."

To take it to the queen, so it was taken,
Unrolled and understood. (p. 148)

Remember too this old woman, whose servant status belies her importance as a conveyor of the tale. Having comprehended her sister's woven story, Procne enacts a dreadful punishment. She slaughters, stews,
and skewers her beloved son Itys as a fitting banquet for the lustful
defiler of flesh, Tereus, doomed to feast greedily "on the flesh of his
own flesh" (p. 150). As we know, the gods intervene to thwart a further
cycle of vengeance by transforming Tereus into a bird of prey (the
hoopoe or a hawk), Philomela into the onomatopoetic image of the
quivering tongue as a twittering swallow, and Procne into the nightingale. The Romans (with greater sense of poetic justice) transposed the
names, making Philomela into the nightingale who sings eternally the
melancholy tale of betrayal, rape, and maternal sorrow. As such, she
comes down to us as the archetypal tale-teller, one who not only weaves
the revelatory tapestry but also sings the song which Ovid appropriates
as his myth.[5]

Ovid's account forces upon us the analogy between weaving or spinning and tale-telling. Classicist Edith Hamilton elaborates upon this
connection by noting that "Philomela's case looked hopeless. She was
shut up; she could not speak; in those days there was no writing. . . .
However, although people then could not write, they could tell a story
without speaking because they were marvelous craftsmen. . . . The
women . . . could weave, into the lovely stuffs they made, forms so lifelike anyone could see what tale they illustrated. Philomela accordingly
turned to her loom. She had a greater motive to make clear the story
she wove than any artist ever had."[6] And when Procne "unrolled the
web . . . with horror she read what had happened, all as plain to her
as if in print." What is notable about Hamilton's account is the ease
with which she elides the acts of weaving or spinning, narrating a tale
in pictorial or "graphic" terms, and writing that is to be read and understood by the comprehending audience. But Hamilton's elisions find
their basis in the semiotics of Greek itself, which Ann Bergren brilliantly analyzes in her study "Language and the Female in Early Greek
Thought."[7] Bergren argues cogently that "the semiotic[8] activity peculiar

5. See also Cheryl Walker, *The Nightingale's Burden: Women Poets and American Culture Before
1900* (Bloomington: Indiana University Press, 1982), pp. 21–22.
6. Edith Hamilton, *Mythology: Timeless Tales of Gods and Heroes* (New York: New American
Library, 1940), pp. 270–71.
7. Ann L. T. Bergren, "Language and the Female in Early Greek Thought," *Arethusa* 16, nos.
1 and 2 (Spring and Fall 1983): 71. See also Ann L. T. Bergren, "Helen's Web: Time and
Tableau in the Iliad," *Helios*, n.s. seven, no. 1 (1980): 19–34. For discussions of the shifting
aesthetic theories of the relationship between art and literature, picture and poesy, see Wendy
Steiner, *The Colors of Rhetoric: Problems in the Relation between Modern Literature and
Painting* (Chicago: University of Chicago Press, 1982); and Richard Wendorf, ed., *Articulated
Images: The Sister Arts from Hogarth to Tennyson* (Minneapolis: University of Minnesota Press,
1983).
8. Pertaining to signs [*Editor*].

to women throughout Greek tradition is not linguistic. Greek women do not speak, they weave. Semiotic woman is a weaver. Penelope is, of course, the paradigm," to which we might add, among others, Helen, Circe, the Fates, and Philomela. But the semiotic relationships are far more complicated. For if women weave and use the woven object, be it tapestry or robe, as a medium for narrating the truth, it must also be recalled that Greek culture inherited from Indo-European culture a tradition in which poets metaphorically defined their art as "weaving" or "sewing" words. Having appropriated the terms of what was "originally and literally woman's work par excellence," as Bergren illustrates, Greek poets "call their product, in effect, a 'metaphorical web.' " Bergren's emphasis falls upon the male appropriation of women's peculiar craft of spinning as a semiotic equivalent for the art of creating Greek poetry itself. For my purposes, the intimate connection, both literal and metaphoric, between weaving and telling a story also establishes the cultural and literary frameworks within which women transmit not only tapestries that tell stories, but also later folklore and fairy tales. In this respect, Bergren's analysis of Philomela again becomes germane, for she writes: "Philomela, according to Apollodorus (3.14.8), *huphēnasa en peplōi grammata* 'wove pictures / writing (*grammata* can mean either) in a robe' which she sent to her sister. Philomela's trick reflects the 'trickiness' of weaving, its uncanny ability to make meaning out of inarticulate matter, to make silent material speak. In this way, women's weaving is, as *grammata* implies, a 'writing' or graphic art, a silent, material representation of audible, immaterial speech." Similarly, when later women become tale-tellers or *sages femmes*, their "audible" art is likewise associated with their cultural function as silent spinners or weavers, and they employ the folk or fairy tale as a "speaking" (whether oral or literary) representation of the silent matter of their lives, which is culture itself.

What then are the multiple levels through which Philomela's tale is told, that is, in which the silent tapestry is made to speak so graphically? First, we might acknowledge the actuality of Tereus' rape itself, the truth of an act which is re-presented to us in various forms. When Philomela threatens to seek an audience to whom she will tell her story, Tereus belatedly recognizes the terrible power of the woman's voice to speak, and by a possible psychological displacement, of the fear he harbors that the woman's body will reveal the foul ravishment by generating illegitimate offspring. This double recognition that both tongue and body may speak of his unspeakable act explains why Tereus must not only sever Philomela's tongue but imprison her in the woods as well, removed from society and unable to communicate her sorry fate in either way.

Second, Philomela turns in her agony to the mainstay of women's

domestic life, the spinning enjoined upon women both by ancient practice and by the later biblical portrait in Proverbs (31:10–31) of the
virtuous woman. She who spins is the model of the good woman and
wife and, presumably, in many cultures of the subservient woman who
knows her duty—that is, to remain silent and betray no secrets. Philomela, tongueless though she may be, creates a tapestry that becomes
her voice. Ironically, Philomela, the innocent woman who spins, becomes the avenging woman who breaks her enforced silence by simply
speaking in another mode—through a craft presumed to be harmlessly
domestic, as fairy tales would also be regarded in later centuries. What
is significant, however, is that Philomela's tapestry becomes the first
"telling," a *grammata* (woven picture/writing) that fulfills the verbal
threat previously uttered, yet so cruelly foreshortened. It is the first remove from the actual rape as an event, done this time through a medium which "writes" (*graphein*) that truth in a style governed by the
conventions of pictorial narration.

   Third, the tapestry, woven strand by strand, becomes itself a metaphor for Ovid's patiently detailed rendering of the myth in words. Ovid,
the skilled craftsman of Roman storytelling, in a sense semiotically re-
sembles Philomela, whose distinctive female craft is weaving. Ovid further stylizes the tale in one further remove from the act when he
attaches the transformation or metamorphosis of Philomela into a swallow and Procne into a nightingale. That metamorphosis presents us
with another way of envisioning the relationship of Philomela's story to
Ovid's. We might conclude that Ovid himself has heard the nightingale's singing (as the emperor would later do in Hans Christian Andersen's "The Nightingale") and has articulated it for us, as part of his
sequence of tales which comprise the *Metamorphoses*. Nonetheless, the
event and threatened telling, the tapestry that speaks, and the eternal
song of lament that retells all originate with Philomela, though we know
them only through the crafted version of Ovid's poetic art.

   The paradigm that I envision is, therefore, twofold. First, Philomela
as a woman who weaves tales and sings songs becomes the prototype
for the female storytellers of later tradition, those *sages femmes* whose
role is to transmit the secret truths of culture itself. It is critical to note,
as I hinted earlier, that the conveyor of the tapestry is herself an old
and trusted servant woman, who takes the tapestry through which the
voiceless Philomela speaks to the sister, Procne, who reads and understands the depiction. Similarly, I might suggest that in the history of
folktale and fairy tale, women as storytellers have woven or spun their
yarns, speaking at one level to a total culture, but at another to a sis-
terhood of readers who will understand the hidden language, the secret
revelations of the tale. Second, Ovid, the male poet, by appropriating
Philomela's story as the subject of his myth also metaphorically re-

inforces the connection between weaving and the art of storytelling. Through his appropriation, he lays claim to or attempts to imitate the semiotic activity of woman par excellence—weaving, by making his linguistic recounting an equivalent, or perhaps implicitly superior version of the original graphic tapestry. Like Zeus, as Ann Bergren details, who incorporates his wife, Metis, and gives birth to the virgin Athena, so too Ovid seeks to control the female power of transformative intelligence, that power which enabled Metis to shift and change shapes. Despite its primacy as a literary text, Ovid's account is nonetheless a retold version, having already been truthfully represented through the peculiarly female medium of weaving, and only imitatively represented to us through the creative, transformative power of poetic art—the weaving of a tale in a second sense. In Ovid's tale itself, Tereus more brutally attempts to usurp speech, not only by cutting out the female tongue with which Philomela threatens to "speak" of his crimes, but also by contriving a false story of her death in a duplicitous and ultimately fatal misrepresentation of reality. To appropriate the tongue/text and the fictive-making function, for both Tereus and Ovid, is fraught with triumph *and* terror, for both only approximate the truth and can do no more than render a twice-old tale.

When the French scholar Antoine Galland first translated *The Book of the Thousand Nights and a Night* from Arabic into French (1704–17), he retitled them *Arabian Nights Entertainments*, no doubt heightening the appeal to the French court's sophisticated taste for exotic delights.[9] When we conjure up *The Arabian Nights*, we are also likely to think first of discrete tales, primarily masculine adventures ("Ali Baba and the Forty Thieves," "Aladdin; or, The Wonderful Lamp," or "Sinbad"), recalling neither the narrative framework nor the stated function which is not only to entertain but also to instruct. But who tells the tales? And for what reason? The frame story identifies Scheherazade as the tale-spinner and the purpose as a double deliverance, of virgins from slaughter and of an aggrieved king from his mania.

The frame plot of *The Arabian Nights* may thus seem straightforward. King Shahryar of India surprises his adulterous wife as she torridly copulates with a blackamoor slave. He executes his wife and swears "himself by a binding oath that whatever wife he married he would abate her maidenhead at night and slay her next morning to make sure of his honour; 'For,' said he, 'there never was nor is there one chaste woman upon the face of the earth'" (p. 14). Scheherazade, the "wise and witty" daughter of the King's Wazir, steps in to break this cycle of silent sacrifice by offering herself as a "ransom for the virgin daughters of Moslems [*sic*] and the cause of their deliverance" (p. 15). Her

9. *Tales from the Arabian Nights Selected from "The Book of the Thousand Nights and a Night,"* trans. Richard F. Burton, ed. David Shumaker (New York: Avenel Books, 1978). See David Shumaker's "Introduction" for comments on the presumed authorship that follow.

counterplot requires, however, the complicity of her sister. Admitted to the bedchamber, Dunyazad, foreshadowing each evening's formulaic plea, appeals, "Allah upon thee, O my sister, recite to us some new story, delightsome and delectable, wherewith to while away the waking hours of our latter night," so that Scheherazade in turn might " 'tell thee a tale which shall be our deliverance, if so Allah please, and which shall turn the King from his blood-thirsty custom' " (p. 24). Tale after tale, Scheherazade ceases just before "the dawn of day . . . to say her permitted say," thereby cannily suspending each tale mid-way and luring the King into a three-year reprieve—or a thousand and one Arabian nights (p. 29).

*Historia interrupta* may be sufficient to stave off execution, but it is clearly not to be recommended as a contraceptive, for within three years' time Scheherazade has "borne the King three boy children" (p. 508). Craving release "from the doom of death, as a dole to these infants," Scheherazade elicits repentant tears from the king, who readily responds: "I had pardoned thee before the coming of these children, for that I found thee chaste, pure, ingenuous and pious!" (p. 508). Sexuality and marital fidelity are here intimately linked with the act of tale-telling, strikingly resembling the same motifs in the story of Procne and Philomela. Whereas in Ovid's myth, the tapestry becomes a medium for communicating Tereus' adulterous rape and instigating a proper vengeance, in *The Arabian Nights* the two sisters conspire together to cure King Shahryar by telling admonitory stories of past times and by demonstrating Scheherazade's chaste fidelity. Scheherazade's purity, signified by the legitimate product of her womb, converts the king from his "blood-thirsty custom." But it is likewise Scheherazade's wise telling of tales that instructs the king in precisely how to interpret his good fortune: " 'Thou marvelledst at that which befell thee on the part of women,' " Scheherazade allows, " 'and indeed I have set forth unto thee that which happened to Caliphs and Kings and others with their women . . . and in this is all-sufficient warning for the man of wits and admonishment for the wise' " (pp. 508–9). Like an analyst upon whom the patient projects his murderous jealousy, so Scheherazade's stories function for King Shahryar, who with reasoning powers restored and heart cleansed returns from mania to sanity.

Scheherazade's power to instruct derives from three kinds of special knowledge attributed to women: the knowledge of sexual passion, the knowledge of healing, and the wisdom to spin tales. More a model of the intellectual and literate storyteller than, like Philomela, of the domestic spinner and singer, Scheherazade, it is written, "had perused the books, annals and legends of preceding Kings, and the stories, examples and instances of by-gone men and things; indeed it was said that she had collected a thousand books of histories relating to antique races and departed rulers. She had perused the works of the poets and knew them by heart; she had studied philosophy and the sciences, arts and accomplishments; and she was pleasant and polite, wise and witty, well read and well bred" (p. 15). The description might apply as well to those later "learned Ladies" of the French court, Madame d'Aulnoy and Mlle. L'Héritier, or to well-bred English governesses (Madame de Beaumont, Charlotte Brontë, Jane Eyre).[1] And one stands amazed at the immense repertoire of Scheherazade's stories, sufficient we might imagine for another one thousand and one nights of delectation and delight. Scheherazade paradigmatically reinforces our concept of female storytellers as transmitters of ancient tales, told and remolded in such a way as to meet the special needs of the listener—in this case, King Shahryar and all men who harbor deep fears of the sexual woman and the dual power of her body and voice. As readers of *The Arabian Nights*, we participate as eavesdroppers in the bedchamber, together with the King and Dunyazad, whom Scheherazade initiates into the mysterious truths of sexuality and folklore. Similar to Procne, who unrolled the tapestry and understood its *grammata*, Dunyazad comes to signify the community of all women to whom the female narrator tells tales.

The voice to tell "marvellous stories and wondrous histories," the wisdom to shape them rightly, the procreative and imaginative generativity belong to Scheherazade. But in *The Arabian Nights* we find another instance of male appropriation (p. 515). No doubt a remarkably quick student, King Shahryar retells "what he had heard from" Scheherazade during three years' time to his brother Shah Zaman, who is afflicted with the same jealous mania (p. 510). He is also miraculously redeemed and conveniently wed to Dunyazad. Having usurped the storytelling and curative power originally possessed by Scheherazade, the King further summons "chroniclers and copyists and bade them write all that had betided him with his wife, first and last; so they wrote this and named it 'The Stories of the Thousand Nights and a Night' " (p. 515). A succeeding, equally "wise ruler," who "keen-witted and accomplished . . . loved tales and legends, especially those which chronicle the doings of Sovrans and Sultans," promptly "bade the folk copy them and dispread them over all lands and climes; wherefore their report was bruited abroad" (pp. 515–16). As the basis for a theory of the origin and dissemination of *The Arabian Nights*, this account may be as fictional as the frame story of Scheherazade; nevertheless, it usefully suggests the manner in which tales told by a woman found their way into royal circles, then were dispersed to the "folk," where pre-

1. Marie-Catherine d'Aulnoy (1650–1705) and Marie-Jeanne L'Héritier (1664–1734): French authors who specialized in fairy tales; Jeanne-Marie Leprince de Beaumont (1711–80): French author of many fairy tales, including "Beauty and the Beast," who worked in England as a governess; Charlotte Brontë (1816–55): English author, who worked as a governess, as did her fictional character Jane Eyre [*Editor*].

sumably oral recountings insured their descent to the present day. Even the narrator hesitates to push this theory too hard, disclaiming that "this is all that hath come down to us of the origin of this book, and Allah is All-knowing" (p. 516).

Beyond this intratextual story that establishes Scheherazade as the frame tale-teller, the question of authorial identity becomes yet murkier. Scholars have suggested that Scheherazade's story appeared in the tenth-century *Hezar Afsane*, attributed to the Persian Princess Homai, daughter of Artaxerxes I, whose female authorship I would like to believe. But the alternative of a fifteenth-century Arabian collection, compiled by a professional storyteller in Cairo, sex unspecified, leaves us with no firm indication. We do know that in later centuries *The Arabian Nights* have come down to us (the folk) through French and English translations by savants, such as Galland, Henry Torrens (1838), E. W. Lane, John Payne (1882–84), and Richard Burton (1885–88), whose sixteen-volume English edition has been praised for its "exceptional accuracy, *masculine vitality*, and literary discernment" (emphasis added). Reinforcing the paradigm set by Ovid's *Metamorphoses*, Scheherazade's story and *The Arabian Nights* exemplify further the appropriation of text by a double narration in which a presumably male author or collector attributes to a female the original power of articulating silent matter. But having attributed this transformative artistic intelligence and voice to a woman, the narrator then reclaims for himself (much as Tereus and the King assert dominion over body and voice within the tales) the controlling power of retelling, of literary recasting, and of dissemination to the folk—a folk that includes the female community of tale-tellers from which the stories would seem to have originated.

Subsequent European collections of folk and fairy tales often assert a similarly double control over voice and text, whether as a mere literary convention or as a reflection of the actual informants and contexts of tale-telling. *The Book of the Seven Wise Masters*, or *Seven Sages*, probably of ninth-century Persian origin, but known in Europe, practically inverts the frame story of *The Arabian Nights Entertainments*.[2] Not a wazir's daughter, but instead a king's son, under notice of death, is saved from execution by the tales of seven philosophers, who tell stories of female deceptions, while a woman vehemently defends her sex from these slanders. Gianfrancesco Straparola (c. 1480–c. 1557), in his sixteenth-century Italian collection, *Le piacevoli Notti* or *The Delightful Nights* (1550–53), excuses the crude jests and earthy telling of tales by claiming (perhaps falsely?) to have heard them "from the lips of ten young girls." And Giambattista Basile's (1575–1632) famous *Lo Cunto*

2. Peter Opie and Iona Opie, "Introduction," *The Classic Fairy Tales* (London: Oxford University Press, 1974), pp. 20–21.

*de li Cunti* (1634–36) or the *Pentamerone* (1674) contains a frame story attributing the fifty tales to common townswomen. Charles Perrault, borrowing perhaps from *les contes de vieilles* told by his son's nurse or repeated by his son Pierre, creates in *Histoires ou Contes du tems passé: Avec des Moralitez* (1697) the style of restrained simplicity that set the literary standard for subsequent fairy tale collections and *Kunstmärchen*.[3]

Madame d'Aulnoy (c. 1650–1705) may be the female exception that proves the rule of male appropriation, for as the author of eleven volumes she becomes notable for her elegantly ornamented fairy tales, designed to delight the adult aristocratic tastes of Louis XIV's court. As Dorothy R. Thelander establishes in "Mother Goose and Her Goslings: The France of Louis XIV as Seen through the Fairy Tale," these "fairy tales formed a distinct socioliterary genre," whose "roots lay in stories that peasant nursemaids and servants told children left in their charge, yet they were shaped for an adult and relatively sophisticated audience," that "shared the ideals of the Paris salons, particularly those which cultivated the refinement of language and manners associated with the précieux."[4] It is perhaps a sign of how removed Madame d'Aulnoy is from *les vieilles* as hearth-side tale-tellers that in one volume of her *contes de fées*, she imagines them to be narrated by some women during a short carriage trip. I do not intend to dispute the issues of the Ancien Régime and salon tales, or of Perrault's authorship, or of his style. My argument underscores, however, the observation of how regularly the tales are assumed and asserted to have their origins in a province definably female, and how the literary *contes de fées* become geared to an increasingly large circle of women readers—aristocratic ladies, mothers and nursemaids, governesses, young girls, and ironically the folk.

What surfaces during the period of the seventeenth century in which fairy tales become part of Western Europe's literary as well as oral tradition are "tell-tale" signs of a twofold legacy. First, we have noted already how insistently literary raconteurs, both male and female, validated the authenticity of their folk stories by claiming to have heard them from young girls, nurses, gossips, townswomen, old crones, and wise women. The female frame narrator is a particularly significant indicator, because it converts into literary convention the belief in women as truth-sayers, those gifted with memory and voice to transmit the culture's wisdom—the silent matter of life itself. Consider, for example, the term *conte de fées*. The terms *fées* and *faerie* derive originally from the Latin *Fatum*, the thing spoken, and *Fata*, the Fates who speak

---

3. *Lo Cunto de li Cunti: The Tale of Tales*; Kunstmärchen: literary fairy tale in German [*Editor*].
4. Dorothy R. Thelander, "Mother Goose and Her Goslings: The France of Louis XIV as Seen Through the Fairy Tale," *The Journal of Modern History* 54 (1982): 467–96. [*Précieux*: literati (*Editor*).]

it. According to Andrew Lang, in his "Introduction" to *Perrault's Popular Fairy Tales* (1888), "the *Fées* answered, as in Sleeping Beauty, to Greek *Moirai* or Egyptian *Hathors*. They nursed women in labour: they foretold the fate of children."[5] And Katherine Briggs, in *An Encyclopedia of Fairies*, cites the derivation from "the Italian *fatae*, the fairy ladies who visited the household of births and pronounced on the future of the baby."[6] These Italian, French, and English derivatives from the Greek and Latin, compel us to see the origin of fairy as closely related to female acts of birthing, nursing, prophesying, and spinning —as ancient myth makes plain. Recall the three Fates: Klōthō, the spinner, spins the thread of life; Lachēsis, draws it out, thereby apportioning one's lifespan and destiny; and the dread Atropos, she who cannot be kept from turning the spindle, is "the blind *Fury* with th'abhorred shears," who "slits the thin-spun life."[7] *Contes de fées* are, therefore, not simply tales told about fairies; implicitly they are tales told by women, descendents of those ancestral Fates, who link once again the craft of spinning with the art of telling fated truths. In these women's hands, literally and metaphorically, rests the power of birthing, dying, and tale-spinning.

Second, it is not just the nature of the female raconteur, but also the context within which she tells tales in France, Germany, and England that reinforces associations between the literal and metaphorical spinning of yarns. Edward Shorter, among other historians of French popular culture, documents how in the *veillées*, those weekly gatherings of farm families, the women would "gather closely about the light of the nut-oil lamp," not only to "spin, knit, or darn to keep their own family's clothes in shape," but also to "tell stories and recite the old tales. Or maybe, as one disgusted observer reported of the late-nineteenth century, they just 'gossip.' "[8] The *veillée* in some parts of France became sex segregated, often a gathering exclusively of women with their marriageable daughters, in which both generations carded wool, spun, knitted, or stitched, thus enacting the age-old female rituals. As Abel Hugo, one of Shorter's nineteenth-century antiquarians, portrays it, "the women, because of the inferiority of their sex, are not admitted at all to conversation with their lords and masters. But after the men have

---

5. Andrew Lang, ed., *Perrault's Popular Tales* (Oxford: Clarendon Press, 1888; repr. New York: Arno, 1977).
6. Katherine Briggs, *An Encyclopedia of Fairies* (New York: Pantheon, 1976), p. xi, as quoted in Thelander, "Mother Goose," p. 487.
7. Bergren, "Language and the Female in Early Greek Thought," p. 87, n. 5, suggests this provocative emphasis on Atropos, who otherwise might be translated "she who does not turn." Bergren cites Thompson as the source of "she who cannot be kept from turning" the spindle itself.
8. Edward Shorter, "The 'Veillée' and the Great Transformation," in *The Wolf and the Lamb: Popular Culture in France from the Old Regime to the Twentieth Century*, ed. Jacques Beauroy, Marc Bertrand, and Edward T. Gargan (Saratoga, California: Anma Libri, 1977), pp. 127–40. The first long quotation is taken from p. 129.

retired, the women's reign begins. . . ."[9] Within the shared esprit of these late-evening communes, women not only practiced their domestic crafts, they also fulfilled their role as transmitters of culture through the vehicle of "old tales," inherited from oral tradition or the filtered down versions from the *Bibliothèque bleue*, those cheaply printed, blue-covered penny dreadfuls sold by traveling colporteurs.[1]

✻   ✻   ✻

To have the antiquarian Grimm Brothers regarded as the fathers of modern folklore is perhaps to forget the maternal lineage, the "mothers" who in the French *veillées* and English nurseries, in court salons and the German *Spinnstube*, in Paris and on the Yorkshire moors, passed on their wisdom. The Grimm brothers, like Tereus, Ovid, King Shahryar, Basile, Perrault, and others reshaped what they could not precisely comprehend, because only for women does the thread, which spins out the lore of life itself, create a tapestry to be fully read and understood. Strand by strand weaving, like the craft practiced on Philomela's loom or in the hand-spinning of Mother Goose, is the true art of the fairy tale—and it is, I would submit, semiotically a female art. If we then recognize the continuity of this community of female storytellers, then perhaps Madame d'Aulnoy or her carriage trade ladies differ only in status and style from Basile's townswomen, the French *vieilles*, or English old wives and middle-class governesses. We may also wish to re-conceptualize Madame d'Aulnoy, Mlle. L'Héritier, and Madame de Beaumont, not as pseudomasculine appropriators of a folkloric tradition, but as reappropriators of a female art of tale-telling that dates back to Philomela and Scheherazade. As such, they foreshadow, indeed perhaps foster, the eighteenth- and nineteenth-century emergence of a passion for romantic fictions, particularly among women writers and readers. Moreover, the "curious" socio-literary genres of the salon tale and Perrault's nursery tales (*contes naïfs*) may be reperceived as a mid-stage, linking the ancient oral repertoire of folktales to the later, distinctively literary canon that embraces collections of folk and fairy tales as well as *Kunstmärchen*, moral and didactic stories, and romantic novels in which fairy tale motifs, structures, and frame narrators exert a shaping influence.

---

9. Abel Hugo, from *La France pittoresque*, 3 vols. (Paris, 1835), 1:238, as quoted in Shorter, "The 'Veillée,' " p. 131. In *Ethnologie et langage: La parole chez les Dogon* (Paris: Gallimard, 1965), Geneviève Calame-Griaule similarly observes the "parole cachée" (concealed speech) among the Dogon women, who while spinning cotton whisper the stories of their men. It is also while mother and daughter spin that the mother teaches her daughter the necessary knowledge of marriage and sexual relations. These "confidences" are a mode dear to the Dogon women ("une parole féminine"), and as we have seen in European cultures, here too in an African tribe of the French Sudan the associations turn around the ideas of spinning yarn and of a secret, both skills and truths passed from mothers to daughters.
1. Peddlers of books [*Editor*].

# MARINA WARNER

## The Old Wives' Tale†

\* \* \*

Plato in the *Gorgias* referred disparagingly to the kind of tale—*mythos graos*, the old wives' tale—told by nurses to amuse and frighten children. This is possibly the earliest reference to the genre. When the boys and girls of Athens were about to embark for Crete, to be sacrificed to the Minotaur, old women are described coming down to the port to tell them stories, to distract them from their grief. In *The Golden Ass*, Charite, a young bride, is captured by bandits, forcibly separated from her husband and thrown into a cave; there, a disreputable old woman, drunken and white-haired, tells her the story of Psyche's troubles before she reaches happiness and marriage with Cupid: 'The old woman sighed sympathetically. "My pretty dear," she said, ". . . let me tell you a fairy tale or two to make you feel a little better." ' The picture of another's ordeals will console Charite and distract her from her own distress. William Adlington published his exuberant translation of 'sondrie pleasant and delectable Tales, with an excellent Narration of the Marriage of Cupide and Psiches . . .' in 1566; it is most improbable that a writer like George Peele would not have known this earliest recognizable predecessor of 'Cinderella' and 'Beauty and the Beast'.

In Latin, the phrase Apuleius uses is literally 'an old wives' tale' (*anilis fabula*); the type of comic romance to which 'Cupid and Psyche' belongs was termed 'Milesian', after Aristides of Miletus, who had compiled a collection of such stories in the second century A.D.; these were translated into Latin, but are now known only through later retellings. The connection of old women's speech and the consolatory, erotic, often fanciful fable appears deeply intertwined in language itself, and with women's speaking roles, as the etymology of 'fairy' illuminates.

The word 'fairy' in the Romance languages indicates a meaning of the wonder or fairy tale, for it goes back to a Latin feminine word, *fata*, a rare variant of *fatum* (fate) which refers to a goddess of destiny. The fairies resemble goddesses of this kind, for they too know the course of fate. *Fatum*, literally, that which is spoken, the past participle of the verb *fari*, to speak, gives French *fée*, Italian *fata*, Spanish *hada*, all meaning 'fairy', and enclosing connotations of fate; fairies share with Sibyls knowledge of the future and the past, and in the stories which feature them, both types of figure foretell events to come, and give warnings.

Isidore of Seville (*d. 636*), in the *Etymologies*, gives a famous, sceptical definition of the pagan idea of fate and the Fates: 'They say that fate is whatever the gods declare, whatever Jupiter declares. Thus they say that fate derives from *fando*, that is, from speaking. . . . The fiction is that there are three Fates, who spin a woollen thread on a distaff, on a spindle, and with their fingers, on account of the threefold nature of time: the past, which is already spun and wound onto the spindle; the present, which is drawn between the spinner's fingers; and the future, which lies in the wool twined on the distaff, and which must still be drawn out by the fingers of the spinner onto the spindle, as the present is drawn to the past.' These classical Fates metamorphose into the fairies of the stories, where they continue their fateful and prophetic roles. But fairy tales themselves also fulfil this function, quite apart from the fairies who may or may not make an appearance: 'Bluebeard' or 'Beauty and the Beast' act to caution listeners, as well as light their path to the future.

Although they do not have the same root, 'fairy' has come under strong semantic influence from 'fay' and 'fair', both of which may be derived ultimately from the Middle English '*feyen*', Anglo-Saxon '*fegan*', meaning to agree, to fit, to suit, to join, to unite, to bind. Thus the desirable has the power to inspire—even compel—agreement, as well as to bind. Binding is one of the properties of decrees, and of spells. Interestingly, this root also gives 'fee', as in payment, for transferrals of money too arise from agreed bonds, as a response to a desire, a need.

Although the ultimate origin, in time and place, of a fairy tale can never really be pinned down, we do sometimes know the teller of an old tale in one particular variation, we can sometimes identify the circle of listeners at a certain time and place. The collectors of the nineteenth century occasionally recorded the name of their sources when they took down the story, though they were not as interested in them as historians would be now. One salient aspect of the transmission of fairy tales has not been looked at closely: the female character of the storyteller.

Italo Calvino, in his 1956 collection of Italian *Fiabe*, or Tales, the Italian answer to the Grimms, drew attention to this aspect of the tradition, noticing that several of the nineteenth-century folklore anthologies he drew on and adapted cited female sources. Agatuzza Messia, the nurse of the Sicilian scholar and collector of tales Giuseppe Pitré, became a seamstress, and, later, a quilt-maker in a section of Palermo: 'A mother, grandmother, and great-grandmother, as a little girl, she heard stories from her grandmother, whose own mother had told them having herself heard countless stories from one of her grandfathers. She had a good memory so never forgot them.' The *Kalevala*, the national poem of Finland, was collected from different oral sources and reshaped by Elias Lönnrot in the mid-nineteenth century in the form in which it is read today; Sibelius, who would compose many pieces inspired by the *Kalevala's* heroes and heroines, heard the epic in part direct from Larin Paraske, a woman bard, who held eleven thousand lines of such folk material in her head. Karel Čapek, the utopian Czech writer most famous for his satire *RUR* (which introduced the concept of Robots), wrote an acute essay about fairy tale in 1931, in which he decided:

> A fairy story cannot be defined by its motif and subject-matter, but by its origin and function. . . . A true folk fairy tale does not originate in being taken down by the collector of folklore but in being told by a grandmother to her grandchildren, or by one member of the Yoruba tribe to other members of the Yoruba tribe, or by a professional storyteller to his audience in an Arab coffeehouse. A real fairy tale, a fairy tale in its true function, is a tale within a circle of listeners. . . .

He himself remembered his mother and his grandmother telling him stories—they were both millers' daughters, as if they had stepped out of a fairy tale. The *traditio* does literally pass on, as the word suggests, between the generations, and the predominant pattern reveals older women of a lower status handing on the material to younger people, who include boys, sometimes, if not often, of higher position and expectations, like future ethnographers and writers of tales.

So although male writers and collectors have dominated the production and dissemination of popular wonder tales, they often pass on women's stories from intimate or domestic milieux; their tale-spinners often figure as so many Scheherazades, using narrative to bring about a resolution of satisfaction and justice. Marguerite de Navarre, in the *Heptaméron*, gives the stories to ten speakers, five of whom are women: they too, like the narrator of *The Arabian Nights*, put their own case, veiled in entertaining and occasionally licentious fantasy. Boccaccio, and his admirer and emulator (to some degree) Chaucer, voiced the stories of women, and some contain folk material which makes a strong showing in later fairy stories; the Venetian Giovan Francesco Straparola (the 'Babbler') reported the stories told by a circle of ladies in his entertaining and sometimes scabrous fantasies, filled with fairytale motifs and improbabilities, called *Le placevoli notti* (The Pleasant Nights), published in 1550; the Neapolitan Giambattista Basile, in *Lo cunto de li cunti* (The Tale of Tales), also known as *Il Pentamerone* (The Pentameron), published posthumously in 1634–6, featured a group of wizened and misshapen old crones as his sources.

The women who inaugurated the fashion for the written fairy tale, in Paris at the end of the seventeenth century, consistently claimed they had heard the stories they were retelling from nurses and servants. Mme de Sévigné, writing to her daughter, revealingly reported a metaphor borrowed from the kitchen to describe the new enthusiasm: '*cela s'appelle les [contes] mitonner. Elle nous mitonna donc, et nous parla d'une île verte, où l'on élevait une princesse plus belle que le jour'* (it's called simmering them [tales]; so she simmered for us, and talked to us about a green isle where a princess grew up who was more beautiful than the day).

Charles Perrault's collection of 1697 bore the alternative title of *Contes de ma Mère l'Oye* (Mother Goose Tales); in an earlier preface, to the tale '*Peau d'Ane*' (Donkeyskin), Perrault also placed his work in the tradition of Milesian bawdy, like the tale of 'Cupid and Psyche', but he added that he was passing on 'an entirely made up story and an old wives' tale', such as had been told to children since time immemorial by their nurses. While referring to a written canon, he thus disengaged himself from its élite character to invoke old women, grandmothers and governesses as his true predecessors. He was quick to add, however, that unlike the moral of 'Cupid and Psyche' ('*impénétrable*'), his own was patently clear, which made it far superior to its classical predecessors:

> These Milesian fables are so puerile that it is doing them rather an honour to set up against them our own Donkeyskin tales and Mother Goose tales, or [they are] so filled with dirt, like *The Golden Ass* of Lucian or Apuleius . . . that they do not merit that we should pay them attention.

Perrault may have had his tongue in his cheek when he protested that 'Donkeyskin', a tale of father-daughter incest, was morally impeccable. But a contemporary pedant, the Abbé de Villiers, took his argument at face value, and rounded in outrage on Perrault and the writers of fairy tales, penning a pamphlet against the genre, 'As a preventive measure against bad taste.' There he lumped women and children together as the perpetrators of the new fad: 'Ignorant and foolish, they have filled the world with so many collections, so many little stories, and in short with these reams of fairy tales which have been the death of us for the last year or so.' The diminutive form of the nouns (*sornettes, bagatelles, historiettes*) recurs in the rhetoric of detractors and supporters alike; the former branding fairy stories as infantile, the latter praising them as childlike. This tension between opposing perceptions of the child informs the development of the tales and continues to do so.

Villiers sets up an imaginary debate between a fashionable Parisian and a sensible visitor from the provinces. The provincial calls them *sottises imprimées* (follies in print) and compares them derogatorily to fables, scorning them as 'Tales to make you fall asleep on your feet, that nurses have made up to entertain children'. The Parisian counters that nurses have to be highly skilled to tell them. To which the provincial retorts that if such tales ever contained a coherent moral purpose, they would not be considered in the first place 'the lot of ignorant folk and women'. The battle was joined, over the value of fairy tales; their female origin was not really contested.

Villiers's Parisian was putting forward the views of poets and literati like Mlle Marie-Jeanne L'Héritier de Villandon (1664–1734), a cousin and close friend of Perrault, who defended the form with fighting spirit precisely because it conveyed the ancient, pure wisdom of the people from the fountainhead—old women, nurses, governesses. In her preface to the story '*Marmoisan, ou l'innocente tromperie*' (Marmoisan, or the innocent trick) of 1696, she declared herself a partisan of women and their stories, remembering: 'A hundred times and more, my governess, instead of animal fables, would draw for me the moral features of this surprising story. . . . Why yes, once heard, such tales are far more striking than the exploits of a monkey and a wolf. I took an extreme pleasure in them—as does every child.'

L'Héritier could never rid her praise of its defensive tone ('the moral features'), and for good reason. The phrase 'old wives' tale' was superficially pejorative when Apuleius used it on the lips of his hoary-headed crone of a storyteller; it remained so, in the very act of authenticating the folk wisdom of the stories by stressing the wise old women who had carried on the tradition. It is still, in English, an ambiguous phrase: an old wives' tale means a piece of nonsense, a tissue of error, an ancient act of deception, of self and others, idle talk. As Marlowe writes in *Dr Faustus*, 'Tush, these are trifles and mere old wives' tales'. On a par with trifles, 'mere old wives' tales' carry connotations of error, of false counsel, ignorance, prejudice and fallacious nostrums—against heartbreak as well as headache; similarly 'fairy tale', as a derogatory term, implies fantasy, escapism, invention, the unreliable consolations of romance.

But the idealistic impulse is also driven by dreams; alternative ways of sifting right and wrong require different guides, ones perhaps discredited or neglected. Women from very different social strata have been remarkably active in the fields of folklore and children's literature since the nineteenth century. The Grimm Brothers' most inspiring and prolific sources were women, from families of friends and close relations, like the Wilds—Wilhelm married Dortchen, the youngest of four daughters of Dorothea Wild, who possessed a rich store of traditional tales, and she provided thirty-six for the collection. Dorothea, the Grimms' sister, married Ludwig Hassenpflug, and his three sisters passed on forty-one of the tales. From the Romantic literary circle of the artistic aristocratic von Haxthausens (who contributed collectively no fewer than sixty-six of the Grimms' tales) Annette von Droste-Hülshoff, the poet, and her sister Jenny were among the women who eagerly took part in telling the brothers the stories they had heard as children and more recently from their local area of Westphalia. Oscar

Wilde's father, a doctor in Merrion Square, Dublin, in the mid-nineteenth century, used to ask for stories as his fee from his poorer patients: his wife Speranza Wilde then collected them. Many of these were told to him by women, and in turn influenced their son's innovatory fairy tales, like 'The Selfish Giant' and 'The Happy Prince'. At the end of the century, the omnivorous Scottish folklorist Andrew Lang relied on his wife Leonora Alleyne, as well as a team of women editors, transcribers and paraphrasers, to produce the many volumes of fairy stories and folk tales from around the world, in the immensely popular *Red, Yellow, Green, Blue, Rose Fairy Books*, which he began publishing in 1890. The writer Simone Schwarz-Bart stitched her memories of Creole stories from her Martinique childhood into her poetic, adventurous, linguistically hybrid fictions. The grandmother Reine Sans Nom (Queen-With-No-Name) in *Pluie et vent sur Télumée Miracle* (1972) embodies survival and history, and keeps the memory of slave culture, and of Africa before that. With the help of her friend, a sorceress, she passes on lore, fables, fairy tales, ghost stories to her granddaughter. As Simone Schwarz-Bart once said in an interview, 'The tale is, in large part, our capital. I was nourished on tales. It is our bible. . . . I don't have a technique, but I know. I'm familiar. I've heard. I've been nourished. . . . When an old person dies, a whole library disappears.'

It would be absurd to argue that storytelling was an exclusively female activity—it varies from country to country, from one people to another, and from place to place within the same country, among the same people—but it is worth trying to puzzle out in what different ways the patterns of fairytale romancing might be drawn when women are the tellers.

The pedagogical function of the wonder story deepens the sympathy between the social category women occupy and fairy tale. Fairy tales exchange knowledge between an older voice of experience and a younger audience, they present pictures of perils and possibilities that lie ahead, they use terror to set limits on choice and offer consolation to the wronged, they draw social outlines around boys and girls, fathers and mothers, the rich and the poor, the rulers and the ruled, they point out the evildoers and garland the virtuous, they stand up to adversity with dreams of vengeance, power and vindication.

The *veillées* were the hearthside sessions of early modern society, where early social observers, like Bonaventure des Périers and Noël du Fail in the sixteenth century, describe the telling of some of today's most familiar fables and tales, like 'Donkeyskin' and 'Cinderella'. These gatherings offered men and women an opportunity to talk—to preach —which was forbidden them in other situations, the pulpit, the forum, and frowned on and feared in the spinning rooms and by the wellside. Taking place after daylight hours, they still do not exactly anticipate the leisure uses of television or radio today—work continued, in the

form of spinning, especially, and other domestic tasks: one folklore historian recalled hearing the women in her childhood tell stories to the
rhythm of the stones cracking walnuts as they shelled them for bottling
and pickling. As Walter Benjamin wrote in his essay on 'The Storyteller':

> [The storyteller's] nesting places—the activities that are intimately
> associated with boredom—are already extinct in the cities and are
> declining in the country as well. With this the gift for listening is
> lost and the community of listeners disappears. . . .

Benjamin never once imagines that his storytellers might be women,
even though he identifies so clearly and so eloquently the connection
between routine repetitive work and narrative—storytelling is itself 'an
artisan form of communication', he writes. And later, again, it is 'rooted
in the people . . . a milieu of craftsmen'. He divides storytellers into
stay-at-homes and rovers—tradesmen and agriculturalists, like the tailors
and the shoemakers who appear in the stories, on the one hand; on
the other, the seamen who travel far afield adventuring, like the quest-
ing type of hero. He neglects the figure of the spinster, the older woman
with her distaff, who may be working in town and country, in one place
or on the move, at market, or on a pilgrimage to Canterbury, and who
has become a generic icon of narrative from the frontispiece of fairytale
collections from Charles Perrault's onwards. The Scottish poet Liz
Lochhead, who has drawn on much fairytale imagery in her work, has
written:

> No one could say the stories were useless
> for as the tongue clacked
> five or forty fingers stitched
> corn was grated from the husk
> patchwork was pieced
> or the darning was done . . .
>
> And at first light . . .
> the stories dissolved in the whorl of the ear
> but they
> hung themselves upside down
> in the sleeping heads of the children
> till they flew again
> into the storyteller's night.

Spinning a tale, weaving a plot: the metaphors illuminate the relation; while the structure of fairy stories, with their repetitions, reprises,
elaboration and minutiae, replicates the thread and fabric of one of
women's principal labours—the making of textiles from the wool or the
flax to the finished bolt of cloth.

Fairy tales are stories which, in the earliest mentions of their existence, include that circle of listeners, the audience; as they point to
possible destinies, possible happy outcomes, they successfully involve
their hearers or readers in identifying with the protagonists, their mis-
fortunes, their triumphs. Schematic characterization leaves a gap into
which the listener may step. Who has not tried on the glass slipper? Or
offered it for trying? The relation between the authentic, artisan source
and the tale recorded in book form for children and adults is not simple;
we are not hearing the spinsters and the knitters in the sun whom
Orsino remembers chanting in *Twelfth Night*, unmediated. But the
quality of the mediation is of great interest. From the mid-seventeenth
century, the nurses, governesses, family domestics, working women living in or near the great house or castle in town and country existed in
a different relation to the élite men and women who may have once
been in their charge, as children. The future Marquise de la Tour du
Pin recalled in her memoirs how her nurse was her mainstay and that,
when she turned eleven and a governess was appointed instead, 'I used
to escape whenever I could and try to find her [the nurse], or to meet
her about the house.' Another noblewoman, Victorine de Chastenay,
also wrote that her own mother alarmed her and dominated her, and
that she took refuge with her nurse and her nurse's family. The rapports
created in *ancien régime* childhood shape the matter of the stories, and
the cultural model which places the literati's texts on the one side of a
divide, and popular tales on the other, can and should be redrawn: fairy
tales act as an airy suspension bridge, swinging slightly under different
breezes of opinion and economy, between the learned, literary and
print culture in which famous fairy tales have come down to us, and
the oral, illiterate, people's culture of the *veillée*; and on this bridge the
traffic moves in both directions.

Women writers like Marie-Jeanne L'Héritier and Marie-Catherine
d'Aulnoy mediated anonymous narratives, the popular, vernacular culture they had inherited through fairy tale, in spite of the aristocratic
frippery their stories make at a first impression. Indeed, they offer rare
and rich testimony to a sophisticated chronicle of wrongs and ways to
evade or right them, when they recall stories they had heard as children
or picked up later and retell them in a spirit of protest, of polite or not
so polite revolt. These tales are wrapped in fantasy and unreality, which
no doubt helped them entertain their audiences—in the courtly salon
as well as at the village hearth—but they also serve the stories' greater
purpose, to reveal possibilities, to map out a different way and a new
perception of love, marriage, women's skills, thus advocating a means
of escaping imposed limits and prescribed destiny. The fairy tale looks
at the ogre like Bluebeard or the Beast of 'Beauty and the Beast' in
order to disenchant him; while romancing reality, it is a medium deeply
concerned with undoing prejudice. Women of different social positions

have collaborated in storytelling to achieve true recognition for their subjects: the process is still going on.

                                   *    *    *

# ZOHAR SHAVIT

## The Concept of Childhood and Children's Folktales: Test Case—"Little Red Riding Hood"†

                                   *    *    *

Children's literature today enjoys centrality in cultural awareness and constitutes such a sizeable proportion of new educational materials that it is hard to imagine publishing activity without it. However, although children's literature is today a "natural" phenomenon taken for granted in any national literature, it is a relatively new development—less than two hundred years old. Books written especially for children were virtually unknown until the eighteenth century, and the children's book industry did not begin to flourish until the second half of the nineteenth century, when adult literature (in the modern sense) had already been established for at least one hundred years.

The reasons contributing to the late development of children's literature are diverse, but undoubtedly among the most important was the total absence of the concepts of "child" and "childhood" as we perceive them today. Before children's literature could be written, "childhood" itself had to come into existence and receive recognition and legitimation as a distinct time period in the life of the individual, or in the words of Townsend: "Before there could be children's books, there had to be children—children, that is, who were accepted as beings with their own particular needs and interests, not only as miniature men and women."[1]

In this article I will analyze along general lines and only in their principal features the creation and crystallization of the prerequisites for the development of Western children's literature—the development of the concept of the "child" in culture—and I will examine the relationships between this concept and texts written for children. In other words, I will ask how the nature of the concept of the child in literature and the meaning that has been given to the nature have to a large extent determined the character and the structure of texts for children, and how the changes that occurred in this concept were largely responsible for the changes that came about in texts for children. In

---

† From *Little Red Riding Hood: A Casebook,* ed. Alan Dundes (Madison: U of Wisconsin P, 1989) 129–52, 156–58. Originally published in Hebrew in *Jerusalem Studies in Jewish Folklore* 4 (1983): 93–124. Reprinted by permission.

1. J. R. Townsend, *Written for Children* (London: Penguin, 1977), 17.

attempting to answer these questions, I will use as a test case different versions of the folktale "Red Riding Hood."

The twentieth century is characterized by the almost obsessive use of the concept of childhood: issues about psychological, physical, and sexual problems of the child do not cease to concern adults. The period of childhood is considered the most important period in one's life, and an adult's behavior is often explained by his childhood experiences. But such a perception of childhood is completely different from the cultural outlook that prevailed two hundred years ago—the concept of childhood as we know it today did not exist then.

In his classic work, Philippe Ariès[2] proposes the argument, supported by later research as well,[3] that from the Middle Ages until the seventeenth century a different view of childhood dominated social consciousness, a view which began to develop and to change along lines familiar to us today beginning in the seventeenth century, passing through several transformations as one of the basic concepts of Western civilization.

## The Concept of Childhood up to the Seventeenth Century

Up to the seventeenth century the child was not perceived as an entity distinct from the adult, and consequently he was not recognized as having special needs. One of the results of this outlook was the lack of an established educational system for children, and of books written specifically for them.

In the Middle Ages and the ensuing period neither the living conditions nor the prevailing theological standpoint allowed for the concept of childhood. In the conceptual outlook of the day there was no room for the concept of childhood because of the identification between man and nature, as a result of which the life cycle was described as analogous to that of nature, including only the periods of birth, life, and death. In such a system there was no place for the period of childhood, the lack of which in the conceptual framework was no doubt strengthened by the poor chances of survival of children and their high mortality rate, which rendered their continued existence utterly uncertain. In addition, the basic living conditions were a contributing factor: people were wed at a relatively young age, and therefore "left childhood"—in the modern sense of the term—at a very tender age. Upper-class children took an active part in society from an extremely young age (10–13), whereas children of the lower classes were needed in the work force, and began working at a tender age. Consequently, children who successfully survived the first dangerous years of life could not remain

2. P. Ariès, *Centuries of Childhood* (New York: Vintage, 1962).
3. I. Weber-Kellermann, *Die Kindheit: Eine Kulturgeschichte* (Frankfurt a/M.: Insel Verlag, 1979); M.-L. Plessen and P. von Zahn, *Zwei Jahrtausende Kindheit* (Köln: VSG, 1979).

children for long, and were quickly forced to enter the adult world and to become part of it.

## Relations between the Child's World and the Adult's World: From Unity to Polarization

Up to the seventeenth century children were an integral part of adult society, sharing clothing, lodging, games, and work. Unity prevailed between children and adults in regard to all physical and psychic needs. A process of polarization began to undermine this unity from the seventeenth century on, as can be seen, for instance, from a discussion about the nature of the dress of children and adults of the upper class.[4] Up to the seventeenth century it was customary for children to wear a miniature version of the adults' clothing as soon as they stopped wearing swaddling clothes, which occurred at a relatively late age (3–5 years). With the development of the concept of childhood, the designing of special clothes for children also began. In general it can be said that the child's new wardrobe was characterized by items of attire which formerly belonged to the realm of adult wear and lost their function as such. Children's clothes became systematized through a process of reduction and at times also of simplification, and in the new system they also acquired a new function: they became a symbol of the separation of the world of children from that of the adult. Soon after certain items became children's clothing, they were used exclusively for children, such as breeches, which formerly had been a standard item of adult attire, but later became a trademark of children's dress. Moreover, various items of dress designated different stages of childhood, and permission to wear a certain item marked another stage in a child's maturation, until finally he entered the adult world and began to dress as a full-fledged adult.

The process of the transformation of childhood was expressed in other aspects of daily life, such as children's games, the educational system of the child, and even the fact that there was a special room in the house set aside for children, just as there were special rooms for the parents, for dining, and the like. As Ariès points out, an interesting example of this process of the transformation of elements from the adult's world to the world of the child and their consequent evolution into a trademark of the child's world is the case of the wooden rocking horse. The horse, which had been a primary medium of transportation, lost this function for the adult world at the end of the nineteenth century. It did not disappear from the culture, but rather evolved through a process of reduction and simplification into the wooden horse of the nursery, where it acquired a new function as a toy. Moreover, in ad-

---

4. For an exhaustive discussion about this aspect, see Ariès, *Centuries of Childhood*, 50–61; Plessen and von Zahn, *Zwei Jahrtausende Kindheit.*

dition to this function it became a symbol differentiating the children's room from the adults' room, and a sine qua non in nursery furnishings. (For a similar phenomenon, other dolls and miniature toys can be pointed to which originally had a ritual function for adults and children alike, but which later lost their ritual function, becoming not only part of the child's world, but his exclusive monopoly.)

Hence, in the process of the formation of the concept of "child," there occurred a polarization between the adult's and the child's world. The system of childhood began to be characterized by a series of elements which migrated from the adult system to the child's system, and took on the function of differentiating between the two systems.

### The Spread of the Concept of Childhood into Society: Two Concepts

The polarization between the adult's and the child's world and the spread of the concept of childhood were the result of many processes which occurred in Western society, especially the changes in social and material processes. The Industrial Revolution, the decrease in infant mortality, and the increase in life expectancy undoubtedly all played an important part in the development of the child concept, but changes in man's perception of the world during the Renaissance and the Enlightenment contributed considerably to the fact that the concept of "child" began to rise to consciousness before the physical conditions justified it, that is, before any change occurred in living conditions, and the change in these conditions later aided in the dissemination of the child concept among the middle class as well.

The first signs of the formation of this child concept, and the recognition that the child is a creature distinct from the adult, were already apparent at the end of the sixteenth century in the realm of painting. Here the child served a religious purpose—the infant Jesus, Jesus and the Angels, and the like—being depicted for the first time as sweet, angelic, and innocent, qualities which were also to characterize the image of the child at a later date. In time this iconography acquired a decorative character (viz. the paintings of Putt) beyond its original religious nature, and images of children gradually began to undergo a process of secularization and to hold a dominant position in the realms of painting and iconography. These pictures were the expression of a perception of the child as different from the adult by virtue of the former's innocence, sweetness, and angelic appearance. Gradually depictions of children began to acquire their own legitimacy, and painting children's portraits became more and more common. Thus the depiction of children aided in the spread of the new concept of the child as possessing the qualities portrayed in the paintings, qualities which from the seventeenth century onward made children a source of amusement for adults.

Regarding the child as a source of entertainment began to develop within the family circle. People no longer hesitated to acknowledge the diversion which children provided, and delighting in children, as well as in their sweetness, beauty, and witticisms, became fashionable among the upper classes. Children were invited to the parlor so that adults might be amused by them: the attitude towards children greatly resembled that assumed for cherished pet animals. Fleury described this attitude as follows: "It is as if the poor children had been made only to amuse the adults, like little dogs or little monkeys."[5]

This attitude began to arouse resistance among extrafamilial groups, such as moralists and pedagogues, who were opposed to the fashion which prevailed in relation to children. Nevertheless, they accepted the principal concept of considering the innocent child who is closer to God as distinct from the adult. They used this very concept to justify their demand for separating children from the corrupt adult society.

In contrast to the perception that was developing within the extended family circle, which saw the child as a source of amusement, a second perception of the child arose among groups which stood in opposition to the family: the church, the moralists, and the pedagogues, who, because of their awareness of his different nature, felt responsible for the spiritual development of the child. They believed that children need education and discipline, and simultaneous with the new interest in the psychology of the child, they drafted a demand for an educational system that would satisfy these needs. Henceforth the child was perceived as a delicate creature who must be protected, educated, and molded in accordance with the current educational beliefs and goals.

The way to shape children along these lines was first and foremost by means of books, which were considered the primary tool in achieving these "pedagogical" goals. This new "educational" perception of society, unlike the "amusement" perception which preceded it, created for the first time the need for children's books, and became the frame of reference in which the first books were written whose intended audience was specifically children. From then on official children's books were written, based on an understanding of the child as the audience and of his needs, which were different from those of adults. When a change in this understanding came about, texts written for children changed as well.

In order to investigate the relationship between the cultural concept of the child and the norms governing literature for children, I shall analyze as a test-case different versions of "Little Red Riding Hood."

---

5. Quoted in Ariès, *Centuries of Childhood*, 131.

The text of "Little Red Riding Hood" has been chosen not only because it is a "classic" of children's literature, but also for reasons of methodological convenience, as there is an extraordinary correspondence between the periods in which the different versions of the text were produced and the parallel developments in the child concept and the changes which occurred in it. Examining this text may therefore shed light on the link between the changes that took place in the child concept in Western civilization at different periods and the changes that occurred in the versions of the text in at least two ways: (1) understanding the child's needs and his comprehension capacity, and (2) seeing the manner in which the child and his world are presented in the texts themselves.

The examination of versions of "Little Red Riding Hood" will deal therefore with these questions and the way in which the "amusement" perception served as a basis for Perrault's version, its transformation into the "educational" version of the Brothers Grimm, and the further transformation of this version to the "protective" version of the twentieth century.

### "Little Red Riding Hood": A Test Case of Attitudes towards Folktales from the Seventeenth Century On

We have seen how, in the process of the creation of the child concept, elements from the adult world have passed over to the child's world, becoming the exclusive property of the child, after previously being shared by adults and children alike. This process characterized modes of dress, games children played, and folktales, which gradually entered the child's world, until in the twentieth century they were considered an essential component in his development (unlike the first half of the nineteenth century, when they were considered too dangerous for children and were removed from the canon of juvenile literature).

Up until the nineteenth century, folktales were told and read, as were romances, by adults (even among the upper classes). Children, who constituted part of adult society, were acquainted with them in the same way, although the tales were not considered meant for them. However, starting from the second half of the seventeenth century a change occurred in the attitude of the upper class vis-à-vis folktales. This was part of a general change in the prevailing literary fashions. Members of the literary elite, whose tastes were becoming more "sophisticated," regarded folktales as too "simple" and "childish," suitable, in their estimation, only for children and members of the lower classes (who were seen as social equals by the class-conscious of the time).[6] Despite this, it became fashionable to be interested in folktales and to write tales modeled after oral tales, at times pretending to be setting down an oral

6. Ibid., 95–98.

tale in written form (which was in some cases true). Yet in spite of the fact that folktales were in vogue, the writing and acceptance of them were based on the assumption that they were meant for children and the lower classes. Thus members of high society could enjoy them only vicariously through children, but since the child was perceived in any case as a source of amusement, adults could enjoy elements of the child's world while openly or covertly considering them part of the world of children, part of a culture different from that of the upper classes.

## Perrault's Version

\*    \*    \*

### MANIPULATING THE MODEL: THE AMBIGUITY OF "LITTLE RED RIDING HOOD"

\* \* \* Perrault was the first person to set down "Little Red Riding Hood" in writing. Scholars are still undecided on the question of whether or not Perrault's text is based on an existing folktale, mainly because of the atypical tragic ending of his text, a phenomenon unheard of in folktales. At any rate, even those scholars who believe that his text is based on an original folktale agree that Perrault doctored the text, altering part of its formal structure in order to make it more sophisticated.

For instance, Perrault changed the formulaic structure of the dialogue, which is generally characterized by completely symmetrical repetitions. Perrault violated this semi-sacred symmetry in the following manner:

> The *better* to embrace you,—
> The *better* to run with,—
> The *better* to hear with,—
> The *better* to see with,—
> To eat *you* with.[7]

Nevertheless, Perrault took pains to create the illusion of a folktale, mainly by means of stylistic devices, as Soriano asserts: "An attentive study of vocabulary shows that many of the turns of phrase utilized by the tale-teller were already considered old at that time—it is in sum a reconstitution, a sort of "in the manner of."[8]

The function of the stylizing of the text was not only to lend it the qualities of "authenticity" and "antiquity," but also, and perhaps primarily, to emphasize who its official audience was. The desire to stress the intended audience, that is, the child, would explain why Perrault

7. Gilbert Rouger, ed., *Contes de Perrault* (Paris: Garnier, 1967–1972), 115. Italics are mine.
8. Marc Soriano, *Les Contes de Perrault* (Paris: Gallimard, 1968), pp. 154–55.

used in the text words which were at that time considered to belong exclusively to the language of children, words such as *la bobinette* and *la chevillette*, which were not part of the accepted written language.[9] The very act of inserting such vocabulary items into the texts was a striking departure from the norm, thus serving an important stylistic function.

However, together with the attempt to characterize the work as "authentic" and as intended for children through the use of elements whose stylistic identity was clear, Perrault did not hesitate to deviate from the formulas of the folktale even at key points, such as the addition of a tragic ending, or in typical structures, such as the repetitions. In this manner he created a text which cannot be considered unequivocally either a folktale or a literary tale, possessing instead an ambiguous nature.

### THE BASIS FOR THE AMBIGUOUS NATURE OF THE TEXT

It seems that the ambiguous nature of the text can be explained by its official and unofficial audience. This ambiguity enabled Perrault to address two different audiences at one and the same time. On the one hand, he was able to take advantage of the current perception regarding the appropriateness of folktales for children in order to direct the text officially to them, while at the same time availing himself of the common conception of the child as a source of amusement in order to orient the text to the literary elite. However, in order to ensure that the upper classes would read his work, he felt obliged to "equip" it with signs that would indicate who the true audience was, while also making possible the duplicity of the text. While the folktale formulas designated the official audience, the breaking of such formulas—in addition to lending an ironic and satirical aspect to the text—marked the unofficial audience, the literary elite. Numerous accounts from the period testify to Perrault's success in attracting his unofficial audience to reading these texts—perhaps even more so than their officially intended audience—as Muir states:

> A feature of these salons, male and female alike, was the reading aloud of pasquinades, vaudevilles, sonnets à bouts-rimés, and similar short pieces: and the Comtesse d'Aulnoy seems to have introduced the telling of fairy-stories in the female salons. The idea caught on and became the rage. The fashion eventually extended to the male writers—The curious point to be taken is that the stories were devised or adapted from ancient originals, for the amusement not of children but of adults. The consequence is that,

9. La bobinette: (wooden) latch; la chevillette: page [*Editor*].

although the characters and the background belong superficially to fairy-tales, most of them are too sophisticated for children.[1]

It is therefore evident that Perrault, like many of his contemporaries, did not write his famous tales for children alone, but also, or perhaps mainly, for the pleasure of his friends. It seems that the following quotation about his contemporary Mlle l'Héritier also applies to Perrault himself: "Mademoiselle l'Héritier wrote for the amusement of her friends and all of her writings bear the imprint of her 'salon wit.' "[2]

### THE FUNCTION OF THE DUALITY OF THE INTENDED AUDIENCE

Perrault had to emphasize the fact that children were the official audience of his work because this was a condition for its acceptance by high society. Even scholars who see the text as meant primarily for children agree that at least part of it is aimed at adults, as Soriano, for example, says: "It is always addressed to an audience of children, no doubt, but at the same time allowing a wink in the direction of the adult."[3]

Whether the text was intended entirely for adults or only partially so, there is no disagreement that the ironic and satirical tone of the text, particularly as it is expressed in the tragic ending of the tale, is meant for adults, and not for children. By means of the tragic ending, Perrault created a satire about the city gentleman who does not hesitate to take advantage of the poor village girl. The text's satirical nature depends primarily on the moral, which comes at the end. From this ending it is made clear that the wolf is not a real wolf, but rather represents all sorts of people whom an innocent village girl must beware of:

> Who does not know that these gentle wolves
> Are of all such creatures the most dangerous.[4]

The depiction of the gentleman abusing the innocent village girl is further strengthened in the text by the erotic elements that accompany her description: her beauty, the color red which is her symbol, and of course the erotic bed scene, in which she is surprised to discover what "grandmother" looks like in bed, after the latter asks her to undress and to come lie with her: "Little Red Riding Hood took off her cloak, but when she climbed up on the bed she was astonished to see how her grandmother looked in her nightgown."[5] It is clear that the erotic aspect encourages the reading of the text as the story of a gentleman exploiting the innocence of a village girl and enjoying her charms, rather than simply as the story of a little girl who is devoured by a wolf.

1. P. Muir, *English Children's Books* (New York: Frederick A. Praeger, 1969), 36.
2. Soriano, 65.
3. Ibid., 155.
4. Rouger, *Contes de Perrault*, 115.
5. Ibid., 114–115.

The child concept of Perrault's day provided the background for *Les Contes* and the mask necessary for their acceptance by the literary elite. However, in addition to the changes that later took place in the conception of the child, the nature of the texts meant for him also changed, as well as in the way the child himself was depicted in different texts. These changes were among the factors causing the transformation of "Little Red Riding Hood" from Perrault's version to the later one that the Brothers Grimm collected and committed to writing—along with their own revisions and alterations—a century later.

### Differences between Versions of "Little Red Riding Hood": Perrault vs. the Brothers Grimm

Folktale research has dealt at length with the differences between the tales of Perrault and different versions of tales similar to his published by the Brothers Grimm. Scholars are divided regarding the origins of the texts and their degree of "originality," accounting for the similarities and differences in them by various methods. Some explain them using the historic-geographic method,[6] while others prefer to look at cross-cultural relationships[7] or the crossover from one national culture to another.[8] Other researchers deny the possibility of a direct connection between Perrault's tales and those of the Brothers Grimm, attributing the similarities and differences to the intermediary influences of Tieck, whom the Brothers Grimm refer to in their commentary on "Little Red Riding Hood": "Perrault's 'Little Red Riding Hood' which Tieck elegantly reworked in his romantic drama . . ."[9]

Rather than getting involved in this complex argument, or refuting the conclusions of this or that researcher, I would like to propose an alternative way of accounting for the differences between Perrault's version and that of the Brothers Grimm: One could also regard the differences between the two as the result of the different perceptions of the concept of childhood which prevailed in each of the two periods in question, thereby yielding differing assumptions concerning the intended audience and the manner in which the child is presented in the texts.

In the hundred years that had passed since Perrault's days, a revolutionary change had taken place in the child concept. The "amusement" perception of the child was replaced in the Grimm Brothers' day by an "educational" perception which gave primary importance to

6. Reference to the Finnish School of folklore, which studies the origins and dissemination of tales.
7. J. Bolte and G. Polívka, *Anmerkungen zu den Kinder- und Hausmärchen der Brüder Grimm*, vol. 4 (Hildesheim: Georg Olms, 1963 reprint of 1913 edition), 261–277.
8. H. V. Velten, "The Influence of Charles Perrault's Contes de ma Mère l'Oie on German Folklore," *Germanic Review* 5 (1930), 4–18.
9. Brüder Grimm, *Kinder- und Hausmärchen*, vol. 3 (Stuttgart: Reclam, 1890), 59.

a new and heretofore unheard of concept: that of educating the child. Consequently, an educational system evolved, the needs of which largely dictated both the nature of works written for children, and above all the literary models then dominating the literary scene.

The Brothers Grimm, like other writers of the mid-nineteenth century, adopted the new image of the child, stressing his straightforwardness and the ability, uniquely his, to look at the world in a special way. They expressed this view in the introduction to *Kinder- und Hausmärchen*, claiming to transmit the text from the child's point of view: "There runs throughout these narratives that quality of purity which makes children appear to us so wonderful and happy. The tales have, so to speak, the selfsame shining eyes open as far as they can possibly be while the rest of the body is still fragile, weak and unskilled for earthly labor."[1]

However, in contradistinction to Perrault, whose official audience was the child, the Brothers Grimm did not intend their text for children at first, although the book's title indicates the origin of the texts: they were collected from household members—maidservants—and children. The tales were first intended for adult members of the literary elite, for the accepted literary tastes—a return to the primary sources and to nature were in vogue—enabled them to enjoy such texts. The Brothers Grimm did not have the option of directing their works to adults and children at one and the same time, for according to the current child concept, the child was seen as an entity distinct from the adult, with different needs and capabilities of understanding. In order nevertheless to enable children to read their tales, the Brothers Grimm thought it necessary to revise them, gearing them to a child's level of understanding, particularly from a stylistic point of view. This they did starting with the second edition, in the introduction to which they outlined the principles that guided them in their endeavor to render the texts suitable for children.

In spite of this, the Brothers Grimm still recognized the possibility that there would be parents who would deem the book inappropriate for their children, forbidding them to read it: "Therefore we have taken care to leave out of this new edition expressions which were not suitable for children. Yet there may be objections. One or another parent may find material embarrassing or offensive, so that they would not be comfortable putting the book into the hands of children. In such well-founded individual cases, the parents have an easy choice to make."[2] In this introduction, two new ideas are evident which apparently were a major part of the changes that occurred in the text since Perrault's time. As stated above, one idea expressed the supposition that the child

1. Ibid., 16.
2. Ibid., 17.

is an entity distinct from the adult. The other expressed the belief that the adult is responsible for satisfying the child's needs, and that the latter must be under his direct and constant supervision.

The differences between the versions of Perrault and the Brothers Grimm thus consist of more than just different assumptions about the audience and the fact that in the Grimm text there is no trace of the protracted game which Perrault played with his audience. Another striking difference between the texts is the distinctive way the child and everything connected with him is presented in each. In the Grimm version of "Little Red Riding Hood" the two beliefs that were combined in the child concept of the time are evident, particularly in the portrayal of intrafamilial relations, the simple honesty of the child, and the need to guide and instruct him. These viewpoints will be treated here through an examination of the differing tones of the two texts, and their divergent endings, as well as less salient differences.

### DIFFERENCES IN TONE AND ENDING

As many scholars have asserted, the most salient differences between Perrault and the Brothers Grimm lie in the tone of the texts, ironic versus naive, and in the ending, happy versus tragic.

It seems that the difference in tone is due to the differing intentions of the authors. Whereas Perrault used satire and irony to address the literary elite, the Brothers Grimm made a noticeable effort to preserve the illusion of the naive narrator, considered crucial to the "authenticity" of the text. Although they freely admitted reworking the oral text —the written version is probably very different from it and closer to Tieck's[3]—they still took pains to keep intact the naive character of the narrator, mainly by preserving the naive tone.

The other striking difference is, as noted earlier, the ending. In Perrault's version, the story ends when the wolf devours the girl, followed by a moral in rhyming verse. The Grimm version, on the other hand, offers two alternative endings, the common denominator between them being that the girl is not harmed in the end. In the first alternative, she is punished—the grandmother and the girl are at first devoured by the wolf, but are later rescued by the hunter, who also kills the wolf; however in the second alternative the wolf is drowned before it has a chance to harm the girl or her grandmother.

The drastic change in the nature of the tale's ending, completely changing its significance, raises the question why there was the need to insert such an ending at all, apart from the question of whether or

3. R. Hagen, "Perraults Märchen und die Brüder Grimm," *Zeitschrift für Deutsche Philologie* 74 (1955), 392–410.

not it was organic to the text.[4] In other words, what function did the addition of this ending to the text serve?

It is clear that turning the tragic ending into a happy one was first and foremost the result of the need to fit the story into the pattern of the folktale. The happy ending is considered an indispensable component of the folktale; it can be said to be a distinctive feature which differentiates folktales from literary tales. Hence the Brothers Grimm, or the anonymous narrator who added the happy ending (from the point of view of the function of the ending it is immaterial who was responsible for the addition, rather it is important to understand why it was necessary) could not deviate from the pattern, unlike Perrault, who intentionally departed from it at decisive points in the story. However, the selection of this specific ending has implications above and beyond the folktale pattern, reflecting also the educational views of the day. According to these views, the child must derive a moral lesson from every event, experience, or story to which he is exposed. Punishment was itself perceived as an integral part of the educational process—and in this respect the "Red Riding Hood" of the Brothers Grimm was no different. It is interesting to note that the Brothers Grimm themselves were pleased with the "educational" nature of the tales, seeing it as further proof that the text was suitable for children.[5]

Bolte and Polívka[6] suggest that this specific ending was chosen because it already existed in the folktale inventory in the tale "The Wolf and the Seven Young Kids." Because the wolf's role as protagonist is common to both tales, its choice presented a "natural" and ready-made solution. Even if we accept this explanation, it does not contradict the one offered above. Moreover, we must not ignore the fact that in the tale "The Wolf and the Seven Young Kids" the element of learning a lesson is absent. This is a feature which exists only in the text of "Red Riding Hood," which strengthens the assumptions made about the text regarding the education of the child and the process of reward and punishment.

This difference between the versions of Perrault and the Brothers Grimm changed not only the ending of the text, but also its meaning and moral. Unlike Perrault's Little Red Riding Hood, the Grimms' Little Red Riding Hood has the opportunity to learn a lesson, and indeed avails herself of the opportunity. Whereas Perrault's moral emphasizes the wolf, thereby pointing to the gentleman from the city, the moral of the Brothers Grimm's version stresses Little Red Riding Hood's learning a lesson. Thus the tale was transformed from a satire to a tale about reward and punishment and learning a lesson.

4. On this question see Velten, "The Influence of Charles Perrault's Contes de ma Mère l'Oie."
5. See their introduction to the Kinder- und Hausmärchen, 17.
6. Bolte and Polívka, Anmerkungen, vol. 1, 234–237.

The difference in emphasis in the two versions and in their general significance explains the total omission of the erotic scene and the erotic elements from the Grimm version, and was probably also the reason for some less obvious changes. In Perrault's version there are only slight hints as to the relationship between family members, while in the Grimm version they are quite explicit. Examples include the grandmother's love for the girl, the mother's feeling of responsibility for the grandmother, and the girl's love for her grandmother.

While in Perrault's version the grandmother's love for the girl is not mentioned at all, in the Grimm version her love for Little Red Riding Hood is boundless, and she makes her the red hood as a symbol of her love. Hence the hood serves a different function in each of the two versions: for Perrault it symbolizes the girl's eroticism, whereas for the Brothers Grimm it is an expression of the grandmother's deep love.

| *Perrault* | *The Brothers Grimm* |
|---|---|
| The good woman made her a little red hood, which became her so well that everywhere she went by the name of Little Red Riding Hood.[7] | But it was her grandmother who loved her most. She could never give the child enough. One time she made her a present, a small, red velvet cap, and since it was so becoming and the maiden insisted on always wearing it, she was called Little Red Cap.[8] |

In the Grimm version, the mother's feeling of responsibility for the grandmother is far greater than in Perrault's version. Whereas in Perrault's, the girl is sent to the grandmother's house because the mother has baked flat cakes and because she has heard that the grandmother is sick, in the Grimm version the mother has precise knowledge of the grandmother's condition, and consequently sends the girl to help her. In the Grimm version family ties are much stronger than in Perrault's:

| *Perrault* | *The Brothers Grimm* |
|---|---|
| One day her mother, who had just made and baked some cakes, said to her: "Go and see how your grandmother is, for I have been told that she is ill. Take her a cake and this little pot of butter."[9] | One day her mother said to her, "Come, Little Red Cap, take this piece of cake and bottle of wine and bring them to your grandmother. She's sick and weak, and this will strengthen her.[1] |

7. Rouger, *Contes de Perrault*, 113.
8. Brüder Grimm, *Kinder- und Hausmärchen*, 156–157.
9. Rouger, *Contes de Perrault*, 113.
1. Brüder Grimm, *Kinder- und Hausmärchen*, 157.

The bond between the girl and her grandmother is also less haphazard in the Grimm version. In Perrault's version, the girl picks flowers for her own enjoyment alone, while in the Grimm version she picks them to bring as a gift to her grandmother:

| Perrault | The Brothers Grimm |
|---|---|
| . . . and the little girl continued on her way by the longer road. As she went she amused herself by gathering nuts, running after the butterflies, and making nosegays of the wild flowers which she found.[2] | Little Red Cap looked around and saw how the rays of the sun were dancing through the trees back and forth and how the woods were full of beautiful flowers. So she thought to herself, If I bring Grandmother a bunch of fresh flowers, she'd certainly like that.[3] |

Family ties and the great amount of attention paid to children—a phenomenon which was nonexistent in Perrault's time[4]—took on a central importance in the century following Perrault, and were apparently also among the reasons for the discrepancy between the texts in the presentation of family ties. Similarly, different assumptions regarding the rearing of children are discernible in the two versions.

In Perrault's day there was no educational system in the modern sense of the term, nor was the need for the systematic education of the child recognized. In the time of the Brothers Grimm, on the other hand, not only was an educational system already established, but it was seen as an essential condition for the normal development of the child, and as part of the adult's responsibility toward him. Views about children's education are expressed in the Grimm version first and foremost in the directions which the mother gives the little girl about how she should conduct herself at her grandmother's house, direction which are totally absent from the Perrault version. The mother instructs the girl to behave nicely: "And when you enter her room, don't forget to say good morning, and don't go peeping in all the corners."[5] She admonishes her not to turn off the path: "Get an early start, before it becomes hot, and when you're out in the woods, be nice and good and don't stray from the path, otherwise you'll fall and break the glass, and your grandmother will get nothing."[6]

The girl does not obey, and is therefore punished. However, she ultimately learns her lesson. What is even more important from an

---

2. Rouger, *Contes de Perrault*, 114.
3. Brüder Grimm, *Kinder- und Hausmärchen*, 158.
4. For a discussion of the development of the nuclear family, see Ariès, *Centuries of Childhood*, 339–407.
5. Brüder Grimm, *Kinder- und Hausmärchen*, 157.
6. Ibid.

educational standpoint is the alternative ending of the text, which furnishes proof that the lesson has indeed been learned: "Meanwhile, Little Red Cap thought to herself, Never again will you stray from the path by yourself and go into the forest when your mother has forbidden it."[7]

Although the notion that adults are duty-bound to guide their children and that they are responsible for the behavior of the latter did not yet exist in Perrault's time, it became the basis for the mother-daughter relationship in the Grimm version. Moreover, the school, an institution lacking in Perrault's day, became not just a recognized institution, but a hated one. In the version of the Grimm Brothers, when the wolf encounters Little Red Riding Hood in the woods, he says something that could not have appeared in Perrault's version: she looks as sad as if she were going to school: "You march along as if you were going straight to school."[8]

In the century following Perrault's lifetime, the concept of children's education took definite shape. This new concept, which struck deep roots in the educational system developed during the same period, lent a great deal of importance to children's reading material, thus creating an intellectual climate suitable for the composition of an official children's literature. * * *

\* \* \*

# JACK ZIPES

## Breaking the Disney Spell†

It was not once upon a time, but at a certain time in history, before anyone knew what was happening, that Walt Disney cast a spell on the fairy tale, and he has held it captive ever since. He did not use a magic wand or demonic powers. On the contrary, Disney employed the most up-to-date technological means and used his own "American" grit and ingenuity to appropriate European fairy tales. His technical skills and ideological proclivities were so consummate that his signature has [obscured] the names of Charles Perrault, the Brothers Grimm, Hans Christian Andersen, and Carlo Collodi. If children or adults think of the great classical fairy tales today, be it *Snow White*, *Sleeping Beauty*, or *Cinderella*, they will think Walt Disney. Their first and perhaps lasting impressions of these tales and others will have emanated from a

7. Ibid., 159.
8. Ibid., 157–158.
† From *From Mouse to Mermaid: The Politics of Film, Gender, and Culture*, ed. Elizabeth Bell, Lynda Haas, and Laura Sells (Bloomington: Indiana UP, 1995) 21–42. Reprinted by permission.

Disney film, book, or artifact. Though other filmmakers and animators produced remarkable fairy-tale films, Disney managed to gain a cultural stranglehold on the fairy tale, and this stranglehold has even tightened with the recent productions of *Beauty and the Beast* (1991) and *Aladdin* (1992). The man's spell over the fairy tale seems to live on even after his death.

But what does the Disney spell mean? Did Disney achieve a complete monopoly on the fairy tale during his lifetime? Did he imprint a particular *American* vision on the fairy tale through his animated films that dominates our perspective today? And, if he did manage to cast his mass-mediated spell on the fairy tale so that we see and read the classical tales through his lens, is that so terrible? Was Disney a nefarious wizard of some kind whose domination of the fairy tale should be lamented? Wasn't he just more inventive, more skillful, more in touch with the American spirit of the times than his competitors, who also sought to animate the classical fairy tale for the screen?

Of course, it would be a great exaggeration to maintain that Disney's spell totally divested the classical fairy tales of their meaning and invested them with his own. But it would not be an exaggeration to assert that Disney was a radical filmmaker who changed our way of viewing fairy tales, and that his revolutionary technical means capitalized on American innocence and utopianism to reinforce the social and political status quo. His radicalism was of the right and the righteous. The great "magic" of the Disney spell is that he animated the fairy tale only to transfix audiences and divert their potential utopian dreams and hopes through the false promises of the images he cast upon the screen. But before we come to a full understanding of this magical spell, we must try to understand what he did to the fairy tale that was so revolutionary and why he did it.

## The Oral and Literary Fairy Tales

The evolution of the fairy tale as a literary genre is marked by dialectical appropriation that set the cultural conditions for its institutionalization and its expansion as a mass-mediated form through radio, film, and television. Fairy tales were first *told* by gifted tellers and were based on rituals intended to endow with meaning the daily lives of members of a tribe. As *oral folk tales*, they were intended to explain natural occurrences such as the change of the seasons and shifts in the weather or to celebrate the rites of harvesting, hunting, marriage, and conquest. The emphasis in most folk tales was on communal harmony. A narrator or narrators told tales to bring members of a group or tribe closer together and to provide them with a sense of mission, a *telos*. The tales themselves assumed a generic quality based on the function that they were to fulfill for the community or the incidents that they were to report, describe, and explain. Consequently, there were tales of initiation, worship, warning, and indoctrination. Whatever the type may have been, the voice of the narrator was known. The tales came directly from common experiences and beliefs. Told in person, directly, face-to-face, they were altered as the beliefs and behaviors of the members of a particular group changed.

With the rise of literacy and the invention of the printing press in the fifteenth century, the oral tradition of storytelling underwent an immense revolution. The oral tales were taken over by a different social class, and the form, themes, production, and reception of the tales were transformed. This change did not happen overnight, but it did foster discrimination among writers and their audiences almost immediately so that distinct genres were recognized and approved for certain occasions and functions within polite society or cultivated circles of readers. In the case of folk tales, they were gradually categorized as legends, myths, fables, comical anecdotes, and, of course, fairy tales. What we today consider fairy tales were actually just one type of the folk-tale tradition, namely the *Zaubermärchen* or the magic tale, which has many sub-genres. The French writers of the late seventeenth century called these tales *contes de fées* (fairy tales) to distinguish them from other kinds of *contes populaires* (popular tales), and what really distinguished a *conte de fée*, based on the oral *Zaubermärchen*, was its transformation into a literary tale that addressed the concerns, tastes, and functions of court society. The fairy tale had to fit into the French salons, parlors, and courts of the aristocracy and bourgeoisie if it was to establish itself as a genre. The writers, Mme D'Aulnoy, Charles Perrault, Mlle L'Héritier, Mlle de La Force, etc., knew and expanded upon oral and literary tales. They were not the initiators of the literary fairy-tale tradition in Europe (cf. Zipes 1989). Two Italian writers, Giovanni Francesco Straparola and Giambattista Basile, had already set an example for what the French were accomplishing.[1] But the French writers created an institution, that is, the genre of the literary fairy tale was institutionalized as an aesthetic and social means through which questions and issues of *civilité*, proper behavior and demeanor in all types of situations, were mapped out as narrative strategies for literary socialization, and in many cases, as symbolic gestures of subversion to question the ruling standards of taste and behavior.

While the literary fairy tale was being institutionalized at the end of the seventeenth and beginning of the eighteenth century in France, the oral tradition did not disappear, nor was it subsumed by the

1. See Straparola's *Le piacevoli notti* (1550–53), translated as *The Facetious Nights* or *The Delectable Nights*, and Basile's *Lo Cunto de li Cunti* (*The Story of Stories*, 1634–36), better known as *The Pentamerone*. The reason that the Italians did not "institutionalize" the genre is that the literary culture in Italy was not prepared to introduce the tales as part of the civilizing process, nor were there groups of writers who made the fairy-tale genre part of their discourse.

new literary genre. Rather, the oral tradition continued to feed the writers with material and was now also influenced by the literary tradition itself. The early chapbooks (cheap books), known as the *Bibliothèque Bleue*, that were carried by peddlers or *colporteurs* to the villages throughout France contained numerous abbreviated and truncated versions of the literary tales, and these were in turn told once again in these communities. In some cases, the literary tales presented new material that was transformed through the oral tradition and returned later to literature by a writer who remembered hearing a particular story.

By the beginning of the nineteenth century when the Brothers Grimm set about to celebrate German culture through their country's folk tales, the literary fairy tale had long since been institutionalized, and they, along with Hans Christian Andersen, Carlo Collodi, Ludwig Bechstein, and a host of Victorian writers from George MacDonald to Oscar Wilde, assumed different ideological and aesthetic positions within this institutionalization. These writers put the finishing touches on the fairy-tale genre at a time when nation-states were assuming their modern form and cultivating particular types of literature as commensurate expressions of national cultures.

What were the major prescriptions, expectations, and standards of the literary fairy tale by the end of the nineteenth century? Here it is important first to make some general remarks about the "violent" shift from the oral to the literary tradition and not just talk about the appropriation of the magic folk tale as a dialectical process. Appropriation does not occur without violence to the rhetorical text created in the oral tales. * * * Such violation of oral storytelling was crucial and necessary for the establishment of the bourgeoisie because it concerned the control of desire and imagination within the symbolic order of western culture.

Unlike the oral tradition, the literary tale was written down to be read in private, although, in some cases, the fairy tales were read aloud in parlors. However, the book form enabled the reader to withdraw from his or her society and to be alone with a tale. This privatization violated the communal aspects of the folk tale, but the very printing of a fairy tale was already a violation since it was based on separation of social classes. Extremely few people could read, and the fairy tale in form and content furthered notions of elitism and separation. In fact, the French fairy tales heightened the aspect of the chosen aristocratic elite who were always placed at the center of the seventeenth- and eighteenth-century narratives. They were part and parcel of the class struggles in the discourses of that period. To a certain extent, the fairy tales were the outcome of violent "civilized" struggles, material representations, which represented struggles for hegemony. As Nancy Armstrong and Leonard Tennenhouse have suggested,

> a class of people cannot produce themselves as a ruling class with-
> out setting themselves off against certain Others. Their hegemony
> entails possession of the key cultural terms determining what are
> the right and wrong ways to be a human being.[2]

No matter where the literary tale took root and established itself—
France, Germany, England—it was written in a standard "high" language that the folk could not read, and it was written as a form of
entertainment and education for members of the ruling classes. Indeed,
only the well-to-do could purchase the books and read them. In short,
by institutionalizing the literary fairy tale, writers and publishers violated
the forms and concerns of non-literate, essentially peasant communities
and set new standards of taste, production, and reception through the
discourse of the fairy tale.

   The literary fairy tales tended to exclude the majority of people who
could not read, while the folk tales were open to everyone. Indeed, the
literary narratives were individualistic and unique in form and exalted
the power of those chosen to rule. In contrast, the oral tales had themes
and characters that were readily recognizable and reflected common
wish-fulfillments. Of course, one had to know the dialect in which they
were told. From a philological standpoint, the literary fairy tale elevated the oral tale through the standard practice of printing and setting
grammatical rules in "high French" or "high German." The process of
violation is *not* one of total negation and should not be studied as one-
dimensional, for the print culture enabled the tales to be preserved and
cultivated, and the texts created a new realm of pleasurable reading that
allowed for greater reflection on the part of the reader than could an
oral performance of a tale. At the beginning, the literary fairy tales were
written and published for adults, and though they were intended to
reinforce the mores and values of French *civilité*, they were so symbolic
and could be read on so many different levels that they were considered
somewhat dangerous: social behavior could not be totally dictated, prescribed, and controlled through the fairy tale, and there were subversive
features in language and theme. This is one of the reasons that fairy
tales were not particularly approved for children. In most European
countries it was not until the end of the eighteenth and early part of
the nineteenth century that fairy tales were published for children, and
even then begrudgingly, because their "vulgar" origins in the lower
classes were suspect. Of course, the fairy tales for children were sani-
tized and expurgated versions of the fairy tales for adults, or they were
new moralistic tales that were aimed at the domestication of the imagination, as Rüdiger Steinlein has demonstrated in his significant study.[3]

2. Nancy Armstrong and Leonard Tennenhouse, eds., *The Violence of Representation: Literature
   and the History of Violence* (New York: Routledge, 1989), 24.
3. Cf. *Die Domestizierte Phantasie: Studien zur Kinderliteratur, Kinderlektüre und Literaturpä-
   dagogik des 18. und frühen 19. Jahrhunderts* (Heidelberg: Carl Winter, 1987).

The form and structure of the fairy tale for children were carefully regulated in the nineteenth century so that improper thoughts and ideas would not be stimulated in the minds of the young. If one looks carefully at the major writers of fairy tales for children who became classical and popular in the nineteenth century,[4] it is clear that they themselves exercised self-censorship and restraint in conceiving and writing down tales for children.

This is not to argue that the literary fairy tale as institution became one in which the imagination was totally domesticated. On the contrary, by the end of the nineteenth century the genre served different functions. As a whole, it formed a multi-vocal network of discourses through which writers used familiar motifs, topoi, protagonists, and plots symbolically to comment on the civilizing process and socialization in their respective countries. These tales did not represent communal values but rather the values of a particular writer. Therefore, if the writer subscribed to the hegemonic value system of his or her society and respected the canonical ideology of Perrault, the Grimms, and Andersen, he/she would write a conventional tale with conservative values, whether for adults or children. On the other hand, many writers would parody, mock, question, and undermine the classical literary tradition and produce original and subversive tales that were part and parcel of the institution itself.

The so-called original and subversive tales have kept the dynamic quality of the dialectical appropriation alive, for there has always been a danger that the written word, in contrast to the spoken word, will fix a structure, image, metaphor, plot, and value as sacrosanct. For instance, for some people the Grimms' fairy tales are holy, or fairy tales are considered holy and not to be touched. How did this notion emanate?

To a certain extent it was engendered by the Grimms and other folklorists who believed that the fairy tales arose from the spirit of the folk. Yet, worship of the fairy tale as holy scripture is a petrification of the fairy tale that is connected to the establishment of correct speech, values, and power more than anything else. This establishment through the violation of the oral practices was the great revolution and transformation of the fairy tale.

By the end of the nineteenth century the literary fairy tale had the following crucial functions as institution in middle-class society:

(1) It introduced notions of elitism and separatism through a select canon of tales geared to children who knew how to read.

(2) Though it was also told, the fact that the fairy tale was printed

4. This list would include the Grimms, Wilhelm Hauff, Ludwig Bechstein, Hans Christian Andersen, and Madame De Ségur. In addition, numerous collections of expurgated folk tales from different countries became popular in primers by the end of the nineteenth century. Here one would have to mention the series of color fairy books edited by Andrew Lang in Great Britain.

and in a book with pictures gave it more legitimacy and enduring value than an oral tale that disappeared soon after it was told.

(3) It was often read by a parent in a nursery, school, or bedroom to soothe a child's anxieties, for the fairy tales for children were optimistic and were constructed with the closure of the happy end.

(4) Although the plots varied and the themes and characters were altered, the classical fairy tale for children and adults reinforced the patriarchal symbolic order based on rigid notions of sexuality and gender.

(5) In printed form the fairy tale was property and could be taken by its owner and read by its owner at his or her leisure for escape, consolation, or inspiration.

(6) Along with its closure and reinforcement of patriarchy, the fairy tale also served to encourage notions of rags to riches, pulling yourself up by your bootstraps, dreaming, miracles, etc.

(7) There was always tension between the literary and oral traditions. The oral tales have continued to threaten the more conventional and classical tales because they can question, dislodge, and deconstruct the written tales. Moreover, within the literary tradition itself, there were numerous writers such as Charles Dickens, George MacDonald, Lewis Carroll, Oscar Wilde, and Edith Nesbit who questioned the standardized model of what a fairy tale should be.

(8) It was through script by the end of the nineteenth century that there was a full-scale debate about what oral folk tales and literary fairy tales were and what their respective functions should be. By this time the fairy tale had expanded as a high art form (operas, ballets, dramas) and low art form (folk plays, vaudevilles, and parodies) as well as a form developed classically and experimentally for children and adults. The oral tales continued to be disseminated through communal gatherings of different kinds, but they were also broadcast by radio and gathered in books by folklorists. Most important in the late nineteenth century was the rise of folklore as an institution and of various schools of literary criticism that dealt with fairy tales and folk tales.

(9) Though many fairy-tale books and collections were illustrated (some lavishly) in the nineteenth century, the images were very much in conformity with the text. The illustrators were frequently anonymous and did not seem to count. Though the illustrations often enriched and deepened a tale, they were generally subservient to the text.

However, the domination of the word in the development of the fairy tale as genre was about to change. The next great revolution in the institutionalization of the genre was the film, for the images now imposed themselves on the text and formed their own text in violation of print but also with the help of the print culture. And here is where Walt Disney and other animators enter the scene.

## Disney's Magical Rise

By the turn of the twentieth century there had already been a number of talented illustrators, such as Gustave Doré, George Cruikshank, Walter Crane, Charles Folkard, and Arthur Rackham, who had demonstrated great ingenuity in their interpretations of fairy tales though their images. In addition, the broadside, broadsheet, or *image d'Epinal* had spread in Europe and America during the latter part of the nineteenth century as a forerunner of the comic book, and these sheets with printed images and texts anticipated the first animated cartoons that were produced at the beginning of the twentieth century. Actually, the French filmmaker Georges Méliès began experimenting as early as 1896 with types of fantasy and fairy-tale motifs in his *féeries* or trick films.[5] He produced versions of *Cinderella, Bluebeard,* and *Little Red Riding Hood* among others. However, since the cinema industry itself was still in its early phase of development, it was difficult for Méliès to bring about a major change in the technological and cinematic institutionalization of the genre. As Lewis Jacobs has remarked,

> this effort of Méliès illustrated rather than re-created the fairy tale. Yet, primitive though it was, the order of the scenes did form a coherent, logical, and progressive continuity. A new way of making moving pictures had been invented. Scenes could now be staged and selected specially for the camera, and the movie maker could control both the material and its arrangement.[6]

During the early part of the twentieth century Walter Booth, Anson Dyer, Lotte Reiniger, Walter Lantz and others all used fairy tale plots in different ways in trick films and cartoons, but none of the early animators ever matched the intensity with which Disney occupied himself with the fairy tale. In fact, it is noteworthy that Disney's very first endeavors in animation (not considering the advertising commercials he made) were the fairy-tale adaptations that he produced with Ub Iwerks in Kansas City in 1922–23: *The Four Musicians of Bremen, Little Red Riding Hood, Puss in Boots, Jack and the Beanstalk, Goldie Locks and the Three Bears,* and *Cinderella.*[7] To a certain degree, Disney identified so closely with the fairy tales he appropriated that it is no wonder his name virtually became synonymous with the genre of the fairy tale itself.

However, before discussing Disney's particular relationship to the fairy-tale tradition, it is important to consider the conditions of early

5. Lewis Jacobs, "George Méliès: Scenes," in *The Emergence of Film Art: The Evolution and Development of the Motion Picture as an Art, from 1900 to the Present,* 2d ed., ed. Lewis Jacob (New York: Norton, 1979).
6. Jacobs, "George Méliès," 13.
7. Cf. Russell Merrit and J. B. Kaufman, *Walt in Wonderland: The Silent Films of Walt Disney,* for the most complete coverage of Disney's early development.

animation in America and role of the animator in general, for all this has a bearing on Disney's productive relationship with the fairy tale. In his important study, *Before Mickey: The Animated Film 1898–1928*, Donald Crafton remarks that

> the early animated film was the location of a process found else-where in cinema but nowhere else in such intense concentration: self-figuration, the tendency of the filmmaker to interject himself into his film. This can take several forms, it can be direct or in-direct, and more or less camouflaged. . . . At first it was obvious and literal; at the end it was subtle and cloaked in metaphors and symbolic imagery designed to facilitate the process and yet to keep the idea gratifying for the artist and the audience. Part of the an-imation game consisted of developing mythologies that gave the animator some sort of special status. Usually these were very flat-tering, for he was pictured as (or implied to be) a demigod, a purveyor of life itself.[8]

As Crafton convincingly shows, the early animators before Disney literally drew themselves into the pictures and often appeared as char-acters in the films. One of the more interesting aspects of the early animated films is a psychically loaded tension between the artist and the characters he draws, one that is ripe for a Freudian or Lacanian reading, for the artist is always threatening to take away their "lives," while they, in turn, seek to deprive him of his pen (phallus) or creative inspiration so that they can control their own lives. (Almost all the early animators were men, and their pens and camera work assume a dis-tinctive phallic function in early animation.) The hand with pen or pencil is featured in many animated films in the process of creation, and it is then transformed in many films into the tail of a cat or dog. This tail then acts as the productive force or artist's instrument through-out the film. For instance, Disney in his Alice films often employed a cat named Julius, who would take off his tail and use it as stick, weapon, rope, hook, question mark, etc. It was the phallic means to induce action and conceive a way out of a predicament.

The celebration of the pen/phallus as ruler of the symbolic order of the film was in keeping with the way that animated films were actually produced in the studios during the 1920s. That is, most of the studios, largely located in New York, had begun to be run on the Taylor system by men who joined together under the supervision of the head of the studio to produce the cartoons. After making his first fairy-tale films in close cooperation with Ub Iwerks in Kansas City, Disney moved to Hollywood, where he developed the taylorized studio to the point of perfection. Under his direction, the films were carefully scripted to

8. Donald Crafton, *Before Mickey: The Animated Film 1898–1928* (Cambridge: MIT Press, 1982), 11.

project his story or vision of how a story should be related. The story-line was carried by hundreds of repetitious images created by the artists in his studios. Their contribution was in many respects like that of the dwarfs in *Snow White and the Seven Dwarfs:* they were to do the spade-work, while the glorified prince was to come along and carry away the prize.

It might be considered somewhat one-dimensional to examine all of Disney's films as self-figurations, or embodiments of the chief desig-ner's[9] wishes and beliefs. However, to understand Disney's importance as designer and director of fairy-tale films that set a particular pattern and model as the film industry developed, it does make sense to elab-orate on Crafton's notion of self-figuration, for it provides an important clue for grasping the further development of the fairy tale as animated film or film in general.

We have already seen that one of the results stemming from the shift from the oral to the literary in the institutionalization of the fairy tale was a loss of live contact with the storyteller and a sense of com-munity or commonality. This loss was a result of the social-industrial transformations at the end of the nineteenth century with the *Ge-meinschaft* (community-based society) giving way to the *Gesellschaft* (contract-based society). However, it was not a total loss, for industri-alization brought about greater comfort, sophistication, and literacy in addition to new kinds of communication in public institutions. There-fore, as I have demonstrated, the literary fairy tale's ascent corresponded to violent and progressive shifts in society and celebrated individualism, subjectivity, and reflection. It featured the narrative voice of the edu-cated author and publisher over communal voices and set new guide-lines for freedom of speech and expression. In addition, proprietary rights to a particular tale were established, and the literary tale became a commodity that paradoxically spoke out in the name of the unbridled imagination. Indeed, because it was born out of alienation, the literary fairy tale fostered a search for new "magical" means to overcome the instrumentalization of the imagination.

By 1900 literature began to be superseded by the mechanical means of reproduction that, Walter Benjamin declared, were revolutionary:

> the technique of reproduction detaches the reproduced object from the domain of tradition. By making many reproductions it substitutes a plurality of copies of a unique existence. And in per-mitting the reproduction to meet the beholder or listener in his own particular situation, it reactivates the object reproduced.

9. I am purposely using the word designer instead of animator because Disney was always de-signing things, made designs, and had designs. A designer is someone who indicates with a distinctive mark, and Disney put his mark on everything in his studios. A designing person is often a crafty person who manages to put his schemes into effect by hook or by crook. Once Disney stopped animating, he became a designer.

> These two processes lead to a tremendous shattering of tradition which is the obverse of the contemporary crisis and renewal of mankind. Both processes are intimately connected with the contemporary mass movements. Their most powerful agent is the film. Its social significance, particularly in its most positive form, is inconceivable without its destructive, cathartic aspect, that is, the liquidation of the traditional value of the cultural heritage.[1]

Benjamin analyzed how the revolutionary technological nature of the film could either bring about an aestheticization of politics leading to the violation of the masses through fascism, or a politicization of aesthetics that provides the necessary critical detachment for the masses to take charge of their own destiny.

In the case of the fairy-tale film at the beginning of the twentieth century, there are "revolutionary" aspects that we can note, and they prepared the way for progressive innovation that expanded the horizons of viewers and led to greater understanding of social conditions and culture. But there were also regressive uses of mechanical reproduction that brought about the cult of the personality and commodification of film narratives. For instance, the voice in fairy-tale films is at first effaced so that the image totally dominates the screen, and the words or narrative voice can only speak through the designs of the animator who, in the case of Walt Disney, has signed his name prominently on the screen. In fact, for a long time, Disney did not give credit to the artists and technicians who worked on his films. These images were intended both to smash the aura of heritage and to celebrate the ingenuity, inventiveness, and genius of the animator. In most of the early animated films, there were few original plots, and the story-lines did not count. Most important were the gags, or the technical inventions of the animators ranging from the introduction of live actors to interact with cartoon characters, to improving the movement of the characters so that they did not shimmer, to devising ludicrous and preposterous scenes for the sake of spectacle. It did not matter what story was projected just as long as the images astounded the audience, captured its imagination for a short period of time, and left the people laughing or staring in wonderment. The purpose of the early animated films was to make audiences awestruck and to celebrate the magical talents of the animator as demigod. As a result, the fairy tale as story was a vehicle for animators to express their artistic talents and develop their technology. The animators sought to impress audiences with their abilities to use pictures in such a way that they would forget the earlier fairy tales and remember the images that they, the new artists, were creating for them. Through these moving pictures, the animators appropriated lit-

1. Walter Benjamin, "The Work of Art in the Age of Mechanical Reproduction," in *Illuminations*, trans. Harry Zohn (New York: Harcourt, Brace, and World, 1968), 223.

erary and oral fairy tales to subsume the word, to have the final word, often through image and book, for Disney began publishing books during the 1930s to complement his films.

Of all the early animators, Disney was the one who truly revolutionalized the fairy tale as institution through the cinema. One could almost say that he was obsessed by the fairy-tale genre, or, put another way, Disney felt drawn to fairy tales because they reflected his own struggles in life. After all, Disney came from a relatively poor family, suffered from the exploitative and stern treatment of an unaffectionate father, was spurned by his early sweetheart, and became a success due to his tenacity, cunning, courage, and his ability to gather around him talented artists and managers like his brother Roy.

One of his early films, *Puss in Boots* (1922), is crucial for grasping his approach to the literary fairy tale and understanding how he used it as self-figuration that would mark the genre for years to come. Disney did not especially care whether one knew the original Perrault text of *Puss in Boots* or some other popular version. It is also unclear which text he actually knew. However, what is clear is that Disney sought to replace all versions with his animated version and that his cartoon is astonishingly autobiographical.

If we recall, Perrault wrote his tale in 1697 to reflect upon a cunning cat whose life is threatened and who manages to survive by using his brains to trick a king and an ogre. On a symbolic level, the cat represented Perrault's conception of the role of the *haute bourgeoisie* (his own class), who comprised the administrative class of Louis XIV's court and who were often the mediators between the peasantry and aristocracy. Of course, there are numerous ways to read Perrault's tale, but whatever approach one chooses, it is apparent that the major protagonist is the cat.

This is not the case in Disney's film. The hero is a young man, a commoner, who is in love with the king's daughter, and she fondly returns his affection. At the same time, the hero's black cat, a female, is having a romance with the royal white cat, who is the king's chauffeur. When the gigantic king discovers that the young man is wooing his daughter, he kicks him out of the palace, followed by Puss. At first, the hero does not want Puss's help, nor will he buy her the boots that she sees in a shop window. Then they go to the movies together and see a film with Rudolph Vaselino as a bullfighter, a reference to the famous Rudolph Valentino. This spurs the imagination of Puss. Consequently, she tells the hero that she now has an idea that will help him win the king's daughter, provided that he will buy her the boots. Of course, the hero will do anything to obtain the king's daughter, and he must disguise himself as a masked bullfighter. In the meantime Puss explains to him that she will use a hypnotic machine behind the scenes so he can defeat the bull and win the approval of the king. When the day of the bullfight arrives, the masked hero struggles but eventually manages to defeat the bull. The king is so overwhelmed by his performance that he offers his daughter's hand in marriage, but first he wants to know who the masked champion is. When the hero reveals himself, the king is enraged, but the hero grabs the princess and leads her to the king's chauffeur. The white cat jumps in front with Puss, and they speed off with the king vainly chasing after them.

Although Puss as cunning cat is crucial in this film, Disney focuses most of his attention on the young man who wants to succeed at all costs. In contrast to the traditional fairy tale, the hero is not a peasant, nor is he dumb. Read as a "parable" of Disney's life at that moment, the hero can be seen as young Disney wanting to break into the industry of animated films (the king) with the help of Ub Iwerks (Puss). The hero upsets the king and runs off with his prize possession, the virginal princess. Thus, the king is dispossessed, and the young man outraces him with the help of his friends.

But Disney's film is also an attack on the literary tradition of the fairy tale. He robs the literary tale of its voice and changes its form and meaning. Since the cinematic medium is a popular form of expression and accessible to the public at large, Disney actually returns the fairy tale to the majority of people. The images (scenes, frames, characters, gestures, jokes) are readily comprehensible by young and old alike from different social classes. In fact, the fairy tale is practically infantilized, just as the jokes are infantile. The plot records the deepest oedipal desire of every young boy: the son humiliates and undermines the father and runs off with his most valued object of love, the daughter/wife. By simplifying this oedipal complex semiotically in black-and-white drawings and making fun of it so that it had a common appeal, Disney also touched on other themes:

(1) Democracy—the film is very *American* in its attitude toward royalty. The monarchy is debunked, and a commoner causes a kind of revolution.

(2) Technology—it is through the new technological medium of the movies that Puss's mind is stimulated. Then she uses a hypnotic machine to defeat the bull and another fairly new invention, the automobile, to escape the king.

(3) Modernity—the setting is obviously the twentieth century, and the modern minds are replacing the ancient. The revolution takes place as the king is outpaced and will be replaced by a commoner who knows how to use the latest inventions.

But who is this commoner? Was Disney making a statement on behalf of the masses? Was Disney celebrating "everyone" or "every man"? Did Disney believe in revolution and socialism? The answer to all these questions is simple: no.

## *Casting the Commodity Spell with* Snow White

Disney's hero is the enterprising young man, the entrepreneur, who uses technology to his advantage. He does nothing to help the people or the community. In fact, he deceives the masses and the king by creating the illusion that he is stronger than the bull. He has learned, with the help of Puss, that one can achieve glory through deception. It is through the artful use of images that one can sway audiences and gain their favor. Animation is trickery—trick films—for still images are made to seem as if they move through automatization. As long as one controls the images (and machines) one can reign supreme, just as the hero is safe as long as he is disguised. The pictures conceal the controls and machinery. They deprive the audience of viewing the production and manipulation, and in the end, audiences can no longer envision a fairy tale for themselves as they can when they read it. The pictures now deprive the audience of visualizing their own characters, roles, and desires. At the same time, Disney offsets the deprivation with the pleasure of scopophilia[2] and inundates the viewer with delightful images, humorous figures, and erotic signs. In general, the animator, Disney, projects the enjoyable fairy tale of his life through his own images, and he realizes through animated stills his basic oedipal dream that he was to play out time and again in most of his fairy-tale films. It is the repetition of Disney's infantile quest—the core of American mythology—that enabled him to strike a chord in American viewers from the 1920s to the present.

However, it was not through *Puss in Boots* and his other early animated fairy tales that he was to captivate audiences and set the "classical" modern model for animated fairy-tale films. They were just the beginning. Rather, it was in *Snow White and the Seven Dwarfs* (1937) that Disney fully appropriated the literary fairy tale and made his signature into a trademark for the most acceptable type of fairy tale in the twentieth century. But before the making of *Snow White*, there were developments in his life and in the film industry that are important to mention in order to grasp why and how *Snow White* became the first definitive animated fairy-tale film—definitive in the sense that it was to define the way other animated films in the genre of the fairy tale were to be made.

After Disney had made several Laugh-O-Gram fairy-tale films, all ironic and modern interpretations of the classical versions, he moved to Hollywood in 1923 and was successful in producing fifty-six *Alice* films, which involved a young girl in different adventures with cartoon characters. By 1927 these films were no longer popular, so Disney and Iwerks soon developed Oswald the Lucky Rabbit cartoons that also

---

2. The gaining of sexual pleasure by looking at erotic images [*Editor*].

found favor with audiences. However, in February of 1928, while Disney was in New York trying to renegotiate a contract with his distributor Charles Mintz, he learned that Mintz, who owned the copyright to Oswald, had lured some of Disney's best animators to work for another studio. Disney faced bankruptcy because he refused to capitulate to the exploitative conditions that Mintz set for the distribution and production of Disney's films.[3] This experience sobered Disney in his attitude to the cutthroat competition in the film industry, and when he returned to Hollywood, he vowed to maintain complete control over all his productions—a vow that he never broke.

In the meantime, Disney and Iwerks had to devise another character for their company if they were to survive, and they conceived the idea for films featuring a pert mouse named Mickey. By September of 1928, after making two Mickey Mouse shorts, Disney, similar to his masked champion in *Puss in Boots*, had devised a way to gain revenge on Mintz and other animation studios by producing the first animated cartoon with sound, *Steamboat Willie*, starring Mickey Mouse. From this point on, Disney became known for introducing new inventions and improving animation so that animated films became almost as realistic as films with live actors and natural settings. His next step after sound was color, and in 1932 he signed an exclusive contract with Technicolor and began producing his *Silly Symphony* cartoons in color. More important, Disney released *The Three Little Pigs* in 1933 and followed it with *The Big Bad Wolf* (1934) and *The Three Little Wolves* (1936), all of which involved fairy-tale characters and stories that touched on the lives of people during the Depression. As Bob Thomas has remarked, "*The Three Little Pigs* was acclaimed by the Nation. The wolf was on many American doorsteps, and 'Who's Afraid of the Big Bad Wolf?' became a rallying cry."[4] Not only were wolves on the doorsteps of Americans but also witches, and to a certain extent, Disney, with the help of his brother Roy and Iwerks, had been keeping "evil" connivers and competitors from the entrance to the Disney Studios throughout the 1920s. Therefore, it is not by chance that Disney's next major experiment would involve a banished princess, loved by a charming prince, who would triumph over deceit and regain the rights to her castle. *Snow White and the Seven Dwarfs* was to bring together all the personal strands of Disney's own story with the destinies of desperate Americans who sought hope and solidarity in their fight for survival during the Depression of the 1930s.

Of course, by 1934 Disney was, comparatively speaking, wealthy. He hired Don Graham, a professional artist, to train studio animators at the Disney Art School, founded in November 1932. He then embarked

3. Leonard Mosley, *Disney's World* (New York: Stein and Day, 1985), 85–140.
4. Bob Thomas, *Disney's Art of Animation: From Mickey Mouse to Beauty and the Beast* (New York: Hyperion, 1991), 49.

on ventures to stun moviegoers with his ingenuity and talents as organizer, storyteller, and filmmaker. Conceived some time in 1934, *Snow White* was to take three years to complete, and Disney did not leave one stone unturned in his preparations for the first full-length animated fairy-tale film ever made. Disney knew he was making history even before history had been made.

During the course of the next three years, Disney worked closely with all the animators and technicians assigned to the production of *Snow White*. By now, Disney had divided his studio into numerous departments, such as animation, layout, sound, music, storytelling, etc., and had placed certain animators in charge of developing the individual characters of Snow White, the prince, the dwarfs, and the queen/crone. Disney spent thousands of dollars on a multiplane camera to capture the live-action depictions that he desired, the depth of the scenes, and close-ups. In addition, he had his researchers experiment with colored gels, blurred focus, and filming through frosted glass, while he employed the latest inventions in sound and music to improve the synchronization with the characters on the screen. Throughout the entire production of this film, Disney had to be consulted and give his approval for each stage of development. After all, *Snow White* was his story that he had taken from the Grimm Brothers and changed completely to suit his tastes and beliefs. He cast a spell over this German tale and transformed it into something peculiarly American. Just what were the changes he induced?

(1) Snow White is an orphan. Neither her father nor her mother are alive, and she is at first depicted as a kind of "Cinderella," cleaning the castle as a maid in a patched dress. In the Grimms' version there is the sentimental death of her mother. Her father remains alive, and she is never forced to do the work of commoners such as wash the steps of the castle.

(2) The prince appears at the very beginning of the film on a white horse and sings a song of love and devotion to Snow White. He plays a negligible role in the Grimms' version.

(3) The queen is not only jealous that Snow White is more beautiful than she is, but she also sees the prince singing to Snow White and is envious because her stepdaughter has such a handsome suitor.

(4) Though the forest and the animals do not speak, they are anthropomorphized. In particular the animals befriend Snow White and become her protectors.

(5) The dwarfs are hardworking and rich miners. They all have names—Doc, Sleepy, Bashful, Happy, Sneezy, Grumpy, Dopey—representative of certain human characteristics and are fleshed out so that they become the star attractions of the film. Their actions are what counts in defeating evil. In the Grimms' tale, the dwarfs are anonymous and play a humble role.

(6) The queen only comes one time instead of three as in the Grimms' version, and she is killed while trying to destroy the dwarfs by rolling a huge stone down a mountain to crush them. The punishment in the Grimms' tale is more horrifying because she must dance in red-hot iron shoes at Snow White's wedding.

(7) Snow White does not return to life when a dwarf stumbles while carrying the glass coffin as in the Grimms' tale. She returns to life when the prince, who has searched far and wide for her, arrives and bestows a kiss on her lips. His kiss of love is the only antidote to the queen's poison.

At first glance, it would seem that the changes that Disney made were not momentous. If we recall Sandra Gilbert and Susan Gubar's stimulating analysis in their book, *The Madwoman in the Attic* (1979), the film follows the classic "sexist" narrative about the framing of women's lives through a male discourse. Such male framing drives women to frustration and some women to the point of madness. It also pits women against women in competition for male approval (the mirror) of their beauty that is short-lived. No matter what they may do, women cannot chart their own lives without male manipulation and intervention, and in the Disney film, the prince plays even more of a framing role since he is introduced at the beginning while Snow White is singing, "I'm Wishing for the One I Love To Find Me Today." He will also appear at the end as the fulfillment of her dreams.

There is no doubt that Disney retained key ideological features of the Grimms' fairy tale that reinforce nineteenth-century patriarchal notions that Disney shared with the Grimms. In some way, they can even be considered his ancestor, for he preserves and carries on many of their benevolent attitudes toward women. For instance, in the Grimms' tale, when Snow White arrives at the cabin, she pleads with the dwarfs to allow her to remain and promises that she will wash the dishes, mend their clothes, and clean the house. In Disney's film, she arrives and notices that the house is dirty. So, she convinces the animals to help her make the cottage tidy so that the dwarfs will perhaps let her stay there. Of course, the house for the Grimms and Disney was the place where good girls remained, and one shared aspect of the fairy tale and the film is about the domestication of women.

However, Disney went much further than the Grimms to make his film more memorable than the tale, for he does not celebrate the domestication of women so much as the triumph of the banished and the underdogs. That is, he celebrates his destiny, and insofar as he had shared marginal status with many Americans, he also celebrates an American myth of Horatio Alger: it is a male myth about perseverance, hard work, dedication, loyalty, and justice.

It may seem strange to argue that Disney perpetuated a male myth through his fairy-tale films when, with the exception of *Pinocchio*

(1940), they all featured young women as "heroines": *Sleeping Beauty* (1959), *Cinderella* (1950), and *The Little Mermaid* (1989). However, despite their beauty and charm, these figures are pale and pathetic compared to the more active and demonic characters in the film. The witches are not only agents of evil but represent erotic and subversive forces that are more appealing both for the artists who drew them and the audiences.[5] The young women are helpless ornaments in need of protection, and when it comes to the action of the film, they are omitted. In *Snow White and the Seven Dwarfs*, the film does not really become lively until the dwarfs enter the narrative. They are the mysterious characters who inhabit a cottage, and it is through their hard work and solidarity that they are able to maintain a world of justice and restore harmony to the world. The dwarfs can be interpreted as the humble American workers, who pull together during a depression. They keep their spirits up by singing a song "Hi ho, it's home from work we go," or "Hi ho, it's off to work we go," and their determination is the determination of every worker, who will succeed just as long as he does his share while women stay at home and keep the house clean. Of course, it is also possible to see the workers as Disney's own employees, on whom he depended for the glorious outcome of his films. In this regard, the prince can be interpreted as Disney, who directed the love story from the beginning. If we recall, it is the prince who frames the narrative. He announces his great love at the beginning of the film, and Snow White cannot be fulfilled until he arrives to kiss her. During the major action of the film, he, like Disney, is lurking in the background and waiting for the proper time to make himself known. When he does arrive, he takes all the credit as champion of the disenfranchised, and he takes Snow White to his castle while the dwarfs are left as keepers of the forest.

But what has the prince actually done to deserve all the credit? What did Disney actually do to have his name flash on top of the title as "Walt Disney's Snow White and the Seven Dwarfs" in big letters and later credit his coworkers in small letters? As we know, Disney never liked to give credit to the animators who worked with him, and they had to fight for acknowledgment.[6] Disney always made it clear that he was the boss and owned total rights to his products. He had struggled for his independence against his greedy and unjust father and against fierce and ruthless competitors in the film industry. As producer of the

---

5. Solomon cites the famous quotation by Woody Allen in *Annie Hall*: "You know, even as a kid I always went for the wrong women. When my mother took me to see 'Snow White,' everyone fell in love with Snow White; I immediately fell for the Wicked Queen" [Charles Solomon, "Bad Girls Finish First in Memory of Disney Fans," *Milwaukee Journal* 17 August 1980, 28].

6. Bill Peet, for example, an "in-betweener" in the early Disney studio, worked for a year and a half on *Pinocchio* (1940). Peet relates that, after watching the film in his neighborhood theatre, "I was dumbfounded when the long list of screen credits didn't include my name" (*Bill Peet: An Autobiography* [Boston: Houghton Mifflin, 1989] 108).

fairy-tale films and major owner of the Disney studios, he wanted to figure in the films and sought, as Crafton has noted, to create a more indelible means of self-figuration. In *Snow White*, he accomplished this by stamping his signature as owner on the title frame of the film and then by having himself embodied in the figure of the prince. It is the prince Disney who made inanimate figures come to life through his animated films, and it is the prince who is to be glorified in *Snow White and the Seven Dwarfs* when he resuscitates Snow White with a magic kiss. Afterward he holds Snow White in his arms, and in the final frame, he leads her off on a white horse to his golden castle on a hill. His golden castle—every woman's dream—supersedes the dark, sinister castle of the queen. The prince becomes Snow White's reward, and his power and wealth are glorified in the end.

There are obviously mixed messages or multiple messages in *Snow White and the Seven Dwarfs*, but the overriding sign, in my estimation, is the signature of Disney's self-glorification in the name of justice. Disney wants the world *cleaned up*, and the pastel colors with their sharply drawn ink lines create images of cleanliness, just as each sequence reflects a clearly conceived and preordained destiny for all the characters in the film. For Disney, the Grimms' tale is not a vehicle to explore the deeper implications of the narrative and its history.[7] Rather, it is a vehicle to display what he can do as an animator with the latest technological and artistic developments in the industry. The story is secondary, and if there is a major change in the plot, it centers on the power of the prince, the only one who can save Snow White, and he becomes the focal point by the end of the story.

7.  Karen Merritt makes the interesting point that "Disney's *Snow White* is an adaptation of a 1912 children's play (Disney saw it as a silent movie during his adolescence) still much performed today, written by a male Broadway producer under a female pseudonym; this play was an adaptation of a play for immigrant children from the tenements of lower East Side New York; and that play, in turn, was a translation and adaptation of a German play for children by a prolific writer of children's comedies and fairy-tale drama. Behind these plays was the popularity of nineteenth- and early twentieth-century fairy-tale pantomimes at Christmas in England and fairy-tale plays in Germany and America. The imposition of childish behavior on the dwarfs, Snow White's resulting mothering, the age ambiguities in both Snow White and the dwarfs, the 'Cinderella' elements, and the suppression of any form of sexuality were transmitted by that theatrical tradition, which embodied a thoroughly developed philosophy of moral education in representations for children. . . . By reading Disney's *Snow White* by the light of overt didacticism of his sources, he no longer appears the moral reactionary disdained by contemporary critics. Rather, he is the entertainer who elevates the subtext of play found in his sources and dares once again to frighten children" [Karen Merritt, "The Little Girl/Little Mother Transformation: The American Evolution of 'Snow White and the Seven Dwarfs,'" in *Storytelling in Animation: The Art of the Animated Image*, ed. John Canemaker (Los Angeles: American Film Institute, 1994), 106]. Though it may be true that Disney was more influenced by an American theatrical and film tradition, the source of all these productions, one acknowledged by Disney, was the Grimms' tale. And, as I have argued, Disney was not particularly interested in experimenting with the narrative to shock children or provide a new perspective on the traditional story. For all intents and purposes his film reinforces the didactic messages of the Grimms' tale, and it is only in the technical innovations and designs that he did something startlingly new. It is not the object of critique to "disdain" or "condemn" Disney for reappropriating the Grimms' tradition to glorify the great designer, but to understand those cultural and psychological forces that led him to map out his narrative strategies in fairy-tale animation.

In Disney's early work with fairy tales in Kansas City, he had a wry and irreverent attitude toward the classical narratives. There was a strong suggestion, given the manner in which he and Iwerks rewrote and filmed the tales, that they were "revolutionaries," the new boys on the block, who were about to introduce innovative methods of animation into the film industry and speak for the outcasts. However, in 1934, Disney was already the kingpin of animation, and he used all that he had learned to reinforce his power and command of fairy-tale animation. The manner in which he copied the musical plays and films of his time, and his close adaptation of fairy tales with patriarchal codes, indicate that all the technical experiments would not be used to foster social change in America but to keep power in the hands of individuals like himself, who felt empowered to design and create new worlds. As Richard Schickel has perceptively remarked, Disney

> could make something his own, all right, but that process nearly always robbed the work at hand of its uniqueness, of its soul, if you will. In its place he put jokes and songs and fright effects, but he always seemed to diminish what he touched. He came always as a conqueror, never as a servant. It is a trait, as many have observed, that many Americans share when they venture into foreign lands hoping to do good but equipped only with knowhow instead of sympathy and respect for alien traditions.[8]

Disney always wanted to do something new and unique just as long as he had absolute control. He also knew that novelty would depend on the collective skills of his employees, whom he had to keep happy or indebted to him in some way. Therefore, from 1934 onward, about the time that he conceived his first feature-length fairy-tale film, Disney became the orchestrator of a corporate network that changed the function of the fairy-tale genre in America. The power of Disney's fairy-tale films does not reside in the uniqueness or novelty of the productions, but in Disney's great talent for holding antiquated views of society *still* through animation and his use of the latest technological developments in cinema to his advantage. His adaptation of the literary fairy tale for the screen led to the following changes in the institution of the genre:

(1) Technique takes precedence over the story, and the story is used to celebrate the technician and his means.

(2) The carefully arranged images narrate through seduction and imposition of the animator's hand and the camera.

(3) The images and sequences engender a sense of wholeness, seamless totality, and harmony that is orchestrated by a savior/technician on and off the screen.

(4) Though the characters are fleshed out to become more realistic, they are also one-dimensional and are to serve functions in the film.

8. Richard Schickel, *The Disney Version* (New York: Simon and Schuster, 1968), 227.

There is no character development because the characters are stereotypes, arranged according to a credo of domestication of the imagination.

(5) The domestication is related to colonization insofar as the ideas and types are portrayed as models of behavior to be emulated. Exported through the screen as models, the "American" fairy tale colonizes other national audiences. What is good for Disney is good for the world, and what is good in a Disney fairy tale is good in the rest of the world.

(6) The thematic emphasis on cleanliness, control, and organized industry reinforces the technics of the film itself: the clean frames with attention paid to every detail; the precise drawing and manipulation of the characters as real people; the careful plotting of the events that focus on salvation through the male hero.

(7) Private reading pleasure is replaced by pleasurable viewing in an impersonal cinema. Here one is brought together with other viewers not for the development of community but to be diverted in the French sense of *divertissement* and American sense of diversion.

(8) The diversion of the Disney fairy tale is geared toward nonreflective viewing. Everything is on the surface, one-dimensional, and we are to delight in one-dimensional portrayal and thinking, for it is adorable, easy, and comforting in its simplicity.

Once Disney realized how successful he was with his formula for feature-length fairy tales, he never abandoned it, and in fact, if one regards the two most recent Disney Studio productions of *Beauty and the Beast* (1991) and *Aladdin* (1992), Disney's contemporary animators have continued in his footsteps. There is nothing but the "eternal return of the same" in *Beauty and the Beast* and *Aladdin* that makes for enjoyable viewing and delight in techniques of these films as commodities, but nothing new in the exploration of narration, animation, and signification.

There is something sad in the manner in which Disney "violated" the literary genre of the fairy tale and packaged his versions in his name through the merchandising of books, toys, clothing, and records. Instead of using technology to enhance the communal aspects of narrative and bring about major changes in viewing stories to stir and animate viewers, he employed animators and technology to stop thinking about change, to return to his films, and to long nostalgically for neatly ordered patriarchal realms. Fortunately, the animation of the literary fairy tale did not stop with Disney, but that is another tale to tell, a tale about breaking Disney's magic spell.

# DONALD HAASE

## Yours, Mine, or Ours? Perrault, the Brothers Grimm, and the Ownership of Fairy Tales†

\*    \*    \*

### The Revered Place of Folklore

In 1944 W. H. Auden decreed that Grimm's fairy tales are "among the few indispensable, common-property books upon which Western culture can be founded . . . [I]t is hardly too much to say that these tales rank next to the Bible in importance."[1]

Auden was in one sense right. Like the Bible, fairy tales—especially the classic tales of Charles Perrault and the Brothers Grimm—hold a revered if not sacred place in modern Western culture. Often thought to reach back like sacred works to "times past," to some ancient, pristine age in which their original tellers spoke mythic words of revelation, folk tales and fairy tales are endowed by many readers with unassailable moral and even spiritual authenticity.

Because such tales had their genesis in an oral tradition, we are tempted to imagine their original tellers as simple folk endowed with infallible wisdom and, in some cases, divine inspiration. As a consequence of that belief, tampering with the classic texts of Perrault or the Brothers Grimm is considered by some to be tantamount to sacrilege, similar to revising the text of the Holy Scriptures. As one of my undergraduate students remarked in a journal he kept while studying fairy tales in the winter term of 1990: "I am not a deeply religious person. However, I have a vague feeling that questioning the origin of fairy tales is somehow sacrilegious." Some traditionalists even go so far as to argue that the common practice of replacing *Sneewittchen*, the Grimms' original German spelling of Snow White, with the more modern orthographical form *Schneewittchen* constitutes "monument desecration."[2]

When classic stories are changed unacceptably, the blame is often placed on the culture industry—publishers, advertisers, merchandisers, and even pedagogues who have capitalized on the mass appeal of the traditional tales and emptied them of their original vigor and truth.

---

† From Donald Haase, "Yours, Mine, or Ours? Perrault, the Brothers Grimm and the Ownership of Fairy Tales," *Once Upon a Folklore: Capturing the Folklore Process with Children*, ed. Gloria T. Blatt (New York: Teachers College, Columbia Univ., 1993) 63–75. Copyright © 1993. Reprinted by permission of Teachers College, Columbia University.

1. W. H. Auden, "In Praise of the Brothers Grimm," *The New York Times Book Review* (12 Nov. 1944): 1, 28.

2. Hermann Bausinger, "Anmerkungen zu Schneewittchen," in *Und wenn sie nicht gestorben sind: Perspektiven auf das Märchen*, ed. H. Brackert (Frankfurt a.M.: Suhrkamp, 1980), 46.

Disney's Americanized and romanticized fairy-tale movies, for example, have been severely criticized for trivializing and betraying the original themes, thus enfeebling an important cultural possession.[3] As the civilized entrepreneur and creator of the fairy tale as consumer romance,[4] Disney is the absolute antithesis of the mythic peasant or Ice Age storyteller, from whom we have supposedly inherited this allegedly sacred possession.

While this religious or quasi-religious reverence is certainly appealing and even reassuring, it is dangerously misleading. As an antidote to it, consider two of the twenty-four theses offered by the German writer Wolfdietrich Schnurre in a piece he aptly entitled "Heretical Thoughts on the Treasury of Fairy Tales." In a sardonic letter to the long deceased Brothers Grimm, Schnurre seeks to explain why he thinks fairy tales have lost their value for us. "The primary guilt for the decline of the fairy tale," he claims, "rests with those who [originally] made them. They forgot to impress on them the stamp of copyright."[5] In this case, not the culture industry, but the folk themselves are held responsible for the fairy tale's bankruptcy. Ironically, the fairy tale's status as communal property is proposed as the very cause of its neglect and demise. It is a fairy tale, Schnurre asserts, to believe "that fairy tales are the property of the *Volk*—the people. Property is cared for. The *Volk*," he asserts, "has ruined fairy tales."[6]

These statements are heretical to established views that tell us not only why folktales are still relevant but to whom they belong. However we might feel about the tales of the Brothers Grimm or Perrault, Schnurre's provocative assertions raise intriguing questions about the reception and cultural ownership of fairy tales. Who are the folk, that anonymous group we often view as the originators and owners of the fairy tale? And if the tales do not belong to the folk, then to whom do they belong? And, finally, why does the issue of ownership matter at all?

## The Nationalistic View of Folklore

The concept of "the folk" is a slippery one. To some, the folk are an ethnic or national group sharing common traditions, lore, and social or cultural traits. In general parlance, "the folk" are the common folk, that is, the working or peasant classes. But as the Italian folklorist Giuseppe Cocchiara has suggested, the identity of the folk transcends classes and "is the expression of a certain vision of life, certain attitudes

3. Bruno Bettelheim, *The Uses of Enchantment: The Meaning and Importance of Fairy Tales* (New York: Knopf, 1976), 210.
4. Donald Haase, "Gold into Straw: Fairy Tale Movies for Children and the Culture Industry," *The Lion and the Unicorn* 12 (1988): 193–207.
5. Wolfdietrich Schnurre, "Ketzerisches zum Märchenschatz: 24 kurzweilige Thesen," in *Grimmige Märchen: Prosatexte von Ilse Aichinger bis Martin Walser* (Frankfurt: Fischer, 1986), 23.
6. Schnurre, "Ketzerisches," 23.

of the spirit, of thought, of culture, of custom, of civilization, which appear with their own clearly delineated characteristics."[7] While Cocchiara's definition avoids the class bias of earlier definitions, Alan Dundes excises the ethnic and national emphasis by defining the folk as "*any group of people whatsoever* who share at least one common factor."[8]

However, for the Grimms and many early folklorists, it was the so-called common people who best embodied a nation's folk life. It was their lore—including their folktales—that was to become the reservoir and model of national character. As the product of the German folk, the tales were thought to contain the scattered fragments of ancient Germanic myth, which—when collected—would provide the German people with a magic mirror in which they could discern and thus reassert their national identity. In this way, the Grimms' collection of folktales was conscripted into nationalistic service and became a political weapon in the Grimms' intellectual resistance to the Napoleonic occupation of their beloved Hessian homeland.

To define the folk in nationalistic terms establishes fairy tales as national property. They are either yours, or they are mine. Following—and, it must be emphasized, grossly exaggerating—the Grimms' nationalistic understanding of fairy tales, many Germans were only too ready to exercise their right of ownership by advocating the Grimms' tales as a national primer, after 1871, for the newly unified nation. In 1899, for instance, Carl Franke gave this explanation of the close link between the Grimms' tales and the education of a nation:

> To the spirit of German schoolchildren the tales have become what mother's milk is for their bodies—the first nourishment for the spirit and the imagination. How German [are] Snow White, Little Briar Rose, Little Red Cap, the seven dwarfs! Through such genuine German diet must the language and spirit of the child gradually become more and more German. . . .[9]

Given the Grimms' precedent and given the need of every new state to authenticate its self-image, we can understand such remarks; just as we can understand the lamentable exploitation of the Grimms' tales under National Socialism, which points up all too clearly the dangers inherent in viewing fairy tales as the property of a single group or nation. * * *

But there is another, hidden danger in this nationalistic view. Ironically, the abuse of the Grimms' tales by the culture industry of National Socialism has reinforced prejudice against the Grimms' tales. So

---

7. Giuseppi Cocchiara, *The History of Folklore in Europe*, trans. J. N. McDaniel (Philadelphia: Institute for the Study of Human Issues, 1981), 4.
8. Alan Dundes, *The Study of Folklore* (Englewood Cliffs, N.J.: Prentice Hall, 1965), 2.
9. L. L. Snyder, "Cultural Nationalism: The Grimm Brothers' Fairy Tales," in *Roots of German Nationalism* (Bloomington: Indiana UP, 1978), 51.

...ling was the German identification of Germanic folktales with
...nal identity that the Grimms' stories have very often been accepted
... belonging uniquely to the Germans. But instead of identifying fa-
vorable cultural traits in the tales, some readers have discerned more
ambiguous characteristics. In 1939, Vincent Brun accused the Germans of perverting the fairy tale by exploiting its rude primitive instincts
to educate and not to amuse children. By the end of World War II,
the German fairy tale had fallen into such disrepute that during the
Allied occupation of Germany fairy tales were viewed with serious sus-
picion and banned from the public school curriculum. Evidently, Auden's reclamation of the Grimms' tales as common property in 1944
was not universally accepted; in 1947 T. J. Leonard let loose with his
infamous attack on German fairy tales, which he unequivocally condemned as relics of Germanic barbarism, and blamed for promoting
German nationalism and sadistic behavior among Germans. The reverberations of such attacks on Germanic folktales and German national character can still be felt. In 1985, Siegfried Heyer published an
abridged German translation of Leonard's attack, and Jörg Becker, in
response, reflected on the enduring image of the "ugly German." That
the alleged connection between German national character and fairy
tales should occupy scholars forty years after the war is not surprising
given that Germans, as well as their former adversaries, have kept this
essentially postwar issue alive.

In 1978, Louis Snyder repeated the thesis he first put forth in the
1950s that the Grimms' tales, having played a role in the development
of modern German nationalism, emphasize "such social characteristics
as respect for order, belief in the desirability of obedience, subservience
to authority, respect for the leader and the hero, veneration of courage
and the military spirit, acceptance without protest of cruelty, violence,
and atrocity, fear of and hatred for the outsider, and virulent anti-
Semitism."[1] Readers like Snyder clearly relinquish title to the tales and
deed them back to their owners. The nationalism implicit in the message is clear: these tales are yours (German), not mine (American).

Differentiating between tales belonging to different countries, and
thus differentiating between the countries themselves, has become standard practice. In his study of the French folktale during the Old Regime, the historian Robert Darnton has insisted on the unique
characteristics of the French folktale that distinguish it from its German
counterpart. Darnton summarizes the differences in this way:

> Where the French tales tend to be realistic, earthy, bawdy, and
> comical, the German [tales] veer off toward the supernatural, the
> poetic, the exotic, and the violent. Of course, cultural differences

1. Snyder, "Cultural Nationalism," 51.

cannot be reduced to a formula—French craftiness versus German cruelty—but the comparisons make it possible to identify the peculiar inflection that the French gave to their stories, and their way of telling stories provides clues about their way of viewing the world.[2]

Although Darnton tries to avoid stereotyping national character by adding a disclaimer and by referring instead to differing world views, in the final analysis his implicit notion of fairy tales as culturally defined property makes this difficult. However, he is at least aware of the danger of idealizing the national ethos. In pointing to the similarity between the tales of French peasants and those of Perrault, Darnton says that both groups of "tales communicated traits, values, attitudes, and a way of construing the world that was peculiarly French. To insist upon their Frenchness," he notes, "is not to fall into romantic rhapsodizing about national spirit, but rather to recognize the existence of distinct cultural styles, which set off the French . . . from other peoples identified at the time as German, Italian, and English."[3] Perhaps it is easy for Darnton to avoid rhapsodizing because he is not French. That is, the tales he discusses are "theirs," not his.

Although the French are not immune to praising the unique nature of their national fairy tales, they seem to be less dependent on the tales for the codification of their self-image than are the Germans. France lacked—indeed, did not need—strong nationalistic voices such as those of the Brothers Grimm, who set the German precedent for folktale worship. Moreover, because the French enjoyed a strong literary heritage, they were perhaps more likely to find models of the national ethos in their classical canon than in popular folk literature. After all, unlike the Grimms' tales, Perrault's stories are usually considered not so much examples of the folk culture as part of the elevated literary tradition of the Old Regime. Although Robert Darnton might find the French popular tale characterized by the earthy and bawdy, Paul Hazard praises Perrault's fairy tales for their expression of such typically French characteristics as logic, wit, and refined femininity.[4] Fernand Baldensperger, not without irony, has even observed that Perrault's fairies are charming Cartesian fairies.[5]

The pride the French take in their tales rarely gets more impassioned than this. Perhaps this also has something to do with the influential essay on Perrault written by Sainte-Beuve in 1851, in which he stressed

2. Robert Darnton, "Peasants Tell Tales: The Meaning of Mother Goose," in *The Great Cat Massacre and Other Episodes in French Cultural History* (New York: Basic Books, 1984), 50–51.
3. Darnton, *Great Cat Massacre*, 63.
4. Paul Hazard, *Books, Children and Men*, trans. Marguerite Mitchell (Boston: Horn Book, 1947), 121–24.
5. Cited in Hazard, *Books*, 122.

not only the naivete and simplicity, but also the universal appeal of the French stories.[6]

Such a view draws on another interpretation of the folk that does not rely on national or ethnic identity and consequently proposes an alternative ownership for the fairy tale. This view of the folk is informed by a universalizing tendency that completely disregards social, historical, and cultural factors. It is the view espoused in particular by psychoanalytic, archetypal, and anthroposophical-spiritualist (Waldorf school) readers of fairy tales.[7] It is best summed up in this amazingly wrongheaded passage taken from the book *Fairy Tales and Children* by psychologist Carl-Heinz Mallet:

> Fairy Tales are popular poetry, for they originated and developed among the people [the folk]. They were born in fusty spinning rooms. Simple people told them to simple people. No one else was interested in these "old wives' tales." No superior authority, whether profane or ecclesiastic, exerted any influence. Fairy tales developed outside the great world, beyond the centers of political and cultural power. They absorbed nothing from these areas, no historical events, no political facts, no cultural trends. They remained free of the moral views, behavioral standards, and manners of the various epochs. . . . Human beings *per se* are the focal point of fairy tales, and people are pretty much alike no matter when or where they have lived.[8]

This is in striking contrast to the opinions discussed earlier in this chapter. Here the folk constitute not a national group bound together by a common culture, but an ill-defined population of idyllic innocents whose sole characteristic is simplicity. Rousseau is responsible for this model. But both this mythical peasant and the ensuing notion of a fairy tale untouched by its social or historical context are ridiculous. Yet these are the very premises upon which very influential and popular theories of the fairy tale have been built. Their unfortunate success lies in their reassuring appeal to our humanity, to the soothing promise that both human beings and values transcend time and space. In other words, as vessels of purportedly universal human truths, fairy tales belong to us all. The classic example of this view is Bruno Bettelheim, whose popular psychoanalytic interpretations of fairy tales by the Brothers Grimm and Perrault have been widely and enthusiastically embraced.

6. C.-A. Sainte-Beuve, "Charles Perrault," in *Causeries du lundi* (Paris: Garnier, 1944), V, 273.
7. Readers who follow the teachings of Rudolf Steiner, who was deeply influenced by Jungian psychology [*Editor*].
8. Carl-Heinz Mallet, *Fairy Tales and Children: The Psychology of Children Revealed through Four of Grimms' Fairy Tales*, trans. J. Neugroschel (New York: Schocken, 1984), 38.

*Bettelheim's Psychoanalytic Interpretations of Fairy Tales*

From Bettelheim's psychoanalytic perspective, fairy tales address "essential human problems" and "have great psychological meaning."[9] Through fairy tales, Bettelheim argues, both children and adults can find their way through life's existential dilemmas. Bettelheim can come to these conclusions because he assumes that fairy tales transcend the specific time and place of their origin and give us insight into "manifold truths . . . which can guide our lives; . . . truth as valid today as it was once upon a time."[1] Thus, fairy tales, whether German or French, for example, would seem to belong to us all, not simply by virtue of our sharing a common Western culture, but because the fairy tale's transcendent nature addresses our common humanity. However, Bettelheim's point of view is problematic because what he believes to be universal truths ultimately turn out to be the values of nineteenth-century Europe.

The repressive moralizing inherent in Bettelheim's readings of fairy tales has been solidly criticized before, but I mention the issue again here because his understanding of fairy tales remains influential, especially among teachers and children's librarians who often rely on his work. * * * Jack Zipes's criticism of Bettelheim's "Use and Abuse of Folk and Fairy Tales with Children,"[2] in particular, deserves reading or rereading in light of the recent, sobering allegations by one of Bettelheim's former patients at the Orthogenic School that the author of *The Uses of Enchantment* was an authoritarian who physically and emotionally abused children in his care.[3] The values that Bettelheim views as timeless and common to us all frequently turn out to be those of the authoritarian, patriarchal society in which he was raised.[4]

Some of Bettelheim's influence has been mitigated by recent studies that reveal the specific sociocultural roots of many tales and thus expose their historically determined values. In fact, for the last fifteen years the Grimms' tales have been the center of considerable discussion and controversy as a result of renewed interest in evidence that the Grimms did not give us authentic, unaltered folktales transcribed from the mouths of simple people, but instead drew many of their tales from highly educated informants or printed literary texts. * * * That Wilhelm

9. Bettelheim, *Uses*, 17.
1. Bettelheim, *Uses*, 310.
2. Jack Zipes, "On the Use and Abuse of Folk and Fairy Tales with Children: Bruno Bettelheim's Moralistic Magic Wand," in *Breaking the Magic Spell: Radical Theories of Folk and Fairy Tales* (New York: Methuen, 1984), 160–82.
3. C. Pekow, "The Other Dr. Bettelheim: The Revered Psychologist Had a Dark, Violent Side," *Washington Post* (26 Aug. 1990), C1, C4; and Jack Zipes, *The Brothers Grimm: From Enchanted Forests to the Modern World* (New York: Routledge, 1988), 110–34.
4. Donald Haase, " 'Verzauberungen der Seele': Das Märchen und die Exilanten der NS-Zeit," in *Begegnungen mit dem "Fremden": Grenzen—Traditionen—Vergleiche: Akten des VIII. Internationalen Germanisten-Kongresses, Tokyo 1990* (Munich: iudicium 1991), 44–50.

Grimm had freely revised, edited, added to, and basically rewritten many of the classic tales to reflect his own aesthetic and moral values renders the universal, transcendent view of these tales untenable.

But the discrediting of theories has affected not only those who, like Bettelheim, believe in the universal nature of fairy tales. The nationalists have had to confront the discovery that many of the best known and most cherished of the Grimms' tales are not purely German. They are in many cases of mixed origin. Some of the Grimms' most significant informants have turned out to be educated bourgeois women from families of French Huguenots who had settled in Germany after the revocation of the Edict of Nantes. Of course, to say that these oral sources spoke French and were familiar with the tales of Perrault is not to say that what the Grimms have given us is a collection of French tales. They did not. But it is enough to undermine the view that makes fairy tales the possession of a single nationality.

We are left, however, with a question. If fairy tales are not the universal possession of an all-encompassing, undifferentiated humanity, and if they are not the sole property of any single national group, then to whom do fairy tales belong? This question can be best answered by turning first to the question: Why does it matter at all to whom fairy tales belong?

## The Question of Ownership

The question of ownership is not an idle question. As we've seen, our specific views on the origin and nature of fairy tales necessarily imply that we have, implicitly or explicitly, a specific attitude toward their ownership. And these attitudes, in turn, have an impact on the reception of fairy tales insofar as they determine how we both read and use fairy tales. The problem—indeed, the danger—with both the nationalistic/ethnic and universal views of fairy tales is that they prescribe forms of thought and behavior, and modes and models of humanity, that are meant to be normative. That is, they stereotype us—either as members of a nationalistic or ethnic group, or as human beings defined by a certain concept of what is or is not normal. This is why fairy tales have been so frequently utilized by *both* nationalists and universalists in the socialization of children. In both cases, fairy tales are supposed to depict or prescribe for us what is true, as well as what forms of behavior are typical, normal, and acceptable. Whether we view them as yours and mine or as ours, fairy tales—read from these perspectives —confine and limit us, narrowing our views of reality while allegedly giving us greater insight into the other, into ourselves, or into humanity. From these perspectives, fairy tales own us, we don't own them.

An important twist was added to the question of ownership with the proliferation of both printed texts and copyright law in the nineteenth century. While folktales remain in the public domain because of their anonymous origin in the oral tradition (which accounts in part for their popularity among publishers), there has been a growing tendency to stress private ownership by individuals or even corporations. This is evident in the way we speak about fairy tales. With deference to the folk's public ownership of fairy tales, the Grimms claimed only to have *collected* the stories in their famous edition. Yet we refer to them as "Grimms' fairy tales." Contemporary storytellers, who work for a fee and are cautious about allowing audio or video recordings of their performances, frequently talk of making a traditional folktale their own. Although this is in one sense an artistic claim, the vocabulary of ownership clearly implies the expectation to control and profit from the tale in question. When Disney called his animated fairy tales by his own name—*Walt Disney's Snow White and the Seven Dwarfs, Walt Disney's Sleeping Beauty,* and so on—he was not simply making an artistic statement, but also laying claim to the tales in what would become their most widely known, public versions. In 1989, when the Academy of Motion Picture Arts and Sciences used the figure of Snow White in its televised award ceremonies, the Walt Disney Company filed a lawsuit claiming "unauthorized use of its Snow White character," which the corporation felt had been treated in an unflattering manner in the comical and mildly satirical sketch.[5] When the Walt Disney Company spent $1 million for the videocassette rights to the "Rocky and Bullwinkle" series—including the "Fractured Fairy Tales" that sometimes parody the Disney versions and Walt Disney himself—its corporate ownership and control of the fairy tale were extended to even the subversive fairy tale.[6] If the Walt Disney Company cannot completely prevent unflattering parodies of its fairy-tale movies and their creator, at least it will now be able to control and profit from their distribution.

The Disney case demonstrates that the question of ownership is important because it is ultimately a question of control. So who owns fairy tales? To be blunt: I do. And you do. We can each claim fairy tales for ourselves. Not as members of a national or ethnic folk group—as French, German, or American. Not as nameless faces in a sea of humanity. And not in the Disney model as legal copyright holders. We claim fairy tales in every individual act of telling and reading. If we avoid reading fairy tales as models of behavior and normalcy, they can become for us revolutionary documents that encourage the development of personal autonomy.

As some revisionist writers and storytellers have already recognized, the removal of the fairy tale from the service of nationalism and uni-

5. "Disney Company Sues over Snow White Use," *New York Times* (31 March 1989), C33; A. Harmetz, "An Apology to Disney," *New York Times* (7 April 1989), C30.
6. D. A. Kaplan, "Vatch out Natasha, Moose and Squirrel Are Back," *Detroit Free Press* (7 May 1989), 3F.

versalism requires the subversion of traditional tales. Thus we find contemporary literary versions of "Little Red Riding Hood," for instance, that offer alternative visions. In one version, by the Merseyside Fairy Story Collective, a young girl overcomes her fear and slays the wolf who threatens her grandmother.[7] In another, by Angela Carter, a young woman, far from becoming the wolf's innocent victim, accepts her animal nature—her sexuality—and actually leaves her family and village to join the company of wolves.[8] In other media, such as film, video, and music, attempts have also been made to reclaim the fairy tale. In fact, Angela Carter's Red Riding Hood story, "The Company of Wolves," has itself been remade as a movie.[9] And some of the irreverent video adaptations in Shelley Duvall's *Fairie Tale Theatre*[1] go a long way toward offsetting the saccharine Disney model of the Consumer Romance. Even in popular music the Disney claim on meaning has been challenged by authorized remakes of the songs from Walt Disney's fairytale movies. Sinéad O'Connor's subtly ironic rendering of "Someday My Prince Will Come," Betty Carter's sensual subversion of "I'm Wishing," and Tom Waits's industrialized "Heigh Ho" give us the opportunity to reinterpret Disney and "his" tales for ourselves and our time.[2]

## Discovering Individual Ownership of Fairy Tales

The opportunity to reclaim fairy tales is as crucial for children as it is for adults. But the right to ownership of the tales may in some ways be more difficult for children to claim. After all, teachers, librarians, parents, and powers in the culture industry exert a certain control over the popular reception of fairy tales by determining to a great extent not only the nature of the tales that are made accessible to children, but also the context of their reception. A storyteller who buys into myths about the pristine origin of fairy tales assumes an unearned mantle of authority and shrouds the stories not only in mystery but in error. A parent under Bruno Bettelheim's spell uses time-bound tales to justify a timeless moral authority. And a teacher concerned about the so-called crisis of cultural literacy will emphasize canonized fairy-tale texts and treat them as sacred cultural artifacts. In each case, children's responses are expected to conform to the external authority of the tales they read or hear. It is no accident that parents and educators so often praise fairy tales because of their ability to enchant children. Stripped of sentimen-

7. Jack Zipes, *The Trials and Tribulations of Little Red Riding Hood: Versions of the Tale in Sociocultural Context* (South Hadley, Mass.: Bergin & Garvey, 1984), 239–46.
8. Zipes, *Trials*, 272–80.
9. Angela Carter and N. Jordan (Screenwriters), *The Company of Wolves*, Vestron Video, 1984–85.
1. Shelley Duvall (Producer), *Fairie Tale Theater*, Playhouse Video, 1982–85.
2. H. Willner. *Stay Awake: Various Interpretations of Music from Vintage Disney Films*, A & M, 1988.

tality, enchantment—that is, being spellbound and powerless—is also a curse. We applaud the rescue of a Frog King or a Sleeping Beauty who is powerless to break the spell of a malevolent force, but when a moralistic text "enchants" and has a child in its spell, we apparently have that child exactly where we want her or him.

There are at least two ways in which children can be awakened from this form of enchantment and helped to discover their individual ownership of fairy tales. First, teachers and parents can offer children a wider variety of fairy tales than is usually proffered. Complementing the classic tales and anthologies with newer or lesser-known stories and variants places the traditional tales in a context that encourages diverse responses, questions, and significant comparisons—even among elementary school children. When I read my own daughter the Grimms' "Little Red Riding Hood" and the version of the Merseyside Fairy Story Collective, for example, she announced that she liked the second version better "because the little girl was smarter."

\* \* \*

Beyond presenting children with a variety of fairy tales, adults can also encourage the creative reception of fairy tales. In other words, children can make fairy tales their own by creating and re-creating their own versions. There is good evidence that given the opportunity, children will take fairy tales into their own hands in any case. In his book on the Brothers Grimm, Jack Zipes has recounted how fifth- and sixth-grade girls combined the character of Peter Pumpkin-Eater and the story of Cinderella into a new tale that explicitly reflects their developing sexuality and consciousness.[3] And Kristin Wardetzky has shown how the storytelling of children in the former East Germany does not always succumb to the dominant cultural models and re-creates the fairy tale in ways that express the children's power over the genre.[4]

At the end of his list of heresies Wolfdietrich Schnurre wonders, "Can the fairy tale be saved?" His answer: "Perhaps. If specialists expose the roots of the tales and tell them in a way that is thoroughly new and which expresses their essence."[5] Writers and professional storytellers retelling tales and making them their own can indeed renew the fairy tale. But readers, too—including children—can reread and reinterpret the tales in new ways. By experiencing a wide variety of tales, they can view the stories of the classical canon in new context. By actively selecting, discussing, enacting, illustrating, adapting, and retelling the tales they experience, both adults and children can assert their own proprietary rights to meaning. It is no heresy to re-appropriate the tales

3. Jack Zipes, *Don't Bet on the Prince: Contemporary Feminist Fairy Tales in North America and England* (New York: Methuen, 1986), 146.
4. Kristin Wardetzky, "The Structure and Interpretation of Fairy Tales Composed by Children," *Journal of American Folklore*, 103 (1990): 157–76.
5. Schnurre, "Ketzerisches," 25.

from either tradition or the culture industry. "They are not," as Auden knew, "sacred texts."[6] If the fairy tale needs saving and if we are to save it, then we need to abandon the untenable views of its ownership that put us in its power. We must take possession of it on our own terms. Saving the fairy tale in this way is nothing less than saving our very selves.

# MARIA TATAR

## Sex and Violence: The Hard Core of Fairy Tales†

For many adults, reading through an unexpurgated edition of the Grimms' collection of tales can be an eye-opening experience. Even those who know that Snow White's stepmother arranges the murder of her stepdaughter, that doves peck out the eyes of Cinderella's stepsisters, that Briar Rose's suitors bleed to death on the hedge surrounding her castle, or that a mad rage drives Rumpelstiltskin to tear himself in two will find themselves hardly prepared for the graphic descriptions of murder, mutilation, cannibalism, infanticide, and incest that fill the pages of these bedtime stories for children. In "The Juniper Tree," one of the most widely admired of the tales, a woman decapitates her step-son, chops his corpse into small pieces, and cooks him in a stew that her husband devours with obvious gusto. "Fledgling" recounts a cook's attempt to carry out a similar plan, though she is ultimately outwitted by the boy and his sister. Frau Trude, in the story of that title, turns a girl into a block of wood and throws her into a fire. "Darling Roland" features a witch who takes axe in hand to murder her stepdaughter but ends by butchering her own daughter. Another stepmother dresses her stepdaughter in a paper chemise, turns her out into the woods on a frigid winter day, and forbids her to return home until she has harvested a basket of strawberries.

Lest this litany of atrocities lead to the mistaken view that women are the sole agents of evil in German fairy tales, let us look at examples of paternal and fraternal cruelty. Who can forget the miller who makes life miserable for his daughter by boasting that she can spin straw to gold? Or the king of the same tale who is prepared to execute the girl if her father's declarations prove false? In another tale a man becomes so irritated by his son's naiveté that he first disowns him, then orders him murdered by his servants. The singing bone, in the tale of that title, is whittled from the remains of a fratricide victim; when the bone

6. W. H. Auden, "Praise," 28.
† From *The Hard Facts of the Grimms' Fairy Tales* by Maria Tatar. Copyright © 1987 by Princeton University Press. Reprinted by permission of Princeton University Press. Footnotes have been edited for this Norton Critical Edition.

reveals the secret of the scandalous murder to the world, the surviving brother is sewn up in a sack and drowned. The father of the fairy-tale heroine known as Thousandfurs is so bent on marrying his own daughter that she is obliged to flee from her home into the woods. Another father is so firm a believer in female ultimogeniture that he prepares twelve coffins for his twelve sons in the event that his thirteenth child turns out to be a girl. One monarch after another punishes wicked females by forcing them to disrobe and to roll down hills in kegs studded with nails.

In fairy tales, nearly every character—from the most hardened criminal to the Virgin Mary—is capable of cruel behavior. In "The Robber Bridegroom," a young woman watches in horror as her betrothed and his accomplices drag a girl into their headquarters, tear off her clothes, place her on a table, hack her body to pieces, and sprinkle them with salt. Her horror deepens when one of the thieves, spotting a golden ring on the murdered girl's finger, takes an axe, chops off the finger, and sends it flying through the air into her lap. Such behavior may not be wholly out of character for brigands and highwaymen, but even the Virgin Mary appears to be more of an ogre than a saint in the Grimms' collection. When the girl known as Mary's Child disobeys an injunction against opening one of thirteen doors to the kingdom of heaven and tries to conceal her transgression, the Virgin sends her back to earth as punishment. There the girl marries a king and bears three children, each of whom is whisked off to heaven by the Virgin, who is annoyed by the young queen's persistent refusal to acknowledge her guilt. The mysterious disappearance of the children naturally arouses the suspicions of the king's councilors, who bring the queen to trial and condemn her to death for cannibalism. Only when the queen confesses her sin (just as flames leap up around the stake to which she is bound) does Mary liberate her and restore the three children to her. Compassion clearly does not number among the virtues of the Virgin Mary as she appears in fairy tales.

The Grimms only occasionally took advantage of opportunities to tone down descriptions of brutal punishments visited on villains or to eliminate pain and suffering from their tales.[1] When they did, it was often at the behest of a friend or colleague rather than of their own volition. More often, the Grimms made a point of adding or intensifying violent episodes. Cinderella's stepsisters are spared their vision in the first version of the story. Only in the second edition of the *Nursery and Household Tales* did Wilhelm Grimm embellish the story with a

1. Jost Hermand mistakenly claims that the Grimms deleted violent episodes from the tales ("Biedermeier Kids: Eine Mini-Polemik," *Monatshefte* 67 [1975]: 59–66). John Ellis, by contrast, finds that the Grimms actually *"increased* the level of violence and brutality when, for example, those in the tales who suffered it deserved it according to their moral outlook." See his *One Fairy Story Too Many: The Brothers Grimm and Their Tales* (Chicago: University of Chicago Press, 1983), p. 79.

vivid account of the doves' revenge and with a somewhat fatuous jus-
tification for the bloody tableau at the tale's end: "So both sisters were
punished with blindness to the end of their days for being so wicked
and false." Rumpelstiltskin beats a hasty retreat on a flying spoon at the
end of some versions of his tale, but the Grimms seem to have favored
violence over whimsy. Their Rumpelstiltskin becomes ever more in-
furiated by the queen's discovery of his name; in the second edition of
the *Nursery and Household Tales*, he is so beside himself with rage that
he tears himself in two. Briar Rose sleeps for a hundred years while a
hedge peacefully grows around the castle in the first recorded version
of the story. In successive editions of the Grimms' collection, we not
only read about the young prince who succeeds in penetrating the
thorny barrier, but also learn the grisly particulars about Briar Rose's
unsuccessful suitors. They fail because "the briar bushes clung together
as though they had hands so that the young princes were caught in
them and died a pitiful death."

The changes made from the first to the second edition in "The
Magic Table, the Gold Donkey, and the Cudgel in the Sack" show
just how keen the Grimms must have been to give added prominence
to violent episodes. In the first edition of the *Nursery and Household
Tales*, we read about the encounter between the story's hero and an
innkeeper who confiscates the property of the hero's brothers.

> The turner placed the sack under his pillow. When the innkeeper
> came and pulled at it, he said: "Cudgel, come out of the sack!"
> The cudgel jumped out of the sack and attacked the innkeeper,
> danced with him, and beat him so mercilessly that he was glad to
> promise to return the magic table and the gold donkey.[2]

The second edition not only fills in the details on the crime and its
punishment, but also puts the innkeeper's humiliation on clearer
display.

> At bedtime [the turner] stretched out on the bench and used his
> sack as a pillow for his head. When the innkeeper thought his
> guest was fast asleep and that no one else was in the room, he
> went over and began to tug and pull very carefully at the sack,
> hoping to get it away and to put another in its place. But the turner
> had been waiting for him to do exactly that. Just as the innkeeper
> was about to give a good hard tug, he cried out: "Cudgel, come
> out of the sack!" In a flash the little cudgel jumped out, went at
> the innkeeper, and gave him a good sound thrashing. The inn-
> keeper began screaming pitifully, but the louder he screamed the
> harder the cudgel beat time on his back, until at last he fell down
> on the ground. Then the turner said: "Now give me the magic

2. *Die Kinder- und Hausmärchen der Brüder Grimm: Vollständige Ausgabe in der Urfassung*, ed.
Friedrich Panzer (Wiesbaden: Emil Vollmer, 1953), p. 155.

table and the gold donkey, or the dance will start all over again."
"Oh no!" said the innkeeper. "I'll be glad to give you everything,
if only you'll make that little devil crawl back into his sack." The
journeyman answered: "This time I will, but watch out for further
injuries." Then he said: "Cudgel, back in the sack" and left him
in peace.

What the brothers found harder to tolerate than violence and what
they did their best to eliminate from the collection through vigilant
editing were references to what they coyly called "certain conditions
and relationships." Foremost among those conditions seems to have
been pregnancy. The story of Hans Dumm, who has the power (and
uses it) of impregnating women simply by wishing them to be with
child, was included in the first edition but failed to pass muster for the
second edition of the *Nursery and Household Tales*. "The Master
Hunter," as told by Dorothea Viehmann, the Grimms' favorite exhibit
when it came to discoursing on the excellence of folk narrators, must
have struck the Grimms as unsatisfactory. Viehmann's version, which
was relegated to the notes on the tales, relates that the story's hero enters
a tower, discovers a naked princess asleep on her bed, and lies down
next to her. After his departure, the princess discovers to her deep distress and to her father's outrage that she is pregnant. The version that
actually appeared in the *Nursery and Household Tales* made do instead
with a fully clothed princess and a young man who stands as a model
of restraint and decorum.[3]

Pregnancy, whether the result of a frivolous wish (as in "Hans
Dumm") or of an illicit sexual relationship (as in "The Master
Hunter"), was a subject that made the Grimms uncomfortable. In fact,
any hints of premarital sexual activity must have made Wilhelm Grimm
in particular blush with embarrassment. A quick look at the "Frog King
or Iron Heinrich" (the first tale in the collection and therefore the most
visible) reveals the tactics he used to cover up the folkloric facts of the
story. When the princess in that celebrated tale dashes the hapless frog
against the wall, he "falls down into her bed and lies there as a handsome young prince, and the king's daughter lies down next to him."
No printed edition of the *Nursery and Household Tales* contains this
wording. Only a copy of the original drafts for the collection, sent to
the Grimms' friend Clemens Brentano in 1810 and recovered many
years later in a Trappist monastery, is explicit about where the frog
lands and about the princess's alacrity in joining him there. In the first
edition, the frog still falls on the bed. After his transformation, he becomes the "dear companion" of the princess. "She cherished him as
she had promised," we are told, and *immediately* thereafter the two fall

---

3. Dorothea Viehmann's tale is printed in volume 3 of Heinz Rölleke's edition of the 1856
version of the Grimms' collection: *Brüder Grimm: Kinder- und Hausmärchen* (Stuttgart: Reclam, 1980), pp. 192–93.

"peacefully asleep." For the second edition, Wilhelm Grimm deprived the frog king of his soft landing spot and simply observed that the transformation from frog to prince took place as soon as the frog hit the wall. In this version, the happy couple does not retire for the evening until wedding vows are exchanged, and these are exchanged only with the explicit approval of the princess's father. The Grimms' transformation of a tale replete with sexual innuendo into a prim and proper nursery story with a dutiful daughter is almost as striking as the folkloric metamorphosis of frog into prince.[4]

Another of the "conditions and relationships" that the Grimms seem to have found repugnant, or at least inappropriate as a theme in their collection, was incest and incestuous desire. In some cases, incest constituted so essential a part of a tale's logic that even Wilhelm Grimm thought twice before suppressing it; instead he resorted to weaving judgmental observations on the subject into the text. The father of Thousandfurs may persist in pressing marriage proposals on his daughter throughout all editions of the Nursery and Household Tales, but by the second edition he receives a stern reprimand from his court councilors. "A father cannot marry his daughter," they protest. "God forbids it. No good can come of such a sin." In later editions, we learn that the entire kingdom would be "dragged down to perdition" with the sinful king. * * *

When a tale was available in several versions, the Grimms invariably preferred one that camouflaged incestuous desires and Oedipal entanglements. The textual history of the tale known as "The Girl without Hands" illustrates the Grimms' touchy anxiety when it came to stories about fathers with designs on their daughters. That story first came to the Grimms' attention in the following form: A miller falls on hard times and strikes a bargain with the devil, promising him whatever is standing behind his mill in exchange for untold wealth. To his dismay, he returns home to learn that his daughter happened to be behind the mill at the moment the pact was sealed. She must surrender herself to the devil in three years. But the miller's pious daughter succeeds in warding off the devil, if at the price of bodily mutilation: the devil forces the father, who has not kept his end of the bargain, to chop off his daughter's hands. For no apparent reason, the girl packs her severed hands on her back and decides to seek her fortune in the world, despite her father's protestations and his promises to secure her all possible creature comforts at home. The remainder of the story recounts her further trials and tribulations after she marries a king. This is the tale as it appeared in the first edition of the Grimms' collection.

4. For the original manuscript version of "The Frog King or Iron Heinrich," see Die älteste Märchensammlung der Brüder Grimm: Synopse der handschriftlichen Urfassung von 1810 und der Erstdrucke von 1812, ed. Heinz Rölleke (Cologny-Genève: Fondation Martin Bodmer, 1975), pp. 144–46.

The brothers subsequently came upon a number of versions of that story, one of which they declared far superior to all the others. So impressed were they by its integrity that they could not resist substituting it for the version printed in the first edition of the *Nursery and Household Tales*. Still, the opening paragraph of the new, "superior" version did not quite suit their taste, even though it provided a clear, logical motive for the daughter's departure from home. Instead of leaving home of her own accord and for no particular reason, the girl flees a father who first demands her hand in marriage, and then has her hands and breasts chopped off for refusing him. There is no mention of devils in this version; the girl's father is the sole satanic figure. The Grimms found it easy, however, to reintroduce the devil by mutilating the folk-loric text whose authenticity they so admired. The original introduction detailing the father's offenses was deleted from the tale and replaced by the less sensational account of a pact with the devil.

Even without reading Freud on the devil as a substitute for the father, it is easy to see how the devil became mixed up in this tale. Just as God, Saint Peter, and Christ came to stand in for various benefactors in folktales, so Satan in his various guises was available for the role of villain and could incarnate forbidden desire. "The Poor Man and the Rich Man," "The Devil and His Grandmother," and "The Carnation" are among the many other texts in the *Nursery and Household Tales* that mobilize divinities and devils as agents of good and evil. The Grimms seemed, in general, to have favored tales with a Christian cast of characters over their "pagan" counterparts, although there was no compelling folkloristic reason for them to do so. For "The Girl without Hands," they chose to graft the introduction from what they considered an inferior version of the tale (but one that had the advantage of de-monizing Satan instead of a father) onto a "superior (and complete)" variant. Clearly the Grimms were not particularly enamored with the idea of including plots concerned with incestuous desire in a collection of tales with the title *Nursery and Household Tales*. Incest was just not one of those perfectly natural matters extolled in their preface to the tales.

Sex and violence: these are the major thematic concerns of tales in the Grimms' collection, at least in their unedited form. But more important, sex and violence in that body of stories frequently take the perverse form of incest and child abuse, for the nuclear family furnishes the fairy tale's main cast of characters just as the family constitutes its most common subject. When it came to passages colored by sexual details or to plots based on Oedipal conflicts, Wilhelm Grimm exhibited extraordinary editorial zeal. Over the years, he systematically purged the collection of references to sexuality and masked depictions of incestuous desire. But lurid portrayals of child abuse, starvation, and exposure, like fastidious descriptions of cruel punishments, on the whole escaped censorship. The facts of life seemed to have been more disturbing to the Grimms than the harsh realities of everyday life.

How is one to explain these odd editorial practices? The Grimms' enterprise, we must recall, began as a scholarly venture and a patriotic project. As early as 1811, the brothers proclaimed that their efforts as collectors were guided by scholarly principles, and they therefore implied that they were writing largely for academic colleagues. Theirs was an idealistic effort to capture German folk traditions in print before they died out and to make a modest contribution to the history of German poetry. As Jacob Grimm pointed out during his search for a publisher, the main purpose of the proposed volume was not so much to earn royalties as to salvage what was left of the priceless national resources still in the hands of the German folk. The Grimms therefore were willing to forgo royalties for the benefit of appearing in print. Still, the brothers expressed the hope that the volume in the offing would find friends everywhere—and that it would entertain them as well.

Weighed down by a ponderous introduction and by extensive annotations, the first edition of the *Nursery and Household Tales* had the look of a scholarly tome, rather than of a book for a wide audience. Sales, however, were surprisingly brisk, perhaps in part because of the book's title. Several of the Grimms' contemporaries had already registered respectable commercial successes with collections of stories for children, and the appearance of the *Nursery and Household Tales* coincided to some extent with a developing market for collections of fairy tales. By 1815 nearly all 900 copies of the first volume had been sold, and Wilhelm Grimm began talking about a second edition in light of the "heavy demand" for the collection. The Grimms had every reason to be pleased, particularly when one calculates that thirty years later (when literacy was more widespread and the demand for children's literature greater) a book such as the popular *Struwwelpeter* had a first printing of only 1,500. With their reputation for "revering trivia" and their endless struggles to get things published, they must also have been growing hungry for a measure of commercial success or at least for some indication of strong interest and support for their literary efforts. Before preparations were even set in motion for publication of the second edition of the *Nursery and Household Tales*, Wilhelm Grimm had already calculated exactly what the appropriate royalties would be for the first and second editions.

The projected royalties for the collection were by no means inconsequential. These were lean years for the Grimms, and their letters to each other are sprinkled with references to financial pressures and to indignities visited on them owing to their impecunious circumstances. From Vienna, Jacob grumbled that he was short of cash and that his clothes were shabby and his shoes worn out. In 1815, Wilhelm Grimm complained that there was not a chair in the house that could be used without imperiling the physical welfare of its occupant. Books were often borrowed and copied out by hand because they were too dear an item in a household where the number of daily meals was limited to two. Thus the 500 talers that Savigny and Wilhelm Grimm had established as appropriate royalties for the first edition of the *Nursery and Household Tales* certainly must have been a welcome prospect. And the 400 talers that Wilhelm Grimm expected to receive for the second edition would have been a substantial addition to the household budget, particularly if we bear in mind that in 1816 Jacob Grimm drew an annual salary of 600 talers as librarian in Kassel, while Wilhelm received an annual salary of 300 talers. It is thus not surprising that the royalties for the *Nursery and Household Tales* would go a long way toward paying their many debts.

*   *   *

The Grimms may never have made or even hoped to make a financial killing on the *Nursery and Household Tales*, but the profit motive was certainly not wholly absent from their calculations and to some extent must have guided their revisions of the first edition. Still, the potential financial benefits to be reaped from strong sales of the collection counted merely as a secondary gain. What really mattered, particularly in the years immediately following publication of the first edition, were the views of the larger literary world. Both brothers monitored reviews with special interest, and here one disappointment followed another. Jacob, on the road much of the time from 1813 to 1815 in diplomatic service, repeatedly asked his brother for news about the collection's reception. But none of the people who counted seemed to take much interest in reviewing the book, and those who actually did review it rarely had anything good to say. *   *   *

*   *   *

For many observers, the *Nursery and Household Tales* fell wide of the mark and missed its potential market because the brothers had let their scholarly ambitions undermine the production of a book for children. The Grimms' seemingly slavish fidelity to oral folk traditions—in particular to the crude language of the folk—came under especially heavy fire. August Wilhelm Schlegel and Clemens Brentano felt that a bit of artifice would have gone a long way toward improving the art of the folk and toward making the tales more appealing. "If you want to display children's clothing, you can do that quite well without bringing out an outfit that has buttons torn off it, dirt smeared on it, and the shirt hanging out of the pants," Brentano wrote to Arnim. Arnim candidly told the Grimms that they would be wise to add, in the form of a subtitle, a consumer warning to the collection. Future editions ought to state that the book was "for parents, who can select stories for retelling." Other readers were less tactful. Heinrich Voß described the collection (with the exception of a few tales) as "real junk."

*   *   *

* * * In successive editions of the collection, [Wilhelm Grimm] fleshed out the texts to the point where they were often double their original length, and he so polished the prose that no one could complain of its rough-hewn qualities. He also worked hard to clean up the content of the stories. Both A. L. Grimm and Friedrich Rühs singled out "Rapunzel" as a tale particularly inappropriate to include in a collection of tales that children could get their hands on. "What proper mother or nanny could tell the fairy tale about Rapunzel to an innocent daughter without blushing?" Rühs gasped. Wilhelm Grimm saw to it that the story was rewritten along lines that would meet with both critics' approval. Jacob Grimm may have responded to criticism by asserting that the collection had never been intended for young audiences, but his brother was prepared to delete or revise tales deemed unsuitable for children. He was encouraged in such efforts by his brother Ferdinand, who was all for eliminating anything that might offend the sensibilities (*Feingefühl*) of the reading public.

* * * Consider the following passage from the first edition of the *Nursery and Household Tales* (Rapunzel's daily romps up in the tower with the prince, we learn, have weighty consequences).

> At first Rapunzel was frightened, but soon she came to like the young king so much that she agreed to let him visit every day and to pull him up. The two lived joyfully for a time, and the fairy did not catch on at all until Rapunzel told her one day: "Tell me, Godmother, why my clothes are so tight and why they don't fit me any longer." "Wicked child!" cried the fairy.[5]

In the second edition of the *Nursery and Household Tales*, Wilhelm Grimm made the passage less "lewd"—and in the bargain a good deal less colorful. Here, Rapunzel's "wickedness" has a very different cause.

> At first Rapunzel was frightened, but soon she came to like the young king so much that she agreed to let him visit every day and to pull him up. The two lived joyfully for a time and loved each other dearly, like man and wife. The enchantress did not catch on at all until Rapunzel told her one day: "Tell me, Godmother, why is it that you are much harder to pull up than the young prince?" "Wicked child," cried the enchantress.

It is easy to leap to the conclusion that Teutonic prudishness or the Grimms' delicate sense of propriety motivated the kinds of changes made in "Rapunzel." That may well be the case. But it is far more

5. *Die Kinder- und Hausmärchen der Brüder Grimm*, ed. Friedrich Panzer, p. 85.

logical to assume that Wilhelm Grimm took to heart the criticisms leveled against his volume and, eager to find a wider audience, set to work making the appropriate changes. His nervous sensitivity about moral objections to the tales in the collection reflects a growing desire to write for children rather than to collect for scholars.

In the years that intervened between the first two editions of the *Nursery and Household Tales,* Wilhelm Grimm charted a new course for the collection. His son was later to claim that children had taken possession of a book that was not theirs to begin with, but Wilhelm clearly helped that process along. He had evidently already done some editing behind Jacob's back but apparently not enough to satisfy his critics. The preface to the second edition emphasized the value of the tales for children, noting—almost as an afterthought—that adults could also enjoy them and even learn something from them. The brothers no longer insisted on literal fidelity to oral traditions but openly admitted that they had taken pains to delete "every phrase unsuitable for children." Furthermore, they expressed the hope that their collection could serve as a "manual of manners" *(Erziehungsbuch).*

\* \* \*

# ANTTI AARNE and STITH THOMPSON

## *From* The Types of the Folktale: A Classification and Bibliography†

Listed below are models for some of the tale types included in this volume. Each tale type is assigned a number, preceded by the standard designation AT (Aarne/Thompson). Note that the type is defined by a series of episodes that constitute the full version of a tale. Most variants will not contain a complete elaboration of each episode.

AT311 *Rescue by the Sister,* who deceives the ogre into carrying the girls in a sack (chest) back to their home. \* \* \*

    I. *The Forbidden Chamber.* (a) Two sisters, one after the other, fall into an ogre's power, and are taken into a subterranean castle. (b) They are forbidden entrance into one room or (b$^1$) to see souls in torment or (b$^2$) to eat a human bone. (c) They disobey and an egg or key becomes bloody.

    II. *Punishment.* The ogre kills them for disobedience.

† From Antti Aarne, *The Types of Folktale: A Classification and Bibliography,* trans. and enlarged by Stith Thompson (Helsinki: Academia Scientiarum Fennica, 1964). Reprinted by permission.

III. *Rescue by youngest sister.* (a) The youngest sister finds the bodies and (b) resuscitates them by putting their members together or (c) otherwise, and hides them.

VI. *Carrying the Sacks.* (a) The girls are put into sacks and the ogre is persuaded to carry the sacks home without looking into them.

V. *Disguise as Bird.* (a) The youngest sister leaves a skull dressed as a bride to deceive the ogre. (b) She smears herself with honey and feathers and escapes as a strange bird.

VI. *Punishment of the Murderer.*

AT312 *The Giant-killer and his Dog (Bluebeard).* The brother rescues his sisters. The youngest sister threatened with death for disobedience asks respite for prayer. Her brother with the aid of animals kills the ogre and rescues his sister.

AT327 *The Children and the Ogre.*

I. *Arrival at Ogre's House.* (a) Children are abandoned by poor parents in a wood (b) but they find their way back by cloth shreds or pebbles that they have dropped; (c) the third time birds eat their breadcrumbs, or grain clue and (d) they wander until they come to a gingerbread house which belongs to a witch; or (e) a very small hero (thumbling) and his brothers stay at night at the ogre's house; or (f) the ogre carries the child home in a sack; (g) the child substitutes a stone in the sack twice but is finally captured.

II. *The Ogre Deceived.* The ogre smells human flesh and has the children imprisoned and fattened. (b) When his finger is to be cut to test his fatness the hero sticks out a bone or piece of wood. (c) The exchange of caps, (d) the ogre's wife or child burned in his own oven, * * * or (e) the hero by singing induces the ogre to free them, or (f) the hero to be hanged feigns ignorance and has ogre show him how, or (g) hero feigns inability to sleep until ogre brings certain objects and escapes while ogre hunts the object.

III. *Escape.* (a) The children are carried across the water by ducks (or angels), or (b) they throw back magic objects which become obstacles in the ogre's path, or (c) they transform themselves, or (d) the ogre (ogress) tries to drink the pond empty and bursts, or (e) the ogre is misdirected and loses them.

327A *Hansel and Gretel.* The parents abandon their children in the wood. The gingerbread house. The boy fattened; the witch thrown into the oven. * * *

327B *The Dwarf and the Giant.* The dwarf and his brother in the giant's house. The nightcaps of the children are exchanged. * * *

327C *The Devil (Witch) Carries the Hero Home in a Sack.* The wife or daughter are to cook him, but are thrown into the oven themselves. * * *

327D *The Kiddelkaddelkar.* The children in the ogre's house are protected by his wife but discovered. They are to be hanged, but the ogre is persuaded to show them how it is done. He is released only when he promises them a "kiddelkadderlkar" and much treasure. They flee. The ogre is misdirected and defeated. * * *

327E *Abandoned Children Escape from Burning Barn.* Return after long time and astonish parents.* * *

327F *The Witch and the Fisher Boy.* Witch has her tongue made thin by a blacksmith so as to change her voice. * * * She thus entices the fisher boy. * * *

327G (formerly 327) *The Boy at the Devil's (Witch's) House.* The daughters are to cook him, but are killed by him. The devil is then killed. With his corpse the robbers are frightened from the tree. * * *

123 *The Wolf and the Kids.* The wolf comes in the absence of the mother and eats up the kids. * * * The old goat cuts the wolf open and rescues them. * * *

Motifs: * * * Disguise by changing voice. * * * Thief disguises voice and is allowed access to goods (children). * * * Wolf puts flour on his paws to disguise himself. * * * Well-trained kid does not open door to wolf. * * * Victims rescued from swallower's belly.

* * *

AT425 *The Search for the Lost Husband.* * * *
   I. *The Monster as Husband.* (a) A monster is born because of a hasty wish of the parents. (b) He is a man at night. (c) A girl promises herself as bride to the monster, (c[1]) to recover stolen clothes or jewels, (c[2]) to escape from captivity in spring or well (c[3]) or a girl seeks out or accidentally discovers a supernatural husband, (d) or her father promises her (d[1]) in order to secure a flower (lark) his daughter has asked him to bring from journey, (d[2]) to pay a gambling debt, or (d[3]) to escape from danger. (e) The father and daughter try in vain to send another girl as the monster's bride.
   II. *Disenchantment of the Monster.* (a) The girl disenchants the monster (dwarf, bear, wolf, ass, snake, hog, hedgehog, frog, bird, or tree) by means of a kiss and tears, or (b) by burning the animal skin or (c) by decapitation, or (d) by other means.
   III. *Loss of the Husband.* (a) But she loses him because she has burned the animal's skin too soon, or (b) has revealed his secret to her

sisters, or (c) has broken other prohibitions, (c¹) looking at him, (c²) kissing him, or (c³) staying too long at home.

IV. *Search for Husband.* (a) She undergoes a sorrowful wandering in iron shoes, (b) gets magic objects from an old woman or from her own child, (c) asks her directions from the wind and stars, (d) climbs a steep glass mountain, (e) takes service as maid with witch who gives her impossible or dangerous tasks to perform, or (f) deceives importunate suitors.

V. *Recovery of Husband.* (a) She buys with three jewels three nights by the side of her lost husband, and wins him back, or (b) disenchants him by affectionate treatment. (c) Sometimes she must go on a journey * * * and be compassionate to people and objects.

AT425A *The Monster (Animal) as Bridegroom* (Cupid and Psyche). The maiden on quest for her vanished bridegroom. Various introductions: Present from journey, father promises daughter or daughter promises self. Jephthah's vow. Attempt to evade promise. Sometimes: louse fattened. Sometimes the husband is a vivified image. Tabu: looking, skin burning, gossip. Long wearisome search. Buying three nights to sleep with husband. Formula: old and new key.

AT425B *The Disenchanted Husband: the Witch's Tasks.* Present from journey or other promise to supernatural husband, marriage. Tabu broken. Search for vanished husband leads to house of witch who has enchanted him. Heroine as servant, given difficult or impossible tasks. Sometimes visits to second witch where objects or beings are to be treated with kindness. Box not to be opened. Disenchantment by kiss or affectionate treatment.

AT425C *Beauty and the Beast.* Father stays overnight in mysterious palace and takes rose. Must promise daughter to animal (or she goes voluntarily). Tabu: overstaying at home. She finds the husband almost dead. Disenchants him by embrace. (No search, no tasks.)

AT510 *Cinderella and Cap o' Rushes*

AT510A *Cinderella.* The two stepsisters. The stepdaughter at the grave of her own mother, who helps her (milks the cow, shakes the apple-tree, helps the old man * * *). Three-fold visit to church (dance). Slipper test.

AT510B *The Dress of Gold, of Silver, and of Stars* (Cap o' Rushes). Present of the father who wants to marry his own daughter. The maiden as servant of the prince, who throws various objects at her. The three-fold visit to the church and the forgotten shoe. Marriage.

AT511 *One-Eye, Two-Eyes, Three-Eyes.* Two-Eyes (or a stepdaughter) is abused by her mother. She has to act as goatherd and she becomes hungry. A wise old woman provides the maiden with a magic table and food. The sisters spy upon her. Gold-producing tree from animal's entrails. The wonderful tree whose fruit Two-Eyes alone can pluck. She becomes the wife of a lord.

AT511A *The Little Red Ox.* A stepbrother of One-Eye, Two-Eyes and Three-Eyes is cruelly treated by his stepmother and stepsisters. He is assisted by a magic ox which furnishes him food from its removable horn. The stepsisters try to spy on him, but he puts them to sleep except for a single eye. The stepmother feigns illness and demands the meat of the ox. The ox carries the boy on his horns through woods of copper, silver, and gold, where they pick twigs and must fight successive animal guardians. The ox is eventually killed. The boy takes the ox's horn, which furnishes him with property and leads to success.

AT709 *Snow-White.* The wicked stepmother seeks to kill the maiden. At the dwarfs' (robbers') house, where the prince finds the maiden and marries her.
    I. *Snow-White and her Stepmother.* (a) Snow-White has skin like snow, and lips like blood. (b) A magic mirror tells her stepmother that Snow-White is more beautiful than she.
    II. *Snow-White's Rescue.* (a) The stepmother orders a hunter to kill her, but he substitutes an animal's heart and saves her, or (b) she sends Snow-White to the house of the dwarfs (or robbers) expecting her to be killed. The dwarfs adopt her as sister.
    III. *The Poisoning.* (a) The stepmother now seeks to kill her by means of poisoned lace, (b) a poisoned comb and (c) a poisoned apple.
    IV. *Help of the Dwarfs.* (a) The dwarfs succeed in reviving her from the first two poisonings but fail with the third. (b) They lay the maiden in a glass coffin.
    V. *Her Revival.* A prince sees her and resuscitates her. The stepmother is made to dance herself to death in red hot shoes.

AT720 *My Mother Slew Me; My Father Ate Me. The Juniper Tree.* The boy's bones transformed into a bird. The bird lets the millstone fall on the mother. Becomes a boy again.
    I. *The Murder.* (a) The little boy is slain by his cruel stepmother, who closes the lid of a chest on him. (b) She cooks him and serves him to his father who eats him unwittingly.
    II. *The Transformation.* (a) His little stepsister gathers up his bones and puts them under the juniper tree. (b) From the grave a bird comes forth.

III. *The Revenge.* (a) The bird sings of his murder. (b) He brings presents to his father and sister and the millstone for the mother.

IV. *The Second Transformation.* At her death he becomes a boy.

# VLADIMIR PROPP

## Folklore and Literature†

*   *   *

Folklore is the product of a special form of verbal art. Literature is also a verbal art, and for this reason the closest connection exists between folklore and literature, between the science of folklore and literary criticism. Literature and folklore overlap partially in their poetic genres. There are genres specific to literature (for example, the novel) and to folklore (for example, the charm), but both folklore and literature can be classified by genres, and this is a fact of poetics. Hence there is a certain similarity in some of their tasks and methods.

One of the literary tasks of folklore is to single out and study the category of genre and each particular genre. Especially important and difficult is to study the inner structure of verbal products, their composition and makeup. The laws pertaining to the structure of the folktale, epic poetry, riddles, songs, charms, etc., are little known. In epic genres consider, for example, the opening of the poem, the plot, and the conclusion. It has been shown that works of folklore and literature have different morphologies and that folklore has specific structures. This difference cannot be *explained*, but it can be *discovered* by means of literary analysis. Stylistic and poetical devices belong here too. Again we will see that folklore has devices specific to it (parallelisms, repetition, etc.) and that the usual devices of poetical language (similes, metaphors, epithets) have a different content in folklore and literature. This too can be determined by literary analysis.

In brief, folklore possesses a most distinctive *poetics*, peculiar to it and different from the poetics of literary works. Study of this poetics will reveal the incomparable artistic beauty of folklore.

Thus, not only is there a close tie between folklore and literature, but folklore is a literary phenomenon. Like literature, it is a verbal art.

In its descriptive elements the study of folklore is the study of literature. The connection between these disciplines is so close that folklore and literature are often equated; methods of literature are extended to folklore, and here the matter is allowed to rest. However, as just pointed out, literary analysis can only *discover* the phenomenon and the law of

† From Vladimir Propp, *Theory and History of Folklore*, trans. Ariadana Y. Martin and Richard P. Martin, ed. Anatoly Liberman (Minneapolis: U of Minnesota P, 1984) 5–9. Copyright © 1984. Reprinted by permission of University of Minnesota Press.

folklore poetics, but it is unable to *explain* them. To avoid the error of equating folklore with literature, we must ascertain not only *how literature and folklore are alike*, related, and to a certain extent identical in nature, but also *how they differ*. Indeed, folklore possesses a number of features so sharply differentiating it from literature that methods of literary research are insufficient for solving all its problems.

One of the most important differences is that literary works invariably have an author. Folklore works, on the contrary, never have an author, and this is one of their specific features. The situation is quite clear: either we acknowledge the presence of *folk art* as a phenomenon in the social and cultural history of peoples or we do not acknowledge it and claim that it is a poetical or scientific fiction and that only individuals and groups can create poetry.

We believe that folk art is not a fiction, that it really exists and that the study of it is the basic objective of scientific folklore. * * * What older scholarship felt instinctively and expressed naively, awkwardly, and not so much scientifically as emotionally must now be purged of romantic errors and elevated to the height of modern scholarship, with its consistent methods and exact techniques.

Brought up in the traditions of literature, we are often unable to conceive that a poetical work can have arisen not as a literary work arises when created by an individual. It always seems to us that someone must have been the first to compose it. Yet it is possible for poetical works to arise in completely different ways, and the study of those ways is one of the most fundamental and complex problems of folklore. I cannot go into this problem here and will only mention that in its origin folklore should be likened not to literature but to language, which is invented by no one and which has neither an author nor authors. It arises everywhere and changes in a regular way, independently of people's will, once there are appropriate conditions for it in the historical development of peoples. Universal similarity does not present a problem. It is rather its absence that we would have found inexplicable. Similarity indicates a regular process; the similarity of works of folklore is a particular case of the historical law by which identical forms of production in material culture give rise to identical or similar social institutions, to similar tools, and, in ideology, to the similarity of forms and categories of thought, religion, rituals, languages, and folklore. All of these live, influence one another, change, grow, and die.

With regard to the problem of conceiving *empirically* the origin of folklore, it will suffice to note that in its beginnings folklore can be an integral part of ritual. With the degeneration or decline of a ritual, folklore becomes detached from it and continues to live an independent life. * * *

The distinction discussed here is so important that it compels us to single out folklore as a special type of verbal art and the science of folklore as a special discipline. A literary historian interested in the origin of a work looks for its author. The folklorist, with the aid of broad comparative material, discovers the conditions that brought forth a plot. But the difference between folklore and literature is not confined to this distinction; they are differentiated not only by their origin but also by their forms of existence.

It has long been known that literature is transmitted through writing and folklore by word of mouth. Until now this distinction has been considered to be purely technical. However, it captures the innermost difference between the functioning of literature and folklore. A literary work, once it has arisen, no longer changes. It exists only when two agents are present: the author (the creator of the work) and the reader. The mediating link between them is a book, manuscript, or performance. A literary work is immutable, but the reader always changes. Aristotle was read by the ancient Greeks, the Arabs, and the Humanists, and we read him too, but all read and understand him differently. True readers always read creatively. A work of literature can bring them joy, inspire them, or fill them with indignation. They may wish to interfere in the heroes' fortunes, reward or punish them, change their tragic fate to a happy one, put a triumphant villain to death. But the readers, no matter how deeply they are aroused by a work of literature, are unable and are not allowed to introduce any changes to suit their own personal tastes or the views of their age.

Folklore also presupposes two agents, but different agents, namely, the performer and the listener, opposing each other directly, or rather without a mediating link.

As a rule, the performers' works are not created by them personally but were heard earlier, so performers can in no way be compared with poets reciting their own works. Nor are they reciters of the works of others, mere declaimers reproducing someone else's work. They are figures specific to folklore, and all of them, from the primitive chorus to the folktale narrator * * * , deserve our closest attention. Performers do not repeat their texts word for word but introduce changes into them. Even if these changes are insignificant (but they can be very great), even if the changes that take place in folklore texts are sometimes as slow as geological processes, what is important is the fact of *change-ability of folklore compared with the stability of literature*.

If the reader of a work of literature is a powerless censor and critic devoid of authority, anyone listening to folklore is a potential future performer, who, in turn, consciously or unconsciously, will introduce changes into the work. These changes are not made accidentally but in accordance with certain laws. Everything that is out-of-date and in-congruous with new attitudes, tastes, and ideology will be discarded. These new tastes will affect not only what will be discarded but also what will be reworked and supplemented. Not a small (though not the decisive) role is played by the narrator's personality, taste, views on life, talents, and creative abilities. A work of folklore exists in constant flux, and it cannot be studied in depth if it is recorded only once. It should be recorded as many times as possible. We call each recording a variant, and these variants are something completely different from a version of a work of literature made by one and the same person.

Folklore circulates, changing all the time, and this circulation and changeability are among its specific characteristics. Literary works can also be drawn into the orbit of this circulation. For example, Mark Twain's *Prince and the Pauper* is told as a folktale. * * *

What do we have in this instance: folklore or literature? The answer is fairly simple. If, for example, a story from a chapbook, a saint's life, or the like, is recited from memory with no changes from the original, or if "The Black Shawl" or an excerpt from *The Peddlers* are sung exactly as Pushkin and Nekrásov wrote them, this case differs little from a performance on the stage or anywhere else. But as soon as such songs begin to change, to be sung differently, as soon as they begin to form variants, they become folklore, and the process of their change is the folklorist's domain. To be sure, there is a difference between folklore of the first sort, which often originated in prehistoric times and has variants all over the world, and poets' verses, freely used and transmitted by word of mouth. In the first case, we have pure folklore, that is, folklore both by origin and by transmission; in the second case, folklore of literary origin, that is, folklore by transmission but literature by origin. This distinction must always be kept in mind. A song that we consider pure folklore can turn out to be literary, can have an author. * * * Such examples are numerous, and ties between literature and folklore, as well as the literary sources of folklore are among the most interesting subjects both in the history of literature and in folklore.

This case again brings us to authorship in folklore. We have taken only two extreme cases. The first is folklore that was created by no one individual and arose in prehistoric times within the framework of some ritual or in some other way and that has survived through oral transmission to the present. The second case is obviously an individual's recent work circulating as folklore. In the development of both literature and folklore, between these two extremes occur all sorts of intermediate forms, each of which is a special problem. Modern folklorists are well aware that such problems cannot be solved descriptively, synchronically, but should be studied in their development. The genetic study of folklore is just one part of *historical* study, for folklore is not only a literary but also a historical phenomenon and the science of folklore not only a literary but also a historical discipline.

# VLADIMIR PROPP

## *From* Morphology of the Folktale†

### *The Method and Material*

Let us first of all attempt to formulate our task. As already stated in the foreword, this work is dedicated to the study of *fairy* tales. The existence of fairy tales as a special class is assumed as an essential working hypothesis. By "fairy tales" are meant at present those tales classified by Aarne under numbers 300 to 749. This definition is artificial, but the occasion will subsequently arise to give a more precise determination on the basis of resultant conclusions. We are undertaking a comparison of the themes of these tales. For the sake of comparison we shall separate the component parts of fairy tales by special methods; and then, we shall make a comparison of tales according to their components. The result will be a morphology (i.e., a description of the tale according to its component parts and the relationship of these components to each other and to the whole).

What methods can achieve an accurate description of the tale? Let us compare the following events:

1. A tsar gives an eagle to a hero. The eagle carries the hero away to another kingdom.
2. An old man gives Súčenko a horse. The horse carries Súčenko away to another kingdom.
3. A sorcerer gives Iván a little boat. The boat takes Iván to another kingdom.
4. A princess gives Iván a ring. Young men appearing from out of the ring carry Iván away into another kingdom, and so forth.

Both constants and variables are present in the preceding instances. The names of the dramatis personae change (as well as the attributes of each), but neither their actions nor functions change. From this we can draw the inference that a tale often attributes identical actions to various personages. This makes possible the study of the tale *according to the functions of its dramatis personae*.

We shall have to determine to what extent these functions actually represent recurrent constants of the tale. The formulation of all other questions will depend upon the solution of this primary question: how many functions are known to the tale?

---

† From Vladimir Propp, *Morphology of the Folktale*, trans. Laurence Scott (Austin: U of Texas P, 1968) 19–24. Copyright © 1968. Reprinted by permission of University of Texas Press.

Investigation will reveal that the recurrence of functions is astounding. Thus Bába Jagá, Morózko, the bear, the forest spirit, and the mare's head test and reward the stepdaughter. Going further, it is possible to establish that characters of a tale, however varied they may be, often perform the same actions. The actual means of the realization of functions can vary, and as such, it is a variable. Morózko behaves differently than Bába Jagá. But the function, as such, is a constant. The question of *what* a tale's dramatis personae do is an important one for the study of the tale, but the questions of *who* does it and *how* it is done already fall within the province of accessory study. The functions of characters are those components which could replace Veselóvskij's "motifs," or Bédier's "elements." We are aware of the fact that the repetition of functions by various characters was long ago observed in myths and beliefs by historians of religion, but it was not observed by historians of the tale. * * * Just as the characteristics and functions of deities are transferred from one to another, and, finally, are even carried over to Christian saints, the functions of certain tale personages are likewise transferred to other personages. Running ahead, one may say that the number of functions is extremely small, whereas the number of personages is extremely large. This explains the two-fold quality of a tale: its amazing multiformity, picturesqueness, and color, and on the other hand, its no less striking uniformity, its repetition.

Thus the functions of the dramatis personae are basic components of the tale, and we must first of all extract them. In order to extract the functions we must define them. Definition must proceed from two points of view. First of all, definition should in no case depend on the personage who carries out the function. Definition of a function will most often be given in the form of a noun expressing an action (interdiction, interrogation, flight, etc.). Secondly, an action cannot be defined apart from its place in the course of narration. The meaning which a given function has in the course of action must be considered. For example, if Iván marries a tsar's daughter, this is something entirely different than the marriage of a father to a widow with two daughters. A second example: if, in one instance, a hero receives money from his father in the form of 100 rubles and subsequently buys a wise cat with this money, whereas in a second case, the hero is rewarded with a sum of money for an accomplished act of bravery (at which point the tale ends), we have before us two morphologically different elements—in spite of the identical action (the transference of money) in both cases. Thus, identical acts can have different meanings, and vice versa. *Function is understood as an act of a character, defined from the point of view of its significance for the course of the action.*

The observations cited may be briefly formulated in the following manner:

1. *Functions of characters serve as stable, constant elements in a tale, independent of how and by whom they are fulfilled. They constitute the fundamental components of a tale.*
2. *The number of functions known to the fairy tale is limited.*

If functions are delineated, a second question arises: in what classification and in what sequence are these functions encountered?

A word, first, about sequence. The opinion exists that this sequence is accidental. Veselóvskij writes, "The selection and *order* of tasks and encounters (examples of motifs) already presupposes a certain *freedom*." Śklóvskij stated this idea in even sharper terms: "It is quite impossible to understand why, in the act of adoption, the *accidental* sequence [Śklóvskij's italics] of motifs must be retained. In the testimony of witnesses, it is precisely the sequence of events which is distorted most of all." This reference to the evidence of witnesses is unconvincing. If witnesses distort the sequence of events, their narration is meaningless. The sequence of events has its own laws. The short story too has similar laws, as do organic formations. Theft cannot take place before the door is forced. Insofar as the tale is concerned, it has its own entirely particular and specific laws. The sequence of elements, as we shall see later on, is strictly *uniform*. Freedom within this sequence is restricted by very narrow limits which can be exactly formulated. We thus obtain the third basic thesis of this work, subject to further development and verification:

3. *The sequence of functions is always identical.*

As for groupings, it is necessary to say first of all that by no means do all tales give evidence of all functions. But this in no way changes the law of sequence. The absence of certain functions does not change the order of the rest. We shall dwell on this phenomenon later. For the present we shall deal with groupings in the proper sense of the word. The presentation of the question itself evokes the following assumption: if functions are singled out, then it will be possible to trace those tales which present identical functions. Tales with identical functions can be considered as belonging to one type. On this foundation, an index of types can then be created, based not upon theme features, which are somewhat vague and diffuse, but upon exact structural features. Indeed, this will be possible. If we further compare structural types among themselves, we are led to the following completely unexpected phenomenon: functions cannot be distributed around mutually exclusive axes. This phenomenon, in all its concreteness, will become apparent to us in the succeeding and final chapters of this book. For the time being, it can be interpreted in the following manner: if we designate with the letter A a function encountered everywhere in first position, and similarly designate with the letter B the function which (if it is at all present) *always follows* A, then all functions known to the tale will arrange themselves within a *single* tale, and none will fall out of order, nor will any one exclude or contradict any other. This is, of course, a completely unexpected result. Naturally, we would have expected that where there is a function A, there cannot be certain functions belonging to other tales. Supposedly we would obtain several axes, but only a single axis is obtained for all fairy tales. They are of the same type, while the combinations spoken of previously are subtypes. At first glance, this conclusion may appear absurd or perhaps even wild, yet it can be verified in a most exact manner. Such a typological unity represents a very complex problem on which it will be necessary to dwell further. This phenomenon will raise a whole series of questions.

In this manner, we arrive at the fourth basic thesis of our work:

4. *All fairy tales are of one type in regard to their structure.*

We shall now set about the task of proving, developing, and elaborating these theses in detail. Here it should be recalled that the study of the tale must be carried on strictly deductively, i.e., proceeding from the material at hand to the consequences (and in effect it is so carried on in this work). But the *presentation* may have a reversed order, since it is easier to follow the development if the general bases are known to the reader beforehand.

Before starting the elaboration, however, it is necessary to decide what material can serve as the subject of this study. First glance would seem to indicate that it is necessary to cover all extant material. In fact, this is not so. Since we are studying tales according to the functions of their dramatis personae, the accumulation of material can be suspended as soon as it becomes apparent that the new tales considered present no new functions. Of course, the investigator must look through an enormous amount of reference material. But there is no need to inject the entire body of this material into the study. We have found that 100 tales constitute more than enough material. Having discovered that no new functions can be found, the morphologist can put a stop to his work, and further study will follow different directions (the formation of indices, the complete systemization, historical study). But just because material can be limited in quantity, that does not mean that it can be selected at one's own discretion. It should be dictated from without. We shall use the collection by Afanás'ev, starting the study of tales with No. 50 (according to his plan, this is the first fairy tale of the collection), and finishing it with No. 151.[1] Such a limitation of material will undoubtedly call forth many objections, but it is theoretically justified. To justify it further, it would be necessary to take into account

---

1. Propp bases his analyses on one hundred tales from Alexander Afanasev's *Russian Fairy Tales*, trans. Norbert Guterman (New York: Pantheon, 1945) [*Editor*].

the degree of repetition of tale phenomena. If repetition is great, then one may take a limited amount of material. If repetition is small, this is impossible. The repetition of fundamental components, as we shall see later, exceeds all expectations. Consequently, it is theoretically possible to limit oneself to a small body of material. Practically, this limitation justifies itself by the fact that the inclusion of a great quantity of material would have excessively increased the size of this work. We are not interested in the quantity of material, but in the quality of its analysis. Our working material consists of 100 tales. The rest is reference material, of great interest to the investigator, but lacking a broader interest.

\* \* \*

## Propp's Thirty-One Functions

1. One of the members of a family absents himself from home (*absention*).
2. An interdiction is addressed to the hero (*interdiction*).
3. The interdiction is violated (*violation*).
4. The villain makes an attempt at reconnaissance (*reconnaissance*).
5. The villain receives information about his victim (*delivery*).
6. The villain attempts to deceive his victim in order to take possession of him or his belongings (*trickery*).
7. The victim submits to deception and thereby unwittingly helps his enemy (*complicity*).
8. The villain causes harm or injury to a member of the family (*villainy*).
8a. One member of a family either lacks something or desires to have something (*lack*).
9. Misfortune or lack is made known; the hero is approached with a request or command; he is allowed to go or he is dispatched (*mediation, the connective incident*).
10. The seeker agrees to or decides upon counteraction (*beginning counteraction*).
11. The hero leaves home (*departure*).
12. The hero is tested, interrogated, attacked, etc., which prepares the way for his receiving either a magical agent or helper (*the first function of the donor*).
13. The hero reacts to the actions of the future donor (*the hero's reaction*).
14. The hero acquires the use of a magical agent (*provision or receipt of a magical agent*).
15. The hero is transferred, delivered, or led to the whereabouts of an object of search (*spatial transference between two kingdoms, guidance*).

16. The hero and the villain join in direct combat *(struggle)*.
17. The hero is branded *(branding, marking)*.
18. The villain is defeated *(victory)*.
19. The initial misfortune or lack is liquidated *(liquidation)*.
20. The hero returns *(return)*.
21. The hero is pursued *(pursuit, chase)*.
22. Rescue of the hero from pursuit *(rescue)*.
23. The hero, unrecognized, arrives home or in another country *(unrecognized arrival)*.
24. A false hero presents unfounded claims *(unfounded claims)*.
25. A difficult task is proposed to the hero *(difficult task)*.
26. The task is resolved *(solution)*.
27. The hero is recognized *(recognition)*.
28. The false hero or villain is exposed *(exposure)*.
29. The hero is given a new appearance *(transfiguration)*.
30. The villain is punished *(punishment)*.
31. The hero is married and ascends the throne *(wedding)*.

\* \* \*

# Propp's *Dramatis Personae*

1. Villain
2. Donor or provider
3. Helper
4. Princess (a sought-for person) and her father
5. Dispatcher
6. Hero
7. False Hero

# Selected Bibliography

## ANTHOLOGIES

Abrahams, Roger D., comp. *African Folktales.* New York: Pantheon, 1983.
Afanasev, Alexander, comp. *Russian Fairy Tales.* Trans. Norbert Guterman. New York: Pantheon, 1945.
Andersen, Hans Christian. *Eighty Fairy Tales.* Trans. R. P. Keigwin. New York: Pantheon, 1976.
*Arabian Nights.* Trans. Richard F. Burton. Ed. David Shumaker. New York: Avenel Books, 1978.
Asbjørnsen, Peter Christian, and Jörgen Møe, comps. *Popular Tales from the Norse.* Trans. Sir George Webbe Dasent. New York: D. Appleton, 1859.
———. *Norwegian Folktales.* New York: Pantheon, 1960.
Basile, Giambattista. *The Pentamerone of Giambattista Basile.* Trans. Benedetto Croce. Ed. N. M. Penzer. 2 vols. London: John Lane the Bodley Head, 1932.
Blecher, Lone Thygensen, and George Blecher. *Swedish Tales and Legends.* New York: Pantheon, 1993.
Briggs, Katharine M. *A Dictionary of British Folk-Tales in the English Language.* 4 vols. London: Routledge and Kegan Paul, 1970–71.
———, and Ruth L. Tongue. *Folktales of England.* Chicago: U of Chicago P, 1965.
Bushnaq, Inea, comp. *Arab Folktales.* New York: Pantheon, 1986.
Calvino, Italo, comp. *Italian Folktales.* Trans. George Martin. New York: Pantheon, 1980.
Carter, Angela. *The Bloody Chamber and Other Stories.* Harmondsworth: Penguin, 1979.
———, ed. *The Second Virago Book of Fairy Tales.* London: Virago Press, 1992.
———, ed. *The Virago Book of Fairy Tales.* London: Virago Press, 1990.
Chase, Richard, comp. *American Folk Tales and Songs.* New York: Signet, 1956.
Clarkson, Atelia, and Gilbert B. Cross, comp. *World Folktales: A Scribner Resource Collection.* New York: Charles Scribner's Sons, 1980.
Crossley-Holland, Kevin, comp. *Folktales of the British Isles.* New York: Pantheon, 1988.
Dahl, Roald. *Revolting Rhymes.* London: Jonathan Cape, 1982.
Dasent, George Webbe, comp. *East o' the Sun and West o' the Moon.* Toronto: Dover, 1970.
Datlow, Ellen, and Terri Windling, eds. *Black Thorn, White Rose.* New York: Avon, 1994.
———. *Snow White, Blood Red.* New York: William Morrow, 1993.
Dawkins, R. M., comp. *Modern Greek Folktales.* Oxford: Clarendon, 1953.
Delarue, Paul, comp. *Borzoi Book of French Folk Tales.* New York: Knopf, 1956.
Dorson, Richard M., comp. *American Negro Folktales.* New York: Fawcett Publications, 1968.
———. *Buying the Wind: Regional Folklore of the United States.* Chicago: U of Chicago P, 1964.
———. *Folktales Told Around the World.* Chicago: U of Chicago P, 1975.
Eberhard, Wolfram, comp. *Folktales of China.* Chicago: U of Chicago P, 1965.
Erdoes, Richard, and Alfonso Ortiz, comps. *American Myths and Legends.* New York: Pantheon, 1984.
Feldmann, Susan, comp. *The Storytelling Stone: Myths and Tales of the American Indians.* New York: Dell, 1965.
Grimm, Jacob, and Wilhelm Grimm. *The Complete Fairy Tales of the Brothers Grimm.* Trans. Jack Zipes. Toronto: Bantam, 1987.

Hallett, Martin, and Barbara Karasek, comp. *Folk and Fairy Tales.* Peterborough, Ont.: Broadview Press, 1991.

Hearn, Michael Patrick, comp. *Victorian Fairy Tale Book.* New York: Pantheon, 1988.

Jacobs, Joseph, comp. *Celtic Fairy Tales.* London: D. Nutt, 1892.

——. *English Fairy Tales* (1890). London: Bodley Head, 1968.

Lang, Andrew, comp. *The Blue Fairy Book* (1889). New York: Dover Publications, 1974.

——. *The Green Fairy Book* (1892). New York: Dover Publications, 1974.

——. *The Pink Fairy Book* (1897). New York: Dover Publications, 1974.

——. *The Red Fairy Book* (1890). New York: Dover Publications, 1974.

——. *Yellow Fairy Book* (1894). New York: Dover Publications, 1974.

Lurie, Alison, comp. *Clever Gretchen and Other Forgotten Folktales.* New York: Crowell, 1980.

——. *The Oxford Book of Modern Fairy Tales.* Oxford: Oxford UP, 1993.

Massignon, Geneviève, comp. *Folktales of France.* Trans. Jacqueline Hyland. Chicago: U of Chicago P, 1968.

Mieder, Wolfgang, ccmp. *Disenchantments: An Anthology of Modern Fairy Tale Poetry.* Hanover, N.H.: UP of New England, 1985.

Minard, Rosemary. *Womenfolk and Fairy Tales.* Boston: Houghton Mifflin, 1975.

Montgomerie, Norah, and William Montgomerie, comps. *The Well at the World's End: Folk Tales of Scotland.* Toronto: The Bodley Head, 1956.

Noy, Dov, comp. *Folktales of Israel.* Trans. Gene Baharav. Chicago: U of Chicago P, 1963.

Opie, Peter, and Iona Opie, comp. *The Classic Fairy Tales.* London: Oxford UP, 1974.

Perrault, Charles. *Perrault's Complete Fairy Tales.* Trans. A. E. Johnson et al. New York: Dodd, Mead, 1961.

Phelps, Ethel Johnston, comp. *The Maid of the North: Feminist Folk Tales from Around the World.* New York: Holt, Rinehart and Winston, 1981.

——. *Tatterhood and Other Tales.* Old Westbury, N.Y.: Feminist Press, 1978.

Philip, Neil, comp. *The Cinderella Story: The Origins and Variations of the Story Known as "Cinderella".* London: Penguin, 1989.

Pourrat, Henri, comp. *French Folktales.* Trans. Royall Tyler. New York: Pantheon, 1989.

Ramanujan, A. K., comp. *Folktales from India.* New York: Random House, 1991.

Randolph, Vance, comp. *Pissing in the Snow and Other Ozark Folktales.* Urbana: U of Illinois P, 1976.

——. *Sticks in the Knapsack and Other Ozark Folk Tales.* New York: Columbia UP, 1958.

Ranke, Kurt, comp. *Folktales of Germany.* Trans. Lotte Baumann. Chicago: U of Chicago P, 1966.

Rugoff, Milton A., comp. *A Harvest of World Folk Tales.* New York: Viking, 1949.

Simpson, Jacqueline, comp. *Icelandic Folktales and Legends.* Berkeley: U of California P, 1972.

Straparola, Giovanni Francesco. *The Facetious Nights of Straparola.* Trans. W. G. Waters. 4 vols. London: Society of Bibliophiles, 1901.

Thompson, Stith, comp. *One Hundred Favorite Folktales.* Bloomington: Indiana UP, 1968.

——. *Tales of the North American Indians.* Bloomington: Indiana UP, 1929.

Travers, P. L., comp. *About the Sleeping Beauty.* New York: McGraw-Hill, 1975.

Walker, Barbara G. *Feminist Fairy Tales.* New York: Harper Collins, 1996.

Weinrich, Beatrice Silverman, comp. *Yiddish Folktales.* New York: Pantheon, 1988.

Williams, Jay. *The Practical Princess and Other Liberating Fairy Tales.* New York: Parents Magazine Press / London: Chatto and Windus, 1979.

Yolen, Jane. *Favorite Folktales from Around the World.* New York: Pantheon, 1986.

Zipes, Jack, comp. *Beauties, Beasts and Enchantment: Classic Fairy Tales.* New York: New American Library, 1989.

——. *Don't Bet on the Prince: Contemporary Fairy Tales in North America and England.* New York: Methuen, 1986.

——. *The Outspoken Princess and the Gentle Knight: A Treasury of Modern Fairy Tales.* New York: Bantam, 1994.

——. *Spells of Enchantment: The Wondrous Fairy Tales of Western Culture.* New York: Viking, 1991.

——. *Victorian Fairy Tales. The Revolt of the Fairies and Elves.* New York: Routledge, 1987.

CRITICAL STUDIES

•indicates works included or excerpted in this Norton Critical Edition.

•Aarne, Antti, and Stith Thompson. *The Types of the Folktale. A Classification and Bibliography*. Helsinki: Academia Scientiarum Fennica, 1961.

Bacchilega, Cristina. *Postmodern Fairy Tales: Gender and Narrative Strategies*. Philadelphia: U of Pennsylvania P, 1997.

Barchilon, Jacques. "Beauty and the Beast: From Myth to Fairy Tale." *Psychoanalysis and the Psychoanalytic Review* 46 (1959): 19–29.

——, and Peter Flinders. *Charles Perrault*. Boston: Twayne Publishers, 1981.

Barzilai, Shuli. "Reading 'Snow White': The Mother's Story." *Signs* 50 (1990): 515–34.

Behlmer, Rudy. "They Called It 'Disney's Folly': Snow White and the Seven Dwarfs (1937)." *America's Favorite Movies: Behind the Scenes*. New York: Ungar, 1982.

Bell, Elizabeth, Lynda Haas, and Laura Sells, eds. *From Mouse to Mermaid: The Politics of Film, Gender, and Culture*. Bloomington: Indiana UP, 1995.

•Bettelheim, Bruno. *The Uses of Enchantment: The Meaning and Importance of Fairy Tales*. New York: Knopf, 1976.

Bottigheimer, Ruth B. "Fairy Tales and Children's Literature: A Feminist Perspective." In *Teaching Children's Literature: Issues, Pedagogy, Resources*. Ed. Glen Edward Sadler. New York: Modern Language Association of America, 1992.

——. *Fairy Tales and Society: Illusion, Allusion, and Paradigm*. Philadelphia: U of Pennsylvania P, 1986.

——. *Grimms' Bad Girls and Bold Boys*. New Haven: Yale UP, 1987.

Briggs, Katharine. *An Encyclopedia of Fairies: Hobgoblins, Brownies, Bogies, and Other Supernatural Creatures*. New York: Pantheon, 1976.

Bronfen, Elisabeth. *Over Her Dead Body: Death, Femininity and the Aesthetic*. New York: Routledge, 1992.

Bryant, Sylvia. "Re-Constructing Oedipus through 'Beauty and the Beast.' " *Criticism* 31 (1989): 439–53.

Canham, Stephen. "What Manner of Beast? Illustrations of 'Beauty and the Beast.' " In *Image and Maker: An Annual Dedicated to the Consideration of Book Illustration*. Ed. Harold Darling and Peter Neumeyer. La Jolla: Green Tiger Press, 1984.

Carter, Angela, ed. "About the Stories." In *Sleeping Beauty and Other Favourite Fairy Tales*. Boston: Otter Books, 1991.

Cech, Jon. "Hans Christian Andersen's Fairy Tales and Stories: Secrets, Swans and Shadows." In *Touchstones: Reflections on the Best in Children's Literature*. Vol. 2. West Lafayette, Indiana: Children's Literature Assn., 1983.

Cox, Marian Roalfe. *Cinderella: Three Hundred and Forty-five Variants of Cinderella, Catskin, and Cap o' Rushes*. Ed. Andrew Lang. London: David Nutt, 1893.

•Darnton, Robert. "Peasants Tell Tales: The Meaning of Mother Goose." In *The Great Cat Massacre and Other Episodes in French Cultural History*. New York: Basic Books, 1984.

Dégh, Linda. *Folktales and Society: Storytelling in a Hungarian Peasant Community*. Trans. Emily M. Schossberger. Bloomington: Indiana UP, 1969.

Delarue, Paul. "Les Contes merveilleux de Perrault et la tradition populaire." *Bulletin folklorique de l'Ile-de-France* (1951): 221–28, 251–60, 283–91; (1953): 511–17.

Dobay Rifelj, Carol de. "Cendrillon and the Ogre: Women in Fairy Tales and Sade." *Romanic Review* 81 (1990): 11–24.

Dorson, Richard. *Folklore*. Bloomington: Indiana UP, 1972.

Dowling, Colette. *The Cinderella Complex: Women's Hidden Fear of Independence*. New York: Summit Books, 1981.

Dundes, Alan. "Bruno Bettelheim's Uses of Enchantment and Abuses of Scholarship." *Journal of American Folklore* 104 (1991): 74–83.

——. *Cinderella: A Casebook*. New York: Garland, 1982; Madison: U of Wisconsin P, 1988.

——. *Little Red Riding Hood: A Casebook*. Madison: U of Wisconsin P, 1989.

——. *The Study of Folklore*. Englewood Cliffs: Prentice Hall, 1965.

Edelson, Maria. "The Language of Allegory in Oscar Wilde's Tales." In *Anglo-Irish and Irish Literature*. Ed. Birgit Bramsbäck and Martin Croghan. Stockholm: Almqvist and Wiksell and Bromsbäck, 1988.

Edwards, Carol L. "The Fairy Tale 'Snow White.'" In *Making Connections across the Curriculum: Readings for Analysis.* New York: St. Martin's Press, 1986.

Edwards, Lee R. "The Labors of Psyche: Toward a Theory of Female Heroism." *Critical Inquiry* 6 (1979): 33–49.

Ellis, John. *One Fairy Story Too Many: The Brothers Grimm and Their Tales.* Chicago: U of Chicago P, 1982.

Farrer, Claire, ed. *Women and Folklore.* Austin: U of Texas P, 1975.

Franz, Marie-Luise von. *Archetypal Patterns in Fairy Tales.* Toronto: Inner City Books, 1997.

———. *Problems of the Feminine in Fairy Tales.* New York: Spring Publications, 1972.

•Gilbert, Sandra M., and Susan Gubar. "The Queen's Looking Glass." In *The Madwoman in the Attic: The Woman Writer and the Nineteenth-Century Literary Imagination.* New Haven: Yale UP, 1979.

Girardot, N. J. "Initiation and Meaning in the Tale of Snow White and the Seven Dwarfs." *Journal of American Folklore* 90 (1977): 274–300.

Grønbech, Bo. *Hans Christian Andersen.* Boston: Twayne, 1980.

•Haase, Donald. "Yours, Mine, or Ours? Perrault, the Brothers Grimm and the Ownership of Fairy Tales." In *Once Upon a Folktale: Capturing the Folklore Process with Children.* Ed. Gloria T. Blatt. New York: Teachers College, Columbia University, 1993.

———, ed. *The Reception of Grimms' Fairy Tales: Responses, Reactions, Revisions.* Detroit: Wayne State UP, 1993.

Hanks, Carole, and D. T. Hanks, Jr. "Perrault's 'Little Red Riding Hood': Victim of the Revisers." *Children's Literature* 7 (1978): 68–77.

Hartland, E. Sidney. "The Forbidden Chamber." *Folk-Lore Journal* 3 (1885): 193–242.

Hearne, Betsy. *Beauty and the Beast: Visions and Revisions of an Old Tale.* Chicago: U of Chicago P, 1989.

Holbek, Bengt. *The Interpretation of Fairy Tales: Danish Folklore in a European Perspective.* Helsinki: Academia Scientiarum Fennica, 1987.

Holliss, Richard, and Brian Sibley. *Walt Disney's "Snow White and the Seven Dwarfs" and the Making of the Classic Film.* New York: Simon and Schuster, 1987.

Johnson, Faye R., and Carole M. Carroll. "'Little Red Riding Hood': Then and Now." *Studies in Popular Culture* 14 (1992): 71–84.

Jones, Steven Swann. "On Analyzing Fairy Tales: 'Little Red Riding Hood' Revisited." *Western Folklore* 46 (1987): 97–106.

———. *The New Comparative Method: Structural and Symbolic Analysis of the Allomotifs of "Snow White".* Helsinki: Academia Scientiarum Fennica, 1990.

Kamenetsky, Christa. *The Brothers Grimm and Their Critics: Folktales and the Quest for Meaning.* Athens: Ohio UP, 1992.

Kolbenschlag, Madonna. *Kiss Sleeping Beauty Good-bye: Breaking the Spell of Feminine Myths and Models.* New York: Doubleday, 1979.

Laruccia, Victor. "Little Red Riding Hood's Metacommentary: Paradoxical Injunction, Semiotics and Behavior." *Modern Language Notes* 90 (1975): 517–34.

Lewis, Philip. *Seeing through the Mother Goose Tales: Visual Turns in the Writings of Perrault.* Stanford: Stanford UP, 1996.

Lieberman, Marcia. "Some Day My Prince Will Come: Female Acculturation through the Fairy Tale." *College English* 34 (1972): 383–95.

Lurie, Alison. *Don't Tell the Grown-ups: Subversive Children's Literature.* Boston: Little, Brown, 1990.

Lüthi, Max. *The European Folktale: Form and Nature.* Trans. John D. Niles. Philadelphia: Institute for the Study of Human Issues, 1982.

———. *The Fairy Tale as Art Form and Portrait of Man.* Trans. Jan Erickson. Bloomington: Indiana UP, 1984.

———. *Once Upon a Time: On the Nature of Fairy Tales.* Bloomington: Indiana UP, 1970.

Mallet, Carl-Heinz. *Fairy Tales and Children: The Psychology of Children Revealed through Four of Grimms' Fairy Tales.* New York: Schocken Books, 1980.

Maranda, P., ed. *Soviet Structural Folkloristics.* The Hague: Mouton, 1974.

Marin, Louis. *Food for Thought.* Trans. Mette Hjort. Baltimore: The Johns Hopkins UP, 1989.

McGlathery, James, ed. *The Brothers Grimm and Folktale.* Urbana: U of Illinois P, 1988.

McMaster, Juliet. "Bluebeard: A Tale of Matrimony." *A Room of One's Own* 2 (1976): 10–19.
Mieder, Wolfgang. "Survival Forms of 'Little Red Riding Hood' in Modern Society." *International Folklore Review* 2 (1982): 23–41.
Monaghan, David M. "The Literary Fairy-Tale: A Study of Oscar Wilde's 'The Happy Prince' and 'The Star-Child.' " *Canadian Review of Comparative Literature* 1 (1974): 156–66.
Panttaja, Elisabeth. "Going Up in the World: Class in 'Cinderella.' " *Western Folklore* 52 (1993): 85–104.
Preston, Cathy Lynn. " 'Cinderella' as a Dirty Joke: Gender, Multivocality, and the Polysemic Text." *Western Folklore* 53 (1994): 27–49.
•Propp, Vladimir. *Morphology of the Folktale*. Trans. Laurence Scott. Austin: U of Texas P, 1975.
•———. *Theory and History of Folklore*. Trans. Ariadna Y. Martin and Richard P. Martin. Ed. Anatoly Liberman. U of Minnesota P, 1984.
Quintus, John Allen. "The Moral Prerogative in Oscar Wilde: A Look at the Fairy Tales." *Virginia Quarterly Review* 53 (1977): 708–17.
Rooth, Anna Birgitta. *The Cinderella Cycle*. Lund: C. W. K. Gleerup, 1951.
Rose, Ellen Cronan. "Through the Looking Glass: When Women Tell Fairy Tales." In *The Voyage In: Fictions of Female Development*. Ed. Elizabeth Abel, Marianne Hirsch, and Elizabeth Langland. Hanover: UP of New England, 1983.
•Rowe, Karen E. "To Spin a Yarn: The Female Voice in Folklore and Fairy Tale." In *Fairy Tale and Society: Illusion, Allusion, and Paradigm*. Ed. Ruth B. Bottigheimer. Philadelphia: U of Pennsylvania P, 1986.
———. "Feminism and Fairy Tales." *Women's Studies: An Interdisciplinary Journal* 6 (1979): 237–57.
Sale, Roger. *Fairy Tales and After: From Snow White to E. B. White*. Cambridge: Harvard UP, 1978.
Schectman, Jacqueline. "Hansel and Gretel." In *The Stepmother in Fairy Tales: Bereavement and the Feminine Shadow*. Boston: Sigo, 1991.
Scherf, Walter. "Family Conflicts and Emancipation in Fairy Tales." *Children's Literature*, 3 (1974): 77–93.
Schickel, Richard. *The Disney Version: The Life, Times, Art and Commerce of Walt Disney*. New York: Simon and Schuster, 1968.
Schwartz, Emanuel K. "A Psychoanalytic Study of the Fairy Tale." *American Journal of Psychotherapy* 10 (1956): 740–62.
Seifert, Lewis Carl. *Fairy Tales, Sexuality, and Gender in France, 1690–1715: Nostalgic Utopias*. New York: Cambridge UP, 1996.
Sendak, Maurice. "Hans Christian Andersen." In *Caldecott and Co.: Notes on Books and Pictures*. New York: Farrar, Straus and Giroux, Michael di Capua Books, 1988.
•Shavit, Zohar. "The Concept of Childhood and Children's Folktales: Test Case—'Little Red Riding Hood.'" *Jerusalem Studies in Jewish Folklore* 4 (1983): 93–124.
Sheets, Robin Ann. "Pornography, Fairy Tales, and Feminism: Angela Carter's 'The Bloody Chamber.' " *Journal of the History of Sexuality* 1 (1991): 633–57.
Snider, Clifton. "Eros and Logos in Some Fairy Tales by Oscar Wilde: A Jungian Interpretation." *Victorian Newsletter* 84 (1993): 1–8.
Soriano, Marc. "Le petit chaperon rouge." *Nouvelle Revue Française* 16 (1968): 429–43.
Stone, Kay F. "The Misuses of Enchantment: Controversies on the Significance of Fairy Tales." In *Women's Folklore, Women's Culture*. Ed. Rosan A. Jordan and Susan J. Kalcik. Philadelphia: U of Pennsylvania P, 1985.
———. "Things Walt Disney Never Told Us." *Journal of American Folklore* 88 (1975): 42–49.
Sullivan, Paula. "Fairy Tale Elements in *Jane Eyre*." *Journal of Popular Culture* 12 (1978): 61–74.
Swahn, Jan-Ojvind. *The Tale of Cupid and Psyche (Aarne-Thompson 425 and 428)*. Lund, Sweden: Gleerup, 1955.
•Tatar, Maria. *The Hard Facts of the Grimms' Fairy Tales*. Princeton: Princeton UP, 1987.
———. *Off with Their Heads! Fairy Tales and the Culture of Childhood*. Princeton: Princeton UP, 1992.
Thompson, Stith. *The Folktale*. New York: Holt, Rinehart and Winston, 1946.
———. *Motif Index of Folk-Literature*. 6 vols., rev. and enlarged ed. Bloomington: Indiana UP, 1955–58.

Tolkien, J. R. R. "On Fairy-Stories." In *The Tolkien Reader*. New York: Ballantine, 1966.

Travers, P. L. *About the Sleeping Beauty*. London: Collins, 1977.

——. "The Black Sheep." In *What the Bee Knows: Reflections on Myth, Symbol, and Story*. Wellingborough, Northamptonshire: Aquarian, 1989.

Verdier, Yvonne. "Grands-mères, si vous saviez, . . . le Petit Chaperon Rouge dans la tradition orale." *Cahiers de Littérature Orale* 4 (1978): 17–55.

Waelti-Walters, Jennifer. *Fairy Tales and the Female Imagination*. Montreal: Eden Press, 1982.

Waley, Arthur. "The Chinese Cinderella Story." *Folk-Lore* 58 (1947): 226–38.

Walker, Mary. "Wilde's Fairy Tales." *Unisa English Studies: Journal of the Department of English* 14 (1976): 30–41.

•Warner, Marina. *From the Beast to the Blonde: On Fairy Tales and Their Tellers*. New York: Farrar, Straus and Giroux, 1994.

Weber, Eugen. "Fairies and Hard Facts: The Reality of Folktales." *Journal of the History of Ideas* 42 (1981): 93–113.

Weigle, Marta. *Spiders and Spinsters*. Albuquerque: U of New Mexico P, 1982.

Wilson, Sharon R. "Bluebeard's Forbidden Room: Gender Images in Margaret Atwood's Visual and Literary Art." *American Review of Canadian Studies* 16 (1986): 385–97.

——. *Margaret Atwood's Fairy-Tale Sexual Politics*. Jackson: UP of Mississippi, 1993.

Yolen, Jane. "America's Cinderella." *Children's Literature in Education* 8 (1977): 21–29.

——. *Touch Magic: Fantasy, Faerie and Folklore in the Literature of Childhood*. New York: Philomel, 1981.

Zipes, Jack. *Breaking the Magic Spell: Radical Theories of Folk and Fairy Tales*. Austin: U of Texas P, 1979.

——. *The Brothers Grimm: From Enchanted Forests to the Modern World*. New York: Routledge, Chapman and Hall, 1988.

——. *Fairy Tales and the Art of Subversion: The Classical Genre for Children and the Process of Civilization*. New York: Wildman, 1983.

•——. *Happily Ever After: Fairy Tales, Children, and the Culture Industry*. New York: Routledge, 1997.

——, ed. *The Trials and Tribulations of Little Red Riding Hood*. 2d ed. New York: Routledge, 1993.